STANDARD
C++ IOSTREAMS
AND LOCALES

STANDARD
C++ IOSTREAMS
AND LOCALES

Advanced Programmer's Guide and Reference

Angelika Langer
and
Klaus Kreft

ADDISON–WESLEY

Boston • San Francisco • New York • Toronto • Montreal
London • Munich • Paris • Madrid
Capetown • Sydney • Tokyo • Singapore • Mexico City

The publisher offers discounts on this book when ordered in quantity for special sales. For more information, please contact:

Corporate, Government, and Special Sales
Addison Wesley Longman, Inc.
One Jacob Way
Reading, Massachusetts 01867
(781) 944-3700

Library of Congress Cataloging-in-Publication Data

Langer, Angelika.
    Standard C++ IOStreams and locales : advanced programmer's guide and reference /
  Angelika Langer, Klaus Kreft.
      p.   cm.
    Includes bibliographical references and index.
    ISBN 0-201-18395-1
    1. C++ (Computer program language)   I. Kreft, Klaus.   II. Title.

QA76.73C153   L37   1999
005.13'3—dc21

                                                                        99-047625

ISBN 0-201-18395-1
Text printed on recycled paper

  2 3 4 5 6 7 8 9 10–CRW–04030201
First printing, January 2000

CONTENTS

PART II: INTERNATIONALIZATION

REFERENCE GUIDE

FOREWORD

I began working on C++ input/output libraries around 1986. I started by fixing a bug I had noticed in the stream library that was part of the internal Bell Labs distribution of C++. I decided to also add some of the functionality that was present in the C stdio library but was not in the stream library. As I looked at the stream library, I realized that the architecture of an input/output library in C++ raised interesting issues about C++ design, and I conceived what became the IOStream library. Originally I thought of this as a personal library that could be used for experimentation and had no intention of replacing the stream library. But at some point, Bjarne Stroustrup encouraged the product organization that was responsible for C++ to replace the stream library with the IOStream library. They did so, and what started out as an exercise that I expected to last a few months became an effort that would span more than ten years, including the ANSI/ISO standardization effort.

A major goal in my original design was that it be extensible in interesting ways. In particular, in the stream library the streambuf class was an implementation detail, but in the IOStream library I intended it to be a usable class in its own right. I was hoping for the promulgation of many streambufs with varied functionality. I wrote a few myself, but almost no one else did. I answered many more questions of the type "How do I make my numbers look like this?" than "How do I write a streambuf?" And textbook authors also tended to ignore streambufs. Apparently they did not share my view that the architecture of the input/output library was an interesting case study.

Another common question addressed to me was "Why weren't the members of the stream classes virtual?" On further discussion it usually became clear that what the questioner needed to do was write a streambuf with some particular functionality. Or sometimes what was needed was to write an alternative top-level class that used streambufs for transport. When I would explain this, they frequently lost interest.

All this led to a sense of frustration and disappointment that the library was not being used to its best advantage. Several friends encouraged me to address this frustration by writing a book, the theory being that the extensibility features were hard to understand but that a book explaining them clearly would encourage people to use them. As the C++ standardization effort went on and the library became more complicated, the need for such a book increased. I started on the project several times, but never organized the time and energy required of an author.

During this period, when I heard about books on the IOStream library I approached them with mixed feelings. On the one hand I was always glad to see the IOStream library getting attention, on the other I worried that this book would beat me to the punch. But my fears were groundless: None of them addressed the issues of architecture and C++ design that were my major concern.

None, that is, until the present book. Not only does it address the kinds of questions that concern me, but also it does so with concrete examples that will enable readers to quickly adapt the ideas to their own requirements. I am no longer contemplating writing a book on the library so I have only positive feelings about this book.

—Jerry Schwarz
November 1999

PREFACE

Since 1998, the programming language C++ has been formally specified in the form of the ISO/IEC International Standard 14882, a document that for historical reasons is often referred to as the *ANSI C++ Standard*. Integral to this standard is a rich set of abstractions known as the *C++ Standard Library*. In fact, half of the standard is devoted to the library. This book covers two major domains of the standard library: IOStreams and locales.

During the process of standardization from 1989 to 1998, the new language features and the standard library created a fair amount of interest in the C++ community. To address this need for information, several books were published during and after the standardization. Some cover standard C++ in general, typically including a brief introduction to some of the library abstractions; one textbook is devoted exclusively to the standard library. However, the only part of the library that has been discussed in depth so far is the STL, a set of collections and algorithms that was developed at Hewlett-Packard independent of the standardization effort and was later integrated into C++ standard library. While the STL is, without doubt, the most popular part of the standard library, it represents less than a third of the library as a whole (counting the pages in the standards document and considering the time that the committee spent on it), whereas IOStreams and locales form another third of the library.

When we got involved with the standardization of C++ through our professional occupations in 1993, hardly anything had been published about IOStreams, and C++ locales had not yet been invented. The only book on IOStreams was the *C++ IOStreams Handbook* by Steve Teale, which describes the classic, prestandard IOStreams; and there was a definite lack of information regarding the standardized IOStreams. The situation has not radically changed since then. Even now, at the time of this writing in 1999, little has been published about the standardized IOStreams, and even less about C++ locales. The few books that exist about IOStreams are out of date; they all cover the classic, prestandard IOStreams. The C++ textbooks provide introductory information about IOStreams but rarely anything about locales. For this reason, we felt the need for a book exclusively devoted to these topics that begins where the tutorials leave off.

TARGET AUDIENCE

This book is a programmer's guide to the standard IOStreams and locales, together with a complete reference of all relevant classes, functions, templates, headers, etc. It is neither a tutorial nor a textbook. It does not aim to teach the reader C++ or the basics of IOStreams. We expect of the readers that they know, at least roughly, what happens when they type a line of C++ code such as

```
cout << "Hello world" << endl;
```

Hence this book is not for absolute beginners, but rather for C++ programmers who have been studying a C++ textbook, or have comparable practical experience, and who intend to use IOStreams and locales in more than a casual way.

As locales are an abstraction that is new to C++, as opposed to IOStreams, which has been around for more than a decade, we cover locales from the ground up. Some knowledge of locales in C will aid understanding, but it is not required. We do not aim to cover internationalization in a comprehensive way. Internationalization is too broad a topic, and an adequate discussion of it would fill another whole book. However, IOStreams and locales are closely related, and for this reason the book explains the concept of C++ locales, with emphasis on usage of locales in conjunction with IOStreams.

Regarding IOStreams, we acknowledge the fact that the classic IOStreams library has been in existence since the early days of C++. We assume that readers are familiar with the basic features as they are explained in every C++ textbook. Instead of repeating the basics, we aim to go beyond that introductory level. For instance, we demonstrate advanced features—such as user-defined shift operators and manipulators, extending streams by use of iword/pword, and derivation of new stream and stream buffer classes—as well as less ambitious topics like format control and error handling.

Overall, the goal of this book is to provide as much information about the general principles as is needed to enable readers to accomplish their concrete programming tasks using IOStreams and locales. The focus is on the underlying concepts and the more advanced programming techniques that IOStreams and locales support, rather than on the details of each and every interface. For this reason we refrain from presenting extensive and lengthy case studies and code examples. IOStreams and locales are general purpose tools and can be used to solve a sheer abundance of problems. It would have been impossible to find a representative and comprehensive set of case studies. Instead, we concentrate on a few condensed examples that we use to explain programming techniques and concepts, and we deliberately refrain from blowing them up to full applications in order to avoid unnecessary distractions. We trust that readers will be astute enough to figure out concrete applications once the principles are clear.

ABOUT THE STANDARD

We have received a considerable number of queries such as "Why is this and that so and so?" seeking an explanation of why IOStreams and locales are designed the way they are. Where we know of an underlying rationale, we explain it. Yet there are inconsistencies and "interesting" design decisions that can be explained only by "historical reasons" or "design by committee." Where we feel that certain features introduce potential pitfalls, we point them out, so that the reader can avoid them. Beyond that, we neither aim to defend the standard nor intend to discuss alternative designs. We describe it as it is.

ACKNOWLEDGMENTS

Writing this book took us more than three years, and during this long period many people helped us to endure and finish the task. As with any book, the authors are only part of the story, and we would like to thank all those people who contributed in one way or another.

At Addison-Wesley, we would like to thank Mike Hendrickson, Deborah Lafferty, and in particular Marina Lang; they believed in the value of this book and accompanied us through the entire process from proposal to print. Our thanks also to Beth Burleigh Fuller and John Fuller for their support during the production process of the book.

We would like to thank all those knowledgeable and patient people at the standards committee and elsewhere who answered our countless and sometimes stupid questions: Nathan Myers, who invented the C++ locales and proposed them to the standards committee, told us everything about locales and helped us understand his proposal as well as any resulting discussions. Jerry Schwarz, who is the "father of IOStreams," that is, the author of the first version of IOStreams (or "streams" as they were called in C++ 1.0), gave us invaluable insights into the intent of many of the IOStreams features, and we thank him for his patience and support. Bill Plauger, author of the Microsoft version of the C++ standard library, helped us distinguish between bugs in the implementation and misunderstandings on our side; he was also invaluable in helping us understand and interpret the standard correctly. Philippe LeMouel, a former colleague at RogueWaveSoftware, implemented IOStreams there and explained his implementation to us. So did Joe Delaney, who worked on RogueWave's implementation of locales. Dietmar Kühl worked on the implementation of IOStreams and locales for the gnu compiler and answered numerous questions. John Spicer of EdisonDesignGroup and Erwin Unruh of Siemens answered questions regarding templates and other language features. Beman Dawes, who maintains the library issue list for the standards committee, helped clarify countless open issues in the standard.

Thanks also to our reviewers, some of whom spent a considerable amount of effort and time compiling thorough and helpful comments: (in alphabetical order) Chuck Allison,

Stephen Clamage, Mary Dageforde, Amelia Lewis, Stan Lippman, Dietmar Kühl, Werner Mossner, and Patrick Thompson, as well as others who preferred to stay anonymous.

—Angelika Langer
Klaus Kreft

I would like to thank Bernd Eggink, author of a book about the classic IOStreams written in German. Our email correspondence about IOStreams spawned the idea of a joint book project on the standard IOStreams. The original idea had been to translate his book into English and upgrade to the standard, but his sudden, serious illness thwarted our plans.

I would like to thank Thomas Keffer, the founder of RogueWaveSoftware, for coming up with the idea of writing a book of my own and for supporting and encouraging me ever since. I had been working at his company when he suggested the book project. I was a German alien working at a U.S. corporation when he proposed that I write a book about internationalization in C++. I would like to thank Roland Hartinger, my former supervisor and head of the C++ compiler construction group at Siemens Nixdorf, who threw me into the library project and encouraged me to join the standards committee.

Last, but not least, I thank Klaus Kreft for joining me on this project. Without him this book would have never been finished, and not much is worth doing without him.

—Angelika Langer

First of all, I would like to thank my parents for recognizing and fostering my interest and talent in mathematics and natural sciences. Without their support I would not be who I am.

Next, I thank two individuals whom I met through my professional work who were true sources of inspiration and insight: Gerhard Draxler, whom I miss tremendously since he retired from his professional life, and Werner Mossner, with whom I had my first contact with IOStreams. Together we implemented a logging facility by derivation from the IOStreams classes.

Finally, I thank Angelika Langer, who is a constant source of ideas and an overwhelmingly persistent worker. Without her effort this book would not have been finished, yet the significance of her contribution is nothing compared to what she means to me in my private life.

—Klaus Kreft

CONTACT INFORMATION

If you would like to provide feedback on the book, report errors, ask questions, or if you just want to share your thoughts on IOStreams and locales with us, feel free to e-mail us at: langer@camelot.de.

GUIDE FOR READERS

ORGANIZATION OF THIS BOOK

This book on internationalization and stream input and output components from the C++ standard library consists of the following parts:

Users' Guide:

Part I: Stream Input and Output

Part II: Internationalization

Reference Guide

Appendices

Both the users' guide and the reference guide are organized in a way that allows lookup of information as needed. The users' guide is organized around topics, architectural concepts, and certain types of usage rather than discussing each class and interface one by one. For instance, in the users' guide you find sections such as Error Indication in IOStreams and Creation of Locale Objects. The reference guide, on the other hand, is organized in terms of classes and interfaces, with an entry for every header, class, function, and so forth.

ORGANIZATION OF THE USERS' GUIDE

Parts I and II each have the following sections:

- general introduction to the problem domain
- usage and description of the API

• architecture: structure, design concepts, and idioms of the component

• extending the framework

These are "virtual" sections. Each such section can consist of several subsections. Also, the section's titles differ from the abstract titles suggested above. For example, the usage and API description section in Part II on internationalization consists of two sections called Locales and Standard Facets, and the advanced usage section is called User-Defined Facets. The usage and API description in Part I on stream I/O consists of several subsections on format control, error indication, manipulators, and so on. However, the overall structure follows the pattern shown above.

The general introduction is for readers that are not at all familiar with the problem domain. The introduction to stream input and output is more concise than the one on internationalization because we assume that numerous readers are familiar with stream I/O, but that more information is needed on internationalization since it is unlikely that readers have expertise in this area.

Both IOStreams and locales can be seen in two ways:

1. They can serve as a foundation library that provides a number of ready-to-use interfaces.

2. They are also frameworks that can be customized and extended.

The section on usage focuses on the foundation library aspect. It describes the most common and straightforward ways of using the respective components' API. Each of the sections can in principle be read independently.

The section on architecture explains the "guts" of each component, that is, various aspects of the internal structure. In this section you will find class diagrams and discussions of interesting details and certain design issues. The section should be reviewed before reading the subsequent section on advanced usage and extending the component. You can also skip the entire section and return to certain subsections later once the information is needed for better understanding of the advanced usage section.

The section on advanced usage explores ways of extending the components and focuses on the framework aspect of each component. Again, the subsections can be read independently of each other. For demonstration of the techniques for extending IOStreams, we use the same example—namely, insertions and extraction of date objects—throughout several sections. To a minor extent, the later sections build on source code that was explained in the earlier sections. Still, for understanding the later sections it is not necessary to read all the preceding sections. There are cross references pointing to the relevant part of an earlier section, so that the reader can jump back and forth between sections as needed.

ORGANIZATION OF THE REFERENCE GUIDE

The reference guide is designed to allow lookup of function signatures and class interfaces. It is divided into five major sections:

1. locale

2. character traits

3. IOStreams

4. stream iterators

5. other I/O operations

Within each section there are the following entries:

• header files

• global type definitions

• global objects

• global functions

• one entry per class, in alphabetical order

More about the organization of the reference guide can be found in section R.0, Introduction, at the beginning of the reference guide itself.

CLASS DIAGRAMS

As notation for class diagrams we use the standard object modeling language UML. For those who are not familiar with the UML notation, here is a brief overview of the elements we use in this book.

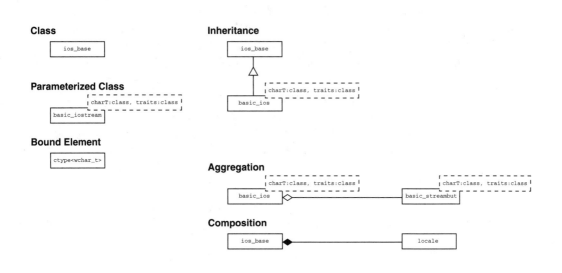

Translated to C++ terminology, these are:

class	=	class
parameterized class	=	class template
bound element	=	template class, i.e., an instantiation of a class template
inheritance	=	inheritance, i.e., "is a" relationship (no distinction between virtual and nonvirtual inheritance)
aggregation	=	reference or pointer to an object
composition	=	containment of an object, i.e., "has a" relationship

CODE EXAMPLES

Please note that the source code examples in this book might not compile in all development environments. At the time of this writing, scarcely any C++ compiler understands the full range of language features defined by the C++ standard. Neither does any compiler come with a complete standard-compliant C++ library.

We tried to compile the code examples in this book using Microsoft's MVC 6.0 compiler. As expected, some of our sample programs could not be compiled and tested successfully in this development environment. Despite this discouraging situation, we made our best effort to show you standard C++ programs as they are supposed to work under a standard-compliant C++ compiler.

While this is less than ideal, and we really wish that we could have verified all of our code examples, we still decided to include examples. The danger is that the sample code might not compile in your environment, because your compiler, like ours, does not comply with the standard yet. Another hazard is that minor mistakes might have sneaked into the code and stayed undetected. The safe alternative would have been to omit certain techniques entirely, because today they do not compile. However, we wanted to demonstrate the full range of techniques that standard C++ will support. Hence, this book is written with an eye to the standard C++ developments environments of the (hopefully near) future. Compilers and libraries will catch up, and techniques that do not work with your current compiler will work once you will have a true standard-compliant C++ compiler available. We feel that including these techniques contributes to the usefulness of this book.

All code examples are simplified. We did this to make the examples as concise and focused as possible, rather than endlessly repeating the same code fragments. Simplifications include:

- *Include statements*. The necessary `#include< ... >` statements for standard library header files are omitted. An overview of the header files can be found in this book's reference guide. You can find out which header files you have to include by looking up the item (object, class, function, type, etc.) in the reference guide; each entry has a section that mentions the required header file.

- *Standard namespace.* The entire standard C++ library resides inside the reserved global namespace std. For the sake of readability we generally omit the scope operator for the standard library namespace. Hence, instead of writing

```
::std::cout << "Hello world" << ::std::endl;
```

we simply write

```
cout << "Hello world" << endl;
```

It is common practice to insert a `using` statement at the beginning of each translation unit that uses standard library components, so that you can omit the namespace. Therefore, to make the latter line of source code compile one has to add the necessary `#include` statements as well as a `using` statement. The complete example would look like this:

```
#include <iostream>
using namespace ::std;
int main()
{
    cout << "Hello world" << endl;
    return 0;
}
```

- *Error handling.* IOStreams operations indicate failure by setting certain flags in the so-called stream state. Optionally, they can also throw exceptions in case of failure. In principle, it is advisable to check failure of operations by checking the stream state or catching exceptions. To keep examples in this book focused on the usage and functionality of the IOStreams operation under discussion, we omit the error handling in most examples. The exceptions are section 8, Input/Output of User-Defined Types, and section 9, Manipulators; they include extended and comprehensive source code examples, which among other aspects also demonstrate the proper use of error-checking strategies in IOStreams.

TERMINOLOGY

The standard C++ library consists mostly of class and function templates. In this book we use the following notations and abbreviations for class templates:

- Fully qualified class template names. An example is: `template <class charT, class Traits> class basic_fstream`

- A short form of class template name. The short form corresponding to the example above would be: `basic_fstream <class charT, class Traits>`

- Sometimes, if we intend to describe properties common among the class template and all its instantiations, we only use the class template's identifier. In the example above this would be: `basic_fstream`

- If we talk of instantiations of class templates for certain template arguments we use the following notation: `basic_fstream <char, char_traits<char> >`

In addition to abbreviations for class templates, you will find certain contrived technical terms. An example is *file stream*. It stands for the abstract notion of the file stream class template `basic_fstream <class charT, class Traits>` and its instantiations.

Also, we omit the class scope if it is unmistakable. An example would be `badbit` standing for `ios_base::badbit`. Another example is `facet`, which stands for `class locale::facet`, a class type nested into class locale.

The term *facet* is a hybrid one. It can also be used as a technical term designating all of the following:

- a class template, e.g., `template <class charT> class ctype`

- classes and class templates derived from such a class template, e.g., `ctype_byname<class charT>`

- the class template instantiation for a certain type, e.g., `ctype<char>`

- the instance of a class template instantiation, e.g., an object of type `ctype<char>`

Considering the context it will always be clear what the intended meaning is.

IMPLEMENTATION-SPECIFIC FEATURES

In many places throughout the book the term *implementation-specific* is used. It is a technical term from the ISO/ANSI standardization, which denotes features that are not standardized, but may differ between implementations of the standard C++ library. Each library implementor has to provide a list of these properties specific to his or her implementation of the standard C++ library.

An example of an implementation-specific feature is the type `streamsize` that is used in IOStreams. It is an implementation-specific integral type. This means that it can be an `int` in one implementation of the standard library and a `long` in another standard library. If you aim for portability of your programs, you should never rely on implementation-specific features. If in this example you take advantage of the knowledge that a `streamsize` object is an `int` in a particular implementation of the standard library, then your code will break once you port it to a standard library where a `streamsize` object is a `long`.

PART I

Stream Input and Output

INTRODUCTION

This part of the book explains *IOStreams,* the stream input and output component in the standard C++ library. In its chapters, we will repeatedly refer to part II of this book, which explains locales and facets, the means for internationalization in the standard C++ library. The reason for these references is that IOStreams have been internationalized using standard C++ locales and facets. We suggest either reading part II first or being prepared to look up the topics referenced in part II as needed.

Part I falls into three major categories:

Chapter 1, "IOStreams Basics," describes how features that are predefined in IOStreams can be used effectively. This is the most basic component of part I. It explains the formatting features of IOStreams in detail, including all format flags and predefined manipulators. It also shows how input and output can be written to files and in-memory locations, how I/O operations indicate errors, and how unformatted I/O can be done.

Chapter 2, "The Architecture of IOStreams," explains the underlying concepts of the IOStreams framework such as the class hierarchies, the transport layer with its stream buffer classes, special purpose features such as additional stream storage, stream callbacks, character types and traits, and stream and stream buffer iterators. This chapter provides information that is not used every day and is meant as preparation for chapter 3.

Chapter 3, "Advanced IOStreams Usage," discusses techniques for extending the IOStreams framework. It explains user-defined input and output operations, along with user-defined manipulators. The chapter also describes techniques for implementing extended stream and stream buffer classes.

CHAPTER 1

IOStreams Basics

1.1 Input and Output

This chapter introduces *IOStreams*, the stream input and output component of the ISO/ANSI standard C++ library. IOStreams has quite a history, since it was introduced along with the advent of the C++ programming language itself. The first C++ compilers that appeared in the marketplace were equipped with a small class library that, among other components, included I/O classes called *streams. IOStreams* came with C++ 2.0 in 1989. The ISO/ANSI standardization used this existing stream input and output component as a foundation for defining a new, improved, more powerful, and standardized stream component.

In this book we refer to the "new" IOStreams as the *standard IOStreams* and to the old IOStreams as the *classic IOStreams.*

The standard IOStreams component is mostly compatible with the classic IOStreams; the overall architecture is retained, as are the most commonly used interfaces. However, significant changes were introduced, the most obvious of which is the templatization of all IOStreams classes. If you are familiar with the classic IOStreams and interested in the differences between it and the standard IOStreams, see appendix E, "Differences Between the Classic and the Standard IOStreams"; it explains deviations and deprecated features in greater detail.

In this chapter we give you a first idea of stream input and output in C++, what IOStreams actually is, and what kinds of problems it helps to solve. If you are already familiar with the concept of C++ IOStreams, feel free to skip this chapter.

WHAT IS STREAM INPUT AND OUTPUT?

Generally, input and output are the transfer of data between a program and any kind of external device. Examples of external devices are files, communication channels, display windows, and so on.

The transport to and from an external device can be organized in different ways:

- *Stream I/O.* The transferred data can be seen as an unstructured stream of bytes, characters, or any other kind of small units of equal size. Input and output are conceptually seen as a stream of data flowing between the program and the external device. In this case we talk of stream I/O.

- *Record or block I/O.* Alternatively, a certain structure might be imposed on the transferred data, such as a record, block, or message structure. In that case, larger chunks of data, i.e., records, blocks, or messages, are transported. These chunks may also contain information additional to the actual data. For instance, if you read from an ISAM[1] file, you receive a data record that consists of the actual data plus a record identification. In such cases of structured I/O we talk of record or block I/O. The main difference from stream I/O is that input and output are structured and additional information is transported along with the actual data.

The standard C++ IOStreams, as the name already implies, supports stream I/O. This does not mean, however, that the actual external device may not have any structure, only that the concept of IOStreams is that of stream I/O, and that the specifics of the actual external device are hidden behind the IOStreams interfaces. For a user of IOStreams, input and output to and from an external device are streams of characters. Note that they are streams of characters, as opposed to streams of bits or bytes. This is because IOStreams facilitates text I/O.

So far we have seen *how* data are transported by IOStreams. We have not yet considered *what* kind of data are transported. What is the content of the transferred data? How is it represented?

In order to discuss the data representation in IOStreams, let us get back to the definition of input and output given above: Input and output are the transfer of data between a program and any kind of external device. The representation of data in a program and on an external device may differ. We distinguish between an *internal* and an *external* representation.

The *internal representation* of data is of a form that is convenient for data processing in a program. Common examples are the binary format of integral numbers, the IEEE representation of floating-point numbers, or the ASCII or Unicode encoding of a string.

The *external representation* varies depending on the type of device and the intended use of the data. Here are some examples:

---

1. ISAM stands for Index Sequential Access Method. ISAM files are record oriented, i.e., they are not streams.

- If the data are to be displayed on a screen or printout, the external representation is in a human-readable form as a sequence of characters.

- If the data are to be sent to other components in different system environments via a communication channel, they might be represented in a portable data exchange format. In this case the external data are not in human-readable form but are understandable to any recipient on the other end of a communication channel.

- If the data are to be stored on a storage device and it is important to conserve storage space, then a compressed data representation, which is also not in human-readable form, is appropriate.

Depending on the type of external representation, we distinguish between *text I/O* and *binary I/O*.

If the external data representation is a sequence of human-readable characters, we talk of *text I/O*. In all cases in which the external representation is different from a sequence of human-readable characters, we talk of *binary I/O*. The main purpose of the standard C++ IOStreams is to facilitate text I/O. Binary I/O is not directly supported.

In sum, the standard C++ IOStreams is designed as a means of stream input and output of text. IOStreams thus performs conversion between external data represented as a sequence of characters and an internal data representation. It also transports such character sequences as a coherent stream between the program and the external device.

THE STAGES OF STREAM TEXT I/O VIA IOSTREAMS

In IOStreams input and output involve four activities:

1. formatting/parsing
2. buffering
3. code conversion
4. transport

Formatting/parsing is the transformation between a byte sequence representing the internal data and a character sequence. Consider an integral number, for instance. It is represented as a sequence of bytes internally and is converted to a sequence of digit and sign characters for display externally. The diagram below shows an example:

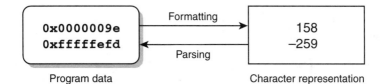

Program data   Character representation

Figure 1-1: Formatting/parsing is the conversion between an internal representation and a sequence of characters.

Buffering is the maintenance of character sequences between formatting/parsing and transport to/from the external device. For output, smaller character sequences are compiled into a buffer after formatting, until they are eventually transported to the external device as a larger block of data. Conversely, larger amounts of input are read from an external device, stored in a buffer, and made available for parsing in smaller portions. By default, input and output operations in IOStreams are buffered. However, buffering is optional and can be suppressed.

Code conversion is the process of translating one character representation into another. Code conversion is necessary if the character representation that results from formatting is different from the external character representation, or if the external representation differs from the representation that can be parsed by IOStreams. An example is the processing of multibyte text files. In that case the external representation of data on the file is as so-called multibyte characters. Multibyte characters have different sizes; some are represented as one byte, others as two or more bytes. This mix of sizes is inconvenient for internal data processing. For this reason, the internal representation is different; it is in an encoding where all characters are the same size, called wide characters. Hence, in the processing of multibyte text files the internal and the external character representation differ and a code conversion is needed. (See section 4.2.7, Character Encodings, for detailed explanations of character encodings and code conversions.)

Figure 1-2 shows an example of a code conversion from a multibyte character sequence read from a multibyte file into a wide-character sequence to be used internally. The conversion involves, among other tasks, blowing up one-byte characters like *J, a,* etc. to wide characters, and recognizing, interpreting, and eliminating control sequences like "<ESC> $ B".

Code conversion is not needed in most cases. Whenever the internal character representation matches the character representation on the external device, no conversion is performed.

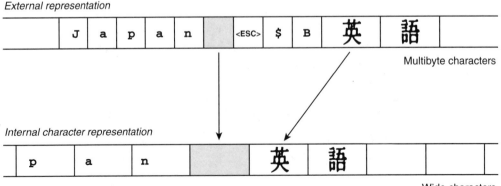

External representation

Multibyte characters

Internal character representation

Wide characters

Figure 1-2: Code conversion between multibytes and wide characters.

Transport involves access to the external device for reading and writing data. It manages the physical transfer of character sequences to the device after formatting, buffering, and code conversion, as well as extracting data from the device and making the received data available as a sequence of characters for subsequent code conversion, buffering, and parsing.

THE LAYERS OF IOSTREAMS

The IOStreams component has a layered architecture that consists of two layers (see figure 1-3): (1) *the formatting layer,* which handles the formatting and parsing, i.e., the transformation of data from an internal representation into a character representation; (2) *the transport layer,* which is responsible for buffering, code conversion, and transport of characters to and from an external device.

The *formatting layer* is responsible for the parsing of character sequences received as input read from an external device and for the formatting and production of a character sequence for output to an external device. Both transformations take various factors into account. Here are a couple of features involved in parsing and formatting in IOStreams:

- Skipping of whitespace characters in the input. For instance, when you read an integral number, you usually want to ignore leading blanks, because they are not relevant to the number's value.

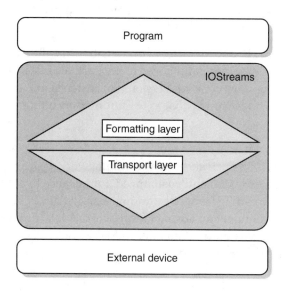

Figure 1-3: The layers of IOStreams.

- Field width for output. IOStreams is capable of inserting fill characters in order to adjust fields in the output.

- Precision and notation of floating-point numbers. You might want to control how many digits should be printed as fractional parts of a floating-point value.

- Hexadecimal, octal, or decimal representation of integers. IOStreams can produce and recognize integral values to various bases.

- Adapting of number formatting to local conventions. A number like 1,000,000 in the United States is represented as 1.000.000 in other countries. IOStreams has the ability to adjust its formatting and parsing of numerical values to local conventions.

The transport layer's main task is transporting character sequences to and from an external device. It encapsulates all the necessary knowledge about the properties of a specific external device. This knowledge can include several aspects:

- Access to the external device. Typically, a connection must be established before characters can be transported to and from an external device. For instance, the transport layer knows how to open and close files.

- Buffering. Transport of data to and from an external device might be most efficient when done in blocks of a certain size. The transport layer knows how to do block-wise output to files through system calls. In such a case the actual output is delayed, and character sequences received from the formatting layer are buffered until the block size is reached. Conversely, input from the external device is received in larger chunks and made available to the formatting layer, which requests smaller character sequences.

- Code conversion. If the character representation on the external device differs from the character representation used by the formatting layer, the transport layer performs the necessary code conversion. For instance, the transport layer knows how to convert wide-character codes to multibyte encodings.

STREAM CONCEPTS IN IOSTREAMS

In principle, IOStreams is an open and extensible framework. It defines a layered architecture. Both layers can be extended and customized, for instance by adding input and output operations to the formatting layer or by adding external devices to the transport layer. However, IOStreams is not only an abstract framework. A lot of concrete functionality is already provided by the Standard IOStreams and is ready for use. In particular, the following concepts are already supported:

- file streams and string streams

- narrow- and wide-character streams

FILE STREAMS AND STRING STREAMS. Files and strings are two categories of external devices. File I/O involves the transfer of data to and from an external device that conforms to the file abstraction. The device need not necessarily be a file in the usual sense of the word. It could just as well be a communication channel like sockets or pipes, or another device that exhibits a file-like behavior. In contrast, neither string I/O nor in-memory I/O involves an external device. The source and destination of in-memory I/O is a memory location in your program's storage space and can be retrieved in the form of a C++ string.

NARROW- AND WIDE-CHARACTER STREAMS. These two types of streams differ in the type of character sequence passed between the formatting and transport layers. In narrow-character streams the character sequences produced by the formatting layer and consumed by the transport layer are sequences of characters of type char, which is the built-in C++ character type. For instance, a unit of type char can hold a character literal like x, Ü, or \n; arrays of such narrow characters can hold string literals like Hello world\n. In wide-character streams the character sequences passed between the formatting and transport layers are arrays of units of type wchar_t, which is a type defined in C++ for storage of wide characters. For instance, a unit of type wchar_t can hold a character literal like L'A' or L'英'; arrays of such wide characters can hold string literals like L"Hello world\n" or L"します". Note that in C++, wide-character literals are prefixed with an uppercase L to distinguish them from narrow-character literals.

The concepts of external devices on the one hand and the character type used for streaming on the other hand are orthogonal, i.e., there are narrow and wide file streams as well as narrow and wide string streams. The concept of external devices is implemented by means of inheritance; the variation on the character type of a stream is achieved via templates. The next section gives an overview of classes and templates in IOStreams.

CLASSES IN IOSTREAMS

Here is a brief overview of the stream classes in IOStreams. There are two *stream base classes* that encapsulate information and functionality common to all stream classes. Class ios_base encapsulates all information that is independent of the character type handled by a stream. Class basic_ios is a class template taking the character type as a template argument.[2] It contains character-type dependent information common to all stream classes.

Then there are the *general input and output stream classes* that implement the concepts of input, output, and bidirectional I/O. They provide the entire functionality for parsing of input and formatting for output. However, they do not contain any information that is specific to the external device associated with the stream.

---

2. For the sake of brevity and simplicity, we omit the more "exotic" template parameters of the IOStreams classes in this introduction. Class basic_ios, like all class templates in the standard C++ library that take the character type as a template argument, has a second template parameter called traits, which is associated with the first template parameter. The traits type contains information about the character type, such as the end-of-file value or the way characters are compared or copied. A detailed discussion of the template parameters of the IOStreams classes is deferred until section 2.3, Character Types and Character Traits.

For each direction two derived classes implement the concepts of file and string I/O respectively. The *file stream classes* support input and output to and from files. They add functions for opening and closing files. The *string stream classes* support in-memory I/O, that is, reading and writing to a string held in memory. These classes add functions for getting and setting the string to be used as a buffer.

Figure 1-4 shows the class hierarchy of all stream classes and their base classes.

Almost all classes are template classes, parameterized on the character type and a related traits type.[3] Instances of these class templates are provided for the character types `char` and `wchar_t`; they represent narrow and wide character streams. Additionally, for convenience and for compatibility to the classic IOStreams, there are type definitions for those instantiations. Here are some examples:

narrow-character file streams:

```
typedef basic_ifstream<char> ifstream;
typedef basic_ofstream<char> ofstream;
typedef basic_fstream<char>  fstream;
```

wide-character file streams:

```
typedef basic_ifstream<wchar_t> wifstream;
typedef basic_ofstream<wchar_t> wofstream;
typedef basic_fstream<wchar_t>  wfstream;
```

There are equivalent type definitions for string streams and all other streams classes in IOStreams.

IOSTREAMS AS A FRAMEWORK

IOStreams is not only a set of ready-to-use classes, like `fstream` or `stringstream`. You can also think of the Standard IOStreams as a framework that is intended to be customized and extended. Just to give you an idea of the power of this framework, here is a list of means for extending the Standard IOStreams. We will explore them in greater detail later in this book (in section 3, Advanced IOStreams Usage).

- You can add input and output operations for user-defined types. IOStreams already provides input and output operations for all built-in types and many types in the Standard C++ Library. Still, you can add operations for types you defined for your application. We discuss techniques for building such I/O operations in section 3.1, Input and Output of User-Defined Types.

- You can add new concepts for transport, i.e., new categories of external devices, such as communication channels in a network or display fields in a graphical user

---

3. The `traits` template parameter is a type that contains information about the character type `charT`. See section 2.3, Character Types and Character Traits, for details on the template parameters of IOStreams classes. All IOStreams classes define a default for the traits template parameter; hence the traits argument can usually be omitted.

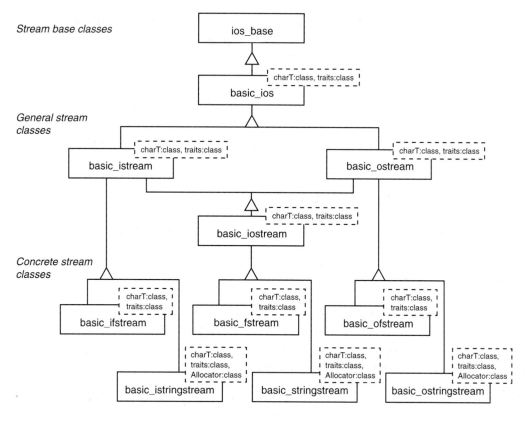

Figure 1-4: *The Stream Classes.*

interface. IOStreams supports I/O to files and strings. Other concepts may be added. We discuss this in section 3.4, Adding Stream Buffer Functionality.

- The IOStreams classes are templatized on the character type. IOStreams already facilitates narrow- and wide-character streams by provided instantiations for the built-in character types char and wchar_t. However, you can instantiate the standard IOStreams classes for user-defined character types. An example of a user-defined type could be a type Jchar for Japanese characters that contains additional information about each character. More information about user-defined character types in IOStreams can be found in section 2.3.3, Character Types.

- Localization and code conversion are factored out into separate abstractions called *locales*.[4] Locale objects are attached to streams and used by IOStreams' input and

---

4. See part II for further information on class locale.

output operations for adapting their behavior to cultural conventions. Locales can be replaced, and as a result the I/O operations exhibit an adjusted behavior. Also, locales can be extended by adding new categories of information about cultural dependencies. An example of such an addition would be information about time zones or rules for address formats. You can attach extended locales to streams, and you can add I/O operations that use this additional culture-dependent information to adapt their behavior. For instance, you can add operations for culture-dependent formatting of an `address` data type. Techniques for extending locales and IOStreams in this way are explained in part II.

1.2 Formatted Input/Output

This section describes the parsing and formatting facilities of IOStreams. We begin with an introduction to global streams that are predefined in IOStreams. Then we move on to simple input and output using IOStreams' I/O operators before we explore in detail how to control parsing and formatting.

1.2.1 The Predefined Global Streams

There are eight predefined global stream objects, which are automatically created and initialized at program start.[5] These global stream objects are associated with the C standard files `stdin`, `stdout`, and `stderr`, as shown in table 1-1.

Table 1-1: Predefined Global Streams with Their Associated C Standard Files

NARROW-CHARACTER STREAM	WIDE-CHARACTER STREAM	ASSOCIATED C STANDARD FILES
cin	wcin	stdin
cout	wcout	stdout
cerr	wcerr	stderr
clog	wclog	stderr

Like the C standard files, these streams are all associated by default with the terminal.

The predefined streams have certain special behaviors. Details can be found in section 1.8.2, Synchronizing the Predefined Standard Streams. Here are the most important features:

- `cin` is "tied" to `cout`. This means that whenever input is requested from `cin`, `cout` is first flushed, i.e., `cout` writes output to the external device before any input operation on `cin`.

---

5. Like all other abstractions from the IOStreams, the global streams reside in the namespace `std`.

- Both `cerr` and `clog` are associated with `stderr`. The difference between `clog` and `cerr` lies in their synchronization with the associated external device. Output to `cerr` is written to the external device immediately after formatting, i.e., `cerr`'s buffer is flushed after each output operation. Flushing of `clog`'s buffer either has to be explicitly invoked or happens automatically, depending on the internal buffering mechanism.

- `cerr` and `clog` are used for different purposes: `cerr` is preferred for error output to the terminal; `clog` is typically used for error output that is redirected to a file.

- The wide-character counterparts `wclog` and `wcerr` have the same buffering characteristics.

- The predefined global streams are by default synchronized with their associated C standard files. This means, for instance, that you can write output to the same C standard file, say `stdout`, via C stdio functions like `printf()` and via IOStreams output operations to `cout`. Although you mix output operation from the C and the C++ library, the output is not garbled, but appears in the order in which the respective instructions were executed.

1.2.2 The Input and Output Operators

The IOStreams component defines shift operators for formatted stream input and output. The output operator is the shift operator `operator<<()`, also called the *inserter*. It writes text to an output stream.[6] Here is an example:

```
cout << "result: " << x << '\n';7
```

A possible output is (under the assumption that x is a variable of an integral type and contains the value 10):

```
result: 10
```

Input is done through the other shift operator `operator>>()`, often referred to as the *extractor*. It reads text from an input stream. Here is an example of how this is done:

```
cin >> x >> y;
```

---

6. All examples in this section are restricted to the use of predefined global streams. This is because we defer the discussion of creating other stream objects to subsequent sections: section 1.4, File Input/Output, and section 1.5, In-Memory Input/Output.

7. Note that code examples in this book are simplified: Both the necessary `#include` statements and the `using` statement for the standard library namespace `::std` are omitted. See the Guide for Readers for more information.

The two variables x and y are filled with valid values of their respective type, if the input extracted from the stream can be parsed according to the rules for those types. For instance, if x is a variable of a type `int` and the input is a sequence of digits, the variable x is filled with the integral value that is equivalent to the extracted sequence of digits.

OPERATORS VERSUS FUNCTIONS

Operators were chosen for input and output operations to avoid the verbosity that would have resulted from using input or output *functions* instead. Imagine IOStreams had a `put()` function for output instead of the shift operator. Compare the following:

```
put(cerr, "x = ");
put(cerr,x);
put(cerr, '\n');
```

to

```
cerr << "x = " << x << '\n';
```

The latter is more compact, because the shift operators permit the printing of several units in one expression. Source code like the line above is also more readable, because one line of output inserted to the stream corresponds to one line of source code in the program.

Among operators that can be overloaded in C++ the operators << and >> were chosen because their precedence is low enough to allow arithmetic expressions as operands without using parentheses. You can, for example, write

```
cout << "a*b+c=" << a*b+c << '\n';
```

without a need for parentheses around the arithmetic expression `a*b+c`. Still, parentheses must be used to write expressions containing operators of lower precedence, such as bit operations, for instance:

```
cout << "a^b|c=" << (a^b|c) << '\n';
```

CONCATENATION OF SHIFT OPERATORS

All the above examples demonstrate that it is possible to print several units in one expression. For example, we have seen that the following statement is permitted:

```
cout << "result: " << x;
```

It is equivalent to the following:

```
(cout.operator<<("result: ")).operator<<(x);
```

The concise notation is possible thanks to the use of operators as input/output operations instead of functions. Another prerequisite for the concatenation of the shift operators is that each operator return a reference to the respective stream. In the example above, the subexpression `cout << "result: "` is equivalent to `cout.operator<< ("result: ")`, i.e., it invokes the inserter for C strings. This inserter, `operator<<(const char*)`, returns a reference to the stream it was invoked on, in this case `cout`. Hence, the subexpression `cout << "result: "` evaluates to a reference to `cout`. Consequently, the whole expression `cout << "result: " << x` is equivalent to `cout << x` after evaluation of the first subexpression. The remaining subexpression `cout << x` again results in a call to an inserter, which also returns a reference to `cout`. Thanks to the convention that all shift operators return a reference to the stream object they were invoked on, concatenation of I/O operation is possible.

OVERLOADED SHIFT OPERATORS

Note also that the shift operator is overloaded. In the example above we invoked the version of `operator<<()` for C strings and the version for integral numbers. IOStreams provides shift operators for all built-in types in C++, as well as for some of the types defined in the standard C++ library. Here are some examples:

```
cout << int(10) << '\n';
cout << complex<float>(1.0,2.5) << '\n';
cout << bool(false) << '\n';
cout << string("Hello world\n") << '\n';
cout << "Hello world\n" << '\n';
```

There are inserters and extractors for `bool`, `char`, `int`, `long`, `float`, `double`, C strings, C++ strings, complex numbers, etc. You can also add shift operators for user-defined types (see section 3, Advanced IOStreams Usage, for details). When you insert or extract a value to or from a stream, the C++ function overload resolution chooses the appropriate operator, based on the value's type. This makes C++ IOStreams type-safe and superior to C stdio, where you can produce unpredictable results by mismatching format specifier and value type, as in

```
printf("%d %s \n","Hello world\n", 10);
```

which can result in a program crash.

FORMAT CONTROL

Simple input and output of data as shown in the examples above are useful, yet insufficient in many cases. For example, others ways of formatting output or parsing input may be needed. IOStreams allows control over many features of its input and output operators, for example:

- the width of an output field and the adjustment of the output within this field

- the precision and format of floating point numbers, and whether or not the decimal point should always be included

- whether you want to skip whitespace when reading from an input stream

- whether integral output values are displayed in decimal, octal, or hexadecimal format

Contained in each stream are a number of *format parameters* that control such details of formatting and parsing. The following sections discuss format parameters; format flags, which are predefined values to be stored in a format parameter variable; and manipulators, which provide convenient access to the format parameters.

1.2.3 The Format Parameters of a Stream

Format parameters are data members of a stream that store information for controlling the details of formatting and parsing. Format parameters are defined as private data members of one of the stream's base classes, either `ios_base` or `basic_ios<charT,Traits>`. The types of these data members differ.

The majority are of type `ios_base::fmtflags`, which is a nested type defined in class `ios_base`. The type `fmtflags` is a bitmask type (see section G.1, Bitmask Types, in appendix G). Those format parameters that can take numeric values are of type `streamsize`, which is an implementation-specific[8] global type.

Those that take values of the stream's character type form yet another category of format parameters; they are of type `basic_ios<charT,Traits>::char_type`, which is a synonym for the first template argument `charT`.

Some format parameters can have an *arbitrary value*, others can vary according to a *predefined set of values*. Both categories of format parameters differ in the way they are set and retrieved.

FORMAT PARAMETERS WITH AN ARBITRARY VALUE

The value of a format parameter is stored as a private data member in one of the base classes, and it is set and retrieved through public member functions inherited from that base class. There are three such parameters, described in table 1-2.

The first three columns list the access function used to set or get a particular parameter's current value, the return and parameter type of that function, and the base class that defines the access function.

Each access function is overloaded. There is a version without a parameter for retrieval of the current parameter value; the version that takes a parameter is for setting the value.

---

8. *Implementation-specific* means that a feature is not standardized but may differ between implementations of the standard C++ library.

The remaining columns, Effect and Default, show the purpose and effect of the format parameter and list the default value, which is used if you do not explicitly set the flag.

Table 1-2: Format Parameters with Arbitrary Values

ACCESS FUNCTION	ARGUMENT AND RETURN TYPE	DEFINED IN BASE CLASS	EFFECT	DEFAULT
width()	streamsize	ios_base	Minimal field width	0
precision()	streamsize	ios_base	Precision of floating-point values	6
fill()	basic_ios <charT, Traits> ::char_type	basic_ios <charT, Traits>	Fill character for padding	The space character

Here are some examples showing how to use the access functions:

You can set the field width by calling

```
cout.width(10);
```

You can retrieve the current field width setting by

```
streamsize wid = cout.width();
```

You can set the fill character by calling

```
cout.fill('.');
```

You can retrieve the current fill character setting by

```
char fll = cout.fill();
```

FORMAT PARAMETERS WITH A PREDEFINED SET OF VALUES

Parameters with a predefined set of values are stored in a data member of class ios_base; the data member is of type ios_base::fmtflags, which is a bitmask type (see also section G.1, Bitmask Types, in appendix G). Associated with a bitmask type is a set of predefined values, each of which represents the abstraction of a *bit* or *flag* (the two terms are synonymous in this context). Such a bit can be set or cleared or tested. Combinations of bits are valid values that can be stored in an object of the bitmask type.

The bits associated with the bitmask type fmtflags are usually called *format flags*. They are listed in table 1-3. You can set format flags using the setf() function. You can clear bits using unsetf(), and you can retrieve them through the flags() function. These functions are member functions defined in class ios_base. Here are some examples of their usage:

You can set the `boolalpha` flag, which controls alphabetic representation of `bool` values, by calling

```
cout.setf(ios_base::boolalpha);
```

You can retrieve the current setting of the `boolalpha` flag by saying

```
bool boolalpha_set = cout.flags() & ios_base::boolalpha;
```

You can remove the `boolalpha` flag from the current format flag setting by saying

```
cout.unsetf(ios_base::boolalpha);
```

BIT GROUPS

Some format flags are mutually exclusive; for example, output within an output field can be adjusted to the left or to the right, or to an internally specified adjustment. Only one of the corresponding three format flags—`left`, `right`, or `internal`—can be set.[9] If you want to set one of these bits, you need to clear the other two bits. To make this easier, there are *bit groups* defined whose main function is to reset all bits in one group. A bit group is the combination of all valid flags that mutually exclude each other. For instance, the bit group for adjustment in an output field is `adjustfield`; it is defined as `left | right | internal`. The operation *bitfield &= ~bitgroup;* clears all flags in the bit field. Hence the operation *bitfield = (bitfield & ~bitgroup) | (flag & bitgroup);* clears all flags and then sets one particular flag only. Those bit operations that are necessary for setting mutually exclusive flags are encapsulated into the `setf()` function. You do not have to perform them manually. Instead, there is an overloaded version of the `setf()` function. We have seen the one-argument version of `setf()` before. In addition to the format flag, the overloaded version takes the corresponding bit group as an argument. It clears all format flags belonging to the bit group and sets the specified format flag, basically performing the bit operations described above.

Here is an example: You can set the `right` adjustment flag and clear all other flags in that bit group by calling

```
cout.setf(ios_base::right, ios_base::adjustfield);
```

LIST OF FORMATTING FLAGS

Table 1-3 gives an overview of all format flags and their effect on input and output operators.[10]

---

9. IOStreams does not prevent you from setting other, invalid combinations of these flags, however. Use of illegal combinations results in undefined behavior of the program.

10. For details on how the format flags affect input and output operations, look up `ios_base` in the reference section and in appendices A and B.

The Group column lists the name of the group for flags that are mutually exclusive. The groups are defined in class `ios_base` too.

The second column, Format flag, lists the flag names. All values are defined in class `ios_base`. The class scope is omitted, e.g., `showpos` stands for `ios_base::showpos`.

The third column, Effect, gives a brief description of the effect of setting the flag.

The last column, Default, lists the setting that is used if you do not explicitly set the flag.

Table 1-3: Format Flags and Their Effects on Operators

GROUP	FORMAT FLAG	EFFECT	DEFAULT
adjustfield		Adds fill characters to certain generated output for adjustment:	right[11]
	left	left	
	right	right	
	internal	Adds fill characters at designated internal point.	
basefield		Converts integer input or generates integer output in	dec
	dec	decimal base	
	oct	octal base	
	hex	hexadecimal base	
floatfield		Generates floating-point output in	not set[12]
	fixed	fixed-point notation	
	scientific	scientific notation	
	boolalpha	Inserts and extracts `bool` values in alphabetic rather than numeric format.	not set
	showpos	Generates a + sign in non-negative numeric output.	not set
	showpoint	Always generates a radix separator in floating-point output.	not set
	showbase	Generates a prefix indicating the numeric base of a generated integer output.	not set
	skipws	Skips leading whitespace before certain input operations.	set
	unitbuf	Flushes output after each formatting operation.	not set[13]
	uppercase	Uses uppercase letters where letters are generated during numeric formatting.	not set

---

11. The `adjustfield` does not have a default value, but if none of the flags `right`, `left`, or `internal` is set, all predefined inserters behave as though the `adjustfield` were set to `right`.

12. If none of the `floatfield` flags is set, the formatting depends on the value that is to be formatted: Scientific notation is produced if the exponent is less than −4 or greater than or equal to the precision; otherwise, the result is in fixed-point notation. Details regarding the formatting of floating-point values can be found in appendix B.

13. For the predefined standard stream `cerr`, the `unitbuf` format flag is set by default. For other streams, it is not set.

EXAMPLE: USE OF FORMATTING FLAGS

The example below shows how you can control formatting by using some of the parameters. We retrieve the current format flag setting, modify the setting, do some output under the new setting, and eventually restore the original setting.

```
ios_base::fmtflags original_flags = cout.flags();

cout<< 812 <<'|';
cout.setf(ios_base::left,ios_base::adjustfield);
cout.width(10);
cout<< 813 << 815 << '\n';

cout.unsetf(ios_base::adjustfield);
streamsize original_precision = cout.precision(2);
cout.setf(ios_base::uppercase|ios_base::scientific);
cout << 831.0 << ' ' << 8e2;

cout.flags(original_flags);
cout.precision(original_precision);
```

First we retrieve the current format flag setting via the stream's `flags()` function, in order to restore the original setting later on.

After output of 812 and '|' we modify the setting: We set the adjustment to `left`, which means that padding characters will be inserted after the actual output. Also, we set the field width from its default 0 to 10. (A field width of 0 means that no padding characters are inserted, and this is the default behavior of all insertions.) The effect of these settings can be seen in the resulting output:

```
812|813        815
```

No padding characters are inserted after 812 and '|', because the field width was 0 at the time of this output. 813 is written after the modification of adjustment and field width. Hence, padding characters are inserted after 813 so that the field width of 10 is reached.

Then we clear the adjustment flags and change the precision for floating-point values from its default 6 to 2. Also, we set some format flags that affect the formatting of floating-point values (`ios_base::uppercase` and `ios_base::scientific`). The resulting output is

```
8.31E+02 8.00E+02
```

Eventually we restore the original flags by calling the `flags()` function again.

PECULIARITIES OF THE FIELD WIDTH

The effect of setting a format parameter is usually permanent; that is, the parameter setting is in effect until the setting is explicitly changed. The only exception to this rule is the field width, which is automatically reset to its default value 0 after each input or output operation *that uses the field width.* Such operations fall into two categories:

All inserters. All output operators provided by IOStreams use the field width and hence reset the width after output.

String extractors. Among input operators only those for strings (both C and C++ strings) use the field width and reset it after input. All other extractors neither use nor reset the field width; they extract as many characters as belong to the item.

Here are examples that demonstrate that the extractor for integers does not reset the field width, whereas the inserter for integers does. Consider the following program fragment in which characters are extracted from an input device:

```
// input
int i; string s;

cin.width(10);
cin >> i >> s;
```

If the input sequence is

```
12345 abcdefghijklmnopqrstuvwxyz
```

the program extracts the 5 digits and places the value 12345 into the integer variable i; it then skips the separating whitespace character; and it subsequently extracts another 10 characters, namely abcdefghij, and places them into the character array s followed by the end-of-string character '\0'. Hence the result would be

```
i: 12345
```

and

```
s: "abcdefghij"
```

Let us see how and why it happens this way. Extracting an integer is independent of the specified field width. The extractor for integers always reads as many digits as belong to the integer. As extraction of integers does not use the field width setting, the field width of 10 is still in effect after evaluation of the subexpression cin >> i. When a character sequence is subsequently extracted, only 10 characters will be extracted in this case, because the field width setting is still in effect. After the extraction of the character sequence, however, the field width is reset to 0. This is because the extractor for C strings uses the field width setting and resets it after use.

In contrast to the extractor for integers, the inserter for integers uses the field width and resets it. To understand the difference, let us consider the following program fragment in which characters are inserted to an output device:

```
// output
int i; char s[11];

cout.width(10);
cout.fill ('.');
cout <<i << s;
```

If the variables i and s have the following values

```
i: 123
```

and

```
s: "abc"
```

then the output is

```
.......123abc
```

that is, seven dots followed by the three digits representing the value of i, followed by the character sequence contained in s.

This is because the inserter for integers uses the specified field width and fills the field with padding characters if the integral value has less than ten digits. As the inserter uses the field width setting, it resets the field width to 0. Hence, after evaluation of the subexpression cout <<i, the field width is reset. (Note the difference: On input the field width setting was still in effect after extraction of the integer.) Hence the subsequent insertion of the string s will not fill the field with padding characters for a string of less than ten characters.

1.2.4 Manipulators

Format control requires calling a stream's member functions. Each such call interrupts the respective shift expression. But what if you want to change formats within a shift expression? This is possible in IOStreams. Instead of writing

```
cout.setf(ios_base::left,ios_base::adjustfield);
cout << 813;
```

you can write

```
cout << left << 813;
```

In this example, an expression like `left` is called a *manipulator*. You can think of a manipulator as an object you can insert into or extract from a stream, in order to manipulate that stream.

THE EFFECT OF MANIPULATORS

Most manipulators set just one of the format flags described in section 1.2.3, The Format Parameters of a Stream, or do some other kind of stream manipulation. The `left` manipulator used in the code snippet above is an example of such a manipulator. Nothing is inserted into the stream. The only effect is that the format flag for adjusting the output to the left is set.

Other manipulators really insert or extract items into or out of a stream. For instance, the manipulator `endl` inserts the new-line character to the stream and flushes the underlying stream buffer. The expression

```
cout << endl;
```

is equivalent to

```
cout << '\n'; cout.flush();
```

Some manipulators also take arguments, like `setw(int)`. The `setw` manipulator sets the field width. The expression

```
cout << setw(10);
```

is equivalent to

```
cout.width(10);
```

LIST OF MANIPULATORS

Table 1-4 gives an overview of all manipulators defined by IOStreams. Further details about the standard manipulators can be found in this book's reference guide. The information, however, is spread over several entries in the reference guide, because manipulators with and without arguments are implemented in different ways. (Section 3.2, User-Defined Manipulators, explains these differences in greater detail, describes how manipulators work, and shows how you can implement your own manipulators.)

Manipulators *with arguments* construct an object of a class derived from the implementation-specific type `smanip`. These manipulators are listed under a special entry: *manipulators*.

Manipulators *without* arguments take and return a reference either to class `ios_base`, class `basic_istream <charT, traits>`, or class `basic_ostream <charT, traits>`. Because they are so closely coupled to one of the classes, they are described under the entry of the corresponding class.

Table 1-4, which describes manipulators in IOStreams, has the following entries:

The first column, Manipulator, lists its name. As usual, we omit the scope operator for the namespace `::std`.

The second column, Affects, indicates whether the manipulator is intended to be used with istreams (`i`), ostreams (`o`), or both (`io`).

The third column, Purpose, summarizes the effect of the manipulator.

The fourth column, Equivalent, lists the corresponding call to the stream's member function.

The last column, Ref, indicates where further information can be found in the reference guide:

```
O       = basic_ostream <charT,traits>,
I       = basic_istream <charT,traits>,
B       = ios_base,
M       = manipulators.
```

Table 1-4: Manipulators

MANIPULATOR	AFFECTS	PURPOSE	EQUIVALENT	REF
flush	o	Flushes stream buffer.	`o.flush()`	O
endl	o	Inserts newline and flushes buffer.	`o.put(o.widen('\n'));` `o.flush()`	O
ends	o	Inserts end-of-string character.	`o.put(o.widen('\0'))`	O
ws	i	Extracts whitespaces.		I
boolalpha	io	Sets flags for input/output of `bool` values in alphabetic format.	`io.setf` `(ios_base::boolalpha)`	B
noboolalpha	io	Resets the above.	`io.unsetf` `(ios_base::boolalpha)`	B
showbase	o	Sets flags for generation of a prefix indicating the numeric base of an integer.	`o.setf` `(ios_base::showbase)`	B
noshowbase	o	Resets the above.	`o.unsetf` `(ios_base::showbase)`	B
showpoint	o	Sets flags for always generating a radix separator for floating-point values.	`o.setf` `(ios_base::showpoint)`	B
noshowpoint	o	Resets the above.	`o.unsetf` `(ios_base::showpoint)`	B
showpos	o	Sets flags for generation of a + sign for non-negative numeric values.	`o.setf` `(ios_base::showpos)`	B
noshowpos	o	Resets the above.	`o.unsetf` `(ios_base::showpos)`	B
skipws	i	Sets flag for skipping of leading whitespace.	`i.setf` `(ios_base::skipws)`	B

Table 1-4: Manipulators (*continued*)

MANIPULATOR	AFFECTS	PURPOSE	EQUIVALENT	REF
noskipws	i	Resets the above.	i.unsetf (ios_base::skipws)	B
uppercase	o	Sets flag for use of uppercase letters where letters are generated during numeric formatting.	o.setf (ios_base::uppercase)	B
nouppercase	o	Resets the above.	o.unsetf (ios_base::uppercase)	B
unitbuf	o	Sets flags for flushing output after each formatting operation.	o.setf (ios_base::unitbuf)	B
nounitbuf	o	Resets the above.	o.unsetf (ios_base::unitbuf)	B
internal	o	Sets flags for adding fill characters at a designated internal point.	o.setf (ios_base::internal, ios_base::adjustfield)	B
left	o	Sets flags for adding fill characters for adjustment to the left.	o.setf(ios_base::left, ios_base::adjustfield)	B
right	o	Sets flags for adding fill characters for adjustment to the right.	o.setf(ios_base::right, ios_base::adjustfield)	B
dec	io	Sets flags for converting integers to/from decimal notation.	io.setf(ios_base::dec, ios_base::basefield)	B
hex	io	Sets flags for converting integers to/from hexadecimal notation.	io.setf(ios_base::hex, ios_base::basefield)	B
oct	io	Sets flags for converting to/from octal notation.	io.setf(ios_base::oct, ios_base::basefield)	B
fixed	o	Sets flags for formatting of floating point values in fixed-point notation.	o.setf (ios_base::fixed, ios_base::floatfield)	B
scientific	o	Sets flags for formatting of floating-point values in scientific notation.	o.setf (ios_base::scientific, ios_base::floatfield)	B
setiosflags (ios_base:: fmtflags mask)	io	Sets format flags according to mask.	io.setf(mask)	M
resetiosflags (ios_base:: fmtflags mask)	io	Clears format flags according to mask.	io.setf ((ios_base::fmtflags)0, mask)	M
setbase (int base)	io	Sets base for integer notation (base = 8, 10, 16).	io.setf (base == 8 ? ios_base::oct : base == 10 ? ios_base::dec : base == 16 ? ios_base::hex : ios_base::fmtflags(0) , ios_base::basefield)	M

continued

Table 1-4: Manipulators (*continued*)

MANIPULATOR	AFFECTS	PURPOSE	EQUIVALENT	REF
setfill (charT c)	io	Sets fill character for padding.	io.fill(c)	M
setprecision (int n)	o	Sets precision of floating-point values.	io.precision(n)	M
setw(int n)	io[14]	Sets minimal field width.	io.width(n)	M

EFFECT ON BIDIRECTIONAL STREAMS

Note that the second column indicates only the *intended* use of a manipulator. In many cases it is possible to apply an output manipulator to an input stream, and vice versa. Generally, this kind of unintended manipulation is harmless because it has no effect. For instance, if you apply the output manipulator showpoint to an input stream, the format parameter setting will simply be ignored. However, if you use an output manipulator on a bidirectional stream during input, the manipulation will not affect current input operations but *will* affect subsequent output operations.

REMARK ON THE MANIPULATOR endl

The manipulator endl is often used for inserting the end-of-line character into a stream. However, endl additionally flushes the output stream. Flushing a stream is a time-consuming operation that decreases performance, and it is unnecessary in most common situations. In the standard example

```
cout << "Hello world" << endl;
```

flushing is not necessary, because the standard output stream cout is *tied*[15] to the standard input stream cin, which means that input and output to the standard streams are synchronized anyway. Since no flush is required, the intent is probably to insert the end-of-line character. If you consider typing '\n' more trouble than typing endl, you can easily add a simple manipulator nl that inserts the end-of-line character but refrains from flushing the stream.[16]

MANIPULATORS AND STREAM STATE

It is a convention among operations in IOStreams that they shall have no effect if the stream is not in working order. Section 1.3, The Stream State, explains what is meant by a

---

14. The field width controls input and output. However, on input it is relevant only for extraction of strings (see section 1.2.7, Peculiarities of Formatted Input) and is otherwise ignored.

15. See section 1.8.1.3, Synchronization by Tying Streams, for further details.

16. See section 3.2, User-Defined Manipulators, to learn how you can define such a manipulator.

stream in "working order." Note that some of the manipulators conform to this rule; others do not. The `endl` manipulator, for instance, has no effect on out-of-order streams. Manipulators that set format flags like `setw`, `setprecision`, etc., do have an effect: They set the respective format parameter whether the stream is in working order or not.[17]

1.2.5 The Locale of a Stream

In the previous sections we saw how formatting can be controlled by manipulating a stream's format state. The other mechanism that has an impact on formatting is localization through a stream's locale.

Cultural conventions influence the formatting of numeric values. In particular, the *radix separator character,* sometimes also called the *decimal point,* varies among cultures. A period is used in the United States, for instance, but a comma is used in most of Europe. Hence, the equivalent to the U.S. notation 19.99 would be 19,99 in Germany. The grouping of digits and the group separator character, also called the *thousands separator,* depend on cultural conventions as well. For instance, the equivalent of 1,000,000 in the United States is 1.000.000 in Germany and 10,00,000 in Nepal.

Cultural dependencies like the ones mentioned above are factored out into a separate object, a so-called *locale.* (See part II for further information on locales.) A locale is a container of so-called *facets.* A facet encapsulates information about related local conventions together with a set of services for adapting to those conventions. Each locale contains, for instance, numeric facets that handle parsing and formatting of numbers in the way outlined above. They contain information about the radix character, the grouping rules, the thousands separator, etc.

Each stream has such a locale object attached. The stream's input and output operations relay the task of formatting and parsing numbers to the numeric facets of the locale that is attached to the stream.

The source snippet below shows an example of adapting the output of numbers to German formatting rules. The stream classes have a member function `imbue()` for attaching a locale. In the example below, a German locale, whose name is `German_Germany`, is attached:

```
cout.imbue(locale("German_Germany"));
cout << 19.99 << '\t' << fixed << 1000000 << endl;
```

The resulting output is

```
19,99   1.000.000
```

Naturally, the radix character is relevant to the formatting and parsing of floating-point numbers, because floating-point numbers usually have a fractional part.

---

17. Section 3.2.2.4.1, Manipulator Base Template with Error Handling, explains the reason for this.

The thousands separator, on the other hand, is relevant only for integral values.[18] You cannot produce output of a floating-point number that contains thousands separators, i.e., there is no such output as 1,000,000.50.

1.2.6 Comparison Between Formatted Input and Output

There is a significant difference between input and output in principle. For output you control the precise format of the inserted character sequence, whereas for input the rules for extracting a value are more relaxed. This is for practical reasons. You may, for example, want to extract the next floating-point value from a stream, no matter what its exact format is. You want it whether it is signed or not, or in exponential notation with a small or capital *E* for the exponent, etc. All of the following character sequences—"+1.5E+000" or "+1.5" or "1.50" or "0.15e+1"—shall be recognized as the floating-point value 1.5. For this reason, extractors accept an item in any format permitted for its type. In contrast, an item to be formatted and inserted is described unambiguously by the various format parameter settings.

Input and output operators also have things in common. Certain format parameters influence both parsing and formatting. For instance, if you set the boolalpha flag for alphabetical format of bool values, then input and output operations handle Boolean values in their alphabetical form.

Parsing and formatting also always obey the rules specified by the locale attached to the stream. For instance, the bool value false is inserted as the character sequence "falsch" if the boolalpha format flag is set and a German locale is attached to the stream. The extractor exhibits symmetric behavior: It does not recognize the character sequence "falsch" as the bool value false, once the attached locale is not a German one or the boolalpha flag is not set.

The precise rules for parsing and formatting are described in appendices A and B.

1.2.7 Peculiarities of Formatted Input

This section discusses issues specific to input, namely:

Skipping of characters. Preceding whitespace characters are skipped by default when input is parsed. This automatic skipping can be suppressed. Also, there are means for explicitly ignoring *any kind* of characters on input.

Input of strings. The extraction of strings differs from the extraction of other types of items. Also, there are subtle differences between extraction of a C string and of a C++ string.

Both issues are discussed in greater detail below.

WHITESPACE SKIPPING

All extractors by default ignore whitespace characters that precede the item to be extracted. Imagine that an input sequence contained " \t46sec", and we read an inte-

---

18. Numerous formatting options can be switched on and off by setting or clearing corresponding format flags. However, the insertion of thousands separators to integral values cannot be suppressed once the locale specifies rules for thousands grouping.

gral value from that input sequence via an IOStreams extractor. The shift operator would extract, but then discard, all preceding whitespace characters (blanks, tabs, newlines). When it found the first relevant character, i.e., the digit character "4" in our example, it would accumulate the characters until it encountered one that did not belong to the item. In this case the separator would be the alphabetical character "s" after the digit sequence. The separator would remain in the input sequence and become the first character extracted in a subsequent read operation.

You can switch off the default behavior of skipping preceding whitespace characters by means of the manipulator `noskipws` or the equivalent stream operation `unsetf (ios_base::skipws)`. This may be useful if you expect the input to have a certain format and the whitespace characters to be part of the format specification; then you need to extract the whitespace characters rather than silently ignoring them, so that you can check for violations of the format requirements.

Here is an example. It extracts one line of input that is supposed to consist of a list of floating-point numbers separated by commas; no whitespace is permitted.

```
cin >> noskipws;
char c;
do {
    float fl;
    c = ' ';                        // clear character
    cin >> fl >> c;                 // extract number and separator
    if (c == ',' || c == '\n')      // next char is ',' or newline ?
        process(fl);                // yes: use the number
} while (c == ',');
if (c != '\n') error();             // no: error!
```

IGNORING CHARACTERS

If you have to skip a sequence of characters other than whitespace, you can use the `ignore(streamsize n, int_type delim)` function. Its functionality is to read and discard characters until a certain number of characters are extracted or a separator is found. If you want to use the `ignore()` function for skipping any number of characters until a particular character is found, simply set the limit to the largest possible number of characters in a file so that the maximum number of extracted characters will never be reached. Only the occurrence of the separator will stop the extraction. Here is an example:

```
cin.ignore(numeric_limits<streamsize>::max(),'\n');
```

In this call the function `ignore()` reads and discards all characters until the end of the line. The constant `numeric_limits<streamsize>::max()` is the largest possible number of characters in a stream.

Note that the example relies on the fact that `cin` is a stream for narrow characters. For a wide-character input stream the equivalent to the call above would be

```
wcin.ignore(numeric_limits<streamsize>::max(), wchar_t('\n'));
```

The main difference from the case of narrow-character streams is the end-of-line character. Different character types can have different end-of-line characters. The equivalent of `'\n'` for any given character type `charT` can be created via the character type's constructor, i.e. `charT('\n')`.

INPUT OF STRINGS

IOStreams supports extraction of character sequences into strings. String extractors are slightly different from extractors for other types, because there is no particular format specification. Instead, all characters except whitespace characters are considered part of a string. Hence the only separator that can stop the extraction of a string is a whitespace character. In contrast, the extraction of items of other types stops once a character is found that does not belong to the format for that type. For instance, the extraction of an integral number from the sequence `"5ft"` stops once the letter "f" is found, because an "f" is not considered part of an integral number.

The field width setting, too, can stop the extraction of characters into a string. More precisely, when you extract strings from an input stream, characters are read until (1) a whitespace character is found, (2) an end-of-string character[19] is found, (3) the end of the input is reached, or (4) a certain number of characters are extracted if `width() != 0`.

This maximum number of extracted character is the field width `width()` for C++ strings and `width()-1` for C strings.

Note that the field width will be reset to 0 after the extraction of a string.

DIFFERENCES BETWEEN EXTRACTION OF C STRINGS AND C++ STRINGS

There are subtle differences between the operation that extracts a character sequence into a C-style string and the operation that extracts it into a `basic_string` object. For example:

```
// extraction of C string
char buf[SZ];
cin >> buf;
```

is different from

```
// extraction of C++ string
string s;
cin >> s;
```

When characters are extracted into a `basic_string` object you need not worry whether the number of extracted characters might exceed the string's capacity.

---

19. See appendix G.12, C++ Strings, for an explanation of the end-of-string character.

`basic_string` objects dynamically allocate additional storage and adjust their size as necessary. C-style strings, on the other hand, are character arrays, which have fixed size and cannot dynamically extend their capacity. If more characters are available from the input than the character array can hold, the extractor writes beyond the end of the array. To prevent this, you must set the field width to the array size each time you extract a C string:

```
char buf[SZ];
cin >> setw(SZ) >> buf;
```

1.3 The Stream State

Each stream has a state reflecting failure of operations and loss of integrity. In this section we explain the stream state and its state flags, ways and means for accessing the stream state for detecting error situations, and error indication via exceptions thrown by IOStreams.

The stream state is stored in a state variable, which is a private data member of the stream base class `basic_ios <class charT, class Traits>`. The data member is of type `iostate`, which is a nested bitmask type[20] in class `ios_base`. The corresponding bits are defined in class `ios_base`, too.

1.3.1 The Stream State Flags

Each of the state bits represents a certain category of error state. These flags and their error categories are summarized in table 1-5.

Table 1-5: Flags and Corresponding Error Categories

IOSTATE FLAG	ERROR CATEGORY
`goodbit`	Everything's OK.
`eofbit`	An input operation reached the end of an input sequence.
`failbit`	An output operation failed to generate the desired characters, or an input operation failed to read the expected character, or any other kind of operation failed to produce the desired result.
`badbit`	Indicates the loss of integrity of the stream.

THE STATE FLAG `goodbit`

The flag `ios_base::goodbit` has the value 0 and indicates the absence of any error flag. It means the stream is OK.

---

20. More information about bitmask types can be found in appendix G.1, Bitmask Types.

THE STATE FLAG `eofbit`

The flag `ios_base::eofbit` indicates the end of the input sequence, i.e., it is set when there is an attempt to read past the end of an input sequence. Here are two typical situations in which the `eofbit` is set:

1. *Characterwise extraction.* Assume you read input character by character. Eventually, you will extract the last available character. Once the last character is read, the stream is still in good state; `eofbit` is not yet set. Any subsequent extraction, however, will try to extract a character from a stream that does not have any more characters available. This extraction will be considered an attempt to read past the end of the input sequence. Thus, `eofbit` will be set as a result of the subsequent extraction.

2. *Extraction of an item other than a single character.* If you do not read characterwise but extract an integer or a string or any other kind of multicharacter item, you might read past the end of the input sequence. This is because the input operators read characters until they find a separator, or hit the end of the input sequence. Imagine the input sequence contained in `"... 912749<eof>"`. Also, assume that an integer is supposed to be extracted. The respective extractor will read all digit characters until it receives the information that it hit the end of the input. Then the extraction will be terminated and `eofbit` will be set, because there was an attempt to read past the end of the input sequence.

THE STATE FLAG `failbit`

The flag `ios_base::failbit` is generally set as the result of an operation that fails. For example, if you try to extract an integer from an input sequence that contains nothing but whitespace, the extraction of an integer fails, because no integral value can be produced. As a result of that extraction, the `failbit` is set. Not only input and output operations can set the `failbit`. Additional failure situations can arise in operations like `open()` in file streams. If the `open()` operation fails to open the requested file, it sets `failbit`.

THE RELATIONSHIP BETWEEN THE STATE FLAGS `eofbit` AND `failbit`

The flags `eofbit` and `failbit` have distinct meanings: `ios_base::eofbit` indicates the end of an input sequence; `ios_base::failbit` indicates failure of a stream operation. Stream input operations often set *both flags at a time*. Therefore, `eofbit` and `failbit` are sometimes mixed up. Let us see how they differ and how they relate.

In input operations situations of failure often correspond to the situation of hitting the end of the input sequence. Let us reexamine the previous examples and see whether `failbit` would be set in addition to `eofbit`.

1. *Characterwise extraction.* After reading the last available character, the stream is still in good state; neither `eofbit` nor `failbit` is set. Any subsequent extraction not only reads past the end of the input sequence, which results in setting the `eofbit`, but also fails to extract the requested character. Hence, `failbit` is set in addition to `eofbit`.

2. Extraction of an item other than a single character. Here it is different. Let us again imagine the input sequence contained `"912749<eof>"` and an integer was supposed to be extracted. Although the end of the input sequence is reached by extracting the integer, which results in setting the `eofbit`, the input operation does not fail. The desired integer can be extracted. Hence in this situation `failbit` is not set; only the `eofbit` is set.

THE STATE FLAG `badbit`

The flag `ios_base::badbit` indicates loss of integrity of the stream. Typical problems of that category include the following:

- *Memory shortage.* There is no memory available to create or resize the internal buffer or other internal data.

- *Transport layer problems.* The transport layer might indicate problems, as in memory shortage, or code conversion failure, or an unrecoverable read error from the external device.

- *Exceptions.* Components used by a stream operation might raise an exception, which indicates a fatal error. Such an exception is caught by the stream operation and results in setting the `badbit` in the stream's state.

THE STREAM STATE'S EFFECT ON INSERTION AND EXTRACTION

The stream state affects the behavior of the IOStreams operations. By convention, all IOStreams operations have no effect once the stream state indicates an error situation. More specifically, I/O operations do nothing if the initial stream state at the time of their invocation includes either `failbit`, `badbit`, or `eofbit`, and input and output operations stop as soon as one of the stream state flags is set.

Note the interesting effect of the `eofbit`: Extractions do not only stop in case of an error (`failbit` or `badbit`), but also when the end of the input stream is reached (`eofbit`). Insertions typically stop only in case of an error, because no output operation ever sets the `eofbit`. If, however, the `eofbit` has been set before the output operation is invoked, then the attempted insertion will fail and have no effect. This can happen in bidirectional streams when an extraction that reached the end of the input is followed by an insertion to the stream, which then has the `eofbit` set due to the preceeding extraction. For this reason the `eofbit` in addition to the error flags `failbit` and `badbit` stops operations on input and bidirectional streams, but is irrelevant for operations on output streams.

Extractors read a value from an input stream and place it into a variable. If an extraction fails, what is the content of that variable? Unfortunately, there is no unambiguous answer to this question. Some inserters (e.g., for `int`, `long`, `bitset`) leave the variable unaltered in case of a failure; others clear its content. For some extractors (e.g., for `complex`) it's not defined in the standard, so it will depend on your version of the library implementation. With yet another set of extractors (e.g., for `string`, `char`, `char*`) it depends on the nature of the failure within the extractor. In sum, there is no consistent concept for the output of a failed extraction in IOStreams. Therefore, don't make any assumptions about the value contained in the output variable of a failed extractor.

The stream state does not influence only the IOStreams operations. As a user of IOStreams, you will want to react to I/O errors as well. What would be a reasonable strategy? The rule of thumb is that `badbit` indicates an error situation that is likely to be unrecoverable, whereas `failbit` indicates a situation that might allow you to retry the failed operation. The flag `eofbit` simply indicates that the end of the input sequence has been reached, which need not be considered an error at all.

However, before you react to any stream error, you need to detect it. How can you do this? There are two possibilities:

1. You can actively access the streams state after each stream operation and check for errors. This is the default.

2. You can declare that you want to have an exception raised once an error occurs in any stream operation.

We will explore these possibilities in the next two sections.

1.3.2 Checking the Stream State

A stream has several member functions, which give you access to the stream's state so that you can check for error situations. These access functions are defined by the base class `basic_ios<class charT, class Traits>`. They are summarized with their effects in table 1-6.

Table 1-6: Stream Member Functions for Error Checking[21]

ACCESS FUNCTION	EFFECT
`bool good()`	True if no error flag is set
`bool eof()`	True if `eofbit` is set.
`bool fail()`	True if `failbit` or `badbit` is set.
`bool bad()`	True if `badbit` is set.
`bool operator!()`	As `fail()`.
`operator void*()`	Null pointer if `fail()` and non-null value otherwise.

The following examples show how you would use these functions.

CHECKING THE STREAM STATE VIA `operator ! ()`

In order to check the stream state in some central place, one writes:

```
if (!cout) // error!
```

The state of `cout` is examined with `operator!()`, which will return `true` if `failbit` or `badbit` are set, i.e., if the stream state indicates an error has occurred.

---

21. There are three further access functions: `rdstate()`, `clear()`, and `setstate()`. `rdstate()` returns the value of the stream state. `clear()` and `setstate()` allow you to modify the stream state. Their main purpose is for modifications of the stream state, not for checking the state flags.

CHECKING THE STREAM STATE VIA `operator void* ()`

An output stream can also appear in a Boolean position to be tested as follows:

```
if (cout << x) // okay!
```

The magic here is the `operator void* ()` in conjunction with standard conversion sequences implicitly performed by the compiler. In particular, the compiler implicitly converts an expression of a given type when used in the condition of an `if` statement; the destination type of such a conversion is `bool`. In the example above the expression `cout << x` is used in a condition, and therefore a sequence of implicit conversion is applied: Initially, the expression `cout << x` evaluates to a reference to a stream, because shift operators generally return a reference to the stream on which they are invoked. The compiler then performs the following conversions:

1. A cast from a reference of a stream to a pointer of type `void*` using the stream's cast operator `operator void* ()`.

2. A promotion from the pointer type `void*` to type `bool`.

The cast operator `operator void* ()` returns a zero pointer value if `failbit` or `badbit` are set, and nonzero otherwise. Hence, the value of `cout << x` is `false` in case of an error situation, and `true` if the stream is in a good state.

CHECKING THE STREAM STATE VIA `good()`, `eof()`, `fail()`, OR `bad()`

Eventually, the explicit member functions can also be used. Here is an example:

```
cout << x;
if (cout.good()) // okay!
```

or, more concise:

```
if (cout << x, cout.good()) // okay!
```

The value of the comma expression `cout << x, cout.good()` is the return value of `good()`. This is because a comma expression always evaluates to the value of the right-hand side of the comma operator; i.e., the rightmost expression in a sequence of comma operators determines the value of the entire expression.

A final note on subtle differences between `good()` and the other access functions: The function `good()` takes *all* flags into account, the `eofbit` included, whereas `fail()`, `operator !()`, and `operator void* ()` ignore `eofbit`. In other words, a stream that is not in a good state according to `good()` need not be in a state of failure according to `fail()`; it may just have the `eofbit` set.

Recommendation: Considering the meaning of the state flags, we recommend checking for *error situations* via `fail()`, `operator!()`, or `operator void* ()`, and checking for *failure of input operations* via `!good()`.

1.3.3 Catching Stream Exceptions

By default none of the stream operations throws an exception. You have to explicitly declare that you want a stream to throw exceptions. For this purpose every stream contains an *exception mask,* which consists of several exception flags. Each flag in this mask corresponds to one of the stream state flags `failbit`, `badbit`, and `eofbit`. For example, once the `badbit` flag is set in the exception mask, an exception will be thrown each time the `badbit` flag gets set in the stream state.

The exception mask is a private data member in class `basic_ios<class charT, class Traits>`. It is of the same type as the stream state, i.e., of the bitmask type `ios_base::iostate`. The member function `exceptions()`, defined in class `basic_ios<class charT, class Traits>`, allows getting and setting the exception mask value.

The exception that is thrown can be of any type. However, one can distinguish the two following typical cases:

1. `ios_base::failure`. If the exception is raised due to an error situation discovered by any of the IOStreams operations, it is of the type `failure`. `failure` is a nested class in the base class `ios_base` and is derived from class `exception`, which is the base class of all standard exceptions in C++. (See appendix G.10, Standard Exceptions, for further details on class `exception`.)

2. *Otherwise.* The IOStreams operations propagate exceptions that are thrown by expressions or functions used to implement the operation. This propagation is useful, because it can be expected that the original exception type provides more information about the source of the problem than `ios_base::failure` would do. An example is the `bad_alloc` exception that can occur during allocation of memory for a stream's internal data. Such a `bad_alloc` exception is caught by the operation, classified as a `badbit` situation, and rethrown, if the exception mask allows it.

In principle you must be prepared to receive an exception of unknown type from most IOStreams operations. To catch such exceptions, wrap the critical I/O operations into a `try` block and activate the relevant exceptions, usually `badbit` and `failbit`, in the exception mask. The first statement in the `try` block that fails raises either an exception of the type `ios_base::failure` or a propagated exception of unknown type. The following code demonstrates activation and catching of exceptions on an input stream:

```
try {
    cout.exceptions(ios_base::badbit | ios_base::failbit);
    cout << x;
    // do lots of other stream output
}
catch(...)
{   if (cout.bad())
    {   // unrecoverable error
        ...
```

```
        throw;
    }
    else if(cout.fail())
    {   // retry
        ...
        return;
    }
}
```

In calling the exceptions() function, you specify what flags in the stream's state will cause an exception to be thrown. In this example we want an exception thrown each time either badbit or failbit gets set in the stream state. It is generally recommended to set badbit *and* failbit for output streams, because this conforms to the checking for error situations via fail(), operator!(), and operator void*(). Similarly, you would set badbit, failbit, and eofbit for input streams, because it is equivalent to checking for input errors via !good(). Note also that the call to exception() raises an exception, if the respective state flag is already set. For this reason, the activation of exceptions is in itself a critical operation that has to be called inside the try block.

The catch clause catches any exception raised by one of the previously invoked I/O operations. As the exception object itself does not contain any information about the state flag that triggered the exception, you must also check the stream state. If the stream state is bad, the error situation is unrecoverable. Otherwise, it was just a failure of a certain operation, and a retry might make sense.

An alternative to wrapping the critical operations into a try block is to suppress exceptions, execute all critical operations, and activate them afterwards. Here is an example:

```
cout.exceptions(ios_base::goodbit);
cout << x;
// do lots of other stream I/O
try {cout.exceptions(ios_base::badbit | ios_base::failbit);}
catch(ios_base::failure& exc)
{   if (cout.bad())
    {
        // unrecoverable error
        ...
        throw;
    }
    else if(cout.fail())
    {
        // retry
        ...
        return;
    }
}
```

The call to `cout.exceptions(ios_base::goodbit)` clears the exception mask and deactivates all exceptions. All of the subsequent statements are executed, because no exception can be thrown. Eventually, the call to `cout.exceptions (ios_base:: badbit | ios_base::failbit)` is wrapped into a `try` block and raises an `ios_base::failure` exception in case any of the previously executed operations failed.

Note that only an `ios_base::failure` exception can be raised, which is different from the previous, alternative example, where the exception thrown could also be a propagated exception of unknown type. Hence, when exceptions are activated after all critical operations have been executed, the distinction between IOStreams-specific error situations and errors caused by other sources gets lost.

1.3.4 Resetting the Stream State

As a convention, all of the stream's I/O functionality is disabled when its stream state is not good, i.e., `str.good() != true`. That means that a stream's stream state has to be reset to `goodbit` whenever it should be used again for input or output operations after an error occurred.

The stream offers two member functions to change its stream state explicitly:

`void clear(iostate state = goodbit)` sets the stream state to the value of the argument `state`. The default argument is `goodbit`, which means that a call to clear with no argument sets the stream state to `goodbit`.

`void setstate(iostate addstate)` adds state bits from `addstate` to the existing stream state, i.e., the new stream state will be `old_stream_state | addstate`.

To reset the stream state to good after an error has occurred, either `clear()` or `clear(goodbit)` can be used. Let's add a call to `clear()` to the example above where we suggest retrying I/O processing. The code changes to

```
cout.exceptions(ios_base::goodbit);
cout << x;
// do lots of other stream I/O
try {cout.exceptions(ios_base::badbit | ios_base::failbit);}
catch(ios_base::failure& exc)
{   if (cout.bad())
    {
        // unrecoverable error
        ...
        throw;
    }
```

```
    else if(cout.fail())
    {
        cout.clear();
        // redo those stream I/O operations that do not cause failure
        return;
    }
}
```

1.4 File Input/Output

File streams allow input and output to *files* or, more generally, to external devices that exhibit file-like behavior. Files share the feature that they must be *opened* before the actual input or output can be performed, and have to be *closed* afterward. The file to be opened is specified by a *file name*. The syntax and semantics of such file names are not standardized but are system- and implementation-dependent. This section explains the handling of file streams.

In IOStreams there are three file stream class templates: `basic_ifstream` for input, `basic_ofstream` for output, and `basic_fstream` for bidirectional I/O. Their template parameters are the character type and the associated traits type, i.e., the complete template specification is `basic_(i/o)fstream<class charT, class Traits>`. There are typedefs defined for instantiations of the three class templates for the character types `char` and `wchar_t`. The type names are identical to the corresponding class names in the Classic IOStreams and are provided for convenience and for compatibility with the Classic IOStreams: `ifstream`, `ofstream`, and `fstream` perform narrow-character I/O; their wide-character counterparts—`wifstream`, `wofstream`, and `wfstream`—are for input and output of wide-character sequences. The file connected to a wide-character stream is supposed to be a multibyte character file.[22] There are no stream classes in IOStreams for I/O to files that contain wide characters.

1.4.1 Creating, Opening, Closing, and Destroying File Streams

A file stream object can be in two states, open or closed.

CLOSED. A closed file stream object is not yet connected to a file. Before invoking any input or output operation, the file must be opened and a connection to the stream established. This is done by calling the stream's member function `open()`, as in the example below.

```
ifstream file;          // create closed file stream
...;
file.open("src.cpp");   // "open" the file stream
```

---

22. See section 4.2.7, Character Encodings, for information on multibyte character files.

OPEN. Open file streams are fully functioning file stream objects that are ready to perform input and output operations, because they are connected to an open file. A closed file stream can be turned into an open file stream by invoking `open()`, which is demonstrated in the example above. The converse can be achieved by calling `close()`. The `close()` member function closes the file and disconnects it from the file stream.

The file stream classes additionally have a constructor that allows creation of an open file stream by providing a file name. The constructor implicitly opens the file and connects it to the stream (see example below).

```
ifstream source("src.cpp");  // create "open" file stream
```

One can check whether a file stream is connected to an open file by means of the `is_open()` member function.

When a file stream object is destroyed, the connected file is automatically closed by the file stream's destructor.

Calls to `open()` and `close()` cannot be nested; a file stream must be closed before it can be opened again. Attempts to open an already open file stream fail. Similarly, you cannot close a file that is already closed. Every call to `open()` must be matched by a call to `close()` (see example below):

```
{
  ofstream fil("src.cpp");  // fil is implicitly opened at construction time
  // ...
  if (fil.is_open())
     fil.close();

  fil.open("dst.cpp");      // connect to another file
}                           // fil goes out of scope here and is automatically
                            // closed
```

The functions `open()` and `close()`, as well as the file stream constructors, indicate failure by setting `failbit` in the stream state in case they cannot open or close the external file (see also section 1.3.2, Checking the Stream State).

ERROR STATE VERSUS CONNECTION STATE

Checking `is_open()` should not be confused with checking the stream state after a call to `open()`. The member function `is_open()` indicates whether a file stream is connected to an open file or whether it is closed. Functions like `good()`, `fail()`, `operator!()`, on the other hand, check the stream's error state, which reflects success or failure of previous operations on the stream. In the case of the `open()` operation this might at times seem a little confusing. Let us take a look at an example:

Normally, after a successful call to `open()`, `is_open()` yields `true` and `fail()` yields `false`, because a connection to an open file is established and the previous operation was successful. However, a call to `open()` can fail even if the file stream is open, for example, if you attempt to reopen an already open file stream. As expected, the call to `open()` fails, and as a result `fail()` yields `true`; at the same time `is_open()` yields `true`, because the stream is connected to an open file due to a previous successful call to `open()`. The code below shows such a situation:

```
ofstream fil("src.cpp");    // file stream is connected to "src.cpp"

fil.open("dst.cpp");        // attempt to connect to another file; will fail
if (fil.fail())
{  /* open operation failed */  }

if (fil.is_open())
{  /* connected to an open file, namely "src.cpp" */  }
```

1.4.2 The Open Modes

Opening a file stream can involve

- creation of the external file, if it does not exist

- truncating its content, if it exists and its content is to be replaced

- positioning to the end of the file, if the file exists and its content is to be extended rather than replaced

By default, an output file is created if it does not yet exist; and if it does exist its content is discarded. The situation is radically different for input file streams, however. An attempt to open an input file stream fails if the file does not exist. In addition, the content of an input file is never discarded.

File streams support the notion of an *open mode* that allows specification of certain properties of the stream, among them the way in which the underlying file is opened. For instance, we might need to deviate from the default behavior outlined above and want to preserve the content of an output file. To achieve this, the open mode can be set so that output operations append to the end of a file rather than overwriting the existing file content.

The open mode can be set when the file stream is created or when it is connected to a file. Both the file stream constructor and the `open()` function take the open mode as a second argument. Here is an example:

```
fstream Str("inout.txt",ios_base::in|ios_base::out|ios_base::app);
```

Both functions store the open mode setting in one of the stream's data members, and subsequent input and output operations adjust their behavior according to the current setting. The open mode setting is always determined when the file stream is connected to a file. The setting cannot be changed afterwards. Also, the current setting cannot be retrieved after it has been set.

OPEN MODE FLAGS

We have already seen an example of an open mode setting above. The open mode argument of the constructor and the `open()` function are of type `ios_base::openmode`, which is a bitmask type.[23] The following bits, also defined in class `ios_base`, are associated with the bitmask type:

Table 1-7: Flag Names and Effects

FLAG NAMES	EFFECTS
`in`	Opens file for reading.
`out`	Opens file for writing.
`ate`	Indicates start position is at file end.
`app`	Appends file, i.e., always writes to the end of the file.
`trunc`	Truncates file, i.e., deletes file content.
`binary`	Binary mode.

Table 1-7 shows the flag names and effects. The open mode flags control how the file is opened and in which way it is used later on. More specifically, the open mode flags have an impact on the initial file position and the initial file length. The open mode determines whether system-specific conversions are performed or suppressed and whether the file to be opened must exist or shall be created. Here are the details:

THE INITIAL FILE POSITION. Each file maintains a *file position* that indicates the position in the file where the next byte will be read or written. When a file is opened, the initial file position is by default at the beginning of the file. The open modes `ate` (meaning *at end*) and `app` (meaning *append*) change this default to the end of the file. There is a subtle difference between `ate` and `app` mode.

If the file is opened in *append mode,* all output to the file will be done at the current end of the file, regardless of intervening repositioning. Even if you modify the file position[24] to a position before the file's end, you do not write there.

With *at-end mode,* only the initial file position is at the end of the file. You can reposition to a position before the end of file and write to that position.

THE INITIAL FILE LENGTH. The open mode `trunc` (meaning *truncate*) sets the initial file length to zero, which has the effect of discarding the file content. The `trunc` flag is included in the default open mode of output file streams, so you can omit the `trunc` flag and think of the open mode `out` as being equivalent to `out|trunc`. This only holds true for output file streams. For bidirectional file streams, the `trunc` flag must always be explicitly specified, i.e., you must say `in|out|trunc`, if the file content is to be discarded.

---

23. See section G.1, Bitmask Types, in appendix G for further information on bitmask types.

24. The file position can be changed via the `seekpos()` member function of a stream. See section 1.7, Stream Positioning, for reference.

If an output file is to be extended rather than having its content replaced, we must omit the `trunc` flag and include the at-end or append flag instead. These flags move the initial file position to the file's end; the missing trunc flag causes the initial file length not to be set to zero but retained; and as a result of these open mode settings, the file is extended rather than overwritten.

CREATING FILES. When the open mode contains `in` (meaning that the file is opened for *input*), the attempt to open the file fails if the file does not exist. When the open mode is the `out` flag (meaning that the file is opened for *output*), the file will be created if it does not yet exist. In that case, the attempt to open the file fails only if the file cannot be created.

SYSTEM-SPECIFIC CONVERSIONS. The open mode flag `binary` has the effect of suppressing automatic conversions performed by underlying system services. The representation of text files varies among operating systems. For example, the end of a line in a UNIX environment is represented by the *linefeed* character `'\n'`, whereas on Microsoft operating systems the end of the line consists of two characters, *carriage return* `'\r'` and *linefeed* `'\n'`. An operating system's I/O functions therefore perform automatic conversions, such as converting between `"\r\n"` and `'\n'`.

The open mode flag `binary` has the effect of suppressing such automatic conversions. Basically, the `binary` mode flag is passed on to the respective operating system's service function, which means that in principle *all* system-specific conversions will be suppressed, not just the carriage return / linefeed handling. The effect of the binary open mode is frequently misunderstood. It does *not* put the inserters and extractors of IOStreams into a binary mode in the sense of suppressing the formatting they usually perform. Binary input and output, in the sense of unformatted I/O, is done via certain member functions of the stream classes: `basic_istream <charT> ::read()` and `basic_ostream<charT> ::write()`.

VALID OPEN MODE COMBINATION

Not all combinations of the open mode flags are allowed. Table 1-8 lists all permitted combinations of open modes for text files. The at-end flag and/or the binary flag can be added to either of the combinations listed below.

Combinations of modes that are not listed in the table (such as both `trunc` and `app`) are invalid, and the attempted construction or `open()` operation fails due to the invalid open mode.

DEFAULT OPEN MODES

The open mode parameter in constructors and the `open()` function of the file stream classes have a default value. The default open mode is `ios_base::in` for input file streams, `ios_base::out` for output file streams (which is equivalent to `ios_base::out|ios_base::trunc`), and `ios_base::in|ios_base::out` for bidirectional file streams. Hence, instead of creating a bidirectional output file stream as

```
fstream BiStr("poem.txt", ios_base::in|ios_base::out);
```

Table 1-8: Open Modes and Their Effects[25]

OPEN MODE	EFFECT	+ AT-END FLAG	+ BINARY FLAG
`in`	Opens text file for reading only.	Initial file position is at the end of the file.	Suppresses conversions.
`out|trunc` `out`	Truncates to zero length, if existent, or creates text file for writing only.	Initial file position is at the end of the file.	Suppresses conversions.
`out|app`	Appends; opens or creates text file only for writing at end of file.	Initial file position is at the end of the file.	Suppresses conversions.
`in|out`	Opens text file for update (reading and writing).	Initial file position is at the end of the file.	Suppresses conversions.
`in|out|trunc`	Truncates to zero length, if existent, or creates text file for update.	Initial file position is at the end of the file.	Suppresses conversions.

you can simply say

```
fstream BiStr("poem.txt");
```

In order to make sure that an output stream is opened in output mode and an input stream is opened in input mode, the default open modes are always implicitly added to the mode argument. This way, you cannot inadvertently open an input file for output, or vice versa. The correct open mode would be added implicitly, and the wrong open mode would have no effect. Moreover, the implicit addition of the default open mode for input and output streams is convenient to use. For instance, instead of writing

```
ofstream OStr("out.txt", ios_base::out|ios_base::app);
ifstream IStr("in.txt", ios_base::in|ios_base::binary);
```

you can simply say

```
ofstream OStr("out.txt", ios_base::app);
ifstream IStr("in.txt", ios_base::binary);
```

For bidirectional streams, the default open mode is not added implicitly, because a bidirectional stream need not always be opened for both transport directions. You can open a bidirectional stream for just reading or just writing. A bidirectional file stream is

---

25. Some of the open modes correspond to the file open modes used in the C stdio (for invocation of the `fopen()` function). See section D.1, File Open Modes, in appendix D for details.

opened in exactly the modes that are provided to its constructor or `open()` function, without implicit additions. The result is that we always have to fully specify a bidirectional file stream's open mode, as in the examples below:

```
// bidirectional file stream opened only for input
fstream BiFil("poem.txt", ios_base::in);
```

or

```
// bidirectional file stream opened only for output
fstream OutFil("out.txt", ios_base::out|ios_base::app);
```

1.4.3 Bidirectional File Streams

If a bidirectional file stream is opened for input and output, in principle both read and write operations can be applied to the stream. Switching between reading and writing must follow certain rules. These rules stem from the C stdio and are basically the same rules as those that apply to input and output to and from bidirectional files in the C stdio.

SWITCHING FROM OUTPUT TO INPUT

When output has been written to the bidirectional file stream, a read attempt immediately after writing to the file stream will lead to "undefined results." This means that almost anything can happen: The read operation might fail without indicating this failure in any way; it might lead to a program crash; it might work; or something else might happen. Whatever the result under a particular implementation of the standard IOStreams, a read attempt immediately after writing to a bidirectional file stream is neither predictable nor portable.

Before any read attempt, the file stream must be flushed or the file position must be reset. Both flushing and repositioning trigger the stream to empty its internal buffer and write its content to the external file. In the case of repositioning, the file position indicator of the external file is adjusted. In the case of flushing, the file position indicator remains unchanged. Subsequent read operations will read input from the external file beginning at the respective file position.

Below is an example of output to a bidirectional file stream followed by repositioning to the beginning of the file and subsequent input from the file stream:

```
fstream fstr("test2.txt", ios_base::in|ios_base::out);
char buf[32]; buf[31] = '\0';
char puf[] = "hello world";

// write output to the file stream
fstr << puf;
if (!fstr.good())
    cout << "stream status: " << fstr.rdstate() << endl;
```

```
// reposition to the begin of the file stream
fstr.seekg(0, ios_base::beg);
if (!fstr.good())
    cout << "stream status: " << fstr.rdstate() << endl;

// read input from the file stream
fstr.get(buf, sizeof(buf)-1);
if (!fstr.good())
    cout << "stream status: " << fstr.rdstate() << endl;
```

The call seekg(0, ios_base::beg) has the effect of emptying the internal buffer to the external file and resetting the file position indicator to the beginning of the file. Subsequent read attempts start reading from the beginning of the file. In the example above, we read what we had previously written to the file.

Instead of repositioning, we can flush the internal buffer by invoking the flush() member function instead of seekg(). In that case the file position remains unchanged and in the example above the subsequent read attempt fails because the file position is at the end of the file where there is nothing to read.

SWITCHING FROM INPUT TO OUTPUT

Similar rules apply for the switch from input to output operations on a bidirectional file stream. If we first read from a bidirectional file stream, we cannot immediately afterwards write output to the file stream. A write attempt immediately after reading from the file stream will lead to undefined results and hence must be avoided. Before we can safely write to the file stream, we must reposition the file position indicator.

An exception to that rule is the situation in which the file has been entirely read and input has reached the end of the file. In that case, output operations need not be preceded by resetting the file position indicator.

Below is an example where the entire content of the file is read before output is written to the bidirectional file stream:

```
fstream fstr("test1.txt", ios_base::in|ios_base::out);
char buf[32];  buf[31] = '\0';
char puf[] = "hello world";

// read from the file stream
fstr.get(buf, sizeof(buf)-1);
if (!fstr.good())
{ cout << "stream status: " << fstr.rdstate() << endl;
   if (fstr.eof())
      fstr.clear();  // needed to allow subsequent output
}
```

```
// write to the file stream
fstr << puf;
if (!fstr.good())
   cout << "stream status: " << fstr.rdstate() << endl;
```

Note that after reading the entire content of the file, the stream status indicates that the end of file has been reached. When any of the stream state bits is set, all stream operations refuse to do anything. Before we can successfully write to the file stream, we must clear the stream state. As we did not reposition the file position indicator, the output appears at the end of the file. Had we reset the position, we would have overwritten part of the file content.

1.5 In-Memory Input/Output

String streams allow in-memory input and output. The source and sink of the characters read or written are a buffer in memory. The in-memory buffer can be initialized from a string object and can be made available in the form of a string object.

In IOStreams there are three string stream class templates: `basic_istringstream` for input, `basic_ostringstream` for output, and `basic_stringstream` for bidirectional I/O. Their template parameters are the character type, the associated traits type, and the allocator type. The complete template specification is `basic_(i/o) stringstream<class charT, class Traits, class Allocator>`. The `Allocator` template parameter determines which type of string is accepted and produced; the strings are of type `basic_string <class charT, class Traits, class Allocator>`.

For convenience, there are typedefs defined for instantiations of three class templates for the character types `char` and `wchar_t`: `istringstream`, `ostringstream`, and `stringstream` perform narrow-character I/O; their wide-character counterparts, `wistringstream`, `wostringstream`, and `wstringstream`, are for input and output of wide-character sequences.

String streams can be created with or without an initial content. If no initial string is provided, the string stream has no content after construction. Naturally, read attempts from an empty input string stream fail. Output string streams are filled or extended by repeated insertions to the stream. String streams are dynamic, which means that the in-memory location grows as necessary for holding all characters written to it. Bidirectional string streams maintain a read and a write position, which can be moved independent of each other. The only restriction is that read operations can extract only what was previously written or initially provided to the string stream. Switching between input and output operations is no problem and can be done at any time.

Typically, in-memory I/O is used if the information to be read is already available in the form of a string, or if the formatted result will be processed as a string. For example, to interpret the contents of a string as an integer value, the code might look like this:

```
int i;
if (istringstream("4711") >> i)
{
    // i has the value: 4711
}
```

The equivalent operation in C would be a call to the `sscanf()` function. However, string streams are more powerful than `sscanf()` and `sprintf()` because they use the full set of formatting facilities of IOStreams, including internationalization, for instance.

RETRIEVAL AND REPLACEMENT OF THE STRING STREAM CONTENT

The current content of a string stream can be retrieved via the `str()` member function. A copy of the internal buffer is created and returned as a string. Here is an example:

```
ostringstream oBuf;
oBuf.imbue("German_Germany");
oBuf << setprecision(2) << fixed;

float DeutschMark = 19.99;
string Amount;

oBuf << DeutschMark << " DM";
if (oBuf)
    Amount = oBuf.str();   // Amount now contains: "19,99 DM"
```

The current content of a string stream can be replaced via an overloaded version of the `str()` member function that takes a string. The string is copied to the internal buffer and from then on serves as the source or sink of characters to subsequent insertions and extractions.

THE OPEN MODES

The only open modes that have an effect on string streams are `in`, `out`, `ate`, and `app`. They have the same meaning that they have with file streams (see section 1.4.2, Open Modes).

The `binary` open mode is irrelevant, because there are no system-specific conversions. The `trunc` open mode is simply ignored.

1.6 Unformatted Input/Output

IOStreams is typically used for formatted input and output of text. In addition to the shift operators that perform formatted input and output, the stream classes also provide a set of functions for unformatted input and output.

UNFORMATTED INPUT

Unformatted input differs from formatted input as follows:

Leading whitespaces are not skipped. They are extracted and delivered as part of the extracted character sequence.

The input operations read as many characters as are requested, or until a delimiter or the end of file is found. Otherwise, they do not interpret the extracted characters in any way.

There are several types of unformatted input functions:

- read a single character, e.g., via `int_type get()`

- read a specified number of characters, e.g., via `read(char_type*, streamsize)`

- read characters until a delimiter is found or a maximum number of characters is read, e.g., via `getline(char_type*, streamsize, char_type delim)`

- read a line, e.g., via `getline(char_type*, streamsize)`

Each of these functions comes in several flavors. They differ in the criteria that stop the extraction of characters. Details can be found in the reference part of this book. The extracted characters are stored into successive locations of an array that is passed to the operation. The operation adds a terminating null character to the extracted character sequence.

Like the formatted input operations, the unformatted input operations return the stream for which they are invoked, with the exception of `int_type get()`, which returns the extracted character. The unformatted input functions indicate failure in the same way as the formatted input functions do, namely, by setting the stream state bits and/or raising exceptions.

In order to find out how many characters were read, the function `gcount()` can be called. It returns the number of characters extracted by the last unformatted input operation called for the stream. This number can be different from the number of characters that are stored in the provided character array. For instance, a delimiter is read and counted, but not stored.

Below is an example where input is read line by line into a fixed-size character buffer. If a line is longer than the buffer size, the line must be read in several steps until it is completely consumed.

```
// character buffer; can store lines of length 99
// note: input adds a terminating null character
const int line_buffer_size = 100;
char buffer[line_buffer_size];
```

```
int line_number = 0;
while (cin.getline(buffer, line_buffer_size, '\n')      // stream still good() ?
    || cin.gcount())                                    // any characters read ?
{
  int count = cin.gcount();

  if (cin.eof())
      // end of file found; last line extracted
      cout << "Partial final line";
  else if (cin.fail())
  {   // max number of chars was reached; line was longer 99 chars
      cout << "Partial long line";
      // clear stream state so that we can continue reading
      cin.clear(cin.rdstate() & ~ios::failbit);
  } else {
      // don't include newline in count
      // mind: delimiter was extracted and counted, but not stored
      count--;
      cout << "Line " << ++line_number;
  }
  cout << " (" << count << " chars): " << buffer << endl;
}
```

Note that there is an additional getline() function defined in the header file
<string>, which is substantially more convenient to use than the stream member func-
tion getline() that was used in the example above. While the stream member function
reads a line into a character array of fixed size, the string getline() function reads a line
into a string object of dynamic size. We need not worry whether the line will fit into the
buffer or not, because the string will grow as needed. Let us compare use of the two
getline() functions. The stream member function would be called as

```
const int line_buffer_size = 100;
char buffer[line_buffer_size];
cin.getline(buffer, line_buffer_size, '\n');
```

and would indicate failure if the line is longer than the buffer size. In contrast, the string
getline() function would be called as

```
string buffer;
getline(cin, buffer, '\n');
```

and would fail if the line is longer than the maximum string size, which is an implementation-dependent size that can be obtained via buffer.max_size().

   In addition to the unformatted input functions, there are related functions for the
following:

- skipping characters, i.e., reading and discarding them, via `ignore()`

- look ahead, i.e., reading a character without consuming it, via `int_type peek()`. The character remains in the input sequence and is available to subsequent input operations.

- putback, i.e., putting characters back into the input sequence, via `putback (char_type)` or `unget()`. The characters that are put back are available to subsequent input operations.

UNFORMATTED OUTPUT

Unformatted output differs from formatted output in that the characters are written as they are, without any interpretations, additions, or modifications.

There are two categories of functions for unformatted output:

1. Write a single character; an example is `put(char_type)`.

2. Write a specified number of characters; an example is `write(const char_type*, streamsize)`.

Like the formatted output operations, the unformatted output operations return the stream for which they are invoked. The unformatted output functions indicate failure in the same way as the formatted output functions do, namely, by setting the stream state bits and/or raising exceptions.

1.7 Stream Positioning

Streams maintain a stream position. This is the position where the next input or output operation will start reading or writing. The stream position changes during input and output operations. Unidirectional streams (input or output streams) naturally have exactly one stream position. Bidirectional streams can maintain two independent stream positions: a read position for input operations and a write position for output operations. Bidirectional string streams work by distinguishing between a read and a write stream position. Bidirectional file streams, in contrast, maintain only one joint stream position; both input and output operations move the joint stream position indicator.

The stream position can be modified explicitly, that is, independent of any input or output operation. The input and output stream classes `basic_istream` and `basic_ostream` provide member functions that allow retrieval of the current stream position and modification of the stream position. They are explained in the following sections.

RETRIEVING THE CURRENT STREAM POSITION

The current stream position can be inquired after via the member functions `tellg()` for input streams and `tellp()` for output streams. Both functions return an object of type `pos_type` that represents the current stream position. The type `pos_type` is a nested type defined in each stream class.[26] For bidirectional file streams, `tellp()` and `tellg()` yield the same joint stream position. For bidirectional string streams, the two stream positions can differ: `tellg()` provides the read position and `tellp()` provides the write position.

A call to `tellg()`/`tellp()` can fail under the following circumstances:

- If the stream has the fail bit set as a result of any previous operation.

- (For file streams:) If the file stream is not connected to a file, i.e., `is_open()` yields `false`.

- If the file stream performs a code conversion and the encoding of the external file is either state-dependent or the number of external characters needed to produce an internal wide character is not constant.

- If the call to `tellg()`/`tellp()` fails then `pos_type(-1)` is returned to indicate the failure.

MODIFYING THE STREAM POSITION

The stream position can be reset via the member functions `seekg()` for input streams and `seekp()` for output streams. There are two overloaded versions of each of these functions: `seek(p/g)(pos_type)` and `seek(p/g)(off_type, ios_base::seekdir)`.

The first version takes an object of type `pos_type` that was obtained by a previous successful call to `tellg()`/`tellp()` and resets the stream position accordingly. Any subsequent input or output operations will start at the newly set stream position. For bidirectional file streams, `seekp()` and `seekg()` modify the joint stream position, whereas for bidirectional string streams, `seekp()` resets the write position and `seekg()` modifies the read position.

The other overloaded version of the functions `seekg()` and `seekp()` is called with a predefined symbolic stream position, explained in table 1-9, and an offset to be added to this position. The stream is then repositioned relative to these predefined positions. The symbolic stream position is of type `ios_base::seekdir`, which is an enumerated type that has the following three values:

Table 1-9: Predefined Stream Positions Defined by Type `ios_base::seekdir`[27]

SYMBOLIC STREAM POSITION	REPRESENTS
beg	the beginning of the stream
cur	the current position within the stream
end	the current end of the stream

---

26. The `pos_type` is defined in the stream's character traits and contains all information necessary to represent the stream position and, in the case of file streams, also the current state of the character conversion that is performed on input and output.

27. The symbolic stream positions correspond to the argument that is passed to the C stdio function `fseek()`. See section D.2, Stream Positions, in appendix D for details.

The offset is an object of type `off_type`, which is a nested type defined in each stream class. Stream offsets can be created from integral values[28] and represent the number of characters between two stream positions. Stream offsets are compatible with stream positions in the sense that offsets can be added to and subtracted from stream positions; the distance between two stream positions is an offset; and stream positions are convertible to stream offsets and vice versa.[29]

Here is an example where the joint stream position of a bidirectional file stream is manipulated in various ways:

```
fstream fstr("filnam.txt", ios_base::in|ios_base::out);

... do some output to the file stream ...

// reset the joint file position to the begin of the file stream
fstr.seekg(0, ios_base::beg);

... read from the file stream ...

// move the joint stream position 3 positions back
fstr.seekp(-3,ios_base::cur);

... write to the current stream position  ...

// memorize the current joint stream position for later use
fstream::pos_type pos = fstr.tellg();

... write to the file stream ...

// reposition to a location 2 positions after the previously memorized position
fstr.seekg(pos+fstream::off_type(2));
```

The error handling is omitted from the example. The functions `tellp()`/`tellg()` indicate failure by returning the invalid stream position `pos_type(-1)`; and `seekp()`/ `seekg()` indicate failure by setting the stream state.

---

28. To be more precise, stream offsets can be created from values of the type `streamsize`, and the type `streamsize` is a synonym for one of the signed basic integral types. The type `streamsize` is used to represent the number of characters transferred in an I/O operation.

29. Note that an offset represents a number of characters and not a number of bytes. For wide-character streams, the distance between two stream positions is calculated as the number of wide characters between the two positions. This is slightly confusing in the case of wide-character file streams, because they are typically connected to multibyte files. The distance between two file stream positions is expressed as a number of wide characters, whereas the distance between the corresponding file positions on the external multibyte file is usually expressed in terms of bytes or tiny characters (for instance, when the C stdio function `fseek()` is called).

For bidirectional file streams, it is basically irrelevant whether `seekp()` or `seekg()` is invoked. They both have the same effect. Similarly, `tellp()` and `tellg()` retrieve the same joint stream position too. This is different for bidirectional string streams, because they maintain read and write stream positions independent of each other.

1.8 Synchronization of Streams

Streams do not directly access their associated external devices. Instead, they buffer character sequences between formatting/parsing and actual transport to the external device. The internal buffer is maintained by the stream buffer classes. Please refer to section 2.2, The Stream Buffer Classes, for a detailed description and an explanation of related terms. Streams can be forced to *synchronize* their internal buffers with the external device. In the following section we explain stream synchronization in general, as well as special aspects concerning the predefined standard streams.

1.8.1 Means of Synchronization

Streams are automatically synchronized when the internal buffers of a stream need to be emptied or refilled. The semantics of this implicit synchronization are determined by the stream buffer classes and their `underflow()` and `overflow()` member functions. Also, a stream is synchronized before it is destroyed.

In addition to automatic synchronization, there are ways of triggering synchronization on demand. This can be achieved by either explicitly calling the stream member functions `flush()` and `sync()` or setting certain stream properties such as the `unitbuf` format flag or *tying* the streams.

1.8.1.1 Synchronization via `flush()` and `sync()`

The abstract idea of stream synchronization is synchronizing the content of the internal buffer with the content of the external device. For an output stream this means writing the content of its internal buffer to the associated external device. For an input stream, the notion of synchronization is not defined in general, but depends on the specific kind of input stream.

Output streams have a member function called `flush()` for synchronization. The counterpart for input streams is called `sync()`. Both functions delegate the task of synchronization to the stream buffer's member function `pubsync()`, which calls a protected virtual member function called `sync()`. Concrete stream buffer classes, such as file stream buffers and string stream buffers, are supposed to override the virtual `sync()` function and define the actual meaning of synchronization.

In IOStreams, only the file stream buffers override the virtual `sync()` function. For output files synchronization is defined as emptying the internal buffer by writing the buffer content to the file, performed by a call to `overflow()`. For input files, the meaning of synchronization is not defined by the standard, but depends on the implementation of the IOStreams library.

String stream buffers do not define synchronization at all; i.e., they do not override the virtual `sync()` function. This is because string streams do not distinguish between the internal buffer and the external device; they maintain only one memory location that plays the role of both. Hence the synchronization functions of string streams have no effect.

User-defined stream buffer classes need not override the virtual `sync()` function, if synchronization has no meaning for the new stream buffer type. Otherwise, the semantics of the newly defined synchronization should conform to the abstract idea of synchronization defined above.

1.8.1.2 Synchronization Using the `unitbuf` Format Flag

You can achieve repeated, automatic synchronization for output files by using the format flag `ios_base::unitbuf`. The flag affects all output operations defined in the IOStreams library and causes an output stream to flush its buffer at the end of each output operation. The effect of

```
ofstream ostr("/tmp/fil");
int i=10;
ostr << unitbuf;
while (i--)
{ ostr << i; }
```

is the same as in

```
ofstream ostr("/tmp/fil");
int i=10;
while (i--)
{ ostr << i;
  ostr.flush();
}
```

Synchronization via the `unitbuf` format flag is intended for output to logbook files. The idea is that output should be written to the file as soon as possible, so that no information gets lost in case of a system crash.

1.8.2.3 Synchronization by Tying Streams

Another mechanism for repeated, automatic synchronization is *tying* a stream to an output stream. Both input and output streams can be tied to an output stream. The effect of tying is that the stream memorizes the output stream it is tied to. In all its input and output operations it flushes the memorized output stream prior to the actual operation. Here is an example:

```
ofstream ostr("/tmp/fil");
ifstream istr("/tmp/fil");
string s;
```

```
ostream* old_tie = istr.tie(&ostr);       .
ostr << "Hello world\n";
istr >> s;
istr.tie(old_tie);
```

The input stream `istr` is tied to the output stream `ostr`. The `tie()` function returns a pointer to the previously tied output stream, which is memorized for restoring the tie afterwards. The effect of tying `istr` to `ostr` is the same as in

```
ofstream ostr("/tmp/fil");
ifstream istr("/tmp/fil");
string s;

ostr << "Hello world\n";
ostr.flush();
istr >> s;
```

Ties are intended for terminal I/O. If you read from a stream that is connected to a terminal, then it is useful for output to be flushed to the stream, i.e., written to the terminal, before input is read from the terminal. In such a case you would tie the terminal input stream to the terminal output stream.

1.8.2 Synchronizing the Predefined Standard Streams

The predefined standard streams are associated with the C standard files `stdin`, `stdout`, and `stderr`, as shown in table 1-10:

Table 1-10: Predefined Global Streams with Their Associated C Standard Files

NARROW-CHARACTER STREAM	WIDE-CHARACTER STREAM	ASSOCIATED C STANDARD FILES
cin	wcin	stdin
cout	wcout	stdout
cerr	wcerr	stderr
clog	wclog	stderr

Like the C standard files, these predefined standard streams are all associated by default with the terminal.

The predefined standard streams are of type `istream`, `ostream`, `wistream`, and `wostream`. These are the general stream classes, and the consequence is that the type of their stream buffer is not specified. The predefined standard streams are allowed to use an implementation-specific, special purpose, concrete stream buffer type. Little can be said about its behavior beyond what is defined for the stream buffer abstraction in general (see section 2.2, The Stream Buffer Classes, for details). Especially, the semantics of synchronization are mostly undefined for abstract stream buffer types, but fully depend on each concrete type. The concrete stream buffer type of the predefined standard streams is not known; consequently, the synchronization of the predefined standard streams is highly implementation-specific.

Several aspects are, however, defined by the standard. Four are discussed in the following sections:

1. Synchronization among the predefined standard streams.

2. Synchronization of a predefined standard stream with its associated C standard file.

3. Synchronization of a predefined standard stream with its associated external device.

4. Synchronization between wide and narrow counterparts.

1.8.2.1 Synchronization Among the Predefined Standard Streams

cin is tied to cout. This means that the output stream cout is forced to flush its buffer before any input operation on cin. The wide-character counterparts wcin and wcout are synchronized in the same way.

cerr is synchronized using the unitbuf format flag. The result is that the buffer is flushed after each output to cerr.

The wide-character counterparts wclog and wcerr have the same buffering characteristics.

A NOTE ON DIFFERENCES BETWEEN cerr AND clog

Both cerr and clog are associated with stderr. The difference between clog and cerr is in their synchronization with the associated external device. cerr has the unit-buf flag set, i.e., cerr's buffer is flushed after each output operation. clog, in contrast, exhibits default stream behavior: Output is stored in the internal buffer, and written to the external device only when the buffer is full. In this way, output to the actual external device is delayed. This delay is intended, because it reduces the number of accesses to the external device.

For error reporting, however, the delay is detrimental. In case of a program crash the error message, which might explain the crash, will still sit in the internal buffer and will never be written to the actual output device. In such cases, cerr is preferable because it flushes its buffer after each formatting, i.e., the error messages are buffered only between two subsequent formatting operations.

1.8.2.2 Synchronization with the C Standard I/O

The predefined C++ streams cin, cout, cerr, and clog are associated with the standard C files stdin, stdout, and stderr, as we have seen above. This means that, for instance, insertions into cout via C++ IOStreams go to the same file as output to stdout via C Standard I/O.[30] By default input and output to the predefined streams are synchronized with read or write operations on the standard C files. The effect is that input and

---

30. The C Standard I/O is often abbreviated as C Stdio.

output operations are executed in the order of invocation, independent of whether the operations were using the predefined C++ streams or the standard C files.

This synchronization is time-consuming and therefore might not be desirable in all situations. You can switch it off by calling

```
ios_base::sync_with_stdio(false);
```

where sync_with_stdio() is a static stream member function defined in base class ios_base.

After such a call, the predefined streams will operate independent of the C standard files, with possible performance improvements in your C++ stream operations.

The standard recommends that you call `sync_with_stdio()` prior to any input or output operation on the predefined streams if you want to switch off the synchronization between C and C++ I/O. The effect of calling `sync_with_stdio()` later is not standardized, but implementation-defined.

1.8.2.3 Synchronization with the External Device

We mentioned earlier that the predefined standard streams may use implementation-specific, special purpose stream buffer types whose synchronization characteristics are not standardized. In particular, the requirements regarding synchronization with the C standard files have an impact on synchronization with the external device. Synchronization with the C I/O can be switched off; for this reason we have to distinguish between the following two cases:

NO SYNCHRONIZATION WITH C STDIO. If the predefined standard streams are not synchronized with the C standard files, the buffering mechanism is fully implementation-specific. Most likely, the operations will be buffered using the stream buffer's put and get area, like operations on ordinary files, but this is not guaranteed. The input/output operations can also be unbuffered, line-buffered, or anything else.

SYNCHRONIZATION WITH C STDIO. In case of synchronization of the predefined standard streams with the C standard files, the IOStreams operations are guaranteed to coordinate input and output to the associated external device with the C Stdio operations that also access the same external device. Both I/O components usually maintain independent buffers. In case of `sync_with_stdio(true)`, both I/O components must synchronize the transfer of buffered characters to the external device. How this is achieved is fully implementation-specific. Most likely, IOStreams operations will pass characters to the C Stdio for buffering and will not maintain a buffer of their own. However, other implementation techniques, like sharing a buffer among IOStreams and C Stdio, are conceivable.

In both situations, virtually no statement can be made about synchronization of the IOStreams operations with the external device.

1.8.2.4 Synchronization Between Predefined Standard Streams for Narrow and Wide Characters

Mixing operations on corresponding wide- and narrow-character streams follows the same semantics as mixing such operations on corresponding wide- and narrow-character files in the C Standard I/O: The C files have an *orientation:* they can be *byte oriented* or *wide oriented.* A byte-oriented C file handles narrow characters of type char; a wide-oriented C file works with wide characters of type wchar_t. Wide-character input and output functions should not be applied to byte-oriented files, and vice versa. Initially, a C file is without an orientation. The first operation that is performed on a C file determines its orientation. The net effect is that you cannot mix operations on corresponding wide- and narrow-character streams.[31]

---

31. This does not only hold for the predefined standard streams, but for all situations where a narrow character stream has a wide character counterpart, i.e. whenever a narrow character stream and a wide character stream are associated to the same external file.

CHAPTER 2

The Architecture of IOStreams

In chapter 1, we demonstrated the principles of using stream objects for formatted input and output, but we did not pay much attention to the internal organization of the IOStreams component. More sophisticated usage of IOStreams (chapter 3), however, requires a thorough understanding of the structure of the IOStreams framework. Some background information is needed to understand this chapter, because it is organized around typical examples of using and extending IOStreams rather than explaining the internals of IOStreams. The necessary background information is provided in this chapter. It explains aspects of the software architecture of IOStreams, including a general description of all IOStreams classes; their responsibilities, relationship, and collaboration; and a couple of related topics. The focus in this chapter is on the principles used inside IOStreams rather than on detailed descriptions of all classes and functions. The goal is to provide an understanding of the way the pieces work together. Detailed and complete references can be found in the reference section of this book.

Not all of the subjects addressed in this chapter are needed to understand the rest of the book. Feel free to skip what is of no interest to you now and return later once you feel you need some background information. Here is an overview of the topics covered in this chapter.

As explained in chapter 1, IOStreams has two layers, one for parsing and formatting and another for buffering, code conversion, and transport of characters to and from the external device. As a reminder, figure 2-1 repeats the previous illustration of the IOStreams layers.

STREAM AND STREAM BUFFER CLASSES. Related to each layer is a separate hierarchy of classes: Classes that belong to the formatting layer are often referred to as the *stream classes*. Classes of the transport layer are often referred to as the *stream buffer classes.*[1] The stream classes and their internals are explained in section 2.1, The Stream Classes, along with their relationship to stream buffers and locales. A description of the stream buffer classes can be found in section 2.2, The Stream Buffer Classes. Locales are explained in part II of this book.

CHARACTER TYPE AND TRAITS TYPE. Almost all stream and stream buffer classes are class templates that take two template arguments, the character type and the traits type. Section 2.3, Character Types and Character Traits, is devoted to these type parameters.

`iword/pword` AND STREAM CALLBACKS. IOStreams provides a hook for adding information to a stream that can be used for arbitrary purposes. This additional stream storage is also known as *`iword/pword`*, which are the names of the respective data members holding the information. Section 2.5, Additional Stream Storage and Stream Callsbacks, explains this special feature of IOStreams. The stream callbacks are often needed for proper maintenance of such additional stream storage. Stream callbacks are also relevant for imbuing locales.

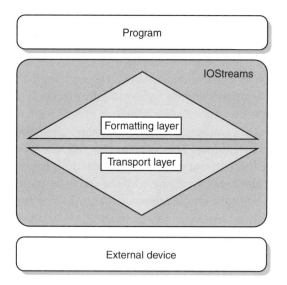

Figure 2-1: *The layers of IOStreams.*

---

1. We use "the stream classes" as a synonym for "the formatting layer" and "the stream buffer classes" as a synonym for "the transport and buffering layer."

2.1 The Stream Classes

We take two approaches for discussion of the stream classes:

1. We describe the formatting layer's static structure, in particular the inheritance relationship among the stream classes, and the maintenance of objects used by the stream classes, i.e., the handling of stream buffers and locales. This section explains which classes belong to the formatting layer, how they are related, and what their purpose and responsibilities are. It also gives an overview of the classes' interfaces in order to facilitate looking up details in the reference section of this book.

2. We explain the formatting layer's dynamic structure, i.e., the collaboration among streams, stream buffers, and locales. In this section we discuss who delegates which tasks to whom and how the various components work together.

2.1.1 Class Hierarchy

All stream classes belong to the same class hierarchy. According to their characteristics, the classes fall into three main categories (see figure 2-2): (1) the stream base classes, (2) the general stream classes, and (3) the concrete stream classes.

2.1.1.1 The Stream Base Classes

The base of the stream class hierarchy consists of two stream base classes: (1) a common, character-type-independent part: `ios_base`, and (2) a character-type-dependent class template: `basic_ios<class charT, class Traits>`, having the character type and the character traits type as template parameters.[2] They represent functionality and properties common to all streams, such as error handling, formatting control, etc.

THE CHARACTER-TYPE-INDEPENDENT IOSTREAMS BASE CLASS `ios_base`
The class `ios_base` encapsulates information that is needed by all types of streams and is independent of the character type. Below we give an overview of the information and functionality encapsulated into class `ios_base`. Further details can be found in the reference section of this book. Additionally, there are numerous references to other sections of this book that explain how the information and functionality can be used. The names in parentheses, e.g., (`fmtflags`) or (`flags()`), are the names of types or functions defined in `ios_base`. They can serve as a hook for looking up the relevant section of the reference part of this book. Here is what class `ios_base` provides:

- Type definitions for bitmask types representing the format state (`fmtflags`), the stream error state (`iostate`), the file open modes (`openmode`), stream positions (`seekdir`), and the definitions of flag values associated with those bitmask types.

---

2. See section 2.3, Character Types and Character Traits, for details on these template parameters.

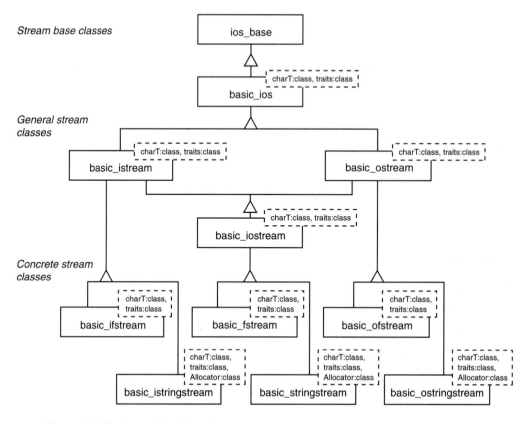

Figure 2-2: *The stream class hierarchy.*

- Type definitions of the IOStreams exception (`failure`).

- The format state, i.e., control information for parsing and formatting, and functionality for setting and getting the format state (`flags()`, `setf()`, `unsetf()`, `precision()`, `width()`).[3]

- Storage, which can be allocated by the stream user, and functionality for accessing it (`xalloc()`, `iword()`, `pword()`).[4]

---

3. This was previously discussed in section 1.2.3, The Format Parameters of a Stream.

4. The additional stream storage is called `iword/pword` and its concept is explained in section 2.5, Additional Stream Storage and Stream Callbacks. Section 3.3.1, Using Stream Storage for Private Use: `iword`, `pword`, and `xalloc`, demonstrates how `iword/pword` can be used for extending IOStreams.

- The locale imbued on the stream, as well as functionality for retrieving and imbuing the locale (getloc() and imbue()).[5]

- Callback functions related to certain events (e.g., the destruction of the stream), plus functionality for their registration (register_callback()), as well as related type definitions.[6]

THE CHARACTER-TYPE-DEPENDENT IOSTREAMS BASE CLASS basic_ios<>

Class basic_ios<class charT, class Traits = char_traits<charT> > is derived from class ios_base and serves as a virtual base class for the general and concrete stream classes. It maintains information common to all stream classes, such as the following:

- A pointer to the stream buffer, and functions for retrieving it (rdbuf()).[7]

- Functionality for error indication:[8]

- The stream state, plus functionality for access to the stream state (rdstate(), setstate(), clear(), good(), bad(), fail(), eof(), etc.).

- The exception mask, plus functionality for access to the exception mask (exceptions()).

Character-type-dependent formatting functionality:

- The fill character for field adjustment in output operations, and functionality for accessing it (fill()).[9]

- A function for copying a stream's data members except the stream state and the stream buffer pointer (copyfmt()).[10]

- A function for stream synchronization by tying streams together (tie()).[11]

---

5. See section 2.1.4, How Streams Maintain Their Locale, for details on locales in IOStreams, and chapter 5 of this book for locales in general.

6. See section 2.5, Additional Stream Storage and Stream Callbacks, for details.

7. See section 2.1.2, How Streams Maintain Their Stream Buffer, for details on how stream buffers are maintained by streams, and 2.2, The Stream Buffer Classes, for an explanation of the internal principles of stream buffers.

8. This was previously discussed in section 1.3, The Stream State.

9. The fill character is the only character-type-dependent formatting information. It was previously discussed in conjunction with the format state in section 1.2.3, The Format Parameters of a Stream.

10. See section 2.1.3, Copying and Assignment, for details.

11. See section 1.8, Synchronization of Streams, for details.

- Character- and locale-dependent functionality for converting character representations (`narrow()` and `widen()`).[12]

RESPONSIBILITY FOR ERROR HANDLING

One might expect that the error handling would be contained in `ios_base` because error indication is character-independent. However, the functionality for access to the stream state and the exception mask is located in class `basic_ios<class charT, class Traits>`. Class `ios_base` contains only the definition of all stream state flags, such as `badbit`, `eofbit`, etc. Access to the stream state and the exception mask is via member functions of class `basic_ios<class charT, class Traits>`, by invoking functions like `exception()`, `good()`, `bad()`, `setstate()`. The reason for this design is that `ios_base` is also used in the locale section of the standard library, where it serves as an abstraction for passing formatting information to the locale. If `ios_base` contained the error indication, which includes throwing exceptions, these exceptions could also be raised by functions of the locale. This effect is neither intended nor acceptable.

This has the interesting side effect that stream functionality can be invoked via an `ios_base` reference or pointer, but the result of such calls cannot be checked, because the caller is deprived of access to the stream state, which can be accessed only via a class derived from `ios_base`. Here is an example of such a situation:

```
void foo(ios_base& str)
{
    int idx = str.xalloc();  // might set badbit in case of memory shortage

    if (str.fail())          // does not work; no access to the stream state here
        ...
}
```

Generally, all functions taking a reference or pointer to an `ios_base` object as a parameter are incapable of performing any kind of error checking or error reporting via the stream state. Also, they cannot obey the IOStreams' policy for raising exceptions in conformity with the exception mask, because the exception mask cannot be accessed either. The callback functions, for instance, fall into this category of functions.

2.1.1.2 The General Stream Classes

The general input and output stream classes provide the entire functionality for parsing input and formatting output. However, they do not contain any information that is specific to the external device associated with the stream. The following are the three general stream classes for input and output:

---

12. See section 2.3.1, Character Representations, for more information on character representations, and section 6.1.1, Character Classification, for more information on the `ctype` facet, to which the task of character transformation is eventually delegated.

```
basic_istream <class charT, class traits=char_traits<charT> >
basic_ostream <class charT, class traits=char_traits<charT> >
basic_iostream<class charT, class traits=char_traits<charT> >
```

Class `basic_istream` handles input, while class `basic_ostream` is for output. Class `basic_iostream` represents a *bidirectional* stream; it is derived from `basic_istream` and `basic_ostream` by multiple inheritance and deals with input *and* output.

The general stream classes provide functions for formatted input and output as well as for unformatted input and output.

FORMATTED I/O. Overloaded versions of `operator>>()` for input, called *extractors*, and overloaded versions of `operator<<()` for output, called *inserters*. The shift operators' overloaded versions for built-in types such as `bool`, `int`, `long`, `float`, `double`, etc. are contained in the general stream classes as member functions. The exceptions to that rule are the inserters and extractors for characters and character sequences; they are implemented as global functions. The versions for abstractions defined in the standard library, such as `string`, `complex`, etc., are provided by global functions.[13]

UNFORMATTED I/O. Member functions like `get()`, `getline()`, `read()`, `peek()`, `put()`, `write()`, etc. They read and write character sequences without parsing or formatting them.

The general stream classes typically serve as base classes for deriving new stream types. They define the way parsing and formatting is done, but do not have knowledge about any specific external device. Derived classes typically reuse the parsing and formatting machinery and just add device-specific functionality. Reuse of the parsing and formatting functionality is facilitated by decoupling parsing and formatting from buffering and transport to the external device. A separate class of objects, the stream buffers, provides device-specific operations. Every stream object refers to a stream buffer object, to which it delegates the task of transporting character to and from the external device.

Like the stream classes, the stream buffer classes are organized in a class hierarchy. The stream buffer base class `basic_streambuf<class charT, class traits = char_traits<charT> >` defines an "abstract" stream buffer interface. The derived stream buffer classes implement the stream buffer interface by overwriting virtual functions as needed.

The operations of the general streams are implemented solely in terms of functions of the stream buffer base class `basic_streambuf`. The "abstract" stream buffer interface is accessed through a pointer to a stream buffer object, which allows polymorphism, so that derived stream classes can delegate to specialized stream buffers derived from the stream buffer base class.

A new stream type can provide access to a new external device via a specialized stream buffer class. This way it reuses all the parsing and formatting functionality, and

---

13. See also section 1.2, Formatted Input/Output.

adds only new device-specific operations such as open() and close() for files, for instance.

2.1.2.3 The Concrete Stream Classes

The concrete stream classes encapsulate formatted input and output to external devices. They contain concrete stream buffer objects, which perform the actual access to the respective device. There are two categories of concrete stream classes: (1) file streams and (2) string streams.

THE FILE STREAM CLASSES

The file stream classes, listed below, support input and output to and from files.[14]

```
basic_ifstream<class charT, class traits=char_traits<charT> >
basic_ofstream<class charT, class traits=char_traits<charT> >
basic_fstream <class charT, class traits=char_traits<charT> >
```

They are derived from the general input and output stream classes and add functions for opening and closing files (open() and close()).

Internally, they contain and use a file buffer object to control the transport of characters to/from the associated file. File buffers are specialized stream buffers that encapsulate the knowledge about reading and writing to the underlying file system.[15]

THE STRING STREAM CLASSES

The string stream classes, listed below, support in-memory I/O, that is, reading and writing to a string held in memory.[16]

```
basic_istringstream<class charT, class Traits=char_traits<charT>
                 ,class Allocator=allocator<charT> >
basic_ostringstream<class charT, class Traits=char_traits<charT>
                 ,class Allocator=allocator<charT> >
basic_stringstream <class charT, class Traits=char_traits<charT>
                 ,class Allocator=allocator<charT> >
```

These classes, too, are derived from the general input and output stream classes. The source and destination of parsing and formatting is a string held in memory. This string also serves as an internal buffer. This means that the string stream buffer and the external

---

14. File streams were previously explained in section 1.4, File Input/Output.

15. See also section 2.2.4, File Stream Buffers.

16. String streams were previously explained in section 1.5, In-Memory Input/Output.

device are identical. The string stream classes add functions for getting and setting the string to be used as a buffer (`str()`).

Internally, a string stream buffer is used; this is a specialized stream buffer that encapsulates reading and writing to the string in memory.[17]

2.1.2 How Streams Maintain Their Stream Buffer

Stream buffers encapsulate buffering, code conversion, and transport of characters to an external device. Each stream object has a stream buffer object to which it delegates all tasks that are specific to the external device.

In the following, we describe how the various stream classes maintain their stream buffer object. Details of how the stream buffer interface is used by the stream classes to implement their functionality are provided in section 3.4.1, Deriving from the Stream Buffer Base Class. The stream buffer interface itself is explained in section 2.2.2, The Stream Buffer Abstraction.

Figure 2-3 shows the static associations between the various stream classes and the stream buffer classes.

The association between streams and stream buffers is as follows:

The stream base class `ios_base` does not refer to stream buffers at all, because `ios_base` is character type independent, whereas the stream buffer is not.

The stream base class `basic_ios <class charT, class Traits>` holds a pointer to a stream buffer object. The pointer is a pointer to the stream buffer base class `basic_streambuf <class charT, class Traits>`. Class `basic_ios<>` is responsible for storing the stream buffer base class pointer but does not access the stream buffer pointed to.

The general stream classes inherit this stream buffer base pointer. They make sure that the stream buffer base class pointer is properly initialized. In contrast to the base class, the general stream classes really access the stream buffer pointed to. All input and output operations defined by the general stream classes are implemented by calling stream buffer functions via the stream buffer base class pointer.

The concrete stream classes eventually provide a stream buffer object. It is contained in a concrete stream object as a data member and is of a type derived from the stream buffer base class; e.g., a string stream contains a string buffer and a file stream has a file buffer. The inherited stream buffer base class pointer is initialized so that it refers to the contained concrete stream buffer object. The concrete stream classes do not add any input or output functionality, only device-specific operations; for instance, file streams have additional `open()` and `close()` functions.

---

17. See also section 2.2.3, String Stream Buffers.

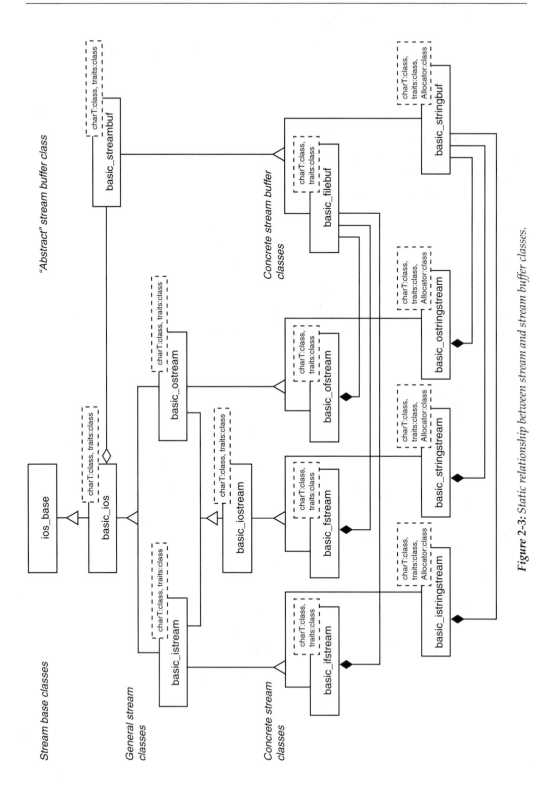

Figure 2-3: Static relationship between stream and stream buffer classes.

The various stream classes offer different functionality for maintaining the stream buffer depending on their responsibilities:

STREAM BASE CLASSES

INITIALIZATION. A stream buffer pointer can be provided when a `basic_ios<>` object is created; for instance, class `basic_ios<class charT, class Traits>` has a public constructor that takes a stream buffer pointer. It also has a protected default constructor that creates a `basic_ios` object with uninitialized members and, in particular, without a valid stream buffer pointer. Such an uninitialized `basic_ios` object must be initialized and provided with a stream buffer by calling the protected member function `init(basic_streambuf <charT, Traits>* sb)` later on.

RETRIEVAL AND REPLACEMENT. Class `basic_ios<class charT, class Traits>` has a function `rdbuf()` for retrieving the current stream buffer pointer. An overloaded version of this function takes a stream buffer pointer and allows replacement of the internal stream buffer pointer.

GENERAL STREAM CLASSES

INITIALIZATION. The general stream classes request a stream buffer pointer at construction time; i.e., their only constructor takes a stream buffer pointer as argument. This pointer is handed over to the base class `basic_ios<>`, which then maintains it as described above. It is allowed that this pointer is 0 and that a later call to `rdbuf(basic_streambuf <charT,traits>* sb)` provides the actual stream buffer that should be used. The stream state is set to `ios_base::badbit` as long as the stream's stream buffer pointer is 0.

RETRIEVAL AND REPLACEMENT. This functionality is inherited from class `basic_ios<>`.

CONCRETE STREAM CLASSES

INITIALIZATION. The concrete stream classes contain a derived stream buffer object as a data member. For example, a file stream contains a file buffer; hence the stream buffer object is automatically created at construction time. A pointer to the contained stream buffer object is handed over to the base classes. The effect is that a concrete stream object contains a stream buffer object and additionally refers to it via the stream buffer base class pointer inherited from class `basic_ios<>`.

RETRIEVAL AND REPLACEMENT. The concrete stream classes also add another version of the retrieval function `rdbuf()`, which hides the `rdbuf()` function inherited from class `basic_ios<>`. The two functions differ in their return type. The inherited version returns a pointer to the stream base class `basic_streambuf<char charT, class Traits>`. The added version returns a pointer to a concrete stream buffer type, such as `basic_filebuf<char charT, class Traits>`. This is the pointer to the contained concrete stream buffer object. The subsequent section explains the subtle differences in more detail.

rdbuf() SUBTLETIES

Note the subtle difference between a concrete stream class's `rdbuf()` function and the inherited version of `rdbuf()`: The inherited `rdbuf()` function `basic_ios<charT, traits>::rdbuf()` returns the pointer to the stream buffer that is maintained by the base class. The concrete stream class's `rdbuf()` function returns a pointer to its contained stream buffer object.

For a newly constructed concrete stream object, both functions return the same pointer. However, after the stream buffer pointer is replaced by a call to `basic_ios<charT,traits>:: rdbuf(basic_streambuf<charT, Traits>* sb)` the base class's `rdbuf()` function returns the newly set pointer, whereas the concrete stream class's `rdbuf()` function keeps on returning the pointer to its contained stream buffer object.

Here is an example that illustrates the difference between the two versions of `rdbuf()`:

```
basic_filebuf<char> buf;
buf.open("in.txt");

basic_ifstream<char> ifstr;             // ifstr by default contains a file buffer object
ifstr.basic_ios<char>::rdbuf(&buf);     // here the file buffer pointer is replaced using the
                                        // hidden base class version of the rdbuf() function

basic_streambuf<char>* bp;
bp = ifstr.rdbuf();                     // redefined rdbuf() returns pointer to contained, but
                                        // unused file buffer
bp = ifstr.basic_ios<char>::rdbuf();    // base class version of the rdbuf() function returns
                                        // pointer to newly assigned and actually used file buffer
```

After replacement of the stream buffer pointer, the buffer object contained in the stream object is unused, because all operations are invoked via the stream buffer pointer, which now refers to a different stream buffer object.

Note, however, that both the member functions `open()` and `close()` of the file stream classes and the member function `str()` of the string stream classes are invoked via their overridden version of `rdbuf()`. The effect is that calls to these functions work only on the embedded stream buffer object, not on the stream buffer that was later assigned and is actually used. For this reason, calls to `open()`, `close()`, and `str()` after replacement of the stream buffer behave in an extremely counterintuitive way.

2.1.3 Copying and Assignment of Streams

Streams can neither be copied nor assigned, because their copy constructor and copy assignment operator are inaccessible.[18] These operations are prohibited because there is

---

18. This is achieved by declaring the copy constructor and copy assignment operator of the stream base class `basic_ios` private.

no common understanding of what the "right" semantics of copying or assigning streams should be. As described above, stream objects contain a pointer to a stream buffer object. After copying or assignment, both copies would be pointing to the same stream buffer object. Whether sharing of the stream buffer is desirable is questionable because lifetime and ownership questions are raised as a result. For example, how long must the stream buffer live? Who owns the stream buffer and will eventually delete it? An alternative approach could be to actually copy the stream buffer object instead of sharing it. At least for string streams, this kind of value semantics would make sense. For file streams, it is hard to imagine anyway what a copy of a file stream buffer should be, because each file stream buffer represents an external file. Should copying a file stream buffer result in copying the actual file? Probably not.

As the semantics of copying and assignment of streams cannot be easily and unanimously defined, they are prohibited, so that streams are not inadvertently copied or assigned.[19] If you need to create copies of streams for any reason, you can do this by copying the parts of a stream separately. Streams have the following member functions defined in their base class `basic_ios`, which can be used for this purpose:

- `iostate rdstate()`, which allows retrieval of the stream state, and

- `void clear(iostate state = goodbit)`, which allows setting of the stream state.

Note that `clear()` can raise exceptions when the stream state is assigned.

`basic_streambuf<class charT, class Traits>* rdbuf()` and `basic_streambuf<class charT, class Traits>* rdbuf(basic_streambuf <class charT, class Traits>* sb)` allow retrieval and setting of the stream buffer pointer.

Mind the difference described in the preceding chapter between the base class version of `rdbuf()` and the hiding version in the concrete stream classes. The base class version returns the stream buffer object referred to by the stream buffer pointer; the derived class version returns a pointer to the embedded stream buffer object. After resetting of the stream buffer pointer, the results of calling the two `rdbuf()` functions differ from one another.

`basic_ios<class charT, class Traits>& copyfmt(basic_ios<class charT, class Traits>& rhs)` allows setting of all other data members of `rhs`.

The following function template shows the use of these functions in an example. Similar to the assignment operator or functions like `strcpy()`, its first parameter is the destination and its second parameter is the source:

---

19. Interestingly, stream buffers, which contain pointers to their get and put areas, *can* be copied and assigned; the semantics of this process are not even defined by the standard. As neither the copy constructor nor the copy assignment for any of the stream buffer classes is specified by the standard, they will most likely not be implemented, which means that the compiler-generated default functionality for copying and assignment will apply; that is, all pointers are copied. Two stream buffer objects that are copies of each other would operate on the same character array without any coordination. The results are likely to be unpredictable. Avoid inadvertent copies or assignments of stream buffer objects.

```
template<class Stream>
void streamcpy(Stream &dest, const Stream& src)
{
    // clear exception mask
    dest.exceptions(ios_base::goodbit);

    dest.clear(src.rdstate());

    typedef basic_ios< Stream::char_type
                    , Stream::traits_type> StreamBase ;
    (static_cast<StreamBase&>(dest))
      .rdbuf((static_cast<const StreamBase&>(src)).rdbuf());
    // call copyfmt after all other actions because it copies
    // the exception mask, which might result in any exceptions thrown
    dest.copyfmt(src);
}
```

First, we must disable all exceptions because we want to invoke `clear()` in order to copy the stream state. This is done as follows: We suppress all exceptions for the time being, because the function `clear()` might otherwise raise exceptions depending on the current exception mask. As we have not yet copied the exception mask of the source stream at this point, the old, incorrect exception mask would be taken into account. Raising exceptions according to the old exception mask would not be correct, and in order to avoid this effect, we disable all exceptions by calling `exceptions(ios_base::goodbit)`. The exceptions will implicitly be enabled again when the exception mask of the source stream is later copied to the destination stream when `copyfmt()` is invoked.

After these preliminaries, we do the actual work and copy the stream state via `rdstate()` and `clear()`, the stream buffer pointer via `rdbuf()`, and eventually the rest of the stream data members (including the exception mask) via `copyfmt()`.

Keep in mind that the issues that led to the prohibition of copy and assignment operations in the stream classes still apply. The stream buffer object, whose pointer is held by both copies of the stream, is a shared object. The caller of `streamcpy()` must make sure that lifetime and ownership issues are handled correctly. We generally do not recommend copying streams, even using a function like `streamcpy()`, unless you are sure you really need the copy and can handle all the resulting pitfalls. Here are two examples of how the `streamcpy()` function could be used and what the resulting surprises would be.

In the code below, we assign all properties of one string stream to another string stream by means of the `streamcpy()` function. Afterwards, the two string streams share the second stream's buffer object so that output via both string streams goes to the same buffer:

```
ostringstream o2, o1;
streamcpy(o1,o2);
o1 << "... something ...";
```

```
o2 << "... something else ...";
cout << o1.str(); // prints nothing
cout << o2.str(); // prints the combined output
```

As expected, the second string buffer will contain the combined output of both output operations, namely:

```
... something ...... something else ...
```

Yet here are the pitfalls:

A little unexpectedly, retrieval of the string streams' content via `str()` yields different results depending on whose `str()` function is called. `o1.str()` accesses its own embedded buffer object, which is not used by any of the output functions anymore, because `o1` uses `o2`'s stream buffer since the call to `streamcpy()`. If, on the other hand, we invoke `o2.str()`, it yields the expected combined output produced by the preceding two output operations. This is because `o2`'s stream buffer is the one that is used by both string streams' output operations, whereas `o1`'s stream buffer is ignored by `o1`'s output operations but is used by `o1`'s `str()` function.

Another pitfall is that the lifetime of the shared stream buffer object must exceed the lifetime of the two string streams that share it. Hence the stream buffer is a data member of the string stream, which means that in the example the string stream `o2`, whose embedded buffer is shared, must not be destroyed before `o1`. For this reason, it is essential that we define the object `o2` prior to `o1`. Naturally, this kind of code is not very robust, and inadvertent reordering of the object definitions would introduce a bug.

Here is another even more deterrent example. The need for assigning streams originally stemmed from the wish to redirect standard output (or any of the other standard I/O objects) by assigning a valid stream object to it, so that any output to the standard stream would actually go to the assigned stream. Here is how you could achieve that by using the `streamcpy()` function:

```
ofstream log("log.txt");

streamcpy(cerr,static_cast<ostream&>(log));

cerr << " ... " << endl;
```

As desired, any output to `cerr` will actually be written to the file `log.txt` that the file stream `log` represents. Here is the snag:

The stream buffer used by `cerr` after the call to `streamcpy()` is that of the file stream object `log`. Now, the standard streams, including `cerr`, are global objects that are destroyed after exit from `main()`. As a consequence, the file stream object `log` is destroyed before `cerr` will be destroyed. Unfortunately, the destructor of `cerr` will `flush()` the stream buffer, which is the shared stream buffer that belonged to the already destroyed file stream `log`. An access violation due to the attempted invocation of `flush()` will occur.

As a rule of thumb, reassignment of the stream buffer pointer should be done with care. As the examples above illustrate, lifetime dependencies and surprises due to the overridden version of `rdbuf()` are likely to create problems.

2.1.4 How Streams Maintain Their Locale

A locale contains culture-dependent information and functionality. A locale object can be seen as a container of facet objects. A facet encapsulates a certain set of culture-dependent information. Examples are the numeric facets that provide functionality for the proper parsing and formatting of numeric values, and the code conversion facets that enable code conversion between different character encodings.[20]

Each stream object "has a" locale object because it delegates the task of parsing and formatting numeric values to the numeric facets of its locale.[21]

A stream buffer object, too, "has a" locale object. File stream buffers use their locale object for code conversion. Figure 2-4 shows the static associations between the various stream classes and the stream buffer classes and the locale and its facets.[22]

The association between streams, stream buffers, and locales is as follows:

FORMATTING LAYER. A locale object is contained and maintained by the base class `ios_base`. The formatting and parsing functions of the general stream classes inherit and access the locale for retrieving its *numeric facets* for culture-dependent parsing and formatting of numeric values, and indirectly the *ctype facet* for determining whitespace characters that have to be skipped on input.

BUFFERING/TRANSPORT LAYER. An additional locale object is contained and maintained by the stream buffer base class `basic_streambuf<class charT,class Traits>`. The stream buffer's locale object is usually a copy of the stream's locale object. Some concrete stream buffer classes access the inherited locale for code conversions. String stream buffers do not access their locale, because they do not perform any culture-dependent operations. File buffers, however, use the *code conversion facet* of their locale for the code conversion between the external and internal character type.

A stream object has two locale objects: one maintained by class `ios_base`, and the other maintained by the stream buffer. Usually, these two locale objects are copies of each other,[23] but they need not be. Let us see how the two locale objects are maintained:

---

20. See part II for details on locales and facets.

21. See also section 2.1.5, Collaboration among Streams, Stream Buffers, and Locales.

22. See section 2.3.1, Character Representations, which motivates the necessity of code conversions. See also section 4.2.7, Character Encodings, for character encodings and code conversions in general.

23. Copying locale objects is a cheap operation. You need not be concerned that the numerous copies of locale objects create any significant overhead. Copies of locales internally refer to the same container of facets. For details see chapter 7, "The Architecture of the Locale Framework."

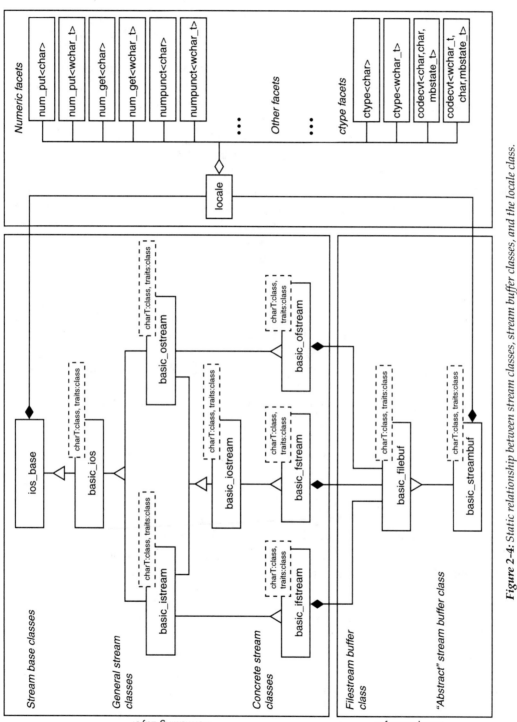

Figure 2-4: *Static relationship between stream classes, stream buffer classes, and the locale class.*

INITIALIZATION. When a stream object is constructed, a copy of the current global C++ locale is used to initialize the stream's locale. The same locale object is used to initialize the stream buffer's locale.

RETRIEVAL. A copy of the stream's locale object can be obtained by calling the `getloc()` member function of the stream base class `ios_base`. Retrieval of the stream buffer's locale object is via the `getloc()` member function of stream buffer base class `basic_streambuf<class charT, class Traits>`.

REPLACEMENT. The locale objects can be replaced independently of each other, or they can both be consistently replaced by the same new locale.

For independent replacement the following functions have to be invoked: The function `ios_base::imbue(const locale& loc)` replaces the stream's locale object. The stream buffer base class's `pubimbue()` function replaces the stream buffer's locale object.

For consistent replacement of both locale objects, the stream base class `basic_ios<>` defines an additional `imbue()` function that implicitly invokes the two functions for separate replacement. The subsequent section explains the details.

IMBUING LOCALES

In choosing the name `imbue()` for the locale replacement function in IOStreams, the standards committee coined a new technical term: *imbuing a stream with a locale,* which means replacing a stream's locale object(s).

The straightforward way of imbuing a stream with a new locale is to replace both locale objects consistently, so that the change affects formatting, parsing, and code conversion. This is easily achieved by calling a stream's `imbue()` function. Here is an example. If `str` is a stream object and `loc` a locale object, then `str.imbue(loc);` is a call to `basic_ios<charT,Traits>::imbue()`, which replaces both locales consistently.

If, for whatever reason, a new locale is to be set only for formatting and parsing, this can be done by calling `ios_base::imbue()` explicitly:

```
((ios_base&)str).imbue(loc);
```

This call replaces only the stream's locale object.

If a new locale is to be set only for code conversion, this can be done by calling the stream buffer's `pubimbue()` member function:

```
if (str.rdbuf() != 0)
   str.rdbuf()->pubimbue(loc);
```

This call replaces only the stream buffer's locale object.

A NOTE ON PROPER IMBUING

In principle, you can attach a new locale to a stream or stream buffer object at any time during the stream's lifetime. However, replacing the locale of a stream or stream buffer is a delicate task. Consider, for example, an input stream that has numeric data waiting to be extracted and parsed. If the stream's locale is replaced, the remaining numeric data might no longer conform to the parsing rules defined by the locale, which might lead to surprising results when the data are eventually extracted.

There is no indication of whether or not it is safe and sensible to switch locales. Neither the stream nor the stream buffer can indicate this. Hence, proper replacement of a locale is completely under the control of the user code, and the user has to come up with a concept that makes locale changes safe.

INDICATION OF LOCALE REPLACEMENT

Streams and stream buffers can be extended in various ways, as described in subsequent chapters. Such extensions might rely on the locale of the stream or stream buffer to perform their operations. Often, it is essential that these functions be informed whenever the current locale object is replaced.

IOStreams uses two different mechanisms for indicating that a locale switch has happened:

FORMATTING LAYER. For a stream object a callback function can be registered; this is invoked with an `imbue_event` indication in case a new locale imbues the stream. For details about callback functions, see section 2.5.2, Stream Callbacks.

BUFFERING/TRANSPORT LAYER. Stream buffer classes have a virtual protected member function `void imbue(const locale& loc)`, which is invoked when a new locale is imbued to the stream buffer. A derived stream buffer class that wants to perform certain activities when the locale changes should override this virtual member function accordingly.

2.1.5 Collaboration Among Streams, Stream Buffers, and Locales

Streams, stream buffers, and locales work closely together. Streams delegate transport, code conversion, and buffering of characters to their stream buffer object. Stream buffers, again, delegate code conversion to their locale object's code conversion facet. Also, streams delegate the parsing and formatting of numeric values to the numeric facets of their locale object. The numeric facets, again, directly collaborate with the stream buffer for transport and buffering via stream buffer iterators.

This section explains the principles of the collaboration of streams, stream buffers, and locales in terms of a typical example: formatted input and output of an integral value.

FORMATTING AND PARSING NUMERICAL VALUES

Here is the implementation of an inserter and an extractor for an integral value. Note that many details are omitted to keep the example focused on the principles. In particular, error handling is left out. The point is that a stream's inserters delegate the task of formatting an integral value to the `put()` function of the stream locale's `num_put` facet, and the task of parsing an integral value is taken over by the `get()` function of the stream locale's `num_get` facet.

The general scheme for an inserter is retrieval of the stream's locale via a call to getloc(), retrieval of the locale's num_put facet, and invocation of the facet's put() function. Here is a simplified version of an inserter for integral values:

```
template<class charT, class Traits>
basic_ostream<charT, Traits>&
basic_ostream<charT, Traits>::operator<<(int n)
{
  use_facet<num_put<charT,ostreambuf_iterator<charT,Traits> > >
  (this->getloc()).put(*this, *this, basic_ios<charT,Traits>::fill(),n);
  return *this;
}
```

The extractor does basically the same. It retrieves the stream's locale, retrieves the locale's num_get facet, and invokes the facet's get() function. Here is a simplified version of an extractor for integral values:

```
template<class charT, class traits>
basic_istream<charT, traits>&
basic_istream<charT, traits>::operator>>(int& n)
{
  ios_base::iostate err = 0;

  use_facet<num_get<charT,istreambuf_iterator<charT,traits> > >
  (this->getloc()).get(*this,istreambuf_iterator<charT,traits>(),*this,err,n);
  return *this;
}
```

We do not want to discuss all of the arguments provided to the calls of the put() and get() functions. The details can be looked up in appendix A, Parsing and Extraction of Numerical and bool Values, appendix B, Formatting of Numerical and bool Values, and section 6.2.1, Numeric and Boolean Values. Certain principles, however, are worth exploring here, because they aid understanding of the intended ways of using parsing and formatting facets in general.

Consider the functions' signatures:

```
iter_type put(iter_type out,
              ios_base& fmt, char_type fill,
              long val) const;
```

and

```
iter_type get(iter_type in, iter_type end,
              ios_base& fmt,
```

```
ios_base::iostate& err,
long& val) const;
```

In the following, we examine access to source and destination of input and output, access to formatting information, and error reporting, in particular:

ITERATORS. The operations of parsing and formatting facets take iterators as arguments. `put()` functions take an output iterator that designates the destination for output; `get()` functions take an input iterator range that designates the character sequence to be parsed. Both operations return an iterator that points to the position after the sequence written to or read from.

FORMATTING INFORMATION. Parsing and formatting facets retrieve formatting information from an `ios_base` object that is provided as an argument to their operations.

ERROR INDICATION. `get()` functions store error information in an `ios_base::iostate` object; `put()` functions report failure indirectly via the iterator they return.

USE OF STREAM BUFFER ITERATORS[24]

Formatting and parsing facets used in IOStreams access the stream buffer directly via a *stream buffer iterator*. Formatting operations, like `num_put<charT>::put()`, take one iterator, the iterator to the beginning of the output sequence. Parsing operations like `num_get<charT>::get()` take an iterator range designating beginning and end of the subsequence of characters to be parsed.

Let us study a typical use of the stream buffer iterators by reexamining the previously shown example of an extractor for integral values:

```
template<class charT, class traits>
basic_istream<charT, traits>&
basic_istream<charT, traits>::operator>>(int& n)
{
  ios_base::iostate err = 0;

  use_facet<num_get<charT,istreambuf_iterator<charT,traits> > >
  (this->getloc()).get(*this,istreambuf_iterator<charT,traits>(),*this,err,n);
  return *this;
}
```

The source of input is described as the iterator range [`*this`, `istreambuf_iterator <charT,traits>()`).[25]

---

24. Stream buffer iterators are described in greater detail in section 2.4.3, Stream Buffer Iterators.

25. We are going to use the mathematical notation [ ), which indicates a half-open interval, whenever we need to specify an iterator range.

The *begin iterator* is the stream buffer iterator pointing to the current position of the input sequence; it is created from the stream itself. This is possible because stream buffer iterators can be constructed from a stream itself by providing `*this` as the first argument. The implicit conversion mechanism for function arguments in C++ cares for construction of the input stream buffer iterator from `*this` by calling the iterator's converting constructor, which takes a reference to a stream as an argument.

The *end iterator* is an input stream buffer iterator designating the end of the input sequence. It is created via the default constructor for input stream buffer iterators. Default constructors of iterators by convention always create an iterator pointing to the position one step past the end of the sequence.

A NOTE ON FORMATTING AND PARSING FACETS IN GENERAL

The formatting and parsing facet templates are even more general than the example above suggests. In fact, the type of iterator is a template parameter of the facet type. The `num_put` facet, for instance, is a class template defined as

```
template <class charT, class OutputIterator = ostreambuf_iterator<charT> >
class num_put;
```

This means that you can instantiate formatting facets so that they can output their results to any kind of container, as long as the container is accessible via an output iterator. Parsing facets do exactly the same, using input iterators for receiving the character sequence to be parsed. Only when used in IOStreams do these facets use stream buffer iterators and in this way achieve direct access to the stream buffer.

ACCESS TO FORMATTING CONTROL

The formatting and parsing facets need access to the formatting information, such as the precision of floating-point values, or whether an integral value is represented as decimal, octal, or hexadecimal. Such information is held in the stream's base class `ios_base`. For this reason both parsing and formatting facets take a reference to an `ios_base` object as an argument.

The formatting facets additionally take a character argument, which is the fill character used for padding. It cannot be taken from the `ios_base` object, because the stream's fill character is contained in the `basic_ios<class charT, class Traits>` base class of the stream.

The formatting and parsing facets also use the `ios_base` object for access to its formatting information, but also for access to its locale. This is necessary because the numeric facets rely on other facets. For instance, the `num_put` facet takes the radix character from the `numpunct` facet; the `num_get` facet takes the information about whitespace characters to be skipped from the `ctype` facet. When a facet's operation must access other facets, it needs an explicit reference to the locale object that contains those required facets, even if they are contained in the same locale. In the case of parsing and formatting facets,

this reference to a locale object containing related facets is accessible via the `ios_base&`
argument to its operations.

This means that the `ios_base` object provided to parsing or formatting operations
should contain a compatible, if not identical, locale object. In the code fragment from the
example above

```
use_facet<num_get<charT,istreambuf_iterator<charT,traits> > >
  (this->getloc()).get(*this,istreambuf_iterator<charT,traits>(),*this,err,n);
```

the compatibility is achieved by providing `*this` as an `ios_base` argument. (It is the
third argument to the call of `get()`.) In fact, the locale objects are the same: The parsing
facet `num_get` is retrieved from the stream's locale object via `this->getloc()`. The
same locale object is contained in the `ios_base` part of `*this`. This way all facets are
guaranteed to be retrieved from the same locale object.

INDICATING ERRORS

Two different techniques are applied for indicating failure of a facet's parsing or formatting operation.

The parsing facets take a reference to an `ios_base::iostate` object as an argument to their `get()` function. They set `ios_base::failbit` in case of parse error and
`ios_base::goodbit` in case of success.

The formatting facets do not make provisions for error reporting. Instead, the iterator returned by their `put()` function can be checked for failure.

Let us revisit the previous examples of an extractor and an inserter for integral values. This time the error checks are added to the calls of `put()` and `get()`.

The extractor provides a reference to an `iostate` object to the `get()` function and
checks it for failure after parsing:

```
template<class charT, class traits>
basic_istream<charT, traits>&
basic_istream<charT, traits>::operator>>(int& n)
{
 ios_base::iostate err = 0;

 use_facet<num_get<charT,istreambuf_iterator<charT,traits> > >(this->getloc())
   .get(*this,
       istreambuf_iterator<charT,traits>(),
       *this,
       err,                          // provide an iostate object to the facet
       n);
 if ( err ) this->setstate(err);    // set the stream's state accordingly
 return *this;
}
```

The inserter checks for failure of the formatting by checking the iterator that is returned by the `get()` function. Output stream buffer iterators have a `failed()` member function that reports whether output was possible:

```
template<class charT, class Traits>
basic_ostream<charT, Traits>&
basic_ostream<charT, Traits>::operator<<(int n)
{
  if (
      use_facet<num_put<charT,ostreambuf_iterator<charT,traits> > >
      (this->getloc()).put(*this,*this,basic_ios<charT,traits>::fill(),n)
      .failed()          // check the returned iterator's state
      )
    this->setstate(ios_base::badbit); // set the stream's state accordingly
  return *this;
}
```

Note that the error reporting of an inserter slightly differs from that of an extractor: The extractor sets the stream state to whatever the parsing facet's `get()` function decided to report in the `iostate` object. This can be `eofbit` (if the end of the input sequence was found), `failbit` (if the extracted character sequence violates the parsing rules, i.e., does not have the format of an integer), and/or `badbit` (in case reading from the external device failed). The inserter, on the other hand, always sets `badbit`, because problems during output can occur only if writing to the external device fails.

A NOTE ON CHECKING FORMATTING FAILURE VIA THE RETURNED ITERATOR

Above, we have considered parsing and formatting facets only in the context of stream inserters and extractors. In those cases, stream buffer iterators were used. However, the type of iterator is a template parameter of a facet type, and formatting facets like `num_put<class charT, class OutputIterator>` can be instantiated on any kind of output iterator. Error checking after formatting is possible only if the output iterator is capable of indicating errors, as output stream buffer iterators do via their `failed()` member function.

2.2 The Stream Buffer Classes

The stream buffer classes represent the abstraction of a connection to an external device. The main task of the stream buffer is transport of characters to and from this external device, and buffering of these characters in an internal buffer.

The external devices are seen as sequences of characters. In the following, we will therefore simply talk of *sequences* when we mean the abstraction of an external device.

Stream buffers are used by streams for actual transport of characters to and from a device, whereas the streams themselves are responsible for parsing and formatting the text input and output.

2.2.1 Class Hierarchy

Like the stream classes, the stream buffer classes are organized in a class hierarchy (see figure 2-5).

Class `basic_streambuf<class charT, class Traits>` acts as an "abstract" stream buffer class. All concrete stream buffer classes, such as file stream buffers and string stream buffers, are derived from that "abstract" stream buffer class. The concrete stream buffer classes encapsulate knowledge that is specific to the external device connected to the stream, whereas the stream base class is independent of the specific device and defines the general buffering and transport interface and functionality that has to be provided by a stream buffer.

Class `basic_streambuf<class charT, class Traits>` is an "abstract" base class in the sense that no instances of this class can be constructed. Its constructor is protected and hence accessible only to derived classes. A number of member functions are virtual and meant to be overwritten by a derived class. However, none of the virtual functions is purely virtual. Rather, all virtual member functions implement a sensible default behavior so that they need not be overwritten in a derived class if the default behavior already meets the derived class's needs.

The file buffer classes `basic_filebuf<class charT, class Traits>` allow input and output to files. They have additional member functions `open()` and `close()` that are necessary for file handling, and they override several virtual functions that perform the actual transport of characters to and from the file.

The string stream buffer classes `basic_stringbuf<class charT, class Traits, class Allocator>` implement the in-memory I/O, i.e., they associate the input and output sequences with a memory location.

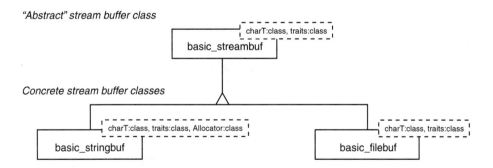

Figure 2-5: *The stream buffer classes.*

The following sections describe first the principles of the stream buffer abstraction in general and then the concrete mechanisms for each of the derived stream buffer classes. We concentrate on the main functionality of stream buffers, namely input, output, and putback. Other aspects such as positioning and locale management are omitted, but can be looked up in the reference part of this book if needed.

2.2.2 The Stream Buffer Abstraction

Two character sequences are associated with a stream buffer: the input sequence and the output sequence, which represents the external device. Internally a stream buffer maintains a character array for buffering the input and/or output sequence. If the entire sequence does not fit into this character array, which naturally is of limited length, the buffer represents a subsequence of the input and/or output sequence. This way the internal buffer can be seen as a window to the input and/or output sequence (see figure 2-6).

The input (sub)sequence, which is kept in the character array, is called the *get area*; the output (sub)sequence is called the *put area*. Each (sub)sequence, the input as well as the output sequence, is described by three pointers: (1) the *begin_pointer*, which is the address of the lowest element in the area, (2) the *next_pointer*, which is the address of the element that is the next candidate for reading or writing, and (3) the *end-pointer*, which is the address of the next element beyond the end of the area.

If an area is not available, the next_pointer is null. The way in which input and output areas are related is unspecified for the stream buffer base class. All you know is that there are two areas, each of which is described by three pointers and represents a (sub)sequence of the external device.

The interface of the stream buffer base class falls into three parts:

1. *Public.* These functions are used by the streams for implementing their functionality on top of the stream buffer.

2. *Protected nonvirtual.* These functions are used for implementing the stream buffer's public interface.

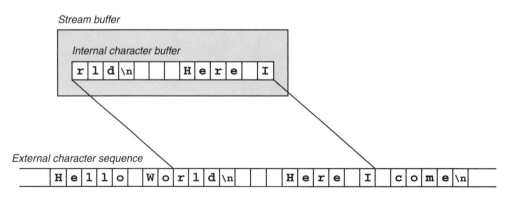

Figure 2-6: *The stream buffer represents a subsequence of the external character sequence.*

3. _Protected virtual._ These functions are meant to be overridden by any derived stream buffer classes.

The protected virtual interface of a stream buffer class provides operations that access the external character sequence.[26] Such operations

- perform reads directly on the associated input (sub)sequence (`xsgetn()`, `underflow()`, `uflow()`, etc.), or

- perform writes directly on the associated output (sub)sequence (`xsputn()`, `overflow()`),

- make put back positions available in the input (sub)sequence (`pbackfail()`), and

- alter "the stream position" and conversion state (`seekoff()`, `seekpos()`).

The protected nonvirtual interface of a stream buffer class provides operations that manipulate one or both of the internal sequences. Such operations

- retrieve the values of the pointers (the get area's begin_, next_, and end_pointer via `eback()`, `gptr()`, `egptr()`, and the put area's begin_, next_, and end_ pointer via `pbase()`, `pptr()`, `epptr()`),

- alter the value of the pointers (by assigning new pointers via `setg()`, `setp()`, or by incrementing the next_pointer via `gbump()`, `pbump()`).

The public interface is built on top of the protected interface and is used by the stream layer to implement its operations. The stream buffer's public interface includes operations for extraction and insertion of characters from/to the get/put area, stream positioning, and other functionality:

- extract characters from the get area (`sgetc()`, `sgetn()`, `sbumpc()`, etc.)

- insert characters to the put area (`sputc()`, `sputn()`, etc.)

- put back characters to the get area (`sputbackc()`, `sungetc()`)

- stream positioning (`pubseekoff()`, `pubseekpos()`).

In addition to the functions mentioned above, stream buffers have a couple of other member functions. Only the most important and typical functions are listed above. For a complete description of the stream buffer base class's interface, see the reference section. Also, section 3.4, Adding Stream Buffer Functionality, provides more details on the protected interface.

---

26. The list of stream buffer operations is not meant to be complete. Only the most important and typical functions are listed. For a complete description of the stream buffer base class's interface, see the reference section. Also, section 3.4, Adding Stream Buffer Functionality, provides more details on the protected interface.

A note on the stream buffer classes' constructors and destructors:

- The stream buffer base class's destructor is public and virtual, as is usual for a class that is designed to serve as a base class.

- The stream buffer base class has only one constructor, which is a protected default constructor. This is to ensure that only derived stream buffer objects may be constructed. The concrete stream buffer classes, of course, have public constructors.

Neither the copy constructor nor the copy assignment for any of the stream buffer classes is specified by the standard. In particular, it is not required that they are inaccessible. They will most likely not be implemented at all, which means that the compiler-generated default functionality for copying and assignment will apply. As a consequence, stream buffers, which contain pointers to their get and put areas, *can* be copied and assigned, meaning that the internally held pointers will be copied. Two stream buffer objects that are copies of each other would operate on the same character array without any coordination. The results are likely to be unpredictable. For this reason, avoid inadvertent copies or assignments of stream buffer objects.

Let's return to the stream buffer's core functionality and look at the principles of handling character input and output in the stream buffer classes.

EXTRACTING INPUT FROM THE INPUT SEQUENCE

A character can be requested from the input sequence by calling the stream buffer's public member function sgetc(). If the get area exists and is not empty, i.e., next_pointer != 0 and next_pointer < end_pointer, the next character from the get area is returned. If the get area does not exist or is empty, the protected virtual member function underflow() is called.

Alternatively, a character can be requested from the input sequence via the stream buffer's public member function sbumpc(). In addition to the functionality of sgetc(), namely, extraction of a character from the input sequence, sbumpc() also advances the read position. The effect is that the character extracted after a call to sbumpc() is the character at the next read position, whereas after a call to sgetc() the same character will be returned again. Roughly speaking, sgetc() means "looking at the available character" and sbumpc() means "consuming the available character." If the get area does not exist or is empty, then sbumpc() invokes the protected virtual member function uflow(), which is the counterpart to underflow() in the case of sgetc().

In the stream buffer base class basic_streambuf, the virtual function uflow() is implemented in terms of underflow(): It invokes underflow() and increments the get area's next pointer. This is a sensible default behavior that works nicely for stream buffers that have an internal character buffer. In fact, neither file buffers nor string buffers override this default behavior of uflow(), but only redefine underflow(). For this reason, we focus on the functionality of underflow() in the rest of this section.

The general purpose of underflow() is to make additional characters from the external sequence available in the internal buffer; in other words, it fills (all or part of) the get area with characters taken from the external device.

BASE CLASS. For the stream buffer base class, `basic_streambuf`, `underflow()` is in a nonoperational mode; its implementation returns `traits::eof()`, which indicates that the end of the stream is reached. Any useful behavior of `underflow()` fully depends on the characteristics of the external device, and `underflow()` is well defined for the derived stream buffer classes, which redefine this virtual function. The functionality of `uflow()` is that of `underflow()` plus advancing the read position.

STRING BUFFER. A string buffer cannot make additional characters available from an external device, because string streams are not connected to an external character sequence.[27] A string stream buffer can make characters available for reading only when they have previously been stored in the internal buffer, for instance, as a result of a previous output operation. Such characters are made accessible by adjusting the get area pointers; more precisely, the get area's end pointer must be moved forward to include additional positions. This pointer adjustment can be done in `underflow()` or `uflow()` as part of an input operation. Alternatively, it can be performed during `overflow()` as part of an output operation. The standard allows both implementations.

FILE BUFFER. A file buffer's `underflow()` function makes additional characters available by reading new characters from the file. It then converts them to the internal character representation (if necessary), writes the result of the conversion into the get area, and returns the first newly read character.

INSERTING OUTPUT TO THE OUTPUT SEQUENCE

A character is written to the output sequence via the public member function `sputc()`. As an argument to `sputc()` the stream buffer receives a character to be inserted into the output sequence. If the put area exists and it is not already full, i.e., next_pointer != 0 and next_pointer < end_pointer, then the character is put to the position the next_pointer is referring to, and the next_pointer is incremented. If the put area does not exist or is full, then the protected member function `overflow()` is called, taking the character as an argument.

The general notion of `overflow()` is to make positions in the internal buffer available by writing characters to the external sequence, in other words, it empties (all or part of) the put area by writing characters to the external device. If the character received as an argument to `overflow()` does not equal end-of-file, this character is placed into the "fresh" internal buffer; otherwise no additional character is placed into the put area.

BASE CLASS. For the stream buffer base class, `basic_streambuf`, `overflow()` is in a nonoperational mode; its implementation returns `traits::eof()`, which indicates that the end of the stream is reached. Any useful behavior of `overflow()` fully depends on the characteristics of the external device, and `overflow()` is well defined for the derived classes, which override this virtual function.

STRING BUFFER. String buffers make positions in their internal buffer available by extending the buffer. The `overflow()` function reallocates a new, larger character array.

---

27. Section 2.2.3, String Stream Buffers, explains in greater detail why this is.

Then the character passed to `overflow()` as an argument is added to the put area, and the get area's end pointer might be adjusted to include this new character.[28]

FILE BUFFER. A file buffer makes positions in its internal buffer available by writing to the external file. To be precise, it converts the characters contained in the put area to the external character representation (if necessary) and writes the result of the conversion to the file. After that it puts the character that was received as an argument to `overflow()` into the (fully or partly) emptied put area, unless it was equal to end-of-file.

PUTTING BACK CHARACTERS TO THE INPUT SEQUENCE

The stream buffer's public interface provides two function for putting back characters to the input sequence: `sputbackc()` and `sungetc()`.

`sputbackc()` receives a character as an argument. This character is to be put back to the input sequence, that is, stored in the input sequence before the current read position. If the get area exists and characters have already been read, i.e., next_pointer != 0 and begin_pointer < next_pointer, a putback position is available. In this case, the character is stored in the position before the one the next_pointer currently refers to, and the next_pointer is decreased so that it points to this previous position.

`sungetc()` does not take an argument, but simply decrements the current read position, which has the effect of putting back the previously extracted character. No actual write access to the input sequence takes place, only the next_pointer is moved one position back.

`pbackfail()` is a protected member function that stores a character at the previous position in the input sequence and makes available additional putback positions.

Both `sputbackc()` and `sungetc()` call the protected member function `pbackfail()`. `sungetc()` uses the second functionality of `pbackfail()` and invokes it, if the get area does not exist (i.e., next_pointer == 0) or if no putback position is available (i.e., begin_pointer == next_pointer). `sputbackc()` uses both features of `pbackfail()`. It invokes `pbackfail()` when no putback position is available and when a character is put back that is different from the previously extracted one, that is, when an actual write access to the input sequence is required.

The general notion of `pbackfail()` is: (1) to store the character received as argument at the previous position, and to adjust the get area pointers so that the next read request will return the character that was put back, and (2) to make a putback position available in the internal buffer.

BASE CLASS. For the stream buffer base class `basic_streambuf`, `pbackfail()` is in a nonoperational mode; its implementation returns `traits::eof()`, which indicates failure. Any useful behavior fully depends on the characteristics of the external device, and `pbackfail()` is well defined for the derived classes, which override this virtual function.

---

28. The adjustment of the get area's end pointer might alternatively be deferred to the next input operations and would then be performed during `underflow()`.

STRING BUFFER. For string stream buffers, only the functionality (1) of pbackfail(), storing a character in the input sequence, is implemented. The next_pointer is decreased, and if the character to be put back is not the previously extracted one, the new character is stored at that position.

Functionality (2), making available additional putback positions, does not make sense for a string stream buffer. Putback positions are available only if characters have previously been extracted from the string. When there are no previously extracted characters, pbackfail() cannot make any available either.

FILE BUFFER. For file stream buffers, functionality (1), storing a character in the input sequence, is implemented in the same way as for string stream buffers. The next_pointer is decreased, and if the character to be put back is not the previously extracted one, the new character is stored at that position. A file buffer might fail to actually store the character, because the associated file was opened only for input and does not allow write access.

Functionality (2), making available additional putback positions, is implemented-dependent. For a file stream buffer it is conceivable that additional putback positions are made available by reloading characters from the external file. The standard, however, does not specify any implementation details.[29]

The subsequent two sections describe the behavior of the string buffers and file buffer in terms of an example. We explain in detail how input and output sequence, the internal character buffer, and the get and put areas are related to each other for these two derived classes. The third section describes the principle of the putback area, which is basically the same for string buffers and file buffers.

In order to show the principles, we make assumptions about the implementation of these classes. Standard compatible implementations, however, are allowed to differ and may work in a slightly different way than demonstrated in the following. Still, the general principles will be the same. The implementations of string buffers and file buffers override the virtual functions discussed above in order to achieve the results that we are going to describe. In the following, we do not aim to explain exactly how each of the virtual functions is redefined, but we intend to explain the overall net effect. Details of how to redefine which of the virtual functions, and under which circumstances, are discussed in section 3.4, Adding Stream Buffer Functionality.

2.2.3 String Stream Buffers

A string stream buffer maintains an internal buffer that is large enough to hold the entire external sequence; the get area contains the entire input sequence, and the put area represents the entire output sequence.

The get and put areas are related and available simultaneously. Figure 2-7 shows a typical situation:

---

29. Details of a typical implementation are described in section 2.2.4, File Stream Buffers.

String stream buffer

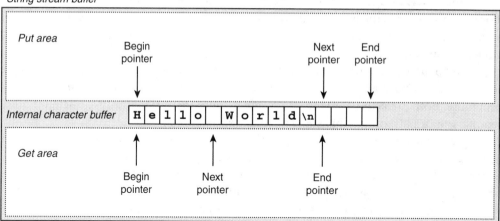

Figure 2-7: Get and put area of a string stream buffer.

In this example the capacity of the internal character buffer is 16 characters, which is utterly unrealistic for real implementations. We do this on purpose, in order to keep the example simple yet demonstrate the crucial case of what happens if the buffer is full or empty.

The character sequence `Hello World\n` has been written to the output sequence, and the pointers of the put area are assigned in the following way:

begin_pointer to the beginning of the character array

next_pointer to the next empty position behind the text written to the output sequence

end_pointer to the next position behind the character array

The character sequence `Hello` has already been read from the input sequence, and the pointers of the get area are assigned in the following way:

begin_pointer to the beginning of the character array

next_pointer to the next position behind the text already read from the input sequence

end_pointer to the same positions as the put area's next_pointer, because it is not possible to read text that has not already been written

Let us discuss the effect of input and output operations on the string stream buffer starting from the situation described above.

OUTPUT

"NORMAL" SITUATION. In this situation we write an additional character to the string stream buffer. The put area's next_pointer refers to the next available position in the put area.

Hence the additional character is put to the position the put area's next_pointer refers to. Afterwards the next_pointer is incremented, so that it points to the next available position.

"OVERFLOW" SITUATION. If we keep on adding characters to the string stream buffer, the put area will eventually be full. When the internal buffer is full, the put area's next_pointer points to the end of the buffer area, i.e., next_pointer == end_pointer. Figure 2-8 illustrates this situation:

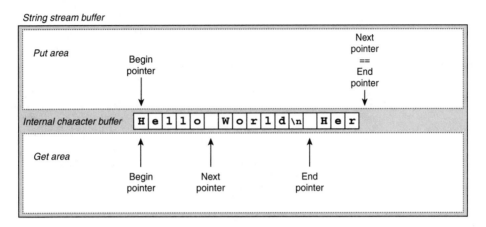

Figure 2-8: String stream buffer is full after output.

This situation is special, because the internal buffer is full. If we want to write an additional character, the string stream buffer needs to make available a new position in the put area. This is achieved by calling overflow(). The function overflow() acquires a new character array that can hold more characters. Figure 2-9 shows the situation after the call to overflow():

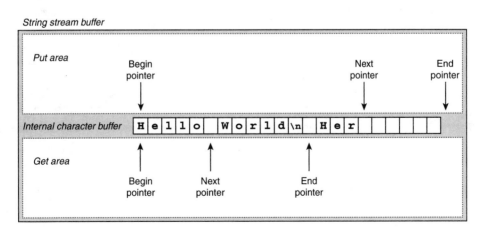

Figure 2-9: String stream buffer after call to overflow().

Afterwards the new character is put into the new position in the put area and the put area's next_pointer is incremented as always.

INPUT

During all these output operations on the string stream buffer the input area basically did not change. After the reallocation of the internal buffer due to the `overflow()`, the get area's pointers are reassigned to the same positions relative to each other.

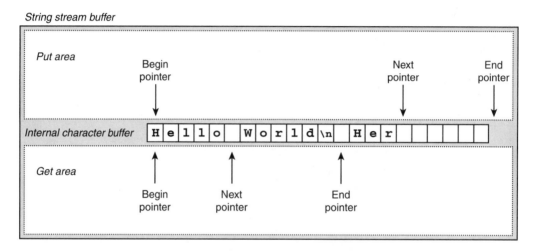

Figure 2-10: String stream buffer before input.

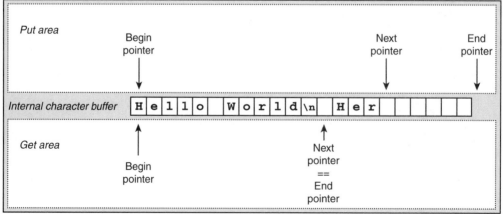

Figure 2-11: String stream buffer with exhausted get area.

"NORMAL" SITUATION. If we read a character from the string stream buffer, we receive the character that the get area's next_pointer refers to. Considering the situation in figure 2-10, this is a whitespace character. Afterwards the get area's next_pointer is incremented.

"UNDERFLOW" SITUATION. Let us assume that we keep on extracting characters from the string stream buffer and there is no intervening insertion; i.e., the put area does not change. We will ultimately reach the end of the get area, i.e., next_pointer == end_pointer, as shown in figure 2-11.

If we now try to read a new character from the string stream buffer, underflow() is called in order to make additional characters available for reading. underflow() adjusts the get area's end_pointer so that it points to the same positions as the put area's next_pointer. In this way, all previously written characters are made available for subsequent read attempts. If all previously written characters have already been read and the get area's end_pointer equals the put area's end pointer, underflow() fails. In the situation shown in figure 2-11, additional characters can be made available, and underflow() adjusts the get area's end_pointer as shown in figure 2-12:

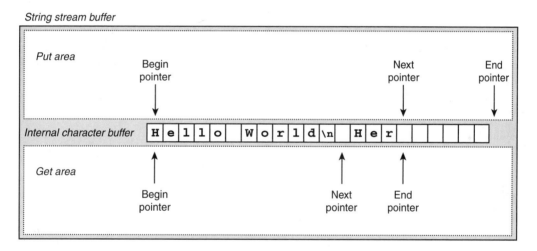

String stream buffer

Figure 2-12: *String stream buffer after call to* underflow().

DISCLAIMER. The model explained above is just one of many ways to implement a string buffer. As an alternative, overflow() could allocate a new buffer area that holds exactly one additional position and adjusts not only the put area's pointers but also the get area's end_pointer. In this way each character written is immediately available for reading, without any pointer adjustment performed via underflow() as in the example above. In this alternative model, underflow() need not be redefined at all. Naturally, this solution is less efficient than the one described before, because the internal character buffer is always full and must be reallocated for each single character written to the string stream.

PUTBACK

Figure 2-13 shows a typical situation in which a number of characters have already been read from the input sequence. In this situation, characters can be put back to the input sequence.

Only the get area is relevant to our discussion of the putback support; the pointers of the put area are not affected at all. The string `Hello` has been extracted, and the get area's next_pointer points to the next available read position. If a character is now requested via `sbumpc()`, the next character (the blank between `Hello` and `World\n`) is extracted and afterwards the next_pointer points to the character `W`.

"NORMAL" SITUATION. Let us see what happens if we then call `sungetc()`, with the intention of putting back the just extracted character, which was the blank. In this case the get area's next_pointer is simply decremented and points to the blank again. The next extraction would again return the blank character, which means that the previous extraction was reversed by the call to `sungetc()`. A further call to `sungetc()` would decrement the next_pointer even further and make available the character `o` for a subsequent read operation.

"PBACKFAIL" SITUATION. What if, in that situation, `sputbackc('l')` is called instead of `sungetc()`? The function `sungetc()` is supposed to make available the character `o`, whereas `sputbackc('l')` should override the character `o` and put back the character `l` in its position. As the character that is put back is different from the character that was extracted from this position, the function `pbackfail()` is called, and

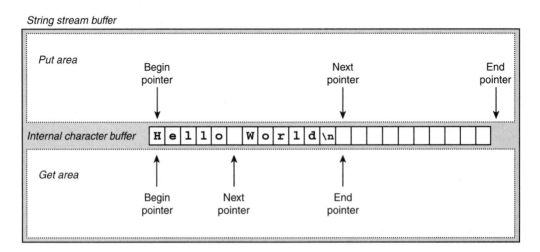

Figure 2-13: String stream buffer before putback.

String stream buffer

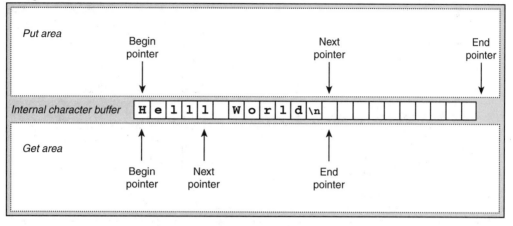

Figure 2-14: String stream buffer after putting back the character l.

pbackfail() performs the write access to the get area and overrides the character o.[30] The situation after sputbackc('l') looks like the one in figure 2-14.

ANOTHER "PBACKFAIL" SITUATION. We can keep on putting back characters via sputbackc() or sungetc() until we hit the beginning of the get area, as shown in figure 2-15.

The next attempt to put back a character triggers pbackfail(), which is supposed to make further putback positions available. The get area's next_pointer cannot be decremented any further, and pbackfail() indicates failure. Only if characters are read from the get area will putback positions become available again.

Note that the put area's pointers are not affected by any of the putback operations. However, overwriting characters in the get area by means of sputbackc() changes the content of the internal buffer, much like an output operation. The modifications will be visible when the content of the string buffer is retrieved via str(), for instance.

2.2.4 File Stream Buffers

For a file buffer the internal character buffer is usually smaller than the external sequences; i.e., the internal buffer normally holds only subsequences of the external sequence as get and put areas.[31]

It is implementation-defined, how large the internal buffer is, whether the file stream buffer maintains two separate character arrays to represent the get and put areas

---

30. Positions in the internal sequence are overwritten only if the stream buffer's open mode allows it. A stream buffer whose open mode does not include output mode will not allow any write access to the internal sequence.

31. Only in rare situations, when the file size is less than or equal to the buffer size, can the internal buffer hold the whole file.

String stream buffer

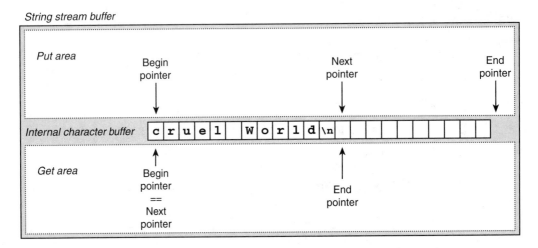

Figure 2-15: *String stream buffer with the putback position available.*

respectively, or whether there is a shared internal character array for both areas. The assumed sample implementation we present in the following sections is one of a variety of conceivable implementations of a file stream buffer. Your particular implementation might have implemented a different scheme.

In our assumed implementation, the file stream buffer maintains only one internal character array, which is of a fixed size and too small to hold the entire content of the external character sequences. For this reason, the internal character array holds only a subsequence of the input sequence in the get area and a subsequence of the output sequence in the put area. Logically, both the put and get areas are present simultaneously; in practice only one of them can be active at a time, because the file stream buffer has only one internal character buffer: During output operations, the internal character array represents the put area, and the get area is inactive; during input operations, the internal character array represents the get area, and the put area is inactive.

The respective inactive area does logically exist, but it may not be immediately accessible. If, for instance, the get area is active, no output operation should be triggered, because it would need access to the currently inactive put area. An output operation can only follow an input operation if the file is repositioned in between, which puts the file stream buffer into a neutral state, from which it can reactivate the put area and make its content available in the internal buffer.

Let us first explore input and output separately before we discuss the scheme for exchanging the get and put areas while switching from input to output and vice versa.

OUTPUT

Initially, neither the put nor the get area is available. An area is considered unavailable when its next_pointer is zero. The begin_pointer and the end_pointer are undefined when the next_pointer is zero; they can also be zero or have any other arbitrary value. The content of the internal character buffer is undefined, too, in this situation; it might be empty, filled with garbage, or not even allocated. Figure 2-16 shows this neutral situation.

Any output request in that neutral situation triggers overflow(), which activates the put area, places the first character into the internal character buffer, and adjusts the put area's pointers. Afterwards, the internal buffer area is filled with the remaining characters that were passed to the output operation, and the next_pointer is advanced accordingly. Figure 2-17 shows the situation after output of the string Hello World\n.

If we keep on writing output to the file stream buffer, the put area's next_pointer will eventually hit the end_pointer. Then overflow() is called again in order to make available additional put positions. overflow() achieves this by transferring data from the internal buffer via code conversion (if necessary) to the external file. It is implementation-dependent whether all or only parts of the data in the internal buffer are transferred to the external file. The standard requires only that overflow() make "enough" positions available in the buffer; it does not specify how many positions. For our sample implementation, we assume that the entire internal character buffer is written to the external file. Afterwards, overflow() stores the first character in the internal character buffer and adjusts the put area pointers as shown in figure 2-18.

Now there is plenty of room in the put area for further output, and the output request that triggered overflow() can be completed.

The character sequence that is transferred from the internal character buffer to the external file during overflow() is placed into successive locations on the external file

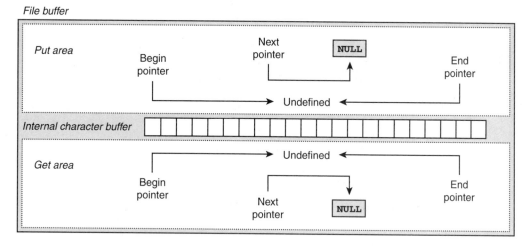

Figure 2-16: File stream buffer in neutral state.

File buffer

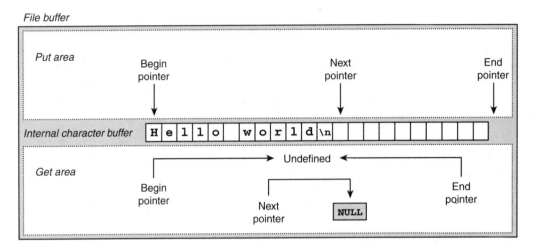

Figure 2-17: *File stream buffer after an output operation.*

File buffer

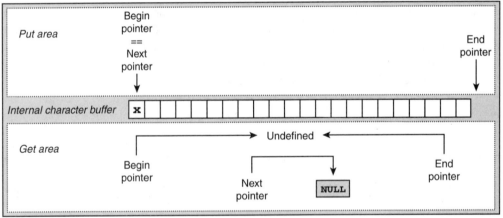

Figure 2-18: *File stream buffer immediately after* `overflow()`.

starting at the current external file position. Where the external file position indicator stands depends on the circumstances.

Immediately after a file stream buffer is connected to an external file (via `open()`), the external file position indicator is either at the beginning of the file, which is the default situation, or at the end of the file, if the open mode included the at-end flag.

After preceding output operations (via `sputc()`, `sputn()`), the external file position indicator stands where the last output operation left it.

After an explicit repositioning of the stream position (via `seekoff()`, `seekpos()`), the external file position indicator is reset to a corresponding position in the external file.

If the open mode includes the append flag, the external file position indicator stands at the end of the file and cannot be repositioned to any other position.

INPUT

Input, like output, starts with a neutral situation, in which neither get nor put areas are active. Figure 2-19 shows this neutral situation.[32]

An input request in this situation triggers `underflow()` in order to make available get positions for reading. This is achieved by transferring data from the external file via code conversion (if necessary) to the internal character buffer. It is implementation-dependent whether `underflow()` fills the entire internal buffer or only a part of it with characters transferred from the external file. In our sample implementation we assume that `underflow()` fills the entire internal buffer if possible. The get area is activated, and the get area's pointers are adjusted. Figure 2-20 shows the situation after the invocation of `underflow()`.

This is the situation after requesting the first character from the file stream via `sgetc()`. Had we extracted the character via `sbumpc()` instead of `sgetc()`, `uflow()` would have been called instead of `underflow()`, with basically the same result. The only difference would be that the put area's next_pointer would be advanced by one position and point the next available read position.

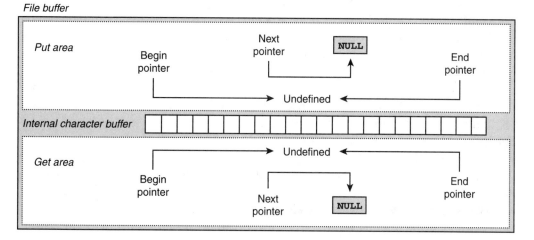

File buffer

Figure 2-19: *File stream buffer in neutral state.*

---

32. Whether the initial neutral state exists in practice is implementation defined. An implementation can also activate the get area right away and fill it with characters transferred from the external file before any actual input request.

File buffer

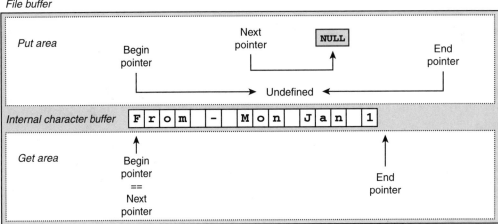

Figure 2-20: *File stream buffer immediately after* `underflow()`.

If we keep on requesting input from the file stream buffer, the get area's next_ pointer will eventually hit the end of the internal buffer. `underflow()` or `uflow()` will then be triggered again. These operations discard the current content of the internal character buffer and transfer the next sequence of characters from the external file into the internal buffer.

The character sequence that is transferred from the external file to the internal character buffer during `underflow()` or `uflow()` is taken from successive locations on the external file starting at the current external file position. Where the external file position indicator stands depends on the circumstances.

Immediately after a file stream buffer is connected to an external file (via `open()`), the file position indicator is either at the beginning of the file, which is the default situation, or at the end of the file, if the open mode included the at-end flag.

After preceding input operations (via `sgetc()`, `sbumpc()`), the external file position indicator stands where the last input operation left it.

After an explicit repositioning of the stream position (via `seekoff()`, `seekpos()`), the external file position indicator is reset to a corresponding position in the external file.

SWITCHING BETWEEN INPUT AND OUTPUT

On bidirectional file streams, input *and* output operations are allowed, and for this reason, a bidirectional file stream uses its file stream buffer's put *and* get areas. Switching between input and output operations must obey certain rules, which are described in section 1.4.3, Bidirectional File Streams. A brief recap:

> After output, the file stream must be flushed or repositioned before any input
> is permitted.

After input, the file stream must be repositioned before any output is allowed, unless the preceding input operations have reached end-of-file, in which case output can immediately follow input.

In our example, where the file stream buffer has only one internal character array, which represents either the put or the get area, the file stream buffer must exchange the get and put areas with every switch between input and output operations. Again, the following explanations are based on our sample implementation; your particular implementation might work differently.

SWITCHING FROM OUTPUT TO INPUT

Let us assume that the last operation on the file stream buffer was an output operation, in which case the put area is active and the get area is inactive. An example is shown in figure 2-21.

Before any input operation can follow, the file stream must be flushed or repositioned, due to the rules for file stream operations. Both operations trigger the file stream buffer to transfer the content of its internal character buffer to the external file. After this transfer, the file stream buffer is in its neutral state again, that is, both areas are inactive, as shown in figure 2-22.

If the requested operation was a request for repositioning, the file stream buffer not only transfers the content of the internal buffer to the external file but also resets the file position indicator of the external file as requested. Resetting the external file position indicator only affects the external file but has no direct effect on the get or put areas.

An input operation following the flush or repositioning works as described earlier for input in general: The get area is not available. As a result, `underflow()` or `uflow()` is called, characters are transferred from the external file to the internal character buffer,

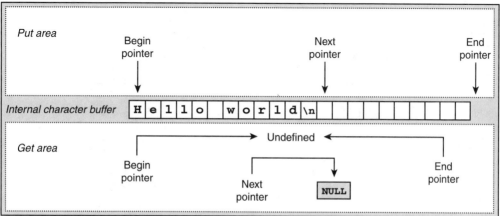

Figure 2-21: *File stream buffer after an output operation.*

File buffer

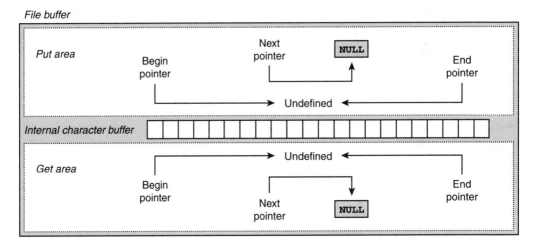

Figure 2-22: *File stream buffer in neutral state after flush or repositioning.*

and the get area's pointers are adjusted accordingly. The character sequence transferred from the external file starts at the current external file position. Depending on whether the preceding operation was a flush or a repositioning, the external file position is either the last write position or the position to which the file position indicator was repositioned. Figure 2-23 shows the situation after a successful input operation.

SWITCHING FROM INPUT TO OUTPUT

After this input operation, the get area is active and the put area is inactive. The situation is exactly as shown in figure 2-23. An output operation can follow only if the input opera-

File buffer

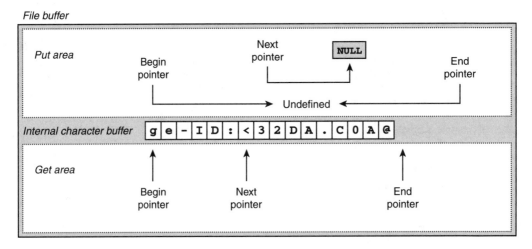

Figure 2-23: *File stream buffer after an input operation.*

tion reached the end of the file. Otherwise, before any output operation can follow, the file stream must be repositioned.

Reaching the end of the file during input puts the file stream buffer into its neutral state, because the entire file content has been consumed, and further input is not possible without any intervening output or repositioning. For that reason, the content of the internal character buffer can be discarded and both areas deactivated. As expected, the file position indicator of the external file stands at the end of the external file in this case.

Repositioning, too, involves the file stream buffer's discarding the content of its internal character buffer and putting itself into the neutral state, in which both areas are inactive. The file position indicator of the external file is reset accordingly, which affects only the external file but has no immediate effect on the get or put areas.

No matter whether the file stream is repositioned or whether the preceding input operation has reached the end of the file, the file stream buffer is put into its neutral state, as shown in figure 2-24.

An output operation in this situation works as described earlier for output in general: First, `overflow()` is invoked, which activates the put area. Then the respective character sequence that was passed to the output operation is stored in the internal buffer area, and the put area's pointers are adjusted. Figure 2-25 shows the situation after successful output of `Hello World\n`.

DISCLAIMER. The explanations given above regarding the management of a file stream buffer's put and get areas are not to be taken literally. An implementation is free to achieve the same effect in a different way. In particular, the neutral state can be expressed in a different way, but it always exists logically. The neutral state serves as the initial state of a file stream buffer, but it is also logically reached when input operations hit the end of

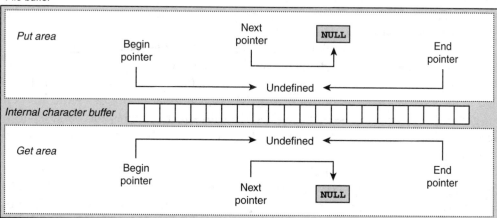

Figure 2-24: *File stream buffer in neutral state after repositioning or reaching end of file during input.*

File buffer

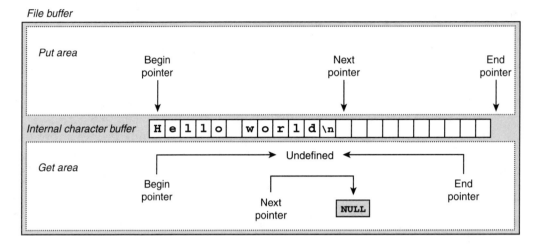

Figure 2-25: *File stream buffer after an output operation.*

the file or when the stream position is reset. A file stream buffer may also put itself into the neutral state for other reasons, such as error situations. How the neutral state is expressed or how exactly an implementation of a file stream buffer uses its internal character buffer(s) to represent the put and get areas is an implementation detail left open by the standard.

PUTBACK

Putting back characters to the input sequence via `sungetc()` or `sputbackc()` can be successful only following preceding input operations. Let us consider such a situation. As a result of the preceding input operations, the get area is active, and the file stream buffer might look like the one shown in figure 2-26.

Putting back the previously read character means decrementing the get area's next_pointer. Putting back a character different from the previously read one means decrementing the get area's next_pointer and storing the different character at that location in the internal character buffer. `pbackfail()` is responsible for this write access to the get area. The write access will be rejected if the file stream buffer is not connected to an open file. Figure 2-27 shows the situation after three previously read characters have successfully been put back.

If we keep on putting back characters, we will eventually hit the begin_pointer. Then the next_pointer cannot be decreased any further, and `pbackfail()` is triggered in order to make further putback positions available. What `pbackfail()` does in such a situation is implementation-dependent. In our example, the attempt to put back any further characters will fail, because we consider it unusual that a large number of characters is put back into the input sequence, and for that reason we do not support it. Alternatively, a file

File buffer

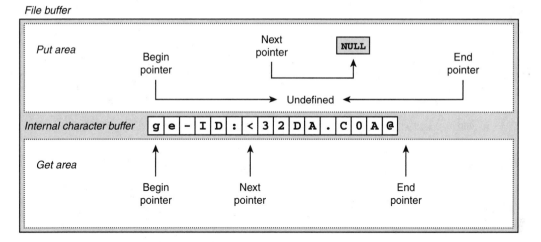

Figure 2-26: *File stream buffer after an input operation.*

File buffer

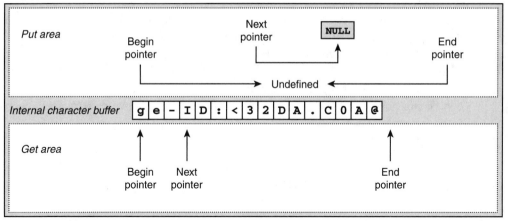

Figure 2-27: *File stream buffer after some putback operations.*

buffer implementation could make additional putback positions available by extracting previously read characters from the external file, if the underlying file system allows that.

Let us discuss another situation. After successive input operations, the get area's next_pointer will eventually hit the end_pointer. Figure 2-28 shows a situation in which the get area is entirely consumed.

The next input operation triggers underflow() or uflow(), which then refills the internal buffer from the external file. In order to allow putback of characters even immediately after underflow() or uflow(), we can keep the first four positions in the internal

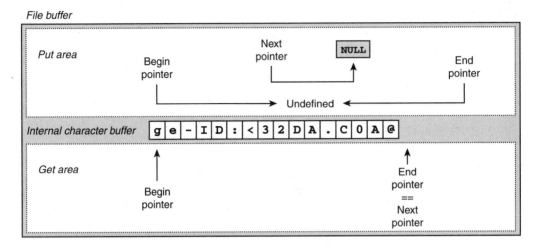

Figure 2-28: *File stream buffer with consumed get area.*

character buffer reserved as putback positions in our sample implementation. The number of putback positions a file stream buffer reserves, if any, is implementation defined. In our sample implementation, underflow() or uflow() copies the last four characters of the consumed get area to the first four locations of the internal character buffer before they fill the rest of the internal buffer with characters transferred from the external file. Figure 2-29 shows the file stream buffer after invocation of underflow().

Now it is possible to put back four characters into the get area even if it has just been refilled from the external sequence.

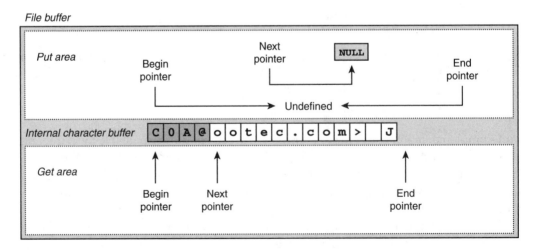

Figure 2-29: *File stream buffer after overflow(), showing the reserved putback positions.*

In general, putting back characters is possible only if the get area is active, which means that for bidirectional file streams putback cannot immediately follow an output operation. The same rules as for input following output apply, that is, the file stream must be flushed or repositioned before any characters can be put back into the input sequence after an output operation.

If an output operation is performed after putting characters back into the input sequence, the entire get area, including the putback positions, is discarded to make room for the put area. As a result, any changes made to the putback positions are lost.

2.3 Character Types and Character Traits

Almost all IOStreams classes are class templates. One template parameter is the character type `charT`. The other parameter is the character traits type associated with the character type. In this section we discuss the meaning of the character type and the character traits type, their purpose, how they are used in IOStreams, requirements imposed on these types, and related issues.

2.3.1 Character Representations

The purpose of IOStreams is to transfer data between a program and an external device. The previous sections of this chapter on the IOStreams' architecture explained that the main components involved in this process are the stream objects, representing the formatting layer, and the stream buffer objects, representing the transport layer. Data are exchanged between the program and the formatting layer, in IOStreams internally between the two layers, and between the transport layer and the external device.

Character sequences play an important role in this data flow. Items received from and returned to the program can be any kind of C++ data; in particular, they can be a character sequence. Inside IOStreams input and output data is always represented in the form of character sequences. Finally, the data transferred to the external device are a character sequence, too. It is important to understand how these character sequences are represented. As data are exchanged between the main components described above, we distinguish among three data representations, shown in figure 2-30.

WHAT IS A CHARACTER?

Before we discuss the data representations used in IOStreams in further detail, we want to take a look at character representations in general. Many issues regarding characters are

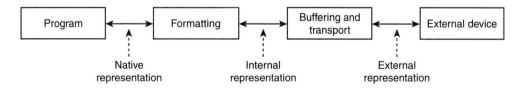

Figure 2-30: *Representations of data exchanged in IOStreams.*

frequently confused. First, there is the *abstraction* of a character. This is what we intuitively associate with a shape. It has numerous properties: visual representations (glyphs), binary representations (codes), and many more. Then we deal with characters inside our C++ programs. Here the character is an *object.* Like other objects in our program, character objects are instances of a certain type and have an individual object state. The most commonly known character types in (C and) C++ are type `char` for narrow characters and type `wchar_t` for wide characters. A character object's state is the content of the character, i.e., its binary representation. It is the bit pattern stored inside a storage unit of type `char` or `wchar_t`, for instance. The content of a character is also called a character code. A code usually belongs to a character encoding, which is a set of character codes along with rules for their interpretation. In this book we talk of character objects. Keep in mind that whenever we mention a "character" in the following text, we mean a "character object inside a C++ program."

CHARACTER TYPE VERSUS CHARACTER ENCODING

A character has two aspects that are relevant in IOStreams: its type and its encoding.[33] In principle, both aspects are independent of each other. In practice, they are related and sometimes even mixed up. Consider an example: an ASCII character sequence. ASCII is a one-byte character encoding. An ASCII character can be stored in a storage unit of type `char`, because no ASCII character takes more than one byte, and the built-in type `char` is large enough to hold a one-byte character. Hence it is customary to store a character sequence encoded in ASCII in an array of type `char`. However, `char` is not synonymous with ASCII. A storage unit of type `char` can as well hold a character encoded in EBCDIC, which is another one-byte character encoding. Also, an ASCII character could be stored in a larger storage unit than a `char`, but this would be wasteful and is rarely done in practice.

As you can see, there is no 1 : 1 relationship between the character type used for storing a character and the character encoding used to represent the code contained in that storage unit. Instead, a character sequence of a given encoding is stored in an array of units that have the minimum size required to hold any character of the encoding. The types typically used in IOStreams for storage of characters are the built-in character types `char` and `wchar_t`; single-byte character encodings are stored as `char`, and wide-character encodings are stored as `wchar_t`. The table below shows examples of single- and wide-character encodings and the character type that is typically used for storing and processing them:

CHARACTER TYPE	CHARACTER ENCODING
char	ASCII
char	EBCDIC
char	ISO 8859-2

---

33. For further information on character encodings, please refer to section 4.2.7, Character Encodings.

wchar_t	Unicode
wchar_t	ISO 10646

Let us now return to the character representations in IOStreams and find out which type and encoding they have.

THE NATIVE REPRESENTATION

Data exchanged between the program and the formatting layer of IOStreams can be of any type that can be represented in C++. Consider, for instance, the following code fragment:

```
int i;
cout << "Number of elements is: " << i;
```

In this example a character sequence and an integral value are passed from the program to the formatting layer.

In both cases the data representation depends on the programming environment's internal encoding. It is the compiler that decides whether an integral value, for instance, has a 32-bit or 64-bit binary representation, or whether a string literal is represented as a sequence of one-byte ASCII characters or two-byte Unicode characters. With regard to character representations, the C++ programming language supports the data types char for narrow characters and wchar_t for wide characters. However, both the size of these types and the encoding of narrow and wide characters may vary between different programming environments.

In sum, the native character representation is that of characters or character sequences exchanged between the program and the formatting layer, while its character type and encoding are determined by the programming environment.

THE INTERNAL REPRESENTATION

Data exchanged between the formatting and transport layers are always in the form of a character sequence. The formatting layer receives input from the program in the native representation; parses it; and transforms it into a character sequence, which it then passes on to the stream buffer. The stream buffer eventually stores these characters in its internal buffer area.

CHARACTER TYPE. The type of character exchanged between the formatting and transport layers is the stream's character type, i.e., the template argument charT. In a narrow-character stream, i.e., a stream instantiated on type char, the formatting layer produces narrow characters of type char, and the transport layer buffers these kinds of characters. In a wide-character stream, sequences of characters of type wchar_t are exchanged. Consider a stream instantiated on an arbitrary, user-defined character type, say Jchar. The formatting layer would produce characters of type Jchar, and the transport layer would maintain a buffer of Jchars. In general, the stream's character type charT is the type of character produced by the formatting layer and buffered in the transport layer.

CHARACTER ENCODING. The encoding of characters exchanged between the formatting and transport layers is the programming environment's internal character encoding. The formatting layer produces characters in the native encoding, and the transport layer buffers them as they are.

To sum up, the internal character representation is that of the units produced and consumed by the formatting layer and is identical to the representation of the units buffered in the transport layer. Its character type is determined by the stream's character type `charT`, and the encoding is dictated by the programming environment.

THE EXTERNAL REPRESENTATION

Data exchanged between the transport layer and the external device depends entirely on the external device. IOStreams support I/O to two devices: in-memory I/O and file I/O. In the case of in-memory I/O, no real external device is involved, because source and destination are a memory location in the program's storage space, which also serves as the buffer area. In the case of file I/O the external device is a single- or multibyte file. User-defined stream classes can in principle support any kind of external device that conforms to the stream abstraction. Hence, little can be said about the representation of data exchanged between the transport layer and external devices in general. As string streams do not have an external device and nothing can be said about arbitrary stream types, we restrict the discussion of the external representation to file streams.

File streams are designed to handle either single-byte or multibyte text files.[34] The narrow file streams usually work with single-byte files, the wide-character file streams typically operate on multibyte files. If the representation of characters on the external file differs from the internal representation, file streams perform a code conversion.

SINGLE-BYTE FILES

CHARACTER TYPE. Single-byte text files contain characters of a one-byte character encoding. A narrow file stream extracts data from the file in portions of one byte each. One-byte characters can be stored in units of type `char`. Hence, the type of characters exchanged between the transport layer and a single-byte file is `char`.

CHARACTER ENCODING. By default, the character encoding of characters stored in the single-byte text file is supposed to be the same as used inside IOStreams; i.e., it is the programming environment's native encoding. Single-byte text files accessed via IOStreams in a programming environment that internally encodes characters in ASCII, for instance, are supposed to contain ASCII characters. This is the default for narrow file streams in IOStreams.

However, file streams are designed to be flexible and adaptable. A narrow file stream can also handle single-byte files that contain different character encodings. If the encoding of characters contained in a text file differs from the native encoding, a conversion between

---

34. Input and output to wide-character files, such as Unicode file, are not directly supported by IOStreams.

the internal and the external encoding is performed. File streams delegate such code conversions to their locale object—to be precise, to their stream buffer's locale's code conversion facet. Hence, in imbuing a narrow file stream with a locale that has an appropriate code conversion facet, the file stream can be made capable of handling EBCDIC files in an ASCII environment for example. Such narrow-character code conversion facets are not provided by the standard library though, but have to be provided otherwise.

In sum, the external character representation of narrow file streams is that of units transferred to and from a single-byte text file. Its character type is `char`, and the encoding depends on the stream's code conversion facet. By default the encoding is the programming environment's native encoding.

MULTIBYTE FILES

CHARACTER TYPE. Multibyte files contain characters in a multibyte encoding. Different from one-byte or wide-character encodings, multibyte characters do not have the same size. A single multibyte character can have a length of 1, 2, 3, or more bytes. Obviously, none of the built-in character types, `char` or `wchar_t`, is large enough to hold any character of a given multibyte encoding. For this reason, multibyte characters contained in a multibyte file are chopped into units of one byte each. The wide-character file stream extracts data from the multibyte file byte by byte, interprets the byte sequence, finds out which and how many bytes form a multibyte character, identifies the character, and translates it to a wide-character encoding.

Due to the decomposition of the multibytes into one-byte units, the type of characters exchanged between the transport layer and a multibyte file is `char`.

CHARACTER ENCODING. The encoding of characters exchanged between the transport layer and a multibyte file can be any multibyte encoding. It depends wholly on the content of the multibyte file. As wide-character file streams internally represent characters as units of type `wchar_t` encoded in the programming environment's wide-character encoding, a code conversion is always necessary. The code conversion is performed by the stream buffer's code conversion facet. There is no default conversion defined. It all depends on the code conversion facet contained in the stream buffer's locale object, which initially is the current global locale.

In sum, the external character representation of wide-character file streams is that of the units transferred to and from a multibyte file. Its character type is `char`, and the encoding depends on the stream's code conversion facet.

SUMMARY

Let's summarize the character representations used in IOStreams:

The *native* character representation is that of characters or character sequences exchanged between the program and the formatting layer. Its character type and encoding are determined by the programming environment's internal conventions.

The *internal* character representation is that of the units produced and consumed by the formatting layer and is identical to the representation of the units buffered in the transport layer. Its character type is determined by the stream's character type `charT`, and the encoding is the programming environment's internal encoding for narrow and wide characters.

Character sequences in the internal representation are produced and consumed by the formatting layer, and in particular they are produced and consumed by the formatting and parsing facets of the stream's locale. Hence, a `charT` stream has a `charT` stream buffer and uses the `charT` numeric and ctype facets of its locale.

Character sequences in the internal representation are also produced and consumed by the stream's code conversion facet. A `charT` file stream uses a code conversion facet of type `codecvt <charT, char, stateT>`.[35]

The *external* character representation of file streams is that of the units transferred to and from a single-byte or multibyte text file.[36] Its character type is `char`; the encoding varies and depends on the file's encoding. The stream buffer's code conversion facet converts between the external and internal character representation.

2.3.2 Character Traits

Character traits were invented in the process of templatizing IOStreams and strings. Both IOStreams and strings are capable of handling characters of a generic character type `charT`. The character type alone does not suffice for proper handling of arbitrary character types, because it describes only the storage unit of a character. Related information, such as special character values like the end-of-file value, or related functionality for comparing or copying characters, is needed for IOStreams and strings, but it cannot be provided by built-in character types like `char` or `wchar_t`. Character traits were introduced as a solution to this problem, and both IOStreams and string class templates have a traits type parameter in addition to their character type parameter.

2.3.2.1 Requirements of a Character Traits Type

Naturally, certain requirements are imposed on a character traits type. It is supposed to provide the necessary information, i.e., it must define a number of nested types and several static member functions. Some of the details are needed mainly in the string classes of the standard C++ library; others are relevant for IOStreams. The requirements relevant for IOStreams are described below (grouped by topics).

2.3.2.1.1 The End-of-File Character

The end-of-file character is a character that must be different from all other character values. It marks the end of a file. Historically, the end-of-file value was `EOF`, which is a constant of type `int`, which is different from all character values of type `char`. Note that its type is different from the type of all other characters. In the standard IOStreams this principle was generalized. The end-of-file character is a character value different from all other character values; it is determined by the static traits member function `eof()`. Also,

---

35. For an explanation of the state type stateT, see section 2.3.2.1.3, Conversion State.

36. Transport of units of type `wchar_t` is not supported by any of the concrete streams in the standard library.

its type differs from the character type: the end-of-file value's type is defined as a type nested in the character traits called `int_type`, whereas the character type is a different type: `char_type`. For convenience reasons each stream class contains a nested typedef `int_type`, defined as `traits::int_type`.

The end-of-file value and its type are used by numerous operations of IOStreams. Typically, stream operations receive or return characters, which can either be valid characters of type `char_type` or the end-of-file value of type `int_type`. In order to handle both cases, these functions receive or return values of type `int_type`, which is large enough to hold valid characters *and* the end-of-file value.

This leads to situations in which one needs to translate between `char_type` and `int_type`. For this purpose, the character traits provide conversion functions:

`int_type` **to_int_type** (char_type)	which blows a valid character up to a value of type `int_type`, and
`char_type` **to_char_type**(int_type)	which extracts a valid character from a value of type `int_type`.

Here is an example that demonstrates their use. The stream buffer's member function `sgetc()` is invoked. It returns the next available character, or the end-of-file value if no characters are available. In the example below, the returned value is checked and converted to its character equivalent in case it is different from the end-of-file value.

```
template <class charT, class Traits>
void foo(basic_streambuf<charT,Traits>* sbuf)
{
        Traits::char_type c;
        Traits::int_type i;
        i = sbuf->sgetc();                   // get the next value
                                             // see whether it's end-of-file
        if (!Traits::eq_int(i,Traits::eof()))
                                             // if not, convert it to a character
        {  c = Traits::to_char_type(i);
        ...                                  // pass on the character
        }
}
```

Note that two values of type `int_type` cannot simply be compared by means of the built-in equality operator, because `int_type` can be any arbitrary type. Instead they are compared via the `eq_int_type()` member function provided by the character traits.[37] Similarly, two character values are compared by means of the traits member function `eq()`.

---

37. In the Classic IOStreams this would simply have been a comparison of two integral values. Also, the explicit conversion from `int_type` to `char_type` was not needed in Classic IOStreams, because the compiler automatically converted `int` to `char`.

Related to the end-of-file value is another function in the character traits, `not_eof()`. It returns an `int_type` value that is guaranteed to be different from the end-of-file value. It takes an `int_type` value as an argument. If the received value is different from the end-of-file value, it returns the same value; if the value is end-of-file value, a value different from the end-of-file value is returned. This is a convenience function used by stream operations that indicate success by returning a value different from the end-of-file value.

2.3.2.1.2 Copying, Finding, and Comparing Characters

The character traits provide a number of member functions for typical operations on characters and character sequences. Examples are `compare()`, `assign()`, `move()`, `copy()`, `find()`, and `length()`. They are mostly used by the string classes in the standard C++ library and are not especially relevant to IOStreams.

2.3.2.1.3 Conversion State

The wide-character file stream classes in IOStreams are designed to convert between the internal wide-character encoding used inside the stream and the external multibyte character encoding of the file content. Some multibyte encodings are state-dependent,[38] which means that the interpretation of a byte depends on its context. Such state-dependent multibyte encodings typically contain so-called shift sequences, which are byte sequences that indicate a context switch. In order to keep track of the current context, a stream has to maintain a conversion state. Parsing, for instance, starts with an initial conversion state. Each time an escape sequence is found, the conversion state changes.

The conversion state is maintained in a variable of appropriate type. The type is defined in the character traits as `state_type`. It depends on the code conversion and its needs. As code conversion in IOStreams is done by a stream buffer's code conversion facet, the state type defined in the character traits corresponds to the state type parameter of the code conversion facet's type: A file stream instantiated with the types `charT` and `Traits` has a code conversion facet of type `codecvt<charT, char, typename Traits::state_type>`.

The state type is also associated with the stream's position type (see section 2.3.2.1.4, Stream Positions, below). The position type `pos_type` must be able to hold all the information necessary to reposition a stream buffer. Part of this information is the code conversion state related to the position.

2.3.2.1.4 Stream Positions

IOStreams allows for repositioning of a stream. This means that you can change the current read or write position and continue input or output at another position in the stream. For instance, you can position back to the beginning of the stream and reread the stream's content. Repositioning is done via seek functions. Input streams have a `seekg()` operation that allows manipulation of stream positions; output streams have an equivalent `seekp()` function. These functions take either an absolute stream position or a speci-

---

38. See section 4.2.7.5, Code Conversion, for a detailed explanation of state-dependent code conversions.

fied position together with an offset. The functions for retrieving stream positions are `tellg()` and `tellp()`.

ABSOLUTE STREAM POSITIONS. An absolute stream position is a position that has been obtained by a previous successful call to a tell function. When a seek function is provided with an absolute stream position, it alters the stream buffer so that the provided position becomes the current position. Positions that have not been obtained by previous successful calls to a tell function on the same external device are not valid and lead to undefined results.

The type of absolute stream position is defined in the stream's character traits as `pos_type`. It is a type that is able to hold all the information necessary to reposition a stream buffer, which in the case of file streams includes a code conversion state. This is because file streams are designed to perform state-dependent code conversions. (See section 2.3.2.1.3, Conversion State.) Associated with each position is not only the actual information about the position itself but also the information about the conversion state at that position.

The position type of a file stream is always `fpos<Traits::state_type>`, where `fpos<class stateT>` is a predefined class template in IOStreams for defining position types that carry a conversion state. This requirement is mandatory only for file streams because they are the only stream that performs code conversions and hence need to maintain a conversion state. Other types of stream can have a different position type.

SPECIFIED STREAM POSITIONS. A specified stream position is either the beginning of the external sequence, the current position, or the end. Specified stream positions are of type `ios_base::seekdir`, and the three options are represented by the constants `ios_base::beg`, `ios_base::cur`, and `ios_base::end`.

A specified position is always accompanied by an offset. Offsets represent a signed displacement, measured in characters, from a specified position within the external character sequence. When a seek function is provided with a specified position and an offset, it repositions the stream buffer by a displacement calculated in terms of bytes as the product of character size[39] and offset. The direction of the repositioning is determined by the offset's value. If the value is positive, the current position moves toward the stream's end; if it is negative, it moves toward the beginning.

Not all external sequences can be repositioned. If the external sequence is a multibyte sequence, it is impossible to calculate the displacement in bytes from the offset, because each character can be of different size. Another typical exception is external sequences that are connected to display devices.

---

39. The character size of an encoding can be obtained via the code conversion facet's member function `encoding()`. If `encoding() >0`, then the returned value is the character size. Otherwise, the encoding does not have a fixed character size, and positioning is not possible.

The type of an offset is defined in the stream's character traits as `off_type`. It is usually a synonym for one of the signed, built-in integral types.

The values `off_type(-1)` and `pos_type(-1)` have a special meaning. They designate an invalid position or offset and are used as error indicators in IOStreams.

There are a couple of additional requirements that describe the relationship between the position and the offset type:

- `pos_type` must be convertible to `off_type`, and vice versa.

- Instances of both types can be constructed from an integral value.

- Positions must be comparable for equality and inequality; the same holds for offsets.

- Some arithmetics are required, for example:
  The difference between two positions must be an offset of type `off_type`, and adding an offset to a position must yield a new position.

Here is the sketch of an example of repositioning an input string stream buffer:

```
istringstream buf;
// fill string stream
// read input until a position of interest and memorize the position
istringstream::pos_type p = buf.tellp();
if (p != istringstream::pos_type(-1))
{  // tellp() was successful
   // read further input
   ...
}
// return to the point of interest
buf.seekp(p);
// return to beginning of stream
buf.seekg(0,ios_base::beg);
```

For convenience reasons each stream class contains a nested typedef `pos_type` and `off_type` defined as `traits::pos_type` and `traits::off_type`.

2.3.2.2 The Predefined Standard Character Traits

The standard library provides two predefined traits types for the built-in character types `char` and `wchar_t`. These two types are specialization[40] of a class template called `char_traits<class charT>`. Here are the declarations of these predefined traits types as they appear in the header file `<string>`:

---

40. See section G.4, Template Specialization, in appendix G for an explanation of template specialization in general.

```
template<class charT> struct char_traits;
template struct char_traits<char>;
template struct char_traits<wchar_t>;
```

The traits types char_traits<char> and char_traits<wchar_t> are the default traits types associated with the built-in character types char and wchar_t. If you never specify character traits, the standard library classes will use these defaults.

Interestingly, the char_traits<class charT> template itself is an empty class template. Its sole purpose is to provide a name. It is not supposed to be instantiated for any character types. A traits type for a user-defined character type would be a specialization, not an instantiation of the char_traits template. The purpose of this empty character traits class template is to serve as a default template argument for the class templates requiring a traits type argument. Let's take a look at a typical example:

```
template <class charT, class traits = char_traits<charT> >
class basic_fstream;
```

The traits type parameter of string and IOStreams classes has a default value, so that users of these classes need not specify the traits type argument. The default value for the traits type naturally depends on the character type. It is a specialization of the predefined character traits class template char_traits. In this way the predefined specializations for char and wchar_t are used as defaults, and even for user-defined types there is a natural default value.

Imagine you would define a new character type myChar. Then you would have to provide an associated traits type. If you defined it as a specialization of the char_traits template, i.e., as char_traits<myChar>, the default would apply, and a myChar-file-stream would be of type basic_fstream<myChar>. Alternatively, you could give the traits type a name of its own, say myCharTraits. In that case the traits type argument could not be omitted, i.e., you would have to say basic_fstream<myChar, myCharTraits> instead of just basic_fstream<myChar>. For this reason it is recommended that you define the traits type associated with a character type as a specialization of the char_traits template. There is only one situation in which you would want to define traits types that are not specializations of the char_traits template: when you define more than one traits type for the same character type.

2.3.3 Character Types

Let us return to the character types. They are a template parameter of strings, IOStreams, and facets in the standard library. Potential candidates for the character type are, of course, the built-in types char and wchar_t. User-defined types are allowed, too. The Japanese delegation on the ISO committee standardizing C++ brought up the notion of Jchar, a character type that encapsulates information specific to processing of Japanese character representations. Jchar would be a user-defined type that can be used for instantiation of class templates like basic_string, basic_fstream, ctype, etc.

2.3.3.1 Requirements for Character Types

Naturally, not just any type can serve as a character type. User-defined character types have to exhibit "characterlike" behavior and must meet the following requirement:

- A character type must be a POD (=plain old data structure).

- Construction of a character from the numeric value 0 must yield an end-of-string character.

PODs are C-style `structs`, i.e., classes without base classes, virtual member functions, etc. They do not require explicit construction or destruction and allow bitwise copy and assignment. See appendix G.2, POD—Plain Old Data, for further details.

For certain purposes (details below) the character type must provide additional functionality:[41]

- An `operator==()` to compare elements.

If a character type meets the first set of requirements, i.e., the "weak" requirements, it can then be used for instantiation of the string template classes. The second requirement, the "strong" one, is needed for instantiation of facet and IOStreams template classes, since strings and IOStreams rely on different parts of the character traits and facets do not rely on the character traits at all, but rather make additional requirements to the character type. To aid understanding of these differences, let us get a rough impression of the way the character traits are used in the implementation of strings, IOStreams, and facets.

REQUIREMENTS IMPOSED BY STRINGS

The implementation of the `basic_string` class template uses the traits member typedefs and function, whenever it manipulates characters and character sequences. Here are some examples that illustrate the use of character traits in string implementations: `traits::eq()` is used for comparison in string functions such as `find()` and `rfind()`; `traits::compare()` is used for implementation of string `compare()` functions; functions like `traits::copy()` and `traits::assign()` are used to implement the `append()` and `insert()` member functions of `basic_string`. No assumptions are made about the character type itself or the way objects of that type are copied and assigned. One assumption that *is* made is that the end-of-string character can be obtained by constructing a character object from the numeric value 0. This is one of the requirements for the character type imposed by strings.

---

41. Note that some implementations require even more of a character type, such as

- a conversion to the character type `char` to allow conversion of a character of user-defined type to its corresponding one-byte character code, or `'\0'` if no such code exists

- a conversion from the character type `char` to convert a `char` value to its corresponding character code of the user-defined character type

- an `operator!=()` to compare elements

- a guarantee that construction from the character `'\n'` yields the end-of-line character

Implementations with such additional requirements are not strictly standard conforming.

REQUIREMENTS IMPOSED BY IOSTREAMS

IOStreams classes rely on the character traits, too. They use the traits member typedefs and functions that have to do with the end-of-file value. Below is a typical example. Numerous member functions of stream and stream buffer classes return the end-of-file value in case of failure and a valid character in case of success. The `get()` functions for unformatted input of characters show the principle:

```
template<class charT, class traits>
class basic_istream : virtual public basic_ios<charT, traits> {
public:
    typedef typename traits::int_type int_type;

    int_type get()
    {int_type c;
     ...
     if (!_Ok)          c = traits::eof();
     else {...          c = rdbuf()->sbumpc();   ... }
     return (c);
    }

    basic_istream<charT, traits>& get(charT& x)
    {int_type c = get();
     if (!traits::eq_int_type(traits::eof(), c))
        x = traits::to_char_type(c);
     return (*this);
    }
};
```

You can see that the first `get()` function has to return a value of type `traits::int_type`,[42] because the return value is either the end-of-file value, which is of type `traits::int_type`, or a character of type `charT`. The second `get()` function demonstrates the need for conversions between both types and for comparison of values of those types.

IOStreams classes additionally use the traits members that relate to stream positioning and code conversion.

Note that the standard does not guarantee that IOStreams classes restrict themselves to the traits member typedefs and functions related to the end-of-file value and stream positioning and code conversion. They are also allowed to make use of member functions like `compare()`, `assign()`, etc. Similarly, strings could theoretically use `eof()`, `not_eof()`, `pos_type`, `off_type`, etc., although this is unlikely in practice. The principle is that strings and IOStreams are permitted to rely on the full set of properties that are required of character types and their traits.

---

42. See section G.7, The `typename` Keyword, in appendix G for further information.

REQUIREMENTS IMPOSED BY FACETS

The facet class templates do not have a traits parameter. This is because many of the facets really do not manipulate characters. Think of the ctype facet, for instance: It classifies characters according to their properties, i.e., whether they are digits, whitespace, printable, lowercase, or uppercase letters, etc. There is no need ever actually to touch a character object, copy it, or compare it.

The situation is different for parsing and formatting facets like num_get, num_put, money_get, money_put, time_get, and time_put. They have to compare characters. Just think of parsing numeric values: The num_get facet has to recognize that an input character is the radix character or the thousands separator. It will therefore compare an input character to the respective symbols defined in the numpunct facet. Comparison is defined by the character traits in the form of the eq() function, but the facets do not know anything about the associated traits type. Instead of using traits::eq(), they perform the comparison of two characters by means of operator==(). Here is a code snippet that could be part of the num_get facet's do_get() function:

```
template <class charT, class InputIterator = istreambuf_iterator<charT> >
class num_get : public locale::facet {
protected:
   virtual iter_type
   do_get(iter_type beg, iter_type end, ios_base& iob,ios_base::iostate& err,
          long& v) const
   {
    ...
    char_type ct = *beg;
    char c;
    if ( ct == use_facet<numpunct<charT> >(iob.getloc()).decimal_point() )
       c = '.';
    bool discard =
        ( ct == use_facet<numpunct<charT> >(iob.getloc()).thousands_sep()
        &&
        use_facet<numpunct<charT> >(iob.getloc()).grouping().length() != 0 );
    ...
   }
};
```

As you can see, the comparison of a character of type charT is performed using an operator==() for that character type. This explains why facets impose additional requirements on the character type.

An interesting side effect is that IOStreams classes generally use the traits::eq() function for comparison of characters, but for parsing and formatting numeric values they use operator==(), because the parsing and formatting of numeric values are delegated to the stream's locale's numeric facets. We've seen above that facets do not use character traits. It follows that one should better implement an operator==() for a user-defined character type that has the same semantics as the character type's `traits::eq()` function. One problem remains: You can have only one `operator==()` for a given character type, but several character traits types associated with that character type. What if the traits types have different `eq()` functions? IOStreams might yield "interesting" results under these circumstances. However, this problem is unlikely to occur in practice.

Consider also that IOStreams classes do not only rely on certain properties of the character type and the character traits type, but additionally require facets for that character type. IOStreams needs the numeric facets, as we've mentioned above. It also needs conversions between the character type and the built-in type `char`, which have to be defined in the `ctype` facet in the form of member functions `narrow()` and `widen()`. Character classification functions from the `ctype` facet are also needed in order to identify whitespace characters. A code conversion facet is needed for file streams. In turns out that eventually you have to provide *all* standard facets for a new character type, because facets are generally allowed to be interdependent.

To sum up, character types are used as template arguments to strings, IOStreams, and facets. Such character types have to meet certain requirements (listed in section 2.3.2.1, Requirements for a Character Traits Type) and must be accompanied by both an associated character traits type (described in section 2.3.2, Character Traits) and the standard facets for that character type (described in section 6.3.1.4, Mandatory Facet Types).

2.4 Stream Iterators and Stream Buffer Iterators

The prestandard IOStreams library did not have any iterators. The idea for iterators came up when the standards committee adopted Hewlett-Packard's STL as part of the standard library. The STL is based on the idea of generic programming: Iterators are provided by containers, and algorithms use these iterators to access the container elements. At first it looked as if the standard library would contain two entirely unrelated domains: the IOStreams abstraction, refined and reworked from the classic IOStreams, and the STL, with its concept of generic programming. Then stream and stream buffer iterators were built as a bridge between both domains.

Before we delve into the details of stream iterators and stream buffer iterators in sections 2.4.2 and 2.4.3, let's briefly review the concepts of iterators and generic programming in the standard library. If you are already familiar with these concepts, skip the following introductory section, 2.4.1.

2.4.1 The Concepts of Iterators in the Standard Library

With the adoption of Hewlett-Packard's STL as part of the standard library, the concept of *generic programming* was introduced into the standard library. The essential idea of generic programming is to separate a data structure (container) from the operations (algorithms) performed on the data structure. Iterators are provided by the container and used to connect the algorithm with the container. Iterators are pointerlike objects that provide an interface allowing the algorithm to traverse the container and to access and mutate the container's elements. The following code shows an example. The `find`-algorithm is applied to a list of integers to see whether one of the list's elements is 0:

```
void foo(list<int>& myList)
{
  if (find(myList.begin(), myList.end(), 0) != myList.end())
      cout << "Found a 0 in the list." << endl;
}
```

The member function `begin()` yields an iterator that refers to the first element of the list, while `end()` yields an iterator one past the end of the list. The `find`-algorithm traverses this iterator range checking if any of the elements of the list match the value specified by the last parameter (see implementation of `find` below). If it reaches the iterator specified by the second parameter without finding any match, it returns this iterator, which refers past the end of the list. Otherwise, when `find` has found a matching element in the list, it returns an iterator referring this element.

```
template <class Iterator, class T>
Iterator find ( Iterator first, Iterator end, const T& value)
{
  while (first != end && *first != value)
        first++;
  return first;
}
```

There are two aspects in `find` that are typical for standard library algorithms and their relation to iterators: (1) the way iterator ranges are used and (2) the way algorithms are implemented generically based on the iterators' types.

We will explore both aspects in greater detail now. Let's start with iterator ranges.

ITERATOR RANGES

An iterator range is specified by two iterators. The first indicates the beginning of the range and the second one the end. All iterator positions in that range can be reached by consecutively applying ++ (either postfix or prefix) to the first iterator until ++ yields the end iterator. The end iterator is excluded from the iterator range (denoted as [first, last)). It need not even refer to a valid container element; it only has to be reachable. This past-the-end iterator can be used to indicate failure: When an algorithm normally returns a valid iterator from the iterator range as the result of its task, it can return the past-the-end iterator to indicate that it failed to accomplish the task. The `find`-algorithm shown above does so when it cannot find the specified value. Hence, iterator ranges specify sequences of elements that an algorithm can step through, and the end iterator can also be used by an algorithm as an error indication.

USE OF ITERATORS IN ALGORITHMS

Algorithms are generic with respect to the types of iterators they use. An algorithm is usually implemented as a function template that has one or more iterator types as template parameters.

The interface required of these iterator types is determined by the operations that an algorithm applies to the iterators. These operations can be the public member functions (type when the iterator is a class) plus global functions or function templates that represent operators for this type when the iterator is a class. When the iterator is a built-in type, the operations used are the built-in operations for that type. In the example above, the find-algorithm has only one iterator type template parameter. The operations used from this iterator type's interface are the ! = operator and the * operator in line 1, the postfix ++ operator in line 2, and the copy constructor in line 3. That's all the find-algorithm requires of an iterator type.

The interface supported by an iterator type depends on the kind of container that provides it. Take, for example, the standard library's list, which is a doubly linked list. It can be iterated in a forward and backward direction. Hence, it provides an iterator to whom the pre- and postfix operator++ and operator-- can be applied. A vector, on the other hand, need not be iterated element by element but allows steps of arbitrary size. It provides an iterator to whom the operator+(Distance) and operator-(Distance) can be applied. In other words, the characteristics of a container determine the interface of the iterators it provides.

ITERATOR CATEGORIES

The standard library classifies the iterator types into five categories according to their interfaces, as shown in figure 2-31:

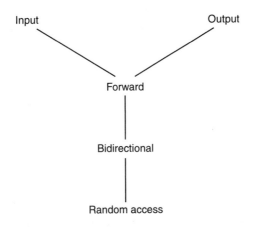

Figure 2-31: Iterator categories.

Note that figure 2-31 does not show inheritance relationships. Iterator categories are just abstractions, which represent a set of requirements to an iterator's interface, listed briefly below:

Input iterators allow algorithms to advance the iterator and give "read only" access to the value.

Output iterators allow algorithms to advance the iterator and give "write only" access to the value.

Forward iterators combine read and write access, but only in one direction (i.e., forward).

Bidirectional iterators allow algorithms to traverse the sequence in both directions, forward and backward.

Random access iterators allow jumps and "pointer arithmetics."

Each category adds new features to the previous one. For detailed explanations of the iterator categories, take a look at a book on the STL. Some references are given in the Bibliography.

2.4.2 Stream Iterators

Stream iterators allow you to treat a stream as a sequence of elements, much like an STL container, and allow you to apply generic algorithms directly to streams. The standard library provides two stream iterator abstractions for this purpose: *istream iterators,* which can be used to read from a stream, and *ostream iterators,* which can be used to write to a stream.

Before we delve into the details of stream iterators, let's first have a look at two examples. They show how powerful the combination of generic algorithms and IOStreams via stream iterators can be in practice. Let's assume we have a text file and want to count how often the word *the* is contained in the text. We can achieve it in the following way:

```
ifstream str("my_text_file");

istream_iterator<string> beginIter(str);
istream_iterator<string> endIter;

cout << "number of _the_: " << count(beginIter, endIter, "the");
```

This solution uses, on one hand, the IOStreams functionality: A stream is constructed from a file name, and formatted input is read from the stream via the `istream_iterator`. On the other hand, it uses STL components: The generic `count`-algorithm determines how often the word *the* can be found inside the iterator range [beginIter, endIter).

The second example we want to look at deals with the problem that standard library containers do not support any stream I/O directly. So the question is, What is the best way to print a container? Here is a solution that prints all container elements separated by a blank. The approach is based on the `ostream_iterator` and the `copy`-algorithm:

```
List<int> myList;

// fill in some elements

copy (myList.begin(), myList.end(), ostream_iterator<int>(cout, " "));
```

Both examples show that stream iterators allow algorithms to see a stream as a container of homogeneous elements. Standard library algorithms can apply their functionality to the stream in the same way as they would do to any other standard library container. We will explore how these examples work in the following section as we take a detailed look at the stream iterators and how they relate to IOStreams.

2.4.2.1 Output Stream Iterator

The ostream iterator is an output iterator, i.e., it allows write access to the position that it refers to and it can be advanced in single steps. While the output iterator's implementation is not specified by the standard, a typical implementation might look like this (details about the `ostream_iterator` base class template `iterator` can be found in the reference section R.4, Stream Iterators.

```
template <class T, class charT=char, class traits=char_traits<charT> >
class ostream_iterator :
                public iterator<output_iterator_tag,void,void,void,void>
{
  public:
    typedef charT char_type;
    typedef traits traits_type;
    typedef basic_ostream<charT,traits> ostream_type;

    ostream_iterator(ostream_type& s, const charT* d = 0)
    : ost(&s), delim(d) {}

    ostream_iterator& operator= (const T& t)
    {
      *ost << t;
      if (delim != 0) *ost << delim;
      return *this;
    }

    ostream_iterator& operator*() { return *this; }
    ostream_iterator& operator++() { return *this; }
```

```
    ostream_iterator& operator++(int) {return *this; }

  private:
    const charT* delim;
    basic_ostream<charT,traits>* ost;
};
```

An ostream iterator is constructed by providing an output stream, to which the iterator gives write access, and an optional delimiter, which is a string that is inserted between subsequent elements assigned to the iterator. Both constructor parameters are directly stored in private data members.

The rest of the ostream iterator's public member functions are implemented in typical fashion for an output iterator: A prefix and postfix increment operator are provided, as is an `operator*()`. These three operators do nothing but return `*this` in order to allow operator chaining.

The only public member besides the constructor that contains actual functionality is the assignment operator. It inserts the element it receives as an argument into the stream, followed by the delimiter if one was provided to the constructor. For insertion of t into the stream, `operator=(const T& t)` uses `T`'s stream inserter. Consequently, the `ostream_iterator` template can be instantiated only for types `T` that have an associated stream inserter defined. Otherwise, a compile time error will occur.

In our example above we used the `copy`-algorithm and the `ostream_iterator` to write a `list<int>` to standard output. This works out nicely. We instantiate the `ostream_iterator` template as `ostream_iterator<int>`. Hence, a stream inserter for `int` is needed, and such an inserter is supplied by the standard library.

Another observation is that each time the `ostream_iterator`'s assignment operator inserts an object into the output stream, the current stream position is advanced. This demonstrates that the `ostream_iterator` is not an artificial abstraction contrived out of the need to combine generic programming and output streams. Instead, it has genuine iteratorlike semantics: It keeps track of the stream position at which the next object should be inserted, and it allows write access to this position via the assignment operator `operator=()`.

ERROR INDICATION

The `ostream_iterator` has no specific feature to indicate that the insertion of an object into the stream failed or caused an error. For error detection, only the error indication mechanisms of the underlying stream are available. (For details of new stream features such as IOStreams exceptions, see section 1.3, The Stream State.) The best idea is perhaps to set `badbit`, `eofbit`, and `failbit` in the output stream's exception mask before the `ostream_iterator` is used. The stream will then throw an `ios_base::failure` exception when an error occurs. Alternatively, the `ostream_iterator`'s state can be checked after the ostream iterator has been used, to see if an error occurred.

2.4.2.2 Input Stream Iterator

While the `ostream_iterator` is an output iterator, the `istream_iterator` naturally is an input iterator. It allows read access to the position that it refers to, and it can be advanced in single steps. Its implementation is straightforward. A private data member (`value`) buffers the next value from the input stream, because the stream does not allow rereading of the value from the stream. Read-only access to this data member is given by `operator*()` and `operator->()`: They return a `const` reference or a `const` pointer to this data member. Here is a conceivable implementation of the `istream_iterator`:

```
template <class T, class charT = char,
          class Traits = char_traits<charT>, class Distance = ptrdiff_t>
class istream_iterator :
      public iterator<input_iterator_tag, T, Distance, const T*, const T&>
{
    friend bool operator==
                   (const istream_iterator<T,charT,traits,Distance>& lhs,
                    const istream_iterator<T,charT,traits,Distance>& rhs)
    {
       return (lhs.istp == rhs.istp);
    }

    friend bool operator!=
                   (const istream_iterator<T,charT,traits,Distance>& lhs,
                    const istream_iterator<T,charT,traits,Distance>& rhs)
    {
       return (!(lhs == rhs));
    }

  public:
    typedef charT char_type;
    typedef Traits traits_type;
    typedef basic_istream<charT,Traits> istream_type;

    istream_iterator() : istp(0) {}
    istream_iterator(istream_type& s) : istp(&s) { readElem(); }

    const T& operator*() const { return value; }
    const T* operator->() const { return &value; }

    istream_iterator& operator++()
    {
      readElem();
      return *this;
    }
```

```
      istream_iterator operator++(int)
      {
        istream_iterator tmp = *this;
        readElem();
        return tmp;
      }

  private:
    void readElem()
    {
      if (istp != 0)
        if (!(*istp >> value))
          istp = 0;
    }

    basic_istream<charT,Traits>* istp;
    T value;
};
```

When we examined the `ostream_iterator`'s implemention, we saw that it is based on `T`'s inserter. Similarly, the `istream_iterator`'s implementation is based on `T`'s extractor. The extractor is used in the private member function `readElem()`. It reads the next object of type `T` from the stream and buffers it in the private data member `value`.

The standard specifies that the next object is extracted from the stream whenever `operator++()` or `operator++(int)` is applied to the `istream_iterator`. It is, however, implementation-specific when the *first* object is read by the `istream_iterator`. According to the standard, this can be done either when the `istream_iterator` is constructed or as a kind of lazy evaluation, when `operator*()` or `operator->()` is used for the first time to access the value buffered in the iterator. The implementation given above extracts the first object in its constructor. Please note that the stream position of the input stream (that is, the position of the read pointer) is moved forward in the stream with every extraction of an object from the stream. This means that an `istream_iterator` has true iteratorlike semantics: It iterates over the input stream, giving read access to the objects contained in the stream.

ERROR INDICATION

What happens if `readElem()` tries to extract the next object of type `T` from the stream and none is available? By IOStreams convention, the `failbit` is set in the stream state to indicate that an extraction has failed. After each extraction `readElem()` checks the stream state. If the stream state is not `good()` anymore, the private member `istp` is set to 0, which indicates that the iterator is detached from its stream. As a consequence, the stream iterator cannot be used to extract any further objects. An `istream_iterator` that is in this state is called an *end-of-stream iterator.*[43] This name might be a bit misleading, because the iterator becomes an end-of-stream iterator whenever the stream state is not good(), i.e., when either failbit, badbit, eofbit, or a combination of them has been set. An input iterator that turns into an end-of-stream iterator either signals an error or indicates that the end of the input stream was reached. As with the output stream iterator, we have to resort to the underlying stream's error indication mechanisms to distinguish between these two situations.

INPUT ITERATOR RANGES

As described above, generic algorithms often receive a pair of input iterators as parameters, which denote an iterator range. By convention, the iterator that specifies the beginning of the range is part of the range, while the iterator that specifies the end is not; that is, the algorithm is not applied to the end iterator. Say we want to apply a generic algorithm to an input stream. How can we specify an according iterator range in terms of istream_iterators?

An istream_iterator constructed from a valid input stream refers to the current stream position of that input stream. Hence, this istream_iterator can be used to specify the beginning of the iterator range. Still, which iterator should be used to specify the end of the range?

Iterator ranges are typically used in while-loops like this:

```
while (beginIter != endIter)
{
    ...             // do something
    beginIter++;    // increment iterator
}
```

As an end iterator, we need an iterator that is reachable from the beginning of the range; that is, successive increments of the first iterator must eventually yield the second iterator.

A word on the while-condition: We silently assumed the existence of an (in)equality operator for istream_iterators. How is that defined? The standard requires the following semantics:

- Two end-of-stream iterators of the same type are always equal.

- An end-of-stream iterator is not equal to a non-end-of-stream iterator.

- Two non-end-of-stream iterators are equal when they are constructed from the same stream.

---

43. In the implementation shown above, the end-of-stream iterator state is expressed by the fact that the private member istp is 0. While this is a valid and efficient implementation (which is also used in all standard library implementations we know of), the standard allows implementation of the end-of-stream state indication in any appropriate way.

From the third requirement it follows that two `istream_iterators` that are equal do not necessarily refer to the same stream position. One might intuitively expect such a property, because it is true for pointers and container iterators. Note that it is *not* true for input stream iterators.

Back to our problem: How do we express an iterator range of `istream_iterators`? For the begin iterator we can simply use the `istream_iterator` constructed from the input stream. It represents the current stream position. If we successively increment this iterator, which means that we successively extract items from the stream, we will eventually hit the end of the stream. For the end iterator we therefore need an input stream iterator in end-of-stream state. How do we get one? The `istream_iterator`'s default constructor creates it.

Note that the only input stream iterator ranges are from the current stream position to the end of the stream. It is not possible to specify a range from one stream position to another stream position, because any two non-end-of-stream iterators referring to the same stream always compare equal.

By comparing an `istream_iterator` to an end-of-stream iterator, it is possible to detect if a stream error has occurred. Yet `istream_iterators` have no feature to reset an iterator that has gone into an end-of-stream state. If the error is not fatal, we can do the following: clear the stream's error state; construct a new `istream_iterator`, which then represents the current stream position; and restart the algorithm with this iterator as the begin iterator.

2.4.2.3 Stream Iterators Are One-Pass Iterators

Stream iterators are *one-pass iterators;* that is, an element referred to by a stream iterator can only be accessed once. For instance, it is not possible to reread elements through a memorized iterator. The following would fail: memorizing the begin position of the stream, then extracting elements from the stream, and later trying to reread the first element through the memorized begin iterator.[44] The reason is that once extracted, the element is consumed and cannot be reread.

The single-pass property can best be understood in terms of I/O from/to a terminal. Once we've read from the terminal stream, the input is consumed. Once we've written to the terminal stream, we cannot reposition and override the output. In contrast, container iterators are multipass iterators. We can repeatedly access any element referred to by any iterator (except the end iterator, of course). The one-pass or multipass property is expressed in the iterator categories. Iterators in the input and output iterator category are one-pass iterators. Iterators in the forward, bidirectional, or random-access iterator categories must be multipass iterators.

Another consequence of the one-pass property is that you would usually not want to have more than one stream iterator operating on the same stream, because they influ-

---

44. "Rereading" through the memorized iterator need not even fail. It will instead extract the "next" element from the stream, should there be one available at the current stream position.

ence each other. If one iterator is incremented, it moves the stream position of the under-lying stream so that the other iterator is affected, too.

Is the single-pass property a restriction? Can all algorithms live with this restriction? Let's see what algorithms typically need of an iterator.

Algorithms that write output via an output iterator usually do not access the same output position twice. That would mean that they override a position they had previously filled. No standard library algorithm we know of does anything like that. Therefore, all algorithms that write output via an iterator require an iterator type of the output iterator category and happily live with its one-pass property. For this reason, an `ostream_iterator` can be used in all standard library algorithms that require an out-put iterator.

Algorithms that read input via an iterator usually take an input iterator range. Not all such algorithms can live with the one-pass restriction of input iterators like the `istream_iterator`. The `find_end()` algorithm, for instance, does a look ahead and for that matter needs the multipass property. In order to explain this, let's take a closer look at the `find_end()` algorithm. It finds a subsequence of equal values in a sequence and returns an iterator to the beginning of the subsequence. Here is an example of how it would be used:

```
string s1 = "abcdefghijk";
string s2 = "def";

string::iterator i = find_end(s1.begin(),s1.end(),s2.begin(),s2.end());
cout << i << endl;
```

The result would be an iterator to the letter *d* in `s1`. The algorithm maintains two iterators: the first refers to the first input sequence, the second to the potential subse-quence. In the beginning the first iterator points to the 'a' in `s1`, the second to the *d* in `s2`. Then the algorithm looks for a match, that is, whether the 'a' is the beginning of the subse-quence `"def"`. It performs this search by successively advancing both iterators and com-paring the characters referred to. When it can't find a match here, it resets both iterators: the first one to the 'b' in `s1` and the second iterator back to the beginning of `"def"`. Then it starts looking for the match again. And so on and so forth. The crux is that the `find_end()` algorithm needs to reread elements from the input sequences. This cannot be done with iterators from the input iterator category, because they only support one-pass access. And indeed, the interface description of the `find_end()` function asks for an iterator from the forward_iterator category:

```
template<class ForwardIterator1, class ForwardIterator2> inline
ForwardIterator1 find_end(ForwardIterator1 first1, ForwardIterator1 last1,
                          ForwardIterator2 first2, ForwardIterator2 last2);
```

Note that the `find_end()` algorithm does not need the entire functionality required of a forward iterator. Forward iterators allow multipass access for reading *and* writing. Write access isn't needed in `find_end()`. Hence, all that this algorithm really needs is a multipass input iterator. However, there is no such iterator category.

Let us hasten to add that there are of course algorithms for whom one-pass input iterators perfectly suffice. The often quoted `find()` algorithm is an example, and so is the `count()` algorithm that we used in our examples. These algorithms read elements successively until they find what they're looking for or until they've counted all relevant elements. No element needs to be accessed twice, no look ahead is needed, no repositioning required. Their interface description asks only for iterators from the input iterator category:

```
template<class InputIterator, class T>
InputIterator find (InputIterator first, InputIterator last, const T& val);

template<class InputIterator, class T>
size_t count(InputIterator first, InputIterator last, const T& val);
```

In sum, where input iterators are required, `istream_iterators` can be provided. When an algorithm asks for a forward iterator, an `istream_iterator` will not suffice.

2.4.3 Stream Buffer Iterators

While the stream iterators can be used as an alternative to inserters and extractors, the stream buffer iterators can be used as an alternative to the stream buffer's I/O functions `sbumpc()` and `sputc()`. An IOStreams user would use stream buffer iterators when an inserter or extractor for a user-defined type is being implemented, and this implementation cannot be based on existing inserters and extractors. In such situations, the stream buffer iterators allow the use of the parsing and formatting functionality of a locale facet to the stream buffer via stream buffer iterators. An example of such a situation can be found in section 3.1, Input and Output of User-Defined Types, and in section 3.1.3, Refined Inserters and Extractors, in particular.

Stream buffer iterators enable a stream buffer to be seen as a sequence of characters. The standard library provides two stream buffer iterator abstractions for this purpose: (1) *ostream buffer iterators,* which can be used to write to a stream buffer, and (2) *istream buffer iterators,* which can be used to read from a stream buffer.

Like stream iterators, stream buffer iterators are one-pass iterators. The ostream buffer falls into the output iterator category, while the istream iterator is an input iterator.

2.4.3.1 Output Stream Buffer Iterator

The ostream buffer iterator is an output iterator, i.e., it allows write access to the position that it refers to, and it can be advanced in single steps. It is implemented in a way typical for output iterators in general. Hence a conceivable implementation is similar to the `ostream_iterator`'s implementation:

```cpp
template <class charT=char, class traits=char_traits<charT> >
class ostreambuf_iterator :
                public iterator<output_iterator_tag,void,void,void,void>
{
  public:
    typedef charT char_type;
    typedef traits traits_type;
    typedef basic_streambuf<charT,traits> streambuf_type;
    typedef basic_ostream<charT,traits> ostream_type;

    ostreambuf_iterator(ostream_type& s) throw()
      : sbuf(s.rdbuf()), failedFlag(false) {}

    ostreambuf_iterator(streambuf_type* sb) throw ()
      : sbuf(sb), failedFlag (false) {}

    ostreambuf_iterator& operator= (const charT& t)
    {
      if (failed() == false && sbuf != 0)
      {
        traits_type::int_type result;

        try
        {
          result = sbuf->sputc(t);
        }
        catch (...)
        {
          failedFlag = true;
          throw;
        }

        if (traits_type::eq_int_type(result, traits_type::eof()))
          failedFlag = true;
      }

      return *this;
    }

    ostreambuf_iterator& operator*() { return *this; }
    ostreambuf_iterator& operator++() { return *this; }
    ostreambuf_iterator& operator++(int) {return *this; }
```

```
   bool failed() const throw()
   {
     return failedFlag;
   }
 private:
   bool failedFlag;
   streambuf_type* sbuf;
};
```

Again, the two increment operators and the `operator*()` do nothing but return `*this`. The real work is done by the assignment operator, which inserts a character into the stream buffer by invoking the stream buffer's public member function `sputc()`. If the call to `sputc()` fails, indicated by either an exception or the return value of `traits_type::eof()`, the private data member `failedFlag` is set to true. `failedFlag` holds the error state of the iterator. Once an error has occurred, the iterator's error state is set to `true`, and the iterator does not insert further characters into the stream buffer.

The iterator's error state can be checked by the iterator's public member function `failed()`. This is the stream buffer iterator's explicit error handling. Here the output stream buffer iterator differs from the output stream iterator, which does not have any explicit error indication. Errors that occur during the use of a stream iterator are reflected in the stream state of the underlying stream object. Errors that occur during the use of a stream buffer iterator cannot be indicated through the underlying stream buffer, because stream buffers, unlike streams, have no explicit error indication mechanism. For this reason, the stream buffer iterator must provide an error indication mechanism on its own.

2.4.3.2 Input Stream Buffer Iterator

The input stream buffer iterator has a lot in common with the input stream iterator. Like the stream iterator, it is an input iterator that can be used only by one-pass algorithms.

Similar to the istream iterator, the istream buffer iterator supports the concept of an end-of-stream-iterator. A non-end-of-stream-iterator turns into an end-of-stream-iterator, when the end of the stream is reached, i.e., when the public stream buffer member function `sgetc()`, which the iterator uses to extract characters from the stream, returns `traits_type::eof()`. An end-of-stream-iterator can be explicitly constructed either by the default constructor or when a stream buffer is constructed with a stream buffer pointer that equals 0.

The only istream iterator range consists of the following two stream buffer iterators: The first iterator is constructed by providing either a stream or a stream buffer pointer different from 0; it refers to the current stream buffer position. The second iterator is an end iterator that is constructed via the default constructor.

The rules for comparison of istream buffer iterators are similar to those of istream iterators: All non-end-of-stream-iterators on the same stream buffer compare equal, as do all end-of-stream-iterators of the same type. The comparison of a non-end-of-stream-iterator and an end-of-stream-iterator yields false.

Despite the fact that input stream buffer iterators and input stream iterators have a lot in common, their implementations can differ significantly. The stream iterator typically has a private data member, where it stores the element that it has extracted from the stream. This is necessary because the underlying stream does not allow this element to be reextracted from the stream. The stream buffer iterator could be implemented in a similar way, i.e., it could buffer the character extracted from the stream buffer. However, it need not do so, because it can get the same character from the current stream buffer position repeatedly by calling `sgetc()`. This way, the implementation of a stream buffer iterator need not buffer the character but can use `sgetc()` in order to save the space for the character.

The implementation of the postfix increment operator needs a nested proxy class, which complicates the implementation a little bit. Here is such an implementation using a proxy class. We will discuss the details of the implementation below.[45]

```cpp
template<class charT, class traits = char_traits<charT> >
class istreambuf_iterator
    : public iterator<input_iterator_tag, charT,
                      typename traits::off_type, charT*, charT&>
{
  public:
    typedef charT                         char_type;
    typedef traits                        traits_type;
    typedef typename traits::int_type     int_type;
    typedef basic_streambuf<charT,traits> streambuf_type;
    typedef basic_istream<charT,traits>   istream_type;

    template <class charT, class traits = char_traits<charT> >
    class proxy
    {
      friend class istreambuf_iterator;

      public:
        charT operator*() { return keep_; }

      private:
        proxy(charT c, streambuf_type * sb) : keep_(c), sbuf(sb) {}

        charT keep_;
        basic_streambuf<charT,traits>* sbuf;

    };
```

---

45. See section G.7, The `typename` Keyword, in appendix G for further information.

```
istreambuf_iterator() throw() : sbuf(0) {}
istreambuf_iterator(istream_type& s) throw() : sbuf(s.rdbuf) {}
istreambuf_iterator(streambuf_type* sb) throw() : sbuf(sb) {}
istreambuf_iterator(const proxy& p) throw() : sbuf(p.sbuf) {}

charT operator*() const
{
  if (sbuf)
    return (sbuf->sgetc());
  else
    return 0;
}

istreambuf_iterator& operator++()
{
  if (sbuf)
  {
    sbuf->sbumpc();
    if ( traits::eq_int_type(sbuf->sgetc(),traits::eof()) )
      sbuf = 0;
  }
  return *this;
}

proxy operator++(int)
{
  if (sbuf)
  {
    proxy temp(sbuf->sgetc(), sbuf);
    sbuf->sbumpc();
    if ( traits::eq_int_type(sbuf->sgetc(),traits::eof()) )
      sbuf = 0;
    return temp;
  }
  else
    return proxy(0,0);
}

bool equal(const istreambuf_iterator& b) const
{
  if( ((sbuf ==0) && (b.sbuf==0)) || ((sbuf !=0) && (b.sbuf !=0)) )
    return true;
  else
    return false;
}
```

```
  private:
    streambuf_type* sbuf;
};


template <class charT, class traits>
bool operator==(const istreambuf_iterator<charT,traits>& lhs,
                const istreambuf_iterator<charT,traits>& rhs)
{
    return lhs.equal(rhs);
}


template <class charT, class traits>
bool operator!=(const istreambuf_iterator<charT,traits>& lhs,
                const istreambuf_iterator<charT,traits>& rhs)
{
    return (!(lhs == rhs));
}
```

As explained before, the iterator does not buffer the character at the current stream buffer position, but rather gets it via `sgetc()` each time it is needed. The postfix increment operator must return the iterator position before the increment. The character referred to before the iterator increment cannot be obtained from the stream buffer anymore after the increment operation has been performed, because the increment operator invoked `sbumpc()` on the underlying stream buffer, which moves the current buffer position forward. In this case it is necessary to save the previously retrieved character temporarily, so that it can be returned in some kind of "pseudo" iterator. This pseudo iterator is represented by the proxy class, which provides an `operator*()` for returning the stored character.

The proxy class has a second data member: the stream buffer pointer. The pointer is needed when a new istream buffer iterator must be constructed from a proxy object. This happens when another operation is applied to the return of a post-incremented istream buffer iterator, as in (`i++ == end`), where a comparison operator follows the postfix increment operation.

The error checking of our implementation might at first sight look a bit overcautious, with a negative impact on the performance. In the postfix increment operator, `sgetc()` is called after `sbumpc()`, only to check if the iterator still refers to a valid character or if it has already reached the end of the stream. The next increment operation or the next call to `operator*()` would detect the end of the stream buffer anyway. Why is this look-ahead necessary? When the character before the increment is the last available character, this character will be stored for later use in the returned proxy object. As we then perform the look-ahead, the istream iterator changes its state and turns into an end iterator, which closely mimics the behavior of pointers to memory. Incrementing a pointer to the last valid position is expected to yield the past-the-end position. That is exactly what happens due to the look-ahead: the istream iterator for the last valid position turns into an end istream iterator.

2.5 Additional Stream Storage and Stream Callbacks

IOStreams provides a hook for adding data fields to a stream object. This additional stream storage can be used by IOStreams users for adding any kind of information to a stream. The additional data fields are also known as *iword/pword*. Section 2.5.1, Additonal Stream Storage, explains how additional stream storage is allocated, used, and maintained.

The stream callbacks play a role in maintaining additional stream storage. Generally, the stream callbacks provide a means of allowing the user to take action when certain events occur. These events are destruction of a stream, copying a stream via `copyfmt()`, and imbuing a stream with a new locale. Section 2.5.2, Stream Callbacks, explains the purpose of these callbacks, how they are registered, and when they are invoked.

2.5.1 Additional Stream Storage

The IOStreams framework allows dynamic addition of data fields to stream objects. This means that new data members can be added to a stream at runtime. An alternative to dynamic addition of data fields is static addition by deriving a new stream class. Hence the usage of iword/pword is an alternative to derivation of new stream classes. Section 3.3.1, Using Stream Storage for Private Use: iword, pword, and xalloc, demonstrates how this functionality can be used. The present section explains the feature in principle.

The additional stream storage is maintained by the stream base class `ios_base` in two arrays, one containing elements of type `long`, the other storing pointers of type `void*`. Functionality for allocating and accessing these arrays is via the following three member functions of class `ios_base`:

```
long&  iword(int index);
void*& pword(int index);
static int xalloc();
```

`iword()` and `pword()` provide read and write access to the arrays: `iword()` to the data fields of type `long`, `pword()` to those of type `void*`. Both functions take an index into the respective array as an argument and return a reference to the associated array element.

Before these functions can be used, a valid index must be acquired, which is achieved by calling the static member function `xalloc()`. Each call to `xalloc()` acquires a different, new index. The data fields associated with this index are guaranteed to be initialized with 0. In principle, there is no limit to the number of indices that can be acquired; class `ios_base` allocates additional storage if necessary. Note that an index once acquired can never be released again; `ios_base` does not have an operation for release of a valid index.

Note that despite the fact that `xalloc()` is a static member function in `ios_base`, each `ios_base` object has its own iword and pword array, which means that every acquired index is valid for *all* stream objects regardless of their type, because all stream types are derived from `ios_base`.

LIFETIME OF THE REFERENCE RETURNED BY `iword()` OR `pword()`

Calls to `iword()` and `pword()` return a reference to the data field associated with a valid index. This reference is used to read and write the data field. Under the following circumstances, the reference may become invalid:

1. After a call to the object's `iword()` or `pword()` with a different index argument. In order to understand this, consider that the iword and pword arrays grow dynamically. The functions `iword()` and `pword()` might reallocate the arrays if an index is provided that is greater then the arrays' current capacity. In such a situation, the operation might allocate new memory for both arrays, copy the old values into the new arrays, initialize the requested data field, and release the old arrays—which would render all references obtained by previous calls invalid.[46]

2. After a call to the object's `copyfmt()` member function. The function `copyfmt()` takes a stream as an argument and copies its data members (except the stream buffer pointer and stream state) to the data members of `*this`. The data members to be copied include the iword and pword arrays. If the arrays of the source stream are longer than the ones of `*this`, additional memory must be allocated. Hence a reallocation similar to the one described above might be performed, by which all references obtained by previous calls to `iword()` or `pword()` would become invalid.[47]

3. When the stream object is destroyed. The dynamic memory used for the iword and pword arrays is freed on destruction of the stream object. Hence all previously obtained references to data fields of the arrays become invalid.

ERROR INDICATION

Calls to `iword()` and `pword()` can fail, for instance due to memory shortage. As usual in IOStreams, failure is indicated by setting `ios_base::badbit` in the stream state and,

---

46. The C++ standard states that a reference to the data field associated with a valid index may become invalid after *any* call to the object's `iword()` or `pword()` with a different index argument. The behavior described above is a *conceivable* strategy, not necessarily the one your IOStreams implementation really chooses. To be portable, you must be prepared to handle invalid references after any call.

47. Again, the C++ standard states that a reference to the data field associated with a valid index may become invalid after *any* call to the object's `copyfmt()` member function. The behavior described above is a *conceivable* strategy, not necessarily the one your IOStreams library implements.

depending on the exception mask, throwing an exception. The reference returned in case of failure refers to a data field containing 0.

Note that `iword()` and `pword()` are member functions of class `ios_base`, whereas the functions for checking the stream state and manipulating the exception mask are contained in the derived class template `basic_ios<>`. This way you can call `iword()` and `pword()` via a reference or pointer to `ios_base`, but in such a case you cannot check for failure afterwards.

CALLBACKS

IOStreams allows registration of callback functions, which are invoked under certain conditions, for instance when the stream object is destroyed. These callback functions increase the usability of `iword()` and `pword()`. For instance, it is common to store a pointer to dynamically allocated memory in a pword data field. Once the stream object is destroyed, the pword array is destroyed too. In order to avoid garbage, one would want to free the memory, which the pointer in the pword field refers to, before the pointer itself is discarded. This kind of cleanup is typically performed by a callback function that is invoked on destruction of a stream object. For details see section 2.5.2, Stream Callbacks.

The callback mechanism completes the iword/pword concept in such a way that both together allow streams to be extended without derivation: The iword/pword arrays provide facilities to store additional data streams, and the callback functions allow the functionality of streams to be extended. Section 3.3.1, Using Stream Storage for Private Use: iword, pword, and xalloc, explores the respective techniques in depth.

2.5.2 Stream Callbacks

IOStreams supports the concept of callback functions, whose invocation is triggered by certain events. In principle, the callback mechanism can be used whenever it is deemed beneficial to the IOStreams user's program. However the mechanism is mostly tailored for the following situations:

- functionality that should be invoked when the stream is imbued with a new locale. The corresponding event is `ios_base::imbue_event`.

- functionality used in combination with `ios_base` member functions `iword()` and `pword()`. The triggering events are `ios_base::erase_event` and `ios_base::copyfmt_event`.

Please see the example from section 3.3.1, Using Stream Storage for Private Use: iword, pword, and xalloc, which uses `iword()`/`pword()` in conjunction with the callback mechanism.

REGISTRATION OF CALLBACK FUNCTIONS

Callback functions are of type `ios_base::event_callback`, which is a type definition for a pointer to a function taking an IOStreams event, a reference to an `ios_base` object, and an index to the iword/pword arrays. A callback function must not throw any exceptions. Here is the complete typedef:

```
typedef void (*event_callback)(ios_base::event, ios_base&, int user_data);
```

Callback functions are registered via the following member function of ios_base:

```
void register_callback(ios_base::event_callback fct, int user_data);
```

A callback function is registered together with an index to the iword/pword arrays. This index is later provided to the function once it will be invoked.

INVOCATION OF CALLBACK FUNCTIONS

Registered callback functions of a stream object are called when one of the three IOStreams events imbue_event, erase_event, or copyfmt_event occurs. When a callback function is invoked, it is provided with the event that triggered the invocation, a reference to the invoking ios_base object, and the index to the iword/pword array that was registered together with the callback function. The event is provided so that the callback function can perform different operations for each type of event. Via the ios_base reference the callback function has access to the stream object by which it is invoked. The iword/pword index serves as a kind of function argument and allows data exchange with the caller.

When an event occurs, all registered functions are invoked, in reverse order of registration. The events have the following meaning.

IMBUE_EVENT. This event occurs when a stream object is imbued with a new locale. Imbuing with the new locale happens prior to the invocation of the callback functions, so that getloc() will already return the newly imbued locale when the callback is invoked.

A callback function for an imbue_event is needed, for instance, if a stream caches information from a locale object. The callback function would then retrieve information from the new locale object and update the stream object's cache.

COPYFMT_EVENT. This event occurs when the copyfmt() member function is called, i.e., when a stream object's data members are replaced by those of another stream. Most of the copying is done before the callback functions are invoked; all data members but the exception mask have already been assigned.

A callback function for a copyfmt_event is needed, for instance, if a stream object has pword data fields that contain pointers to data that will not be shared between stream objects after a call to copyfmt(). The point is that copyfmt() copies only the pword entries, but not the data to which the pword entries point. Hence a callback function could perform the necessary copy operations.

A call to copyfmt() triggers not only a copyfmt_event but also an erase_ event, i.e., all callback functions are also called with ios_base::erase_event. See below for details.

ERASE_EVENT. This event occurs when the stream object is destroyed or when the stream object's copyfmt() member function is called. In the latter case the callback is then invoked before any data members of the stream are assigned.

Callback functions for erase_events are needed, for instance, if pword entries point to dynamically allocated memory. On destruction of the stream object it might be necessary to free the memory pointed to before the pointers stored in the pword array are destroyed.

Invocation of erase_event callback functions on calls to copyfmt() is useful because copyfmt() overwrites the original data members of the stream object. In particular, the iword and pword entries are overwritten. If pword entries point to dynamically allocated memory, it might be desirable to free the memory pointed to before the pointer is discarded. This would typically be done by callback function that handles erase_events.

ERROR INDICATION

Callback functions are not allowed to indicate errors by means of exceptions. Also, they cannot indicate errors by setting error flags in the stream state, because the stream is passed to the callback function as ios_base& and access to the stream state and the exception mask is via the derived class basic_ios<class charT class Traits>. The consequence is that callbacks cannot indicate errors in the same way as other IOStreams functions do. It also means that callback functions must be prepared to catch all conceivable exceptions, because they have to suppress them.

CHAPTER 3

Advanced IOStreams Usage

3.1 Input and Output of User-Defined Types

One of the major advantages of the IOStreams framework is its extensibility. Just as you have predefined inserters and extractors for almost all types defined by the C++ language and library, you can implement and add input and output operations for your own user-defined types. To avoid surprises, user-defined input and output operations should follow the same conventions as the predefined inserters and extractors.

In this section we discuss how inserters and extractors for arbitrary user-defined types can be implemented and which rules they should follow. In several steps, we work through a complete example: insertion and extraction of a date class.

We start off with a simple, straightforward solution: breaking down a user-defined type into its contained data elements and using existing inserters and extractors for those elements. By combining operations that already know how to perform formatted input and output for existing types, we avoid most of the chores associated with formatting and parsing itself.

This first approach can be refined in several ways. We discuss use of format control parameters, internationalization, error indication, and several other IOStreams-specific tasks. For each of the refinements we explain the respective conventions used by the predefined shift operators and recommend applying the same rules for user-defined inserters and extractors. A reimplementation of the first example demonstrates application of these guidelines.

Eventually, we generalize the refined approach by factoring out the IOStreams-specific tasks, which are common to all inserters and extractors, and separating them from the part that is specific to input and output of a particular user-defined type. We put the general pattern into a generic inserter and extractor template and suggest encapsulating the type-specific part in the user-defined type in the form of member functions. This proposed solution has reusable elements that make life easier if you implement a significant number of inserters and extractors.

3.1.1 The Signature of Inserters and Extractors

TEMPLATE ARGUMENTS. Inserters and extractors are typically function templates that take the character type and the character traits type as template arguments. The reason for this is that streams are class templates on the character type and the character traits type, and input and output will be possible for all types of streams. Hence the I/O functions have the same template arguments as the streams they operate on.

FUNCTION ARGUMENTS. Inserters and extractors take a reference to the stream, to/from which the data are to be inserted/extracted, as a function argument and return a reference to the same stream object. This is because shift operators can be concatenated and thus the return value of a shift operator must be appropriate as input to the next shift operator in an expression.[1] The second argument is a reference to an object of the user-defined type that is written or read. Inserters take a constant reference, because the inserter is not supposed to modify the object it prints; extractors take a non-constant reference, because they alter the object by filling it with information extracted from the stream. One question is still left open: Of which type shall the stream argument and the return value be? The natural choice for the argument and return type of inserters and extractors are the general stream classes (see section 2.2.1, Class Hierarchy), either `basic_istream <class charT, class traits>` for extractors or `basic_ostream <class charT, class traits>` for inserters. All predefined inserters and extractors in IOStreams are defined for these stream classes. User-defined inserters and extractors should be in line with common IOStreams practice and do the same. The only sensible exceptions are inserters and extractors for user-defined stream classes, if the I/O operations depend on information that is specific to the new stream class. Section 3.3.2, Creating New Stream Classes by Derivation, gives an example of shift operators for a derived stream class.

3.1.2 First Inserters and Extractors

Let us begin with a straightforward way of implementing inserters and extractors for arbitrary user-defined types. The easiest thing to do when building an inserter or extractor for a new type is to break down the type into its parts and make use of existing input and output operations for the contained elements. For instance, input and output of an

---

1. The concatenation of shift operators is explained in the introductory section 1.2.2, The Input and Output Operators.

array type would be implemented by iterating through the array and using the inserters and extractors of the array element type for reading and writing each single element.

For a class type, input and output of the object would boil down to input and output of the object's data members and base classes.

We intend to explain the technique in terms of an example. Let us start with introducing the type in question—a date class.

```
class date {
public:
   date(int d, int m, int y)
   { tm_date.tm_mday = d; tm_date.tm_mon = m-1; tm_date.tm_year = y-1900; }
   date(const tm& t) : tm_date(t) {}
   date()
   { /* get current date */ }
   // more constructors and useful member functions
private:
   tm tm_date;
};
```

The date class has a private data member of type tm, which is the time structure defined in the C library (in header file <ctime>). It is a type suitable for representing date values and consists of a number of integral values, among them the day of a month, the month of a year, and the year since 1900. In the tm structure, days are counted from 1 to 31, but months are denoted by values 0 to 11.

We want to allow insertion and extraction of date objects in exactly the same way as input and output of built-in types like integers or strings, i.e., via shift operators, as in the following code fragments:

```
date eclipse(11,8,1999);
cout << "solar eclipse on " << eclipse << '\n';
```

and

```
date aDate;
cout << '\n' << "Please, enter a date (day month year):" << '\n';
cin  >> aDate;
cout << "date: " << aDate << '\n';
```

To facilitate this convenient kind of input and output, we need to implement shift operators as inserters and extractors for date objects:

The extractor:
```
template<class charT, class Traits>
basic_istream<charT, Traits>&
operator>> (basic_istream<charT,Traits>& is, date& dat)
{
 int tmp;
 is >> dat.tm_date.tm_mday;
 is.ignore();
 is >> tmp; dat.tm_date.tm_mon = tmp-1;
 is.ignore();
 is >> tmp; dat.tm_date.tm_year = tmp-1900;
 return is;
}
```

The inserter:
```
template<class charT, class Traits>
basic_ostream<charT, Traits>&
operator<< (basic_ostream<charT, Traits >& os, const date& dat)
{
 os << dat.tm_date.tm_mday << '.';
 os << dat.tm_date.tm_mon+1 << '.';
 os << dat.tm_date.tm_year+1900 ;
 return os;
}
```

A `date` object is broken down into its elements, in this case the day, month, and year contained in the `struct tm` data member of the `date` object. Each such element is an integer value and is inserted or extracted by means of the standard shift operator for type `int`.

Note that it usually is a good idea to make insertion and extraction complementary operations: An item should be written in a format that is understood by the input operation, so that you can read what you've written.

The `date` class still needs a minor modification: Both operations access private data members of class `date` and must therefore be declared friend functions to class `date`. Here's a completed version of class `date`:

```
class date {
public:
date(int d, int m, int y)
   { tm_date.tm_mday = d; tm_date.tm_mon = m-1; tm_date.tm_year = y-1900;
     tm_date.tm_sec = tm_date.tm_min = tm_date.tm_hour = 0;
     tm_date.tm_wday = tm_date.tm_yday = 0;
     tm_date.tm_isdst = 0;
   }
   date(const tm& t) : tm_date(t) {}
   date()
   { time_t ltime;
```

```
    time(&ltime);
    tm_date = *localtime(&ltime);
  }
  // more constructors and useful member functions

private:
  tm tm_date;

template<class charT, Traits>
friend basic_istream<charT, Traits>&
operator>> (basic_istream<charT, Traits >& is, date& dat);

template<class charT, Traits>
friend basic_ostream<charT, Traits>&
operator<< (basic_ostream<charT, Traits >& os, const date& dat);
};
```

The default constructor uses the C library functions `time()` for getting the current time from the system and `localtime()` for converting the time value into a `tm` structure.

With the input and output operations implemented as outlined above, we can insert and extract `date` objects via shift operators. The code fragments from above (repeated below for illustration) would behave as follows:

```
date eclipse(11,8,1999);
cout << "solar eclipse on " << eclipse << '\n';
```

would print

```
solar eclipse on 11.8.1999
```

and

```
date aDate;
cout << '\n' << "Please enter a date (day month year):" << '\n';
cin  >> aDate;
cout << "date: " << aDate << '\n';
```

would request a date and accept input as shown below:

```
Please enter a date (day month year):
> 2.6.1952
```

store it as a `date` object and print

```
date: 2.6.1952
```

3.1.3 Refinements

The technique of creating new inserters and extractors by composing existing inserters and extractors is simple and powerful, but it can be refined in several ways: More elaborate format control can be desired, errors might occur and must be handled, the format might depend on cultural conventions. Also, there are several other possibilities for reading and writing data from/to a stream rather than via existing shift operators. We discuss such refinements in the following sections.

The predefined inserters and extractors in IOStreams follow a number of conventions: They report errors in a uniform way, interpret format control parameters consistently, factor out culture-sensitive information into locales and facets, and so on. User-defined I/O operations should apply the same rules. Along with each refinement suggested in the following sections we explain the related conventions and eventually combine all the information in another example: an internationalized date inserter and extractor.

3.1.3.1 Format Control

Our simple inserter from the previous section has a tiny problem with the field adjustment. If the field width is set to a particular value, only the first item printed will be adjusted properly, because the first inserter will reset the field width to zero. The following program snippet:

```
date today;
cout << "today: " << left << setw(10) << setfill('*')
    << today << endl;
```

would print

```
today: 27********.7.1999
```

Probably the expected result after setting the field width prior to insertion of a date object is that the entire date is adjusted, and not just the first part of it. You might want to fix this problem and control the field width yourself. This leads us to the more general discussion of format control in inserters and extractors.

For the sake of consistency, format control facilities defined in IOStreams should generally be interpreted and manipulated by user-defined I/O operations in the same way as the predefined inserters and extractors are. Not all format flags are relevant to input and output of all types of objects. Some format flags apply to insertion and extraction of certain data types only. They are often irrelevant to input and output of user-defined types. For example, the `oct`, `dec`, and `hex` format flags have an impact solely on input and output of integral values and can be ignored for the formatting and parsing of dates, as in our example. Other format flags, such as `unitbuf`, `skipws`, or the field width, are independent of the type of object inserted or extracted. They have an impact on user-defined types, too.

As a rule of thumb, you should first determine all format flags that you want to be relevant to the user-defined type that you intend to parse and format. Once you have identified the relevant format facilities, understand how they are used in the predefined inserters and extractors, and make sure that your user-defined operations interpret and manipulate them in exactly the same way.

Here are some things to keep in mind:

We've already mentioned that the field width is the only format information that is not permanent but is reset to 0 each time it is used. Stick to this rule if you decide to adjust output fields according to the field width, and reset the field width to 0 at the end of your inserter.

Some of the format flags do not have a default value. The `adjustfield`, for instance, is not initialized, so you must cope with the possibility that none of the `adjustfield` flags might be set. In this case, all the predefined inserters behave as though the field were set to `right`, that is, they add padding characters before the actual output. Stick to this rule if you decide to adjust output fields in your inserters.

Note also that typical candidates of relevance for your user-defined inserter or extractor such as `unitbuf` and `skipws` are automatically performed as so-called prefix and suffix operations. If you decide that these format elements are relevant for your inserters and extractors, don't forget to use the sentry objects in your implementation.

3.1.3.2 Prefix and Suffix Operations

It's a convention for stream input and output operations to carry out certain tasks prior (prefix activities) and subsequent (suffix activities) to any actual input or output. The prefix activities include flushing of a tied stream and skipping of whitespace. The suffix activities include flushing the stream if the `unitbuf` flag is set.[2]

In the date inserter and extractor from the previous section, there is a certain performance overhead due to the use of existing inserters and extractors. The flushing, for instance, is performed for each single shift operation, although it would only be necessary for input or output of the entire date. If we want to eliminate the overhead, we have to care about flushing ourselves.

In IOStreams, the prefix and suffix activities are encapsulated into classes called `sentry`, nested into the general stream classes `basic_istream` and `basic_ostream`. The constructors of these classes perform the prefix activities, the destructors carry out the suffix activities. The `sentry` classes have an `operator bool()`, which allows checking for success of construction (i.e., success of the prefix operations).

The standard allows the provider of an IOStreams library to add operations, beyond the ones listed above, to the constructors and destructors of the `sentry` classes. Conceivable additions could be locking and unlocking of mutually exclusive locks for ensuring thread-safety of your IOStreams library, or maintenance of internal caches, etc.

---

2. See section 1.8, Synchronization of Streams, for further information.

Instead of using sentries, you could theoretically manually add the prefix and suffix activities into your shift operators. Such explicitly implemented prefix and suffix activities, however, introduce potential portability problems, because the hidden vendor-specific additions would be missing. If you implement an inserter or extractor, you should use the sentry classes in order to make sure that all necessary prefix and suffix tasks are carried out. When you compose existing shift operators, you implicitly do so anyway, because the predefined inserters and extractors use sentries. If you build shift operators on top of low-level I/O operations, you have to care about prefix and suffix activities yourself.

Here is how you should use the sentry classes in your inserters and extractors:

Create a local sentry object (which receives the stream as parameter) on the stack prior to any other activity in your shift operator. The sentry constructor, which will be the first operation executed in your shift operator, performs all necessary prefix tasks. The local sentry object goes out of scope when the shift operator returns; its destructor will always, even in the presence of exceptions, be called and cares about the suffix tasks.

Check the success of the prefix operations after construction of the sentry object by means of its bool operator. The operator returns false in case of !good(), which means either that an error occurred or that the end of the input was encountered. It's another convention that stream operations stop if the stream state is not good. Following this policy, one should return from the function if the check after construction of the sentry object does not indicate success.

The example in section 3.1.3, Refined Inserters and Extractors, demonstrates the correct use of sentries.

3.1.3.3 Error Indication

Errors can occur during the parsing or formatting of an item. Consider the extractor from the previous section; we might want to check the extracted date's validity and indicate failure if the date is incomplete or incorrect (December 32, for instance). Again, there are rules to follow.

Users of inserters and extractors in IOStreams expect error situations to be indicated by means of the stream state and by throwing exceptions according to the exception mask. The predefined I/O operations for built-in and library types demonstrate the principle; section 1.3, The Stream State, describes it in detail. Here is what a shift operator in IOStreams is expected to do in case of errors:

THE STREAM STATE. Each stream has a state consisting of flags indicating certain types of errors.

The state flags have the following meaning: badbit indicates an error situation that is likely to be unrecoverable, whereas failbit indicates a situation that might allow you to retry the failed operation. The flag eofbit simply indicates the end of the input sequence.

By convention, most IOStreams operations stop and have no further effect once one of the flags is set.

THE EXCEPTION MASK. By default none of the stream operations throws an exception. The user has to declare explicitly that he wants a stream to throw exceptions.

For this purpose every stream contains an *exception mask,* which consists of several exception flags. Each flag in this mask corresponds to one of the stream state flags `failbit`, `badbit`, and `eofbit`. For example, once the `badbit` flag is set in the exception mask, an exception will be thrown each time the `badbit` flag is set in the stream state.

THE OUTPUT VARIABLE OF AN EXTRACTOR. The value of the output variable must be a valid value; it need not be meaningful in the case of a failed extraction. Other than that, there are no requirements imposed by IOStreams. However, common sense indicates that the behavior should be similar at this point for all user-defined extractors.

Inserters and extractors for user-defined types should obey these policies for error indication in IOStreams. Here is what you need to do when implementing input and output operations:

DETECTING ERROR SITUATIONS. Problems can be reported from any component you invoke to accomplish the task of formatted input and output. Examples are a `bad_alloc` exception thrown by an invoked operation due to memory shortage, or failure of an invoked stream operation indicated by a bit set in the stream state. Also, the internal logic of your inserter or extractor can identify error situations, e.g., extraction of incomplete or invalid dates in our example. Therefore:

• Catch all exceptions.

• Check all return codes, the stream state, or other error indications.

• Check the consistency of extracted or inserted data, if possible and necessary.

INDICATING ERROR SITUATIONS. Have your inserter and extractor report errors according to the IOStreams principles, that is, set the stream state flags as follows:

• `ios_base::badbit` to indicate loss of integrity of the stream. Typical problems of that category include memory shortage and errors reported from stream buffer functions.

• `ios_base::failbit` if the formatting or parsing itself fails due to the internal logic of your operation.

• `ios_base::eofbit` when the end of the input is reached.

Raise an exception if the exception mask asks for it. If any of the invoked operations raises an exception, catch the exception and rethrow it, if the exception mask allows it. It is important that you rethrow the original exception rather than raising an IOStreams exception of type `ios_base::failure`. The original exception is likely to convey information that precisely describes the error situation, whereas `ios_base::failure` is a rather nonspecific, general IOStreams error. If you do not retain the original exception, useful information might get lost.

CARE ABOUT THE OUTPUT VARIABLE OF AN EXTRACTOR. Find a concept for the value you return in the output variable of a failed extractor. Ideally, one would retain or restore the original value of the output variable, so that the variable would return unaltered in case of failure. Another strategy is to clear the content and return a nil value in case no valid value can be extracted. This is doable only if there is a nil value for the respective type. Examples of nil values are a zero-length string or a date like 00-00-00.

A concrete example is shown in section 3.1.3, Refined Inserters and Extractors.

3.1.3.4 Internationalization

The textual representation of a date value varies from one cultural area to another. The inserter and extractor from the previous section, however, ignore this fact and are incapable of adjusting the formatting and parsing of dates to cultural conventions. For instance, the order of day, month, and year are hard-coded, and the typical U.S. notation of `12/31/99` instead of the German `31.12.99` can neither be parsed nor produced. Also, textual representations of the month name are not supported; we cannot use dates such as `December 31, 1999` or `31.Dezember 1999`.

We want to eliminate this restriction and intend to internationalize our date inserter and extractor. Users of our shift operators will be allowed to indicate and switch cultural environments, and as a result the formatting and parsing will be adjusted accordingly. In IOStreams, internationalized I/O operations are implemented by factoring out culture-sensitive parsing and formatting into exchangeable components: locales and facets. A short review of locales and facets follows.

The purpose of a locale is to represent a cultural area and contain all the culture-dependent information and services relevant to that area. They are used by components that deal with culture-sensitive data for retrieving information about cultural differences. Inserters and extractors in IOStreams are examples of such components; they need to know how culture-sensitive items like numeric values and dates are formatted.

The services and information in a locale are organized in smaller units, the facets. Often, there is not just a single facet for a certain problem, but rather a group of facet types related to one problem domain. For instance, the standard facets `num_put`, `num_get`, and `numpunct` together represent the knowledge about numeric formats. Each locale object represents a particular cultural area and contains facets for that culture. A German locale, for example, has the numeric facets for German numeric format, and a U.S. locale has the numeric facets for U.S. formats.

Locales are provided to IOStreams on a per stream basis. That is, each stream has a locale of its own. The locale attached to a stream can be replaced. Locale-sensitive I/O operations are expected to use a stream's current locale object in order to achieve adaptability to cultural environments.

If you implement inserters and extractors for culture-sensitive data types, you should take the following steps:

1. Identify the culture dependencies related to the respective data type.
2. Encapsulate relevant culture-dependent rules and services into facets. (This requires implementation of new facet types, if the necessary functionality is not yet available in a locale.)

3. Provide locales that contain the necessary facets, or provide means for creating such locales. (Every locale contains at least all standard facets. If you need nonstandard facets, you must support creation of these locales.)

4. Imbue streams with such locales.

5. Use the stream's locale and its facets for implementing your internationalized inserters and extractors. (Users of your culture-sensitive inserters and extractors must first create locales that contain the necessary facets and then imbue streams with such locales, by which the necessary facets are made available to your inserters and extractors.)

Some of these aspects are demonstrated in the example presented in section 3.1.3, Refined Inserters and Extractors. It shows use of facets for implementation of inserters and extractors. We use existing standard facets in that example, and for this reason we do not explain how new facet types are created and how they become part of a locale. The creation of nonstandard locales is explained in chapter 8, "User-Defined Facets."

The delegation of culture-sensitive parsing and formatting to locales and facets demonstrates a more general design principle: factoring out parsing and formatting into independent, replaceable components. Such a design makes for a high degree of flexibility that can be used for many purposes: We have seen that users of internationalized I/O operations can replace a stream's locale and in this way enable parsing and formatting rules for an unlimited number of cultural areas. The inserters and extractors presented in section 3.1.4, Generic Inserters and Extractors, are another demonstration of the principle. In that example, formatting and parsing rules are decoupled from IOStreams-specific tasks and become part of the data type in the form of member functions. In this way not only can formatting and parsing be replaced, but the entire data type is exchangeable, and the resulting inserters and extractors become entirely generic.

3.1.3.5 I/O Operations

The inserter and extractor from the previous section were built on top of existing shift operators. Composition of existing shift operators is not the only way of implementing new inserters and extractors. Alternatively, you can insert and extract items via stream iterators (see section 2.4, Stream Iterators and Stream Buffer Iterators, for further information). Stream iterators themselves are based on existing shift operators. Hence, the use of stream iterators is another way of building new inserters and extractors on top of formatted I/O operations.

Approaches of a different quality are the use of unformatted I/O operations such as the `read()` and `write()` member functions of a stream or direct access to the stream buffer via stream buffer iterators. Both solutions require explicit implementation of the entire parsing and formatting logic. The guidelines given above for format control, prefix and suffix operations, error indication, and internationalization help you to implement such shift operators correctly. In the next section we reimplement the date inserters and extractors, demonstrating the use of stream buffer iterators.

3.1.4 Refined Inserters and Extractors

Eventually, we return to the example of an inserter and extractor for a date class. We are going to use the same date class that was initially introduced in section 3.1.2, First Inserters and Extractors. There, the inserter and extractor broke down a date object into its elements, inserting and extracting the data elements by means of existing shift operators.

This time we will build internationalized versions of the date inserter and extractor. The task of parsing and formatting a date object is delegated to the time facets `time_get` and `time_put` of the stream's locale. These facets directly access the underlying stream buffer via stream buffer iterators. The example demonstrates several of the techniques discussed in the previous section. It shows use of stream buffer iterators; delegation to facets; use of prefix and suffix operations by means of sentry objects; and, eventually, error indication. We will address each of the topics one by one. Let us start with internationalizing the date inserter and extractor.

3.1.4.1 Internationalization

Let us repeat the list of recommended steps to take for input and output of culture-sensitive data types:

1. Identify the culture dependencies related to the respective data type.

2. Encapsulate relevant culture-dependent rules and services into facets.

3. Provide locales that contain such facets, or provide means for creating such extended locales.

4. Imbue streams with such locales.

5. Use the stream's locale and its facets for implementing your internationalized inserters and extractors.

The format of dates is clearly culture-dependent. Consequently, we need facets that represent the rules for formatting and parsing dates. Fortunately, the standard library already contains the facets `time_put` and `time_get` for this purpose. As a result, we need not create new facet types, but can use standard facets instead. Also, we need not care about equipping locales with the necessary facets or imbuing streams with such extended locales, because every locale object contains at least all standard facets. We can concentrate on step 5: use of facets for implementing an internationalized version of our date inserter and extractor.

Here is the internationalized version of the inserter and extractor:

The extractor:
```
template<class charT, class Traits>
basic_istream<charT, Traits>&
operator>> (basic_istream<charT, Traits >& is, date& dat)
{
 if (!is.good()) return is;

 ios_base::iostate err = 0;

use_facet<time_get<charT,istreambuf_iterator<charT,Traits> > >(is.getloc())
   .get_date(is, istreambuf_iterator<charT,Traits>(),is, err, &dat.tm_date);

 return is;
}
```

The inserter:
```
template<class charT, class Traits>
basic_ostream<charT, Traits>&
operator<< (basic_ostream<charT, Traits >& os, const date& dat)
{
 if (!os.good()) return os;

 use_facet<time_put<charT,ostreambuf_iterator<charT,Traits> > >(os.getloc())
   .put(os,os,os.fill(),&dat.tm_date,'x');
 return os;
}
```

Use of the `time_get` and `time_put` facets is similar to use of the numeric and monetary facets. Section 2.1.5, Collaboration Among Streams, Stream Buffers, and Locales, explains the principle of using parsing and formatting facets. The details specific to time facets are described in section 6.2.3, Date and Time Values. We will not repeat the details here. Let's just get a rough idea of the time facets' interfaces. A time-parsing facet of type `time_get<char_type,iter_type>` has the following parsing function for dates:

```
iter_type get_date(iter_type in, iter_type end,
            ios_base& fmt,
            ios_base::iostate& err,
            tm* time) const;
```

A time-formatting facet of type `time_put<char_type,iter_type>` has the following function for formatting time and date values:

```
iter_type put(iter_type out,
            ios_base& fmt, char_type fill,
            const tm* time,
            char fmtspec, char fmtmodifier = 0) const;
```

Here is a brief description of the function arguments:

ITERATORS. Formatting functions like put() take an output iterator (parameter out) that designates the destination for output. Parsing functions like get_date() take an input iterator range (parameters in and end) that designates beginning and end of the character sequence to be parsed. The operations return an iterator that points to the position after the sequence written to or read from.

The iterators used in our example are input and output stream buffer iterators. The begin iterators are created by converting the stream itself into stream buffer iterators. This is possible because the istreambuf_iterator and the ostreambuf_iterator have converting constructors that take a reference to a stream and convert it into a stream buffer iterator to the current stream position. The end iterator is created by means of the default constructor of class istreambuf_iterator.

FORMATTING INFORMATION. Unlike other formatting facets in the locale, the time_put facet uses neither format information from the ios_base object that is provided as an argument (parameter fmt) nor the provided fill character (parameter fill).[3]

VALUE. Naturally, parsing and formatting functions take a pointer or reference to the value to be written or read. In this case it's a pointer to a time structure (parameter time).

FORMAT SPECIFICATION. The time-formatting function takes a format specifier, plus an optional format modifier (parameters fmtspec and fmtmodifier). These are characters as defined for the C library function strftime() (defined in header <ctime>).

ERROR INDICATION. Parsing functions like get_date() store error information in an ios_base::iostate object (parameter err). Formatting functions like put() do not have an error parameter. If the output iterator returned by the put() function has a failed() member function, you can use this to check for success or failure. If the iterator type does not have means for error indication, you cannot check for error of a put() operation.

3.1.4.2 Prefix and Suffix Operations

We will now add the prefix and suffix operations by means of sentries. As a reminder, here are the recommendations for use of sentry classes in inserters and extractors:

1. Create a sentry object prior to any other activity.

2. Check for success of the prefix operations after construction of the sentry object by means of its bool operator.

3. Return from the function if the check after construction of the sentry object does not indicate success.

---

3. Nonstandard time_put facets, that is, facets that are not required by the standard as part of the standard library, might be using format information from the ios_base object as well as the provided fill character. However, the predefined standard facets time_put<char> and time_put<wchar_t>, which we use in our sample implementation, do not use these arguments.

Below is the previous example, extended by use of sentries.[4]

The extractor:
```
template<class charT, class Traits>
basic_istream<charT, Traits>&
operator>> (basic_istream<charT, Traits >& is, date& dat)
{
  if (!is.good()) return is;

  ios_base::iostate err = 0;
  typename basic_istream<charT,Traits>::sentry ipfx(is);
  if(ipfx)
  {
    use_facet<time_get<charT,istreambuf_iterator<charT,Traits> > >(is.getloc())
      .get_date(is, istreambuf_iterator<charT,Traits>(),is, err, &dat.tm_date);
  }
  return is;
}
```

The inserter:
```
template<class charT, class Traits>
basic_ostream<charT, Traits>&
operator<< (basic_ostream<charT, Traits >& os, const date& dat)
{
  if (!os.good()) return os;

  typename basic_ostream<charT,Traits>::sentry opfx(os);
  if(opfx)
  {
    use_facet<time_put<charT,ostreambuf_iterator<charT,Traits> > >(os.getloc())
      .put(os,os,os.fill(),&dat.tm_date,'x');
  }
  return os;
}
```

3.1.4.3 Format Control

Let us now add format control to the inserter and extractor. The only format control parameter that we want to add is proper use of the field width when date objects are written to output streams. This requires taking into account not only the streams field width

---

4. Class `sentry` is a type that depends on the template arguments of the extractor function and for this reason requires use of the `typename` keyword. If you are not familiar with the use of `typename`, see Section G.7, The typename Keyword, in appendix G, for further information.

setting but also the adjustment flags (right, left, internal) and the fill character. Naturally, we intend to follow the recommendations that we previously explained:

As the field width is not permanent, but is reset to 0 each time it is used, we need to reset the field width to 0 at the end of our inserter.

The adjustfield need not be initialized, so we stick to the rule that all inserters behave as though the field were set to right.

Below you find the inserter from the previous example, with field width adjustment added.

The inserter:
```
template<class charT, class Traits>
basic_ostream<charT, Traits>&
operator<< (basic_ostream<charT, Traits >& os, const date& dat)
{
 if (!os.good()) return os;

 typename basic_ostream<charT,Traits>::sentry opfx(os);
 if(opfx)
 {
   basic_stringbuf<charT,Traits> sb;

   use_facet<time_put<charT,ostreambuf_iterator<charT,Traits> > >(os.getloc())
     .put(&sb,os,os.fill(),&dat.tm_date,'x');

   basic_string<charT, Traits> s = sb.str();
   streamsize charToPad = os.width() - s.length();
   ostreambuf_iterator<charT,Traits> sink(os);
   if (charToPad <= 0)
      {
        sink = copy(s.begin(), s.end(), sink);
      }
   else
      { if (os.flags() & ios_base::left)
          { sink = copy(s.begin(), s.end(), sink);
            fill_n(sink,charToPad,os.fill());
          }
        else
          fill_n(sink,charToPad,os.fill());
            sink = copy(s.begin(), s.end(), sink);
          }
      }
 }
 os.width(0);
 return os;
}
```

3.1.4.4 Error Indication

Finally, we add error handling to the inserter and extractor. Here are the recommendations that were previously explained.

DETECTING ERROR SITUATIONS.

- Catch exceptions.

- Check return codes, the stream state, or other error indications.

- Check the validity of extracted objects and determine other potential errors.

INDICATING ERROR SITUATIONS. Have your inserter and extractor report errors according to the IOStreams principles, and set the stream state flags as follows:

- `ios_base::badbit` to indicate loss of integrity of the stream.

- `ios_base::failbit` if the formatting or parsing itself fails due to the internal logic of your operation.

- `ios_base::eofbit` when the end of the input is reached.

Raise an exception if the exception mask asks for it. If any of the invoked operations raises an exception, catch the exception and rethrow it, if the exception mask allows it.

First, we extend the date class and add a `bool` operator to the `date` class, which checks the validity of the date. We sort out nonsensical input like `Dec 32, 1999`, via a private helper function `valid()`, and we use the C library function `mktime()` for calculation of the data fields `tm_wday` (day of the week) and `tm_yday` (day of the year) of the `tm` structure. `mktime()` also flags date values that cannot be represented[5] in a tm structure, such as dates before January 1, 1970. We will use the `bool` operator of the `date` class for detecting error situations that are due to extraction of invalid objects. Here is the complete declaration of the extended date class:

```
class date {
public:
   date(int d, int m, int y)
   { tm_date.tm_mday = d; tm_date.tm_mon = m-1; tm_date.tm_year = y-1900;
     tm_date.tm_sec = tm_date.tm_min = tm_date.tm_hour = 0;
     tm_date.tm_wday = tm_date.tm_yday = 0;
     tm_date.tm_isdst = 0;
     ok = ( valid() && (mktime(&tm_date)!=time_t(-1)) ) ? true : false;
   }
   date(const tm& t) : tm_date(t)
   { ok = ( mktime(&tm_date)!=time_t(-1) ) ? true : false; }
   date()
   {  time_t ltime;
```

---

5. The range of times representable in `time_t` is implementation-defined. In many implementations of the C library dates befor January 1, 1970 cannot be represented.

```
        tm* tm_ptr;
        time(&ltime);  // get system time
        tm_ptr=localtime(&ltime); // convert to tm struct
        if (tm_ptr != NULL)
        {  tm_date = *tm_ptr;
           ok = true;
        }
        else // is date before 1-1-1970
           ok = false;
     }

     bool operator!()               // check for the date's validity
     {  ok = ( valid() && (mktime(&tm_date)!=time_t(-1)) ) ? true : false;
        return !ok;
     }

private:
   tm tm_date;
   bool ok;

   bool valid()  // check for sensible date; rejects nonsense like 32.12.1999⁶
   {  if (tm_date.tm_mon < 0 || tm_date.tm_mon > 11)    return false;
      if ( tm_date.tm_mday < 1 )                        return false;
      switch (tm_date.tm_mon) {
      case 0: case 2: case 4: case 6: case 9: case 7: case 11:
         if (tm_date.tm_mday > 31)                      return false;
         break;
      case 1:
         if (tm_date.tm_mday > 29)                      return false;
         if (tm_date.tm_mday > 28 && tm_date.tm_year%4) return false;
         break;
      default:
         if (tm_date.tm_mday > 30) return false;
      }
      return true;
   }

template<class charT, Traits>
friend basic_istream<charT, Traits>&
operator>> (basic_istream<charT, Traits >& is, date& dat);

template<class charT, Traits>
friend basic_ostream<charT, Traits>&
operator<< (basic_ostream<charT, Traits >& os, const date& dat);
};
```

---

6. The leap-year rule in date::valid( ) is simplified. For example, 1900 wasn't a leap year and 2100 won't be.

The `operator!()` is used in the extractor below to check whether the extracted date is valid. Here are the previous inserter and extractor, this time with error handling and error indication added:

The extractor:

```
template<class charT, class Traits>
basic_istream<charT, Traits>&
operator>> (basic_istream<charT, Traits >& is, date& dat)
{
 if (!is.good()) return is;

 ios_base::iostate err = 0;
 try
 {
    typename basic_istream<charT,Traits>::sentry ipfx(is);
    if(ipfx)
    {
     use_facet<time_get<charT,istreambuf_iterator<charT,Traits> > >
       (is.getloc()).get_date
           (is, istreambuf_iterator<charT,Traits>(),is, err, &dat.tm_date);

     // check for the date's validity
     if (!dat) err |= ios_base::failbit;

    }
 }
 catch(bad_alloc& )
 {
  err |= ios_base::badbit;
  ios_base::iostate exception_mask = is.exceptions();

  if (    (exception_mask & ios_base::failbit)
     && !(exception_mask & ios_base::badbit ))
  {
     is.setstate(err);
  }
  else if (exception_mask & ios_base::badbit)
  {
     try { is.setstate(err); }
     catch( ios_base::failure& ) { }
     throw;
  }
 }
 catch(...)
 {
  err |= ios_base::failbit;
  ios_base::iostate exception_mask = is.exceptions();
```

```
  if (  (exception_mask & ios_base::badbit)
     && (err & ios_base::badbit))
  {
     is.setstate(err);
  }
  else if(exception_mask & ios_base::failbit)
  {
     try { is.setstate(err); }
     catch( ios_base::failure& ) { }
     throw;
  }
 }
 if ( err ) is.setstate(err);
 return is;
}
```

The inserter:

```
template<class charT, class Traits>
basic_ostream<charT, Traits>&
operator<< (basic_ostream<charT, Traits >& os, const date& dat)
{
 if (!os.good()) return os;

  ios_base::iostate err = 0;
  try
  {
    typename basic_ostream<charT,Traits>::sentry opfx(os);
    if(opfx)
    {
      basic_stringbuf<charT,Traits> sb;

      // formatting the date
      if (use_facet<time_put<charT,ostreambuf_iterator<charT,Traits> > >
         (os.getloc()).put(&sb,os,os.fill(),&dat.tm_date,'x').failed()
         )
         // set the stream state after checking the return iterator
        err = ios_base::badbit;

      // field width adjustment
      if (err == ios_base::goodbit)
      {
        basic_string<charT, Traits> s = sb.str();
        streamsize charToPad = os.width() - s.length();
        ostreambuf_iterator<charT,Traits> sink(os);
```

```
        if (charToPad <= 0)
        {
          sink = copy(s.begin(), s.end(), sink);
        }
        else
        {
          if (os.flags() & ios_base::left)
          {
            sink = copy(s.begin(), s.end(), sink);
            sink = fill_n(sink,charToPad,os.fill());
          }
          else
          {
            sink = fill_n(sink,charToPad,os.fill());
            sink = copy(s.begin(), s.end(), sink);
          }
        }
        if (sink.failed())
            err = ios_base::failbit;
      }
      os.width(0);
    }
  }
// error handling
catch(bad_alloc& )
{
  err |= ios_base::badbit;
  ios_base::iostate exception_mask = os.exceptions();


  if ((exception_mask & ios_base::failbit)
        && !(exception_mask & ios_base::badbit) )
  {
    os.setstate(err);
  }
  else if (exception_mask & ios_base::badbit)
  {
    try { os.setstate(err); }
    catch( ios_base::failure& ) { }
    throw;
  }
}
catch(...)
{
  err |= ios_base::failbit;
  ios_base::iostate exception_mask = os.exceptions();
```

```
  if ((exception_mask & ios_base::badbit)
        && (err & ios_base::badbit))
  {
    os.setstate(err);
  }
  else if(exception_mask & ios_base::failbit)
  {
    try { os.setstate(err); }
    catch( ios_base::failure& ) { }
    throw;
  }
}
if ( err ) os.setstate(err);
return os;
}
```

As recommended, we dutifully keep track of all error situations by catching all exceptions, checking the stream state and other error indications, and detecting invalid dates. We then set the stream state and raise exceptions. Let us group the discussion by topics: (1) the setting of the stream state and (2) the strategy for catching and throwing the exceptions.

SETTING THE STREAM STATE

Both the inserter and the extractor maintain a local stream state object `err`. The failure of any invoked operation is accumulated in this temporary stream state. (Note that accumulation of errors is not required by the IOStreams framework. You can, alternatively, stop when the first error is detected.) Eventually, the temporary stream state replaces the current stream state. Let us see how the various activities contribute to the stream state.

EXTRACTOR. In the extractor, the parsing operation of the `time_get` facet uses the stream state object for reporting its success or failure. The parsing operation might set any of the state flags as appropriate. We then check the extracted date's validity by means of its `bool` operator and add `failbit` to this stream state object if the date is invalid. We set `failbit` instead of `badbit` because we consider extraction of an invalid date a recoverable parsing failure (hence `failbit`) rather than a loss of the stream's integrity (which would have required setting `badbit`).

INSERTER. In the inserter, the result of the formatting operation of the `time_put` facet is checked by calling the returned iterator's `failed()` function. In case of failure, we set the temporary stream state object to `badbit` instead of `failbit`, because a failed formatting operation indicates a broken stream rather than a recoverable formatting failure.

The local stream state object is eventually used to adjust the stream's state if no exceptions have been raised so far. The stream state is set via the `setstate()` function, which takes a new stream state value, replaces the current stream state with the new value, and automatically raises an `ios_base::failure` exception if the exception mask requires it.

CATCHING AND THROWING EXCEPTIONS

All relevant statements are now wrapped into a try block. The reason is that in an inserter and extractor we must catch all exceptions that are thrown by any invoked operation, because we cannot simply let exceptions propagate out of an I/O operation. We must first check whether the exception mask permits the caught exception to be propagated outside the inserter or extractor. Only if the exception mask allows it do we rethrow the exception; otherwise we suppress it. Additionally, we must set the stream state appropriately in order to reflect the error situation that was detected by catching an exception.

Exceptions caught in an I/O operation are best handled as follows:

- The caught exception is qualified as an indication of failure (equivalent to `failbit`) or of loss of integrity (equivalent to `badbit`).

- The exception mask is checked in order to find out whether an exception must be thrown.

- The stream state must be set and, if required, an exception must be raised.

In our example, both the inserter and the extractor handle caught exceptions exactly the same way. They both have two catch clauses: We qualify memory shortage indicated by a `bad_alloc` exception as a loss of the stream's integrity (`badbit`) and all other exceptions as failure of the operation (`failbit`). The respective error flag is added to the local stream state object.

By examining the exception mask and the local stream state object, we determine whether an exception must be raised at all and if so, which exception it must be: either `ios_base::failure` or the originally caught exception.

Due to the accumulation of errors, it can happen that both `badbit` and `failbit` are set in the local stream state object. If both flags are also set in the exception mask, we have to raise two exceptions, so to speak. As only one exception can be thrown, we decide to throw the exception that belongs to the `badbit`, because we consider a `badbit` situation the more severe error situation. The exception associated with the `badbit` is `bad_alloc`, if such an exception was caught, or `ios_base::failure` otherwise.

Depending on the exception mask and the local stream state object, the following actions are taken:

The `setstate()` function is called with the accumulated local stream state as an argument. This call sets the stream state and raises an `ios_base::failure` exception.

The `setstate()` function is called in a `try` block with an empty corresponding `catch` block. As a result, the stream state is set to the accumulated local stream state and the automatically raised `ios_base::failure` exception is caught and discarded. Then the originally caught exception is rethrown.

3.1.4.5 Using the Refined Inserter and Extractor

Finally, let us demonstrate that the suggested implementation of the refined date inserter and extractor indeed exhibits the desired, improved behavior. Specifically:

- The stream's format control parameters are taken into account. Our date inserter adjusts the date output according to the settings of the field adjustment, field width, and fill character.

- Redundant prefix and suffix operations are eliminated. This is an optimization that is not visible in actual input and output of date objects.

- All errors are indicated in an IOStreams-specific way, that is, using the stream state and the stream's exception mask. Specifically, invalid date input is indicated as failure of the extractor.

- The inserter and the extractor are internationalized. Depending on the stream's locale they accept and produce date formats that conform to the respective cultural conventions.

Here are sample programs that use the refined inserter and extractor. First, we demonstrate that the field width is handled correctly. The code snippet below:

```
date eclipse(11,8,1999);
cout << "eclipse (default right adjustment): "        << setw(10)
     << setfill('(') << eclipse << endl;
cout << "eclipse (left adjustment)        : " << left << setw(10)
     << setfill('*') << eclipse << endl;
```

yields the following output, assuming that the standard output stream `cout` uses a U.S. locale:

```
eclipse(default right adjustment): ((08/11/99
eclipse(left adjustment):          08/11/99**
```

Second, the date handling abides cultural conventions. The code snippet below shows that our refined inserter and extractor are internationalized:

```
cout << "A date like Dec 2, 1978" << " is needed: ";
date d;
cin >> d;
cout << "This is the specified date in US notation: " << d << endl;
cout.imbue(locale("German"));
cout << "This is the specified date in German notation: " << d << endl;
```

The program can result in the following dialog, assuming that the standard output stream `cout` initially uses a U.S. locale:

```
A date like Dec 2, 1978" << " is needed:
> Dec 31, 1999
This is the specified date in US notation: 12/31/99
This is the specified date in German notation: 31.12.99
```

Third, we show that our refined inserter and extractor indicate extraction of an invalid date by means of the stream state and the stream exceptions. Consider the following program:

```
cout << "A date like Dec 2, 1978" << " is needed: ";
date d;
cin.exceptions(ios_base::badbit | ios_base::failbit);
try { cin >> d; }
catch (ios_base::failure&)
{ err << "date extraction failed" << endl; throw; }
cout << "This is the specified date in US notation: " << d << endl;
```

We deliberately set the exceptions mask so that `badbit` and `failbit` situations must raise an exception. In particular, extraction of an invalid date should be detected and indicated by means of an exception. The program might lead to the following dialog and output:

```
A date like Dec 2, 1978" << " is needed:
> Dec 32, 1999
date extraction failed
```

We can see that the control flow passes through the exception handler for the `ios_base::failure` exceptions, that is, the result of the extraction of the invalid date `Dec 32, 1999`.

3.1.5 Generic Inserters and Extractors

In conjunction with explaining the example in the previous section, we presented a couple of rules and recommendations for inserters and extractors in general, such as use sentries; catch, qualify, and rethrow exceptions; set the stream state, etc. In this section we will factor out all code that is common to all inserters and extractors into *generic* insertion and extraction functions. These generic inserters and extractions aid implementation of inserters and extractors for arbitrary user-defined types.

The example code is structured in the following way:

The inserter and extractor for our date class, or any other user-defined type, are reimplemented and now call the generic insertion and extraction functions.

The generic inserter and extractor encapsulate error handling, i.e., everything that has to do with exceptions and the stream state as described in the previous section. They also perform the prefix and suffix tasks by using sentries. The actual parsing and formatting of the user-defined type are delegated to member functions of that type.

The user-defined type has two member functions, called `print_on()` and `get_from()`, that represent the knowledge about the type-specific parsing and formatting of an object of that class.

THE DATE INSERTER AND EXTRACTOR

The inserter and extractor boil down to wrappers around the generic functions. In our example the wrapper functions are called `g_inserter()` and `g_extractor()`. Here is the implementation of the shift operators for `date` objects:

```
template <class charT, class Traits>
basic_istream<charT, Traits>& operator>>
  (basic_istream<charT, Traits>& is, date& arg)
{
  if (!is.good()) return is;
  return g_extractor(is,arg);
}

template <class charT, class Traits>
basic_ostream<charT, Traits>& operator<<
  (basic_ostream<charT, Traits>& os, const date& arg)
{
  if (!os.good()) return os;
  return g_inserter(os,arg);
}
```

Note that we did not make the shift operators themselves generic. This would have required adding a third template parameter for the data type that is inserted or extracted. Such templates would be instantiated for any kind of data type that does not have a shift operator of its own. The potential danger is that those shift operator templates might be accidentally instantiated for types that should actually have I/O operations of their own.

THE GENERIC INSERTER AND EXTRACTOR

The generic inserter and extractor are function templates that take the stream's character and traits type, but also the user-defined type, as template arguments. They encapsulate the recommendations given in the previous section for error handling and use of sentries. Naturally, they are very similar to the date inserter and extractor presented in the previous section. The only difference is that actual parsing and formatting are delegated to the user-defined type's member functions `get_from()` and `print_on()`.

The extractor:
```
template <class charT, class Traits, class Argument>
basic_istream<charT, Traits>& g_extractor
  (basic_istream<charT, Traits>& is, Argument& arg)
{
```

```
ios_base::iostate err = 0;
try
{ typename basic_istream<charT,Traits>::sentry ipfx(is);
  if(ipfx)
  { err = arg.get_from(is); }
}
catch(bad_alloc& )
{ err |= ios_base::badbit;
  ios_base::iostate exception_mask = is.exceptions();
  if (   (exception_mask & ios_base::failbit)
      && !(exception_mask & ios_base::badbit))
  {  is.setstate(err);   }
  else if (exception_mask & ios_base::badbit)
  {  try { is.setstate(err); }
     catch( ios_base::failure& ) { }
     throw;
  }
}
catch(...)
{ err |= ios_base::failbit;
  ios_base::iostate exception_mask = is.exceptions();
  if (   (exception_mask & ios_base::badbit)
      && (err & ios_base::badbit))
  {  is.setstate(err);   }
  else if(exception_mask & ios_base::failbit)
  {  try { is.setstate(err); }
     catch( ios_base::failure& ) { }
     throw;
  }
}
if ( err ) is.setstate(err);
return is;
}
```

The inserter:

```
template <class charT, class Traits, class Argument>
basic_ostream<charT, Traits>& g_inserter
  (basic_ostream<charT, Traits>& os, const Argument& dat)
{
 ios_base::iostate err = 0;
 try
 { typename basic_ostream<charT,Traits>::sentry opfx(os);
   if(opfx)
   { err = arg.print_on(os);
     os.width(0);
   }
 }
```

```
catch(bad_alloc& )
{ err |= ios_base::badbit;
  ios_base::iostate exception_mask = os.exceptions();
  if (   (exception_mask & ios_base::failbit)
     && !(exception_mask & ios_base::badbit))
  {  os.setstate(err);  }
  else if (exception_mask & ios_base::badbit)
  {  try { os.setstate(err); }
     catch( ios_base::failure& ) { }
     throw;
  }
}
catch(...)
{ err |= ios_base::failbit;
  ios_base::iostate exception_mask = os.exceptions();
  if (   (exception_mask & ios_base::badbit)
     && (err & ios_base::badbit))
  {  os.setstate(err);   }
  else if(exception_mask & ios_base::failbit)
  {  try { os.setstate(err); }
     catch( ios_base::failure& ) { }
     throw;
  }
}
if ( err ) os.setstate(err);
return os;
}
```

THE MEMBER FUNCTIONS

All the functionality that is specific to the particular user-defined type (the date class in our example) is added to the user-defined type itself in the form of member functions. Their main responsibilities are the actual formatting and parsing, which include internationalization and format control.

These member functions, however, care neither about prefix and suffix tasks and sentries nor about setting the stream state nor about catching and properly rethrowing exceptions according to the exception mask.

Error indication boils down to returning a stream state object that reflect the results of the invoked operations and/or error conditions due to the functions' internal logic.

Exceptions thrown by any of the invoked operations are simply propagated to the generic level if they cannot be handled.

Note that you have to arrange statements in such a way that in the case of exceptions, the object is not left in an inconsistent state. If you need to catch exceptions in order to preserve the object's state, store the exception and rethrow it.

The listing below shows the `date` class, which is basically unchanged but now has two additional public member functions: `print_on()` and `get_from()`.

```cpp
class date {
public:
 date(int d, int m, int y);
 date(const tm& t);
 date();
 bool operator!();

 template <class charT, class Traits>
 ios_base::iostate get_from(basic_istream<charT, Traits>& is)
 {
   ios_base::iostate err = 0;
   use_facet<time_get<charT,Traits> >(is.getloc()).get_date
   (is, istreambuf_iterator<char, char_traits<char> >(),is, err, &tm_date);
   if (!(*this) || err)
      return ios_base::failbit;
   else
      return ios_base::goodbit;
 }


 template <class charT, class Traits>
       ios_base::iostate print_on(basic_ostream<charT, Traits>& os) const
 {
   char const * const patt = "%x";
   char fmt[3];
   basic_stringbuf<charT,Traits> sb;
   ios_base::iostate err = 0;

   use_facet<ctype<charT> > (os.getloc()).widen(patt,patt+2,fmt);
   if (        use_facet<time_put<charT,ostreambuf_iterator<charT,Traits> > >
       (os.getloc()).put(&sb,os,os.fill(),&tm_date,fmt,(fmt+2)).failed()
     )
     err = ios_base::failbit;
   if (err == ios_base::goodbit)
   { basic_string<charT, Traits> s = sb.str();
     streamsize charToPad = os.width() - s.length();
     ostreambuf_iterator<charT,Traits> sink(os);
     if (charToPad <= 0)
       sink = copy(s.begin(), s.end(), sink);
```

```
      else
      { if (os.flags() & ios_base::left)
        { sink = copy(s.begin(), s.end(), sink);
          sink = fill_n(sink,charToPad,os.fill());
        }
        else
        { sink = fill_n(sink,charToPad,os.fill());
          sink = copy(s.begin(), s.end(), sink);
        }
      }
      if (sink.failed())
        err = ios_base::failbit;
    }
    return err;
 }

private:
 tm tm_date;
 bool ok;
 bool valid();
};
```

3.1.6 Simple versus Refined Approach

In this chapter we have discussed several approaches for implementing inserters and extractors for user-defined types. We started out with a simple approach, where we just broke down the user-defined type into its parts and used existing inserters and extractors for each of the parts. We identified areas of potential refinement such as internationalization, format control, and error indication; and we eventually implemented a full-fledged internationalized inserter and extractor for date objects. In addition, we generalized the solution and factored out the IOStreams-specific issues into generic inserters and extractors for reuse in the implementation of inserters and extractors for other user-defined types.

When we look back at the various implementations, we can see that the implementation of the refined inserter and extractor is significantly more complex than the initial simple approach. Let us devote some thought to the trade-off between the simple, straightforward implementation and the full-fledged, refined implementation. When would we prefer one approach over the other?

There is no carved-in-stone rule for the "right" level of refinement for inserters and extractors. The degree of sophistication that must be implemented depends on the situation where these operators shall be used. For instance, if the inserter is predominantly used for writing trace output to a log file for debugging purposes, the simple approach might be quite sufficient. Conversely, the inserters and extractors might be intended to be used for formatting and parsing objects by means of string streams, that is, for conversion between the object representation and a human-readable string representation. If these string representations are to be displayed or printed in an application that is designed for worldwide use, more sophisticated operators are obviously needed.

When we compare the simple inserter and extractor with the refined one, it is evident that these refinements do not come free of charge. Besides the greater effort required for implementation of the refined inserter and the extractor, the refined approach needs significantly more time during the design stage. For the simple approach, you just have to identify the parts that the user-defined type consists of and reuse existing operators. This is easy. For the refined approach, on the other hand, each of the areas of refinement needs a sound design. Take, for example, the error handling. You have to decide which error can occur. Then you have to determine to which error states (bad or failure) each error should be mapped. An equivalent number of considerations is necessary, if format control or internationalization is to be added.

Comparing the implementations presented in this chapter, it is obvious that both approaches differ significantly in the amount of code that is needed for their implementation. Accordingly, both approaches differ in the amount of time needed for the implementation and the performance of the resulting implementation. Let's briefly discuss both issues: runtime performance and implementation effort.

RUNTIME PERFORMANCE. Operators for built-in types, which are predefined in the standard IOStreams library for `basic_istream` and `basic_ostream`, are implemented in much the same way that we suggested in our refined date inserter and extractor above. Almost everything in the standard C++ library is designed for efficiency and optimal runtime performance, and indeed the more sophisticated inserters and extractors can perform better than the simple ones, despite their greater complexity. If the simple approach is taken, the user-defined type is broken down into its parts, and for each of the parts an existing inserter or extractor is invoked. Inevitably, certain functionality, for instance the prefix and postfix operations, is executed redundantly. With a more sophisticated implementation, this overhead can be eliminated.

IMPLEMENTATION EFFORT. Regarding the amount of time needed for implementation of a sophisticated inserter or extractor, it is definitely true that the refined approach requires a greater effort. The implementation effort can, however, be reduced substantially if the IOStreams-specific refinements are implemented once, as a generic inserter and extractor, and the I/O-functionality for each user-defined type is just hooked into the generic operators.

Ultimately, the "right" level of refinement for a user-defined inserter or extractor depends on the requirements for these operations and their intended use. Often, engineers shy away from implementing sophisticated I/O operations for their types, because they assume that inserters and extractors are needed only for terminal and file I/O and are obsolete in an application that uses a graphical user interface for user interaction and an off-the-shelf database system for data storage. This assumption is not quite true. Inserters and extractors, together with the different string streams defined in standard IOStreams, are the foundation of the internationalization of the application. For instance, text entered in a text field of the graphical user interface can be parsed according to local conventions by means of string streams and according to inserters and extractors. Similarly, it might be necessary to convert a wide-character text into a multibyte representation for storage in the narrow-byte text field of a database. IOStreams can be used for this. In general, it might be worth implementing user-defined inserters and extractors, because they extend the existing parsing and formatting mechanisms in C++ in a natural and beneficial way.

3.2 User-Defined Manipulators

Manipulators are objects that can be inserted into or extracted from a stream in order to manipulate that stream. Section 1.2.4, Manipulators, describes the manipulators that are defined in IOStreams. We will henceforth call them the standard manipulators, in contrast to user-defined manipulators.

As a recapitulation, here is a typical example of two standard manipulators:

```
cout << setw(10) << 10.55 << endl;
```

The inserted objects setw(10) and endl are the manipulators. The manipulator setw(10) sets the stream's field width to 10; the manipulator endl inserts the end-of-line character and flushes the output. As you can see, manipulators can take arguments or be parameterless.

Extensibility is a major advantage of IOStreams. We've seen in the previous section how you can implement inserters and extractors for user-defined types that behave like the built-in input and output operations. Similarly, you can add user-defined manipulators that fit seamlessly into the IOStreams framework. In this section, we will explain how to do this.

Manipulators are inserted and extracted via shift operators. To be inserted and extracted in this way, there must be shift operators defined for each type of manipulator. We will denote the type of manipulator object as manipT in the following text. The extractor for a manipulator of type manipT looks like this:

```
template <class charT, class Traits>
basic istream<charT,Traits>&
operator>> (basic_istream<charT,Traits>& istr, const manipT& manip)
{ /*
  ... do the manipulation ...
 */
 return istr;
}
```

With this extractor defined, you can extract a manipulator object Manip of type manipT by saying

```
cin >> Manip;
```

The manipulator inserter is analogous.

The manipulation performed by a manipulator inserter or extractor can be any sequence of operations that leads to the desired change of the stream. This sequence of operations can be encapsulated into a function, which we will call the associated function $f_{manipT}()$ in the following examples. There are several ways to associate a manipulator type $manipT$ and its function $f_{manipT}()$. It turns out that the technique for manipulators with parameters is fundamentally different from that for manipulators without parameters. Some implementation idioms for manipulators can be studied by examining the standard manipulators. Additional techniques might be needed for advanced user-defined manipulators. In the subsequent sections, we explain various ways of implementing manipulators. Let's start with the simpler case of manipulators without parameters.

3.2.1 Manipulators Without Parameters

Parameterless manipulators are the simplest form of manipulator; they are function pointers, and the manipulation is invocation of the function pointed to.

In IOStreams, the following function pointer types serve as manipulator types:

```
(1) ios_base&                    (*pf)(ios_base&)
(2) basic_ios<charT,Traits>&     (*pf)(basic_ios<charT,Traits>&)
(3) basic_istream<charT,Traits>& (*pf)(basic_istream<charT,Traits>&)
(4) basic_ostream<charT,Traits>& (*pf)(basic_ostream<charT,Traits>&)
```

For these four manipulator types, IOStreams already contains the required inserters and extractors. The extractor for parameterless manipulators to input streams, for instance, takes the following form:

```
template<class charT, class traits>
basic_istream<charT, traits>& basic_istream<charT, traits>::operator>>
( basic_istream<charT,traits>& (*pf)(basic_istream<charT,traits>&) )
{ return (*pf)(*this); }
```

It uses a function pointer of type (3) from the list above. Similarly, an inserter for parameterless manipulators to output streams uses a function pointer of type (4) and is already defined in IOStreams as

```
template<class charT, class traits>
basic_ostream<charT, traits>& basic_ostream<charT, traits>::operator<<
( basic_ostream<charT, traits>& (*pf)(basic_ostream<charT, traits>&) )
{ return (*pf)(*this);  }
```

The inserters and extractors for function pointers of type (1) and (2) are also predefined in IOStreams. They allow insertion and extraction of parameterless manipulators that can be applied to input and output streams.

The list of manipulator types is not limited to the examples above. If you have created your own user-defined stream types, you might want to use additional signatures as parameterless manipulators.

EXAMPLES OF MANIPULATORS WITHOUT PARAMETERS

Let's look at the standard manipulator `endl` as an example of a manipulator without parameters. The manipulator `endl`, which can be applied solely to output streams, is a pointer to the following function of type (4):

```
template<class charT, class traits>
inline basic_ostream<charT, traits>& endl(basic_ostream<charT, traits>& os)
{
  os.put( os.widen('\n') );
  os.flush();

  return os;
}
```

Hence an expression like

```
cout << endl;
```

results in a call to the inserter

```
ostream& ostream::operator<< (ostream& (*pf)(ostream&))
```

with `endl` as the actual argument for `pf`. In other words, `cout << endl;` is equal to `cout.operator<<(endl);`

Here is another manipulator, `boolalpha`, that can be applied to input *and* output streams. The manipulator `boolalpha` is a pointer to a function of type (1):

```
ios_base& boolalpha(ios_base& strm)
{
  strm.setf(ios_base::boolalpha);

  return strm;
}
```

In principle, every function that takes a reference to an `ios_base`, a `basic_ios`, a `basic_ostream`, or a `basic_istream`, and returns a reference to the same stream, can be used as a parameterless manipulator.

3.2.2 Manipulators with Parameters

Manipulators with parameters are objects that can be inserted into and extracted from a stream via shift operators and can take arguments that parameterize the manipulation of the stream. Insertion of a manipulator with one parameter would look like this:

```
cout << Manip(x);
```

The expression `Manip(x)` evaluates to a manipulator object of a manipulator type `manipT`, for which an according shift operator is defined. Manipulators with n parameters take the form `Manip(`$x_1, x_2, x_3, \ldots, x_n$`)`. We restrict all consideration in this section to the case of manipulators with one argument. All presented solutions can canonically be applied to the case of any arbitrary number of arguments.

In the subsequent sections we first discuss a simple, straightforward way of implementing manipulators with parameters. We then generalize the technique, discuss the solution chosen for the standard manipulators in IOStreams, and eventually consider ways of extending the manipulator functionality.

3.2.2.1 Straightforward Manipulator Implementations

As a case study, we implement a manipulator called `width`. Its effect is exactly the one produced by the standard manipulator `setw`: It sets the stream's field width when inserted to an output stream. The manipulator `width` is an example of a manipulator with one parameter that can be inserted into output streams only. Here is a possible implementation:[7]

```
class width {
public:
   explicit width(unsigned int i) : i_(i) {}
private:
   unsigned int i_;

   template <class charT, class Traits>
   friend basic_ostream<charT,Traits>& operator<<
   (basic_ostream<charT,Traits>& ib, const width& w)
   {
     // the manipulation: set the stream's width
     ib.width(w.i_);
     return ib;
   }
};
```

The class type `width` is the manipulator type, i.e., it is a concrete example of the type we previously denoted as `manipT`. A width manipulator can be used like this:

```
cout << width(5) << 0.1 << endl;
```

---

7. The constructor of the `width` class is declared as `explicit`. If you are not familiar with explicit constructors, see section G.3, Explicit Constructors, for an explanation of the `explicit` keyword in general.

Here the manipulator expression width(5) is the construction of an unnamed object of the manipulator type width. The argument that is passed to the manipulator expression is used to initialize the private data member i_ of class width. This data member is later used by the shift operator for setting the field width.

Let us consider a second example: a multi-end-of-line manipulator, much like the standard manipulator endl, but with the additional capability of inserting an arbitrary number of end-of-line characters. We will call it mendl and would want to use it like this:

```
cout  << mendl(5);
```

The implementation of mendl would look like this:

```
class mendl {
public:
   explicit mendl(unsigned int i) : i_(i) {}
private:
   unsigned int i_;

   template <class charT, class Traits>
   friend basic_ostream<charT,Traits>& operator<<
   (basic_ostream<charT,Traits>& os, const mendl& w)
   {
     // the manipulation: insert end-of-line characters and flush
     for (int i=0; i<w.i_;  i++)
        os.put(os.widen('\n'));
     return os.flush();
   }
};
```

In the next section we show you a different implementation technique that pays off if you implement several manipulators with the same number of parameters, but with different types of arguments.

3.2.2.2 Generalized Technique: Using a Manipulator Base Template

Manipulators with a parameter vary with respect to the type of their parameter and their respective functionality. We now build a framework that abstracts from those two properties and generally eases the implementation of manipulators with arbitrary functionality and parameters of arbitrary type. Again, we will discuss only the case of one parameter.

The key idea is that the manipulation must not be hard-coded into the shift operators, but factored out into an associated function. A pointer to this function is provided to the constructor of the manipulator type and stored as a data member of the manipulator object for subsequent invocation in the shift operators.

The manipulator type, which was a class type in the straightforward solution, now becomes a class template that takes the types of the manipulator arguments as template parameters. Concrete manipulator types are derived from this base class template.

Here is the suggested base class template called `one_arg_manip`:

```
template <class Argument>
class one_arg_manip
{
public:
 typedef void (* manipFct)(ios_base&, Argument);
 one_arg_manip(manipFct pf, const Argument& arg)
 : pf_(pf), arg_(arg) {}

private:
 manipFct pf_;
 const Argument arg_;

template <class charT, class Traits>
friend basic_istream<charT,Traits>& operator>>
(basic_istream<charT,Traits>& is, const one_arg_manip& oam)
{
 if (!is.good()) return is;
 (*(oam.pf_))(is,oam.arg_);
 return is;
}

template <class charT, class Traits>
friend basic_ostream<charT,Traits>& operator<<
(basic_ostream<charT,Traits>& os, const one_arg_manip& oam)
{
 if (!os.good()) return os;
 (*(oam.pf_))(os,oam.arg_);
 return os;
}
};
```

The core of the shift operators is invocation of the associated manipulator function with the manipulator arguments. Using the base manipulator template `one_arg_manip`, we could reimplement the `width` manipulator from the previous example as follows:

```
class width : public one_arg_manip<unsigned int>
{public:
     explicit width(unsigned int i) : one_arg_manip<unsigned int>(width::fct, i)
  { }
 private:
  static void fct (ios_base& ib, unsigned int i)
  { ib.width(i); }
};
```

The manipulator type `width` is a subclass of the manipulator base template `one_arg_manip` instantiated on the type of the manipulator argument, which is `unsigned int` in this case. The manipulation, previously part of the shift operator, is now factored out into a static member function, called `fct()`, of class `width`.

THE STREAM TYPE

Note that the associated manipulator function has a particular function signature: It takes a reference to the stream base class `ios_base`. A manipulator, however, might need information that is specific to a particular stream type and not accessible via the stream base class `ios_base`. Consider for instance the multi-end-of-line manipulator `mendl`. It calls member functions that are specific to output streams, like `put()` and `flush()`. If you build it using the manipulator base template technique, then the manipulator type itself will be a class template. Let us see why. Here is a tentative implementation of `mendl`:

```
class mendl : public one_arg_manip<unsigned int>
{public:
  explicit mendl(unsigned int i) : one_arg_manip<unsigned int>(mendl::fct, i)
  { }
 private:
  static void fct (ios_base& os, unsigned int n)
  { for (int i=0; i<n; i++)
       os.put(os.widen('\n'));    // error: os is not an output stream,
    os.flush();                   // but a reference to a ios_base object
  }
};
```

The problem is that member functions like `put()` and `flush()` are defined in `basic_ostream` and are not accessible via an `ios_base&` argument. For them to be accessible, we would need an associated manipulator function like this:

```
template <class charT, class Traits>
void fct (basic_ostream<charT,Traits>& os, unsigned int n)
  { for (int i=0; i<n; i++)
       os.put(os.widen('\n'));
    os.flush();
  }
```

Note that `fct()` becomes a function template, because the stream it operates on is templatized. Inevitably, the manipulator type `mendl` and the manipulator base class `one_arg_manip` become templates, too. Here is the correct definition of the manipulator class template, assuming that the function signature in `one_arg_manip` is changed as necessary:

```
template <class charT, class Traits = char_traits<charT> >
class mendl : public one_arg_manip<charT,Traits,unsigned int>
{public:
  explicit mendl(unsigned int i)
  : one_arg_manip< charT,Traits, unsigned int>(mendl::fct,i)
  { }
 private:
  static void fct (basic_ostream<charT,Traits>& os, unsigned int n)
  { for (int i=0; i<n;  i++)
        os.put(os.widen('\n'));
    os.flush();
  }
};
```

Now that `mendl` is a template, the manipulator expression is less convenient than it used to be. Each time we manipulate a stream by inserting a `mendl` object, we need to know the character and traits type of that stream. Instead of simply saying

```
cout  << mendl(5);
wcout << mendl(5);
```

we now have to specify the template arguments and say

```
cout  << mendl<char>(5);
wcout << mendl<wchar_t>(5);
```

We can make the calls more convenient by defining typedefs for each of the instantiations of `mendl`. Then we have different manipulators for each type of stream. It's an improvement because we need not know the character and traits type of the stream. Instead we have to figure out which manipulator type is the right one to be used with a particular stream:

```
typedef mendl<char>    cmendl;
typedef mendl<wchar_t> wmendl;

cout  << cmendl(5);
wcout << wmendl(5);
```

Another idea for making the manipulator calls more convenient relies on automatic function template argument deduction: The compiler is capable of deducing function template arguments from the actual arguments provided to a function call. We can use this language feature to have the compiler figure out the character and traits type of a stream and the respective manipulator: We wrap the construction of a manipulator object into a function that we call `mendl` and rename the manipulator type to `basic_mendl`. In other words, we add the following function template:

```
template <class charT, class Traits>
basic_mendl<charT,Traits> mendl(unsigned int n, basic_ostream<charT,Traits>&)
{ return basic_mendl<charT,Traits>(n); }
```

The manipulator expression would now be a call to the wrapper function instead of the construction of an unnamed object of the manipulator type. We would use the `mendl` function like this:

```
cout  << mendl(5,cout);
wcout << mendl(5,wcout);
```

The downside is that we have to repeat the stream object redundantly in the manipulator expression.

3.2.2.3 Variants of a Manipulator Implementation

As we have seen in the previous sections, there are several ways to implement a manipulator with a parameter. Let us discuss some relevant variations.

ENCAPSULATING THE MANIPULATION

We have to decide where the manipulation shall be encapsulated. In the straightforward approach presented above, the manipulation is performed by the shift operator itself. The manipulator class is responsible only for storing the manipulator argument, not for providing the manipulator functionality. Alternatively, the manipulation can be encapsulated into a function that is invoked by the shift operator. We used this technique for the manipulator base class approach discussed above. If such a function is used, the manipulator type can contain both the manipulator argument and the manipulator functionality as a static member function. Alternatively, the associated manipulator function can be a global or static function. However, we prefer to include the associated function in the manipulator type, because we strive for self-documenting code, and a member function clearly expresses the association of manipulator type and associated function.

THE STREAM TYPE

If the manipulation is encapsulated into an associated manipulator function, then the function often takes a reference to the stream base class `ios_base`. The advantage is that the manipulator type need not be a template if the stream base class is used.

Note that sometimes the associated manipulator function cannot be implemented in terms of the stream base class, because the manipulator uses stream functionality that is defined in a stream class derived from `ios_base`. The manipulator `mendl` discussed earlier is an example of such a case. The associated manipulator function becomes a template because the derived stream type it operates on is a template, and in consequence the manipulator type itself has to be a class template. The example of `mendl` demonstrated related drawbacks and corresponding solutions.

An alternative for implementing manipulators for derived stream classes is the straightforward solution, i.e., putting all the manipulator functionality directly into a shift operator for the derived stream type.

STORING THE MANIPULATOR ARGUMENT

Manipulator types might vary regarding the access rights of their members. The data members of a manipulator type must be accessible to the shift operator or the associated manipulator function.

We prefer to declare the data members `private`, make the associated manipulator function a static member function of the manipulator type, and declare the shift operator a friend of the manipulator type. Alternatively, the data members could be `protected` or even `public`.

The manipulator arguments can be stored as nonconstant data members instead of constant data members as in our solution. The example of advanced manipulators in section 3.2.2.4, Refinements, shows why these alternatives might be needed.

CONSTRUCTOR CALL VERSUS FUNCTION CALL

In a call like `cout << width(5);` the manipulator expression `width(5)` is either the construction of an unnamed object of the manipulator type `width`, where 5 is the constructor argument, or a call to a function called `width()` that takes the manipulator argument as function parameter and returns a manipulator object. Remember, all that is required of a manipulator expression is that it must evaluate to a manipulator object of a type for which the shift operators that perform the manipulation are defined.

In almost all of the examples presented so far, we created unnamed manipulator objects. The only exception was the use of a function for automatic template argument deduction in the example of the `mendl` manipulator.

Also, the function call solution is the technique that was chosen for the standard manipulators in IOStreams. It is a sensible alternative if your compiler is not capable of creating unnamed objects in conjunction with overloaded operators.

CHECKING THE STREAM STATE

It is a convention that most I/O operations in IOStreams do not have any effect if the stream state is not good. The same might be expected of manipulators as well. If the stream is not good, the manipulation will have no effect. To enforce this rule, we might want to check the stream state in the shift operators and explicitly suppress the manipulation if necessary. The shift operator for the manipulator base class `one_arg_manip` discussed in the previous section demonstrates the principle.

However, this design decision is potentially contentious. Consider that not *all* I/O operations in IOStreams are without effect if the stream state is not good. Changes to format control settings, for instance, are typically performed regardless of the stream state, whereas input and output operations have no effect when the stream is not in a good state. The standard manipulators, for instance, reflect these differences. They do not actively check the stream state but simply call one or more stream member functions and exhibit exactly the same behavior. The standard manipulators setw and endl illustrate the difference: The setw manipulator boils down to a call to the width() member function, which changes the width setting regardless of the stream state. Consequently, setw always has an effect. The endl manipulator behaves differently: It inserts the end-of-line character and calls the flush() member function; both activities have no effect on streams that are not in a good state.

We feel that user-defined manipulators are easier to understand and use if they behave consistently. For this reason we decided to check the stream state in the shift operator before invoking the associated manipulator function in the example presented in the previous section.

3.2.2.4 Refinements

The manipulations performed by the previously presented manipulators are relatively simple: usually they consist of the invocation of one or two stream member functions. But manipulators can be much more sophisticated and powerful. In the following two sections we show you some useful examples of extensions: (1) manipulations with error handling, and (2) manipulators that maintain state between subsequent manipulations.

We demonstrate how these refinements can be built into the manipulator base class. The ideas behind these extensions are equally relevant for manipulators without a base template.

3.2.2.4.1 Manipulator Base Template with Error Handling

During the manipulation of a stream, error situations can occur. Section 3.3, Extending Stream Functionality, gives a practical example; it contains a manipulator that has to create a string by calling operator new(). Naturally, this memory allocation can fail, and such a failure needs to be handled by the manipulator. Section 3.1.3, Refined Inserters and Extractors, lists conventions for error reporting, which operations in IOStreams should conform to. I/O operations must not propagate exceptions unless the exception mask permits it, and the stream state must be set according to the errors that occurred. These rules are equally relevant for user-defined manipulators.

Because of their simplicity, the standard manipulators have no need for error handling. All they do is call one or two stream member functions, and each of these functions already handles errors in a way that matches the IOStreams conventions. Consequently, the standard manipulators can fully rely on the invoked functions for error handling. User-defined manipulators, however, might perform any kind of operation and must handle errors if necessary.

We show how to build the necessary error-handling logic into a manipulator base template and a wrapper for the associated manipulator function.

The base idea is to catch all exceptions that are raised during a manipulation and to accumulate information about the respective error situations in a data member of the manipulator. After completion of the manipulation the accumulated error state is used for adjusting the stream state and raising an exception according to the exception mask.

For the purpose of catching exceptions during the manipulation, we wrap the associated manipulator function into a wrapper function that we call do_manip(). The wrapper is responsible for

- invoking the associated manipulator function

- catching all exceptions that are propagated from this function

- adjusting the streams state and raising an exception in accordance with the exception mask

In this way the associated manipulator function itself need not worry much about error handling: If no cleanup is necessary, it can simply propagate all exceptions. Otherwise it catches exceptions, does the cleanup, and rethrows the exception. In any case, it need not worry about adjusting the stream state and raising an exception according to the exception mask.

Here is the proposed solution in detail. Let us start with the manipulator type. As before, a concrete manipulator type is supposed to be derived from a manipulator base template. The manipulator object must now maintain a data member for accumulating error information. This data member, along with access functions, is added to the manipulator base template:

```
template <class Argument>
class one_arg_manip_weh
{
public:
 typedef void (* manipFct)(ios_base&, Argument);
 one_arg_manip_weh(manipFct pf, const Argument& arg)
 : pf_(pf), arg_(arg), error_(ios_base::goodbit) {}

protected:
 void setFail() { error_ |= ios_base::failbit; }
 void setBad()  { error_ |= ios_base::badbit;  }

private:
 manipFct pf_;
 const Argument arg_;
 ios_base::iostate error_;

template <class charT, class traits>
friend void do_manip
(basic_ios<charT,traits>& str, const one_arg_manip_weh& oamw);
};
```

The wrapper function `do_manip()` is responsible for error indication: It retrieves the manipulator's stream state object, sets the stream state properly, and raises exceptions according to the exception mask.

The derived manipulator type is responsible for memorizing error situations: It sets the local stream state object via the protected access functions `setFail()` and `setBad()`. Note that the manipulator's constructor *must* use the local stream state object for memorizing error situations, because it does not have access to the stream and therefore cannot set the stream state or check the exception mask itself. The associated manipulator function can, but need not, use `setFail()` and `setBad()`; it can also raise or propagate exceptions and rely on the shift operators for catching and handling them.

The manipulator type's shift operator invokes the wrapper function `do_manip()`. Here is the inserter:

```
template <class charT, class Traits, class Argument>
basic_ostream<charT,Traits>& operator<<
(basic_ostream<charT,Traits>& os,
 const one_arg_manip_weh<Argument>& oamw)
{
 if(os.good())
    do_manip(os,oamw);
 return os;
}
```

The wrapper function itself is shown below. It first checks the manipulator's error variable in order to find out whether there had been a previously detected error situation, encountered, for instance, during the construction of the manipulator object. If so, it handles the error. Otherwise, the associated manipulator function is invoked, and all exceptions propagated from this function are caught and handled. The error indication policy is exactly the same as in section 3.1.3.4, Error Indication, for user-defined inserters and extractors:

```
template <class charT, class traits, class Argument >
void do_manip(basic_ios<charT,traits>& str,
              const one_arg_manip_weh<Argument>& oamw)
{
 if (oamw.error_ != ios_base::goodbit)
 { str.setstate(oamw.error_); }
 else
 { ios_base::iostate err = oamw.error_;
   try { (*(oamw.pf_))(str,oamw.arg_); }
   catch(bad_alloc& )
   { err |= ios_base::badbit;
     ios_base::iostate exception_mask = str.exceptions();
```

```
  if (   (exception_mask & ios_base::failbit)
      && !(exception_mask & ios_base::badbit))
{   str.setstate(err);   }
else if (exception_mask & ios_base::badbit)
{   try { str.setstate(err); }
    catch( ios_base::failure& ) { }
    throw;
  }
}
catch(...)
{ err |= ios_base::failbit;
  ios_base::iostate exception_mask = str.exceptions();
  if (   (exception_mask & ios_base::badbit)
      && (err & ios_base::badbit))
{   str.setstate(err);    }
else if(exception_mask & ios_base::failbit)
{   try { str.setstate(err); }
    catch( ios_base::failure& ) { }
    throw;
  }
}
if ( err ) str.setstate(err);
}
}
```

An example of a concrete manipulator type that uses the base template with exception handling is presented in section 3.3, Extending Stream Functionality.

3.2.2.4.2 Manipulators with State

All manipulators with parameters that we have considered so far have been stateless objects that are created, used only once, and instantly discarded.

We talk of manipulators with state when the manipulation depends on information that is maintained between subsequent manipulations. A manipulator object with state is created, stays permanent, and is used in multiple ways, memorizing information between uses. As an example, we extend the width manipulator discussed in section 3.2.2.2, Generalized Technique: Using a Manipulator Base Template, so that it restricts acceptable width values to a certain interval. The bounds of this interval are provided when the manipulator is created and all subsequent uses of the manipulator perform a bounds check for the current width value. Here is how the bounded width manipulator would be used:

```
bounded_width width_2_6(2,6);
for (unsigned int i = 0; i< 9; i++)
    cout << width_2_6(i) << 'x' << endl;
```

Compare this to use of the original width manipulator:

```
for (unsigned int i = 0; i< 9; i++)
    cout << width(i) << 'x' << endl;
```

You can see that the stateless width manipulator is created as an unnamed object of type width each time it is used. In contrast, the width manipulator with state is created as a permanent manipulator object width_2_6 and is used several times. The manipulator expression width_2_6(i) is a function call. In our implementation, the manipulator type bounded_width has a function call operator for this purpose. The function call operator takes the manipulator argument, performs the bounds check, and calculates the effective width value. Here is the manipulator type bounded_width:

```
class bounded_width : public one_arg_manip<unsigned int>
{
    public:
        bounded_width(unsigned int min, unsigned int max)
            : one_arg_manip<unsigned int>(bounded_width::fct,min),
              min_(min), max_(max) {}

        one_arg_manip<unsigned int>& operator() (unsigned int i)
        {   if (i < min_)
                arg_ = min_;
            else if (i > max_)
                arg_ = max_;
            else
                arg_ = i;
            return *this;
        }
    private:
        static ios_base& fct(ios_base& ib, unsigned int i)
        {   ib.width(i);
            return ib;
        }
        unsigned int min_;
        unsigned int max_;
};
```

The manipulator base template one_arg_manip is basically the one used in section 3.2.2.2, Generalized Technique: Using a Manipulator Base Template, with one minor modification: The manipulator argument was originally stored as a private constant data member and now has to be nonconstant and protected because it is altered by the function call operator.

3.2.2.5 The Standard Manipulator Base Type `smanip`

The IOStreams library contains a number of predefined standard manipulators with parameters, such as `setw()`, `setfill()`, etc. (see section 1.2.4, Manipulators). They are implemented as functions that return an object of a type called *smanip*. The name *smanip* does not denote an actual type in the library but is a placeholder for one or more implementation-specific types. Each standard manipulator is allowed to return an object of a different type. The standard does not specify any details regarding this/these type(s). It is likely that in most implementations *smanip* is a class template very similar to `one_arg_manip`.

When you aim to implement a manipulator with a parameter, your first impulse might be to take a look at the implementation of a standard manipulator in the library and reuse the base manipulator template *smanip* from the library. You might find that a standard manipulator like `setw` is a function that returns an object of a particular *smanip* type, e.g., called `smanip<unsigned int>` or `_Smanip<int>`. It is advisable not to reuse the *smanip* type(s), because they are implementation-specific, and using them makes your manipulator implementation nonportable. Instead, implement your own manipulator base template similar to `one_arg_manip` or one of its extensions, use that for building user-defined manipulators, and stay independent of library specifics.

3.3 Extending Stream Functionality

In this chapter we discuss techniques for extending streams. We want to reuse the stream classes that already exist in IOStreams and aim to extend them by adding data and functionality to them. Two different techniques are available: use of iword/pword fields and derivation of new stream classes.

IWORD/PWORD. New functionality can be added by implementing inserters, extractors, manipulators, and other stream-related operations, but also by registering user-defined callback functions on a per-stream basis; additional storage for user-defined data can be made available via `xalloc()` and stored in the iword/pword fields of a stream. Section 3.3.1 of this chapter will show how these means for extension can be used.

DERIVATION. Since streams are C++ class templates, the typically object-oriented approach can be taken, and functionality and data can be added by deriving new stream classes from the existing stream classes. Derivation of new stream classes is discussed in section 3.3.2 of this chapter.

We describe both techniques, first in principle and then in detail by applying them and going through an example: formatting input and output of date objects. To allow an easy comparison of the two stream extension techniques, the same example is used for demonstration of both techniques. Along the way, we discuss all relevant technical details. We also discuss trade-offs, compare both techniques, and eventually evaluate them.

After studying this chapter, you will know how both techniques work, what their up- and downsides are, how you can use these techniques to add your own stream extensions to the IOStreams framework, and how to map the presented sample solution to your specific problem.

The sample implementations suggested in the following sections are based on implementations that were discussed in previous chapters. You might consider rereading the respective sections for better understanding of this chapter. Specifically, we suggest reading the following:

> section 3.1, Input and Output of User-Defined Types, for understanding the implementation of the date inserter (which we will use in our example) and in particular, subsection 3.1.4, Generic Inserters and Extractors.

> section 3.2.2.4.1, Manipulator Base Template with Error Handling, for understanding the implementation of a manipulator in the example

If you are not familiar with iword/pword, xalloc, and stream callbacks, you might consider reading section 2.5, Additional Stream Storage and Stream Callbacks, where the underlying concepts are described.

3.3.1 Using Stream Storage for Private Use: iword, pword, and xalloc

In this section we explain how the iword/pword fields of a stream can be used to add data to a stream and how stream callbacks can be used to add functionality to a stream. We first explain the principles of the technique, next describe the example that we will use for demonstration of the technique, and then explain how we map the principles to the sample implementation. In sections 3.3.1.1–3.3.1.5 we walk through the example of formatted input and output of date objects and discuss all relevant aspects of the iword/pword technique in minute detail. If you are not interested in this detailed discussion, you might consider skipping these sections and moving on to the final section, 3.3.1.7, where we evaluate the iword/pword technique.

PRINCIPLES OF THE IWORD/PWORD TECHNIQUE

Extending an existing stream class might require storing additional data in a stream object as well as providing additional functionality, which may or may not use the additional data.

ADDING ATTRIBUTES. The main idea of the iword/pword stream extension technique is use of the iword/pword fields of a stream to store additional attributes in the stream object. The details of iword/pword and related features are explained in section 2.5.1, Additional Stream Storage. Here is a brief summary: Every stream object contains the iword/pword fields, which can be thought of as two arrays. One contains fields of type `long` (the iwords) and the other holds elements of type `void*` (the pwords). The fields are accessible through a numeric index of type `int`. Each index gives access to an iword/pword pair. Access to the fields is via accessor functions defined in `ios_base`: the function `iword()` returns a reference to the data field of type `long`, and `pword()` to the one of type `void*`. Iword/pword indices are valid only when they are acquired via `xalloc()`, which is a static member function in class `ios_base` that makes provision for acquisition of additional memory for an iword/pword pair and returns a valid index as a handle to it.

ADDING FUNCTIONALITY. New functionality that uses the user-defined stream attributes is implemented outside the stream, because it cannot be added to the existing stream classes themselves. Such functionality typically, but not necessarily, has an obvious relationship to IOStreams and is often implemented as inserters, extractors, or manipulators.

If new functionality related to the stream's destruction or invocation of its member functions `copyfmt()` or `imbue()` is needed, the stream's callback mechanism is used to add such functionality. The details of the callback mechanism are explained in section 2.5.2, Stream Callbacks. Here is a summary: Callback functions must be registered per stream and are later automatically invoked when the stream's locale is replaced, when the stream's `copyfmt()` is called, and when the stream is destroyed. Each callback function is registered together with an index to the iword/pword fields. This index is later provided to the function when it is invoked and enables the function to use and manipulate the respective iword/pword field. The callback function is also provided with an `ios_base&` that gives access to the stream's error state and other base class features. It also receives information about the type of event for which it is invoked.

EXAMPLE: FORMATTED OUTPUT OF DATE OBJECTS

The iword/pword extension technique is demonstrated by implementing an example: formatted output of date objects. We have used this example in previous sections. In section 3.1, Input and Output of User-Defined Types, we demonstrated how objects of a user-defined type `date` can be inserted into a stream. In this chapter, we want to add functionality to this insertion; we aim to provide control over the format of the inserted date object. The `date` inserter will be able to print dates as "02-08-79" or as "February 8, 1979" or any other notation.

Our new format control facilities will be in line with the format control features that are predefined in IOStreams. For this reason, let us recall how we usually control the formatting in IOStreams: Every stream contains a number of format control parameters that the user can modify in order to control the actual formatting. The format parameters are typically set by means of manipulators, such as the `setprecision` manipulator for floating-point values. We want to provide a similar feature for the formatting of date objects, so that the date format can be conveniently controlled as shown in the code snippet below:

```
date birthday(8,2,1979);
cout << setfmt("%x") << birthday << endl;
```

`setfmt` would be a manipulator that allows modification of the format information. The manipulator will accept a format specification for a date as an argument. Such format specifications are already used in the standard library, namely, in conjunction with the time-formatting facets that are contained in each locale object. The format specification is a C-style string, such as `"%x"` in the example above. (For further details about these format strings, see appendix C, `strftime()` Conversion Specifiers.)

A manipulator that receives arguments typically stores some information in the stream object, so that any subsequent output operation can access and interpret it and adjust its formatting accordingly. In our example, the manipulator `setfmt` must store the date format specification in the stream object, and the inserter for date objects must read the format specification and put date objects into the appropriate format before actual output.

MAPPING THE TECHNIQUE TO THE EXAMPLE

In order to implement the formatted date insertion as outlined above, we want to apply the iword/pword extension technique. Here is an overview of how we intend to do this.

The stream classes defined in IOStreams must be extended so that they can store and maintain a date format specification. As outlined above, one can add new data to a stream by storing it in the iword/pword data fields of the stream. First, a valid index to an iword/pword pair must be acquired. Then the manipulator will use that index to access the respective iword/pword pair and store the date format there. The date inserter, who also has knowledge of the acquired index, uses it to read and utilize the stored date format. This is shown in figure 3-1.

The date format specification that we must store in the stream is a C-style string. Neither an iword, which is a data field of type `long`, nor a pword, which is a data field of type `void*`, is large enough to hold the date format, especially as the format string can be of any length. For that reason, the manipulator creates a copy of the format string on the heap and stores the pointer to that heap string object in the pword data field.

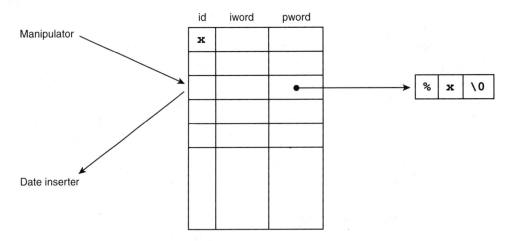

Figure 3-1: Both the manipulator and the date inserter use the same iword/pword field.

Note that use of heap memory adds an additional issue: We must make sure that the allocated heap memory is deallocated correctly, so that no memory leaks are created. When the stream object is destroyed, either because it goes out of scope or because it is explicitly deleted, the stream's destructor properly deletes all of the stream's data members. In particular, the stream's destructor will release the pword entry, but not the string object on the heap the pword entry refers to. Without any further measures, a memory leak is the result. To eliminate the memory leak, we will use the callback mechanism. We will register a function that deletes the format string on the heap when the stream object is destroyed.

3.3.1.1 Initializing and Maintaining the iword/pword Index

Let's assume we create a new format string attribute and want to store it in the stream, using the pword field as outlined above: Who will use this additional stream data in our example? One user is the manipulator `setfmt`; it will fill the pword field with the address of a format string object. The other user is the date inserter; it will access the pword field to read and use the format string. In both cases, the stream storage must have been previously acquired, and the iword/pword index returned as a result of the acquisition must be made available to both the manipulator `setfmt` and the date inserter.

In order to make the iword/pword index available to both the manipulator and the inserter and to ensure that the index is acquired before it is used, we wrap the iword/pword index into an access function `getIdx()`. The C++ language guarantees that static variables in the scope of a function, such as `myIdx` in the example below, are initialized only once before the first use of the variable.

```
int getIdx()
{
    static const int myIdx = ios_base::xalloc();

    return myIdx;
}
```

3.3.1.2 Implementing the Date Inserter

Now that we know how the iword/pword index is initialized and maintained, let us see how the inserter would use it for output of a `date` object. The implementation of the date inserter suggested below is based on the discussions of section 3.1, Input and Output of User-Defined Types, and in particular, section 3.1.4, Generic Inserters and Extractors. The inserter itself relies on a member function of the `date` class, called `print_on()`, which performs the actual output. It is responsible for date formatting and must, of course, use the format string that is stored in the stream. Access to the format string is via the `pword()` function, which returns the address of the date format string object on the heap. `pword()` returns a generic pointer of type `void*`, which must be cast to a pointer of type `basic_string<charT>*` in our case. Here is an excerpt from a tentative implementation of the `print_on()` function:

```
template <class charT, class Traits>
        ios_base::iostate date::print_on(basic_ostream<charT, Traits>& os) const
{
  basic_string<charT> patt =
                 *(static_cast <basic_string<charT>*> (os.pword(getIdx())));
  ...
}
```

In this implementation, the print_on() function assumes that the pointer returned by pword() is a valid address. Is this a safe and sensible assumption? pword() can return a valid address only if a date format string has previously been stored in the pword field. Remember how the pword field is intended to be used: The manipulator setfmt fills the pword field with the address of a format string object, and the date inserter accesses the pword field to read and use the format string. In other words, the manipulator setfmt is responsible for storing a date format in the pword field. What if the inserter is invoked before the manipulator has ever been called? In that case, pword() would return an invalid address. Obviously, our tentative implementation of print_on() is not safe and needs to be fixed.

Fortunately, we can identify such a situation in which the pword field has not yet been filled. We use the fact that iword/pword data fields are guaranteed to be initialized to 0. If no format string has been provided yet, the pointer returned by pword() is the initial value of the pword field, namely 0. When no format string is available, we use a default date format string, which is provided by a function called defaultPatt(). Before we go into the details of defaultPatt(), let us first take a look at the implementation of the print_on() function:

```
template <class charT, class Traits>
ios_base::iostate date::print_on(basic_ostream<charT, Traits>& os) const
{
  void *p;
  basic_string<charT> patt;

  if ((p = os.pword(getIdx())) != 0)
    patt = *(static_cast <basic_string<charT> *> (p));
  else
    patt = defaultPatt(os);

  if (os.good() &&
      ! use_facet<time_put<charT,ostreambuf_iterator<charT,Traits> > >
      (os.getloc()).put(os,os,os.fill(),&tm_date,patt.c_str()
                      ,patt.c_str()+patt.length()).failed()
     )
    return ios_base::goodbit;
```

```
    else
      return ios_base::failbit;
}
```

In contrast to the implementation that was previously shown in section 3.1.4, Generic Inserters and Extractors, all code that deals with field adjustment has been dropped in order to keep the example concise and focused on the additions that are necessary for use of the iword/pword technique.

PROVIDING A DEFAULT DATE FORMAT STRING

We have left open how the default date format string is provided. Here is the implementation of the function template `defaultPatt()`:

```
template <class charT, class Traits>
const basic_string<charT> defaultPatt(basic_ostream<charT,Traits>& str)
{
  static char const * const c_helper = "%x";
  static charT helper[3] = { charT('\0'), charT('\0'), charT('\0') };

  use_facet<ctype<charT> > (str.getloc()).widen(c_helper,c_helper+2,helper);

  return helper;
}
```

This function is a template, because there are different types of date format strings. The background is that date format strings are passed to the `time_put` facet of the stream's locale, as you could see in the implementation of the `print_on()` function. For instance, wide-character streams have a `time_put` facet that requires wide-character strings as a date format string. For that reason, the date format strings are of different types depending on the character type of the stream.

Our idea for the default date format string is to provide `"%x"` as the default. If you study the `time_put` facet in greater detail (see section 6.2.3.1, The time_put Facet), you will find that it takes the format string and narrows it, using the `ctype` facet's `narrow()` function. Here we have to do the opposite: widen the narrow character string `"%x"` in order to provide the result as the default date format string of the required character type.

3.3.1.3 Implementing the Manipulator

The `setfmt` manipulator is responsible for storing the date format string in the stream. More specifically, it has to create a copy of the date format string on the heap and must store its address in the pword field.

For implementation of the manipulator, a technique is used that was described in section 3.2.2.2, Generalized Technique: Using a Manipulator Base Template. The manipulator is a function template that creates a helper object which does the actual work. Here is the manipulator function template:

```
template <class charT>
setfmt_helper<charT> setfmt(const charT* str)
{
    return setfmt_helper<charT>(str);
}
```

In this technique, the really interesting part of the manipulator is the helper object type `setfmt_helper`. It's a typical manipulator class as described in section 3.2.2, Manipulators with Parameters. It's derived from the base class `one_arg_manip_weh` that was suggested in section 3.2.2.4.1, Manipulator Base Template with Error Handling. We do this because the manipulation (i.e., storing the format string in the stream) can fail, and we aim to indicate that failure by setting bits in the stream state and/or raising exceptions. The manipulator base class `one_arg_manip_weh` provides a foundation for this error handling.

The core of the class template `setfmt_helper` is the static function `setfmt_fct()`, which performs the actual manipulation. It creates the copy of the format string on the heap, deletes any previously created format string object, and stores the address of the new format string object in the pword field. Here is the implementation:

```
template <class charT>
class setfmt_helper : public one_arg_manip_weh<const charT*>
{
 public:
  setfmt_helper(const charT* fmt)
  : one_arg_manip_weh<const charT*>(setfmt_fct,fmt) {}

 private:
  static void setfmt_fct(ios_base& str, const charT* fmt)
  {
    void*& formatStringPtr = str.pword(getIdx());
    basic_string<charT>* newFormatStringPtr = new basic_string<charT>(fmt);
    basic_string<charT>* oldFormatStringPtr
       = static_cast<basic_string<charT>*> (formatStringPtr);
    formatStringPtr = newFormatStringPtr;
    delete oldFormatStringPtr;
  }
};
```

Some remarks on the implementation of the function `setfmt_fct()`:

The old format string is deleted unconditionally; that is, there is no check to see if any format string has ever been stored. That might be surprising, but the check is not necessary, because pword fields are initialized to 0. Hence, if no format string has been stored, the pword field would be 0, and deletion of 0 is safe; it is allowed and has no effect.

The introduction of the local variables `formatStringPtr`, `newFormatStringPtr`, and `oldFormatStringPtr` might seem redundant at first sight. However, it is done deliberately for the purpose of exception safety. Let us see why. Consider a straightforward and more compact implementation of the static function `setfmt_fct()`. It could look like this:

```
static void setfmt_fct(ios_base& str, const charT* fmt)
{
    delete static_cast<basic_string<charT> *> (str.pword(getIdx()));
    str.pword(getIdx()) = new basic_string<charT>(fmt);
}
```

The call to `pword()` as well as operator `new` and operator `delete` can raise exceptions. Let us scrutinize the problematic cases:

If the memory allocation via operator `new` fails, a dangling pointer will be left in the pword field. The pointer will point to the already deleted old format string object. This is certainly a problem. If the second call to `pword()` fails, the new string object on the heap will already be created, but its address cannot be stored in the pword field as intended. As a result, the allocated string object can no longer be deleted, and a memory leak will be left.

With the use of additional local variables and the way the statements are arranged in the suggested implementation, the pword entry is kept consistent, and neither the dangling pointer nor the memory leak can occur. The deletion of the old format string is postponed until the very end, after the new format string has successfully been allocated and stored in the pword field.

Note that exceptions that are raised by any of the invoked operations are propagated to the caller and handled there. The caller in this case is the inserter defined for the manipulator base class `one_arg_manip_weh` that was suggested in section 3.2.2.4.1, Manipulator Base Template with Error Handling. This inserter is designed so that it maps any exceptions to the usual error indication for I/O operations, i.e., stream state bits and/or propagation of the exception depending on the stream's exception mask.

Another issue to be considered in this context is the validity of the reference returned by `pword()`. Such a reference is not guaranteed to be valid for ever. The standard specifies:

> The reference returned (by a call to `iword()`/`pword()`) may become invalid after another call to the object's iword/pword member with a different index, after a call to `copyfmt`, or when the object is destroyed.

In our suggested implementation we store the reference returned by `pword()` in the local variable `formatStringPtr`, which we use in the subsequent code sequence. It is safe to do this because there are no intervening calls that could invalidate the reference as long as it is used inside the body of the function `setfmt_fct()`.

3.3.1.4 Using Stream Callbacks for Memory Management

Up to this point, we have seen how the manipulator `setfmt` can be implemented and how it stores a pointer to the format string in the stream's pword field. We have also seen the implementation of the date inserter and the way in which it retrieves the format string from the pword field and uses it for formatting. Everything looks fine so far. There are, however, some minor issues that we have not considered yet.

STREAM DESTRUCTION

What happens when the stream object is destroyed, either because it goes out of scope or because it is explicitly deleted? As expected, the stream's destructor provides proper resource management for all of the stream's data members. In particular, the stream's destructor will release the pword entry itself, but not the string object on the heap the pword entry refers to. Without any further measures, a memory leak is inevitable.

To address this issue, callback functions can be registered for iword/pword entries.[8] These callback functions are triggered under certain conditions, one of which is the destruction of the stream object. The details of callbacks in IOStreams can be found in section 2.5.2, Stream Callbacks. We will be using the callback mechanism here in our example to establish proper resource management for the format string in order to avoid the memory leak. Before we do that, let us see whether there are other resource management problems.

INVOCATION OF `copyfmt()`

It turns out that destruction of the stream object is not the only situation in which a memory leak is likely to occur. Another problematic situation is invocation of the `copyfmt()` function. When the stream's `copyfmt()` function is invoked, data members from one stream are assigned to the stream it is invoked on. The details of `copyfmt()` are described in section 2.1.3, Copying and Assignment of Streams. Among the data members assigned by `copyfmt()` are the iword/pword entries.

In our example, the effect is that the stream's pword field, which holds the pointer to the format string, is overwritten by another stream's pword entry, which points to another format string. One problem here is that the old format string is neither released nor accessible any longer, because the pointer stored in the pword field was overwritten. The result is a memory leak. Another problem is that both streams involved in the call to `copyfmt()` refer to the same date format string on the heap afterwards. Imagine that one stream object receives a new date format string from the `setfmt` manipulator. The other stream object will not be affected by this change and will still be referring to the previous date format string, which both stream objects used to share. Unfortunately, the stream that receives a new date format string will release the old one and will therefore delete the

---

8. The old, classic IOStreams library did not support callback functions, and for that reason there was no solution to this problem at all.

shared date format string. The result is that the other stream will be referring to the previous date format string that is now deleted, and we have a dangling pointer problem.

Again, the callback mechanism can be used to solve the problem. Registered callback functions are triggered not only when the stream is destroyed but also when the stream's `copyfmt()` function is invoked. The case of a `copyfmt()` event is a little more complicated than the case of stream destruction, because the callback functions are triggered twice:

First, the callback functions are called before any stream data members are assigned, in order to allow proper release of any resources that will be replaced by the subsequent assignments performed by `copyfmt()`. In our example, the respective callback function must delete the old format string that the pword entry refers to.

The callbacks are called a second time, after all stream data members—except the exception mask, but including iword/pword and the callback function pointers—have been assigned. We will take advantage of this second invocation to have the callback function care about duplication of the format string object on the heap, so that both streams involved in `copyfmt()` will refer to copies of their own afterwards.

How do we distinguish between both invocations? A callback is always provided with an argument that describes the event that led to its invocation. On destruction, the event is `ios_base::erase_event`; in case of `copyfmt()`, the event is `ios_base::copyfmt_event`. The first invocation of a callback function during `copyfmt()` is called with an `erase_event` argument, much as it would be called on destruction of the stream. The reason for this is that the callback has to care about the exact same issues, namely, proper release of any resources. The second time the callback functions are called with a `copyfmt_event` argument.

Before we delve into the implementation of the callback function, let us recall what it is supposed to do. When it is invoked during destruction or at the beginning of `copyfmt()`, it will delete the format string object that the pword entry refers to. When the callback function is invoked at the end of `copyfmt()`, it will duplicate the date format string and set the pword entry so that it refers to the newly created copy of the date format string.

FAILURE IN CALLBACK FUNCTIONS

Duplication of the format string object requires memory allocation from the heap for the copy of the format string. This memory allocation can fail, and if it does, a `bad_alloc` exception will be propagated out of the callback function. This is not allowed. The standard requires that callback functions must not throw any exceptions. For this reason, we cannot allow the `bad_alloc` exception to propagate out of our callback function. We must find another way to indicate failure of the callback function.

All callback functions receive a reference to the stream on which they shall operate. The most intuitive idea for an alternative error indication is the use of the stream's state. Why not set failbit in the stream state if the callback function fails? This, however, does not work either.

The reference to the stream that the callback function will operate on is passed to the function as a reference of type `ios_base&`. The stream base class `ios_base` does not give access to the stream state, because all members related to the stream state are defined in class `basic_ios`, which is derived from class `ios_base`. As a result, there is no access to the stream state via an `ios_base` reference, and therefore no way to indicate the failure of a callback function by setting the stream state flags.

It turns out that there is no direct way in which a callback function can indicate that it failed. For the time being, we will simply suppress all potential exceptions. In section 3.3.1.5, Error Indication of Stream Callback Functions, at the end of this chapter we will return to this issue and suggest a viable way for error indication from a stream callback function.

IMPLEMENTING THE CALLBACK FUNCTION

At last, here it is: the implementation of the stream callback function that handles the memory management of the format string when the stream is destroyed or `copyfmt()` is invoked:

```
template <class charT>
void callback(ios_base::event ev, ios_base& str, int i)
{
 if (ev == ios_base::erase_event)
 {
  try { delete static_cast<basic_string<charT> *> (str.pword(i)); }
  catch(...) { }
 }
 else if (ev == ios_base::copyfmt_event)
 {
  void*& formatStringPtr = str.pword(i);
  basic_string<charT>* old;
  if ((old = static_cast<basic_string<charT> *> (formatStringPtr)) != 0)
  {
   try { formatStringPtr = new basic_string<charT>(*old); }
   catch (bad_alloc&) { }
  }
 }
}
```

REGISTRATION OF THE CALLBACK FUNCTION

When and how must we register the callback function? Naturally, the callback function must be registered before it is needed. Remember, the purpose of this callback function is to manage the format string object properly. As long as the stream does not hold a format string, we do not need the callback function. For this reason, we will register the callback at the very moment when the manipulator stores a format string in the stream object for the first time in the lifetime of that stream.

We will extend the manipulator function `setfmt_fct()` so that it not only deposits the format string object in the stream but also registers the callback, if this is the first time a format string is installed. How do we recognize that no format string has ever been stored in the stream? We use the same technique as before: The pword fields are guaranteed to be initialized to 0. We will interpret a pword entry of value 0 as indication that there has not yet been a format string installed. Here is the extended version of the `setfmt_fct()` function:

```
template <class charT>
void setfmt_helper<charT>::setfmt_fct(ios_base& str, const charT* fmt)
  {
    void*& formatStringPtr = str.pword(getIdx());

    if (formatStringPtr == 0)
       str.register_callback(callback, getIdx());

    basic_string<charT>* newFormatStringPtr = new basic_string<charT>(fmt);
    basic_string<charT>* oldFormatStringPtr
       = static_cast<basic_string<charT> *> (formatStringPtr);
    formatStringPtr = newFormatStringPtr;
    delete oldFormatStringPtr;
  }
```

PUTTING THE PIECES TOGETHER

So far, the callback function itself is a global function, which it need not be. The only context in which it is needed is the point of registration. This callback function is not intended to be explicitly invoked by anybody. It will be registered and called implicitly by the stream's callback mechanism. For reasons of better encapsulation, we will make the callback function a static member function of the manipulator helper class. Below you see the complete code for the manipulator `setfmt` and its helper class `setfmt_helper`:

```
template <class charT>
setfmt_helper<charT> setfmt(const charT* str)
{
    return setfmt_helper<charT>(str);
}


template <class charT>
class setfmt_helper : public one_arg_manip_weh<const charT*>
{
 public:
  setfmt_helper(const charT* fmt)
  : one_arg_manip_weh<const charT*>(setfmt_fct,fmt) {}
```

```
static void setfmt_fct(ios_base& str, const charT* fmt)
{
  void*& formatStringPtr = str.pword(getIdx());

  if (formatStringPtr == 0)
      str.register_callback(callback, getIdx());

  basic_string<charT>* newFormatStringPtr = new basic_string<charT>(fmt);
  basic_string<charT>* oldFormatStringPtr
      = static_cast<basic_string<charT> *> (formatStringPtr);
  formatStringPtr = newFormatStringPtr;
  delete oldFormatStringPtr;
}

static void callback(ios_base::event ev, ios_base& str, int i)
{
  if (ev == ios_base::erase_event)
  {
    try { delete static_cast<basic_string<charT> *> (str.pword(i)); }
    catch(...) { }
  }
  else if (ev == ios_base::copyfmt_event)
  {
    void*& formatStringPtr = str.pword(i);
    basic_string<charT>* old;
    if ((old = static_cast<basic_string<charT> *> (formatStringPtr)) != 0)
    {
      try { formatStringPtr = new basic_string<charT>(*old); }
      catch (bad_alloc&) { }
    }
  }
}
};
```

3.3.1.5 Error Indication of Stream Callback Functions

In the previous section, one question came up that has been left open: How can a stream callback function indicate that it ran into trouble and failed to accomplish its tasks. In this section we will address this issue and show you a solution.

The C++ standard requires that stream callback functions must not throw any exceptions.[9] However, a callback function, like any other function, can fail. As the excep-

---

9. If a callback function is registered that violates this requirement, the behavior of any IOStreams operations that are subsequently invoked is undefined.

tion mechanism must not be used for error indication, we must find another way of indicating failure. Callback functions are required to have the following signature:

```
void (*event_callback)(ios_base::event, ios_base&, int index);
```

As you can see, callback functions do not have a return code. Consequently, we cannot "return" the error. As the callback function receives a reference to the stream in the form of an `ios_base` reference, one could consider storing the error in the stream's state. Section 3.3.1.4, Using Stream Callbacks for Memory Management, already explained that the callback function cannot set failbit or badbit in the stream's state either, because the stream base class `ios_base` does not give access to the stream state. As the callback function cannot store the error anywhere in the stream, it must store it elsewhere.

A solution is to store the error indication in the not-yet-used iword field. Remember, callback functions are registered per iword/pword index, and each index gives access to an iword/pword pair. In our example, we have been using only the pword entry; we store a pointer to the format string in the pword field. The corresponding iword field has not been used so far. We will now use it for error indication of a callback function. The callback function will store the error information in the iword field, and afterwards the user must check the error indication stored in the iword field. This check need not be done by directly accessing the iword field. The idea is to map the information contained in the iword field to the stream state, so that the error information can then be accessed in the usual way (via `good()`, `bad()`, etc., or in the form of an exception raised if the exceptions mask requires it).

In the following sections we will complete our example of formatted output of date objects as outlined above. We will then show you a more general approach for error indication of callbacks that also works when more than one callback function is registered.

3.3.1.5.1 Extending the Example

If an error occurs in the callback function, a corresponding error indication is stored in the iword field. As described above, this error information is mapped to the stream state in a second step. For this reason, the error information is expressed in terms of an object of type `ios_base::iostate`, because this is the type of the stream state data member of the stream classes; it is a bitmask type that can hold the stream state flags `failbit`, `badbit`, and `eofbit`.

Below is the extended version of the callback function. We catch the `bad_alloc` exception and store a badbit in the iword field.

```
template <class charT>
void setfmt_helper<charT>::callback(ios_base::event ev, ios_base& str, int i)
{
  if (ev == ios_base::erase_event)
  {
   try { delete static_cast<basic_string<charT> *> (str.pword(i)); }
   catch(...) {  }
  }
```

```
else if (ev == ios_base::copyfmt_event)
{
 void*& formatStringPtr = str.pword(i);
 basic_string<charT>* old;
 if ((old = static_cast<basic_string<charT> *> (formatStringPtr)) != 0)
 {
  try { formatStringPtr = new basic_string<charT>(*old); }
  catch (bad_alloc&)
  { ios_base::iostate err = ios_base::badbit;
    str.iword(i) = err | static_cast<ios_base::iostate> (str.iword(i));
  }
 }
}
}
```

Note that we did not do anything about the exception that might be raised in case the callback function was invoked due to an `erase_event`. These situations are either destruction of the stream or the beginning of a `copyfmt()` call. In the case of stream destruction, it would be futile to store any information in the iword field; the error information cannot be retrieved afterwards anyway, because the entire stream has disappeared. In the case of a `copyfmt()` call, the iword field will be overwritten by the subsequent assignment of stream data members performed by `copyfmt()`. Again, it would be futile to store any information in the iword field; it will be overwritten before it can be checked.

While the callback function cares about storing error information in the iword field, it remains the user's responsibility to fetch the error information from the iword field and transfer it to the stream state. To make this more convenient, we provide the function `copyfmtErr()` for this purpose. It must be called by the user after any invocation of the `copyfmt()` function. Here is the implementation of the `copyfmtErr()` function:

```
template <class charT, class Traits>
ios_base::iostate copyfmtErr(basic_ios<charT,Traits>& os)
{
 ios_base::iostate err = static_cast<ios_base::iostate> (os.iword(getIdx()));
 os.iword(getIdx()) = 0L;
 os.setstate(err | os.rdstate());
 return err;
}
```

Note that `copyfmtErr()` can trigger an exception. This is a result of the call to `setstate()`: It throws an exception if the stream's exception mask is configured to react in this way to the newly set stream state.

The function `copyfmtErr()` must be called after any invocation of the `copyfmt()`. The sample code in the next section is an example of how it would be used.

3.3.1.6 Using the New Functionality

Let us now prove that our implementation exhibits the desired behavior. The code snipped below demonstrates that we can specify various formatting strings via the setfmt manipulator and receive correspondingly different formats for a given date. We can also see that the additional format information for date formatting is copied from cerr to cout:

```
date d(11,8,1999);

cout << setfmt("%x is in week %U of year %Y.") << d << endl;
cerr << setfmt("%B %d, %Y was a %A.");
cout.copyfmt(cerr);

if (copyfmtErr(cout) != ios_base::goodbit)
{ /* do the appropriate error handling */ }

cout << d << endl; // now using the date format taken from cerr
```

Assuming a U.S. locale is used, the output of the program above would be

```
The date: 08/11/99 is in week 32 of year 1999.
The date: August 11, 1999 was a Wednesday.
```

3.3.1.7 Evaluation of the iword/pword Approach

Let us step back from the example of date formatting that we have just discussed, and identify the general stream extension technique behind it. We want to differentiate between those parts of the example that are specific to date formatting and those aspects that are typical for stream extension via iword/pword in general.

Stream extensions via the iword/pword technique have the following properties in common:

ADDING ATTRIBUTES. The main idea of this stream extension technique is use of the iword/pword fields of a stream to store additional attributes in the stream object. For this purpose an iword/pword index must be acquired via ios_base::xalloc(), and the index is subsequently used to access the corresponding iword/pword entries.

ADDING FUNCTIONALITY. New functionality that uses the user-defined stream attributes is implemented outside the stream, i.e., it is not added to the stream itself. Such functionality is typically, but not necessarily, implemented as inserters, extractors, or manipulators.

The stream's callback mechanism is used if new functionality related to the stream's destruction or invocation of its member functions copyfmt() or imbue() must be provided.

Listed below are the steps that are typically considered when the iword/pword technique is used. The list is meant to provide a guideline for applying the technique to other problem domains.

1. Using iword or using pword? A good point to start the stream extension is to determine which information should be added to the stream. If the new attribute is of a type that can safely be promoted to `long`, an iword entry can be used to store the value. Otherwise, the attribute can be created on the heap and a pointer referring to the heap object can be stored in a pword entry. (The latter is the approach we used in our example: The manipulator creates a copy of the date format string on the heap and stores a pointer to the heap object in a pword field.)

Another related consideration is the number of iword/pword fields that should be used to store the information. In most cases, one entry will suffice. If, for instance, two integral values should be stored, it is more convenient to use two iword entries rather than one pword entry that points to a heap object containing the two integral values.

2. Acquiring the index. The next step is to determine which part of the program will acquire the index (or the indices) by invoking `ios_base::xalloc()`. It is important to make sure that this is done before the index is used by any other part of the program. (In our example, we wrapped the index into an access function that acquires a valid index immediately before it is accessed for the first time.)

3. Initializing the new attribute(s). Next it must be determined which parts of the program will have read, write, or even read-and-write access to the acquired iword/pword field. (In our example, the manipulator stores the date format string in the pword field, and the inserter retrieves it for formatted output of date objects.)

Depending on the context, it might be necessary for the iword/pword field to be initialized with a sensible value before it is read. This might require coordination between read and write accesses; you must make sure that there is initial write access before any read access to the new attribute(s).

Instead of making provisions for initial write access, a default value can be used. This alternative approach relies on the guarantee that iword/pword fields are initialized to 0. This is a viable solution whenever those parts of the program that read the information can live with an iword/pword set to 0. The 0 value is typically interpreted as an indication that no explicit initialization has been processed so far, and a default for the missing attribute value can be used instead of an explicitly provided attribute value. (We used the latter approach in our example. When the inserter is invoked before any format specification has been provided, a default format is used.)

4. Memory management of the new attribute(s). The use of callbacks is typical of situations where handles to dynamically acquired resources are stored in the iword/pword fields and these resources logically belong to the stream. Destruction of the stream and copying stream data members have a potential for creating a resource leak under such circumstances. The dynamic resource used most often is memory allocated on the heap.

If a pword field is used to store a pointer referring to an object on the heap, the stream's destructor releases only the pword entry itself, but not the object on the heap the pword entry refers to, and a memory leak is the result. Usually, a similar problem arises when the pword entry is copied among other stream data members during `copyfmt()`. To avoid any memory leaks, memory management for the heap object must be installed in the form of a stream callback. The memory management can be implemented by deleting or copying the object on the heap. Alternatively, more sophisticated schemes, such as reference counting, can be used. (In our example, we implemented a callback function that deletes and duplicates the dynamically allocated format string object as needed in case of stream destruction and invocation of `copyfmt()`.)

More generally, the callback function must provide the functionality for situations where the stream is destroyed or its member functions `copyfmt()` or `imbue()` are called.[10] The motivation is usually proper management of a dynamically acquired resource referred to by the iword/pword entries.

5. Indicating callback errors. Errors that occur in the callback function cannot be indicated directly, because the callback function has no access to the stream state and is required not to throw any exceptions. As a workaround, the status information must be stored elsewhere. (In our example, we used the iword field corresponding to the pword field to store the callback's error information. We also provided additional functionality to help the user, who must copy the error information from outside the stream to the stream state after any stream operation that triggers the callback function.)

3.3.2 Creating New Stream Classes by Derivation
The standard IOStreams is organized as a hierarchy of classes, where derived classes extend the functionality of their base classes. This hierarchy was discussed together with the rationale for its structure in section 2.1, The Stream Classes. Following the object-oriented programming paradigm, the canonical approach for adding new stream functionality is deriving new stream classes from the standard stream classes. We discuss this technique for stream extension in the following sections.

Again, the example of date formatting is used for demonstration of the technique. As in the previous solution, an inserter for date objects and a manipulator for setting a date format string must be implemented. It is possible to write code like this:

```
ostr << setfmt("%x") << date(11,8,1999) << endl;
```

The difference from the previous solution is that `ostr` is an output stream of a class type derived from a standard stream class. As before, the format string is passed as an argument to the manipulator `setfmt` and must be stored in the stream object for subsequent use by the `date` inserter. In the previous approach the iword/pword fields were used for this purpose. In this solution, we wrap the format string into a class of its own,

---

10. In our example, we had no need to react to a call of `imbue()` in our callback function. Yet it can be necessary under certain circumstances. Just to give you an idea of when and why a callback function for an `imbue_event` might be needed, here is a conceivable example: If information from the stream's locale is used or may be cached, it might be necessary to update this information when the locale is replaced.

and the new stream class will then inherit the format string handling from the wrapper class. Before we care about the actual stream functionality of the new stream class, let us see how the format string handling can be provided. Here is the date format wrapper class.

THE DATE FORMAT CLASS

The wrapper class for the date format string stores the format string as a private data member and has two public member functions, which allow the format string data member to be acquired and set. Let us call the wrapper class `datefmt`. Class `datefmt` cannot be a simple class but must be a class template with the character type as template parameter, because the character type of the format string can vary.[11] Below is the implementation of class `datefmt`:

```
template<class charT>
class datefmt
{
public:
  datefmt(const charT* f) : myFmt(f) {}

  virtual void fmt(const charT* f)
  { myFmt = f; }

  virtual const basic_string<charT>& fmt() const
  { return myFmt; }

  virtual ~datefmt() {}

private:
  basic_string<charT> myFmt;
};
```

3.3.2.1 Deriving the New Stream Class

Naturally, the new stream class does not care only about storing the date format string. The more important functionality is formatted text output in the way that is typical to IOStreams classes. We do not want to reinvent the wheel, but rather aim to reuse all the functionality that is already provided by the existing stream classes. For this reason, the new stream class will be derived from one of the classes defined in the IOStreams' hierarchy. This class hierarchy contains quite a number of potential base classes, which raises the following question: Which is the appropriate base class for the new abstraction?

---

11. We briefly mentioned the need for different types of format strings before, in section 3.3.1.2, Implementing the Date Inserter, when we discussed the default date format string. There are different types of date format strings, because the format string is passed to the `time_put` facet of the stream's locale, and a wide-character stream's `time_put` facet requires a wide-character format string.

CHOOSING THE RIGHT STREAM BASE CLASS FOR DERIVATION

To answer this question, let us have a look at the IOStreams class hierarchy.

The stream classes from the base layer, `ios_base` and `basic_ios`, do not contain enough functionality to provide the right foundation for our new abstraction. They lack the capability for actual input and output.

The next layer down the class hierarchy comprises the general streams `basic_(i/o)stream`. The inserters and extractors for the standard types are defined in this layer, and for this reason, they are reasonable candidates to serve as base classes for our new stream class.

The lowest layer of the IOStreams hierarchy comprises the concrete streams for in-memory I/O and file I/O: `basic_(i/o)stringstream` and `basic_(i/o)fstream`. They have additional device-specific operations, such as `open()` and `close()`, and they can also serve as base classes.

Let us tentatively consider the general stream classes as base classes. They require a stream buffer to be passed to their constructors. Consequently, the constructor of our derived class would have to provide that stream buffer object to its base class. This leaves us two alternatives for the constructor of the derived stream class:

1. We could hold the user responsible for providing the required stream buffer. In this case, the constructor of our new class would hand over the received stream buffer to its base class constructor. This approach makes the construction of a new stream rather inconvenient for the user.

2. We could make our constructor so smart that it can create a new stream buffer and pass it to its base class constructor. This would require the constructor arguments to describe the device to which the stream buffer is to be connected. Unfortunately, we would have to reimplement functionality that is specific to the device, for instance `open()` and `close()` for files. As device-specific operations are already provided by the concrete stream classes, they are the better candidates for a base class.

For this reason, we will derive our new stream class from one of the concrete stream classes in the IOStreams hierarchy. Which one shall we pick? Since we aim to provide functionality for output of formatted date objects, we consider only the output streams, namely `basic_ofstream`, `basic_fstream`, `basic_ostringstream`, and `basic_stringstream`. All of the four stream classes are equally appropriate as a base class for our new abstraction.

At first sight, it might look as if we had to define four new stream classes, each of which would be derived from one of the concrete output stream classes listed above. Fortunately, C++ supports the powerful language feature of templates, which saves us a lot of work here. Instead of defining four derived classes, we define a class template where the base class type is the template argument of the derived class. Leaving open the question of which stream class shall serve as the base class, our class template can be instantiated for each of the four potential base classes. In this way we defer the decision about the base class to the moment when an object of the new derived class is defined by the user.

Here is a first sketch of the new stream class template, called `ocdatestream`. Note that we use multiple inheritance here, because the new stream class inherits the date format string from the class `datefmt` and the text output functionality from a stream base class.

```
template <class ConcreteOStream>
class ocdatestream
: public ConcreteOStream, public datefmt<typename ConcreteOStream::char_type>
{
public:
  typedef typename ConcreteOStream::char_type   char_type;

  ocdatestream(const char* s, ios_base::openmode mode, const char_type* fmt=0)
  : ConcreteOStream(s,mode),
    datefmt<char_type>(fmt)
  { }


  // ...
};
```

The constructor of class `ocdatestream` takes three parameters.

The first one is a string whose meaning varies depending on the base class. When the base class is a file stream class, that is, `basic_ofstream` or `basic_fstream`, the first argument is interpreted as the name of the file to which the new stream is to be connected. When the base class is a string stream, that is, `basic_ostringstream` or `basic_stringstream`, the first argument specifies the initial content of the string stream. In both cases the string is passed to the stream base class's constructor.

Note that the constructors of the string stream classes require a string object rather than a pointer to a character sequence. The character sequence is implicitly converted by the compiler to a string object before it is handed over to the string stream class's constructor.

The second argument of class `ocdatestream`'s constructor describes the open mode of the stream. It is also forwarded to the stream base class's constructor.

The constructor's third parameter specifies the format string that is initially used for date formatting. It is handed over to `datefmt`'s constructor. As a default, no format string is provided, in which case the inserter will be using a default format string. Details are discussed later in this section.

If we had already implemented all the other missing components, such as the `setfmt` manipulator and the date inserter, we would be capable of writing formatted date objects to `ocdatestreams`. In the example below, the date is written to a file:

```
ocdatestream< basic_fstream<char> > ostr("outfile.txt", ios_base::out);
ostr << setfmt("%B %d, %Y is a %A.") << date(11,8,1999) << endl;
```

AN ADAPTER STREAM TYPE FOR EXISTING STREAM OBJECTS

The solution suggested above has a certain deficiency compared to the iword/pword solution discussed in the previous chapter: We cannot apply the new functionality, namely, date formatting, to existing stream objects such as cout and cerr, because the date-formatting functionality is available only in ocdatestreams. The iword/pword solution, on the other hand, was able to allow date formatting on all stream objects without any restrictions regarding their type, because all stream types have an iword/pword field. How can we eliminate this deficiency and make date formatting available to existing streams?

Our idea is to provide an adapter that adds date-formatting capabilities to existing stream objects. This adapter would be a stream class whose constructor takes an existing stream such as cout and creates an adapted stream that is basically a copy of the existing stream plus the date-formatting functionality. We would then implement all the setfmt manipulator and the date inserter for this adapter stream type, and it could be used like this:

```
adapter_type ostr(cout);
ostr << setfmt("%B %d, %Y is a %A.") << date(11,8,1999) << endl;
```

Let's see how we can design such an adapter stream type. Its constructor is to receive a stream object and create an adapted stream object that is a copy of the original. The first problem is that streams cannot be copied. Both the copy constructor and the copy assignment operator of the stream classes are inaccessible. In section 2.1.3, Copying and Assignment of Streams, we explained a technique for copying the entire state of a stream from one stream to another, piece by piece. The technique uses the following member functions defined in the stream base class basic_ios as copying all relevant parts of a stream:

rdbuf(), which can be used to exchange the stream buffer between streams

clear() and rdstate(), which can be used to exchange the error state between streams

copyfmt(), which can be used to exchange all other data members between streams

We will use this technique to implement the constructor of the adapter stream type and copy the state of the existing stream to the newly constructed stream.

The second question is, Which stream class shall serve a base class for the new adapter stream class?

As before, we want to leave this open and implement the adapter stream class as a class template that takes its stream base class as a template argument. Here is a sketch of the adapter stream type:

```
template <class GeneralOStream>
class ogdatestream
: public GeneralOStream, public datefmt<typename GeneralOStream::char_type>
{
public:
  typedef typename GeneralOStream::char_type   char_type;

  ogdatestream(GeneralOStream& ost, const char_type* fmt)
  : GeneralOStream (ost.rdbuf()),
    datefmt<char_type>(fmt)
  {
    clear(ost.rdstate());
    copyfmt(ost);
  }

  // ...
};
```

Note that in this suggested implementation, only stream classes from the general stream class layer can serve as template arguments. This is because the base classes' constructors must be called when a derived stream object is created. Unfortunately, different stream classes have constructors with different signatures.[12] The moment we decide how we want to invoke the base class constructor, we impose restrictions on the stream type that can be used for instantiation of the adapter stream template. In this case, we decided to allow the general stream classes as base classes.[13]

UNIFYING THE TWO DERIVED STREAM CLASSES

The two derived date-formatting stream classes, ocdatestream and ogdatestream, are almost identical. They differ only in their constructors and in the stream types that they allow for instantiation, i.e., the possible base classes. ocdatestream can be instantiated for the concrete output stream classes basic_ofstream, basic_fstream, basic_ostringstream, and basic_stringstream. ogdatestream can be instantiated for the general output stream classes basic_ostream, and basic_iostream. To avoid redundancies, we decided to combine both class templates, as shown here:

---

12. The concrete stream classes have, among other constructors, a no-argument-constructor, which is convenient, because it need not be explicitly invoked. The general stream classes, in contrast, have only one constructor that requires a stream buffer.

13. A minor disadvantage of this design is that string-and-file stream objects that are adapted lose their device-specific functionality. Consider, for instance, an adapted file stream. Had we allowed the concrete stream classes as base classes, an adapter derived from basic_fstream would have inherited all the file stream–specific operations such as open() and close(). With a general stream class as a base class, the adapter stream type does not inherit the open() and close() member functions. The effect is that a file stream object, which is adapted, cannot be closed via the adapted stream object, but only via its original object.

```
template <class OStream>
class odatestream
: public OStream, public datefmt<typename OStream::char_type>
{
public:
    typedef typename OStream::char_type char_type;

    odatestream(const char_type* s, ios_base::openmode mode
                ,const char_type* fmt);
    odatestream(const OStream& toBeAdapted, const char_type* fmt);

    // ...
};
```

This combined stream class template has two advantages: Only one new abstraction is defined, and any redundant code is eliminated. The downside is that the class might be a little hard to understand. Only one of the constructors will compile. Which one it is depends on the type of the template argument OStream. The first constructor will compile only when OStream is a concrete output stream type, while the second constructor can be used only when OStream is a general output stream type. The combined stream class template odatestream is a highly flexible abstraction. However, it puts the burden of correct usage onto the user.

IMPLEMENTATION OF THE CONSTRUCTORS

Let us now move on to the details of the implementation of odatestream. We start with the two constructors, whose implementation we have already outlined above. So far, we have omitted any error handling. For instance, the initial date format string is passed to the constructors as a pointer to a character sequence. This pointer is handed over to base class datefmt, where it is used to initialize the private string data member. For initialization of the string data member, the compiler must generate a temporary string object from the char* pointer, and this operation can fail and throw a bad_alloc exception. We haven't been concerned about any such failure yet. Here are the two constructors[14] with error handling[15] added:

---

14. A standard compatible compiler can only instantiate those member functions from a template that are really used from the instantiated type. There are still compilers available that do not conform to this rule, i.e., they always instantiate all member functions. Such a nonstandard compatible compiler cannot compile the two odatestream constructors: If the odatestream template parameter is a general stream class, the first constructor cannot be compiled, because a general stream does not provide a constructor that can receive a character string and a mode argument. If the template parameter is a concrete stream class, the second constructor cannot be compiled, because the concrete stream class provides no constructor that can receive a pointer to a stream buffer. Note that no error occurs with a standard compatible compiler, because the constructor that cannot be compiled will not be used and hence will not be instantiated.

15. We use function try blocks for catching exceptions in these contructors. If you are not familiar with function try blocks, see section G.10, Function try Blocks, for further explanation.

```
template <class OStream>
odatestream<OStream>::odatestream(const char_type* s, ios_base::openmode mode,
                                  const char_type* fmt = 0)
  try
  : OStream(s,mode), datefmt<char_type>(fmt ? fmt : defaultPatt(*this)) { }
  catch (...) { setbad(); }
```

And

```
template <class OStream>
odatestream<OStream>::odatestream(const OStream& toBeAdapted,
                                  const char_type* fmt = 0)
  try
  : OStream(toBeAdapted.rdbuf())
  , datefmt<char_type>(fmt ? fmt : defaultPatt(toBeAdapted))
{
  clear(toBeAdapted.rdstate());
  copyfmt(toBeAdapted);
} catch (...) { setbad(); }
```

Both constructors pass their arguments to their respective base classes. The second constructor passes the stream buffer of the stream provided as parameter to its base class constructor and copies the stream state via clear() and the other stream members via copyfmt() from the stream provided as parameter to its newly constructed instance.

Note that we made the format string an optional parameter and use a default when no explicit format string is provided. The default date format string is provided by the function template defaultPatt() as in the previous chapter.

ERROR HANDLING FOR THE CONSTRUCTORS

The try blocks contain the constructors' initialization lists and the constructors' bodies, and this way we catch any exception that occurs during construction. The error handling is factored out into a function called setbad(), which maps any exception that occurs during construction to badbit. The rules for IOStreams error handling are a bit tricky, and they are described in greater detail in section 3.1.22, Error Indication. It is not enough just to add badbit to the stream state. We must also suppress the ios_base::failure exception, which is generated automatically when the exception mask indicates that bad-bit will trigger an exception and must rethrow the original exception instead. Here is the stream error handling function setbad(), which we define as a private member function of class odatestream:

```
template <class OStream>
void odatestream<OStream>::setbad()
{
    if (exceptions() & ios_base::badbit)
    {
        try { setstate(ios_base::badbit | rdstate()); }
        catch( ios_base::failure& ) { }
        throw;
    }
    else
    {
        setstate(ios_base::badbit | rdstate());
    }
}
```

ERROR HANDLING FOR THE INHERITED FUNCTIONS

Now that we have implemented the IOStreams typical error handling for the constructors of class `odatestream`, we should spend a few thoughts on the error handling of the inherited member functions. Do they handle their errors according to IOStreams conventions?

We can safely assume that the member functions that were inherited from the stream base class obey the IOStreams rules. However, is the same true for the member functions inherited from the base class `datefmt`?

To refresh your memory, here is the implementation of class `datefmt`:

```
template<class charT>
class datefmt
{
public:
    datefmt(const charT* f) : myFmt(f) {}

    virtual void fmt(const charT* f)
    { myFmt = f; }

    virtual const basic_string<charT>& fmt() const
    { return myFmt; }

    virtual ~datefmt() {}

private:
    basic_string<charT> myFmt;
};
```

The function that returns the format string does so by returning a `const` reference to a private data member. Consequently, no error can occur and no exception can be thrown.

The function that sets the format string does not explicitly throw an exception, but an exception (most probably a `bad_alloc`) could be raised when the format string argument of type `const charT*` is implicitly converted into a string object of type `basic_string<charT>`. Propagating this `bad_alloc` exception without setting badbit and checking the stream's exception mask violates the error-handling rules in IOStreams.

As this virtual function is inherited by the derived class `odatestream`, which is a stream class and therefore supposed to obey the IOStreams rules, we must redefine this virtual function in the derived class. Here is the redefined function that provides an IOStreams-compliant error handling:

```
template <class OStream>
void odatestream<OStream>::fmt(const char_type* f)
{
    try { datefmt<char_type>::fmt(f); }
    catch (...) { setbad(); }
}
```

3.3.2.2 Implementing the Date Inserter and the Manipulator

Now the derived stream class `odatestream` is complete. It combines date formatting capabilities inherited from class `datefmt` with output stream functionality inherited from either a general or a concrete output stream class. For actual date formatting, we must still implement an inserter that formats and writes date objects to the `odatestreams`. Also, we need to provide the `setfmt` manipulator that allows the setting of the format string that controls the actual formatting. Let us implement the date inserter first, before we turn to the manipulator.

3.3.2.2.1 Implementing the Date Inserter

Inserters usually access the output stream via a base class reference; their first argument is a reference to a `basic_ostream`. This is reasonable, because class `basic_ostream` is a base class of *all* output stream types, and for this reason one inserter can access streams of *any* output stream type via the `basic_ostream` reference. In the previous chapter, where we added date formatting via iword/pword, we implemented the date inserter following this convention. Can we do the same thing here?

We have defined a derived stream class, namely `odatestream`, which provides the date-formatting functionality. The inserter that we want to implement needs access to the date-formatting facilities, but the relevant member functions are not accessible via a reference to the base class `basic_ostream`. If the date inserter took an `odatestream` reference, we would not have that problem. Can we implement the date inserter with a reference to an `odatestream` instead of a reference to a `basic_ostream`?

The answer is no, that would be a fault! To understand why it is wrong, let's look at an example, in which we assume that we had implemented the inserter so that it takes an `odatestream`. The inserter's signature would be

```
template<class OStream>
odatestream<OStream>& operator<< (odatestream<OStream>& ods, const date& dat);
```

Imagine we used this inserter and tried to compile the following lines of code:

```
odatestream<basic_ostream<char> > ods(cout);
ods << "Hello world, today is the: " << date();
```

The compiler would complain that it cannot not find an appropriate `operator<<()` for the insertion of the temporary date object. Why is that? Let's study it step by step. The compiler evaluates the sequence of shift expressions from left to right. First, it looks for an `operator<<()` that allows text of type `const char*` to be inserted into the `odatestream` object `ods`. It finds the following matching global operator, which is already defined in the IOStreams library:

```
template<class charT, class traits>
basic_ostream<charT,traits>& operator<<(basic_ostream<charT,traits>&,
                                        const char*);
```

This operator returns a reference to a `basic_ostream`. Next, the compiler looks for an `operator<<()` that allows insertion of the `date` object into the `basic_ostream` that was returned by the first `operator<<()`. No such operator is available, because the date inserter takes a reference to an `odatestream`, not a `basic_ostream`. The compiler even considers implicit conversions for the arguments, but an implicit conversion from `basic_ostream&` (a base class reference) to `odatestream&` (a derived class reference) is not defined in C++, and as a result the compiler cannot find a matching function and issues an error message.

Obviously, we have a problem with a date inserter that takes a reference to an `odatestream` instead of a `basic_ostream`. The `odatestream` reference is necessary for gaining access to the date-formatting facilities defined in class `odatestream`, but such an inserter is of limited use in a chain of inserters. The problem occurs whenever an object other than a date object is inserted before a date object. The "nondate" inserters can be applied to an `odatestream`, but they always return `basic_ostream` references. Once a `basic_ostream` reference was returned in a chain, the compiler lost the type information necessary to find the date inserter.

This is a typical problem with inserters to derived stream classes and is not limited to our particular example. How does one solve it? As the compiler cannot find an inserter that takes a reference other than a `basic_ostream` reference, we must define the date inserter to take a base class reference. How, then, do we get access to the stream's member functions for date formatting?

The solution takes advantage of a relatively new language feature: the dynamic cast. The idea is to cast the `basic_ostream` reference to an `odatestream` reference so that we gain access to the member functions for date formatting. This kind of cast is called a *downcast* and is performed via the `dynamic_cast` operator. Section G.9, Dynamic Cast, in appendix G explains the dynamic cast and related issues.

At last we are ready to implement the inserter. We use the same framework as before, and again the inserter itself relies on a member function of the `date` class, called `print_on()`, which performs the actual output. (The details of this implementation are described in section 3.1.4, Generic Inserters and Extractors.) This member function has the following signature:

```
template <class charT, class Traits>
ios_base::iostate date::print_on(basic_ostream<charT, Traits>& os) const;
```

If the stream reference `os` refers to an `odatestream` object, we want to perform a downcast in order to gain access to the date-formatting member functions of class `odatestream`. When we consider the details of this cast, we realize that we must cast `os` to an `odatestream<OStream>&`, because `odatestream` is a class template. Unfortunately, we have no way of finding out what the template argument `OStream` is.

Now, do we really need an `odatestream<OStream>&` in order to gain access to the date-formatting functions? These functions are inherited from the other base class `datefmt`. It would suffice if we could cast `os` to a reference to a `datefmt`, or more precisely, to a reference to a `datefmt<charT>`, assuming that the character type of the date format string is the same as the character type of the stream. Such a cast is called a *peer class cast* (see section G.9, Dynamic Cast, in appendix G for further explanations) and can be safely performed via the `dynamic_cast` operator. Using this language feature, the `print_on()` function can be implemented like this:[16]

```
template <class charT, class Traits>
ios_base::iostate date::print_on(basic_ostream<charT, Traits>& os) const
{
 basic_string<charT> formatString;
 datefmt<charT>* p;

 if ((p = dynamic_cast<datefmt<charT>*>(&os)) == 0)
    formatString = defaultPatt(os);
 else
    formatString = p->fmt();

 if (use_facet<time_put<charT,ostreambuf_iterator<charT,Traits> > >
    (os.getloc()).put(os,os,os.fill(),&tm_date,formatString.c_str(),
                     formatString.c_str()+formatString.length()
                     ).failed()
   )
    return ios_base::failbit;
```

---

16. Again, we omitted handling of the field width, in order to keep the example focused.

```
    else
        return ios_base::goodbit;
}
```

The peer cast works the following way: If the dynamic cast of the pointer to the stream to a pointer to `datefmt<charT>` does not yield 0, then we know that the stream object is of a type that supports date format string handling, and the member function `fmt()` can be called. Otherwise, we know that the stream does not support date format string handling, and we use the default string provided by `defaultPatt()` instead.

The rest of `print_on()`'s implementation does not need any further explanations, because it is similar to the implementation discussed in section 3.1.4, Generic Inserters and Extractors, where we used a fixed format string. Also, exceptions are propagated to the calling function and handled there, as in all previously discussed examples.

3.3.2.2.2 Implementing the Manipulator

For implementation of the manipulator `setfmt`, we take the same approach as before, and the entire implementation boils down to providing the manipulator helper class `setfmt_helper`, and in particular its static member function `setfmt_fct()`, which does the actual work. In its implementation we use the dynamic cast in the same way, and for the same reasons, as in the function `print_on()` above: If the pointer to the stream can be cast to a pointer to `datefmt<charT>`, then the manipulator sets the new format string in the stream. Otherwise, the manipulator does nothing. Here is the implementation:

```
template <class charT,class Traits = char_traits<charT> >
void setfmt_helper<charT,Traits>::setfmt_fct(ios_base& str, const charT* f)
{
    datefmt<charT> *p;

    if ((p = dynamic_cast<datefmt<charT>* > (&str)) != 0)
        p->fmt(f);
}
```

3.3.2.2.3 Using the New Functionality

Let us now see how the pieces fit together and try to write date objects to `cout`:

```
cout << "Hello World, this is the year " << setfmt("%Y") << date(1,1,2000)
     << endl;
```

The format string `"%Y"` produces the year with century as a decimal number, yet the output on the terminal is

```
Hello World, this is the year 1/1/00
```

Considering the implementation of the manipulator setfmt explained above, this should not surprise us. The predefined stream cout is not a date-formatting stream, but just a basic_ostream<char>, and in that case the manipulator does nothing. Consequently, setting the format string to "%Y" has no effect.

If we want to see an effect, we must use a date-formatting stream. We can use odatestream's adapting constructor and turn cout into a date-formatting stream, as in the example below:

```
odatestream<basic_ostream<char> > ods(cout);
ods << "Hello World, this is the year " << setfmt("%Y") << date(1,1,2000)
    << endl;
```

Now the expected output appears on the terminal:

```
Hello World, this is the year 2000
```

3.3.2.3 Summary

The stream classes of the standard IOStreams form a typical object-oriented class hierarchy, where derived classes extend the functionality of their base classes. For that reason, it seems only natural to add user-defined stream extensions by derivation. The main idea is to derive from one of the existing stream classes and extend it by adding new data and operations to the derived stream class. Let us recap the main aspects that are typical for stream extension via derivation.

1. Determining the right base class(es). For derivation of a new stream class, we must choose an appropriate base class from the standard IOStreams library. We do this because we want to reuse already existing stream functionality such as the parsing and formatting of numbers and strings, format control, stream-specific error indication, management of the locale, etc. As there is such a variety of stream classes defined in IOStreams, it is quite typical for more than one existing stream class to be extended with the new functionality.

In such a situation, it is a good idea to combine the use of inheritance with templates by making the base class the template argument of the derived class. In this way, the new functionality can be added to all potential base classes, and we gain an extra level of flexibility because the decision about the base class is deferred from the point of implementation to the point of template instantiation. For this reason, not only predefined stream classes, which are known at the time of implementation of the new derived class, but also user-defined stream classes, which are unknown to the implementer of the derived class, can serve as base classes for the new abstraction.

2. Use of dynamic cast. Typically, it is user-defined inserters, extractors, and manipulators, which use the new functionality that was added to the derived stream class, that are implemented. As these new operations will also work with the old stream classes and collaborate with existing operations, they usually take references to stream classes defined in IOStreams. This makes a downcast necessary from the base classes reference to the derived class reference, because otherwise the new functionality would not be accessible. It is advisable to perform the downcast as a dynamic cast rather than a static, reinterpret, or old-style cast. Only the dynamic cast checks whether the downcast is safe; the other casts perform the type conversion unconditionally and can lead to disaster.

Although the dynamic cast is safe, its use is often seen as a symptom of "poor programming style." In general, we agree, because a downcast can almost always be avoided by proper class design and use of virtual functions. In this case here, the design cannot be "fixed," because we derive from base classes that come from a standard library. We cannot add virtual functions to the existing stream classes in the IOStreams library, although we need two versions of an operation—one for the base class and one for the derived class that uses the new functionality. Use of the dynamic cast is the only viable and correct way of implementing the dual functionality.

3.3.3 Comparing Both Solutions—iword/pword versus Derivation

We have now seen two alternative techniques for extending the IOStreams library and adding new stream functionality. In this final section of the chapter, we want to compare these two solutions.

THE IWORD/PWORD TECHNIQUE

The first technique—use of iword/pword—is based on the following hooks that the standard IOStreams provides for stream extension:

- *The iword/pword fields.* They can be seen as a generic way to add new attributes to a stream.

- *The callback mechanism.* It can be seen as a generic way to add new functionality to the stream's destructor, `copyfmt()` (which is comparable to a stream assignment), and `imbue()` member functions.

- *The zero initialization.* The pre-initialization of iword/pword entries to 0 is a hook for explicit initialization, because the zero value can be used as an indicator that a field has not yet been initialized.

The acquisition of a new iword/pword index via `xalloc()` is central to this technique. Since `xalloc()` is a static member function defined in class `ios_base`, which is the base class of all stream classes, the iword/pword entry associated with the acquired index can be accessed by any stream object, independent of its specific type. As a consequence, an extension based on `xalloc()` and iword/pword is always a solution for all stream objects of all stream types. In most cases this can be seen as an advantage, in particular compared with a solution based on inheritance, where the extension is available only for stream objects of the derived type. With the inheritance-based extension technique, we had to use a relatively complex construct to achieve a similarly widespread effect: We had to make the stream base class a template argument of the derived stream class.

There are conceivable situations in which the added functionality will not be available to all streams independent of their type. One example is a manipulator that semantically has an effect on output of objects, but not on input of objects. Yet with the iword/pword technique, such a manipulator is applicable to input streams as well. Such a semantically nonsensical application to an input stream might not do any harm, but it is confusing in the case of bidirectional streams, because extraction of the manipulator from an input stream has no effect on any input operations, but affects subsequent output operations. If functionality is restricted to a certain set of stream types, a dynamic cast can be performed, much as in the inheritance-based solution, in order to check the stream type, and the functionality can be suppressed if necessary.

THE INHERITANCE-BASED TECHNIQUE

The second technique—the inheritance-based approach—is the classical object-oriented solution, which is supported by the C++ language directly:

- *New attributes* are expressed as data members in the derived class.

- *New functionality* is expressed as function members of the derived class.

Inheritance allows the restriction of the extension to a specific stream class, which is often more of a burden than a benefit, as we saw in our example of date formatting. We had to make the base class a template argument of the derived class in order to make the new functionality available to all desired stream types. This template technique renders the user of the new derived class responsible for choosing the "right" base class.

While new functionality can be added by means of derivation, none of the existing stream functionality can be redefined, because all stream member functions except the destructor are nonvirtual functions. As a result, the standard IOStreams framework has carved in stone how stream input and output is done in C++. It is, for instance, impossible to override the inserter for type `int` defined in `basic_ostream`. We cannot generate formats for integers, e.g., a textual representation of a number in words (42 being `"forty-two"`), by overwriting the respective inserter in a derived stream class. In the IOStreams framework, other provisions are made for allowing such variations: in order to print 42 as `"forty-two"` a new `num_put` facet can be defined.[17]

CONCLUSION

The iword/pword technique is the IOStreams-specific way to add new stream functionality. For users who are not familiar with the details of iword/pword and the stream callbacks, this is an unusual and maybe a slightly awkward approach. The inheritance-based technique, in contrast, is the typical object-oriented approach, as supported by C++. It has

---

17. See section 6.2.1, Numeric and Boolean Values, for further information about the facets for parsing and formatting numerical values; and section 8, User-Defined Facets, for an explanation on how to provide special purpose facets.

a certain amount of complexity, too, because the use of dynamic cast is necessary to access the newly added functionality, and the derived class will be templatized taking the base class type as a template argument for greater convenience and flexibility.

3.4 Adding Stream Buffer Functionality

In IOStreams, a stream buffer represents a connection to an external device. In this chapter we explain how additional external devices can be connected by adding new stream buffer classes. Functionality common to all stream buffer classes is factored out into the stream buffer base class template `basic_streambuf <class charT, class Traits>`. For each external device, a concrete stream buffer class must be derived from this base class. Already defined in IOStreams are the stream buffer classes for files and strings: `basic_filebuf` and `basic_stringbuf`. A detailed description of the stream buffer class hierarchy, the base class `basic_streambuf` and the concrete stream buffers `basic_filebuf` and `basic_stringbuf`, can be found in section 2.2, The Stream Buffer Classes. The topics discussed in this chapter require some degree of familiarity with the information contained in that section. We suggest that you read section 2.2 to gain a better understanding of the matters discussed in the following section.

In section 3.4.1, Deriving from the Stream Buffer Base Class, below, we explain how a connection to a new external device can be added to the IOStreams framework by deriving a new stream buffer class from the stream buffer base class `basic_streambuf`. As there are predefined stream buffer classes for files and strings, one might also consider derivation from the concrete stream buffer classes, in particular when their behavior is modified or enhanced in any way. Derivation from the concrete stream buffer classes raises a number of interesting issues that we discuss in section 3.4.2, Deriving from Concrete Stream Buffer Classes.

3.4.1 Deriving from the Stream Buffer Base Class

Deriving from the stream buffer base class `basic_streambuf` is an important extension point in IOStreams. It allows connection of user-specific devices to the IOStreams framework in such a way that the stream layer's rich functionality of formatting and parsing can be reused together with the newly connected device. Not only can additional hardware be made accessible through the stream buffer interface; software abstractions, too, can be hooked into the IOStreams framework. In fact, every abstraction that exhibits streamlike behavior and can serve as a source or sink of characters can be seen as an external device. Examples are (1) output to a certain window in a graphical user interface for display of trace information or input and (2) output to a socket or shared memory for communication between two processes. All that is required of the "device" is that it allow implementation of the required virtual member functions of a stream buffer class in terms of the device's intrinsic functionality.

The stream buffer interface that is known and used by the stream layer consists of the public member functions of the stream buffer base class `basic_streambuf`. These are nonvirtual functions, and they cannot be redefined by any derived class. Instead, the public nonvirtual member functions call protected virtual member functions, which can or must be redefined for a specific external device. The stream buffer base class `basic_streambuf` is not an abstract class, but provides a default functionality for the virtual functions. In general, the implementation of these functions in `basic_streambuf` is a sensible null operation, which can be used by derived stream buffer classes that do not want to override the respective virtual member function.

In the following, we discuss which of the virtual member functions must be redefined under which circumstances when a new stream buffer class is implemented. We start with the mandatory functionality of character transfer to and from the external device in section 3.4.1.1 and move on to the optional stream buffer functionality in section 3.4.1.2. To illustrate the character transfer functionality of a derived stream buffer class, we provide two examples: a buffered and an unbuffered external device. The optional stream buffer functionality is explained only in principle; we do not present any sample implementations.

3.4.1.1 Core Functionality of Stream Buffers: Character Transportation

The ability to transport characters between the stream and the external device is the core functionality of a stream buffer. For a derived stream buffer class, it is often the only functionality implemented. All other functionality is optional and simply inherited from the base class, which exhibits the default behavior of a nonoperational mode.

In principle, a stream buffer can take two different approaches: buffered or unbuffered character transport. An unbuffered stream buffer sounds like a contradiction in terms, but the idea of unbuffered character transport is that characters are transferred directly between the stream and the external device, without being buffered internally in the stream buffer object. The use of unbuffered character transport may well be sensible and can be motivated by comparing it with buffered character transport on the one hand and direct use of the device-specific I/O functionality on the other. In a buffered stream buffer, the internal character buffer represents the get and put areas at the same time, and the stream buffer must coordinate access to both areas. This mechanism is described in greater detail in section 2.2, The Stream Buffer Classes, and is a relatively complicated activity. Alternatively, characters may be transported to an external device independent of IOStreams by direct use of device-specific operations for transfer of characters. The downside of this approach is that all the convenient stream features, such as formatting and parsing, cannot be used, because the external device is not encapsulated into a stream buffer.

Below we explain derivation of user-defined stream buffer classes by discussing two sample implementations: (1) a stream buffer class for unbuffered character transport (in subsection 3.4.1.1.1) and (2) the more typical case of a buffered stream buffer class (in subsection 3.4.1.1.2). Before we turn to these examples, let us first recapitulate the principle of character transportation via stream buffers.

OUTPUT: TRANSPORTING CHARACTERS FROM THE STREAM TO THE EXTERNAL DEVICE

For output, a stream calls its stream buffer's public member function `sputc()`, which inserts a character into the stream buffer's internal character buffer. When the internal buffer is full, `sputc()` calls the protected virtual member `overflow()` to transfer the characters from the internal buffer to the external device. `overflow()` receives a character as an argument, which must also be stored somewhere. It is either written to the (now empty) internal buffer or transferred to the external device along with all the other characters from the internal buffer.

For a stream buffer that does unbuffered character transport, `sputc()` works in a slightly different way. It immediately calls `overflow()`, because there is no internal buffer into which the character could be stored, and `overflow()` transfers the character to the external device.

For flushing, a stream can call its stream buffer's public member function `pubsync()`, which directly calls the protected virtual member `sync()`. For a stream buffer that uses an internal buffer, `sync()` must perform a processing similar to that of `overflow()`, that is, transferring the content of the internal buffer to the external device. A stream buffer that does unbuffered character transport need not do anything in that situation.

A more detailed description of the way in which stream buffers perform output to the external device can be found in section 2.2, The Stream Buffer Classes.

INPUT: TRANSPORTING CHARACTERS FROM THE EXTERNAL DEVICE TO THE STREAM

For input, a stream calls its stream buffer's public member function `sgetc()` in order to receive the next character from the internal buffer. If no character is available in the internal buffer, `sgetc()` calls the protected virtual member `underflow()`, which fills the internal buffer with characters from the external device and returns the first new character in the internal buffer.

For a stream buffer that does unbuffered character transport, `sgetc()` directly invokes `underflow()`, which then fetches the next character from the external device and returns it.

`sgetc()` and `underflow()` do not consume the character that they provide, i.e., the next call to `underflow()` will return the same character as before. The stream buffer class contains a pair of functions similar to `sgetc()` and `underflow()`, which in contrast do consume the character. These functions are `sbumpc()` and `uflow()`. `uflow()` returns a different character each time it is invoked.

For putback support, a stream calls its stream buffer's public member function `sungetc()` or `sputbackc(char_type c)`. `sungetc()` makes an already consumed character available again; `sputbackc(char_type c)` makes the character c available in place of the last consumed character. Both functions have an impact on the input processing of a stream buffer. For instance, a call to `sgetc()`, which means providing the next character without consuming it, must have the same effect as a call to sbumpc() followed by sungetc(), which means first consuming the character and putting it back afterwards.

The stream base class's implementation of sungetc() works without any support from a derived stream buffer, as long as it can reposition the get area's next pointer one step back. This, of course, is not possible if the next pointer is already positioned at the beginning of the internal buffer, or if the stream does not have an internal buffer. In such situations, pbackfail() is invoked and receives traits_type::eof() as an argument. sputbackc(char_type c) calls pbackfail() with c as an argument whenever c does not equal the previously consumed character; otherwise it performs the same operations as sungetc().

A more detailed description of the way in which stream buffers perform input from the external device and support putback of characters can be found in section 2.2, The Stream Buffer Classes.

THE DEFAULT BEHAVIOR PROVIDED BY THE STREAM BASE CLASS

The stream base class basic_streambuf already implements all the functions described above and provides a default behavior for them. Both the base class versions of overflow() and underflow() are implemented so that they do no more than returning traits_type::eof(), which has the semantics of indicating that the end of the stream has been reached. The base class version of uflow() calls underflow(); if that call succeeds, i.e., returns a value other than traits_type::eof(), then uflow() moves the get area's next pointer one step further to indicate that the character has been consumed. The base class version of sync() does nothing but return 0, which indicates that the function executed successfully.

While the behavior of overflow(), underflow(), uflow(), and sync() is obviously not sufficient to establish a working connection between a stream and an external device, it supplies a nonoperational mode implementation, which is in line with the implementation requirements for each of these functions. This way, a unidirectional stream buffer can be built by redefining only the functions relevant for one transport direction; all operations for the other transport direction would automatically be in a well-defined, nonoperational mode.

OVERRIDING THE DEFAULT BEHAVIOR IN USER-DEFINED STREAM BUFFER CLASSES

With this overview of the character transportation functions of the stream buffer classes, together with their default behavior defined in basic_streambuf, we can now determine which protected virtual functions must be redefined for a user-defined stream buffer class. Let us distinguish between stream buffers that do unbuffered character transport and stream buffers that have an internal character buffer.

UNBUFFERED STREAM BUFFER. For an unbuffered stream buffer we must redefine the following protected stream buffer functions:

For the output direction: Only `overflow()` must be redefined. `sync()` need not be redefined, because there is no internal buffer, hence nothing to synchronize.

For the input direction: `underflow()` must be redefined. Also, `uflow()` must be redefined, because the default implementation moves the next pointer of the get area, and this is not possible in the unbuffered case, because there is no internal buffer area and, therefore, no next pointer.

As mentioned above, input functions and putback support are related. A call to `sbumpc()` followed by `sungetc()` must have the same effect as invocation of `sgetc()`. For this reason, we must also implement `pbackfail()`, because it is called by `sungetc()`. The default implementation of `pbackfail()` does not work, because it produces a decrement in the next pointer, which is not possible in the unbuffered case.

BUFFERED STREAM BUFFER. For a buffered stream buffer, we must redefine the following protected stream buffer functions:

For the output direction: `overflow()` and `sync()` must be redefined.

For the input direction: `underflow()` must be redefined. `uflow()` need not be redefined, because the default implementation provided by `basic_streambuf` works perfectly well.

`pbackfail()` must be redefined in order to support `sputbackc(char_type c)` with a character c different from the previously extracted one, that is, when `pbackfail()` must actually write to the internal buffer and a simple decrement of the next pointer does not suffice.

In the following two sections, we show examples for each of the two types of stream buffers discussed above, the unbuffered and the buffered case.

3.4.1.1.1 Stream Buffer for Unbuffered Character Transport

To keep the examples comprehensible and generic, we factored out the device-specific functionality into two functions rather than mixing it into the actual stream buffer implementation. In this way, you can reuse the example for an implementation of an unbuffered stream buffer by simply overwriting these two device-specific functions.

The two functions transport a single character from or to the external device. In our example the external device is a file, and we implement the functions in terms of the operating system functions `read()` and `write()` on UNIX platforms or `_read()` and `_write()` for the Microsoft operating systems. For the sake of simplicity, the example is restricted to character I/O for narrow character, that is, the character type `char`. Also, we did not consider any character code conversion that might be necessary before or after character transport. If needed, they can be included in the implementation of the two functions. Here are the suggested implementations:

```
int char_to_device(char c)
{
    if (write (1, &c, 1) != 1)
        return -1;
```

```
      else
          return 0;
}

int char_from_device(char *c)
{
      if(read(0, c, 1) != 1)
          return -1;
      else
          return 0;
}
```

Below is the definition of the unbuffered stream buffer class:

```
template <class charT, class traits >
class unbuffered_streambuf : public basic_streambuf<charT, traits>
{
      public:
          unbuffered_streambuf() : takeFromBuf(false) {}

      protected:
          int_type overflow(int_type c = traits_type::eof());
          int_type uflow();
          int_type underflow();
          int_type pbackfail(int_type c);

      private:
          char_type charBuf;
          bool takeFromBuf;

          // prohibit copying and assignment18
          unbuffered_streambuf(const unbuffered_streambuf&);
          unbuffered_streambuf& operator=(const unbuffered_streambuf&);
};
```

As discussed above, the virtual functions overflow(), underflow(), uflow(), and pbackfail() must be redefined in the unbuffered case. There are also some private data members needed, whose semantics we will explain later. Let us discuss first output and then input in conjunction with putback support.

---

18. We declare the copy constructor and the copy assignment operator private without defining them in order to make these operations inaccessible. The intent is to prohibit copy operations on stream buffers, because the semantics of the copying stream buffer objects are generally undefined. See also section 2.2.2, The Stream Buffer Abstraction.

CHARACTER OUTPUT

For transport of characters to the external device, `overflow()` must be overridden. Here is its implementation:

```
template <class charT, class traits >
unbuffered_streambuf<charT,traits>::int_type
int_type unbuffered_streambuf<charT,traits>::overflow(int_type c)
{
  if (!traits_type::eq_int_type(c, traits_type::eof()))
  {
    if (char_to_device(traits_type::to_char_type(c)) < 0)
      return traits_type::eof();
    else
      return c;
  }
  return traits_type::not_eof(c);
}
```

When `overflow()` receives a character different from `traits_type::eof()`, it must transfer this character to the external device. It does so by invoking the device-specific function `char_to_device()`, which in our example boils down to invocation of `write()`.[19] Depending on the success of this operation, `overflow()` returns `traits_type::eof()` if the operation failed or any other value (in our implementation the character that has been transported) if the operation succeeded.

When `overflow()` receives a parameter that equals `traits_type::eof()`, it must usually transfer characters contained in the internal buffer to the external device. In this case, where there is no internal buffer, we do nothing, but return `traits_type::not_eof(c)` to indicate that the operation was successful.

Note that the error handling in our sample implementation is only rudimentary. In a real implementation, exceptions should be used to indicate device-specific errors and `traits_type::eof()` should be used only to indicate the end of the stream. Instead, we indicate *all* errors by means of `traits_type::eof()`, because there is little explanatory value in showing a detailed error indication concept for `read()` and `write()` when we aim to explain stream buffer implementations.

CHARACTER INPUT AND PUTBACK SUPPORT

The implementation of the input direction is more complicated than the output direction. Here we must redefine three virtual member functions: `underflow()`, `uflow()`, and

---

19. Note that we convert the character received by means of the traits function `to_char_type()` before we pass it to the device specific output function. This is necessary because the argument that `overflow()` receives can be either a valid character of type `char_type` or `traits_type::eof()`, which is of type `int_type`. For conversion between these two types, the traits provide conversion functions `to_char_type()` and `to_int_type()`. More about the traits member functions can be found in section 2.3.2, Character Traits.

pbackfail(). All three functions work with the private members charBuf and takeFromBuf, whose meaning we have left open so far. Let us see what these two private data members represent.

As we already know, underflow() does not consume the character that it transfers; that is, it does not change the stream position. As a result, successive calls to underflow() must all return the same value referred to by the current stream position. Some external devices might allow the same character to be fetched from the device repeatedly, while others will not. For a device-independent implementation, we assume the worst and store the character in charBuf once we get it from the device, so that we do not have to fetch it twice. takeFromBuf is a Boolean value that is true when the character in charBuf has not been consumed and false otherwise. If takeFromBuf is true, then the next call to underflow() or uflow() must return the character stored in charBuf instead of fetching a new character from the external device.

With these explanations in mind, the implementations of underflow() and uflow() are straightforward. Here is the implementation of underflow():

```
template <class charT, class traits >
unbuffered_streambuf<charT,traits>::int_type
int_type unbuffered_streambuf<charT,traits>::underflow()
{
  if (takeFromBuf)
  {
    return traits_type::to_int_type(charBuf);
  }
  else
  {
    char_type c;

    if (char_from_device(&c) < 0)
      return traits_type::eof();
    else
    {
      takeFromBuf = true;
      charBuf = c;
      return traits_type::to_int_type(c);
    }
  }
}
```

underflow() returns the character stored in charBuf, if takeFromBuf is true. Otherwise, it gets a new character from the external device via the device-specific function char_from_device(), sets takeFromBuf to true, and returns the newly read character.

Here is the implementation of `uflow()`:

```
int_type uflow()
{
  if (takeFromBuf)
  {
    takeFromBuf = false;
    return traits_type::to_int_type(charBuf);
  }
  else
  {
    char_type c;

    if (char_from_device(&c) < 0)
       return traits_type::eof();
    else
    {
       charBuf = c;
       return traits_type::to_int_type(c);
    }
  }
}
```

`uflow()` does the same as `underflow()`, except that it always sets `takeFromBuf` to `false` in order to indicate that the character has been consumed.

Here is the implementation of `pbackfail()`:

```
template <class charT, class traits >
unbuffered_streambuf<charT,traits>::int_type
unbuffered_streambuf<charT,traits>::uflow()
{
  if (!takeFromBuf)
  {
    if (!traits_type::eq_int_type(c, traits_type::eof()))
       charBuf = traits_type::to_char_type(c);

    takeFromBuf = true;

    return traits_type::to_int_type(charBuf);
  }
    else
  {
    return traits_type::eof();
  }
}
```

pbackfail() sets takeFromBuffer to true, if it was false, which makes the character stored in charBuf available again. If the character passed to pbackfail() as an argument does not equal traits_type::eof(), the character is stored in charBuf. If takeFromBuffer has already been true, pbackfail() cannot make a new character available. To indicate this failure, it returns traits_type::eof().

As already mentioned above, the error handling presented here is somewhat rudimentary, in order to keep the example concise. The virtual functions underflow() and uflow() are allowed to throw exceptions. In a real implementation, exceptions should be used to indicate device-specific errors that occur during unsuccessful input operations. traits_type::eof() should be returned only when the end of the stream is reached.

Eventually, here is the code that can be used for testing the new stream buffer. It demonstrates that all the stream facilities like formatting and parsing work with the new stream buffer.

```
int main()
{
  unbuffered_streambuf<char, char_traits<char> > mybuf;
  iostream mystream(&mybuf);

  cout << "Test Begin !!!" << endl;

  mystream << "Hello World !" << endl;

  // Test: extracting numeric value
  cout<< "Type in an integer: ";
  int testInt = 0;
  mystream >> testInt;
  if (!mystream)
      cout << "Error: " << mystream.rdstate() << endl;
  mystream << "Echo: " << testInt << endl;
  mystream.clear();

  // Test: extracting character sequence
  cout<< "Type in a character: ";
  char testChar = '\0';
  mystream >> testChar;
  if (!mystream)
      cout << "Error: " << mystream.rdstate() << endl;
  mystream << "Echo: " << testChar << endl;
  mystream.clear();
```

```
// Test: unformatted input
cout<< "Type in an character: ";
char testC = '\0';
mystream.get(testC);
if (!mystream)
   cout << "Error: " << mystream.rdstate() << endl;
mystream << "Echo: " << testC << endl;
mystream.clear();

cout << "Test End !!!" << endl;
return 0;
}
```

3.4.1.1.2 A Stream Buffer for Buffered Character Transport

Implementing a stream buffer class that uses an internal character buffer is significantly more complex than the unbuffered case. For this reason, we split the discussion of the buffered case into three portions. We discuss first output, then input, and finally bidirectional stream buffers.

Again, we factored out the device-specific functionality into two functions rather than mixing it into the actual stream buffer implementation. The two functions transport a sequence of characters from or to the external device. In our example the external device is a file again, and we implement the functions in terms of the operating system functions read() and write() on UNIX platforms or _read() and _write() for the Microsoft operating systems. For the sake of simplicity, the example is restricted to character I/O for narrow character, that is, the character type char. Also, we did not consider character code conversion, which would be added to the implementation if necessary before or after character transport.

Here are the implementations of the two device-specific functions:

```
int buffer_to_device (const char* c, int n)
{
   if (write(1, c, n) != n)
      return -1;
   else
      return 0;
}

int buffer_from_device (char* c, int n)
{
   return read(0, c, n);
}
```

A UNIDIRECTIONAL STREAM BUFFER FOR BUFFERED OUTPUT

Here is an implementation of a unidirectional buffered stream buffer that supports only the output direction:

```
template <class charT, class traits>
class outbuf : public basic_streambuf<charT, traits>
{
   public:
      outbuf();
      ~outbuf();

   protected:
      streamsize xsputn(const char_type *s, streamsize n);
      int_type overflow (int_type c = traits_type::eof());
      int sync();

   private:
      static const int bufSize = 16;
      char_type buffer[bufSize];

      int buffer_out();

      // prohibit copying and assignment[20]
      outbuf(const outbuf&);
      outbuf & operator=(const outbuf&);
};
```

The essential attribute of a buffered stream buffer is a character array that serves as an internal buffer. It is made a private member together with an integer constant that defines the size of this array.

Let us see what the constructor and destructor must do. Here is the implementation of the constructor:

```
template <class charT, class traits>
outbuf<charT,traits>::outbuf()
{
  setp(buffer, buffer + bufSize);
}
```

The constructor installs the private character array as the internal buffer, so that the functionality implemented in `basic_streambuf` uses this array as the put area. This is achieved by calling `basic_streambuf`'s protected member function `setp(char_type*, char_type*)`. Its two parameters are the beginning and the end of the character array that serve as the put area.[21]

---

20. We declare the copy constructor and the copy assignment operator private without defining them in order to make these operations inaccessible. The intent is to prohibit copy operations on stream buffers because the semantics of the copying stream buffer objects are generally undefined. See also section 2.2.2, The Stream Buffer Abstraction.

21. If no buffer array is installed via `setp()`, the default setting initialized by `basic_streambuf` is used; it indicates that no buffer is available. This is what we implicitly took advantage of in the unbuffered case.

Here is the implementation of the destructor:

```
template <class charT, class traits>
outbuf<charT,traits>::~outbuf()
{
  sync();
}
```

The standard does not specify the functionality of `basic_streambuf`'s destructor. For this reason, we override the base class functionality so that the destructor calls `sync()`. In other words, we force the stream buffer to empty its internal buffer array to the external device before it is destroyed.

Let us see how `sync()` is implemented:

```
template <class charT, class traits>
int outbuf<charT,traits>::sync()
{
  return buffer_out();
}
```

In our example, `sync()` calls the private member function `buffer_out()`, which is implemented as follows:

```
template <class charT, class traits>
int outbuf<charT,traits>::buffer_out()
{
  int cnt = pptr() - pbase();
  int retval = buffer_to_device(buffer, cnt);

  pbump(-cnt);
  return retval;
}
```

`buffer_out()` calculates the number of characters currently stored in the buffer, calls the device-specific I/O function `buffer_to_device()`, and repositions the next pointer of the put area by calling `pbump()`.

Another function besides `sync()` that handles output to the external device is `overflow()`:

```
template <class charT, class traits>
int_type outbuf<charT,traits>::overflow (int_type c)
{
  if (buffer_out() < 0)
  {
    return traits_type::eof();
  }
  else
```

```
    else
    {
      if (!traits_type::eq_int_type(c, traits_type::eof()))
        return sputc(c);
      else
        return traits_type::not_eof(c);
    }
}
```

Like `sync()`, `overflow()` first calls the private member function `buffer_out()` to write the content of the buffer array to the external device. Then it writes the value that it has received as an argument to internal buffer array by calling its own public member `sputc()`, if the value does not equal `traits_type::eof()`; otherwise it returns immediately.

Note that the error handling of both functions, `sync()` and `overflow()`, is again slightly oversimplified. Both functions return `traits_type::eof()` in case of any error. A more specific error handling, which we deliberately omitted to keep the example concise, would return `traits_type::eof()` only when the end of the stream is reached and indicate other errors by throwing appropriate exceptions.

The last virtual function that is redefined is `xsputn()`. While `sync()` and `overflow()` must be redefined for a user-defined buffered output stream buffer, overriding `xsputn()` is optional. A derived stream buffer class can redefine it, when the handling of a character sequence, as opposed to a single character, can be optimized. Here is its implementation:

```
template <class charT, class traits>
streamsize outbuf<charT,traits>::xsputn(const char_type *s, streamsize n)
{
  if (n < epptr() - pptr())
  {
    memcpy(pptr(),s, n * sizeof(char_type));
    pbump(n);
    return n;
  }
  else
  {
    for (streamsize i=0; i<n; i++)
    {
      if (traits_type::eq_int_type(sputc(s[i]), traits_type::eof()))
          return i;
    }
    return n;
  }
}
```

The implementation of xsputn() is not overly sophisticated; if the character sequence received as an argument fits into the stream buffer's internal character array, the sequence is copied to the internal array. Otherwise, the characters from the received sequence are transferred one by one via the public member function sputc().

Here is the code that we used for testing the new buffered output stream buffer class. It demonstrates that the stream features for formatting also work with the new stream buffer class (the integer literal 15 is printed in its hexadecimal representation):

```
int main()
{
  outbuf<char, char_traits<char> > mybuf;
  ostream mystream(&mybuf);

  cout << "Test Begin !!!" << endl;

  mystream << "Hello World !" << endl;
  mystream << "formatting still works: " << hex << 15 << endl;

  cout << "Test End !!!" << endl;
  return 0;
}
```

A UNIDIRECTIONAL STREAM BUFFER FOR BUFFERED INPUT

Let us now explore the input direction. Here is an implementation of a unidirectional buffered stream buffer that supports only the input of character from an external device:

```
template <class charT, class traits>
class inbuf : public basic_streambuf<charT, traits>
{
  public:
      inbuf();

  protected:
      int_type underflow();
      int_type pbackfail(int_type c);

  private:
      static const streamsize bufSize = 16;
      static const streamsize pbSize = 4;
      char_type buffer[bufSize];
```

```
    int buffer_in();

    // prohibit copying and assignment
    inbuf(const inbuf&);
    inbuf & operator=(const inbuf&);
};
```

The private data members are basically the same as for the output stream buffer. A character array is needed to serve as the internal buffer, along with an integer constant that represents the size of the array. For the input buffer, we also need to specify the size of the putback area, that is, the number of characters copied to the beginning of the internal buffer by `underflow()` in order to allow successful calls to `sputbackc()` after refilling the internal buffer. Details of this technique are described in section 2.2.4, File Stream Buffers.

The constructor must install the private character array as the get area. Here is its implementation:

```
template <class charT, class traits>
inbuf<charT,traits>::inbuf()
{
    setg(buffer+pbSize, buffer+pbSize, buffer+pbSize);
}
```

`setg()` is the function that tells the base class which buffer will be used. Its arguments are the beginning of the get area, the next read position in the get area, and the get area's end position.[22]

For the input direction we must redefine the virtual function `underflow()`. Here is its implementation:

```
template <class charT, class traits>
inbuf<charT,traits::int_type inbuf<charT,traits>::underflow()
{
  if (gptr() < egptr())
    return traits_type::to_int_type(*gptr());

  if (buffer_in() < 0)
    return traits_type::eof();
```

---

22. If no buffer array is installed via `setg()`, the default setting initialized by `basic_streambuf` is used; it indicates that no buffer is available. This is what we implicitly took advantage of in the unbuffered case.

```
    else
        return traits_type::to_int_type(*gptr());
}
```

First, `underflow()` checks if the next pointer has reached the end pointer. If not, it returns the character to which the next pointer refers. Otherwise, it must refill the internal character buffer with characters from the external device. In order to do this, `underflow()` calls the private member function `buffer_in()`. Here is the implementation of `buffer_in()`:

```
template <class charT, class traits>
int inbuf<charT,traits>::buffer_in()
{
    // determine number of putback characters
    streamsize numPutbacks = min(gptr() - eback(), pbSize);

    memmove(buffer + (pbSize-numPutbacks) * sizeof(char_type),
            gptr() - numPutbacks * sizeof(char_type),
            numPutbacks * sizeof(char_type));

    int retval = buffer_from_device(buffer + pbSize * sizeof(char_type),
                                    bufSize - pbSize);

    if (retval <= 0)
    {
        setg(0,0,0);
        return -1;
    }
    else
    {
        setg(buffer + pbSize - numPutbacks,
             buffer + pbSize, buffer + pbSize + retval);
        return retval;
    }
}
```

The private member function `buffer_in()` copies the number of characters that will remain in the internal character buffer from the end to the beginning of the array. Afterwards, it fills the rest of the internal buffer with characters from the external device by calling `buffer_from_device()`. Then it adjusts the get area pointer so that the begin position refers to the beginning of the character array, the next position refers to the first character read from the external device, and the end pointer points after the last character read from the external device. If an error is returned from `buffer_from_device()`, `buffer_in()` invalidates the get area by setting all get area pointers to 0.

Again, the error handling in `underflow()` is oversimplified in that it always returns `traits_type::eof()` to indicate failure, regardless of the source of the error. A more sophisticated error handling would return `traits_type::eof()` only when the end of the stream is reached, and in all other cases an exception would be thrown, which describes the error more precisely.

For the input direction, we must also redefine `pbackfail()`:

```
template <class charT, class traits>
int_type inbuf<charT,traits>::pbackfail(int_type c)
{
  if (gptr() != eback())
  {
    gbump(-1);
    if (!traits_type::eq_int_type(c, traits_type::eof()))
        *(gptr()) = traits_type::to_char_type(c);
    return traits_type::not_eof(c);
  }
  else
    return traits_type::eof();
}
```

Our implementation of `pbackfail()` handles a situation where the last consumed character can be made available from the internal buffer array. This is the case if the get area's next pointer does not point to the beginning of the get area. In such a situation, `pbackfail()` sets the get pointer one position back by calling `gbump(-1)` and writes the character received as an argument to this position, unless the character equals `traits_type::eof()`.

In our implementation, `pbackfail()` does not handle the situation where the last consumed stream cannot be made available in the internal buffer area, but must be fetched again from the external device. We refrained from handling this situation, because there is no device-independent solution for this. The canonical approach would be to reload the last consumed character from the external device into the buffer area. However, some devices might not offer such a functionality. Consider, for instance, input from a keyboard device; once a character is read, it cannot be made available again.

Eventually, here is the code that can be used to test the new buffered input stream buffer class.

```
int main()
{
  inbuf<char, char_traits<char> > mybuf;
  istream mystream(&mybuf);
  int testInt = 0;

  cout << "Test Begin !!! - type in an integer: " << endl;
```

```
mystream >> testInt;

if (!mystream)
   cout << "Error: " << mystream.rdstate() << endl;
else
   cout << "Echo: " << testInt << endl;

mystream.putback('3');

mystream >> testInt;

if (!mystream)
   cout << "Error: " << mystream.rdstate() << endl;
else
   cout << "Echo: " << testInt << endl;

cout << "Test End !!!" << endl;
return 0;
}
```

A BIDIRECTIONAL STREAM BUFFER FOR BUFFERED INPUT AND OUTPUT

In order to implement a stream buffer that can handle input and output processing, it is not sufficient to combine all the members shown in the two example implementations above. This is because the get and put areas are not independent of each other, but need some coordination.

There is no general solution for the coordination between the get and put areas. A solution depends on the device as well as on the requirements regarding how and when the stream buffer can be switched from output to input and vice versa. For a more detailed discussion, let us have a look at the standard stream buffers: string buffer and file buffer.

A string buffer can be switched at any time from output operations to input operations and vice versa. Consequently, any character transferred to the string buffer is immediately afterwards available for reading from the same string stream buffer. The string buffer has this property because the external device and the internal character buffer are identical. Both the put and the get areas refer to the same internal character array at the same time. The coordination between the get and the put areas in string stream buffers is described in greater detail in section 2.2.3, String Stream Buffers.

For a user-defined stream buffer that is associated with small external devices, this model can be reused with some minor modifications: The entire device is cached in the buffer's internal character array. Except for explicit synchronization via the public member function pubsync() or when the buffer is deleted and sync() is called implicitly, all input and output operations are performed only on the internal character array.

A file buffer can be switched only under certain conditions from output processing to input processing or vice versa. These conditions put the file buffer into some kind of neutral state, from which I/O processing can be started in any direction. The details are described in section 2.2.4, File Stream Buffers. As a consequence of this usage model, the file buffer's internal character array typically holds, at any given point in time, either the get or the put area, or none of them. When the file buffer is engaged in input processing, it is the get area that is held in the internal array; when the file buffer does output processing, it is the put area; when the file buffer is in the neutral state, the internal character array holds none of the areas. For a user-defined stream buffer, a similar model can be used whenever it is possible to define an adequate set of conditions that put the stream buffer into a neutral state.

These are two examples for the coordination of get and put areas, derived from the models used for the concrete stream buffers of the standard library. Other solutions are possible, as long as they fit into the IOStreams' framework and are in line with proper usage of the respective external device that the new stream buffer class represents.

3.4.1.2 Optional Functionality of Stream Buffers

Having discussed the core functionality of stream buffers, let us now turn to the features that a stream buffer can, but need not, provide. We do not show any example implementations for the optional functionality that we are going to discuss in this section. The reason for this is simply that these features are either highly device-specific (like stream positioning), so that any implementation would not have much explanatory value in general, or that the features are so vaguely specified by the standard (like setbuf()) that any implementation would be misleading.

STREAM POSITIONING—seekoff() AND seekpos()

The member functions that must be redefined in order to activate stream positioning in a derived stream buffer class are seekoff() and seekpos(). As usual, the base class basic_streambuf defines the default behavior for derived stream buffers that do not override these virtual functions. The default behavior is the same for both functions: They do nothing, but return an invalid stream position, which indicates that positioning is not supported.

There is no general rule for the implementation of stream positioning in a stream buffer derived from basic_streambuf. Positioning is a highly device-specific feature; some devices do not support positioning at all, while others do, but only in a very specific way. The C++ standard does not say anything about the way in which stream buffer classes other than basic_filebuf and basic_stringbuf should implement positioning. This degree of latitude means that you are basically free to implement whatever behavior seems reasonable, provided that the underlying device supports any kind of positioning. It also implies that you should document the behavior of your stream buffer implementation, because IOStreams does not establish a common understanding of the way in which positioning works.

ESTIMATING THE CHARACTERS AVAILABLE FOR INPUT—showmanyc()

The virtual member function showmanyc() (pronounced "ess-how-many-see," not "show-manic") returns an estimation of the number of characters that are at least available for input, or -1. If the returned value is positive, then at least the indicated number of characters can be made available by one or more calls to underflow(). If the operation returns -1, calls to underflow() and uflow() will fail. The intent is not only to know in advance that these calls will not return traits_type::eof(), but that they will return "immediately." Or, to put it more simply, the purpose of this operation is to check if characters are available on the external device, which can be read by underflow() or uflow() without waiting.

There is no typical way in which showmanyc() can be implemented, because the required information (the estimate of the characters available for input) is highly device-specific. If you have no idea how to estimate the available characters, it is OK not to redefine basic_streambuf's implementation, which always returns 0.

THE ALMOST SEMANTIC-FREE FUNCTION—setbuf()

The virtual member function setbuf() is a rather peculiar stream buffer member. Its semantics are basically undefined. For string stream buffers, the semantics of setbuf() are implementation-defined, except that setbuf(0,0) has no effect. For file stream buffers, too, only the semantics of setbuf(0,0) are defined: If setbuf(0,0) is called on a stream before any I/O has occurred on that stream, the stream becomes unbuffered, meaning that characters are directly transported to and from the file system. Otherwise the results are implementation-defined.

However, the specifications of setbuf() for basic_filebuf and basic_stringbuf hardly impose any requirements on the semantics of setbuf() in other stream buffer types. At best, the general semantics can be defined as device- and, in the case of user-defined stream buffer types, implementation-specific.

The lack of any requirements frees you to redefine setbuf() for just about any purpose and in any way that fits into the predefined interface of setbuf().

REACTING TO THE ATTACHMENT OF A NEW LOCALE—imbue()

The idea behind imbue() is different from all virtual member functions that we have discussed so far. imbue() is similar to a callback function, and it is called whenever a new locale is attached to the stream buffer via its public member function pubimbue(). The base class implementation of imbue() in basic_streambuf does nothing. A user-derived stream buffer overrides imbue() if it wants to act upon the setting of a new locale. You would only consider redefinition of imbue() when the functionality of the new stream buffer depends on the locale in any way.

3.4.1.3 Providing New Stream Classes Along with New Stream Buffer Classes

When you have defined a new derived stream buffer class, you will usually not want to use it directly. More typical is the indirect use of a stream buffer through a stream object, because streams have a richer and more convenient interface. For this reason you will often construct a new stream buffer object and use this stream buffer to create a new stream. To make this task less tedious, a new stream type can be defined that automatically creates a stream buffer of the newly defined type and uses it.

Additionally, new stream buffer classes sometimes have additional device-specific operations. File stream buffers are a typical example; they have functions for opening and closing the underlying file. A stream class that is defined in relation to a new stream buffer class can act as a facade[23] for the device-specific functionality provided by the stream buffer. For instance, the file stream classes are facades for their file buffers; they offer the same functionality (open and close) in their interface and implement it by forwarding it to the file buffer that they contain.

If you are considering deriving a new stream class along with a new stream buffer class, you might want to take a look at section 3.3.2, Creating New Stream Classes by Derivation.

3.4.2 Deriving from Concrete Stream Buffer Classes

Experience shows that is not at all easy to extend the concrete stream buffer classes in IOStreams, `basic_filebuf` and `basic_stringbuf`, in such a way that the resulting abstraction is portable, that is, independent of any specific implementation of the standard IOStreams library. While the C++ standard precisely specifies the public interface of the concrete stream buffer classes, it does not address issues that are relevant for extending the concrete stream buffer classes. This omission is intentional, because the specification of implementation details would prevent library implementers from building "optimized" solutions. The obverse of the coin is that the concrete stream buffer classes can hardly be extended in a portable way, because different standard library vendors might have implemented their concrete stream buffers in different ways, and it is difficult not to rely on any implementation details.

A typical example of areas where the standard allows variations can be found in `basic_stringbuf`: the memory allocation policy for the internal character buffer and the adjustment of the get area's end pointer are unspecified. For further details see section 2.2.3, String Stream Buffers. Yet a string stream buffer derived from `basic_stringbuf` might need to know about these details. In such situations, it is tempting to examine the IOStreams implementation at hand and mistakenly equate the approach taken there with the standard way of doing it. Keep in mind that hardly anything is specified for the implementation of the concrete stream buffers, and it is prudent to be careful and to avoid false assumptions. Let us try to extract some advice for safely extending the concrete stream buffers in a portable way.

Orthogonal functionality can safely be added to a concrete stream buffer without imposing any portability constraints, because it does not rely on any stream buffer fea-

---

23. A facade is a structural design pattern, described in *Design Patterns—Elements of Reusable Object-Oriented Software* by Gamma, Helm, Johnson, and Vlissides (also known as the gang-of-four [GOF] book).

tures. All nonvirtual member functions defined in `basic_streambuf` are precisely specified and do not allow the library implementers much latitude. Hence, additional functionality does not impair the portability of your stream buffer class, as long as it can be implemented in terms of stream buffer functions that are not redefined in the concrete stream buffer class. In all other situations, it is hard to come up with a comprehensive set of rules for staying independent of any implementation-specific stream buffer features. Often, you have to investigate in detail, whether you are in danger of relying on implementation-dependent features or not.

To understand the portability problem better, let us take a look at a simple example. Say we want to extend the string buffer class so that it is able to determine how often a certain character occurs in the not-yet-consumed input sequence. We derive a new string stream buffer class from `basic_stringbuf` and add a new public member function called `scontainc()`. Here is its implementation:

```
template <class charT,
          class traits = char_traits<charT>,
          class Allocator = allocator<charT> >
class my_stringbuf : public basic_stringbuf<charT, traits, Allocator>
{
   public:
      int_type scontainc(char_type c)
      {
         int_type cnt = 0;

         if (gptr() == egptr())
            underflow();

         for (int_type i = 0; gptr() != 0 && gptr()+i != egptr(); i++)
         {
            if (*(gptr()+i) == c)
               cnt++;
         }
         return cnt;
      }
      my_stringbuf(){}
   private:
      // prohibit copying and assignment
      my_stringbuf(const my_stringbuf&);
      my_stringbuf& operator=(const my_stringbuf&);
};
```

The function `scontainc()` steps through the sequence of available characters in the get area, from the current next pointer to the end of the get area, and examines every single character for counting the occurrences of c. As you can see, it uses only nonvirtual member functions implemented in `basic_streambuf`, namely `gptr()` and `egptr()`, to determine the get area. Both functions are well defined. Yet `scontainc()` is in danger of being implemented in a nonportable way.

For `basic_stringbuf`, it is not specified when and how the get area's end pointer is adjusted. All we know is that characters that have been written to the string stream buffer can be read from the buffer; that is, ultimately the get area's end pointer must point to the same position as the put area's next pointer. In section 2.2.3, String Stream Buffers, we pointed out that the adjustment of the get area's end pointer can be done immediately, during output processing in `overflow()`, or can be delayed to the beginning of input processing in `underflow()`.

For the sake of portability, we must not make any assumptions regarding any implementation details. Consequently, we cannot assume that the get area's end pointer has already been adjusted by a preceding output operation. Instead, we must be prepared to handle a situation in which characters are available, thanks to previous write operations, although the get area's end pointer indicates that the get area is empty because the pointer has not yet been adjusted. To force adjustment of the get area's end pointer, we must call `underflow()`. In this way, we have prepared `scontainc()` for both types of implementations. In an implementation that defers pointer adjustment, we trigger the adjustment by checking for an empty get area and calling `underflow()`; in an implementation that does pointer adjustment immediately, the get area will not be empty if characters are still available, and `underflow()` will not be invoked unnecessarily.

This truly simple extension of a string stream buffer already demonstrates how carefully a derived class must be implemented to be portable. By and large, portable extensions of the concrete stream buffer classes are difficult to achieve.

PART II

Internationalization

This part of the book explains the internationalization and localization features in the standard C++ library. The standard C++ library encompasses *locales* and *facets.* These abstractions are used for internationalization of C++ programs.

Here is an overview of the chapters in this part:

Chapter 4, "Introduction to Internationalization and Localization," introduces internationalization in general. It explains what internationalization is and contrasts it with localization. The paramount problem of internationalization stems from differences in cultural conventions, such as language, numbers, currency, time, date, ordering of words, and character encodings.

This chapter should be read by readers who are not familiar with internationalization and seek a general overview of the problem domain.

Chapter 5, "Locales," describes C++ locales and facets from a conceptual point of view. It explains the major interfaces of class locale, gives a first overview of facets, describes the relationship between locales and facets, and demonstrates the usage of locales in internationalized applications.

This chapter should be read by everyone who wants to understand the concept of C++ locales and facets. It is useful for software developers who want to use C++ locales and facets in their programs.

Chapter 6, "Standard Facets," deals with standard C++ facets in greater detail. There are standard facets for numeric parsing/formatting, parsing/formatting of monetary values, parsing/formatting of time and date, character classification, string collation, character code conversion, and message retrieval from catalogues. For each of the standard facets the chapter gives an overview of its purpose, its main interfaces, and examples of its usage.

This chapter is of interest to readers who want to use the standard C++ facets in their programs.

Chapter 7, "The Architecture of the Locale Framework," describes the framework that is provided by C++ locales and facets. It explains how facets are created, identified, and replaced in a locale object.

This chapter should be read by everyone who strives for a deeper understanding of the locale framework and intends to extend it. It is useful for software developers who want to implement additional facets.

Chapter 8, "User-Defined Facets," presents an example of a user-defined facet. The example is meant as a guideline for implementing novel facets and their usage in conjunction with standard C++ IOStreams.

This chapter is helpful for readers who want to implement a new facet rather than using a standard one.

CHAPTER 4

Introduction to Internationalization and Localization

For reasons of profitability, modern computer programs must be useful and attractive to users all over the world. Naturally, computer users in different countries prefer to interact with their computer in their native language. Ideally, a computer program will be adaptable to all conceivable local languages and cultural conventions. As the developer of a product that aims for high international acceptance, you have to build adaptability to local conventions into your program.

This chapter provides an introduction to internationalization for those readers who want to internationalize their C++ programs but are not yet familiar with internationalization. If you seek an initial overview of the problem domain, this is the right place to begin.

First we will explain what *internationalization* and *localization* mean, how they relate, and where they differ. Then we will show you examples of differences in cultural conventions. These differences are a key problem that has to be dealt with when a program is internationalized. Such cultural conventions include, among others, language, formatting of numbers, currency symbols, formatting of time and date, ordering of words, and character encodings. You will find examples for each of the cultural conventions. Finally, we devote a longer section to character encodings, because they are particularly interesting for software developers. Differences in character encodings are a challenging problem; they are relevant for file input and output and have an impact on the functionality of the standard IOStreams.

4.1 Internationalization and Localization

Internationalization and localization are the two technical terms used most frequently in the area of software development for the world market. Sometimes internationalization[1] is used as a generic term comprising both. In order to be precise about what we mean by internationalization in this book, we will distinguish between *internationalization* and *localization*.[2]

INTERNATIONALIZATION. *Internationalization* is the effort of building into software the potential for worldwide use. It requires provision of means for adaptation to cultural conventions. Software designers and programmers of internationalized software care about this adaptability during software development. They avoid hard-coding elements that need to be localized. For instance, internationalized software never embeds an error message or prompt into its source code; it stores any kind of text that needs to be displayed or printed externally—in a message catalog, for instance. This separation of source code and text to be displayed makes it possible for the text to be translated and exchanged independent of the program. Also, software developers never make assumptions about specific conventions for formatting numeric or monetary values or displays of date and time. Such rules for parsing and formatting numbers and dates are separated from the source code and can be exchanged independently.

LOCALIZATION. *Localization* is the process of adapting software to a certain geographical or cultural area. It includes the translation of message catalogs and the creation of tables that describe the cultural conventions for a certain locality. This is typically the function of people who prepare a given piece of software for distribution in a certain national market. Such message catalogs and tables need to be made available to users of internationalized software. Availability is ensured by the system administrators who use an operating system's facilities for localization of software products. Users of internationalized software can eventually choose their preferred language and local conventions, either before they start an application or even during program execution.

In sum, internationalization is providing the means of adapting to cultural conventions during software development, and localization is using those means for adapting software to a certain cultural area. In this book we will concentrate on internationalization and will ignore localization.

Development of internationalized software is supported in many ways. C and C++ have standardized components for internationalization that accompany every C or C++ runtime system and are part of the respective standard library. Here we will discuss the

---

1. I18N is a common abbreviation for internationalization. The *18* stands for the 18 characters in the word *internationalization* between the first character *I* and the last character *N*.

2. This distinction is not a contrived one; *internationalization* and *localization* are popular terms in the area of software development for the world market.

components that are available in the standard C++ library, so-called *locales* and *facets*. However, before we delve into the details of C++ locales and facets, we want to give you an idea of the relevant cultural differences. The subsequent examples will not be exhaustive; there are many issues that need to be addressed when software is internationalized that we will not mention here. Examples are orientation, sizing and positioning of screen displays, vertical writing and printing, selection of font tables, handling of international keyboards, and so on. The issues we will delineate below are those that can be addressed by using components provided by the standard C++ library.

4.2 Cultural Conventions

People in different geographical and cultural areas use different languages; the representation of numbers and currency can vary; display of time and date can differ; the alphabet and the rules for ordering words might be different. All these factors play a role in internationalizing software. This section will give examples that illustrate these cultural differences.

4.2.1 Language

Different ethnic groups use different *languages,* and of course language is the most apparent difference between cultures. Even within a single country people might prefer different languages. The Swiss, for example, use French, Italian, and German.

Languages also differ in the alphabets they use. Here are a couple of examples of languages and their respective alphabets:

U.S. English:	a–z, A–Z, and punctuation
German:	a–z, A–Z, punctuation, and äöü ÄÖÜ ß
Greek:	α–ω, A–Ω, and punctuation
Japanese:	U.S. English characters, ten of thousands of Kanji characters, Hiragana, and Katakana

4.2.2 Numerical Values

Numbers are represented according to cultural conventions. For example, the symbol used for separation of the integer portion of a number from the fractional portion, the so-called *radix character,*[3] can differ from country to country. In English, this character is a period; in most European countries it is a comma. Conversely, the symbol that groups

---

3. Because the radix character in U.S. English is a period, it is also often referred to as the *decimal point.* However, in other cultures a comma is used as a radix character. Hence the term *decimal point* is misleading. *Radix character* is the correct term for the character separating the integer part of a number from its fractional portion.

numbers with more than three digits, the so-called *thousands separator,* is a comma in English and a period in much of Europe.

Even the grouping of digits varies. In U.S. English, digits are grouped by threes, but in Nepal, for instance, the first group has three digits, while all subsequent groups have two digits.

USA:	10,000,000.00
France:	10.000.000,00
Nepal:	1,00,00,000.00

4.2.3 Monetary Values

Units of currency are represented in different ways. The currency symbol can vary in its placement, as well as in the format of negative currency values.

For example, there are two different ways of representing the same amount in U.S. dollars:

domestic:	$ 99.99
international:	USD 99.99

Here is an example that shows different cultural conventions for placing the currency symbol. It can appear before, after, or within the numeric value:

Germany:	49,99 DM
Japan:	¥ 100
United Kingdom before decimalization:	£13 18s. 5d.

Also, the depiction of negative currency values varies among countries:

Hong Kong:	HK$0.95	(HK$0.95)
Germany:	0,95 DM	–0,95 DM
Austria:	ÖS 0,95	–ÖS 0,95
Switzerland:	SFr. 0.95	SFr. –0.95

4.2.4 Time and Date

Obviously, the representation of time and date too depends on cultural conventions. The names and abbreviations for days of the week and months of the year vary with the language. Also, some countries use a 24-hour clock; others use a 12-hour clock. Even calendars differ; they are based on historical, seasonal, and astronomical events. The official Japanese calendar, for instance, is based on a historical event, the beginning of the reign of the current emperor. Many countries, especially in the Western world, use the Gregorian calendar instead.

Here are examples of representations of the same date in different countries. They differ in order of day, month, and year, the separators between those items, and the use or omission of items such as the weekday in the long form of the date in Hungarian.

	SHORT FORM	LONG FORM
USA:	10/14/97	Tuesday, October 14, 1997
Germany:	14.10.97	Dienstag, 14. Oktober 1997
Italy:	14/10/97	martedì 14 ottobre 1997
Greece:	14/10/1997	Τρίτη, 14 Οκτωβρίου 1997
Hungary:	1997.10.14	1997. október 14.

The same time can have different representations in different cultures. Here is an example of the same time in a 12-hour clock and a 24-hour clock:

Germany:	17:55 Uhr
USA:	5:55 PM

4.2.5 Sorting Words

Different languages have different rules for sorting characters and words. These rules are called _collating sequences._ The collating sequence specifies the ordering of individual characters and other rules for ordering. In some languages, for instance, certain groups of characters are clustered and treated like a single character for the purpose of sorting characters. In other languages it is the other way round; one character is treated as if it were actually two characters.

In software development the order of characters is often determined by the numeric value of the byte(s) representing a character. These are what we call _ASCII rules_ in the examples below. This kind of ordering does not meet the requirements of any language's dictionary sorting.

Here is an example of ASCII sorting compared with dictionary sorting:

ENGLISH RULES	ASCII RULES
alien	American
American	Zulu
zebra	alien
Zulu	zebra

In an ASCII encoding, the numerical values of uppercase letters are smaller than the values of lowercase letters. For this reason, all words with capital letters appear at the beginning of a list sorted according to ASCII rules.

Here is an example of the difference for two-to-one character code pairs:

SPANISH DICTIONARY RULES	ASCII RULES
año	año
cuchillo	chaleco
chaleco	cuchillo
dónde	dónde
lunes	llava
llava	lunes
maíz	maíz

The word *cuchillo* is sorted before the word *chaleco*, because in Spanish *ch* is a digraph; i.e., it is treated as a single character that is sorted after *c* and before *d*. Generally, a digraph is a combination of characters that is written separately but forms a single lexical unit. In the list above there is another example of a two-to-one character code pair, the digraph *ll*, which is sorted after *l* and before *m*.

Here is an example of the difference for one character treated as two:

GERMAN DICTIONARY RULES	ASCII RULES
Musselin	Musselin
Muße	Muster
Muster	Muße

The German character ß, called *sharp s*, is treated as if it were two characters, namely *ss*. This makes a difference in ordering; it is sorted after *ss* and before *st*.

4.2.6 Messages

A program contains many pieces of text that can become visible to a user. Examples are error messages that are displayed in certain situations, labels in a graphical user interface, or standard text in headers and footers of listings and printouts. Internationalized programs never contain any such text strings or messages hard-coded in their source code. The text is separated from the program itself, because these strings and messages depend on the language and have to be translated prior to a product's worldwide distribution.

The state-of-the-art technique for separating language-dependent text from a program is to store all strings that need to be translated in so-called *message catalogs*. Such a message catalog can be a file or a database that can be translated and exchanged independently of the program. The program, rather than using hard-coded strings, accesses the message catalog for a certain language and retrieves the respective localized messages.

4.2.7 Character Encodings

Characters play an important role in text processing. Let's clarify what a character is, what frequently used terms such as *codeset, encoding, multibyte,* and *wide character* mean, and how characters are handled in software development.[4]

4.2.7.1 Terms and Definitions

CHARACTER. A *character* in software development is an abstraction. The natural understanding of a character is that of a written character; one intuitively associates a certain graphic representation with a given character. This is what is called a *glyph:* the actual shape of a character image. A glyph appears on a display or is produced by a printer. Naturally, there can be many such representations. You can represent the characters ABC as: ***ABC*** or **ABC** or **ABC** or ABC. A set of glyphs is called a *font*. So, indeed, one aspect of a character is its graphic representation. However, for the purpose of data processing in software development, a character also needs to have a data representation as a sequence of bits. This is called a *code*.

CHARACTER CODE. A *character code* is a sequence of bits representing a character. Again, there are many such representations. The character *a*, for instance, can be represented as 0×61 in ASCII[5] or as 0×81 in EBCDIC[6] or as 0×0061 in Unicode.[7] From this example you can see that not only the bit pattern but also the number of bits used for representing a character can vary; the bit pattern representing the character *a* has 16 bits in Unicode but only 8 bits in ASCII and EBCDIC.

CHARACTER CODESET. A *character codeset* is a $1 : 1$ mapping between characters and character codes. Here is an excerpt from the ASCII codeset:

Table 4-1: Some ASCII Character Codes

Character	...	?	@	A	B	C	D	E	F	...
Character Code (hexadecimal)	...	0×3F	0×40	×041	0×42	0×43	0×44	0×45	0×46	...

---

4. Section 2.3, Character Types and Character Traits, explains how IOStreams handles character encodings.

5. ASCII stands for "*American standard code for information interchange.*" It is a 7-bit character codeset that is the U.S. national variant of the internationally used ISO646 codeset.

6. EBCDIC stands for "*extended binary coded decimal interchange code.*" It is an 8-bit character codeset developed by IBM.

7. Unicode is a fixed-width, 16-bit worldwide character encoding that was developed and is maintained and promoted by the Unicode Consortium, a nonprofit computer industry organization.

Usually, all character codes in a codeset are of equal size. Examples of character codes are

- the traditional 7-bit ASCII codeset, where every U.S. English character is encoded in 7 bits,

- ISO 8859-1, a character codeset for Western European cultures using one byte per character, and

- Unicode, where each character is represented by 2 bytes.

More information about character codesets is given in section 4.2.7.2, Character Codesets.

CHARACTER ENCODING SCHEME. A *character encoding scheme* is a set of rules for translating a byte sequence into a sequence of character codes. Encoding schemes are necessary in cases where several codesets are used to encode a given set of characters. The Japanese alphabet, for instance, comprises characters from four different writing systems. The characters of these four writing systems are represented by a couple of different character codesets. Some of these character codesets contain one-byte codes, others consist of two-byte codes. It is obvious that for a set of character codesets that consist of a mixture of one- and two-byte characters, rules are needed for parsing a byte stream into a sequence of coded characters. This is because the interpretation of a single byte depends on its context. For instance, a single byte could be the first byte of a two-byte character, or it could represent an entire one-byte character. The rules needed for translating a byte sequence into a sequence of character codes are called a *character encoding scheme*, sometimes simply referred to as *encoding*. We will explain character encoding schemes in greater detail in section 4.2.7.3, Character Encoding Schemes.

4.2.7.2 Character Codesets

Character codesets can be classified by the number of bits or bytes they use for representation of a single character. Here are some examples:

The *7-bit ASCII codeset* is the traditional code for characters from the English alphabet. Using 7 bits you can encode 128 different characters, which is enough to represent all characters from the English alphabet as well as a couple of required additional characters.

The *8-bit codesets* permit the processing of many Eastern and Western European, Middle Eastern, and Asian languages. These languages have alphabets larger than the English language. Some of these 8-bit codesets are strictly extensions of the 7-bit ASCII codeset; these include the 7-bit ASCII codes and additionally support 128-character codes beyond those of ASCII. Such extensions—ISO 8859-1 is an example—meet the needs of Western European users. They represent the U.S. English ASCII characters plus additional characters such as ç, ô, ä, ß, ñ, and š. However, other languages such as Greek or Hebrew have completely different alphabets that do not include the ASCII characters. To encode these languages' alphabets, other 8-bit codesets have been designed, examples of which are ISO 8859-5 (Cyrillic), ISO 8859-6 (Arabic), ISO 8859-7 (Greek), and ISO 8859-8 (Hebrew).

In *wide-character codesets,* all characters are larger than one byte. This format is needed when an alphabet contains more than 256 characters and thus cannot be represented by a one-byte character codeset. The Japanese alphabet is an example; it consists of thousands of characters. There are, for instance, two character codesets defined by the Japanese Industry Standards Committee to represent Japanese characters: JIS X 0208-1990,[8] which contains the most frequently used Japanese characters, and JIS X 0212-1990,[9] which represents the less frequently used characters. Other examples of wide-character codesets are international standards such as Unicode, ISO 10646.UCS-2, and ISO 10646.UCS-4.[10] Unicode and ISO 10646.UCS-2 are two-byte character codesets, ISO 10646.UCS-4 is a four-byte codeset.

4.2.7.3 Character Encoding Schemes

As we have seen before, an encoding scheme is a set of rules for translating a byte sequence into a sequence of character codes.

If all characters in a text belong to *only one character codeset,* the translation is trivial; you have a 1 : 1 mapping between the bit pattern defining the character code and a character. For one-byte codesets you process the byte sequence in portions of one byte, identify the character code defined by the byte's content, and map it to the respective character. For a wide-character codeset you consume the byte sequence in portions of "wide characters of the respective size." For instance, you process two bytes at a time if the text consists of characters from a two-byte character codeset; you would process portions of four bytes at a time in the case of a four-byte character codeset. You examine the bit pattern contained in those two or four bytes, identify the character code, and map it to the respective character.

The translation requires additional considerations if you have to cope with *a mix of character codesets.* Once the characters you have to translate stem from several character codesets, you will not have a 1 : 1 mapping from a character code to a character any longer. Instead, you will have to apply translation rules defined by an encoding scheme. For instance, there might be multiple character codes representing the same character in different codesets. In order to map the character code correctly you need context information, for example, which character codeset the current byte sequence is supposed to belong to.

Matters are even more complicated when the character codesets contain character codes of different sizes. In such cases, it is not even clear how many bytes form a single character code. Translation rules for a mix of character codesets of different size are called *multibyte encoding schemes.* Multibyte character sequences are generally processed in portions of one byte, because this is the smallest unit that can be interpreted.

---

8. The official name for ISO X 0208-1990 is *Code of the Japanese Graphic Character Set for Information Interchange.*

9. The official name for ISO X 02112-1990 is *Code of the Supplementary Japanese Graphic Character Set for Information Interchange.*

10. ISO 10646 is an encoding defined by ISO, the International Standards Organization. ISO 10646-UCS-2 is code-for-code equivalent to Unicode.

Understanding multibyte encoding schemes is easier when they are explained through typical examples. Therefore, the following examples are based on encoding schemes for Japanese text processing.

4.2.7.3.1 Japanese Multibyte Encoding Schemes

In Japan, a single text can be composed of characters from four different writing systems:

- *Kanji,* which has tens of thousands of characters, represented by pictures.

- *Hiragana* and *katakana,* each of which contains about 80 characters, representing syllables.

- *Roman* characters, which include some 95 letters, digits, and punctuation marks.

Figure 4-1 shows a Japanese sentence composed of these four writing system.

The sentence means: "Encoding methods such as JIS can support texts that mix Japanese and English."

The characters from the four writing systems can be represented as follows:

1. One huge, wide-character codeset that encompasses all characters of the Japanese alphabet. This is the approach that is taken by international standards such as Unicode or ISO10646.

2. A mix of several character codesets, some of which are one-byte codesets, others being two-byte codesets. Each of the character codesets represents a subset of characters of the Japanese alphabet. This is the approach standardized by the Japanese industry's standards organization JISC.

Let us consider the second case, because it is an example of where multibyte character encodings are used. The Japanese industry uses national standards for character codesets. The characters from the four Japanese writing systems are represented in a number of character codesets, the most common of which are listed below. Each of these character codesets represents a certain subset of the Japanese alphabet:

Table 4-2: Japanese Character Codesets

CHARACTER CODESET	CHARACTERS CONTAINED	CODE SIZE
JIS X 0208-1990	frequently used kanji characters	2 byte
JIS X 0212-1990	supplementary kanji characters	2 byte
JIS-ROMAN[11]	ASCII and half-width katakana characters	1 byte

There are many ways of translating a byte sequence into a sequence of characters from the character codesets listed above. Consequently, there are several multibyte encodings for Japanese, none of which is universally recognized. Instead, there are three com-

---

11. JIS-ROMAN is a combination of ASCII characters and half-width katakana characters. Katakana and hiragana characters are encoded in one byte, using the 128 character codes left over by the 7-bit ASCII codes.

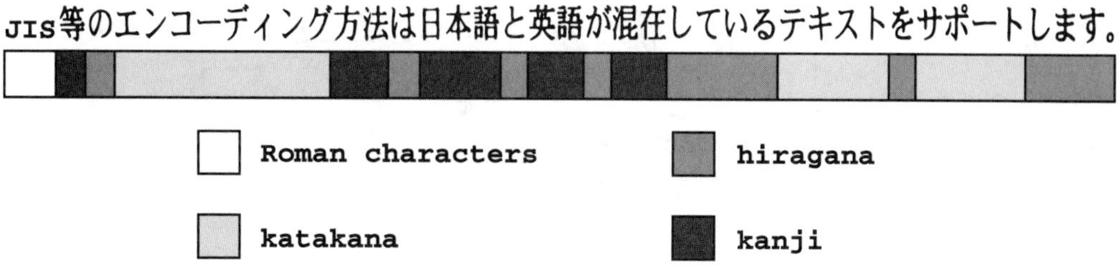

JIS等のエンコーディング方法は日本語と英語が混在しているテキストをサポートします。

| | Roman characters | | hiragana |
| | katakana | | kanji |

Figure 4-1: *A Japanese sentence mixing four writing systems.*

mon multibyte encoding schemes: JIS (Japanese Industrial Standard), Shift-JIS, and EUC (Extended UNIX Code).

The three multibyte encodings just described are typically used in separate areas:

- *JIS* is the primary encoding method used for electronic transmission such as email, because it uses only 7 bits of each byte. This is a required feature, because some network paths strip the eighth bit from characters. Escape sequences are used to switch between one- and two-byte modes, as well as between different character sets.

- *Shift-JIS* was invented by Microsoft for use on its platforms. Each byte is inspected to see if it is a one-byte character or the first byte of a two-byte character. Shift-JIS does not support as many characters as JIS and EUC do.

- *EUC* encoding is implemented as the internal code for most UNIX-based plat- forms available on the Japanese market. It allows for characters containing more than two bytes and is much more extensible than Shift-JIS. EUC is a general method for handling multiple character sets and is not peculiar to Japanese encoding.

To help you gain a better understanding of different types of multibyte encodings, we will take a brief look at the three encoding schemes listed above. As we shall see later, it makes a significant difference whether an encoding is *state-dependent* or not. JIS is a state-dependent, or *modal*, multibyte encoding; Shift-JIS and EUC are *state-independent* encoding schemes.

STATE-DEPENDENT MULTIBYTE ENCODING SCHEMES: THE JIS ENCODING

The *JIS*, or *Japanese Industrial Standard*, defines a number of standard Japanese character sets, some requiring one byte, others two. They include escape sequences, which are required to shift between one- and two-byte modes.

Escape sequences, also referred to as *shift sequences*, are sequences of *control characters.* Control characters do not belong to any of the alphabets. They are artificial characters that do not have a graphic representation. However, they are part of the encoding scheme, where they serve as separators between different character codesets and indicate a switch

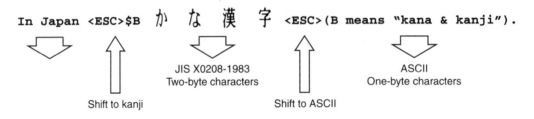

Figure 4-2: An example of a Japanese text encoded in JIS.

in the way a character sequence is interpreted. The use of the shift sequence is demonstrated in figure 4-2.

For encoding schemes containing shift sequences, like JIS, it is necessary to maintain a *shift state* while parsing a character sequence. In the example above, we are in some initial shift state at the start of the sequence. Here it is ASCII. Therefore, characters are assumed to be one-byte ASCII codes until the shift sequence <ESC>$B is seen. This switches us to two-byte mode, as defined by JIS X 0208-1983. The shift sequence <ESC>(B then switches us back to ASCII mode.

STATE-INDEPENDENT MULTIBYTE ENCODING SCHEMES: SHIFT-JIS AND EUC
Shift-JIS and EUC do not use escape sequences. Instead, they inspect each byte and see if it is a one-byte character or the first byte of a two-byte character.

The type of character is determined by reserving a set of byte values for certain purposes. Shift-JIS, for instance, has the following rules:

- Any byte having a value in the range 0×21-7E is assumed to be a one-byte ASCII character.

- Any byte having a value in the range 0×A1-DF is assumed to be a one-byte half-width katakana character.

- Any byte having a value in the range 0×81-9F or 0×E0-EF is assumed to be the first byte of a two-byte character from the set JIS X 0208-1990. The second byte must have a value in the range 0×40-7E or 0×80-FC.

While this encoding is more compact than JIS, it cannot represent as many characters as JIS. In fact, Shift-JIS cannot represent any characters in the supplemental character set JIS X 0212-1990, which contains more than 6,000 additional kanji characters.

The EUC encoding has equivalent encoding rules that rely on interpreting a single byte in order to determine whether it represents an entire character or is the first byte of a two-byte character code. EUC is not peculiar to Japanese encoding. It was developed as a method for handling multiple character sets, Japanese or otherwise, within a single text stream.

4.2.7.4 Uses of Multibyte Encodings and Wide Characters
Now that we understand multibyte encoding schemes, let us consider the role they play in software development. State-dependent multibyte encodings are used primarily as an

external code, because they are compact and save storage space. When used for internal storage or processing in a program, they are not very efficient. For instance, they do not allow random access to arbitrary positions within a character sequence. Instead, wide-character codesets are used because they are more convenient for data processing. The following example will illustrate how wide characters make text processing inside a program.

Consider a filename string containing a directory path with adjacent names separated by a slash, like `/CC/include/locale.h`. To find the actual filename in a single-byte character string, we can start at the back of the string and process the character sequence byte by byte. When we find the first separator, we know where the filename starts. If the string contains multibyte characters, we always have to scan from the front so we don't inspect bytes out of context. However, if we represent the multibyte string as a sequence of wide characters instead, we can treat it like a single-byte character and scan from the back, processing it in portions of "wide-character size."

Multibyte encoding provides an efficient way to move characters around outside programs, and between programs and the outside world. Once inside a program, however, it is easier and more efficient to deal with wide-character codesets where all characters have the same size and format.

4.2.7.5 Code Conversions

Since wide-character codesets are usually used for internal representation of characters in a program and multibyte encodings are used for external representation, converting multibytes to wide characters is a common task during input/output operations. Input to and output from files is a typical example. The external file might contain multibyte characters. When you read such a file, you convert these multibyte characters into wide characters that you store in an internal wide-character buffer for further processing. When you write to a multibyte file, you have to convert the wide characters held internally into multibytes for storage on an external file. Figure 4-3 demonstrates graphically how this conversion during file input is done:

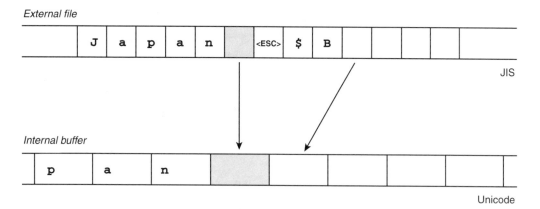

Figure 4-3: *Conversion from a multibyte to a wide-character encoding.*

The conversion from a multibyte sequence into a wide-character sequence requires three elements:

- *Expansion* of one-byte characters into two- or four-byte characters. In the example above the ASCII characters preceding the shift sequence <ESC>$B are "bloated" into their two-byte Unicode equivalents.

- *Elimination of escape sequences.* The sequence <ESC>$B does not have a wide-character equivalent and is thus discarded.

- *Translation* of multibytes that consist of two or more bytes into their wide-character equivalents. The kanji characters following the shift sequence <ESC>$B are converted into their Unicode equivalents. This conversion does not change a kanji character's size, because its representation takes two bytes in both character codesets.

CHAPTER 5

Locales

In the preceding chapter we discussed various areas in which cultural conventions differ from one region to another. For each of these cultural conventions, the standard C++ library provides services that enable you to internationalize your C++ programs. These services are bundled into so-called *facets*. A facet encapsulates data that represent a set of culture and language dependencies and/or offer a set of related internationalization services. Facet objects are maintained by so-called *locales*. Basically, a locale is a container of a facet. In a C++ program, locales are objects of a class type called `locale` and a facet is an object of a facet type. All facet types are derived from a class called `locale::facet`.[1]

Facet types are either predefined in the standard library or user-defined. The predefined facet types are called the *standard facets*. The standard facets provide services and information about the basic set of cultural differences. Such differences concern language and alphabet as well as the formatting of numeric, monetary, date, and time values.[2] *User-defined facets* cover further areas of cultural differences, beyond the basic set provided by the standard facets. User-defined facets are present in a locale only if they are explicitly added to the locale. Standard facets, in contrast, are automatically contained in every

---

1. Details about facet types can be found in section 7.2.1, Facet Identification.

2. Examples of such cultural differences are given in section 4.2, Cultural Conventions.

locale. The idea is that the standard facets provide a basic set of internationalization services that must be available in every locale.[3]

There are two grouping mechanisms for facets in a locale: facet families and locale categories.

FACET FAMILY. A *facet family* is a hierarchy of facet types that are derived from each other. The base class facet defines a facet interface common to all members of the facet family. Some of these facet families are closely related because their base classes are instantiations or specializations of a facet base class template. For instance, `template <class charT> class ctype` is the base class template of the ctype facet families. The facet base classes instantiated or specialized from it are `ctype<char>` and `ctype<wchar_t>`. Any derived classes, such as `ctype_byname<char>` and `ctype_byname<wchar_t>`, are members of their respective facet families.

LOCALE CATEGORY. A *locale category* denotes a group of standard facet families. In a C++ program, a category is a bitmask value of type `locale::category`. For instance, the locale category `locale::ctype` comprises the ctype and codecvt facet families.

Table 5-1 lists the standard facets and shows how they are grouped into categories.

Table 5-1: Standard Facets and Categories

CATEGORY	FACET TEMPLATE	FUNCTIONALITY
ctype	ctype	character classification and conversion
	codecvt	character code conversion
collate	collate	string collation
message	messages	retrieving localized message strings from message catalogs
numeric	numpunct	information about the format and punctuation of numeric and Boolean expressions
	num_get	parsing of character sequences that represent a numeric or Boolean value
	num_put	generation of formatted character sequences that represent a numeric or Boolean value
monetary	moneypunct	information about the format and punctuation of monetary expressions
	money_get	parsing of character sequences that represent a monetary value
	money_put	generation of formatted character sequences that represent a monetary value
time	time_get	parsing of character sequences that represent a date and/or time
	time_put	generation of formatted character sequences that represent a date and/or time

---

3. The predefined standard facets are discussed in section 6, Standard Facets. User-defined, nonstandard facet types are explained in section 8, User-Defined Facets.

Locales have special properties:

- Each locale object contains at most one facet from a given facet family, and for this reason facets in a locale can be identified by means of their family name, that is, their base class type. We see later in section 7.2, Identification and Lookup of Facets in a Locale, why and how this works.

- Locales are immutable, which means that their content does not change during their lifetime. None of the contained facets can be modified or replaced, nor can facets be added or removed from a locale. Section 7.3.2, Immutability of Facets in a Locale, explains why and how this works.

After this first cursory overview of locales and facets, let us take a look at the `locale` class. In the following two sections, we explain how locale objects can be created and how facets can be retrieved from a locale object.

5.1 Creating Locale Objects

Facets are rarely used on a stand-alone basis, that is, independent of a locale. Usually, all facets relevant to a certain cultural area are bundled into a locale object. Such a locale object is created either by providing a locale name (i.e., the name of a certain cultural environment), by combining existing locales, or by adding or replacing facets in an existing locale.

5.1.1 Named Locales

Locale objects are typically created by providing a *locale name.* Such locale names are also used in the standard C library, and C++ uses the same names. Valid locale names are `"C"`, `" "`, and any implementation-defined C locale name.

The name `"C"` stands for the classic U.S. English ASCII locale that is implicitly used in programs that are not internationalized. This locale can be created by providing the name, that is, by saying `locale("C")` or by using a static locale function that yields the same result, namely `locale::classic()`.

The name `" "` stands for the native locale on your system. There is no rule that says which cultural area the native locale represents. It fully depends on your operating system and how it is configured on your particular computer.

The syntax and semantics of other C locale names are not defined by the standard but are entirely implementation-specific. For example, the name `"De_DE"` on an X/Open system denotes the same localization environment as `"German_Germany.1252"` on a Microsoft platform.

The name of a locale can be retrieved via the `name()` member function. Not all locales have a name. Only locales constructed from a name string or from parts of two named locales have a name; all others do not. For instance, a locale object that is created as a combination of a German and a French locale has a name, but a locale that is a German locale with one facet replaced or added is nameless. (Combined locales and replacement of facets are discussed in section 5.1.2, Combined Locales.) Such nonstandard locales do not have a meaningful name and the `name()` member function returns `"*"` in such cases.

In this book we use locale names as they are allowed on Microsoft platforms. Here are a couple of examples:

```
locale native("");
locale usa("American_USA.1252");
locale holland("Dutch");
locale global;

cout << "native : " << native.name() << endl;
cout << "classic: " << locale::classic().name() << endl;
cout << "global : " << global.name() << endl;
cout << "holland: " << holland.name() << endl;
cout << "usa     : " << usa.name() << endl;
```

The resulting printout is

```
native : German_Germany.1252
classic: C
global : C
holland: Dutch_Netherlands.1252
usa     : English_United States.1252
```

From the name of the native locale you can tell that these examples were compiled on a "German" computer. The default constructor creates a snapshot of the so-called global locale. The global locale is discussed in section 5.1.3, The Global Locale.

The locale name can be used for comparing locales. In general, two locales are equal if they are the same locale or one is a copy of the other. If both locales have a name and the names are identical, they are also considered equal. As a result, unnamed locales are equal only to themselves and copies of themselves; in addition, locales are equal to locales with the same name.

5.1.2 Combined Locales

A named locale contains a certain set of predefined facets that represent data and services for a certain cultural area. If additional nonstandard facets are contained in a locale, or if instead of a predefined facet a user-defined facet is contained, a nonstandard locale object is needed. An intuitive first idea for building such nonstandard locales might be simply to add or replace facets in an existing locale object. This, however, is not allowed.

As mentioned earlier, locale objects are immutable, which means that their content does not change during their lifetime. None of the contained facets can be modified or replaced, nor can facets be added or removed from a locale. This guarantee is helpful for components that use locales, because they can rely on the fact that the locale will never change and that references to facets obtained from that locale will stay valid as long as the locale exists.

However, due to the immutability of locale objects, nonstandard locales cannot be created by modifying existing locales, but only as a copy of an existing locale with one or several facets replaced or added. For the creation of such a combined locale, the locale class offers several constructors and member functions. The following two functions allow replacement or addition of exactly one facet.

```
template <class Facet> locale(const locale& other, Facet* fac);
```

This constructor creates a locale that is a copy of an existing locale with exactly one facet replaced or added. Instead of the original facet of type `Facet`, the provided facet `fac` is contained in the locale object. If the original locale does not contain a facet of type `Facet`, the provided facet `fac` is added to the constructed locale.

```
template <class Facet> locale combine(const locale& other);
```

This member function creates a copy of the locale object on which it is invoked, and the copy has the facet of type `Facet` replaced or added by the corresponding facet from the existing locale `other`.

Here are some examples:

```
moneypunct<char>& mfac = ... provide Dutch monetary facet somehow ... ;
locale dutch_german(locale("German"),&mfac);

locale holland("Dutch");
dutch_german = locale("German").combine< moneypunct<char> >(holland);
```

The construction and the invocation of `combine()` yield the same combined locale; it's a German locale that has the moneypunct facet from a Dutch locale. As mentioned before, the resulting combined locale has no name.

Note that the facet to be replaced or added is identified by its family name. As mentioned before, a locale contains at most one member of a given facet family, and for this reason the name of the base class type can be used to identify the respective representative of a family in a locale. Section 7.2, Identification and Lookup of Facets in a Locale, explains the details.

The predefined facets that are required to be contained in each locale are grouped into so-called *categories*. Section 6.3.2, Locale Categories, describes the details of locale categories. A locale category is of type `locale::category`, which is a bitmask type, and values of that type can be combinations of categories. Instead of replacing only one facet, all facets from one or several categories can be exchanged. The following two locale constructors allow replacement of locale categories:

```
locale(const locale& other, const char* std_name, category cats);
```

This constructor creates a locale that is a copy of the existing locale `other`, which has all facets belonging to the specified locale categories replaced by facets taken from a named locale with the name `std_name`.

```
locale(const locale& other, const locale& one, category cats);
```

This constructor creates a locale that is a copy of the existing locale `other`, which has all facets belonging to the specified locale categories replaced by facets taken from another locale.

The resulting combined locales have names, if both source locales are named. The name of the resulting locale is, however, undefined.

Here are some examples:

```
locale polish_german_1(locale("German"),"Polish",locale::monetary);
out << "german_base polish_monetary: " << polish_german_1.name() << endl;
locale polish_german_2(locale("German"),locale("Polish"),locale::time);
out << "german_base polish_time    : " << polish_german_2.name() << endl;
```

The resulting printout on the platform we used is

```
german_base polish_monetary: German_Germany.1252
german_base polish_time    : Polish_Poland.1250
```

At first glance these locale constructors, which copy an existing locale and replace certain facets, look like expensive operations. But we will see in chapter 7, "The Architecture of the Locale Framework," that they are in fact lightweight operations, due to the locale's architecture.

5.1.3 The Global Locale

The C++ standard defines the notion of a *global* locale that is accessible to all components in a program. The global locale typically serves as the default locale to internationalized components, such as IOStreams. If you create a stream object and do not specify which locale the stream will use, the stream uses the global locale, or more precisely, a snapshot of the global locale. A snapshot of the current global locale can be created by calling the default constructor for a locale `locale()`. Snapshots are copies of the current global locale and are not affected if the global locale is later replaced. You can make a given locale object `loc` global by calling `locale::global (const locale& loc)`. Here are some examples:

```
locale global;
out << "global: " << global.name() << endl;
```

```
locale holland("Dutch");
locale::global(holland);
out << "global: " << global.name() << endl;
global = locale(); // get a new snapshot
out << "global: " << global.name() << endl;

locale::global(locale("French-Swiss"));
global = locale();
out << "global: " << global.name() << endl;
```

The resulting output using Microsoft MCV 6.0 on a German PC is

```
global: C
global: C
global: Dutch_Netherlands.1252
global: French_Switzerland.1252
```

The standard does not mandate which locale is the default for the global locale. From the code above, you can see that on our computer the initial global locale is the classic "C" locale.

You can also see that making a locale global does not affect any previously created snapshots of the global locale: The snapshot held in the variable `global` does not change after making a Dutch locale global. A new snapshot must be created to see the effect of having changed the global locale.

The C library also has the notion of a global locale. Setting the global C++ locale might have an effect on the global C locale. The details are described in appendix E, "Relationship Between C and C++ Locales."

Now that we know how locales can be created, let us see how we can access the facets contained in a locale.

5.2 Retrieving Facets from a Locale

Access to the facets contained in a locale is via two functions: `has_facet()` and `use_facet()`. `has_facet()` allows checking of whether a facet of the specified facet type is contained in the specified locale. `use_facet()` returns a reference to the contained facet, if present, and throws a `bad_cast` exception otherwise.

Both functions are function templates and take the facet type as a template argument and the locale object as a function argument. When these functions are invoked, the template argument, that is, the facet type, must be explicitly specified. The explicit function template argument specification is a language feature that is relatively new in C++. Section G.6, Explicit Template Argument Specification, in appendix G explains the details.

Here are some examples that show how `has_facet()` and `use_facet()` would be invoked:

```
locale loc;     // snapshot of the current global locale

if (has_facet<money_put<char> >(loc))       // always yields true
        const money_put<char>& fac1
            = use_facet<money_put<char> >(loc);

if (has_facet<money_put<char,string_inserter<char> > >(loc))
        const money_put<char,string_inserter<char> >& fac2
            = use_facet<money_put<char,string_inserter<char> > >(loc);
```

5.2.1 has_facet

has_facet<Facet>(loc) checks whether the locale loc contains a facet that is of the requested type Facet or any type derived therefrom.

For all mandatory facet types, such as money_put<char> for instance, has_facet() returns true, of course, and the call to has_facet() is really not necessary. For other facet types, in contrast, has_facet() provides valuable information, and one might want to check for a facet's existence before use_facet() is called in order to avoid the exception that use_facet() would throw if the facet could not be found. In our example above, we checked whether a facet of type money_put<char,string_inserter<char>> is contained in the current global locale.[4] The instantiation of money_put for a nondefault iterator type is not automatically contained in every facet, and for this reason, has_facet() might return false for this facet type.

5.2.2 use_facet

use_facet<Facet>(loc) searches the locale loc for a facet that is of the requested type Facet or any type derived therefrom. If a facet of the requested type can be found in the locale, a reference to the found facet is returned. If eventually no matching facet can be found, a bad_cast exception is thrown.

When use_facet() can find a matching facet, it returns a reference to it. References to elements in a container always raise the question: How long do these references stay valid? Often, element references become invalid after the first modifying access to the container. As we've mentioned earlier, locales are immutable objects. There is no such thing as a modifying access to a locale object. For this reason, the reference to the facet returned from use_facet() remains valid as long as the containing locale exists. Actually, the guarantee is even stronger: The reference returned remains valid at least as long as any copy of the containing locale exists. Section 7.3, Memory Management of Facets in a Locale, explains why this is and how it works.

---

4. The facet type money_put<char, string_inserter<char> > is an instantiation of the money_put template for an output iterator other than the default, which is ostreambuf_iterator<charT> and was omitted from the list of template arguments in money_put<char>. Instead of writing the formatted monetary value to an output stream, we've assumed that there is an iterator type string_inserter<char> that enables output to a string. Details about the monetary facets are described in section 6.2.2, Monetary Values.

Yet keep in mind that the validity of the facet reference returned from `use_facet()` is tied to the lifetime of its containing locale and any copies of that locale. In particular, be cautious with passing a temporary locale object as an argument to `use_facet()`. Depending on the context, the facet reference returned might be invalid, because the containing locale has already been destroyed. In the following code snippet, use of a temporary locale object will lead to a program crash:

```
const numpunct<char>& fac = use_facet<numpunct<char> >(locale("German"));
cout << "true in German: " << fac.truename()⁵ << endl; // program crash !!!
```

The temporary German locale lives until the end of the enclosing expression and goes out of scope at the end of the first statement in the code snippet above, which is before the returned reference to the contained `numpunct` facet is used. The facet referred to has already been destroyed along with its containing locale, and a program crash is the result of the second statement.

Use of temporary locale objects does work if the lifetime of the temporary object is taken into account correctly. Below, there is no problem, because the locale and the returned facet reference are temporary objects within the same enclosing expression:

```
cout << "true in German: "
    << use_facet<numpunct<char> >(locale("German")).truename() << endl;
```

The following works, too:

```
const numpunct<char>& fac = use_facet<numpunct<char> >(locale());
cout << "true in " << locale().name() << ": " << fac.truename() << endl;
```

because the temporary locale is a copy of the current global locale, and the facet reference returned by `use_facet()` stays valid as long as any copies of the containing locale exist.

To avoid any confusion, we recommend generally NOT passing temporary locales to `use_facet()`. Typically, locales are objects with a relatively long lifetime. The code below is much safer than any of the examples above:

```
locale german("German");
const numpunct<char>& fac = use_facet<numpunct<char> >(german);
cout << "true in German: " << fac.truename() << endl;
```

---

5. `truename()` and `falsename()` are member functions of the `numpunct` facet that yield the internationalized counterparts to `true` and `false`.

CHAPTER 6

Standard Facets

Facets are objects of a facet type that is either predefined in the standard library or user-defined. The predefined facet types, called the *standard facets,* are discussed in detail in this chapter. User-defined, nonstandard facet types are explained in chapter 8, "User-Defined Facets."

The standard facets provide services and information about the basic set of cultural differences. Such differences concern language and alphabet as well as the formatting of numeric, monetary, date, and time values. Examples of such cultural differences were given in section 4.2, Cultural Conventions. User-defined facets cover further areas of cultural differences, beyond the basic set provided by the standard facets. User-defined facets are present in a locale only if they were explicitly added to that locale. Standard facets, in contrast, are automatically contained in every locale. The idea is that the standard facets provide a basic set of internationalization services that must be available in every locale.

To be more precise, we should say that in every locale there is one representative of each standard *facet family.* Remember, we mentioned before, at the beginning of chapter 5, that facet types are organized in facet families, that is, hierarchies of facet classes derived from each other. Some of these facet families are closely related, because their base classes are instantiations or specializations of a facet base class template. For instance, `template <class charT> class ctype` is the base class template of the ctype facet families.

The facet base classes instantiated or specialized from it are `ctype<char>` and `ctype<wchar_t>`. Each locale object contains one representative from each ctype family, that is, one facet of type `ctype<char>`, or any type derived therefrom, and one facet of type `ctype<wchar_t>`, or any type derived therefrom. A facet of type `ctype<myCharacterType>`, or any type derived therefrom, would not automatically be contained in each locale. This is because although an instantiation or specialization of the ctype facet template for a character type other than `char` or `wchar_t` does introduce a new ctype facet family, the new family is not a mandatory one. We will take a closer look at the facet templates and required instantiations or specializations of these templates in section 6.3.1.4, Mandatory Facet Types, where we provide a complete list of the facet families that are represented in every locale.

In the following sections we review all of the standard facet families and explain their functionality. We discuss alphabet- and language-related facets first; then we explore the parsing and formatting facets; and eventually we take a second look at the standard facet families, their base and derived classes, and the locale categories.

6.1 Alphabet- and Language-Related Facets

Different ethnic groups use different languages. Hence, language constitutes one of the most apparent differences between cultures. Since languages also differ in the alphabet they use, the standard provides four types of facets related to the cultural differences of languages and alphabets. We are going to examine them in the following sections.

6.1.1 Character Classification

Different cultures use different alphabets. For each alphabet one might want to classify its characters into groups like alphabetical character or digit or whitespace character. Also, one might want to determine the uppercase equivalent of a lowercase character and vice versa, if any exists.

The *ctype* facet provides this classification and conversion functionality. The ctype facet is defined by the following class template:

```
template <class charT> class ctype
```

It contains the classification and conversion functionality for a character set that can be represented by the character type `charT`. Two instantiations or specializations of this template are provided by the standard library: a ctype facet for narrow characters of type `char` and one for wide characters of type `wchar_t`.

6.1.1.1 Character Classification

Among other services, the ctype facet provides the functionality to classify the characters of a character set. Criteria for this classification are provided as an enumerated bitmask type,[1] which is called `mask`. It is a nested type in `ctype_base`, the public base class of the ctype facet template. The values of `mask` and their semantics are listed in table 6-1:

Table 6-1: Character Classification Criteria

MASK VALUE	SEMANTICS
alpha	alphabetical character
digit	one of the characters that represent the decimal digits 0–9
cntrl	control character
lower	lowercase character
print	printable character
punct	punctuation characters
space	whitespace characters
upper	uppercase characters
xdigit	one of the characters that represent the hexadecimal digits 0–f
alnum	alpha or digit
graph	alnum or punct

Member functions of the ctype facet provide the functionality

- to check if a certain character conforms to a certain criteria, by means of an overloaded version of the member function `is()`:

```
bool is(mask m, charT c) const;
```

- to determine all criteria to which each character from a range of characters conforms, by means of an overloaded version of the member function `is()`:

```
const charT* is(const charT* beg, const charT* end,
                mask* vec) const;
```

- to find the first element in a range of characters that conforms or does not conform to certain criteria, by means of the member functions:

```
const charT* scan_is(mask m, const charT* beg,
                     const charT* end) const;
```

and

```
const charT* scan_not(mask m, const charT* beg,
                      const charT* end) const;
```

Let's have a look at some examples that show how these member functions can be used. If `loc` is a locale object that contains a `ctype<char>` facet and if `c` is a character of type `char`,

---

1. Bitmask types are explained in section G.1, Bitmask Types, in appendix G.

```
use_facet< ctype<char> >(loc).is(ctype_base::lower, c);
```

returns a `bool` value that indicates if `c` is a lowercase character or not. If we use a variable `m` of type `ctype_base::mask`, then a different overloaded version of `is()`, namely,

```
use_facet< ctype<char> >(loc).is(&c,&c+1,&m);
```

places the bitmask into `m` that contains all classification criteria to which `c` conforms. This second version of `is()` allows for a character range, where the first parameter indicates the beginning and the second parameter points one past the end. The third parameter points to the vector of type `ctype_base::mask[]`, which contains the bitmasks that characterize each character from the range after the operation has finished.

For the sake of convenience, additional global functions, in the namespace `std`, are provided that allow for classification if certain criteria apply to a single character. These are functions like `isspace()`, `isprint()`, `isupper()`, etc. Each function is implemented by calling the ctype facet's member function `is()` with the corresponding mask argument; e.g., `isupper()` is implemented in the following way:

```
template <class charT> bool isupper (charT c, const locale& loc)
{
  return use_facet< ctype<charT> >(loc).is(ctype_base::upper, c);
}
```

6.1.1.2 Character Conversion to Upper- and Lowercase

Besides character classification, the ctype facet provides a means for character conversion. One type of character conversion is supported by the overloaded member functions `toupper()` and `tolower()`. They allow conversion of single characters or character ranges to their corresponding upper- or lowercase representation. For example:

```
use_facet< ctype<char> >(loc).toupper(c);
```

returns the uppercase character representation of `c`, if it exists; otherwise `c`, while

```
use_facet< ctype<char> >(loc).toupper(cp1, cp2);
```

replaces each character in the range `[cp1, cp2)` for which a corresponding uppercase character exists, with that character. The overloaded versions of `tolower()` have analogous behavior.

For convenience, the character conversion from uppercase to lowercase and vice versa is also provided by global functions in the namespace `std`. These functions are

```
template <class charT> charT tolower(charT c, const locale& loc) const;
template <class charT> charT toupper(charT c, const locale& loc) const;
```

Again, the convenience functions are implemented by using `loc`'s ctype member functions `tolower()` and `toupper()`.

6.1.1.3 Character Conversion Between `charT` and `char`

Another type of conversion that ctype supports is the conversion between ctype's template character type `charT` and the built-in character type `char`. This functionality is provided by the member functions `narrow()` and `widen()`. For each function two overloaded versions exist; one that converts single characters:

```
char narrow(charT c, char dfault) const;
charT widen(char c) const;
```

and one that converts character ranges:

```
const charT* narrow(const charT* beg, const charT* end, char dfault,
                char* to) const;
const char*  widen(const char* beg, const char* end,
                charT* to) const;
```

The parameter `dfault` is used by `narrow()` as the return value whenever a wide character to be converted does not have a narrow-character counterpart. Not all wide characters must have a corresponding narrow-character equivalent. The only characters for which the standard requires that `widen()` must provide a unique transformation are those in the basic source character set.[2] For the basic source characters, the following invariant holds:

```
widen(narrow(c), 0) == c
```

6.1.1.4 Special Properties of `ctype<char>`

For the sake of efficiency, the standard requires that `ctype<char>` must be provided as a template specialization; that is, it must not be an instantiation of the ctype template. The difference between the specialization and an instantiation of the ctype template is that the template implements the member functions by calls of virtual protected member functions, whereas the specialization uses a table-driven approach, which is much faster. Let us see how the specialization implements the ctype operations:

The functionality of `narrow()` and `widen()` in the `ctype<char>` facet can be implemented easily and efficiently: The single-character versions do nothing but return their received parameters, and the versions for character ranges behave like `memcpy()`.

---

2. The basic source character set consists of 96 characters: the space character, the control characters representing horizontal tab, vertical tab, form feed, and newline, plus the following characters:

```
a b c d e f g h i j k l m n o p q r s t u v w x y z
A B C D E F G H I J K L M N O P Q R S T U V W X Y Z
0 1 2 3 4 5 6 7 8 9
_ { } [ ] # ( ) < > % : ; . ? * + - / ^ & | ~ ! = , \ " '
```

ctype<char>'s character classification member functions are based on a table, in which the character encoding is the key and a bitmask value of type ctype_base::mask is the value. The bitmask values indicate all classification criteria to which the character conforms. For example, a lowercase letter such as *k* is associated with the bit mask value

```
ctype_base::alpha | ctype_base::lower | ctype_base::print
```

This table-driven approach allows implementation of the character classification member functions as simple and efficient bit operations.

6.1.2 String Collation

Different languages have different rules for sorting characters and words. These rules are called a collating sequence. The collating sequence specifies the ordering of individual characters and other rules for ordering. For example, in some languages certain groups of characters are clustered and treated like a single character for the purpose of sorting characters. In other languages it is the other way round; one character is treated as if it were actually two characters.

Collation services are provided by the *collate* facet, which is defined by the following class template:

```
template <class charT> class collate
```

The collate facet supports the comparison of character sequences according to language-specific rules. Its member function:

```
int compare(const charT* beg1, const charT* end1,
            const charT* beg2, const charT* end2) const;
```

returns an integer value that indicates the order of two character sequences [beg1, end1) and [beg2, end2):

1   indicates that the character sequence [beg1,end1) is greater than the character sequence [beg2,end2),

−1   indicates that the first sequence is less than the second.

0   indicates that both sequences are equal.

The collate facet also supports the functionality to determine a hash value from a character sequence by means of the following member function:

```
long hash(const charT* beg, const charT* end) const;
```

For two strings, for which compare() yields 0, the calculated hash value is the same. With its member function

```
basic_string<charT> transform(const charT* beg, const charT* end) const;
```

the collate facet provides a way to speed up the comparison of one character sequence against many others. `transform()` returns a string that is the transformation of the character sequence represented by the `[beg, end)` to an internal representation. The lexicographic comparison[3] of two strings resulting from `transform()` yields the same result as the comparison of the original character sequences with `compare()`. When one string is compared against n others, using the n+1 calls to `transform()` plus the n lexicographic comparisons can yield a better performance than n calls to `compare()`. This is particularly true when the one string contains characters that cannot be compared on a character-by-character basis, such as strings containing characters that are treated like two characters, such as the character *ß* from the German alphabet. The code below shows an implementation of a one-to-many comparison that uses `transform()`:

```
template <class String>
String* compare1toM (locale loc, String one, String* begin, String* end)
{
    const collate<String::value_type>& collateFacet =
                         use_facet< collate<String::value_type> >(loc);

    String tmpOne =
            collateFacet.transform(one.c_str(),one.c_str()+one.length());

    for (; begin < end ; begin++)
    {
        String tmpMany = collateFacet.transform((*begin).c_str(),
                                 (*begin).c_str()+(*begin).length());

        if (tmpOne == tmpMany)
            return(begin);
    }

    return (end);
}
```

The function template `compare1toM()` compares the string `one` against the strings in the range from `begin` to `end`. An iterator pointing to the first string in this range, which equals the string `one`, is returned; otherwise `end` is returned. The expression `tmpOne==tmpMany` invokes the `operator==()` for `basic_string<charT>`, which is semantically equivalent to a lexicographic comparison of `tmpOne` and `tmpMany` that yields 0.

The fact that the comparison operator for `basic_string<char>` is used to do the lexicographic comparison of two strings reveals that this operation on strings is not

---

3. The lexicographic comparison means that the actual numeric codes are compared, by using the `operator<()` of the character type, which is a fast and efficient operation at least for the built-in character types `char` and `wchar_t`. In particular, it is much faster than the culture-dependent compare.

internationalized. The same is true for all other `basic_string<charT>` operations. For "culture sensitive" string comparison the functionality of the collate facet must be used instead. For convenience, the locale provides culture-dependent string comparison by means of its function call operator `operator()()`, which is declared as

```
template <class charT, class Traits, class Allocator>
bool operator()(const basic_string<charT,Traits,Allocator>& s1,
                const basic_string<charT,Traits,Allocator>& s2) const;
```

Its implementation is based on the collate facet's member function `compare()`. It can be used as a convenient alternative and additionally allows usage of a locale as a comparator argument to the standard containers and algorithms.

6.1.3 Code Conversion

As already explained in detail in section 4.2.7, Character Encodings, there are two possible approaches for encoding large alphabets: character encodings that mix characters of different size (*multibyte-character encodings*) and character encodings where all characters are of the same size (*wide-character encodings*). It is common practice when handling large alphabets to use wide-character encodings inside the program and multibyte-character encodings outside on the external device, which makes it necessary to convert between both encodings whenever characters are transferred from the external device to the program or vice versa.

Code conversion functionality is provided by the *codecvt* facet, which is defined by the following class template:

```
template <class internT, class externT , class stateT> class codecvt
```

Its template parameters are

- `internT`, which is the character type associated with the internal code set

- `externT`, which is the character type associated with the external code set

- `stateT`, which is the state type that is capable of holding the conversion state. It must be maintained during a conversion from the external to the internal character set and vice versa

The codecvt facet contains two types of member functions: those that provide information about the code conversion, and those that perform the conversion. The first category has five member functions:

- `always_noconv()`, which indicates if a code conversion is needed

- `encoding()`, which indicates if a conversion is state dependent, if the ratio between external characters consumed and internal characters produced is fixed, and if it is fixed, what it is

- length(), which determines a subsequence of a given sequence of external characters that produces not more than a given number of internal characters

- max_length(), which returns the maximum number of external characters needed to produce one internal character

- unshift(), which provides the external characters needed in a state-dependent conversion to "unshift" a given state so that the conversion can be terminated

The following member functions perform the conversion:

```
codecvt_base::result in(stateT& state, const externT* from,
           const externT* from_end, const externT*& from_next,
           internT* to, internT* to_limit, internT*& to_next) const;

codecvt_base::result out(stateT& state, const internT* from,
           const internT* from_end, const internT*& from_next,
           externT* to, externT* to_limit, externT*& to_next) const;
```

in() is used to convert from the external to the internal character set; out() is used for the opposite direction. The parameters and usage of both functions are similar.

The first parameter is the conversion state. In section 7.3.2, Immutability of Facets in a Locale, we describe that and explain why facets can have only const member functions: They are immutable objects. A side effect is that the conversion state cannot be a data member of the code conversion facet, because the functions in() and out() change the conversion state during code conversion. Instead, the conversion state must be held outside the facet and must be passed into the facet with each call to in() or out().

The arguments [from, from_end) specify the character sequence that is going to be converted. The resulting converted character sequence is written to [to,to_limit).

The return type codecvt_base::result is a nested enumerated type in codecvt_base, the base class of codecvt. The values of codecvt_base::result and their semantics are listed in table 6-2.

Table 6-2: Return Codes from Code Conversion Operations

RESULT VALUE	SEMANTICS
ok	completed the conversion successfully
partial	last characters from the input interval not converted, additional characters needed
error	encountered one or more character(s) in the input sequence that could not be converted
noconv	no conversion needed

After the return, from_next and to_next point one character past the last character processed by in() or out().

Correct usage of the conversion functions is not completely obvious from studying their signatures. The following example should help to reveal the subtleties. The example shows a situation where multibyte characters are read from a file (accessible via file descriptor fd) and then converted to wide characters via in(). The multibyte characters are read byte by byte from the external file into a buffer. The buffer is an array of bytes, i.e., an array of units of type char. The operating system function read() is used to fill the buffer. The characters resulting from the conversion are wide characters and are accumulated in a wchar_t buffer. The conversion therefore is from the external character type char to the internal character type wchar_t. The type of an appropriate conversion state is assumed to be ConversionState. For error indication there symbolic integral constants defined, namely ReadError, ConversionError, and ResultBufferFull. Here is the source code that does the conversion:

```
ConversionState cs;

const int transBufSize = 32;
char transBuf[transBufSize];
int readSize = transBufSize;
char *readStart = transBuf;

const int resultBufSize = 1024;
wchar_t resultBuf[resultBufSize];
wchar_t *to = resultBuf;
wchar_t const * const toLimit = resultBuf+resultBufSize;

int err = 0;

while (!err)
{
   char *fromNext;
   wchar_t *toNext;
   int readResult;
   codecvt_base::result convResult;

   if ((readResult = read (fd, readStart, readSize)) <= 0)
   {
      if (readResult = 0)
         err = NoMoreInput;
      else
         err = ReadError;

      break;
   }

   convResult = use_facet< codecvt<wchar_t, char, ConversionState> >(loc).in
         (cs, transBuf, transBuf+transBufSize, fromNext, to, toLimit, toNext);
```

```
   to = toNext;

   if (to == toLimit)
      err = ResultBufferFull;
   else if (convResult == codecvt_base::error)
      err = ConversionError;
   else if (convResult == codecvt_base::ok)
   {
      readSize = transBufSize;
      readStart = transBuf;

   }
   else if (convResult == codecvt_base::partial)
   {
      int num = transBuf+transBufSize-fromNext;
      copy(fromNext, transBuf+transBufSize, transBuf);
      readSize = transBufSize - num;
      readStart = transBuf + num;
   }
}
```

The example is straightforward in the way `in()` is invoked: The characters in the byte buffer `transBuf` are used as input, and the resulting output characters are written to wide-character buffer `resultBuf`. After the invocation of `in()`, `toNext` is pointing one behind the last output character and marks the position in the wide-character buffer to which subsequent output can be written. For this reason, `toNext` can be assigned to `to` for the next invocation of `in()`. If the wide-character buffer is full, that is, the new `to` equals `toLimit`, then the conversion is stopped.

The conversion also stops when the call to `in()` has failed, i.e., `codecvt_base::error` has been returned. When `codecvt_base::ok` has been returned, the whole byte buffer `transBuf` is specified to be available for storing new characters from the next `read()`: we set `readSize` to `transBufSize` and `readStart` to `transBuf`.

An interesting situation occurs when the return value from `in()` is `codecvt_base::partial`. It indicates that the last characters of the `transBuf` have not been consumed by `in()`. The reason for this is that more characters from the input are needed to produce an output character. `fromNext` indicates where the not-yet-consumed input starts in the byte buffer transBuf. The leftover bytes are copied to the beginning of `transBuf`. Only the rest of `transBuf` is specified as available for new characters from the next `read()`: We set `readSize` to `transBufSize-num` and `readStart` to `transBuf+num`.

6.1.4 Message Catalogs

The use of different languages makes it necessary to use different message texts for different cultures to provide messages in the user's native language. Such messages are usually maintained in a message catalog.

Services for retrieval of user-defined localized messages from message catalogs are provided by the *messages* facet. It is defined by the following class template:

```
template <class charT> class messages
```

The messages facet provides the following member functions:

```
catalog open(const basic_string<char>& name, const locale& l) const;
```

It opens a message catalog specified by a name and a locale. It returns a catalog identification of type `catalog`, which is typically a typedef for an integral type.

```
basic_string<charT> get(catalog cat_id, int set_id, int msg_id,
                const basic_string<charT> & dfault) const;
```

It retrieves a message specified by two identifications, a `set_id` and a `msg_id`, from a message catalog specified by the catalog identification `cat_id`. The last parameter allows for a string that is returned when the requested message cannot be found.

```
void close(catalog cat_id) const;
```

It closes the message catalog specified by `cat_id`.

The C++ standard describes how message catalogs can be accessed via the messages facet's member functions. Both the syntax of message catalogs and the way message catalogs must be created, installed, and maintained are beyond the scope of the standard and are implementation-specific. Consequently, the `name` for a message catalog provided to the `open()` member function as well as the `set_id` and `msg_id` provided to the get member functions may be different for different platforms.

6.2 Facets for Formatting and Parsing

The representation of numbers, monetary amounts, and date and time values differs widely from country to country. Although the characters used to denote digits are the same in many alphabets, the format of numbers, monetary amounts, and date and time values varies depending on different grouping rules, separators, etc. In the following section we discuss facets for the parsing and formatting of numbers, monetary amounts, and date and time values.

6.2.1 Numeric and Boolean Values

Numbers are represented according to cultural conventions. For example, the *radix character*, the symbol used for separation of the integer portion of a number from the fractional portion, can vary. The localization information and functionality related to numeric and Boolean expressions is handled by three standard facets:

numpunct   defined by `template<class charT> class numpunct,`

num_put   defined by `template<class charT,class OutputIterator` `=ostreambuf_iterator<charT> > class num_put,`

num_get   defined by `template<class charT, class InputIterator` `=istreambuf_iterator<charT> > class num_get.`

The numpunct facet contains the information about the format and punctuation of numeric and Boolean expressions. Based on this information, the facets num_put and num_get provide the functionality to generate a formatted character sequence from a numeric or Boolean value, and the reverse functionality provides the parsing of a character sequence to extract a numeric or Boolean value.

6.2.1.1 The numpunct Facet

The following information is provided by numpunct's member functions:

`decimal_point()` and `thousands_sep()` return the characters that represent the radix separator and the thousands separator respectively. `truename()` and `falsename()` return the strings that represent the Boolean values `true` and `false` respectively.

`grouping()` returns a value of type `string` (= `basic_string<char>`). The semantics of this value are quite tricky. Each character in the string is interpreted as an element of an integer array, which describes the way in which digits of the integral part of a numeric value are grouped. Each integer specifies the number of digits in a group, starting with the rightmost group; the last integer in the string determines the size of all remaining groups. If the last integer is `<= 0` or `== CHAR_MAX`, the described group is unlimited. If the string is empty, there is no grouping.

Let us consider some examples for grouping rules and how they would be represented as a string returned from `grouping()`. In the United States, for example, digits are grouped by threes, so the number 10 million is formatted as 10,000,000. A string s, where `s.length()==1` and `s[0]==3`, describes this grouping.[4] In Nepal, on the other hand, the first group has three digits and all subsequent groups have two digits, so that the same number, 10 million, is formatted as 1,00,00,000. This grouping is described by a two-element string, where the first element is 3 and the second 2.

Please note that an empty string and a string that contains a single 0 describe the same grouping.

6.2.1.2 The num_put Facet

Based on the information contained in the numpunct facet, num_put provides the functionality to generate a formatted character sequence that is the representation of a numeric or a Boolean value. For this reason num_put contains an overloaded version of its member function `put()` for the following types: `bool, long, unsigned long, double, long`

---

4. Note that the required string is `"\003"`, not `"3"`, because the numeric value of `"3"` is that of the character code of the digit 3, which in ASCII would be 51. Hence, the string `"\003"` specifies groups of 3 digits each, and `"3"` probably indicates groups of 51 digits each.

double, void*. At first sight it might look as if versions of put() for short, int, or float values are missing. The intent was to keep the interface of the standard library concise, and a value of type short or int can be handled by the version for long. Similarly, a value of type float can be handled by the put() version for double. Besides the value that should be formatted, put() takes the following additional parameters:

- an output iterator that specifies the location to which the formatted string should be written

- a reference to an ios_base object

- a fill character, which is used for padding

For example, put() for a long value has the following form:

```
OutputIterator put(OutputIterator s, ios_base& fg, char_type fl, long v) const;
```

For formatting of the numeric value, the put() function takes into account the information contained in numpunct, which is obtained from the locale returned by fg.getloc(), the format flags contained in the ios_base object fg, the fill character fl, and the character classification information taken from the ctype facet contained in the locale returned by fg.getloc().

The semantics of the format flags are the same as for the standard IOStreams' output streams, e.g., ios_base::dec, ios_base::hex, ios_base::oct specify if an integer value should be represented to the base 10, 16, or 8 respectively. The fill character is used for padding according to the ios_base::adjustfield specification. The exact details of the formatting are described in appendix B, Formatting Numerical and bool Values. An iterator pointing one beyond the last character written is returned.

The output iterator specifies the location to which the formatted string should be written. The type of output iterator OutputIterator is a template parameter of the num_put class template. As already mentioned above, its default is ostreambuf_iterator<charT>, but any other output iterator type can be used as well. An ostreambuf_iterator writes output to a stream buffer, and such iterators are used by the stream classes in IOStreams when they attempt to output the result of formatting to a file or string stream. In a way, stream buffer iterators are an implementation detail of the IOStreams. More about stream buffer iterators can be found in section 2.4.3, Stream Buffer Iterators.

The put() function makes no provision for error reporting. Any failure during output must be extracted from the returned iterator. Such an error can occur when not enough character positions are available in the output sequence to hold the resulting characters. Output stream buffer iterators have a public member function, failed(), that can be used to check for any previously occurred errors. Other output iterators do not have such a feature, and in that case output errors cannot be detected.

6.2.1.3 The num_get Facet

The num_get facet provides the functionality to parse a character sequence when the representation of a numeric or Boolean value is recognized and extracted. This process is contrary to the functionality provided by num_put. num_get contains overloaded member functions get(), which take the references of one of the following types: bool, long, unsigned long, unsigned int, unsigned short, float, double, long double, void*. Again, as with num_put::put(), the types that are not absolutely necessary are omitted. In particular, there is no parsing function for the integral type int, because an int value can be done by means of the parsing function for long values.

The get() function for a long value has the following signature:

```
InputIterator get(InputIterator in, InputIterator end,
                  ios_base& iob, ios_base::iostate& err, long& v) const;
```

Besides a reference to the value to be extracted, the get() function needs the following arguments:

- two input iterators specifying the character sequence that should be parsed

- a reference to an ios_base object

- a reference to an ios_base::iostate object

The get() function uses the format flags from the ios_base object to control the way in which the character sequence is parsed. The semantics of the flags are the same as for a standard IOStreams, e.g., ios_base::dec, ios_base::hex, ios_base::oct specify if a character sequence should be interpreted as the representation of a numeric value to the base 10, 16, or 8 respectively. The exact details of the parsing algorithm are described in appendix A, Parsing and Extraction of Numerical and bool Values.

The get() function uses the numpunct and ctype facets from the locale attached to the ios_base object. The numpunct facet provides information like the radix character and the thousands separator. The ctype facet is used for character classification, e.g., for distinguishing between digit and nondigit characters.

The reference to the ios_base::iostate object is used for error indication. get() sets the appropriate bitmask elements according to success or failure of the operations. The bitmask elements and their semantics are the same as for the IOStreams (see section 1.3, The Stream State, for details). An iterator pointing one beyond the character read is returned.

Below is an example of how the num_get facet's get() function would be used. The example is that of a function int_get(), which implements parsing of an int value by means of the get() function for long values. The function int_get() takes a string that is parsed in order to extract an int value and indicates failure if the extracted numeric value does not fit into an int value. The three arguments for the function int_get() are the string to be parsed, an ios_base object that carries the formatting flags and a locale with all necessary facets, and an `int` variable in which the parsing result can be stored.

```
template <class String>
ios_base::iostate int_get(const String& s, ios_base& ib, int& i)
{
    typedef String::value_type charT;
    typedef String::const_iterator iterT;
    long l;
    ios_base::iostate err;
    iterT in  = s.begin();
    iterT end = s.end();

    use_facet<num_get<charT,iterT> >(ib.getloc()).get(in, end, ib, err, l);

    if (!(err&ios_base::failbit) && !(err&ios_base::badbit))
    {   if (numeric_limits<int>::min() <= l && l <= numeric_limits<int>::max())
            i = l;
        else
            err |= ios_base::failbit;
    }
    return err;
}
```

6.2.2 Monetary Values

Units of currency are represented differently in different countries. The currency symbol varies, as does its placement, the format of negative currency values, etc. The localization information for monetary values in the standard C++ library is organized in a fashion similar to the information for numeric values. There is one facet, moneypunct, that holds the culture-dependent information. Based on this facet, two facets provide the functionality for formatting and parsing character sequences that represent monetary values. These three facets are defined as follows:

moneypunct	defined by `template<class charT,`
	`bool Inter = false>`
	`class moneypunct`

money_put	defined by `template<class charT,`
	`class OutputIterator=`
	`ostreambuf_iterator<charT> >`
	`class money_put`

money_get	defined by `template<class charT,`
	`class InputIterator= istreambuf_iterator<charT> >`
	`class money_get`

Even in one cultural context, two different currency symbols can be used: either the international symbol, which is a three-letter code defined in ISO 4217, or the domestic symbol. For instance, the international currency symbol for U.S. dollars is USD, while the domestic symbol is $. International currency symbols are useful in applications that handle many different currencies at the same time. Consider the difficulty of distinguishing between U.S. and Canadian dollars if only the domestic currency symbol was used, which in both countries is the $ sign. An application dealing with both currencies will probably use USD and CAD instead of $.

moneypunct's nontype template parameter `Inter` of type `bool` determines whether the international currency symbol (`Inter=true`) or the domestic one (`Inter=false`) should be used. The moneypunct facet has a `static const` data member `intl` that is set at compile time to the value of the template argument. The usage of this data member, which is publicly accessible, is very similar to the usage of a nested typedef for a type template parameter; it allows deduction of the template argument for an instantiated template class.

In contrast to moneypunct, the money_put and money_get facets are not templatized with a specification of the currency symbol. As we will see in detail below, their member functions `get()` and `put()` are parameterized with this specification for each invocation. The consequence of this architecture is that a combination of four facet classes is needed to provide the entire information and functionality for the handling of monetary values: one num_put facet, one num_get facet, and two numpunct facets; one numpunct facet for the international currency symbol; and one for the domestic currency value.

6.2.2.1 The moneypunct Facet

Let's see in detail which information the moneypunct facet provides:

- `decimal_point()`, `thousands_sep()`, and `do_grouping()` behave like the member functions of the same name from the numpunct facet.

- `curr_symbol()` returns the string that represents the currency symbol.[5]

- `positive_sign()` and `negative_sign()` return the strings that indicate a positive or a negative monetary value.

- `frac_digits()` returns the number of digits to be displayed after the radix separator.

- `pos_format()` and `neg_format()` return the pattern that should be used to represent a positive or a negative monetary value. The pattern is a four-element array specifying the order of the parts that form the monetary value representation. Each

---

5. One might wonder why the entire numpunct class is parameterized with the nontype template argument `Inter`. Wouldn't it suffice if the `curr_symbol()` came in two flavors, one for the domestic and one for the international currency symbol? The reason for providing two different numpunct facets for each type of currency symbol is that the type of the currency symbol might have an impact on the rest of the format information. For instance, the format for negative or positive amounts might be different when the international currency symbol is used from the format that is used with the domestic symbol.

element has a value of the enumerated type `money_base::part`. The possible values are `none`, `space`, `symbol`, `sign`, `value`. Each value—`symbol`, `sign`, `value`, and either `space` or `none`—appears exactly once. The value `none`, if present, is not first; the value `space`, if present, is neither first nor last.

The num_put facet uses both `pos_format()` and `neg_format()` for formatting. The num_get facet uses only `neg_format()` for parsing. The following rules apply for the interpretation of the format array:

Where `none` or `space` appears, whitespace is permitted in the input or output sequence. For input, `space` indicates that at least one space is required at that position.

Where `symbol` appears, the sequence of characters returned by `curr_symbol()` is permitted, and can be required. For details, see the subsequent sections on num_put and num_get.

Where `sign` appears, the first (if any) of the sequence of characters returned by `positive_sign()` or `negative_sign()` is required, depending on the monetary value being non-negative or negative. Any remaining characters of the sign sequence are required after all other format components.

Where `value` appears, the absolute numeric monetary value is required.

Let's look at some examples. In Hong Kong, a positive monetary value is written as HK$0.95, while a negative value is written as (HK$0.95). In Germany, a positive value is written as 0,95 DM and a negative one as –0,95 DM. Here are the typical values returned from `pos_format()` and `neg_format()` for these examples:

Hong Kong:

`pos_format()`	sign, symbol, value, none
`neg_format()`	sign, symbol, value, none

Germany:

`pos_format()`	sign, value, space, symbol
`neg_format()`	sign, value, space, symbol

In this case, a positive sign is defined as empty. Note that there are also other valid possibilities to define the format specifications. An alternative for the German `pos_format()` could be value, space, symbol, none.

6.2.2.2 The money_put Facet

money_put contains two overloaded versions of the `put()` member function. One takes a value of type `long double` to be formatted to the representation of a monetary value, the other takes a reference to `basic_string<charT>`:

```
OutputIterator put(OutputIterator s, bool intl, ios_base& fg,
                   charT fill, long double quant) const;
OutputIterator put(OutputIterator s, bool intl, ios_base& fg,
                   charT fill, const basic_string<charT>& quant) const;
```

The first argument is an output iterator that allows output of the resulting character sequence; the iterator's type is a template argument of the money_put class template. The default type is `ostreambuf_iterator<charT>`, but any other output iterator type can be used as well.

The argument `quant` specifies the monetary amount to be formatted. It is interpreted as a value of the smallest currency unit. For instance, 5.00 $ would be expressed in cents and specified as either the numeric value `500` or the string `"500"`. Any fractional parts are ignored.[6] A value of `5.00` or a string like `"5.00"` would yield a monetary amount of 0.05 $. In the string, only the optional leading minus sign and the immediately subsequent digit characters are used; any trailing characters, including digits appearing after a nondigit character, are ignored. In particular, the string must not contain any thousands separators. A string like `"1,000,000"` would yield an amount of 0.01 $. Digit characters are distinguished from nondigit characters by use of the ctype facet that is contained in the locale attached to the `ios_base` argument `fg`.

The `bool` argument `intl` indicates whether the resulting character sequence should contain the international monetary sign (`intl == true`) or the domestic one (`intl == false`). The relevant currency symbol is taken from the moneypunct facets `moneypunct<charT, true>` or `moneypunct<charT, false>` contained in the locale that comes with the `ios_base` object `fg`. Additional formatting information like the character for the radix separator point, number of digits after the radix separator, etc., is also taken from this moneypunct facet.

The format flags are taken from the `ios_base` object `fg` and are interpreted in the following way: A currency symbol is generated if `ios_base::showbase` is set. Fill characters are placed where `none` or `space` appears in the formatting pattern, if `ios_base::internal` is set. If `ios_base::left` is set, they are placed after the other characters; if `ios_base::right` is set, before the other characters.[7] The interpretation of any other format information contained in the `ios_base` object is implementation-defined.

The iterator positioned one beyond the last character written is returned by `put()`. The `put()` function does not report any errors. Failure of output can only be detected by checking the returned iterator's `failed()` function.

If we attempt to use the money_put facet we notice that the formatting of monetary amounts is not supported by IOStreams. Section 6.4.1, Indirect Use of a Facet Through a Stream, demonstrates how the num_put facet can be used with a string stream. Anything comparable is not possible for monetary amounts, unless we define an inserter for monetary amounts ourselves. Section 3.1.4, Refined Inserters and Extractors, in part I explains how such user-defined inserters can be implemented; the example chosen there uses the

---

6. It might seem that the type `long double` for the `quant` argument is inappropriate, because only the integral part is used, but the intent is to allow a maximum range of values, and on most systems this can be achieved by using `long double`, not the integral type `long`.

7. Note that it is possible, with some combination of format patterns and flag values, to produce output that cannot be parsed using `num_get<>::get`.

time_put facet, but the same technique can be applied for use with the monetary facets. If we do not intend to implement an inserter for monetary values, we can resort to direct use of the money_put facet, independent of any streams. Direct use of facets is discussed in section 6.4.2, Use of a Facet Through a Locale, and in section 6.4.3, Direct Use of the Facet Independently of a Locale.

6.2.2.3 The money_get Facet

The money_get facet provides the functionality to parse a character sequence that represents a monetary amount and to extract the numeric value. For this reason it contains overloaded versions of its member function get() for the types long double and basic_string<charT> to store the extracted numeric value:

```
InputIterator get(InputIterator s, InputIterator end, bool intl, ios_base& fg,
                  ios_base::iostate& err, long double& units) const;
InputIterator get(InputIterator s, InputIterator end, bool intl, ios_base& fg,
                  ios_base::iostate& err, basic_string<charT>& digits) const;
```

The first two arguments specify the character sequence, given as input iterator range [s,end), that is to be parsed.

The bool parameter intl specifies which currency symbol should be expected in the character sequence: the international (intl == true) or the domestic (intl == false) symbol. The respective currency symbol is taken from the moneypunct facets moneypunct<charT,true> or moneypunct<charT,false> contained in the locale that comes with the ios_base object fg.

The function get() always uses the neg_format() from the respective numpunct facet to parse the character sequence. The result is returned as an integral value stored in units or as a sequence of digits in the string digits, possibly preceded by a minus sign. For example, the character sequence $1,234.56 parsed with a U.S. locale would yield the value 123456.0 for units, or the string "123456" for digits.

If numpunct's member function grouping() indicates that no thousands separators are permitted, any such characters are not read, and parsing is terminated at the point where the first thousands separator appears. Otherwise, thousands separators are optional; if present, they are checked for correct placement.

Where space or none appears in the format pattern returned by numpunct's neg_format(), except at the end, optional whitespace is consumed after any required space. Whether a character is whitespace or not is determined by using the ctype facet contained in the locale fg.getloc().

The format flags from fg are interpreted in the following way: If ios_base::showbase is not set, the currency symbol is optional and is consumed only if other characters are needed to complete the format; otherwise, the currency symbol is required. For example, if showbase is off, for a neg_format() of "()" and a currency symbol of "L", the L is consumed when the character sequence (100   L) is parsed. If the neg_format() is "-", then the L in -100 L is not consumed.

The reference to the `ios_base::iostate` object is used for error indication. `get()` sets the appropriate bitmask elements according to success or failure of the operations. The bitmask elements and their semantics are the same as for the IOStreams (see section 1.3, The Stream State, for details). An iterator pointing one beyond the last character read is returned.

If we attempt to use the money_get facet, we notice that the parsing of monetary amounts is not supported by IOStreams. In section 6.4.1, Indirect Use of a Facet Through a Stream, we demonstrate how the num_put facet can be used with a string stream. Anything comparable is not possible for monetary amounts, unless we define an extractor for monetary amounts ourselves. Section 3.1.4, Refined Inserters and Extractors, in part I explains how such user-defined extractors can be implemented; the example chosen there uses the time_get facet, but the same technique can be applied for use of the monetary facets. If we do not intend to implement an extractor for monetary values, we can resort to direct use of the money_get facet, independent of any streams. Direct use of facets is discussed in section 6.4.2, Use of a Facet Through a Locale, and section 6.4.3, Direct Use of the Facet Independent of a Locale.

6.2.3 Date and Time Values

The representation of date and time depends on cultural conventions. For example, the names and abbreviations for days of the week and months of the year vary with the language. The localization information for date and time values is organized in two facets:

time_put	defined by `template<class charT, class`
	`OutputIterator = ostreambuf_iterator<charT> >`
	`class time_put`

time_get	defined by `template<class charT, class`
	`InputIterator = istreambuf_iterator<charT> >`
	`class time_get`

Compared with the organization of localization information for numbers and monetary values, the canonical equivalent of numpunct and moneypunct is missing for the localization information for date and time values. The reason for this gap is that the facets time_put and time_get are not based on any common formatting elements, but rather on the C library date- and time-formatting function `strftime()`. Both facets, time_put and time_get, use the structure `tm` that is defined in the C library header file `<ctime>`. The detailed relationship of `strftime()` and the two time facets are explained in the following two chapters; a description of the `tm` structure can be found in the reference part of this book.

6.2.3.1 The time_put Facet

The time_put facet provides two overloaded versions of its `put()` member function. Both differ in the way they allow specification of the formatting pattern.

```
OutputIterator put(OutputIterator s, ios_base& str, char_type fill,
        const tm* t, const charT* pat_begin, const charT* pat_end) const;
OutputIterator put(OutputIterator s, ios_base& str, char_type fill,
        const tm* t, char format, char modifier = 0) const;
```

The first argument is an output iterator that allows output of the resulting character sequence to a character container, and the iterator's type is a template argument of the time_put class template. The default type is `ostreambuf_iterator<charT>`, but any other output iterator type can be used as well.

In the first version of `put()`, the character sequence `[pat_begin, pat_end)` is scanned for any contained format patterns. A format pattern starts with the character `'%'` followed by an optional modifier character and a format specifier character. If no modifier character is present, it is assumed to be zero. The `narrow()` member function from `str.getloc()`'s ctype facet is applied to each character before it is interpreted.

The date or time data contained in the `struct tm t` are formatted according to the found format patterns as if `t` and the respective format pattern were arguments for the C library's function `strftime()` using `fill` for padding. Details about the format patterns of `strftime()` and how they are interpreted can be found in appendix C, `strftime()` Conversion Specifiers used by time_put facet.

Any character from `[pat_begin,pat_end)` that is not part of a format pattern is written to the output iterator s without any interpretation. Thus characters resulting from the formatting of the date/time value and nonformat pattern characters forming the sequence `[pat_begin,pat_end)` are interleaved in the output in the order in which the format pattern and the nonformat pattern characters appeared in sequence `[pat_begin,pat_end)`.

For example, a call to the first version of `put()` with a `struct tm` containing the 25th of December 1993 and the character sequence `"This is %A, day %d of month %B in the year %Y. \n"`, i.e. the following code snippet:

```
ostringstream oss;
locale loc("American_USA.1252");
oss.imbue(loc);
const time_put<char>& tfac = use_facet<time_put<char> >(loc);
struct tm xmas = { 0, 0, 12, 25, 11, 93 };
string fmt("This is %A, day %d of month %B in the year %Y.\n");
time_put<char>::iter_type ret
  = tfac.put(oss,oss,' ',&xmas,
    fmt.c_str(),fmt.c_str()+fmt.length());
cout << oss.str() << endl;
```

will produce the text

```
This is Sunday, day 25 of month December in the year 1993.
```

The second version of `put()` interprets the characters `format` and `modifier` as a format pattern. The date or time value contained in `t` is formatted as if passed to the C library's function `strftime()` (see appendix C, `strftime()` Conversion Specifiers, for details).

Note that neither the first nor the second version of put() interprets the format parameters or the fill character. For the standard facets time_put<char> and time_put<wchar_t>, formatting is controlled by the strftime() format patterns only. The format parameters and the fill character are provided to the put() functions, so that nonstandard facet types derived from time_put may use them in overriding versions of the format functions.

An iterator positioned one beyond the last character written is returned by both versions of put(). The put() function does not report any errors. Failure of output can be detected only by checking the returned iterator's failed() function.

If we attempt to use the time_put facet we notice that the formatting of date and time values is not supported by IOStreams. In section 6.4.1, Indirect Use of a Facet Through a Stream, we demonstrate how the num_put facet can be used with a string stream. Anything comparable is not possible for date and time values, unless we define an inserter for date and time values ourselves. Section 3.1.4, Refined Inserters and Extractors, in part I explains how such user-defined inserters can be implemented; the example chosen there uses the time_put facet. If we do not intend to implement an inserter for date and time values, we can resort to direct use of the time facet, independent of any streams. Direct use of a facet is discussed in section 6.4.2, Use of a Facet Through a Locale, and section 6.4.3, Direct Use of the Facet Independent of a Locale.

6.2.3.2 The time_get Facet
The time_get facet provides the following functions to parse a sequence of characters and determine a contained time or date value:

```
InputIterator get_time(InputIterator begin, InputIterator end,
                       ios_base& fg, ios_base::iostate& err, tm* t) const;
InputIterator get_date(InputIterator begin, InputIterator end,
                       ios_base& fg, ios_base::iostate& err, tm* t) const;
InputIterator get_weekday(InputIterator begin, InputIterator end,
                       ios_base& fg, ios_base::iostate& err, tm* t) const;
InputIterator get_monthname(InputIterator begin, InputIterator end,
                       ios_base& fg, ios_base::iostate& err, tm* t) const;
InputIterator get_year(InputIterator begin, InputIterator end,
                       ios_base& fg, ios_base::iostate& err, tm* t) const;
```

All five member functions behave similarly. They parse the character sequence specified by [begin, end) to determine a time or date value or an element of a date value. If the sequence being parsed matches the correct format, the corresponding members of the struct tm argument t are set to the values used to produce the respective part of the sequence. Otherwise an error is reported via the ios_base::iostate object err[8] or

---

8. The bitmask elements and their semantics are the same as for the IOStreams (see section 1.3, The Stream State, for details).

unspecified values are assigned. As the err object does not necessarily reflect any failure, user confirmation is required for reliable parsing of user-entered dates and times. Only machine-generated formats, produced by time_put, can be parsed reliably. The ios_base object fg is passed to each function to give access to the ctype facet of fg.getloc(), which is needed during parsing. An iterator positioned one beyond the last character read is returned by each of the functions.

The functions differ in the struct tm parts that are extracted from the character sequence.

- get_time() searches for a character sequence that matches a time_put output produced with the format character X.

- get_date() searches for a character sequence that matches a time_put output produced with the format character x.

- get_weekday() and get_monthname() search for a name, perhaps abbreviated, of a weekday or month. If they find an abbreviation that is followed by characters that could match a full name, they continue reading until it matches the full name or fails.

- get_year() searches for an unambiguous year identifier. It is implementation-defined whether two-digit year numbers are accepted and (if so) what century they are assumed to lie in.

Besides the functions that help to extract date and time values from a character sequence, time_get provides a function:

```
dateorder date_order()  const;
```

which indicates the preferred order of components for those date formats that are composed of day, month, and year. date_order() returns values of an enumeration type dateorder nested in time_get. The possible values are no_order, dmy, mdy, ymd, ydm, describing either a certain order or no order. date_order() is intended as a convenience only, for common formats, and may return no_order in valid locales.

If we attempt to use the time_get facet, we notice that the parsing of date and time values is not supported by IOStreams. In section 6.4.1, Indirect Use of a Facet Through a Stream, we demonstrate how the num_put facet can be used with a string stream. Anything comparable is not possible for date and time values, unless we define an extractor for date and time values ourselves. Section 3.1.4, Refined Inserters and Extractors, in part I explains how such user-defined extractors can be implemented; the example chosen there uses the time_put facet. If we do not intend to implement an extractor for date and time values, we can resort to direct use of the time facet, independent of any streams. Direct use of a facet is discussed in section 6.4.2, Use of a Facet Through a Locale, and section 6.4.3, Direct Use of the Facet Independently of a Locale.

6.3 Grouping of Standard Facets in a Locale

In the preceding sections, we described all standard facets with emphasis on their functionality. Let us now take a look at the way in which the standard facets are organized in a locale. As mentioned before, there are two grouping mechanisms: facet families and locale categories.

We will first take a look at the standard facet families and the classes and templates that represent them. In section 6.3.2, Locale Categories, we take a look at the category-grouping mechanism.

6.3.1 The Standard Facet Families

The standard facets are organized in facet families, which are hierarchies of facet classes derived from facet base classes. We have seen in previous chapters that the family name plays a significant role in the usage of locales and facets. In particular, the standard facets contained in a locale are referred to by their family names. This situation is reflected in the signature of the locale constructors as well as in the function templates use_facet <Facet>(loc) and has_facet<Facet>(loc).

The base classes of the standard facet families are instantiations or specializations of a number of facet base class templates, which are listed in section 6.3.1.4, Mandatory Facet Types. In the following section, we look at the architecture of these base class templates and their derived classes.

6.3.1.1 The Standard Facet Base Class Templates

The facet base class templates follow a certain idiom: They have a public interface of non-virtual member functions and a protected interface of virtual functions. Each of the public functions calls a protected virtual counterpart. There is a certain naming convention for these member functions: If a public function is named foo(), its protected counterpart is named do_foo(). For instance, the time_put facet's public put() function calls the protected do_put() function.

Derived classes must override the protected virtual functions. The rationale behind this idiom of providing nonvirtual public functions that call virtual protected functions is that a library implementor might place code for system-specific functionality into the public member functions. A conceivable example for such system-specific functionality is the use of a mutex to support multithreaded environments. A user who derives from such a class need not worry about the system-specific issues, but can simply provide the new functionality by overriding the protected member functions.[9]

The protected virtual interface provides a hook for customization and allows derivation of special versions of the standard facets. The standard library already provides certain derived facet classes—the byname facets.

---

9. The only exception to this rule of public nonvirtual functions calling protected virtual functions is the specialization ctype<char>. Its is() member function does not call any virtual member function, for reasons of efficiency, but takes a table-driven approach; this table can be replaced for the purpose of customizing the facet.

6.3.1.2 The Derived Byname Facets

Some facets contain culture-sensitive data that are specific to each cultural area. Examples are the facets numpunct and moneypunct. They provide data such as the radix character, the thousands separator, the currency symbol, etc., which depend on cultural conventions. Other facets are independent of any cultural area, because they provide only functionality. Examples are the parsing and formatting facets such as money_put, num_put, etc.

For those facets that provide culture-dependent information rather than culture independent functionality, the standard defines so-called *byname* facets. The purpose of a byname facet is that one can pass the name of a localization environment to the facet, and the facet then provides information appropriate for the specified cultural area. These names are the same as those used for construction of named locales (see section 5.1.1, Named Locales).

A byname facet is derived from a base class facet. For instance, there is a byname version of the numpunct facet, defined as

```
template <class charT>
class numpunct_byname : public numpunct<charT>
{
    // class definition
};
```

The byname facets have a constructor that takes the name of a cultural area as a `const char*` argument. A byname facet redefines the protected virtual member functions of its base class with behavior that is appropriate for the specified cultural area.

Byname facets are automatically created when a named locale is constructed. For example:

```
locale loc("US");
```

creates a locale that represents the U.S. localization environment. This locale contains the respective byname versions of those facets that have a byname version, such as the numpunct facet. In the code below, the numpunct facet retrieved from the U.S. locale object is a numpunct_byname facet:

```
char rs = use_facet< numpunct<char> >(loc).decimal_point();
```

As expected, the provided radix character will be '.'.

Note that although the contained facet is a numpunct_byname facet, it can be accessed by its base class type numpunct. Why and how this works is explained in section 7.2, Identification and Lookup of Facets in a Locale.

6.3.1.3 Behavior of the Base Class Facets

None of the standard facet base classes is a pure virtual base class. Instead, the virtual member functions provide functionality, which can be used as a default for those inherited operations that are not redefined by the derived class. Let us see what the respective default behavior is for each of the standard facets.

NUM_PUT, NUM_GET, MONEY_PUT, AND MONEY_GET

No further explanation is needed for these facets. As described above, they define functionality rather than holding locale-sensitive information and the base classes implement this functionality. Note also that for these facets, no byname versions exist.

CTYPE, MESSAGES, MONEYPUNCT, TIME_GET, AND TIME_PUT

The base classes of these facets have implementation-defined behavior. This is because the standards committee, as an international forum, did not want to dictate one nation's preference as a default for all other nations. For instance, there is no pattern that is universally accepted for representing a monetary amount. Consequently, the committee did not define a base class behavior.

NUMPUNCT

The base class for numpunct provides *classic "C"* behavior. Classic "C" behavior is the way C functions used to behave before internationalization was added to the C standard. Obviously, classic "C" describes the behavior only for the character type `char`. The behavior for the character type `wchar_t` is defined in analogy to the classic "C" behavior for `char`. For instance, when `numpunct<char>::decimal_point()` returns `'.'`, then `numpunct<wchar_t>::decimal_point()` returns the wide character equivalent `L'.'`.

COLLATE

In the case of string collation, two collate base class facets must be provided by a standard-compliant library. (See section 6.3.1.4, Mandatory Facet Types, for a list of all the mandatory standard facet types.) Both required base class facets provide classic "C" behavior, which in the case of collation is lexicographic ordering, that is, character and character sequences are ordered according to the numeric values of the character codes.

CODECVT

In the case of code conversion, two codecvt base class facets must be provided by a standard compliant library. (See section 6.3.1.4, Mandatory Facet Types, for a list of all the mandatory standard facet types.) The facet `codecvt<char,char,mbstate_t>` is a degenerated one; it implements "no conversion," so that `in()` and `out()` behave similarly to a `memcpy()`. The behavior of `codecvt<wchar_t,char,mbstate_t>` is implementation-defined.

You may have noticed that some of the standard facet base classes have implementation-dependent functionality. Usually, interfaces with implementation-defined behavior must be avoided by users who strive for portability of their programs. Hence, one might wonder whether it is a problem that the base class behavior of some facets is implementation-defined. The answer is no, not really.

The behavior of a base class facet is of interest only when a specialized version of one of the standard facet interfaces is to be implemented and the existing base class behavior is to be reused. The byname facets are powerful and already provide support for all common localization environments. Only in really special, "exotic" cases is the derivation of a new standard facet necessary at all. In such a case it is likely that the new functionality must be implemented from scratch and cannot be built reusing the base class behavior. Hence, the base class behavior is almost irrelevant, because it will most likely be overridden anyway.

6.3.1.4 Mandatory Facet Types

As mentioned before, the standard C++ library defines a number of facet base class templates for the standard facet families. A certain set of instantiations or specializations of these templates must be contained in every locale. The mandatory facet types are listed in table 6-3, together with their categories, which are explained in section 6.3.2, Locale Categories, later in this chapter.

Table 6-3: Facets Contained in Every Locale

CATEGORY	FACETS CONTAINED IN EVERY LOCALE	
collate	`collate<char>`	`collate<wchar_t>`
ctype	`ctype<char>`	`ctype<wchar_t>`
	`codecvt<char,char,mbstate_t>`	`codecvt<wchar_t,char,mbstate_t>`
monetary	`moneypunct<char>`	`moneypunct<wchar_t>`
	`moneypunct<char,true>`	`moneypunct<wchar_t,true>`
	`money_get<char>`	`money_get<wchar_t>`
	`money_put<char>`	`money_put<wchar_t>`
numeric	`numpunct<char>`	`numpunct<wchar_t>`
	`num_get<char>`	`num_get<wchar_t>`
	`num_put<char>`	`num_put<wchar_t>`
time	`time_get<char>`	`time_get<wchar_t>`
	`time_put<char>`	`time_put<wchar_t>`
messages	`messages<char>`	`messages<wchar_t>`

Whether the mandatory facets are instantiations or specializations of the respective class templates is implementation-dependent. Each locale is guaranteed to contain a facet object of each of the types listed in the table above.

MANDATORY BYNAME FACETS

In addition to the mandatory facet types listed above, the standard library must provide a certain set of byname facet types.[10] The mandatory byname facet types are listed in table 6-4, together with their categories.

---

10. The `codecvt_byname` facets are not required by the final C++ standard. At the time of this writing, the question of whether this situation is a defect in the standard or whether the facets were omitted intentionally is under discussion.

Table 6-4: Mandatory byname Facets

CATEGORY	MANDATORY BYNAME FACETS	
collate	`collate_byname<char>`	`collate_byname <wchar_t>`
ctype	`ctype_byname <char>`	`ctype_byname <wchar_t>`
	`codecvt_byname<char,char,`	`codecvt<wchar_t,char,`
	`mbstate_t>`	`mbstate_t>`
monetary	`moneypunct_byname <char>`	`moneypunct_byname <wchar_t>`
	`moneypunct_byname <char,true>`	`moneypunct_byname <wchar_t,true>`
numeric	`numpunct_byname <char>`	`numpunct_byname <wchar_t>`
time	`time_get_byname <char>`	`time_get_byname <wchar_t>`
	`time_put_byname <char>`	`time_put_byname <wchar_t>`
messages	`messages_byname <char>`	`messages_byname <wchar_t>`

Whether the mandatory byname facets are instantiations or specializations of the respective class template is implementation-dependent. Note that these facets need not be contained in every locale object. Only named locale objects will contain byname facets.

MANDATORY FACET TEMPLATES

The standard facet base class templates need not be instantiable, in the sense that an instantiation of the template would yield a meaningful class. The facet types listed in the tables above are allowed to be specializations of an empty class template instead of instantiations of a template.

However, for some of the facet types, the standard requires that there must be templates available that can be instantiated. These mandatory facet templates are listed in table 6-5, together with their categories.

Table 6-5: Mandatory Facet Templates

CATEGORY	MANDATORY FACET TEMPLATES	
monetary	`money_get<CharT,InputIterator>`	`money_put <CharT,`
		`OutputIterator>`
numeric	`num_get<CharT,InputIterator>`	`num_put<CharT,OutputIterator>`
time	`time_get<char,InputIterator>`	`time_put<char,OutputIterator>`
	`time_get<wchar_t,InputIterator>`	`time_put<wchar_t,`
		`OutputIterator>`
	`time_get_byname<char,`	`time_put_byname<char,`
	`InputIterator>`	`OutputIterator>`
	`time_get_byname<wchar_t,`	`time_put_byname<wchar_t,`
	`InputIterator>`	`OutputIterator>`

The names `InputIterator`, `OutputIterator`, and `CharT` are formal template parameters.

An argument for the formal template parameter `CharT` must satisfy the requirements for a character type, which are described in section 2.3.3, Character Types, in part I.

Types that are used as arguments for the formal parameters `InputIterator` or `OutputIterator` must satisfy the requirements of an input iterator type or an output iterator type respectively. They must be iterators to a character container; that is, the iterator's value type must be compatible with a character type.

Note that instantiations of these facet templates for character types other than `char` and `wchar_t` and iterator types other than `istreambuf_iterator` and `ostreambuf_iterator` are not automatically contained in every locale object and must be explicitly installed.

6.3.2 Locale Categories

The standard facets are grouped into categories. These locale categories stem from the C heritage (see section F.1, Locale Categories in C and C++, in appendix F for further details). In a C++ locale, there are six categories. Each category is expressed as a value of type `locale::category`. For each of the categories there is a predefined value: `locale::collate`, `locale::ctype`, `locale::monetary`, `locale::numeric`, `locale::time`, and `locale::messages`. In addition, there is a value `locale::none`, which represents no category, and `locale::all`, which represents the union of all categories. The type `locale::category` is a bitmask type,[11] which means that combinations of categories yield another valid category value.

The lists in the previous section show the six categories and which standard facets belong to each of them. The categories are used for specifying groups of related facets in locale constructors and member functions. Locale functions expecting a category argument require either a valid `locale::category` value or one of the constants from the C library.

Note that locale categories are a nonextensible grouping mechanism. Let's compare them to the facet families. The grouping mechanism of facet families can be extended by adding further members to a facet family in the form of derived classes or by defining new facet families. (Examples of such extensions can be found in chapter 8, "User-Defined Facets.") In contrast, locale categories cannot be extended. We cannot define any new locale categories beyond the predefined ones. Adding facet families to a locale category is possible only via instantiation of one of the predefined facet base class templates. For instance, the instantiation `time_get <char, string::const_iterator>` would add another facet family to the time category. However, we cannot add any user-defined facet family to any of the predefined locale categories.

For the sake of comprehensiveness, let us mention that the library implementors have some latitude that we do not have. They can in fact add facets to a category, but these additional facets are implementation details and are usually not documented and not visible. For instance, an implementation could have a timepunct facet, which contains information that the time_put and time_get facets might need. Such a timepunct facet would probably belong to the time category as a hidden implementation detail.

---

11. See section G.1, Bitmask Types, in appendix G for further details on bitmask types.

6.3.3 Diagram: Facets and Categories

Figure 6-1 summarizes the relationship of the grouping mechanisms of facets and categories visually:

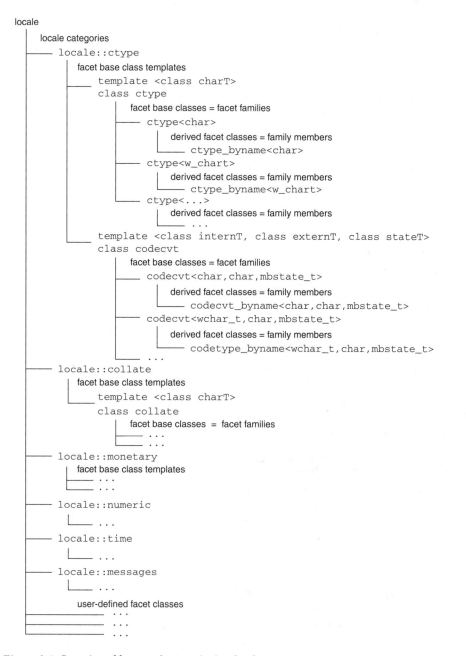

Figure 6-1: *Grouping of facets and categories in a locale.*

6.4 Advanced Usage of the Standard Facets

In this section we discuss how facets can be used. There are basically three possibilities:

- implicit use of a facet through an I/O operation

- use of a facet that is contained in a locale

- use of a facet independent of any locales

6.4.1 Indirect Use of a Facet Through a Stream

The IOStream classes are internationalized, and each stream has a locale attached. Various stream operations use standard facets contained in the stream's locale for performing their tasks. In particular, code conversion facets are used for converting between internal and external character encodings. This is interesting for input and output of wide characters to/from multibyte files. The ctype facets are used for recognition of whitespace characters, digits, etc., during parsing. And most important, the numeric facets are used by the inserters and extractors for numeric values. Inserters and extractors offer a convenient way of using the facets' capabilities.

Here is an example. Let us format a numeric value according to cultural conventions. We can easily achieve this by using a string stream. We attach the desired locale to the string stream, write the numeric value to the string stream, and afterwards extract the resulting string from the string stream.

```
ostringstream ost;
ost.imbue(locale("German"));
ost << "Hello World - " << 12345678L;
string s = ost.str();
```

Afterwards, the string `s` contains the initial string `"Hello World - "` plus the result of formatting the number `12345678L`, that is `"Hello World - 12.345.678"`. The numpunct facet, the format flags, and the fill character used for formatting are those of the German locale, which we attached to the stream via a call to the stream's member function `imbue()`.

Use of formatting and parsing facets through a stream is the most convenient way of using these facets. Predefined in the standard library are inserters and extractors for numeric values, which use the numeric facets, as shown above. Internationalized parsing and formatting of date and time values are not available through the stream classes. This is because there are no standard types for representing date and time values. However, such inserters and extractors can be added. Section 3.1, Input and Output of User-Defined Types, in part I gives an example; it explains how the functionality of the date formatting facet can be made available through a stream.

Other values whose parsing or formatting depends on cultural conventions can be handled in the exact same way. Section 8.2, Defining a New Facet Family, explores the example of address formatting. A facet type for address-formatting rules is defined, corresponding facets are installed in a locale, that locale is attached to a stream, an inserter for address values is defined that uses the address-formatting facet, and eventually addresses can be formatted as easily as the numeric values in the example above.

If for any reason we do not want to use streams for implicit use of a facet, we can call the facets directly. For the sake of comparability, we stick to the example used above: formatting of numeric values, that is, use of the num_put facet. Direct use of the num_put facet might not look terribly useful, but the issues discussed below apply equally well to all other facets. Take, for instance, monetary, date, and time values. There are no inserters and extractors for these entities defined in the standard library, and the monetary and time facets are not used by IOStreams. These facets must be used directly. A facet that we want to use directly can be contained in a locale or it can be used by itself, independent of a locale. In the following section, we discuss both cases, using the num_put facet as an example.

6.4.2 Use of a Facet Through a Locale

Let us try to write the result of formatting a numeric value to a string object of type string. We want to use the num_put facet's put() function for this purpose. The put() function writes to a character container via an output iterator. As we want to write output to a string, we must provide an iterator that allows output to the string. We could use the string's iterator type string::iterator, but we want to make sure that the string grows as needed and can always hold the formatted value's character representation, no matter how long that might be. For this reason, we want to use an insert iterator instead of a normal iterator. Insert iterators add elements to a container rather than overwriting existing positions. We want to use a back_insert_iterator <string>, which is an insert iterator that inserts characters at the end of a string.

Having identified the right iterator type, we know that we want to use a num_put facet of type num_put<char, back_insert_iterator<string> > in order to write the result of formatting directly to a string object. Where do we get such a facet from? Each locale object must contain the standard facets. We saw in section 6.3.1.4, Mandatory Facets, that only certain instantiations of the standard facet templates are automatically contained in every locale. Usually, these are the versions for the two built-in character types char and wchar_t. The parsing and formatting facets, such as num_get and num_put, all have an iterator type as a template argument. Only the instantiations for the stream buffer iterator types are required to be contained in each locale object. In sum, no locale can be expected to contain a facet of the desired type num_put<char, back_insert_iterator<string> >.[12] If the desired facet is to be contained in a

---

12. You might wonder why the entire num_put class template is parameterized by the iterator type if only the member function put() needs the iterator type. An alternative idea could have been to make the member function put() a template function and eliminate the iterator type argument from the num_put class template. Unfortunately, this is not feasible, because the put() function calls a protected virtual do_put() function that has exactly the same signature. This protected virtual member function needs to turn into a function template, too, and virtual member functions are not allowed to be templates in C++.

locale, we must explicitly install it in the locale object that we want to use. Below is an example that shows how the necessary facet is installed and subsequently used in a German locale:

```
locale loc(locale("German"),new num_put<char,back_insert_iterator<string> >);
basic_ios<char> str(0);
str.imbue(loc);
string s("Hello World - ");
use_facet<num_put<char,back_insert_iterator<string> > >(loc)
          .put(back_inserter(s),str,' ',(unsigned long)12345678L);
```

First, we install the num_put facet in a German locale by creating a new locale `loc` that is a copy of the German locale plus the num_put facet for strings.

For invocation of the facet's `put()` function, we need an `ios_base` object.[13] We use a `basic_ios` object here, because the class `ios_base` has a protected constructor, and `ios_base` objects can be created only by friends or derived objects. We could be creating a complete stream instead, but we do not need stream-specific properties such as the stream buffer or the formatting functions of a stream. As we don't need a stream buffer in this context, we create the `basic_ios` objects with a constructor argument of 0, which means that no stream buffer is provided. Then we attach our extended German locale to the `basic_ios` object.

For invocation of the `put()` function, we retrieve the num_put facet from the locale via `use_facet`. We create an insert iterator for the string s, which is appended by the formatted character representation of `12345678L`. The insert iterator for the string is created by using the creator function `back_inserter()` from the standard library.

Then we pass all required arguments to the `put()` function: the iterator (which allows appending characters to the string), the `basic_ios` object (which carries the format flags and the locale that has the German numpunct and ctype facets), a fill character, and the numeric value that is to be formatted. Resulting from the call to `put()` the string s contains the same value as in the previous example: `"Hello World - 12.345.678"`.

The return value of the `put()` function is not checked, because the returned iterator is of type `back_insert_iterator<string>`, which is an iterator type that does not signal failure of output by any means. Failure of output to a dynamically growing string is extremely unlikely anyway. The only failure that can happen would occur when the string cannot be expanded anymore because the entire memory is exhausted. In that case, the allocation inside the string's `insert()` function would probably raise a `bad_alloc` exception anyway.

If another type of output iterator was used that refers to a fixed-sized character container, such as a normal string iterator or a pointer to a character array, a container over-

---

13. The ios_base object is used by the put() function to retrieve the format flags that control the formatting of numeric values. Also, the put() function uses the numpunct and ctype facet from the locale attached to the ios_base object for retrieving information about the radix character, thousands separator, etc., and for recognition of whitespace characters, digits, etc.

flow would escape unnoticed. In such cases, it is advisable to wrap the iterator into a special purpose output iterator that has a `failed()` function like the `ostreambuf_iterator`, so that exhaustion of the character container can be detected.

As you can see from the example above, direct use of a facet is substantially more complicated than use of a facet through a stream operation, as we had shown it before. In the example above, it looks rather stupid to stuff the facet into a locale first and then retrieve it again so that it can be used. It makes sense because the num_put facet needs other facets anyway. Stuffing all of the facets involved in the processing into one locale object makes it easy to pass around all the necessary information in the form of the locale object. Still, we can do it differently. A facet need not necessarily be contained in a locale. Let us see how facets can be used independent of locales.

6.4.3 Direct Use of the Facet Independent of a Locale

If we do not want to create a special purpose locale object that has the facets for nondefault iterators installed, we can also use the num_put facet directly, that is, without stuffing it into a locale first and retrieving it from the locale when it is to be used. A facet need not be contained in a locale, although that is the most common way of using facets.

In fact, facets are designed to be contained in locales. All facet types have a protected destructor, because the facets are usually contained in a locale that manages the facet's memory and lifetime. In particular, the containing locale object takes over responsibility for destroying its facets. The corresponding details are discussed in section 7.3, Memory Management of Facets in a Locale. Objects of a type with an inaccessible destructor cannot be created on the stack or in the data segment; at best they can be created on the heap, in the hope that someone who has access to the destructor will eventually delete the heap object. That is exactly what facets are designed for: We create them on the heap and hand them over to a locale, which is a friend of all facet types and has access to the protected destructor. The locale deletes the facets once it will no longer be used.

If we want to use a facet independent of a locale, then we need an additional abstraction that allows us to create and destroy facet objects. We wrap the original facet in a derived class that has an accessible destructor:

```
template <class Facet>
class StandAloneFacet
  : public Facet
{
 public:
    StandAloneFacet() : Facet(1) {}

    ~StandAloneFacet() {}
};
```

`StandAloneFacet` is a simple wrapper around the actual facet. It is derived from the facet type that it encapsulates and provides the missing public destructor. Note that the base class constructor is called with the value 1 as an argument. This is to indicate that the facet is used "stand alone," i.e., the memory is correctly managed by the base class. For details, see section 7.3, Memory Management of Facets in a Locale. Note also that this wrapper template requires the encapsulated facet type not to take any further constructor arguments. In particular, this wrapper cannot be used for byname facets.

For the sake of comparability with the previous uses of the num_put facet, let us see how the facet wrapper would be used for writing a formatted numeric value to a string:

```
StandAloneFacet<num_put<char,back_insert_iterator<string> > > fac;
basic_ios<char> str(0);
str.imbue(locale("German"));
fac.put(back_inserter("Hello World - "),str,' ',(unsigned long)12345678L);
```

The effect is exactly the same as in the example above, where we installed the num_put facet in a locale first and retrieved it for use later.

CHAPTER 7

The Architecture of the Locale Framework

Locales and facets are designed to form an extensible framework. User-defined internationalization services can be added to the locale framework by providing user-defined facets. Not only can a locale object contain the predefined standard facets that we discussed in the preceding chapter; it can also maintain any kind of user-defined facet. Naturally, such user-defined facets must meet a couple of requirements and constraints in order to fit into the locale framework.

In this chapter we explain these requirements and the overall architecture of the locale framework. The classes representing locales and facets are tightly coupled. We will see what a locale requires of a facet, how a facet is identified, how facet lookup in a locale works, and how a locale manages its facets' lifetime and memory.

7.1 Class Hierarchy

As shown in figure 7-1, all facets are derived from `locale::facet`. The reason for this inheritance is explained in detail in chapter 8.

7.2 Identification and Lookup of Facets in a Locale

In a C++ program, a facet is an object of a facet type. Such facet types can be organized in facet families. The standard facets (see section 6, Standard Facets, for details) are an

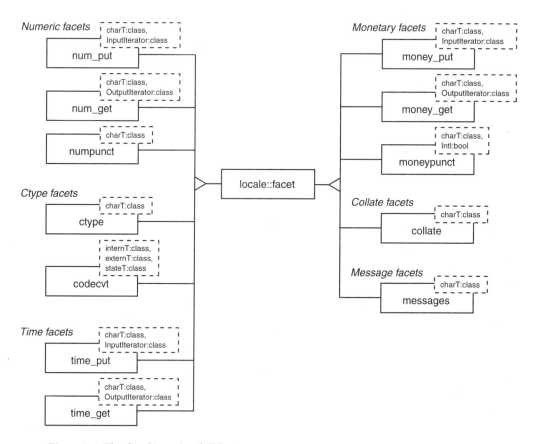

Figure 7-1: *The class hierarchy of all facets.*

example. Facet families are class hierarchies with a facet base class that defines the interface for all its derived facet types. In section 7.2.1, Facet Identification, below, we explain in detail which requirements a type must meet in order to be a facet type, and we also look at the properties that facet base classes must have.

A locale bundles the internationalization services and information for a particular cultural environment. A locale object acts as a container of facet objects and is organized in such a way that it contains at most one facet object out of a given facet family. In section 7.2.2, Facet Lookup, below we explain how this organization is achieved. We saw in previous sections that when `use_facet()` is invoked, we must specify a facet type in order to receive the facet object of the type that is contained in the locale. Section 7.2.2, Facet Lookup, explains how facets contained in a locale are identified and how the facet lookup works.

7.2.1 Facet Identification

Let us start exploring facet types by looking at the C++ standard. Here is what the standard requires of a facet so that it can be contained in a locale (quoted from *International Standard ISO/IEC 14882—Programming Language C++*):

A class is a *facet* if it is publicly derived from another *facet,* or if it is a class derived from `locale::facet` and containing a declaration (in the public section) as follows: `static ::std::locale::id id;`.[1]

The two classes `locale::facet` and `locale::id` obviously play a central role. These classes are defined in the C++ standard as follows:

```
class locale::facet
{
    protected:
      explicit facet(size_t refs = 0);
      virtual ~facet();
    private:
      facet(const facet&);        // not defined
      void operator=(const facet&); // not defined
 };
```

```
class locale::id
{
    public:
      id();
    private:
      void operator=(const id&); // not defined
      id(const id&);             // not defined
};
```

Every facet type must, directly or indirectly, be derived from class `locale::facet`. This is because the locale class uses certain properties of the `locale::facet` class for managing its contained facets. We will look into the functionality of class `locale::facet` in greater detail in section 7.3 where we discuss the memory management of facets in a locale.

The class `locale::id` is designed to provide a unique identification that can be used as an index for facet lookup in a locale. You can imagine a locale object as an indexed container of facets, the index being the facet identification. For each index there is exactly one slot in the locale container. Each index, i.e., each facet identification, provides access to the corresponding contained element, i.e., a facet that is held in that corresponding slot.

Facet identifications are guaranteed to be unique. The `locale::id` class provides this functionality: Each time a new object of type `locale::id` is constructed, a new, unique identification is created. Now it should be clear why the standard requires that a

---

1. As before, we omit the scope `::std` in this book because all names in the standard C++ library are defined within the `::std` namespace. Hence we assume that one would normally add a `using namespace ::std;` statement to each translation unit and avoid full qualification of standard library names.

facet type must define a static `id` member: The locale needs the `id` member of its facets to determine into which slot a facet object belongs.

FACET IDENTIFICATION VERSUS FACET INTERFACE VERSUS FACET FAMILY

Before we go into the details of facet lookup, let's agree on some technical terms.

We call a class derived from `locale::facet`, which defines an `id` member, a *facet base class*. All classes derived from a facet base class share the same static data member `id`. The facet base class is the parent of a *facet family*.

We call the static data member of type `locale::id` the *facet (interface) identification*. As mentioned before, all facet identifications are guaranteed to be unique.

All of the derived classes implement at least the same public interface as the base class; these are the semantics of public derivation in C++. We call this facet base class interface common to all facet types in a facet family a *facet interface*. It represents a set of related localization services and information.

The essence is that all facet classes in a facet family implement the same facet interface as the base class and share the facet identification that the facet base class defines. Hence there is a one-to-one relationship between a facet interface, a facet identification, and a facet family. As a locale has only one slot per facet identification, only one facet out of each facet family can be present in a locale object.

EXAMPLE OF A FACET FAMILY

Let us take a look at an example of a facet family. There is the standard facet numpunct, for instance. The standard library defines a numpunct class template and another derived class template for numpunct_byname facets. The actual facet types are instantiations of these templates. Here is the definition of the numpunct templates:

```
template <class charT>
class numpunct : public locale::facet {
public:
 static locale::id id;
 // ...
protected:
 // ...
};


template <class charT>
class numpunct_byname : public numpunct<charT> {
public:
 // ...
protected:
 // ...
};
```

We can see that instantiations of the numpunct template are facet base classes, because they define the `id` member, whereas instantiations of the numpunct_byname template are facets that belong to the same facet family, because they inherit the `id` member and share the facet identification with their base class.

Note that every instantiation of numpunct for a different character type introduces another facet family with its own facet identification. numpunct<char> has the identification numpunct<char>::id, and numpunct<wchar_t> has the identification numpunct<wchar_t>::id, which is a different static variable with a different value. The derived class numpunct_byname<char> shares the identification numpunct<char>::id with its base class numpunct<char>, and numpunct_byname<wchar_t> has the identification numpunct<wchar_t>::id of its base class.

The locale has one slot per facet identification, which means that a locale can contain one representative of the numpunct<char> family and one representative of the numpunct<wchar_t> family, either a base class object or a derived class object respectively. However, a locale can never contain a numpunct<char> and a numpunct_byname<char> facet, because they have the same facet identification and would compete for the same slot in the locale.

7.2.2 Facet Lookup

When a facet contained in a locale is retrieved from a locale or when a facet is stored in a locale, the slot into which the facet belongs must be determined. In the following sections we explain how the locale uses the identification of a facet interface to store and retrieve its facets.

7.2.2.1 Retrieval of Facets from a Locale

Let us consider an example: Say we are in a situation where we need to access the `decimal_point()` member function of the numpunct<char> facet from a given locale `loc`. The code for this would be the following:

```
use_facet< numpunct<char> >(loc).decimal_point();
```

Let us see what `use_facet` must do so that the contained facet's member function `decimal_point()` is invoked in the end.

IMPLEMENTING `use_facet()`

To understand how `use_facet()` uses the facet identification for retrieval of a facet from a locale, we will study a tentative implementation of the `use_facet()` function. Keep in mind that the C++ standard does not define any implementation issues and that our implementation only demonstrates the principle and is not meant to be a realistic implementation.

For exposition, we assume that the locale contains a facet repository as a private data member. For each facet identification there must be a slot in the facet repository for a representative of the respective facet family. You can think of the facet repository as a map with `locale::id` as the key and `const locale::facet*` as the value. An implementation could use the map class template from the standard, that is, an instantiation `map<size_t, const locale::facet*>`, assuming that `locale::id` is convertible to `size_t`. However, keep in mind that this is only an example; a real implementation probably uses a faster data structure for the facet repository.

Let us further assume that class `locale` has a private member function that implements retrieval of a facet with a given facet identification from the facet repository contained in the locale. This helper function might have the following signature: `const locale::facet* get_facet (const locale::id&)`. Under this assumption, the function `use_facet()` must be a friend of class `locale`, so that it has access to the private member function `get_facet()`.

Here is a tentative implementation of `use_facet()`:

```
template <class Facet>
const Facet& use_facet(const locale& loc)
{
    const locale::facet *pb;
    const Facet *pd;

    // use the Facet identification
    if ((pb = loc.get_facet(Facet::id)) == 0)
      throw(bad_cast("missing locale facet"));

    // use the Facet type
      if ((pd = dynamic_cast<const Facet*>(pb)) == 0)
      throw(bad_cast("missing locale facet"));

    return (*pd);
}
```

The sample code shows that `use_facet()` first tries to retrieve the facet from the locale's facet repository via the interface identification `Facet::id`. The way the locale repository is organized (it does not allow multiple entries for the same key), it can contain no more than one facet with the requested facet identification `Facet::id`. If such a facet can be found, a dynamic cast is performed to check if the found facet can be cast down to the requested facet type `const Facet*`.[2] More about the dynamic cast can be found in section G.8, Dynamic Cast, in appendix G.

`use_facet()` AND FACET HIERARCHIES

We have seen before that a facet type can belong to a facet family, that is, a hierarchy of facet classes with the facet base class defining the facet identification for the entire family.

---

2. An implementation may also perform a downcast to `const Facet&`, which is semantically the same.

What will happen if we invoke `use_facet()` on different classes from such a class hierarchy? Let's assume we have the following situation:

```
class base_facet : public locale::facet
{
// constructors and destructors

   public:
      virtual string bar() { return "this is the base class"; }

      static locale::id id;
};

class derived_facet : public base_facet
{
// constructors and destructors

   public:
      virtual string bar() { return "this is the derived class"; }
      virtual string bar_2() { return "hello world"; }
};
```

To keep the example simple and concise, neither of the two user-defined facets, `base_facet` and `derived_facet`, is meant to contain any realistic localization services or information. For the same reason, we ignore the rule that all standard facets follow, namely, that public member functions of a facet are never virtual, but call protected virtual member functions to do the actual work.

Now let's examine the different possible cases and discuss them in terms of our sample implementation of `use_facet()` above.

EXACT TYPE MATCH. Consider a situation in which the locale object contains a facet of exactly the same type that is requested in the `use_facet()` template specification. Say a locale object `loc` contains a facet object of type `base_facet` and we call

```
cout << use_facet<base_facet>(loc).bar();
```

`use_facet()` will find a facet with the facet interface identification `base_facet::id` in the locale object `loc`, and the dynamic cast to const `base_facet*` will be processed successfully, because the facet is of exactly the required type. The text sent to standard output will be

```
this is the base class
```

BASE REQUESTED, DERIVED AVAILABLE. Let us see what happens when the locale object contains a facet instance of the derived class, and the type requested in the `use_facet()`

template specification is the base class. In terms of our example classes: `loc` contains a facet of type `derived_facet` and we call

```
cout << use_facet<base_facet>(loc).bar();
```

As `derived_facet` is derived from `base_facet`, it has the same facet identification, because `derived_facet::id` and `base_facet::id` refer to the same static data member. `use_facet()` uses `base_facet::id` as a search key for finding a facet in its repository and finds the instance of `derived_facet` that is contained in the locale object `loc`. The dynamic cast to the required facet type `const base_facet*` will be successful, because the object retrieved from the locale is of type `const derived_facet*`. The text sent to standard output will be

```
this is the derived class
```

This effect is really interesting. What we have here is a kind of two-phase polymorphic dispatch.

First, whatever type of derived class object from the facet family is contained in the locale is extracted by specifying the base class type in the `use_facet` template specification.

Second, the invocation of a virtual function of the determined object is dispatched by C++ means, that is, by calling a virtual function through a pointer or reference to the facet.

DERIVED REQUESTED, BASE AVAILABLE. Let's examine the situation in which the locale object contains a facet instance of the base class and the type requested in the `use_facet()` template specification is the derived class, i.e., `loc` contains a facet of type `base_facet` and we call

```
cout << use_facet<derived_facet>(loc).bar_2();
```

With the same argumentation as in the previous situation, `use_facet()` retrieves the instance of `base_facet` from the locale object `loc` when it uses `derived_facet::id` as a search key. The dynamic cast to `const derived_facet*` will fail, because the retrieved object is of type `const base_facet*`. This failure is appropriate, since the base class pointer is not compatible with the derived class pointer, because the base class `base_facet` need not support the full interface of the derived class `derived_facet`. In our example, the base class facet does not have a `bar_2()` member function, and if `use_facet` returned successfully, the subsequent call to `bar_2()` might cause a program crash.

WRONG ID. A call to `use_facet()` also fails with a `bad_cast` exception when the facet repository in the locale object contains no facet with the requested `locale::id`.

As mentioned earlier in section 5.2.1, has_facet, the exception can be avoided by means of the `has_facet()` function. It checks if a locale can satisfy a call to `use_facet()`. The preceding example can be changed to

```
if (has_facet<derived_facet>(loc))
   cout << use_facet<derived_facet>(loc).bar();
```

so that no exception will be thrown.

Finally, let us return to our initial example. We wanted to retrieve a numpunct facet from a locale and invoke the contained facet's member function `decimal_point()`, as shown below:

```
use_facet< numpunct<char> >(loc).decimal_point();
```

What happens? `numpunct<char>` is the base class of a facet family and the representative of that facet family is requested. Depending on the locale, a facet of exactly that type might be contained (*exact type match*) or, if it is a named locale, a facet of the derived type `numpunct_byname<char>` would be contained (*base requested, derived available*). In either case, `use_facet< numpunct<char> >()` will return a reference to the numpunct facet object that is actually contained in the locale (*step 1 of two-phase dispatch*). The member function `decimal_point()` invokes the virtual member function `do_decimal_point()`. Depending on the dynamic type of the contained facet object, either the base class version of `do_decimal_point()` or the more specialized derived class version of it will be called (*step 2 of two-phase dispatch*). The net effect is that due to the two-phase dispatch, the right facet is found and the right member function is invoked, without `use_facet()` having any knowledge of the actual locale and its contained facets.

7.2.2.2 Storing Facets in a Locale

We've seen above that the functions `use_facet()` and `has_facet()` provide the functionality to retrieve facets from a locale object. How are the facets stored in a locale in the first place? It all happens when a locale object is created. A locale fills its facet repository depending on the arguments passed to its constructor, and again the facet identification plays a role. Here is an example of a `locale` constructor:[3]

```
template <class Facet> locale(const locale& other, Facet* f);
```

It creates a locale that is a copy of an existing locale `other`. If the locale `other` contains a facet with the identification `Facet::id`, this facet is replaced in the copy. The replacing facet is the one that the pointer `f` points to. If the locale `other` does not contain

---

3. The different locale constructors are discussed in detail in section 5.1, Creating Locale Objects.

a facet with the identification `Facet::id`, the facet that the pointer f points to is added and extends the copy.

One interesting aspect of this behavior is that it allows the addition of instances of new, user-defined facets in a simple way.

7.2.2.3 The Rationale Behind the Use of the Two-Phase Polymorphism

Until now we have described how the two-phase polymorphism is used by a locale to maintain its facets. Why is this mechanism needed at all? Why is the polymorphism gained by virtual functions insufficient? The answer lies in the extensibility of the locale framework. The goal was to allow user-defined facets, which implement new internationalization services, to be treated by the locale in the same way as predefined standard facets.

Imagine a locale that bases the polymorphic behavior of its facets on the facets' virtual functions alone. Since virtual functions allow polymorphic behavior only for the classes of a single class hierarchy, the standard would have had to define the base classes (i.e., the roots of the hierarchies) for all possible internationalization services. No matter how many conceivable interfaces the standard would have added, the number of interfaces and services would still have been limited. Instead of trying to anticipate all conceivable facet interfaces, the design decision was to use the two-phase polymorphism, because that is an entirely open concept.

The first phase of the dispatch, based on the facet identification, is used to select a certain set of internationalization services. Each set is represented by the interface that the corresponding facet base class defines for its facet family. Further sets of internationalization services can be added by a user in the form of new facet types derived from `locale::facet` defining a static `locale::id` data member. Since the locale framework can generate a (theoretically) unlimited number of unique facet identifications, it is possible to add an unlimited number of new internationalization services to the locale framework.

The second phase of the dispatch, based on virtual functions, is used to select the specific behavior of a service. Each of the services can be implemented differently for each derived facet class in the previously selected facet family. The virtual function dispatch ensures that the service of the facet object actually contained in a given locale is chosen. This way a (theoretically) infinite number of different versions of the same service can be added to the locale framework by means of derivation and redefinition of virtual functions.

An example that shows how a new internationalization service can be implemented is given in section 8.2, Defining a New Facet Family; an address-formatting service is defined as a new facet base class together with two specific implementations of that interface in the form of two derived address facet classes.

7.3 Memory Management of Facets in a Locale

The locale not only provides means for retrieving and storing facets; it is also capable of taking over the memory management of its facets. The idea is that a locale takes over responsibility for the lifetime and memory of all facets that it contains. It will delete its facets once the locale object itself goes out of scope.

In fact, all predefined standard facets are designed for this kind of maintenance by a locale: they have a protected virtual destructor. Objects of classes without a public destructor cannot be created on the stack or as global or static variables; they can be created only on the heap, in the hope that someone who has access to the destructor, such as a friend, will later delete the heap object. Class `locale` is a friend of class `locale::facet` and has access to the protected destructor of the standard facets. As a consequence, standard facets are typically created on the heap and handed over to a locale that later deletes them.

7.3.1 The Facet Reference Counter

The facet base class `locale::facet` offers a control mechanism for the deletion of facet objects: When you create a facet, you can determine whether the facet should later be deleted by the locale or not. This action is implemented by means of an argument passed to the facet constructor. We've briefly shown you the interface of class `locale::facet` in section 7.2.1, Facet Identification. Its only constructor has the following signature:

```
explicit facet(size_t refs = 0);
```

For the values 0 and 1 the `refs` argument has the following effect:

- If `refs == 0`, the locale takes care of deleting the facet. To be more specific: The locale performs `delete static_cast<locale::facet*>(f)`, where f is a pointer to the facet, when the last locale object containing the facet is destroyed. In this case the facet should be used only in conjunction with a locale, because its lifetime is tied to the lifetime of the locales it belongs to.

- If `refs == 1`, the locale does not destroy the facet and the creator of the facet is fully responsible for the facet's lifetime and deletion. In this case, the facet can be used independent of any locale.

The effect of providing values other than 0 or 1 is undefined.

The locale will probably count the references to facets that were constructed with a `refs` argument of value 0, in order to determine how many locale objects refer to the facet, because it must destroy the facet when the last locale referring to the facet is destroyed.

INITIALIZING THE refs ARGUMENT FOR STANDARD FACETS MAINTAINED BY A LOCALE

Here is an example of a standard facet that is created to be used in conjunction with a locale, i.e., with `refs==0`. Since its destructor is protected it must be created on the heap:

```
locale loc(locale("German"), new ctype_byname<char>("US", 0));
```

The American ctype facet, together with the rest of a German locale, forms the locale `loc`. When `loc` goes out of scope, it will delete the American ctype facet on the heap, because `refs` was initialized to 0 when the facet was created. As mentioned above, the locale can delete the facet because it is a friend of the facet base class `locale::facet` so that it can access its virtual destructor.

INITIALIZING THE `refs` ARGUMENT FOR STANDARD FACETS USED STAND-ALONE

Facets that are created with `refs==1` are usually of a type derived from a standard facet, because the standard facets have no public destructor, but a derived facet can provide one. In section 6.4.3, Direct Use of the Facet Independent of a Locale, we have already seen an example of such a facet wrapper that allows a facet to be used stand-alone, that is, outside a locale. Let us revisit the example. The derived facet class was a simple wrapper around the actual facet that provides the missing public destructor:

```
template <class Facet>
class StandAloneFacet : public Facet
{public:
    StandAloneFacet() : Facet(1) {}
    ~StandAloneFacet() {}
};
```

Note that the base class constructor is called with the value 1 as the initial value for the facet's refs argument. Such a facet need not be stuffed into a locale object but can be used independently. Here is the sample usage from section 6.4.3:

```
StandAloneFacet<num_put<char,back_insert_iterator<string> > > fac;
basic_ios<char> str(0);
str.imbue(locale("German"));
fac.put(back_inserter("Hello World - "),str,' ',(unsigned long)12345678L);
```

INITIALIZING THE `refs` ARGUMENT FOR USER-DEFINED FACETS

So far we have been talking only about standard facet types. Nonstandard facets can differ substantially. For instance, they have no need to have the `refs` constructor argument, that was described above for the standard facets. Yet the mechanism used by the locale for managing the lifetime of its facets remains the same. If we provide a user-defined facet to a locale, the locale will still use the facet's `refs` argument to decide whether the facet must be deleted or not. The information about the `refs` argument is already contained in facet base class `locale::facet` and is thus inherited by all facet types, including any user-defined facets. When we design a new facet type, we must decide how the facet shall be used, inside a locale or stand-alone, and must initialize the `refs` argument accordingly.

In the example shown earlier, where we discussed how facets are retrieved from a locale, we presented two user-defined facet types, namely, the classes `base_facet` and `derived_facet`. We omitted the constructors and destructors of these classes. Let us now complete the example.

We decided that the base class should follow the pattern demonstrated by the standard facets in the library, which is to provide the latitude to control deletion of the facet by setting the constructor argument `refs` to 1 if necessary. Such a base class facet can be used either inside a locale or stand-alone, and it allows its derived classes to use both possibilities. It is generally a good idea to provide facet base classes with a `refs` constructor argument in order to keep all options open for the derived classes.

For the derived class we are more restrictive. We decide that derived class facets must not be used independent of any locales, and to ensure this the `refs` argument is 0. Whether this is a wise or not-so-wise decision depends on the circumstances and context. All we want to point out here is that the decision about the `refs` argument is part of the design of a new facet type and has an impact on the way the resulting facets can be used.

Here is the completed example:

```
class base_facet : public locale::facet
{
 public:
  base_facet(size_t refs=0) : locale::facet(refs) {}
  virtual string bar() { return "this is the base class"; }
  static ::std::locale::id id;
 protected:
  ~base_facet() {}
};


class derived_facet : public base_facet
{
 public:
  derived_facet() : base_facet(0) {}
  virtual string bar() { return "this is the derived class"; }
  virtual string bar_2() { return "hello world"; }
 protected:
  ~derived_facet() {}
};
```

HOW THE LOCALE USES THE FACET REFERENCE COUNTER

So far, our focus was on the maintenance of facets by just one locale. However, facets are shared among locales. As we have seen earlier, the facet repository contained in a locale is a mapping between facet identifications and facet pointers. Once a locale is copied, only the facet pointers are duplicated, because it would be wasteful and inefficient to create copies of all contained facets in a locale each time a locale is copied, especially since facets are immutable (see below).

For this reason, there is a more global management scheme: a locale treats its facets as reference-counted resources. It expects each of its facets to be associated with a reference counter, which the locale increments whenever it creates another pointer to the facet and decrements whenever it deletes a pointer to the facet. When a locale deletes the last pointer, it also deletes the facet itself. Again, details of an implementation of the reference counter are not specified by the standard. No matter how the reference-counting scheme is implemented, the entire mechanism should be invisible to a user that uses the locale framework, even when he derives new user-defined facets. Only the `refs` argument must be provided, and the locale uses its value to decide whether or not a facet must be deleted in the end; the rest of the reference-counting scheme is transparent.

For illustration, let us examine an example for the memory management of facets that are shared between locales. Say we have a function that creates a new locale object by combining a given locale with a certain facet.

```
void function(const locale& loc)
{
  locale temp_locale(loc, new type_A(0));

  // do something fancy with temp_locale

} // here temp_locale goes out of scope
```

Figure 7-2 shows an arbitrary locale `loc` provided as an argument to the function.

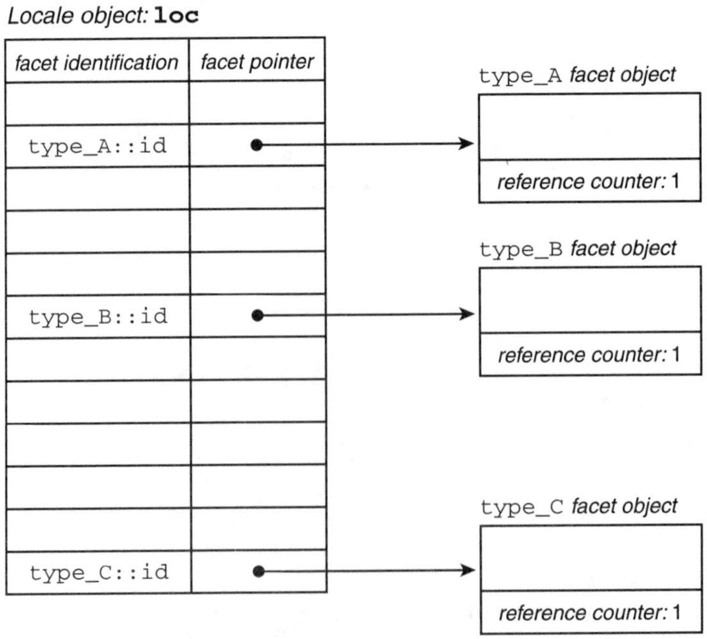

Locale object: **loc**

facet identification	facet pointer
type_A::id	●
type_B::id	●
type_C::id	●

type_A *facet object*

reference counter: 1

type_B *facet object*

reference counter: 1

type_C *facet object*

reference counter: 1

Figure 7-2: The structure of a locale object and its facets.

After creation of the second locale object `temp_locale`, both locale objects share almost all of their facets except the one of type `type_A` that is replaced in the newly constructed locale object (see Figure 7-3).

When the locale object `temp_locale` goes out of scope, its destructor decrements the reference counters of the locale's facets. The reference counter of the new `type_A` object by then will be 0, and consequently the facet will be deleted. After destruction of the locale object `temp_locale`, the situation will be as before.

A REMARK ON THE SEMANTICS OF LOCALES

Locales are designed for being passed around by value. As we have seen in the previous section, internally a locale is nothing more than a handle for a container of facets. As a result, copying and assignment of locales are relatively inexpensive and you can safely pass a locale to a function by value (rather than by reference) without risking substantial overhead.

Although locales behave polymorphically, no references or pointers to locales are needed to make use of this polymorphism. As described in section 7.2.2, Facet Lookup, the polymorphic dispatch works through facet identifications and virtual member functions of the contained facets. Access to the facets' services is through the `use_facet()` function template; the locale class itself has no virtual member functions. As a result, no

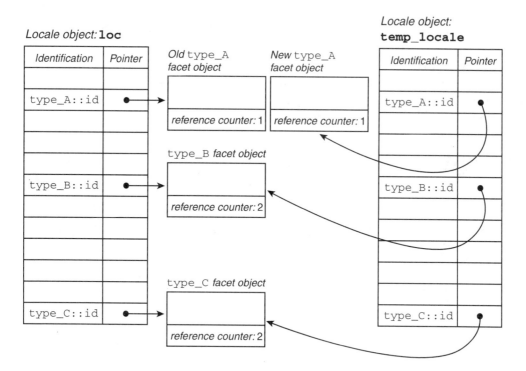

Figure 7-3: Two locale objects sharing facets.

references or pointers to locale objects are required for the polymorphic behavior of the contained facets' services.

Basically, a locale exhibits value semantics to its users, while internally it acts as a reference to a container of facets. It can be passed around as a value at almost no cost. At the same time, a locale object has referencelike properties in that it allows access to polymorphic services of its contained facets through locale objects.

Also, keep in mind that the lifetime of a locale object must exceed the lifetime of its contained facets. With each call to `use_facet()`, a reference to one of its contained facets is provided. References to objects in a container always raise the question of how long the reference to the contained element will stay valid—which leads us to another interesting property of locales.

7.3.2 Immutability of Facets in a Locale

Locales and their contained facets are immutable objects, because they represent information and rules that describe a certain cultural area. Such localization aspects are naturally fixed. Consequently, a locale does not change throughout its lifetime. Apart from this intuitive understanding of a locale, its immutability also has practical reasons. Facets are shared among locales. If it were permitted for a facet to be changed via one locale, all other locales sharing this facet would be affected by this change. Hence notification, coping, or some kind of synchronization between the locales affected would be needed. In any case, this would complicate every program using locales and facets. The design path taken for the locale framework is to make locales and facets immutable. Once created, neither a locale nor its facets can change anymore.

The immutability is reflected in various places. Locales cannot be modified; they can only be built by composition. Also, the member functions of all facets must be declared `const`. This restriction is sensible because the function `use_facet` returns a `const Facet&`. Consequently, only constant operations can be invoked on a facet retrieved from a locale.

CHAPTER 8

User-Defined Facets

Locales and facets form an extensible framework that allows the addition of user-defined internationalization services. Such services can be encapsulated into user-defined facet types, which can have arbitrary interfaces and functionality. In chapter 7, "The Architecture of the Locale Framework," we explained that facet types must have the following two properties: Facets have to be subclasses of class `locale::facet`. Additionally, they must contain a *facet identification* in the form of a static data member that is declared as `static locale::id id;`. This identification is used for maintenance and retrieval of facets from a locale and identifies an entire family of facets: All facets with the same identification belong to the same facet family. A locale cannot contain two facets with identical identification. Hence, facets from the same family can only be replacements of each other.

New types of facets can be added by either deriving from existing facet types, in which case the facet identification is inherited and the new facet belongs to an already existing facet family, or by defining a new facet class that has a facet identification of its own, in which case a new facet family is introduced.

In the following sections we study both cases in terms of examples.

8.1 Adding a User-Defined Facet to an Existing Facet Family

In this section we explain how a facet that is to be added to an existing facet family must be implemented. In section 7.2.1, Facet Identification, we saw that all members of a facet family have the same interface and the same facet identification. If we want to add a user-defined facet type to an existing facet family, we must derive the new facet type from one of the family members so that the new facet type inherits the interface and the facet identification of its base class. The facet families that we use for demonstration are the predefined standard facets, but the technique is the same for other user-defined facet families.

We study two examples: (1) a facet that provides user-defined names for the Boolean values true and false (which will belong to the numpunct facet family), and (2) a facet that recognizes any umlaut in the German alphabet (which will be added to the ctype facet family).

These two examples demonstrate two different techniques. For the implementation of the numpunct facet for user-defined Boolean names, we will override a virtual member function that is inherited from the standard numpunct facet; that is, we redefine existing facet functionality. For the implementation of the umlaut facet, we will add a member function and in this way extend the interface inherited from the standard ctype facet; that is, we add functionality to a facet.

USER-DEFINED NAMES FOR true AND false

Boolean values can be printed in their numeric form, 0 or 1, or their alphanumeric representation can be printed instead. Here is an example:

```
int main(int argc, char** argv)
{
  bool any_args = (argc > 1);
  cout << "Any arguments? " << boolalpha << any_args << endl;
  // ...
}
```

In an Anglo-American environment this might print:

```
Any arguments?  true
```

Say we want to receive an answer like "yes" or "no" instead of "true" or "false". The alphanumeric representations of the Boolean values are contained in a locale's numpunct facet. The numpunct facet has two public member functions, truename() and falsename(), which provide the according strings. Both functions are nonvirtual functions that call protected virtual functions called do_truename() and do_falsename(). In order to solve the problem sketched out above, we derive a new facet type and override the two protected member functions:

```
template <class CharT>
class boolnames : public numpunct_byname<CharT>
{
```

```
protected:
   CharT const * const true_;
   CharT const * const false_;
   basic_string<CharT> do_truename() const {return true_;}
   basic_string<CharT> do_falsename() const {return false_;}
   ~ boolnames() {}
public:
   explicit boolnames(const char* locnam, const CharT* t,
                      const CharT* f, size_t refs = 0)
   : numpunct_byname<CharT>(locnam,refs), true_(t), false_(f) {}
};
```

The new facet type is a byname facet that takes a locale name as a constructor argument. It also takes the string representations of the Boolean values `true` and `false` as constructor arguments. The remaining constructor argument is a reference counter that is passed to the base class and has a default of 0. The reference counter determines whether a containing locale will later delete the facet or not. The new facet type `boolnames` has the same interface and the same facet identification as its base class. When installed in a locale, it will replace the respective numpunct facet that is present in the locale. Note that the new facet must be explicitly installed in a locale. This would be done as follows:

```
int main(int argc, char** argv)
{
   locale loc(locale("US"),new boolnames<char>("US","yes","no"));
   cout.imbue(loc);

   bool any_args = (argc > 1);
   cout << "Any arguments? " << boolalpha << any_args << endl;
   // ...
}
```

A facet of the new facet type `boolnames<char>` is created on the heap. A locale object is created that is a copy of a U.S. locale with the `numpunct<char>` facet replaced by the new `boolnames<char>` facet. This new locale is attached to `cout`, and the subsequent output to `cout` prints:

```
Any arguments?  yes
```

or

```
Any arguments?  no
```

Note that the new facet object is created on the heap and that we used the default value 0 for the `refs` constructor argument. This is typical for facet objects that are placed into a locale, because the locale takes over ownership of its facets and deletes them when it goes out of scope. As already explained in section 7.3, Memory Management of Facets in a Locale, user-defined facets can also be created on the stack or data segment and be used independent of a locale. We demonstrate this in the next example.

CHARACTER CLASSIFICATION FOR UMLAUT

Characters can be classified according to their properties, for instance, whether they are upper- or lowercase letters, digits, whitespace, etc. Character classification is provided by the ctype facet. Let's say we work in a German environment. The German alphabet includes so-called umlaut characters; these are 'ä', 'ö', 'ü', 'Ä', 'Ö', and 'Ü'. We want to provide an extended ctype facet that can identify umlaut characters. The new facet type should belong to the ctype facet family and must be derived from one of the ctype facet types. Here is a conceivable implementation:

```
template <class CharT>
class umlaut : public ctype_byname<CharT>
{
protected:
    virtual bool do_is_umlaut(CharT c) const
    { switch(narrow(c))
      { case 'ä': case 'ö': case 'ü':
        case 'Ä': case 'Ö': case 'Ü': return true;
        default:                      return false;
      }
    }
public:
    explicit umlaut(size_t refs = 0) : ctype_byname<CharT>("German",refs) {}

    bool is_umlaut(CharT c) const { return do_is_umlaut(c); }
};
```

The new umlaut facet can be installed in a locale object, where it would replace the ctype facet. The umlaut facet can be retrieved from the locale and used like any other facet. It has all the functionality of a ctype facet plus the additional is_umlaut() function. The facet can be retrieved as a derived class reference or as a base class reference. In the code snippet below we demonstrate both alternatives:

```
locale loc(locale("German"), new umlaut<char>);

if (has_facet<umlaut<char> >(loc))
{ const umlaut<char>& ufac = use_facet<umlaut<char> >(loc);
  cout << ufac.is(ctype_base::alpha,'Ä') << endl;
  cout << ufac.is_umlaut('Ä') << endl;
}
```

```
const ctype<char>& cfac = use_facet<ctype<char> >(loc);
cout << cfac.is(ctype_base::alpha,'Ä') << endl;
cout << cfac.is_umlaut('Ä') << endl;  // error: is_umlaut() is not accessible
                                      // through a ctype reference
```

When the `umlaut` facet is retrieved via its actual derived class type, the `is_umlaut()` function is accessible. If we use the `umlaut` facet as an ordinary ctype facet and retrieve it by its base class type, only the ctype facet interface is accessible and `is_umlaut()` cannot be invoked. Naturally, we can cast the base class reference down to the derived class type in our example above and then invoke the `is_umlaut()` function. Yet we recommend avoiding downcasts by using a base class reference when only the base class functionality is needed and a derived class reference when the new functionality is accessed.

The `umlaut` facet need not be contained in a locale but can also be used standing alone, that is, independent of any locale. Here is an example of this kind of usage:

```
umlaut<char> fac(1);
cout << fac.is(ctype_base::alpha,'Ä') << endl;
cout << fac.is_umlaut('Ä') << endl;
```

When an `umlaut` facet is created independent of a locale, we construct it with a `refs` argument of 1. As already explained in section 7.3, Memory Management of Facets in a Locale, this is not necessary, but advisable, because the facet object in our example above is not created on the heap and therefore must not be deleted. In case the stand-alone `umlaut` facet is later installed in a locale, the `refs` constructor argument of 1 will make sure that the locale never attempts to delete the facet object.

8.2 Defining a New Facet Family

In the previous sections we explained how existing facet interfaces can be modified or extended. In this section we explore how internationalization services that have no relationship to any of the existing facets can be bundled into a new facet interface and implemented as a new facet family.

Let us first recall what we already know about facet interfaces: In section 7.2.1, Facet Identification, we saw that each facet interface has a facet identification of its own. A facet interface can be provided by just one particular class, but typically there is an entire hierarchy of facet classes that inherit and optionally override the facet interface. All the facet types in such a hierarchy form a facet family. All family members have the same facet identification, and a locale object contains exactly one representative from that facet family.

Equipped with this knowledge, we aim to implement a new facet family. Let us pick a concrete example; let us implement a facet interface for formatting international addresses. First, we define a facet base class that has a new facet interface for address formatting and a new facet identification. We then build two derived address-formatting facets and demonstrate how they can be used in conjunction with IOStreams for implementation of an address inserter. Eventually we explore how the installation of an address-formatting facet in a locale object could be automated and suggest a locale factory for that purpose.

A FACET FOR INTERNATIONAL ADDRESS FORMATS

Imagine a program that prints the address labels for an international mail order service. It should be capable of handling the differences between international address formats. To illustrate the issue, we'll show you two examples of address formats. You might be familiar with the U.S. style of formatting addresses. Here is the general pattern and an example for addresses in private mail exchange:

<FirstName> <SecondName><LastName>	Angelika Sigrid Langer
<Address1>	728 NW 12th Street
[<Address2>]	
<City>, <State> <PostalCode>	Corvallis, OR 97330
[<Country>]	U.S.A.

In Germany addresses have a slightly different format: It is, for instance, not customary to print a person's second name. An optional country code is placed in front of the zip code, separated by a hyphen. States are irrelevant. And so on and so forth. Here is the general pattern and an example of an address in Germany:

<FirstName> <LastName>	Angelika Langer
<Address1>	Weidener Straße 5
[<Address2>]	
<blank line>	
[<CountryCode>-]<PostalCode> <City>	D-81737 München

There is not much explanatory value in showing you how to build a full-fledged address-formatting facet in this chapter. Instead we will drastically simplify matters. We want to focus on the techniques of building a user-defined facet, of integrating it into the standard locale framework, and of using it with standard IOStreams. The address-formatting facet is just an example for a generally applicable technique.

THE ADDRESS CLASS

We start the implementation by introducing a simple address class. Actually it is a class template, because we want the address representation to be so flexible that it can consist of either wide- or narrow-character strings. For instance, it is capable of representing Japanese addresses that contain kanji characters.

```
template<class charT>
class address
{
    friend basic_ostream<charT>&
    operator<<(basic_ostream<charT>& os, const address<charT>& ad);

    typedef basic_string<charT> String;

    public:
        address(const String& firstname, const String& secname,
                const String& lastname,
                const String& address1,  const String& address2,
                const String& town,      const String& zipcode,
                const String& state,     const String& country,
                const String& cntrycode)
          : firstname_(firstname), secname_(secname), lastname_(lastname),
            address1_(address1), address2_(address2),
            town_(town), zipcode_(zipcode), state_(state),
            country_(country), cntrycode_(cntrycode) {}

    private:
        String firstname_;
        String secname_;
        String lastname_;
        String address1_;
        String address2_;
        String town_;
        String zipcode_;
        String state_;
        String country_;
        String cntrycode_;
};
```

The address class contains private data members that hold the various elements of an address. The constructor initializes these elements. An operator<<() prints addresses according to a stream's current locale object. It is a friend function of the address class.[1] We will see its implementation later.

THE ADDRESS-FORMATTING FACET

Now we come to the design and implementation of the address facet. In chapter 7, "The Architecture of the Locale Framework," we explained that facets must have the following

---

1. It would be nicer if the inserter were a template on the same character type, so that output could be written to narrow- and wide-character streams. We restricted the example to narrow-character streams, because our compiler was not capable of coping with friend function templates.

two properties: They have to be subclasses of class `locale::facet`, and they must contain a *facet identification* in the form of a static data member that is declared as `static locale::id id;`

Facet types with the same facet identification belong to the same facet family and replace each other in a locale. A facet class that has a facet identification of its own introduces a new facet family. In our example, address formatting is present in a locale in addition to other internationalization facilities and is not meant to replace any existing information. Hence, we define a new facet family for address formatting by building a new facet type with an identification of its own.

Following the naming conventions of the standard, we call our address facet `address_put` because it handles the formatting of addresses. This is in line with the names of the standard facets `num_put` (formatting of numeric values), `money_put` (formatting of monetary values), and `time_put` (formatting of time and date).[2] The formatting operation is a member function called `put()`.

For the implementation of `address_put` we follow the design and implementation idioms for formatting facets, which are established in the standard library:

OUTPUT ITERATORS. Formatting operations in the standard library, like `num_put <charT>::put()`, take an iterator to the beginning of the output sequence as an argument. This approach allows a flexible solution and fits smoothly into the overall concept of the entire standard library, where iterators are used as generic connectors between independent abstractions. In line with this policy, we too use an output iterator to designate the target location of the formatted address string.

In the standard library, the type of this output iterator is a template argument of the respective facet class template. By default, the output iterator type is an output stream buffer iterator. It allows direct access to a stream buffer and is a sensible default for the use of facets in IOStreams. We adopt this policy for the `address_put` facet and make it a class template taking the output iterator type as a template argument.

PUBLIC AND VIRTUAL PROTECTED INTERFACE. In section 6.3.1.1, The Standard Facet Base Class Templates, we explained that the standard facet types follow a certain idiom: the public interface consists of nonvirtual member functions that delegate all tasks to protected virtual member functions. In other words, a public member function `foo()` calls a protected virtual function `do_foo()`, which does the real work.

In our example, the public interface of the `address_put` class template contains a member function `put()`, which calls a protected virtual function `do_put()`, which does the real work. These functions take the output iterator that specifies the target location, and all elements that form the address (name, city, etc.) as parameters.

---

2. Other naming conventions are

- XXX_get for parsing facets; they typically have a `get()` member function
- XXX_byname for derived facet types that can be constructed from a locale name
- XXXpunct for facets that represent information, rather than functionality

Here is the implementation of the `address_put` facet:

```
template<class charT, class OutIter = ostreambuf_iterator<charT> >
class address_put : public locale::facet
{
    typedef basic_string<charT> String;

    public:
        typedef OutIter iter_type;

        static locale::id id;

        address_put(size_t refs = 0) : locale::facet(refs) {}

        void put(OutIter oi,
            const String& firstname, const String& secname, const String& lastname,
            const String& address1,  const String& address2,
            const String& town,      const String& zipcode, const String& state,
                const String& country,   const String& cntrycode) const
              { do_put(oi, firstname, secname, lastname,
                        address1, address2, town, zipcode, country, cntrycode); }

    protected:
        virtual void do_put (OutIter oi,
            const String& firstname, const String& secname, const String& lastname,
            const String& address1,  const String& address2,
            const String& town,      const String& zipcode, const String& state,
            const String& country,   const String& cntrycode) const;

        void put_string(OutIter oi, String s) const
        {
            typename String::iterator si, end;

            for (si=s.begin(), end= s.end(); si!=end ; ++si, ++oi)
                *oi = *si;
        }
};
```

In the code above, you can see the design decisions made so far:

- The new facet type is a class derived from `locale::facet` with an identification of its own.

- It's a class template taking the character type and the output iterator type as parameters.

- It has a public put() and a protected do_put() function. (The member function put_string() is a helper function that writes strings to an output iterator.)

For the sake of simplicity, we decided against the following design option:

- The patterns for international address formats could have been encapsulated into an addresspunct facet, similar to a numpunct or moneypunct facet. The "punct" facets in the standard library are used by related formatting and parsing facets for finding rules, pattern, and other information. We decided in favor of an alternative technique and put the knowledge about specific address patterns directly into the respective formatting operations rather than factoring it out into a separate facet. This technique can be found in the standard library, too. It is demonstrated by the standard time and date facets time_put and time_get, which, unlike num_put/num_get and money_put/money_get, do not rely on a timepunct facet.

FACETS FOR DIFFERENT CULTURAL AREAS

So far, we've left open how a facet comes to represent the knowledge of a certain cultural area, i.e., what turns our address facet into a German or a U.S. address facet. For many of the standard facets, there are byname versions that accept the name of a localization environment as a constructor argument and then provide information that is typical to the specified cultural area. See sections 6.3.1.2, The Derived Byname Facets, and 5.1.1, Named Locales, for details about these locale names.

To keep our example focused on extending the standard locale framework rather than the maintenance of culture-dependent data, we are going to use a different solution. Instead of putting all the intelligence into a byname facet, which would also force us into dealing with the maintenance of address format patterns in general, we derive an address facet for each specific cultural area from the base class template address_put. Also, we restrict the demonstration to U.S. and German address formatting and ignore other cultural areas.

As we do not prefer any particular way of formatting over others, we refrain from defining a default formatting. For this reason we make the base class template an abstract base class by turning its address_put<>::do_put() function into a pure virtual function with no implementation.

The derived class templates US_address_put and German_address_put are shown below:

```
template<class charT, class OutIter = ostreambuf_iterator<charT> >
class address_put : public locale::facet
{
    ...    // as previously shown
```

```
   protected:
      virtual void do_put (OutIter oi,
                const String& firstname, const String& secname,
                const String& lastname,
                const String& address1,  const String& address2,
                const String& town,      const String& zipcode,
                const String& state,
                const String& country,   const String& cntrycode) const = 0;
};

template<class charT, class OutIter = ostreambuf_iterator<charT> >
class US_address_put : public address_put<charT, OutIter>
{
   public:
      US_address_put(size_t refs = 0) : address_put<charT,OutIter>(refs) {}

   protected:
      void do_put(OutIter oi,
                const String& firstname, const String& secname,
                const String& lastname,
                const String& address1,  const String& address2,
                const String& town,      const String& zipcode,
                const String& state,
                const String& country,   const String& cntrycode) const
      {
         String s(firstname);
         s.append(" ").append(secname).append(" ").append(lastname)
          .append("\n");
         s.append(address1).append("\n");
         if(!address2.empty()) s.append(address2).append("\n");
         s.append(town).append(", ").append(state).append(" ").append(zipcode)
          .append("\n");
         if(!country.empty()) s.append(country).append("\n");

         put_string(oi,s);
      }
};

template<class charT, class OutIter = ostreambuf_iterator<charT> >
class German_address_put : public address_put<charT, OutIter>
{
   public:
      German_address_put(size_t refs = 0) : address_put<charT,OutIter>(refs)
      {}
```

```
protected:
   void do_put(OutIter oi,
              const String& firstname, const String& secname,
              const String& lastname,
              const String& address1,  const String& address2,
              const String& town,      const String& zipcode,
              const String& state,
              const String& country,   const String& cntrycode) const
   {
       String s(firstname);
       s.append(" ").append(lastname).append("\n");
       s.append(address1).append("\n");
       if(!address2.empty()) s.append(address2).append("\n");
       s.append("\n");
       if(!cntrycode.empty()) s.append(cntrycode).append("-");
       s.append(zipcode).append(" ").append(town).append("\n");

       put_string(oi,s);
   }
};
```

The core of these address facets is the implementation of the respective do_put() function. do_put() concatenates the address elements into one large address string, according to U.S. and German address-formatting rules respectively.[3] The helper function address_put<>::put_string() then writes the formatted string to the output iterator.

THE ADDRESS INSERTER

Eventually, we are going to implement the already mentioned stream inserter for the address class. Its implementation, shown below, is a simplified one, focused on the usage of the newly defined address_put facet.

```
template <class charT>
basic_ostream<charT>&
operator<<( basic_ostream<charT>& os, const address<charT>& ad)
{
   locale loc = os.getloc();

   try
   {
     const address_put<charT>& apFacet = use_facet<address_put<charT> > (loc);
     apFacet.put(os, ad.firstname_, ad.secname_, ad.lastname_,
```

---

3. Of course, the repeated invocation of append() is potentially inefficient, because it might lead to reallocation of the string's internal character array with each call to append(). We chose this solution here in order to keep the example concise and simple. In a more realistic implementation, one could create the string with a sufficiently large initial capacity to avoid any reallocation.

```
                    ad.address1_, ad.address2_, ad.town_, ad.zipcode_,
                    ad.state_, ad.country_, ad.cntrycode_);
   }
   catch (bad_cast&)
   {
      // locale does not contain a address_put facet ;
   }
   return (os);
}
```

For culture-sensitive address formatting, the inserter must retrieve the address-formatting facet from the stream's current locale. Streams have a member function getloc() that returns the stream's locale object. From that locale the address facet can be retrieved via the template function use_facet<Facet>(). Note that the user-defined address formatting facet address_put is retrieved in the exactly the same way as it would be for any standard facet.

The inserter then calls the facet's put() function and delegates the actual formatting to it. All the elements of an address are passed as arguments to the put() function. The first argument to put() is expected to be the iterator designating the beginning of the output sequence. A stream buffer iterator pointing to the current position of the output stream can be created from a reference to an output stream. (See section 2.4, Stream Iterators and Stream Buffer Iterators, in part I for more information.) Hence we pass in the stream itself. The implicit conversion mechanism for function arguments in C++ cares for construction of an output stream buffer iterator.

EQUIPPING LOCALES WITH ADDRESS FACETS

We have seen above how an address_put facet is retrieved from a locale object. In addition to retrieval, we need to consider ways and means of storing address facets in locale objects in the first place. In section 7.3.2, Immutability of Facets in a Locale, we explained that locales are immutable objects. Facets are stuffed into a locale when the locale object is created and cannot be replaced or added later on. Locale objects are built by composition: You start off with the copy of an existing locale and replace and add facets to create a new locale object.

In our example, we want to equip a locale that contains all standard facets for a cultural environment (in the following example called a *standard* locale), with an additional address-formatting facet.

A standard locale can be created by means of the following constructor:

```
explicit locale(const char* name);
```

It constructs a locale object that contains all the standard facets for a cultural environment specified by the locale name.

A new locale object containing all the facets from an existing locale object, plus an additional new facet, can be composed via the following locale member template constructor:

```
template<class Facet> locale(const locale& other, Facet* facetPtr);
```

To add a `US_address_put` facet object to the locale that contains all standard U.S. facets, we would have to write

```
locale usLocaleWithAddressPut(locale("En_US"),
                         new US_address_put<char,osIter>);
```

A German locale would be constructed analogously. In general, the construction of a locale object that contains additional facets of user-defined types (in the following example called a *nonstandard* facet) involve the following:

- retrieval or creation of a standard locale object for the cultural area (constructed as an unnamed object via `locale("En_US")` in the example above)

- retrieval or creation of the additional nonstandard facet(s) for that area (constructed via new `US_address_put` `<char, osIter>` in the example above)

- combining both into a new, extended nonstandard locale object

If several nonstandard facets shall be contained in a locale object, the locale is composed step by step: Each time, an object of another nonstandard facet type is added.

A LOCALE FACTORY

For decoupling the potentially troublesome process of locale construction from comparably straightforward locale use, we build a factory[4] that handles the construction of locale objects. The idea is to create locale objects "bynames": they shall all have standard facets for the cultural area specified by the name, plus a number of desired, additional nonstandard facets, such as an address-formatting facet. The extra effort of building such a locale factory might look like overkill in our simple example, but it will definitely pay off in a situation where numerous user-defined facets must be available in every locale object.

We suggest building a hierarchy of locale factories: a base locale factory creating standard locale objects and derived factories for nonstandard locales. The code below shows an implementation of a base locale factory that has a `make_locale()` function that returns a standard locale associated with the cultural environment specified by a locale name:

```
class locale_factory
{
   public:
      virtual locale make_locale (const char* name) const
      { return locale(name); }
};
```

---

4. An in-depth discussion of the factory pattern can be found in *Design Patterns: Elements of Reusable Object-Oriented Software* by Erich Gamma et al. (for details see the bibliography section of this book).

Note that the factory method `make_locale()` usually, according to the general factory pattern, returns a pointer or reference to the created object. This is because derived factories will be allowed to create objects of derived classes, which can have additional members or vary in the behavior of existing member functions. Our factory method `make_locale()` deviates from the general pattern in that it returns a locale *object* rather than a pointer or a reference. This is a general idiom in using locales: They are passed around as objects, but internally they are only a handle to an arbitrary number of facets from arbitrary facet families.[5] No inheritance is involved for creating locales that hold an arbitrary combination of facets. Hence there is no need for returning references or pointers to locales.

The code below shows the implementation of a locale factory that returns a locale containing all standard facets and, if a U.S. or a German locale is requested, additionally an `address_put` facet.

```cpp
class address_locale_factory : public locale_factory
{
    typedef ostreambuf_iterator<char,char_traits<char> > osIter;

    public:
        address_locale_factory()
        {
            facets["En_US"] = new US_address_put<char, osIter>(1);
            facets["De_DE"] = new German_address_put<char, osIter>(1);
        }

        ~address_locale_factory()
        {
            delete facets["En_US"];
            delete facets["De_DE"];
        }

        locale make_locale (const char* name) const
        {
            if (facets.find(name) == facets.end())
                return locale_factory::make_locale(name);
            else
                return locale(locale_factory::make_locale(name),
                              (*(facets.find(name))).second);
        }

    private:
        map<string, address_put<char, osIter>* > facets;
};
```

---

5. The details of the locale architecture were explained in chapter 7, "The Architecture of the Locale Framework."

The implementation of our `address_locale_factory` uses the `map` container from the standard library for mapping a locale name to the respective `address_put` facet, so that nonstandard locale objects can be created. Naturally, this is just a rudimentary implementation of a locale factory.

Conceptually, a locale factory is supposed to encapsulate *all* aspects of creating standard or nonstandard locale objects for any cultural area. Its purpose is to decouple locale creation from locale use.

PUTTING THE PIECES TOGETHER

The code below shows a function that puts all the elements together. It receives an output stream, an address, and a locale. The output stream is temporarily "imbued" with the locale, which is required to have an address facet, before the address is eventually inserted into the stream.

```
void printAddress(ostream& os, const address<char>& address, locale loc)
{
   locale original = os.imbue(loc);
   os << address << endl;
   os.imbue(original);
}
```

A locale that has an address facet installed must be passed to the `printAddress()` function when it is invoked. Here is an example:

```
printAddress(cout,myAddress,address_locale_factory().make_locale("German"));
```

CONCLUSION

In this chapter we demonstrated a technique for adding arbitrary, user-defined facets to the locale framework in the standard library and their usage in conjunction with iostreams. The example of choice was an address-formatting facet. The technique itself, however, is more general and can be applied to arbitrary facet types. Here is a wrapup of the essentials:

MANDATORY. A user-defined facet type must be derived from class `locale::facet` and have a facet identification in the form of a static data member named `id` of type `locale::id`.

RECOMMENDED. We recommend the following: For the sake of consistency, a facet name should follow the naming conventions of the standard facets.

- Formatting and parsing operations should access the source or destination via iterators. Formatting and parsing facets should be templatized on the iterator type and should use stream buffer iterators as a default.

- For the sake of consistency with the standard facets, public member functions should delegate to protected member functions.

REFERENCE GUIDE

INTRODUCTION

The following introduction describes how entries in the reference guide are organized and described.

Entries are grouped into the following sections: locale, character traits, IOStreams, stream iterators, and other I/O operations.

Each section starts with its header files, global type definitions, global objects, and global functions (if they exist), followed by their classes in alphabetical order.

Each class entry describes the header file that contains the class, its base class(es), a general picture of the class, a synopsis, its nested classes and types, its (constant) data members, and its member functions grouped according to access specification (public/protected) and their functionality.

The synopsis and the subsequent descriptions are ordered in the same way: Bold-face comments in the synopsis reappear as entries on the lefthand margin of the descriptions. Within each group, the entries are ordered by meaning in the synopsis and alphabetically in the subsequent descriptions. Below is an example:

SYNOPSIS

```
namespace std {
 template <class charT>
 class numpunct : public locale::facet {
 public:
  // type definitions:
  typedef charT             char_type;
  typedef basic_string<charT> string_type;
```

```
 // data members:
 static locale::id id;
 // constructors:
 explicit numpunct(size_t refs = 0);
 // numpunct operations:
 char_type    decimal_point()    const;
 char_type    thousands_sep()    const;
 string       grouping()         const;
 string_type  truename()         const;
 string_type  falsename()        const;
protected:
 virtual ~numpunct();
 // numpunct operations:
 virtual char_type    do_decimal_point() const;
 virtual char_type    do_thousands_sep() const;
 virtual string       do_grouping()      const;
 virtual string_type  do_truename()      const;
 virtual string_type  do_falsename()     const;
 };
}
```

PUBLIC DATA MEMBERS

```
static locale::id id;
```

numpunct<charT>::id defines the unique identifications of . . .

PUBLIC MEMBER FUNCTIONS

```
explicit numpunct(size_t refs = 0);
```

Constructs an object of type numpunct<charT> . . .

```
char_type decimal_point() const;
...
string_type falsename() const;
...
string grouping() const;
...
...
```

PROTECTED MEMBER FUNCTIONS

```
virtual ~numpunct();
```

Destroys an object of type numpunct<charT>.

```
virtual char_type do_decimal_point()
```
...

...

For virtual functions the base class gives the description of the general semantics and the base class behavior. Derived classes repeat these virtual functions only if they provide new implementations.

Calls to a member function of the same object are always written as `this->foo()`, not simply as `foo()`, to make clear beyond any doubt that `foo` is a member function and not a global function.

In a similar way, scope operators (even if syntactically not necessary) are used to make clear where an item comes from. For instance, constants that are defined as protected or public in a base class and used in a derived class are named `base_class::constant` in the description of the derived class.

To enhance readability, `this` is always used in the text even if `*this` would be correct C++ syntax. Here is an example: *Failures are indicated by the state of* `this`.

The last remark is IOStreams-specific. Member function descriptions of stream classes, e.g., `basic_istream<charT>`, mention only the error bits that are set in case of failure. It is a general principle for the IOStreams that optionally exceptions related to the error bits could be thrown. Hence it is omitted in the reference manual for brevity. For details about the error indication model of IOStreams, see section 1.3, The Stream State.

1
LOCALE

header file <locale>

FILE NAME

<locale>

DESCRIPTION

The header file contains all declarations for class `locale` and all standard facets.

SYNOPSIS

```
namespace std {

//  class locale:
 class locale ;

//  global functions:
//    facet access:
 template <class Facet> const Facet& use_facet(const locale&);
 template <class Facet> bool has_facet(const locale&) throw();
//    character classification:
 template <class charT> bool isspace (charT c, const locale& loc);
 template <class charT> bool isprint (charT c, const locale& loc);
 template <class charT> bool iscntrl (charT c, const locale& loc);
 template <class charT> bool isupper (charT c, const locale& loc);
 template <class charT> bool islower (charT c, const locale& loc);
 template <class charT> bool isalpha (charT c, const locale& loc);
```

```
template <class charT> bool isdigit (charT c, const locale& loc);
template <class charT> bool ispunct (charT c, const locale& loc);
template <class charT> bool isxdigit(charT c, const locale& loc);
template <class charT> bool isalnum (charT c, const locale& loc);
template <class charT> bool isgraph (charT c, const locale& loc);
//    character conversion:
template <class charT> charT toupper(charT c, const locale& loc);
template <class charT> charT tolower(charT c, const locale& loc);


//  ctype (character classification and conversion) facets:
class ctype_base;
template <class charT> class ctype;
template <> class ctype<char>;              //  specialization
template <class charT> class ctype_byname;
template <> class ctype_byname<char>;       //  specialization


//  code conversion facets:
class codecvt_base;
template <class internT, class externT, class stateT> class codecvt;
template <class internT, class externT, class stateT>
                                            class codecvt_byname;


//  numeric facets:
template <class charT, class InputIterator>  class num_get;
template <class charT, class OutputIterator> class num_put;
template <class charT> class numpunct;
template <class charT> class numpunct_byname;


//  collation facets:
template <class charT> class collate;
template <class charT> class collate_byname;


//  date and time facets:
class time_base;
template <class charT, class InputIterator>  class time_get;
template <class charT, class InputIterator>  class time_get_byname;
template <class charT, class OutputIterator> class time_put;
template <class charT, class OutputIterator> class time_put_byname;


//  money facets:
class money_base;
template <class charT, class InputIterator>  class money_get;
template <class charT, class OutputIterator> class money_put;
```

```
template <class charT, bool Intl> class moneypunct;
template <class charT, bool Intl> class moneypunct_byname;

//  message retrieval facets:
class messages_base;
template <class charT> class messages;
template <class charT> class messages_byname;
}
```

global functions

HEADER

header: **<locale>**

FACET ACCESS

template <class Facet> bool **has_facet**(const locale& loc) throw();

Returns true if a facet that can be identified by Facet is available in loc; otherwise returns false.

template <class Facet> const Facet& **use_facet**(const locale& loc);

Makes the facet, which is identified by Facet, available from loc, by returning a reference to this facet. If no such facet can be found there, a bad_cast exception is thrown.

CHARACTER CLASSIFICATION

template <class charT> bool **isalnum**(charT c, const locale& loc);

Checks whether c is an alphanumeric character (i.e., an alphabetical character or a digit) using the ctype facet contained in loc, i.e., calls use_facet<ctype<charT> > (loc).is(ctype_base::alnum,c).

template <class charT> bool **isalpha**(charT c, const locale& loc);

Checks whether c is an alphabetical character, using the ctype facet contained in loc, i.e., calls use_facet<ctype<charT> >(loc).is(ctype_base::alpha,c).

template <class charT> bool **iscntrl**(charT c, const locale& loc);

Checks whether c is a control character, using the ctype facet contained in loc, i.e., calls use_facet<ctype<charT> >(loc).is(ctype_base::cntrl,c).

template <class charT> bool **isdigit**(charT c, const locale& loc);

Checks whether c is a digit, using the ctype facet contained in loc, i.e., calls use_facet<ctype<charT> >(loc).is(ctype_base::digit,c).

locale

```
template <class charT> bool isgraph(charT c, const locale& loc);
```

Checks whether c is a printing character (i.e., either an alphanumeric or punctuation character), using the ctype facet contained in loc, i.e., calls use_facet<ctype<charT> > (loc).is(ctype_base::graph,c).

```
template <class charT> bool islower(charT c, const locale& loc);
```

Checks whether c is a lowercase character, using the ctype facet contained in loc, i.e., calls use_facet<ctype<charT> >(loc).is(ctype_base::lower,c).

```
template <class charT> bool isprint(charT c, const locale& loc);
```

Checks whether c is a lower printable character, using the ctype facet contained in loc, i.e., calls use_facet<ctype<charT> >(loc).is(ctype_base::print,c).

```
template <class charT> bool ispunct(charT c, const locale& loc);
```

Checks whether c is a lower punctuation character, using the ctype facet contained in loc, i.e., calls use_facet<ctype<charT> >(loc).is(ctype_base::punct,c).

```
template <class charT> bool isspace(charT c, const locale& loc);
```

Checks whether c is a lower whitespace character, using the ctype facet contained in loc, i.e., calls use_facet<ctype<charT> >(loc).is(ctype_base::space,c).

```
template <class charT> bool isupper(charT c, const locale& loc);
```

Checks whether c is an uppercase character, using the ctype facet contained in loc, i.e., calls use_facet<ctype<charT> >(loc).is(ctype_base::upper,c).

```
template <class charT> bool isxdigit(charT c, const locale& loc);
```

Checks whether c is a character that represents a hexadecimal digit (i.e., 0–9, a–f, or A–F) using the ctype facet contained in loc, i.e., calls use_facet<ctype<charT> > (loc).is(ctype_base::xdigit,c).

CHARACTER CONVERSION

```
template <class charT> charT tolower(charT c, const locale& loc);
```

Returns the character that represents the lowercase conversion of c, if it exists; otherwise c. Uses the ctype facet contained in loc, i.e., calls use_facet<ctype<charT> > (loc).tolower(c).

```
template <class charT> charT toupper(charT c, const locale& loc);
```

Returns the character that represents the uppercase conversion of c, if it exists; otherwise c. Uses the ctype facet contained in loc, i.e., calls use_facet<ctype<charT> > (loc).toupper(c).

codecvt<internT,externT,stateT>

CLASS TEMPLATE

class template<class internT, class externT, class stateT> **codecvt**
header: **<locale>**
base class(es): **codecvt_base**, **locale::facet**

DESCRIPTION

codecvt is the facet that contains the information about character code conversion and
the functionality to perform the conversions. The following instantiations are required:

codecvt<wchar_t,char,mbstate_t> converts between the native character
sets for narrow and wide characters.

codecvt<char,char,mbstate_t> implements a degenerate conversion; it does
not convert at all.

SYNOPSIS

```
namespace std {
 template <class internT, class externT, class stateT>
 class codecvt : public locale::facet, public codecvt_base {
 public:
  //  type definitions:
  typedef internT  intern_type;
  typedef externT  extern_type;
  typedef stateT   state_type;
  //  data members:
  static locale::id id;
  //  constructors:
  explicit codecvt(size_t refs = 0)
  //  code conversion:
  result in(stateT& state,
          const externT* from, const externT* from_end,
          const externT*& from_next,
          internT* to, internT* to_limit, internT*& to_next) const;
  result out(stateT& state,
          const internT* from, const internT* from_end,
          const internT*& from_next,
          externT*  to, externT* to_limit, externT*& to_next) const;
  //  miscellaneous:
  result unshift(stateT& state,
          externT* to, externT* to_limit, externT*& to_next) const;
  int encoding() const throw();
  bool always_noconv() const throw();
```

```
    int length(const stateT&, const externT* from, const externT* end,
             size_t max) const;
    int max_length() const throw();
protected:
    //  destructor:
    virtual ~codecvt();
    //  code conversion:
    virtual result do_in stateT& state,
                         const externT* from, const externT* from_end,
                         const externT*& from_next,
                         internT* to, internT* to_limit,
                         internT*& to_next) const;
    virtual result do_out(stateT& state,
                         const internT* from, const internT* from_end,
                         const internT*& from_next,
                         externT* to, externT* to_limit,
                         externT*& to_next) const;
    //  miscellaneous:
    virtual result do_unshift(stateT& state,
             externT* to, externT* to_limit, externT*& to_next) const;
    virtual int do_encoding() const throw();
    virtual bool do_always_noconv() const throw();
    virtual int do_length(const stateT&,
             const externT* from, const externT* end, size_t max) const;
    virtual int do_max_length() const throw();
};
}
```

TYPE DEFINITIONS

```
typedef internT  intern_type;
```

The type intern_type is the character type that is associated with the internal code set.


```
typedef externT  extern_type;
```

The type extern_type is the character type that is associated with the external code set.

```
typedef stateT   state_type;
```

The type `state_type` is a type that is capable of holding the conversion state. It must be maintained during a conversion from the external to the internal character set and vice versa and can contain any information that is useful to communicate to or from the `do_in()` and `do_out()` member functions.

PUBLIC DATA MEMBERS

```
static locale::id  id;
```

`codecvt<internT,externT,stateT>::id` defines the unique identifications of the codecvt facet interfaces. Each template instantiation with a different internal or external character type, or different state type, defines a different facet interface with an associated unique `id`.

PUBLIC MEMBER FUNCTIONS

```
explicit  codecvt(size_t refs = 0);
```

Constructs an object of type `codecvt<internT,externT,stateT>`. If `refs==0`, the lifetime of `this` is managed by the locale(s) that contain `this`. If `refs==1`, the memory of this must be explicitly managed. The behavior for `refs>1` is not defined.

CODE CONVERSION

```
result in (stateT& state,
           const externT* from, const externT* from_end,
           const externT*& from_next,
           internT* to, internT* to_limit,
           internT*& to_next) const;
```

Calls `do_in(state, from, from_end, from_next, to, to_limit, to_next)` and returns the result of this call.

```
result out (stateT& state,
            const internT* from, const internT* from_end,
            const internT*& from_next,
            externT* to, externT* to_limit,
            externT*& to_next) const;
```

Calls `do_out(state, from, from_end, from_next, to, to_limit, to_next)` and returns the result of this call.

MISCELLANEOUS

```
bool always_noconv() const throw();
```

Calls do_always_noconv() and returns the result of this call.

```
int encoding() const throw();
```

Calls do_encoding() and returns the result of this call.

```
int length(const stateT& state, const externT* from,
          const externT* end, size_t max) const;
```

Calls do_length(state, from, end, max) and returns the result of this call.

```
int max_length() const throw();
```

Calls do_max_length() and returns the result of this call.

```
result unshift(stateT& state, externT* to,
               externT* to_limit, externT*& to_next) const;
```

Calls do_unshift(state, to, to_limit, to_next) and returns the result of this call.

PROTECTED MEMBER FUNCTIONS

```
virtual ~codecvt();
```

Destroys an object of type codecvt<internT, externT, stateT>.

CODE CONVERSION

```
virtual result do_in (stateT& state,
          const externT* from, const externT* from_end,
          const externT*& from_next,
          internT* to, internT* to_limit,
          internT*& to_next) const;
```

Converts characters from the input represented by the range [from, from_end) and places the result into the output designated by to. Converts no more than (from_end – from) elements from the input and places no more than (to_limit – to) elements into the output. Conversion also stops if it encounters a character that cannot be converted. When the function returns, from_next and to_next are pointing one beyond the last element successfully handled. If no translation is needed (return value `codecvt_base::noconv`), `to_next` is set to `to`, and `from_next` to `from`. Returns one of the values from `codecvt_base::result`.

```
virtual result do_out (stateT& state,
            const internT* from, const internT* from_end,
            const internT*& from_next,
            externT* to, externT* to_limit,
            externT*& to_next) const;
```

Converts characters from the input represented by the range [`from`, `from_end`) and places the result into the output designated by `to`. Converts no more than (`from_end` - `from`) elements from the input and places no more than (`to_limit` - `to`) elements into the output. Conversion also stops if it encounters a character that cannot be converted. When the function returns, `from_next` and `to_next` are pointing one beyond the last element successfully handled. If no translation is needed (return value `codecvt_base::noconv`), `to_next` is set to `to`, and `from_next` to `from`. Returns one of the values from `codecvt_base::result`.

MISCELLANEOUS

```
virtual bool do_always_noconv() const throw();
```

Returns `true` if no conversion is needed, that is, if `this->do_in()` and `this->do_out()` return `codecvt_base::noconv` for all valid parameters.

The required instantiation `codecvt<char,char,mbstate_t>` returns `true`.

```
virtual int do_encoding() const throw();
```

Returns −1 if the encoding of the `externT` sequence is state-dependent. Otherwise, returns the constant number of `externT` characters that are needed to produce one `internT` character, or 0 if this number is not a constant.

```
virtual int do_length(const stateT& state,
    const externT* from, const externT* from_end,
    size_t max) const;
```

Determines a subsequence of a given sequence of external characters that produces not more than a given number of internal characters. Returns *(from_next*-`from`) where *from_next* is the largest value in the range [`from`, `from_end`] such that the sequence of values in the range [`from`, *from_next*) represents `max` or fewer valid complete characters of type `internT`.

locale

The required instantiations codecvt<wchar_t, char, mbstate_t> and codecvt<char, char, mbstate_t> return the lesser of max and (from_end-from).

virtual int **do_max_length**() const throw();

Returns the maximum number of externT characters that can be consumed to produce one internT character, i.e., the maximum value that do_length(st, from, from_end, 1) can return for any valid range [from, from_end) and stateT value st.

result **do_unshift**(stateT& state, externT* to,
                  externT* to_limit, externT*& to_next) const;

Places the characters needed to unshift the conversion state represented by state into the output designated by to. Typically, these characters will be characters to return the state to the initial state stateT().

Places no more than (to_limit - to) elements into the output. When the function returns, to_next is pointing one beyond the last element placed in the output. If no unshift sequence is needed, to_next is set to to. Returns one of the values from codecvt_base::result.

The required instantiations codecvt<wchar_t, char, mbstate_t> and codecvt<char, char, mbstate_t> store no characters.

(The term "unshift" stems from the "shift sequences" that are used in state-dependent multibyte encodings. In this type of encoding scheme, shift (or escape) sequences are used to switch between one- and two-byte modes, as well as between different character sets; "unshift" therefore means "returning to the initial default mode." For further explanation see section 4.2.7.3, Character Encoding Schemes.)

codecvt_base

CLASS

class **codecvt_base**
header: **<locale>**
base class(es): **[none]**

DESCRIPTION

codecvt_base is the base class of all codecvt facets. It provides an enumerated type that represents the result of code conversion operations.

SYNOPSIS

```
namespace std {
 class codecvt_base {
 public:
  enum result { ok, partial, error, noconv };
 };
}
```

TYPE DEFINITIONS

enum **result** { ok, partial, error, noconv };

Enumerated type that represents the result of code conversion operations, such as in(), out(), and unshift().

CONSTANT DEFINITIONS

The following list shows the predefined values and their semantics for the nested enumerated type result. The numeric values are implementation-dependent:

ok

Completed the conversion successfully.

partial

Last characters from the input sequence not converted or additional input characters needed before another output character can be produced (in case of in() and out()) or more characters need to be supplied to complete termination (in the case of unshift()).

error

Encountered one or more character(s) in the input sequence that could not be converted (in the case of `in()` and `out()`) or the state is invalid (in the case of `unshift()`).

noconv

No conversion is needed (in the case of `in()` and `out()`); i.e., this is a nonconverting code conversion facet, or no termination is needed for the state type (in case of `unshift()`); i.e., a stateless encoding scheme is used, which has no shift states, and there is no need to unshift anything.

codecvt_byname<internT,externT,stateT>

CLASS TEMPLATE

class template<class internT,class externT,class stateT> **codecvt_byname**
header: **<locale>**
base class(es): **codecvt<internT, externT, stateT>**

DESCRIPTION

codecvt_byname is the *byname* codecvt facet. It allows the behavior of an object to be specified to conform to a certain localization environment. (See the description of the constructor for more information.)

The following instantiations are required:[1] codecvt_byname<wchar_t,char, mbstate_t> and codecvt_byname<char,char,mbstate_t>.

SYNOPSIS

```
namespace std {
 template <class internT, class externT, class stateT>
 class codecvt_byname : public codecvt<internT, externT, stateT> {
public:
 //  constructors:
  explicit codecvt_byname(const char*, size_t refs = 0);
protected:
 //  destructor:
  virtual ~codecvt_byname();
 //  code conversion:
  virtual result do_out(stateT& state,
        const internT* from, const internT* from_end,
        const internT*& from_next,
        externT* to, externT* to_limit, externT*& to_next) const;
  virtual result do_in(stateT& state,
        const externT* from, const externT* from_end,
        const externT*& from_next,
        internT* to, internT* to_limit, internT*& to_next) const;
```

---

1. At the time of this writing, the question of whether the instantiations of the codecvt_byname facets are required or not is under discussion by the standards committee. The final C++ standard currently does not require them, but there is a corresponding change request pending.

```
// miscellaneous:
virtual result do_unshift(stateT& state,
        externT* to, externT* to_limit, externT*& to_next) const;
virtual int do_encoding() const throw();
virtual bool do_always_noconv() const throw();
virtual int do_length(const stateT&,
        const externT* from, const externT* end, size_t max) const;
virtual result do_unshift(stateT& state,
        externT* to, externT* to_limit, externT*& to_next) const;
virtual int do_max_length() const throw();
};
}
```

PUBLIC MEMBER FUNCTIONS

Implements all public member functions as described for codecvt<internT, externT, stateT>, except

explicit **codecvt_byname**(const char* name, size_t refs = 0);

Constructs an object of type codecvt_byname <internT, externT, stateT>. The implementation-specific name specifies the localization environment to which the constructed object conforms. If refs==0, the lifetime of this is managed by the locale(s) that contain this. If refs==1, the memory of this must be explicitly managed. The behavior for refs>1 is not defined.

PROTECTED MEMBER FUNCTIONS

Implements all protected member functions as described for codecvt<internT, externT, stateT>, except

virtual **~codecvt_byname**();

Destroys an object of type codecvt_byname<charT>.

collate<charT>

CLASS TEMPLATE

template<class charT> class **collate**
header: **<locale>**
base class(es): **locale::facet**

DESCRIPTION

collate is the facet that contains the functionality for string collation (comparison) and hashing.

The following instantiations are required: collate<char> and collate <wchar_t>. They provide classic "C" behavior. Details are given with the description of the virtual protected member functions.

SYNOPSIS

```
namespace std {
 template <class charT>
 class collate : public locale::facet {
public:
  //  type definitions:
  typedef charT             char_type;
  typedef basic_string<charT> string_type;
  //  data member:
  static locale::id id;
  //  constructors:
  explicit collate(size_t refs = 0);
  //. collate operations:
  int compare(const charT* low1, const charT* high1,
            const charT* low2, const charT* high2) const;
  string_type transform(const charT* low, const charT* high) const;
  long hash(const charT* low, const charT* high) const;
protected:
  //  destructor:
  virtual ~collate();
  // collate operations:
  virtual int do_compare(const charT* low1, const charT* high1,
                     const charT* low2, const charT* high2) const;
  virtual string_type do_transform
                     (const charT* low, const charT* high) const;
  virtual long  do_hash (const charT* low, const charT* high) const;
 };
}
```

locale

PUBLIC DATA MEMBERS

static locale::id **id;**

collate<charT>::id defines the unique identifications of the collate facet interfaces. Each template instantiation with a different character type defines a different facet interface with an associated unique id.

PUBLIC MEMBER FUNCTIONS

explicit **collate**(size_t refs = 0);

Constructs an object of type collate<charT>. If refs==0, the lifetime of this is managed by the locale(s) that contain this. If refs==1, the memory of this must be explicitly managed. The behavior for refs>1 is not defined.

int **compare**(const charT* low1, const charT* high1,
        const charT* low2, const charT* high2) const;

Calls do_compare(low1,high1, low2,high2) and returns the result of this call.

long **hash**(const charT* low, const charT* high) const;

Calls do_hash(low,high) and returns the result of this call.

string_type **transform**(const charT* low, const charT* high) const;

Calls do_transform(low,high) and returns the result of this call.

PROTECTED MEMBER FUNCTIONS

virtual ~**collate**();

Destroys an object of type collate<charT>.

virtual int
do_compare(const charT* low1, const charT* high1,
        const charT* low2, const charT* high2) const;

Returns 1, if the character sequence represented by the range [low1,high1) is greater than the character sequence represented by the range [low2,high2), –1, if the first sequence is less than the second, or 0, if they are equal.

The required instantiations `collate<char>` and `collate<wchar_t>` implement a lexicographic comparison; i.e., they compare the sequences element by element by applying the `operator<()` to pairs of corresponding elements. The first pair of unequal elements determines which sequence is less or greater. If all elements of the shorter sequence are equal to the first elements of the longer sequence, the shorter sequence is less than the longer sequence.

```
virtual long do_hash(const charT* low, const charT* high) const;
```

Returns a hash value derived from the character sequence represented by the range `[low,high)`. Character sequences for which `this->compare()` yields 0 will produce the same hash value.

```
virtual string_type do_transform(const charT* low, const charT* high) const;
```

Returns a string that is the transformation of the character sequence represented by the range `[low,high)` to an internal representation. The lexicographic comparison of two strings resulting from `do_transfer()` yields the same result as the comparison of the original character ranges with `do_compare()`. This is helpful when a single character sequence is compared to many other character sequences, because it avoids the transformation of the single character sequence for each comparison.

collate_byname<charT>

CLASS TEMPLATE

class template<class charT> **collate_byname**
header: **<locale>**
base class(es): **collate<**charT**>**

DESCRIPTION

collate_byname is the *byname* collate facet. It allows the behavior of an object to be specified to conform to a certain localization environment. (See the description of the constructor for more information.)

The following instantiations are required: collate_byname<char> and collate_byname<wchar_t>.

SYNOPSIS

```
namespace std {
 template <class charT>
 class collate_byname : public collate<charT> {
 public:
 //  type definitions:
  typedef charT                char_type;
  typedef basic_string<charT> string_type;
  //  constructors:
  explicit collate_byname(const char*, size_t refs = 0);
 protected:
  //  destructor:
  virtual ~collate_byname();
  //  collate operations:
  virtual int do_compare(const charT* low1, const charT* high1,
                       const charT* low2, const charT* high2) const;
  virtual string_type do_transform
                      (const charT* low, const charT* high) const;
  virtual long do_hash  (const charT* low, const charT* high) const;
 };
}
```

locale

PUBLIC MEMBER FUNCTIONS

Implements all public member functions as described for collate<charT>, except

```
explicit collate_byname(const char*, size_t refs = 0);
```

Constructs an object of type collate_byname<charT>. The implementation-specific name specifies the localization environment to which the constructed object conforms. If refs==0, the lifetime of this is managed by the locale(s) that contain this. If refs==1, the memory of this must be explicitly managed. The behavior for refs>1 is not defined.

PROTECTED MEMBER FUNCTIONS

Implements all protected member functions as described for collate<charT>, except

```
virtual ~collate_byname();
```

Destroys an object of type collate_byname<charT>.

ctype<charT>

CLASS TEMPLATE

class template<class charT> **ctype**
header: **<locale>**
base class(es): **ctype_base**, **locale::facet**

DESCRIPTION

ctype is the facet that contains the functionality for character classification and conversion.

The following instantiations are required: ctype<char> and ctype<wchar_t>. They implement character classification appropriate to the implementation's native character set. The type ctype<char> is provided as a specialization of the ctype<charT> template.

SYNOPSIS

```
template <class charT>
 class ctype : public locale::facet, public ctype_base {
public:
 //  type definitions:
 typedef charT char_type;
 //  data members:
 static locale::id id;
 //  constructors:
 explicit ctype(size_t refs = 0);
 //  character classification:
 bool        is(mask m, charT c) const;
 const charT* is(const charT* low, const charT* high, mask* vec) const;
 const charT* scan_is (mask m,
                       const charT* low, const charT* high) const;
 const charT* scan_not(mask m,
                       const charT* low, const charT* high) const;
 //  character conversion:
 charT        toupper(charT c) const;
 const charT* toupper(charT* low, const charT* high) const;
 charT        tolower(charT c) const;
 const charT* tolower(charT* low, const charT* high) const;
 charT        widen(char c) const;
 const char*  widen(const char* low, const char high, charT* to) const;
 char         narrow(charT c, char dfault) const;
 const charT* narrow(const charT* low, const charT*, char dfault,
                     char* to) const;
```

locale

```
protected:
//  destructor:
virtual ~ctype();
//  character classification:
virtual bool         do_is(mask m, charT c) const;
virtual const charT* do_is(const charT* low, const charT* high,
                           mask* vec) const;
virtual const charT* do_scan_is(mask m,
                           const charT* low, const charT* high) const;
virtual const charT* do_scan_not(mask m,
                           const charT* low, const charT* high) const;
//  character conversion:
virtual charT        do_toupper(charT) const;
virtual const charT* do_toupper(charT* low, const charT* high) const;
virtual charT        do_tolower(charT) const;
virtual const charT* do_tolower(charT* low, const charT* high) const;
virtual charT        do_widen(char) const;
virtual const char*  do_widen(const char* low, const char* high,
                           charT* dest) const;
virtual char         do_narrow(charT, char dfault) const;
virtual const charT* do_narrow(const charT* low, const charT* high,
                           char dfault, char* dest) const;
};
}
```

PUBLIC DATA MEMBERS

```
static locale::id id;
```

ctype<charT>::id defines the unique identifications of the ctype facet interfaces. Each template instantiation with a different character type defines a different facet interface with an associated unique id.

PUBLIC MEMBER FUNCTIONS

```
explicit ctype(size_t refs = 0);
```

Constructs an object of type ctype<charT>. If refs==0, the lifetime of this is managed by the locale(s) that contain this. If refs==1, the memory of this must be explicitly managed. The behavior for refs>1 is not defined.

locale

CHARACTER CLASSIFICATION

```
bool is (mask m, charT c) const;
```

Calls do_is(m,c) and returns the result of this call.

```
const charT* is (const charT* low, const charT* high,
                 mask* vec) const;
```

Calls do_is(low,high,vec) and returns the result of this call.

```
const charT* scan_is (mask m, const charT* low,
                      const charT* high) const;
```

Calls do_scan_is(m,low,high) and returns the result of this call.

```
const charT* scan_not (mask m, const charT* low,
                       const charT* high) const;
```

Calls do_scan_not(m,low,high) and returns the result of this call.

CHARACTER CONVERSION

```
char narrow(charT c, char dfault) const;
```

Calls do_narrow(c,dfault) and returns the result of this call.

```
const charT* narrow(const charT* low, const charT* high,
                    char dfault, char* to) const;
```

Calls do_narrow(low,high,dfault,to) and returns the result of this call.

```
charT tolower(charT c) const;
```

Calls do_tolower(c) and returns the result of this call.

```
const charT* tolower(charT* low, const charT* high) const;
```

Calls do_tolower(low,high) and returns the result of this call.

```
charT toupper(charT c) const;
```

Calls do_toupper(c) and returns the result of this call.

```
const charT* toupper(charT* low, const charT* high) const;
```

Calls `do_toupper(low,high)` and returns the result of this call.

```
charT widen(char c) const;
```

Calls `do_widen(c)` and returns the result of this call.

```
const char*  widen(const char* low, const char* high,
                    charT* to) const;
```

Calls `do_widen(low,high)` and returns the result of this call.

PROTECTED MEMBER FCT.

```
virtual ~ctype();
```

Destroys an object of type `ctype<charT>`.

CHARACTER CLASSIFICATION

```
virtual bool do_is (mask m, charT c) const;
```

Returns `true` if c conforms to the classification defined by m. Otherwise returns `false`. (See `ctype_base::mask` for details.)

```
virtual const charT* do_is
 (const charT* low, const charT* high, mask* vec) const;
```

Determines the classification m of type `ctype_base::mask` for each element in the range [low,high) and places m into vec. After the call, the array vec contains the bit masks that characterize each character from the range [low,high). Returns high.

```
virtual const charT* do_scan_is
 (mask m, const charT* low, const charT* high) const;
```

Locates the first element from the range [low,high) that conforms to the classification defined by m. Returns the address of the found element or high, if none was found.

locale

```
virtual const charT* do_scan_not
 (mask m, const charT* low, const charT* high) const;
```

Locates the first element from the range [low, high) that does not conform to the classi-fication defined by m. Returns the address of the found element or high, if none was found.

CHARACTER CONVERSION

```
virtual char do_narrow(charT c, char dfault) const;
```

Returns the char representation that corresponds to c, if it exists; otherwise dfault.

```
virtual const charT* do_narrow
 (const charT* low, const charT* high, char dfault,
  char* to) const;
```

Places the char representation that corresponds to the elements from the range [low, high) into the array designated by to. If an element has no corresponding char representation, dfault is placed into the array alternatively. Returns high.

```
virtual charT do_tolower(charT c) const;
```

Returns the character that represents the lowercase conversion of c, if it exists; otherwise c.

```
virtual const charT* do_tolower
 (charT* low, const charT* high) const;
```

Replaces each element from the range [low, high) with the character that represents the lowercase conversion, if it exists. Returns high.

```
virtual charT do_toupper(charT c) const;
```

Returns the character that represents the uppercase conversion of c, if it exists; otherwise c.

```
virtual const charT* do_toupper
 (charT* low, const charT* high) const;
```

Replaces each element from the range [low,high) with the character that represents the uppercase conversion, if it exists. Returns high.

```
virtual charT do_widen(char c) const;
```

Returns the charT representation that corresponds to c.

```
virtual const char* do_widen
 (const char* low, const char* high, charT* to) const;
```

Places the charT representation that corresponds to the elements from the range [low,high) into the array designated by to. Returns high.

ctype<char>

TEMPLATE SPECIALIZATION

template<> class **ctype**<char>
header: **<locale>**
base class(es): **ctype_base, locale::facet**

DESCRIPTION

For performance reasons, the ctype facet for the character type char is a template specialization. Its implementation is based on a table that uses the character as key and the classification mask that corresponds to the character as value.

SYNOPSIS

```
namespace std {
 template <> class ctype<char> : public locale::facet, public ctype_base{
 public:
 // type definitions:
 typedef char char_type;
 // data members and constant definitions:
 static locale::id id;
 static const size_t table_size =  IMPLEMENTATION_DEFINED;
 // constructors:
 explicit ctype(const mask* tab = 0, bool del = false, size_t refs = 0);
 // character classification:
 bool is(mask m, char c) const;
 const char* is(const char* low, const char* high, mask* vec) const;
 const char* scan_is (mask m, const char* low, const char* high) const;
 const char* scan_not(mask m, const char* low, const char* high) const;
 // character conversion:
 char        toupper(char c) const;
 const char* toupper(char* low, const char* high) const;
 char        tolower(char c) const;
 const char* tolower(char* low, const char* high) const;
 char  widen(char c) const;
 const char* widen(const char* low, const char* high, char* to) const;
 char  narrow(char c, char dfault) const;
 const char* narrow(const char* low, const char* high, char dfault,
                    char* to) const;
 protected:
 // destructor:
 virtual ~ctype();
 // table access:
```

```
const mask* table() const throw();
static const mask* classic_table() throw();
// character conversion:
virtual char         do_toupper(char c) const;
virtual const char* do_toupper(char* low, const char* high) const;
virtual char         do_tolower(char c) const;
virtual const char* do_tolower(char* low, const char* high) const;
virtual char         do_widen(char c) const;
virtual const char* do_widen(const char* low, const char* high,
                             char* to) const;
virtual char         do_narrow(char c, char dfault) const;
virtual const char* do_narrow(const char* low, const char* high,
                              char dfault, char* to) const;
};
}
```

CONSTANT DEFINITIONS

```
static const size_t table_size;
```

Size of the table used for character classification. The value is implementation-defined, but at least 256.

PUBLIC MEMBER FUNCTIONS

Implements all public member functions as described for ctype<charT>, except the following listed:

```
explicit ctype(const mask* tab = 0, bool del = false, size_t refs = 0);
```

Constructs an object of type ctype<char>. If tab==0, the new object uses ctype <char>::classic_table() for character classification. If tab!=0, the new object uses tab for character classification. If tab!=0 and del==true, the table is destroyed via delete[] table() during destruction.

If refs==0, the lifetime of this is managed by the locale(s) that contain this. If refs==1, the memory of this must be explicitly managed. The behavior for refs>1 is not defined.

locale

CHARACTER CLASSIFICATION

```
bool is(mask m, char c) const;
```

Returns true if c conforms to the classification defined by m; otherwise false. Uses the table for classification; that is, returns table()[(unsigned char)c] & m. (See ctype_base::mask for details.)

```
const char* is
  (const char* low, const char* high, mask* vec) const;
```

Determines the classification for each element in the range [low,high) and places it into vec. After the call, the array vec contains the bitmask that characterizes each character from the range [low,high). The classification for an element c is determined as table()[(unsigned char)c]. Returns high.

```
const char* scan_is
  (mask m, const char* low, const char* high) const;
```

Locates the first element from the range [low,high) that conforms to the classification defined by m. The classification for an element c is determined as table() [(unsigned char)c]. Returns the address of the found element or high, if none was found.

```
const char* scan_not
  (mask m, const char* low, const char* high) const;
```

Locates the first element from the range [low,high) that does not conform to the classification defined by m. The classification for an element c is determined as table()[(unsigned char)c]. Returns the address of the found element or high, if none was found.

PROTECTED MEMBER FUNCTIONS

Implements all protected member functions as described for ctype<charT>, except the following listed:

```
virtual ~ctype();
```

Destroys an object of type ctype<char>. If the constructor parameters conform to the following constraint: tab!=0 && del == true, the table is deleted by calling delete[] table().

TABLE ACCESS

`const mask* `**`table`**`() const throw();`

Returns a pointer to the table that is currently used by `this` for character classification, that is, the first constructor argument, if it was nonzero, and otherwise `classic_table()`.

`static const mask* `**`classic_table`**`() throw();`

Returns a pointer to a table that implements a character classification, which conforms to the "C" locale.

ctype_base

CLASS

class **ctype_base**
header: **<locale>**
base class(es): **[none]**

DESCRIPTION

ctype_base is the base class of all ctype facets. It provides a bitmask that represents different character categories.

SYNOPSIS

```
namespace std {
 class ctype_base {
 public:
  enum mask {          //  numeric values are for exposition only.
          space=1<<0, print=1<<1, cntrl=1<<2, upper=1<<3, lower=1<<4,
          alpha=1<<5, digit=1<<6, punct=1<<7, xdigit=1<<8,
          alnum=alpha|digit, graph=alnum|punct
  };
 };
}
```

TYPE DEFINITIONS

enum **mask** {space, print, cntrl, upper, lower, alpha,
          digit, punct, xdigit, alnum, graph}

Enumerated bitmask type that represents the different types of character categories.

CONSTANT DEFINITIONS

The following list shows the predefined values and their semantics for the nested enumerated type mask. The numeric values are implementation-dependent:

alpha

alphabetical characters

digit

characters that represents the decimal digits 0–9

cntrl

control characters

lower

lowercase characters

print

printable characters

punct

punctuation characters

space

whitespace characters

upper

uppercase characters

xdigit

characters that represents the hexadecimal digits, i.e., 0–9, a–f, or A–F

alnum

alphanumeric characters, that is, the union of alphabetical characters and digits; the value equals `alpha|digit`

graph

printing characters, that is, the union of alphanumeric and punctuation characters; the value equals `alnum|punct`

ctype_byname<charT>

CLASS TEMPLATE

template<class charT> class **ctype_byname**
header: **<locale>**
base class(es): **ctype**<charT>

DESCRIPTION

ctype_byname is the *byname* ctype facet. It allows the behavior of an object to be specified to conform to a certain localization environment. (See the description of the constructor for more information.)

The following instantiations are required: ctype_byname<char> and ctype_byname<wchar_t>. The type ctype_byname<char> is provided as a specialization of the ctype_byname<charT> template.

SYNOPSIS

```
namespace std {
 template <class charT>
 class ctype_byname : public ctype<charT> {
 public:
 // type definitions:
  typedef ctype<charT>::mask mask;
 // constructors:
  explicit ctype_byname(const char*, size_t refs = 0);
 protected:
 // destructor:
  virtual ~ctype_byname();
 // character classification:
  virtual bool        do_is(mask m, charT c) const;
  virtual const charT* do_is(const charT* low, const charT* high,
                        mask* vec) const;
  virtual const char*  do_scan_is(mask m,
                        const charT* low, const charT* high) const;
  virtual const char*  do_scan_not(mask m,
                        const charT* low, const charT* high) const;
 // character conversion:
  virtual charT        do_toupper(charT) const;
  virtual const charT* do_toupper(charT* low, const charT* high) const;
  virtual charT        do_tolower(charT) const;
  virtual const charT* do_tolower(charT* low, const charT* high) const;
  virtual charT        do_widen(char) const;
```

```
    virtual const char*   do_widen(const char* low, const char* high,
                                     charT* dest) const;
    virtual char          do_narrow(charT, char dfault) const;
    virtual const charT*  do_narrow(const charT* low, const charT* high,
                                     char dfault, char* dest) const;
  };
}
```

PUBLIC MEMBER FUNCTIONS

Implements all public member functions as described for ctype<charT>, except

explicit **ctype_byname**(const char* name, size_t refs = 0);

Constructs an object of type ctype_byname<charT>. The implementation-specific name specifies the localization environment to which the constructed object conforms. If refs==0, the lifetime of this is managed by the locale(s) that contain(s) this. If refs==1, the memory of this must be explicitly managed. The behavior for refs>1 is not defined.

PROTECTED MEMBER FUNCTIONS

Implements all protected member functions as described for ctype<charT>, except

virtual **~ctype_byname**();

Destroys an object of type ctype_byname<charT>.

locale

CLASS

class **locale**
header: **<locale>**
base class(es): **[none]**

DESCRIPTION

locale encapsulates an abstraction that maintains different facet objects, which together form a certain localization environment. A facet object can be maintained by a locale object only if it is an instance of a class that is either derived from locale::facet and declares a static public member data id of type locale::id or is an instance of a class that is derived from such a class.

Locales can have names. Valid locale names are "C"; ""; and any implementation-defined locale name. "C" stands for the classic U.S. English ASCII locale. "" stands for the native locale on your system. The syntax and semantics of other locale names are not defined by the standard but are entirely implementation-specific. For example, the name "De_DE" on an X/Open system denotes the same localization environment as "German_Germany.1252" on a Microsoft platform.

SYNOPSIS

```
namespace std {
 class locale {
 public:
 //   class definitions:
  class facet;
  class id;
 //   type definitions:
  typedef int category;
 //   constant definitions:
  static const category   //  values assigned are for exposition only
    none     = 0,
    collate  = 0x010, ctype    = 0x020,
    monetary = 0x040, numeric  = 0x080,
    time     = 0x100, messages = 0x200,
    all = collate | ctype | monetary | numeric | time  | messages;
 //   construct/copy/destroy:
  locale() throw()
  locale(const locale& other) throw()
  explicit locale(const char* std_name);
  locale(const locale& other, const char* std_name, category);
```

```
    template <class Facet> locale(const locale& other, Facet* f);
    locale(const locale& other, const locale& one, category);
    ~locale() throw();            //  non-virtual
    const locale& operator=(const locale& other) throw();
    template <class Facet> locale combine(const locale& other);
    // operators:
    bool operator==(const locale& other) const;
    bool operator!=(const locale& other) const;
    template <class charT, class Traits, class Allocator>
    bool operator()
    (const basic_string<charT,Traits,Allocator>& s1,
     const basic_string<charT,Traits,Allocator>& s2) const;
    //  locale operations:
    basic_string<char> name() const;
    //  global locale objects:
    static      locale  global(const locale&);
    static const locale& classic();
  };
}
```

CLASS DEFINITIONS

```
class id {
  public:
     id();
  private:
     void operator= (const id&); // not defined
     id(const id&);              // not defined
};
```

id provides identification of a facet interface. locale objects maintain facets polymorphically via their public data member id of type locale::id.

```
class facet {
   protected:
      explicit facet(size_t refs = 0);
      virtual ~facet();
   private:
      facet(const facet&);         // not defined
      void operator=(const facet&); // not defined
};
```

facet is the base class for all facet instances that can be contained in a locale object. If refs==0, the lifetime of the facet object is managed by the locale(s) that it contain(s). If refs==1, the facet object must be explicitly deleted. The behavior for refs>1 is not defined.

TYPE DEFINITIONS

typedef int **category;**

A category value identifies a set of locale categories.

CONSTANT DEFINITIONS

The following list shows the predefined values and their semantics for the nested bitmask type category. The numeric values are implementation-dependent:

none

Represents the empty set of categories.

collate

Corresponding to the C locale category LC_COLLATE. This category contains at least the facet interfaces associated with collate<char> and collate<wchar_t>.

ctype

Corresponding to the C locale category LC_CTYPE. This category contains at least the facet interfaces associated with ctype<char>, ctype<wchar_t>, codecvt<char,char, mbstate_t>, and codecvt<wchar_t,char,mbstate_t>.

messages

Corresponding to the Posix locale category LC_MESSAGE. This category contains at least the facet interfaces associated with messages<char> and messages<wchar_t>.

monetary

Corresponding to the C locale category LC_MONETARY. This category contains at least the facet interfaces associated with moneypunct<char>, moneypunct<wchar_t>, moneypunct<char,true>, moneypunct<wchar_t,true>, money_get<char>, money_get<wchar_t>, money_put<char>, and money_put<wchar_t>.

numeric

Corresponding to the C locale category LC_NUMERIC. This category contains at least the facet interfaces associated with numpunct<char>, numpunct<wchar_t>, num_get <char>, num_get<wchar_t>, num_put<char>, and num_put<wchar_t>.

time

Corresponding to the C locale category LC_TIME. This category contains at least the facet interfaces associated with time_get<char>, time_get<wchar_t>, time_put <char>, and time_put<wchar_t>.

all = collate | ctype | monetary | numeric | time | messages

Represents the union of all categories corresponding to the C locale category identifier LC_ALL.

PUBLIC MEMBER FUNCTIONS: CONSTRUCT, COPY, DESTROY

locale() throw();

Constructs a snapshot of the current global locale, that is, an object of type locale, which is either a copy of the argument passed into the last call to locale::global (locale&), if this function has been called before, or a copy of the locale returned by a call to locale::classic().

locale(const locale& other) throw();

Constructs an object of type locale, which is a copy of other.

explicit **locale**(const char* name);

Constructs an object of type locale. The name specifies the localization environment to which the constructed object conforms. Valid locale names are "C"; ""; and any implementation-defined locale name. Throws the exception runtime_error if the argument name is not valid, or 0.

locale(const locale& other, const char* name, category c);

Constructs an object of type locale, which is a copy of other, except for the facets identified by the category c. These facets are the same as those in a locale object constructed by `locale(name)`. Throws the exception `runtime_error` if the argument `name` is not valid, or 0. The resulting locale has a name if, and only if, `other` has a name.

```
template<class Facet>
locale(const locale& other, Facet* f);
```

Constructs an object of type `locale`, which is a copy of `other`, except for the facet identified by `Facet`. This facet is the same as `*f`. If `f==0` the newly constructed object is a copy of `other`. The resulting locale has no name.

```
locale(const locale& other,const locale& one,category c);
```

Constructs an object of type `locale`, which is a copy of `other`, except for the facets identified by the category `c`. These facets are taken from `one`. The resulting locale has a name if, and only if, the two source locales have names.

```
const locale& operator= (const locale& rhs) throw();
```

Creates a copy of `rhs` that replaces the current value of `this`. Returns `*this`.

```
template<class Facet>
locale combine(const locale& other);
```

Returns a newly constructed object of type `locale`, which is a copy of `*this`, except for the facet identified by `Facet`. This facet is taken from `other`. Throws the exception `runtime_error` if `has_facet<Facet> (other)` returns `false`. The resulting locale has no name.

```
~locale() throw();
```

Destroys an object of type `locale`.

OPERATORS

```
bool operator== (const locale& rhs) const;
```

Returns `true` if both arguments are the same locale, or one is a copy of the other, or each has a name and the names are identical. Returns `false` otherwise.

```
bool operator!= (const locale& rhs) const;
```

Returns `!(*this == other)`.

```
template <class charT, class Traits, class Allocator>
bool operator()(
const basic_string <class charT, class Traits, class Allocator>& s1,
const basic_string <class charT, class Traits, class Allocator>& s2) const;
```

Compares two strings according to the collate facet of this, i.e., returns

```
(use_facet< collate<charT> > (*this).
          compare(s1.data(), s1.data()+s1.size(),
                  s2.data(), s2.data()+s2.size()) < 0 ).
```

This operator, and therefore locale itself, satisfies the requirements for a comparator predicate for strings. For example, it can be used for instantiation of containers such as map<string,T,locale> or for invocation of algorithms such as sort(begin,end, locale("US"));

LOCALE OPERATIONS

```
basic_string<char> name() const;
```

The name of this, if this has one. Otherwise, the string "*". Valid locale names are "C"; ""; and any implementation-defined locale name.

GLOBAL LOCALE OBJECTS

```
static locale global (const locale& loc);
```

Sets the global locale to loc, which causes future calls to locale() to construct a copy of loc. Returns the previous value set, if this function has been called before, or a copy of the locale returned by a call to locale::classic().

Effects on the C locale: If loc has a name, sets the "C" locale accordingly, i.e., calls setlocale(LC_ALL,loc.name().c_str()). Otherwise the effect on the C locale is implementation-specific.

```
static const locale& classic();
```

Returns a locale object that behaves according to the "C" locale semantics.

messages<charT>

CLASS TEMPLATE

template<class charT> class **messages**
header: **<locale>**
base class(es): **locale::facet**, **messages_base**

DESCRIPTION

messages is the facet that contains the functionality for the retrieval of localized message strings from message catalogs.

The following instantiations are required: messages<char> and messages <wchar_t>. Their behavior is implementation-specific. The standard specifies neither how a message catalog is represented and organized nor what the syntax of the contained messages is.

SYNOPSIS

```
namespace std {
 template <class charT>
 class messages : public locale::facet, public messages_base {
 public:
 //  type definitions:
  typedef charT              char_type;
  typedef basic_string<charT> string_type;
 //  data member:
  static locale::id id;
 //  constructors:
  explicit messages(size_t refs = 0);
  //  messages operations:
  catalog open(const basic_string<char>& fn, const locale&) const;
  string_type  get(catalog c, int set, int msgid,
                  const string_type& dfault) const;
  void    close(catalog c) const;
 protected:
  //  destructor:
  virtual messages();
  //  messages operations:
  virtual catalog do_open(const basic_string<char>&, const locale&) const;
  virtual string_type  do_get(catalog, int set, int msgid,
                             const string_type& dfault) const;
  virtual void    do_close(catalog) const;
 };
}
```

PUBLIC DATA MEMBERS

`static locale::id` **id;**

`messages<charT>::id` defines the unique identifications of the messages facet interfaces. Each template instantiation with a different character type defines a different facet interface with an associated unique `id`.

PUBLIC MEMBER FUNCTIONS

`explicit` **messages**`(size_t refs = 0);`

Constructs an object of type `messages<charT>`. If `refs==0`, the lifetime of `this` is managed by the locale(s) that contain `this`. If `refs==1`, the memory of `this` must be explicitly managed. The behavior for `refs>1` is not defined.

`void` **close**`(catalog c) const;`

Calls `do_close(c)` and returns the result of this call.

`string_type` **get**`(catalog c, int set, int msgid,`
`                const string_type& dfault) const;`

Calls `do_get(c,set,msgid,dfault)` and returns the result of this call.

`catalog` **open**`(const basic_string<char>& fn,`
`                const locale& loc) const;`

Calls `do_open(fn,loc)` and returns the result of this call.

PROTECTED MEMBER FUNCTIONS

`virtual` **~messages**`();`

Destroys an object of type `messages<charT>`.

`virtual void` **do_close**`(catalog c) const;`

Closes the message catalog identified by c. c must be obtained from a previous opening of a catalog that is not yet closed.

locale

```
virtual string_type do_get(catalog c, int set,
             int msgid, const string_type& dfault) const;
```

Retrieves a message identified by set and msgid according to an implementation-defined mapping from the message catalog identified by c. Returns the message if it can be found; otherwise dfault. c must be obtained from a previous opening of a catalog that is not yet closed.

```
virtual catalog do_open(const basic_string<char>& name,
                     const locale& loc) const;
```

Opens the message catalog identified by the name according to an implementation-defined mapping. If the message catalog can be opened, it returns a value >= 0, that is, an identifier for the opened message catalog. Otherwise a value < 0. loc is used, if the messages from the catalog need character set code conversion when they are retrieved via get.

messages_base

CLASS

class **messages_base**
header: **<locale>**
base class(es): **[none]**

DESCRIPTION

messages_base is the base class of the messages facet. It provides a type definition for catalog.

SYNOPSIS

```
namespace std {
 class messages_base {
 public:
  typedef int catalog;
 };
}
```

TYPE DEFINITIONS

```
typedef int catalog;
```

Values of type catalog are usable as arguments to the messages facet's member functions get() and close() and can be obtained only by calling open().

messages_byname<charT>

CLASS TEMPLATE

template<class charT> class **messages_byname**
header: **<locale>**
base class(es): **messages**<charT>

DESCRIPTION

messages_byname is the *byname* messages facet. It allows the behavior of an object to be specified to conform to a certain localization environment. (See the description of the constructor for more information.)

The following instantiations are required: messages_byname<char> and messages_byname<wchar_t>.

SYNOPSIS

```
namespace std {
 template <class charT>
 class messages_byname : public messages<charT> {
 public:
 //  type definitions:
  typedef messages_base::catalog catalog;
  typedef basic_string<charT>     string_type;
  //  constructors:
  explicit messages_byname(const char*, size_t refs = 0);
 protected:
  //  destructor:
 virtual ~messages_byname();
  //  messages operations:
  virtual catalog do_open(const basic_string<char>&,
                        const locale&) const;
  virtual string_type  do_get(catalog, int set, int msgid,
                             const string_type& dfault) const;
  virtual void    do_close(catalog) const;
 };
}
```

PUBLIC MEMBER FUNCTIONS

Implements all public member functions as described for messages<charT>, except

```
explicit messages_byname(const char* name, size_t refs = 0);
```

Constructs an object of type messages_byname<charT>. The implementation-specific name specifies the localization environment to which the constructed object conforms. If refs==0, the lifetime of this is managed by the locale(s) that contain this. If refs==1, the memory of this must be explicitly managed. The behavior for refs>1 is not defined.

PROTECTED MEMBER FUNCTIONS

Implements all protected member functions as described for messages<charT>, except

```
virtual ~messages_byname();
```

Destroys an object of type messages_byname<charT>.

locale

money_base

CLASS

class **money_base**
header: **<locale>**
base class(es): **[none]**

DESCRIPTION

money_base is the base class of all moneypunct facets. It provides the means to store and exchange monetary format patterns.

SYNOPSIS

```
namespace std {
 class money_base {
 public:
   enum part { none, space, symbol, sign, value };
   struct pattern { char field[4]; };
};
```

TYPE DEFINITIONS

enum **part** { none, space, symbol, sign, value };

Enumerated type that represents the elements and their usage of a monetary format.

struct **pattern** { char field[4]; };

Type that is used to store monetary format patterns.

CONSTANT DEFINITIONS

The following list shows the predefined values and their semantics for the nested enumerated type part. The numeric values are implementation-dependent:

none

optional whitespace character for parsing, no character for formatting

sign

the symbol(s) indicating if an amount is positive or negative

space

optional whitespace character for parsing, required whitespace character for formatting

symbol

the currency symbol; usage of the currency symbol also depends on `ios_base::` `showbase` (see `money_put::do_put()` and `money_get::do_get()`)

value

the monetary value

money_get<charT,InputIterator>

CLASS TEMPLATE

template<class charT, class InputIterator = istreambuf_iterator<charT> >
class **money_get**
header: **<locale>**
base class(es): **locale::facet**

DESCRIPTION

money_get is the facet that contains the functionality to parse a character sequence that represents a monetary value. The bool value template parameter Inter specifies whether the currency symbol used should be the international currency symbol (Inter==true) or not (Inter==false).

The following instantiations are required: money_get<char> and money_get <wchar_t>. The money_get template must be instantiable for all character types and input iterator types. The behavior of the instantiations is implementation-specific for character types other than char and wchar_t.

SYNOPSIS

```
namespace std {
 template <class charT,
          class InputIterator = istreambuf_iterator<charT> >
 class money_get : public locale::facet {
 public:
 // type definitions:
 typedef charT             char_type;
 typedef InputIterator     iter_type;
 typedef basic_string<charT> string_type;
 // data members:
 static locale::id id;
 // constructors:
 explicit money_get(size_t refs = 0);
 // parsing operations:
 iter_type get(iter_type s, iter_type end, bool intl, ios_base& f,
               ios_base::iostate& err, long double& units) const;
 iter_type get(iter_type s, iter_type end, bool intl, ios_base& f,
               ios_base::iostate& err, string_type& digits) const;
 protected:
 // destructor:
 virtual ~money_get();
 // parsing operations:
 virtual iter_type do_get(iter_type, iter_type, bool, ios_base&,
                    ios_base::iostate& err, long double& units) const;
```

locale

```
    virtual iter_type do_get(iter_type, iter_type, bool, ios_base&,
                      ios_base::iostate& err, string_type& digits) const;
  };
}
```

PUBLIC DATA MEMBERS

```
static locale::id id;
```

money_get<charT, Inter, InputIterator>::id defines the unique identifications
of the money_get facet interfaces. Each template instantiation with a different character
type, a different bool Inter value, or a different input iterator type defines a different
facet interface with an associated unique id.

PUBLIC MEMBER FUNCTIONS

```
explicit money_get(size_t refs = 0);
```

Constructs an object of type money_get<charT, Inter, InputIterator>. If refs==0,
the lifetime of this is managed by the locale(s) that contain this. If refs==1, the memory of this must be explicitly managed. The behavior for refs>1 is not defined.

```
iter_type get(iter_type s, iter_type end, bool intl,
                    ios_base& f, ios_base::iostate& err,
                            long double& units) const;
```

Calls do_get(s, end, intl, f, err, units) and returns the result of this call.

```
iter_type get(iter_type s, iter_type end, bool intl,
                    ios_base& f, ios_base::iostate& err,
                            string_type& digits) const;
```

Calls do_get(s, end, intl, f, err, digits) and returns the result of this call.

PROTECTED MEMBER FUNCTIONS

```
virtual ~money_get();
```

Destroys an object of type money_get<charT, Inter, InputIterator>.

locale

```
virtual iter_type do_get(iter_type s, iter_type end,
         bool intl, ios_base& f, ios_base::iostate& err,
                              long double& units) const;
```

```
virtual iter_type do_get(iter_type s, iter_type end,
         bool intl, ios_base& f, ios_base::iostate& err,
                              string_type& digits) const;
```

Parses characters in the interval [s, end) to construct a monetary value. The monetary value is constructed according to formatting flags in `f.flags()` and the `moneypunct <charT,intl>` facet from `f.getloc()`. The parsing is done according to `use_facet < moneypunct<charT,intl> >(f.getloc()).neg_format()`.

Digit group separators are optional. If present, digit grouping is checked after all syntactic elements have been read. If no grouping is specified, any thousands separator characters encountered in the input sequence are not considered part of the numeric format.

Where `money_base::space` or `money_base::none` appear in the format pattern, except at the end, optional whitespace is consumed.

The interpretation of all elements from `str.flags()` other than `ios_base:: showbase` is implementation-defined. If `(str.flags() & ios_base::showbase) == false`, the currency symbol is optional. If it appears after all other required syntactic elements, it is not consumed. If `(str.flags() & ios_base::showbase) == true`, the currency symbol is required and always consumed. The expected currency symbol is the international one if `intl == true`; otherwise the domestic one.

If the first character of the sign appears in its correct position, any remaining sign characters are required and consumed.

The result is a pure sequence of digits, representing a count of the smallest unit of currency, which is then stored in `units` or `digits` respectively. If the parsed value is negative, `units` is negated and digits is preceded by `'-'`.

The operation stops when it encounters an error, runs out of character, or has constructed a monetary value. The result of the operation is indicated by `err`.

Returns an iterator pointing immediately beyond the last character recognized as a part of a valid monetary quantity.

locale

moneypunct<charT,Inter>

CLASS TEMPLATE

template<class charT, bool Inter = false> class **moneypunct**
header: **<locale>**
base class(es): **locale::facet**, **money_base**

DESCRIPTION

moneypunct is the facet that contains the information about the format and punctuation
of monetary expressions. The bool value template parameter Inter specifies whether
the currency symbol should be the international currency symbol (Inter==true) or
not (Inter==false).

The following instantiations are required: moneypunct<char>, moneypunct
<char,true>, moneypunt<wchar_t>, and moneypunt<wchar_t,true>. Their
behavior is implementation-specific.

SYNOPSIS

```
namespace std {
 template <class charT, bool International = false>
 class moneypunct : public locale::facet, public money_base {
 public:
 //  type definitions:
  typedef charT              char_type;
  typedef basic_string<charT> string_type;
 //  data members and constant definitions:
  static locale::id id;
  static const bool intl = International;
  //  constructors:
  explicit moneypunct(size_t refs = 0);
  //  moneypunct operations:
  charT       decimal_point() const;
  charT       thousands_sep() const;
  string      grouping()      const;
  string_type curr_symbol()   const;
  string_type positive_sign() const;
  string_type negative_sign() const;
  int         frac_digits()   const;
  pattern     pos_format()    const;
  pattern     neg_format()    const;
  protected:
  //  destructor:
  virtual ~moneypunct();
```

locale

```
  //  moneypunct operations:
  virtual charT        do_decimal_point() const;
  virtual charT        do_thousands_sep() const;
  virtual string       do_grouping()      const;
  virtual string_type  do_curr_symbol()   const;
  virtual string_type  do_positive_sign() const;
  virtual string_type  do_negative_sign() const;
  virtual int          do_frac_digits()   const;
  virtual pattern      do_pos_format()    const;
  virtual pattern      do_neg_format()    const;
};
}
```

PUBLIC DATA MEMBERS

```
static locale::id id;
```

`moneypunct<charT,Inter>::id` defines the unique identifications of the moneypunct facet interfaces. Each template instantiation with a different character type and a different `bool Inter` value defines a different facet interface with an associated unique `id`.

```
static const bool intl = Inter;
```

`intl` holds the bool template value of template parameter `Inter`.

PUBLIC MEMBER FUNCTIONS

```
explicit moneypunct(size_t refs = 0);
```

Constructs an object of type `moneypunct<charT,Inter>`. If `refs==0`, the lifetime of `this` is managed by the locale(s) that contain `this`. If `refs==1`, the memory of `this` must be explicitly managed. The behavior for `refs>1` is not defined.

```
string_type curr_symbol() const;
```

Calls `do_curr_symbol()` and returns the result of this call.

```
charT decimal_point() const;
```

Calls `do_decimal_point()` and returns the result of this call.

`int ` **`frac_digits`**`() const;`

Calls `do_frac_digits()` and returns the result of this call.

`string ` **`grouping`**`() const;`

Calls `do_grouping()` and returns the result of this call.

`pattern ` **`pos_format`**`() const;`

Calls `do_pos_format()` and returns the result of this call.

`string_type ` **`positive_sign`**`() const;`

Calls `do_positive_sign()` and returns the result of this call.

`string_type ` **`negative_sign`**`() const;`

Calls `do_negative_sign()` and returns the result of this call.

`pattern ` **`neg_format`**`() const;`

Calls `do_neg_format()` and returns the result of this call.

`charT ` **`thousands_sep`**`() const;`

Calls `do_thousands()` and returns the result of this call.

PROTECTED MEMBER FUNCTIONS

`virtual ` **`~moneypunct`**`();`

Destroys an object of type `moneypunct<charT, Inter>`.

`virtual string_type ` **`do_curr_symbol`**`() const;`

Returns a string that represents the currency symbol. The `bool` value template parameter `Inter` specifies whether the currency symbol should be the international currency symbol (`Inter==true`) or not (`Inter==false`). The international currency symbol for this is always four characters long, usually three letters and a space.

```
virtual charT do_decimal_point() const;
```

Returns the character that represents the radix separator.

```
virtual int do_frac_digits() const;
```

Returns the number of digits after the radix separator.

```
virtual string do_grouping() const;
```

The returned value of type `string` is interpreted as an array of integral values of size `sizeof(char)`. It describes the way in which digits of the integral part of a numeric value are grouped. Each character in the string is interpreted as an integer and specifies the number of digits in a group, starting with the rightmost group. The last integer in the string determines the size of all remaining groups. If the last integer is <= 0 or CHAR_MAX, the described group is unlimited. If the string is empty, there is no grouping.

    `moneypunct<charT, Inter>` returns the empty string, indicating no grouping.

```
virtual pattern do_pos_format() const;
```

Returns a value of type `money_base::pattern` that is the format pattern for positive monetary values. The pattern specifies the order in which syntactic elements appear in the monetary format. In this four-element array, each value `symbol`, `sign`, `value`, and either `space` or `none` (defined in class `money_base`) appears exactly once. `none`, if present, is not first; `space`, if present, is neither first nor last. Otherwise, the elements may appear in any order.

    For the required instantiations, namely `moneypunct<char>`, `moneypunct<wchar_t>`, `moneypunct<char,true>`, and `moneypunct<wchar_t, true>`, `do_pos_format()` returns the format pattern { `symbol`, `sign`, `none`, `value` }.

```
virtual string_type do_positive_sign() const;
```

Returns a string that represents the indication of a positive monetary value. The first character of the string, if any, is placed at the position where the sign has to appear according to the format pattern (see also the description of `do_pos_format()`). Any remaining characters are placed after all other format elements.

```
virtual string_type do_negative_sign() const;
```

Returns a string that represents the indication of a negative monetary value. The first character of the string, if any, is placed at the position where the sign has to appear according to the format pattern (see also the description of do_neg_format()). Any remaining characters are placed after all other format elements.

virtual pattern **do_neg_format**() const;

Returns a value of type money_base::pattern that is the format pattern for negative monetary values. The pattern specifies the order in which syntactic elements appear in the monetary format. In this four-element array, each value symbol, sign, value, and either space or none appears exactly once. none, if present, is not first; space, if present, is neither first nor last. Otherwise, the elements may appear in any order.

   For the required instantiations, namely moneypunct<char>, moneypunct <wchar_t>, moneypunct<char,true>, and moneypunct<wchar_t, true>, do_neg_format() returns the format pattern { symbol, sign, none, value }.

virtual charT **do_thousands_sep**() const;

Returns the character that represents the thousands separator.

moneypunct_byname<charT,Inter>

CLASS TEMPLATE

template<class charT,bool Inter=false> class **moneypunct_byname**
header: **<locale>**
base class(es): **moneypunct<**charT,Inter**>**

DESCRIPTION

moneypunct_byname is the *byname* moneypunct facet. It allows the behavior of an object to be specified to conform to a certain localization environment. (See the description of the constructor for more information.) The bool value template parameter Inter specifies whether the currency symbol should be the international currency symbol (Inter==true) or not (Inter==false).

The following instantiations are required: moneypunct_byname<char>, moneypunct_byname<char,true>, moneypunct_byname<wchar_t>, and moneypunct_byname<wchar_t,true>.

SYNOPSIS

```
namespace std {
 template <class charT, bool Intl = false>
 class moneypunct_byname : public moneypunct<charT, Intl> {
 public:
  // type definitions:
  typedef money_base::pattern pattern;
  typedef basic_string<charT> string_type;
  // constructors:
  explicit moneypunct_byname(const char*, size_t refs = 0);
 protected:
  // destructor:
  virtual ~moneypunct_byname();
  //   moneypunct operations:
  virtual charT         do_decimal_point() const;
  virtual charT         do_thousands_sep() const;
  virtual string        do_grouping()      const;
  virtual string_type   do_curr_symbol()   const;
  virtual string_type   do_positive_sign() const;
  virtual string_type   do_negative_sign() const;
  virtual int           do_frac_digits()   const;
  virtual pattern       do_pos_format()    const;
  virtual pattern       do_neg_format()    const;
 };
}
```

locale

PUBLIC MEMBER FUNCTIONS

Implements all public member functions as described for moneypunct <charT, Inter>, except

explicit **moneypunct_byname**(const char* name, size_t refs = 0);

Constructs an object of type moneypunct_byname<charT, Inter>. The implementation-specific name specifies the localization environment to which the constructed object conforms. If refs==0, the lifetime of this is managed by the locale(s) that contain this. If refs==1, the memory of this must be explicitly managed. The behavior for refs>1 is not defined.

PROTECTED MEMBER FUNCTIONS

Implements all protected member functions as described for moneypunct <charT, Inter>, except

virtual **~moneypunct_byname**();

Destroys an object of type moneypunct_byname<charT, Inter>.

money_put<charT, OutputIterator>

CLASS TEMPLATE

template<class charT, class OutputIterator = ostreambuf_iterator<charT> >

class **money_put**

header: **<locale>**

base class(es): **locale::facet**

DESCRIPTION

money_put is the facet that contains the functionality to generate a formatted character sequence that represents a monetary value. The bool value template parameter Inter specifies whether the currency symbol used should be the international currency symbol (Inter==true) or not (Inter==false).

The following instantiations are required: money_put<char> and money_put <wchar_t>. The money_put template must be instantiable for all character types and output iterator types. The behavior of the instantiations is implementation-specific for character types other than char and wchar_t.

SYNOPSIS

```
namespace std {
 template <class charT,
           class OutputIterator = ostreambuf_iterator<charT> >
 class money_put : public locale::facet {
 public:
  //  type definitions:
  typedef charT            char_type;
  typedef OutputIterator   iter_type;
  typedef basic_string<charT> string_type;
  //  data members:
  static locale::id id;
  //  constructors:
  explicit money_put(size_t refs = 0);
  //  formatting operations:
  iter_type put(iter_type s, bool intl, ios_base& f,
                char_type fill, long double units) const;
  iter_type put(iter_type s, bool intl, ios_base& f,
                char_type fill, const string_type& digits) const;
 protected:
  //  destructor:
  virtual ~money_put();
```

locale

```
   //  formatting operations:
  virtual iter_type do_put(iter_type, bool, ios_base&, char_type fill,
                           long double units) const;
  virtual iter_type do_put(iter_type, bool, ios_base&, char_type fill,
                           const string_type& digits) const;
 };
}
```

PUBLIC DATA MEMBERS

```
static locale::id id;
```

money_put<charT,Inter,OutputIterator>::id defines the unique identifications of the money_put facet interfaces. Each template instantiation with a different character type, a different bool Inter value, or a different output iterator type defines a different facet interface with an associated unique id.

PUBLIC MEMBER FUNCTIONS

```
explicit money_put(size_t refs = 0);
```

Constructs an object of type money_put<charT,Inter,OutputIterator>. If refs==0, the lifetime of this is managed by the locale(s) that contain this. If refs==1, the memory of this must be explicitly managed. The behavior for refs>1 is not defined.

```
iter_type put(iter_type s, bool intl, ios_base& f,
              char_type fill, long double units) const;
```

Calls do_put(s,intl,f,fill,units) and returns the result of this call.

```
iter_type put(iter_type s, bool intl, ios_base& f,
              char_type fill, const string_type& digits) const;
```

Calls do_put(s,intl,f,fill,digits) and returns the result of this call.

PROTECTED MEMBER FUNCTIONS

```
virtual ~money_put();
```

Destroys an object of type money_put<charT,Inter, OutputIterator>.

locale

```
virtual iter_type do_put(iter_type s, bool intl,
                    ios_base& str, char_type fill,
                    long double units) const;

virtual iter_type do_put(iter_type s, bool intl,
                    ios_base& str, char_type fill,
                    const string_type& digits) const;
```

Produces a formatted character sequence that is a monetary representation of either the value contained in units or the digit string contained in digits. The operation ignores any fractional part of units, or any characters in digits after the (optional) leading '-' and immediately subsequent digit characters. The produced character sequence starts at s.

The formatting is done according to moneypunct<charT,intl> and str. flags(). A currency symbol is generated only if (str.flags() & ios_base:: showbase) == true. The currency symbol is the international one, if intl==true; otherwise the domestic one. Fill characters are placed where money_base::space appears in the formatting pattern, if (str.flags() & ios_base::adjustfield) == ios_base::internal. The interpretation of all other elements from str.flags() is implementation-defined.

Returns an iterator pointing one beyond the last element produced. Failure is not directly reported; the result of the operation must be extracted from the returned iterator.

Note: It is possible, with some combinations of format patterns and flag values, to produce output that cannot be parsed using the num_get facet.

num_get<charT,InputIterator>

CLASS TEMPLATE

```
template<class charT, class InputIterator = istreambuf_iterator<charT> >
```

class **num_get**
header: **<locale>**
base class(es): **locale::facet**

DESCRIPTION

num_get is the facet that contains the functionality to parse a character sequence that represents a numeric or Boolean value.

The following instantiations are required: num_get<char> and num_get <wchar_t>. The num_get template must be instantiable for all character types and input iterator types. The behavior of the instantiations is implementation-specific for character types other than char and wchar_t.

SYNOPSIS

```
namespace std {
  template <class charT, class InputIterator=istreambuf_iterator<charT> >
  class num_get : public locale::facet {
  public:
    //   type definitions:
    typedef charT           char_type;
    typedef InputIterator   iter_type;
    //   data members:
    static locale::id id;
    //   constructors:
    explicit num_get(size_t refs = 0);
    //   parsing operations:
    iter_type get(iter_type in, iter_type end, ios_base&,
                  ios_base::iostate& err, bool& v) const;
    iter_type get(iter_type in, iter_type end, ios_base& ,
                  ios_base::iostate& err, long& v) const;
    iter_type get(iter_type in, iter_type end, ios_base&,
                  ios_base::iostate& err, unsigned short& v) const;
    iter_type get(iter_type in, iter_type end, ios_base&,
                  ios_base::iostate& err, unsigned int& v) const;
    iter_type get(iter_type in, iter_type end, ios_base&,
                  ios_base::iostate& err, unsigned long& v) const;
    iter_type get(iter_type in, iter_type end, ios_base&,
                  ios_base::iostate& err, float& v) const;
```

```
iter_type get(iter_type in, iter_type end, ios_base&,
                        ios_base::iostate& err, double& v) const;
iter_type get(iter_type in, iter_type end, ios_base&,
                        ios_base::iostate& err, long double& v) const;
iter_type get(iter_type in, iter_type end, ios_base&,
                        ios_base::iostate& err, void*& v) const;
```
protected:
```
// destructor:
virtual ~num_get();
// parsing operations:
virtual iter_type do_get(iter_type, iter_type, ios_base&,
            ios_base::iostate& err, bool& v) const;
virtual iter_type do_get(iter_type, iter_type, ios_base&,
            ios_base::iostate& err, long& v) const;
virtual iter_type do_get(iter_type, iter_type, ios_base&,
            ios_base::iostate& err, unsigned short& v) const;
virtual iter_type do_get(iter_type, iter_type, ios_base&,
            ios_base::iostate& err, unsigned int& v) const;
virtual iter_type do_get(iter_type, iter_type, ios_base&,
            ios_base::iostate& err, unsigned long& v) const;
virtual iter_type do_get(iter_type, iter_type, ios_base&,
            ios_base::iostate& err, float& v) const;
virtual iter_type do_get(iter_type, iter_type, ios_base&,
            ios_base::iostate& err, double& v) const;
virtual iter_type do_get(iter_type, iter_type, ios_base&,
            ios_base::iostate& err, long double& v) const;
virtual iter_type do_get(iter_type, iter_type, ios_base&,
            ios_base::iostate& err, void*& v) const;
};
}
```

PUBLIC DATA MEMBERS

```
static locale::id id;
```

num_get<charT,InputIterator>::id defines the unique identifications of the num_get facet interfaces. Each template instantiation with a different character type or a different input iterator type defines a different facet interface with an associated unique id.

PUBLIC MEMBER FUNCTIONS

```
explicit num_get(size_t refs = 0);
```

Constructs an object of type num_get<charT, InputIterator>. If refs==0, the lifetime of this is managed by the locale(s) that contain this. If refs==1, the memory of this must be explicitly managed. The behavior for refs>1 is not defined.

```
iter_type get(iter_type in, iter_type end, ios_base& ib,
                  ios_base::iostate& err, bool& b) const;
```

Calls do_get(in,end,ib,err,b) and returns the result of this call.

```
iter_type get(iter_type in, iter_type end, ios_base& ib,
                   ios_base::iostate& err, long& l) const;
```

Calls do_get(in,end,ib,err,l) and returns the result of this call.

```
iter_type get(iter_type in, iter_type end, ios_base& ib,
            ios_base::iostate& err, unsigned short& s) const;
```

Calls do_get(in,end,ib,err,s) and returns the result of this call.

```
iter_type get(iter_type in, iter_type end, ios_base& ib,
              ios_base::iostate& err, unsigned int& ui) const;
```

Calls do_get(in,end,ib,err,ui) and returns the result of this call.

```
iter_type get(iter_type in, iter_type end, ios_base& ib,
              ios_base::iostate& err, unsigned long& ul) const;
```

Calls do_get(in,end,ib,err,ul) and returns the result of this call.

```
iter_type get(iter_type in, iter_type end, ios_base& ib,
                  ios_base::iostate& err, float& f) const;
```

Calls do_get(in,end,ib,err,f) and returns the result of this call.

```
iter_type get(iter_type in, iter_type end, ios_base& ib,
                 ios_base::iostate& err, double& d) const;
```

Calls do_get(in,end,ib,err,d) and returns the result of this call.

```
iter_type get(iter_type in, iter_type end, ios_base& ib,
          ios_base::iostate& err, long double& ld) const;
```

Calls do_get(in, end, ib, err, ld) and returns the result of this call.

```
iter_type get(iter_type in, iter_type end, ios_base& ib,
              ios_base::iostate& err, void*& p) const;
```

Calls do_get(in, end, ib, err, p) and returns the result of this call.

PROTECTED MEMBER FUNCTIONS

```
virtual ~num_get();
```

Destroys an object of type num_get<charT, InputIterator>.

```
virtual iter_type do_get(iter_type in, iter_type end,
    ios_base& ib, ios_base::iostate& err, bool& b) const;
```

Parses characters in the interval [s, end) to construct a bool value which is then stored in b. The value is constructed according to ib.flags() and the numpunct<charT> facet from ib.getloc(). For details, see appendix A. The result of the operation is indicated by err. Returns an iterator pointing immediately beyond the last character recognized as part of a valid boolean quantity.

```
virtual iter_type do_get(iter_type in, iter_type end,
    ios_base& ib, ios_base::iostate& err, long& l) const;
```

Parses characters in the interval [s, end) to construct a long value, which is then stored in l. The value is constructed according to ib.flags() and the numpunct <charT> facet from ib.getloc(). For details, see appendix A. The result of the operation is indicated by err. Returns an iterator pointing immediately beyond the last character recognized as a part of a valid numeric quantity.

```
virtual iter_type do_get(iter_type in, iter_type end,
                ios_base& ib, ios_base::iostate& err,
                        unsigned short& s) const;
```

Parses characters in the interval [s, end) to construct an unsigned short value, which is then stored in s. The value is constructed according to ib.flags() and the numpunct<charT> facet from ib.getloc(). For details, see appendix A. The result of the operation is indicated by `err`. Returns an iterator pointing immediately beyond the last character recognized as part of a valid numeric quantity.

```
virtual iter_type do_get(iter_type in, iter_type end,
                  ios_base& ib, ios_base::iostate& err,
                            unsigned int& ui) const;
```

Parses characters in the interval [`s`, `end`) to construct an `unsigned int` value, which is then stored in `ui`. The value is constructed according to `ib.flags()` and the `numpunct<charT>` facet from `ib.getloc()`. For details, see appendix A. The result of the operation is indicated by `err`. Returns an iterator pointing immediately beyond the last character recognized as part of a valid numeric quantity.

```
virtual iter_type do_get(iter_type in, iter_type end,
                  ios_base& ib, ios_base::iostate& err,
                            unsigned long& ul) const;
```

Parses characters in the interval [`s`, `end`) to construct an `unsigned long` value, which is then stored in `ul`. The value is constructed according to `ib.flags()` and the `numpunct<charT>` facet from `ib.getloc()`. For details, see appendix A. The result of the operation is indicated by `err`. Returns an iterator pointing immediately beyond the last character recognized as part of a valid numeric quantity.

```
virtual iter_type do_get(iter_type in, iter_type end,
    ios_base& ib, ios_base::iostate& err, float& f) const;
```

Parses characters in the interval [`s`, `end`) to construct a `float` value, which is then stored in `f`. The value is constructed according to `ib.flags()` and the `numpunct<charT>` facet from `ib.getloc()`. For details, see appendix A. The result of the operation is indicated by `err`. Returns an iterator pointing immediately beyond the last character recognized as part of a valid numeric quantity.

```
virtual iter_type do_get(iter_type in, iter_type end,
    ios_base& ib, ios_base::iostate& err, double& d) const;
```

Parses characters in the interval [`s`, `end`) to construct a `double` value, which is then stored in `d`. The value is constructed according to `ib.flags()` and the `numpunct<charT>` facet from `ib.getloc()`. For details, see appendix A. The result of the operation is indicated by `err`. Returns an iterator pointing immediately beyond the last character recognized as part of a valid numeric quantity.

locale

```
virtual iter_type do_get(iter_type in, iter_type end,
                    ios_base& ib, ios_base::iostate& err,
                              long double& ld) const;
```

Parses characters in the interval [s, end) to construct a long double value, which is then stored in ld. The value is constructed according to ib.flags() and the numpunct<charT> facet from ib.getloc(). For details, see appendix A. The result of the operation is indicated by err. Returns an iterator pointing immediately beyond the last character recognized as part of a valid numeric quantity.

```
virtual iter_type do_get(iter_type in, iter_type end,
    ios_base& ib, ios_base::iostate& err, void*& p) const;
```

Parses characters in the interval [s, end) to construct a void* value, which is stored in p. The value is constructed according to ib.flags() and the numpunct<charT> facet from ib.getloc(). For details, see appendix A. The result of the operation is indicated by err. Returns an iterator pointing immediately beyond the last character recognized as part of a valid pointer.

numpunct<charT>

CLASS TEMPLATE

template<class charT> class **numpunct**
header: **<locale>**
base class(es): **locale::facet**

DESCRIPTION

numpunct is the facet that contains the information about the format and punctuation of numeric and boolean expressions.

The following instantiations are required: numpunct<char> and numpunct<wchar_t>. They provide classic "C" behavior. Details are given with the description of the virtual protected member functions.

SYNOPSIS

```
namespace std {
 template <class charT>
 class numpunct : public locale::facet {
 public:
   //  type definitions:
   typedef charT                char_type;
   typedef basic_string<charT> string_type;
   //  data members:
   static locale::id id;
   //  constructors:
   explicit numpunct(size_t refs = 0);
   //  numpunct operations:
   char_type    decimal_point()    const;
   char_type    thousands_sep()    const;
   string       grouping()         const;
   string_type  truename()         const;
   string_type  falsename()        const;
 protected:
   virtual ~numpunct();
   //  numpunct operations:
   virtual char_type    do_decimal_point() const;
   virtual char_type    do_thousands_sep() const;
   virtual string       do_grouping()      const;
   virtual string_type  do_truename()      const;
   virtual string_type  do_falsename()     const;
 };
}
```

locale

PUBLIC DATA MEMBERS

```
static locale::id id;
```

numpunct<charT>::id defines the unique identifications of the numpunct facet interfaces. Each template instantiation with a different character type defines a different facet interface with an associated unique id.

PUBLIC MEMBER FUNCTIONS

```
explicit numpunct(size_t refs = 0);
```

Constructs an object of type numpunct<charT>. If refs==0, the lifetime of this is managed by the locale(s) that contain this. If refs==1, the memory of this must be explicitly managed. The behavior for refs>1 is not defined.

```
char_type decimal_point() const;
```

Calls do_decimal_point() and returns the result of this call.

```
string_type falsename() const;
```

Calls do_falsename() and returns the result of this call.

```
string grouping() const;
```

Calls do_grouping() and returns the result of this call.

```
char_type thousands_sep() const;
```

Calls do_thousand_sep() and returns the result of this call.

```
string_type truename() const;
```

Calls do_truename() and returns the result of this call.

PROTECTED MEMBER FUNCTIONS

```
virtual ~numpunct();
```

Destroys an object of type numpunct<charT>.

```
virtual char_type do_decimal_point() const;
```

Returns the character that represents the radix separator.
>   The base class implementation returns `'.'`.

```
virtual string_type do_falsename() const;
```

Returns a string representing the name of the `bool` value `false`.
>   The base class implementation returns the string `"false"`.

```
virtual string do_grouping() const;
```

The returned value of type `string` is interpreted as an array of integral values of size `sizeof(char)`. It describes the way in which digits of the integral part of a numeric value are grouped. Each character in the string is interpreted as an integer and specifies the number of digits in a group, starting with the rightmost group. The last integer in the string determines the size of all remaining groups. If the last integer is `<= 0` or `CHAR_MAX`, the described group is unlimited. If the string is empty, there is no grouping.
>   The base class implementation returns the empty string, indicating no grouping.

```
virtual char_type do_thousands_sep() const;
```

Returns the character that represents the thousands separator.
>   The base class implementation returns `','`.

```
virtual string_type do_truename() const;
```

Returns a string representing the name of the `bool` value `true`.
>   The base class implementation returns the string `"true"`.

locale

numpunct_byname<charT>

CLASS TEMPLATE

template<class charT> class **numpunct_byname**
header: **<locale>**
base class(es): **numpunct**<charT>

DESCRIPTION

numpunct_byname is the *byname* numpunct facet. It allows the behavior of an object to be specified to conform to a certain localization environment. (See the description of the constructor for more information.)

The following instantiations are required: numpunct_byname<char> and numpunct_byname<wchar_t>.

SYNOPSIS

```
namespace std {
 template <class charT>
 class numpunct_byname : public numpunct<charT> {
 public:
// type definitions:
  typedef charT              char_type;
  typedef basic_string<charT> string_type;
// constructors:
  explicit numpunct_byname(const char*, size_t refs = 0);
 protected:
// destructor:
  virtual ~numpunct_byname();
// numpunct operations:
  virtual char_type    do_decimal_point() const;
  virtual char_type    do_thousands_sep() const;
  virtual string       do_grouping()      const;
  virtual string_type  do_truename()      const;
  virtual string_type  do_falsename()     const;
 };
}
```

locale

PUBLIC MEMBER FUNCTIONS

Implements all public member functions as described for numpunct<charT>, except

explicit **numpunct_byname**(const char*, size_t refs = 0);

Constructs an object of type numpunct_byname<charT>. The implementation-specific name specifies the localization environment to which the constructed object conforms. If refs==0, the lifetime of this is managed by the locale(s) that contain(s) this. If refs==1, the memory of this must be explicitly managed. The behavior for refs>1 is not defined.

PROTECTED MEMBER FUNCTIONS

Implements all protected member functions as described for numpunct<charT>, except

virtual **~numpunct_byname**();

Destroys an object of type numpunct_byname<charT>.

num_put<charT,OutputIterator>

CLASS TEMPLATE

template<class charT, class OutputIterator = ostreambuf_iterator<charT> >
class **num_put**
header: **<locale>**
base class(es): **locale::facet**

DESCRIPTION

num_put is the facet that contains the functionality to generate a formatted character sequence that represents a numeric or Boolean value.

The following instantiations are required: num_put<char> and num_put<wchar_t>. The num_put template must be instantiable for all character types and output iterator types. The behavior of the instantiations is implementation-specific for character types other than char and wchar_t.

SYNOPSIS

```
namespace std {
 template <class charT, class OutputIterator=ostreambuf_iterator<charT> >
 class num_put : public locale::facet {
 public:
  // type definitions:
  typedef charT           char_type;
  typedef OutputIterator  iter_type;
  // data members:
  static locale::id id;
  // constructors:
  explicit num_put(size_t refs = 0);
  // formatting operations:
  iter_type put(iter_type s, ios_base& f, char_type fill, bool v) const;
  iter_type put(iter_type s, ios_base& f, char_type fill, long v) const;
  iter_type put(iter_type s, ios_base& f, char_type fill,
                      unsigned long v) const;
  iter_type put(iter_type s, ios_base& f, char_type fill,
                      double v) const;
  iter_type put(iter_type s, ios_base& f, char_type fill,
                      long double v) const;
  iter_type put(iter_type s, ios_base& f, char_type fill,
                      const void* v) const;
```

```
protected:
  // destructor:
  virtual ~num_put();
  // formatting operations:
  virtual iter_type do_put(iter_type, ios_base&, char_type fill,
                           bool v) const;
  virtual iter_type do_put(iter_type, ios_base&, char_type fill,
                           long v) const;
  virtual iter_type do_put(iter_type, ios_base&, char_type fill,
                           unsigned long) const;
  virtual iter_type do_put(iter_type, ios_base&, char_type fill,
                           double v) const;
  virtual iter_type do_put(iter_type, ios_base&, char_type fill,
                           long double v) const;
  virtual iter_type do_put(iter_type, ios_base&, char_type fill,
                           const void* v) const;
};
}
```

PUBLIC DATA MEMBERS

```
static locale::id id;
```

num_put<charT,OutputIterator>::id defines the unique identifications of the numpunct facet interfaces. Each template instantiation with a different character type or a different output iterator type defines a different facet interface with an associated unique id.

PUBLIC MEMBER FUNCTIONS

```
explicit num_put(size_t refs = 0);
```

Constructs an object of type num_put<charT,OutputIterator>. If refs==0, the life-time of this is managed by the locale(s) that contain(s) this. If refs==1, the memory of this must be explicitly managed. The behavior for refs>1 is not defined.

```
iter_type put(iter_type s, ios_base& ib, char_type fill,
                                         bool b) const;
```

Calls do_put(s,ib,fill,b) and returns the result of this call.

```
iter_type put(iter_type s, ios_base& ib, char_type fill,
                                         long l) const;
```

Calls do_put(s,ib,fill,l) and returns the result of this call.

locale

```
iter_type put(iter_type s, ios_base& ib, char_type fill,
                                 unsigned long ul) const;
```

Calls do_put(s, ib, fill, ul) and returns the result of this call.

```
iter_type put(iter_type s, ios_base& ib, char_type fill,
                                 double d) const;
```

Calls do_put(s, ib, fill, d) and returns the result of this call.

```
iter_type put(iter_type s, ios_base& ib, char_type fill,
                                 long double ld) const;
```

Calls do_put(s, ib, fill, ld) and returns the result of this call.

```
iter_type put(iter_type s, ios_base& ib, char_type fill,
                                 const void* p) const;
```

Calls do_put(s, ib, fill, p) and returns the result of this call.

PROTECTED MEMBER FUNCTIONS

```
virtual ~num_put();
```

Destroys an object of type num_put<charT, OutputIterator>.

```
virtual iter_type do_put(iter_type s, ios_base& ib,
                         char_type fill, bool b) const;
```

Produces a formatted character sequence that is a representation of the Boolean value contained in b. The formatting is done according to numpunct<charT> and ib.flags(). For details, see appendix B. The operation returns an iterator pointing one beyond the last element produced. It makes no provisions for error reporting. Any failures must be extracted from the returned iterator.

```
virtual iter_type do_put(iter_type s, ios_base& ib,
                         char_type fill, long l) const;
```

Produces a formatted character sequence that is a representation of the numeric value contained in l. The formatting is done according to numpunct<charT> and ib.flags(). For details, see appendix B. The operation returns an iterator pointing one

locale

beyond the last element produced. It makes no provisions for error reporting. Any failures must be extracted from the returned iterator.

```
virtual iter_type do_put(iter_type s, ios_base& ib,
                 char_type fill, unsigned long ul) const;
```

Produces a formatted character sequence that is a representation of the numeric value contained in ul. The formatting is done according to numpunct<charT> and ib.flags(). For details, see appendix B. The operation returns an iterator pointing one beyond the last element produced. It makes no provisions for error reporting. Any failures must be extracted from the returned iterator.

```
virtual iter_type do_put(iter_type s, ios_base& ib,
                 char_type fill, double d) const;
```

Produces a formatted character sequence that is a representation of the numeric value contained in d. The formatting is done according to numpunct<charT> and ib.flags(). For details, see appendix B. The operation returns an iterator pointing one beyond the last element produced. It makes no provisions for error reporting. Any failures must be extracted from the returned iterator.

```
virtual iter_type do_put(iter_type s, ios_base& ib,
                 char_type fill, long double ld) const;
```

Produces a formatted character sequence that is a representation of the numeric value contained in ld. The formatting is done according to numpunct<charT> and ib.flags(). For details, see appendix B. The operation returns an iterator pointing one beyond the last element produced. It makes no provisions for error reporting. Any failures must be extracted from the returned iterator.

```
virtual iter_type do_put(iter_type s, ios_base& ib,
                 char_type fill, const void* p) const;
```

Produces a formatted character sequence that is a representation of the pointer value contained in p. The formatting is done according to numpunct<charT> and ib.flags(). For details, see appendix B. The operation returns an iterator pointing one beyond the last element produced. It makes no provisions for error reporting. Any failures must be extracted from the returned iterator.

locale

time_base

CLASS

class **time_base**
header: **<locale>**
base class(es): **[none]**

DESCRIPTION

time_base is the base class of all time_get facets. It provides the means to describe the order of elements that form a date.

SYNOPSIS

```
namespace std {
 class time_base {
 public:
  enum dateorder { no_order, dmy, mdy, ymd, ydm };
 };
}
```

TYPE DEFINITIONS

enum **dateorder** { no_order, dmy, mdy, ymd, ydm };

Enumerated type that represents different types of date ordering.

CONSTANT DEFINITIONS

The following list shows the predefined values and their semantics for the nested enumerated type result:

dmy

order: day, month, year

mdy

order: month, day, year

ydm

order: year, day, month

ymd

order: year, month, day

no_order

none of the above

time_get<charT,InputIterator>

CLASS TEMPLATE

template<class charT, class InputIterator = istreambuf_iterator<charT> >

class **time_get**
header: **<locale>**
base class(es): **locale::facet**, **time_base**

DESCRIPTION

time_get is the facet that contains the functionality to parse a character sequence that represents date and/or time.

The following instantiations are required: time_get<char> and time_get<wchar_t>. The time_get template must be instantiable for all character types and input iterator types. The behavior of the instantiations is implementation-specific for character types other than char and wchar_t.

SYNOPSIS

```
namespace std {
 template <class charT, class InputIterator=istreambuf_iterator<charT> >
 class time_get : public locale::facet, public time_base {
 public:
  // type definitions:
  typedef charT           char_type;
  typedef InputIterator   iter_type;
  // data members:
  static locale::id id;
  // constructors:
  explicit time_get(size_t refs = 0);
  // parsing operations:
  iter_type get_time(iter_type s, iter_type end, ios_base& f,
                     ios_base::iostate& err, tm* t)  const;
  iter_type get_date(iter_type s, iter_type end, ios_base& f,
                     ios_base::iostate& err, tm* t)  const;
  iter_type get_weekday(iter_type s, iter_type end, ios_base& f,
                     ios_base::iostate& err, tm* t) const;
  iter_type get_monthname(iter_type s, iter_type end, ios_base& f,
                     ios_base::iostate& err, tm* t) const;
  iter_type get_year(iter_type s, iter_type end, ios_base& f,
                     ios_base::iostate& err, tm* t) const;
  // miscellaneous:
  dateorder date_order()  const { return do_date_order(); }
```

```
protected:
  virtual ~time_get();
// parsing operations:
  virtual iter_type do_get_time(iter_type s, iter_type end, ios_base&,
                          ios_base::iostate& err, tm* t).const;
  virtual iter_type do_get_date(iter_type s, iter_type end, ios_base&,
                          ios_base::iostate& err, tm* t) const;
  virtual iter_type do_get_weekday(iter_type s, iter_type end, ios_base&,
                          ios_base::iostate& err, tm* t) const;
  virtual iter_type do_get_monthname(iter_type s, ios_base&,
                          ios_base::iostate& err, tm* t) const;
  virtual iter_type do_get_year(iter_type s, iter_type end, ios_base&,
                          ios_base::iostate& err, tm* t) const;
  // miscellaneous:
  virtual dateorder do_date_order()  const;
 };
}
```

PUBLIC DATA MEMBERS

```
static locale::id id;
```

time_get<charT,InputIterator>::id defines the unique identifications of the time_get facet interfaces. Each template instantiation with a different character type or a different input iterator type defines a different facet interface with an associated unique id.

PUBLIC MEMBER FUNCTIONS

```
explicit time_get(size_t refs = 0);
```

Constructs an object of type time_get<charT,InputIterator>. If refs==0, the lifetime of this is managed by the locale(s) that contain(s) this. If refs==1, the memory of this must be explicitly managed. The behavior for refs>1 is not defined.

PARSING OPERATIONS

```
iter_type get_date(iter_type s, iter_type end,
      ios_base& f, ios_base::iostate& err, tm* t) const;
```

Calls do_get_date(s,end,f,err,t) and returns the result of this call.

```
iter_type get_monthname(iter_type s, iter_type end,
      ios_base& f, ios_base::iostate& err, tm* t) const;
```

Calls do_get_monthname(s,end,f,err,t) and returns the result of this call.

```
iter_type get_time(iter_type s, iter_type end,
      ios_base& f, ios_base::iostate& err, tm* t) const;
```

Calls do_get_time(s,end,f,err,t) and returns the result of this call.

```
iter_type get_weekday(iter_type s, iter_type end,
      ios_base& f, ios_base::iostate& err, tm* t) const;
```

Calls do_get_weekday(s,end,f,err,t) and returns the result of this call.

```
iter_type get_year(iter_type s, iter_type end,
      ios_base& f, ios_base::iostate& err, tm* t) const;
```

Calls do_get_year(s,end,f,err,t) and returns the result of this call.

MISCELLANEOUS

```
dateorder date_order() const;
```

Calls do_date_order() and returns the result of this call.

PROTECTED MEMBER FUNCTIONS

```
virtual ~time_get();
```

Destroys an object of type time_get<charT,InputIterator>.

PARSING OPERATIONS

```
virtual iter_type do_get_date(iter_type s, iter_type end,
      ios_base& f, ios_base::iostate& err, tm* t) const;
```

Parses characters in the interval [s,end) to construct the date-related values of struct tm, and store them in t. The interpretation of f.flags() is implementation-defined. The operation stops when it encounters an error, runs out of character, or has read all characters that can be consumed to construct the required date values. The result of the operation is indicated by err. Returns an iterator pointing immediately beyond the last character consumed as part of a valid date value.

```
virtual iter_type
do_get_monthname(iter_type s, iter_type end,
      ios_base& f, ios_base::iostate& err, tm* t) const;
```

Parses characters in the interval [s, end) to construct the month-related value of `struct tm`, and store it in `t`. The interpretation of `f.flags()` is implementation-defined. The operation stops when it encounters an error, runs out of character, or has read all characters that can be consumed to construct the required month value. The input can be the abbreviation of a month name. If it finds an abbreviation that is followed by characters that could match a full name, it continues reading until it matches the full name or fails. The result of the operation is indicated by `err`. Returns an iterator pointing immediately beyond the last character consumed.

```
virtual iter_type do_get_time(iter_type s, iter_type end,
      ios_base& f, ios_base::iostate& err, tm* t) const;
```

Parses characters in the interval [s, end) to construct the time-related values of `struct tm` and store them in `t`. Parsing is done against the time representation known to `this`. The interpretation of `f.flags()` is implementation-defined. The operation stops when it encounters an error, runs out of character, or has read all characters that can be consumed to construct the required time values. The result of the operation is indicated by `err`. Returns an iterator pointing immediately beyond the last character consumed as part of a valid time value.

```
virtual iter_type
do_get_weekday(iter_type s, iter_type end, ios_base& f,
                  ios_base::iostate& err, tm* t) const;
```

Parses characters in the interval [s, end) to construct the weekday-related value of `struct tm` and store it in `t`. The interpretation of `f.flags()` is implementation-defined. The operation stops when it encounters an error, runs out of character, or has read all characters that can be consumed to construct the required weekday value. The input can be the abbreviation of a weekday. If it finds an abbreviation that is followed by characters that could match a full name, it continues reading until it matches the full name or fails. The result of the operation is indicated by `err`. Returns an iterator pointing immediately beyond the last character consumed.

```
virtual iter_type do_get_year(iter_type s, iter_type end,
      ios_base& f, ios_base::iostate& err, tm* t) const;
```

Parses characters in the interval [s, end) to construct the year-related value of struct tm and store it in t. The interpretation of f.flags() is implementation-defined. The operation stops when it encounters an error, runs out of character, or has read all characters that can be consumed to construct the required month value. It is implementation-defined whether or not two-digit year numbers are accepted and, if so, what century they are assumed to lie in. The result of the operation is indicated by err. Returns an iterator pointing immediately beyond the last character consumed.

MISCELLANEOUS

```
virtual dateorder do_date_order() const;
```

Returns one of the values from time_base::dateorder, describing the order of day, month, and year.

time_get_byname<charT,InputIterator>

CLASS TEMPLATE

```
template<class charT, class InputIterator = istreambuf_iterator<charT> >
```

class **time_get_byname**
header: **<locale>**
base class(es): **time_get**<charT,InputIterator>

DESCRIPTION

time_get_byname is the *byname* time_get facet. It allows the behavior of an object to be specified to conform to a certain localization environment. (See the description of the constructor for more information.)

The following instantiations are required: time_get_byname<char> and time_get_byname<wchar_t>. The time_get_byname template must be instantiable for all character types and input iterator types. The behavior of the instantiations is implementation-specific for character types other than char and wchar_t.

PUBLIC MEMBER FUNCTIONS

Implements all public member functions as described for
time_get_byname<charT,InputIterator>, except

```
explicit time_get_byname(const char*, size_t refs = 0);
```

Constructs an object of type time_get_byname<charT, InputIterator>. The implementation-specific name specifies the localization environment to which the constructed object conforms. If refs==0, the lifetime of this is managed by the locale(s) that contain(s) this. If refs==1, the memory of this must be explicitly managed. The behavior for refs>1 is not defined.

PROTECTED MEMBER FUNCTIONS

Implements all protected member functions as described for time_get
<charT,InputIterator>, except

```
virtual ~time_get_byname();
```

Destroys an object of type time_get_byname<charT,InputIterator>.

time_put<charT,OutputIterator>

CLASS TEMPLATE

template<class charT, class OutputIterator = ostreambuf_iterator<charT> >
class **time_put**
header: **<locale>**
base class(es): **locale::facet**

DESCRIPTION

time_put is the facet that contains the functionality to generate a formatted character sequence that represents date and/or time.

The following instantiations are required: time_put<char> and time_put<wchar_t>. The time_put template must be instantiable for all character types and output iterator types. The behavior of the instantiations is implementation-specific for character types other than char and wchar_t.

SYNOPSIS

```
namespace std {
 template <class charT, class OutputIterator=ostreambuf_iterator<charT> >
 class time_put : public locale::facet {
 public:
  // type definitions:
  typedef charT          char_type;
  typedef OutputIterator iter_type;
  // data members:
  static locale::id id;
  // constructors:
  explicit time_put(size_t refs = 0);
  // formatting operations:
  iter_type put(iter_type s, ios_base& f, char_type fill, const tm* tmb,
            const charT* pattern, const charT* pat_end) const;
  iter_type put(iter_type s, ios_base& f, char_type fill,
            const tm* tmb, char format, char modifier = 0) const;
 protected:
  // destructor:
  virtual ~time_put();
  // formatting operations:
  virtual iter_type do_put(iter_type s, ios_base&,char_type, const tm* t,
                       char format, char modifier) const;
 };
}
```

locale

PUBLIC DATA MEMBERS

static locale::id **id;**

time_put<charT,OutputIterator>::id defines the unique identifications of the time_put facet interfaces. Each template instantiation with a different character type or a different output iterator type defines a different facet interface with an associated unique id.

PUBLIC MEMBER FUNCTIONS

explicit **time_put**(size_t refs = 0);

Constructs an object of type time_put<charT,OutputIterator>. If refs==0, the lifetime of this is managed by the locale(s) that contain(s) this. If refs==1, the memory of this must be explicitly managed. The behavior for refs>1 is not defined.

```
iter_type put(iter_type s, ios_base& f, char_type fill,
                   const tm* tmb, const charT* pattern,
                         const charT* pat_end) const;
```

Produces a formatted character sequence that is a representation of the values contained in tm structure pointed to by tmb. Formatting is done according to format specifiers found in [pattern,pat_end). The operation parses characters from that interval and interprets the characters immediately following a '%' as format conversion specifiers used by the C library function strftime. See appendix C for details.

In order to identify '%', the characters are converted using use_facet < ctype<charT> >(f.getloc()).narrow(). No format specifiers are identified, if narrow() has no mapping to '%'.

Each character that is not part of a format specifier is written to s immediately, and for each valid format specifier identified do_put(s, str, fill, t, spec, mod) is called. As a result, format elements and other characters are interleaved in the output in the order in which they appear in the pattern.

The interpretation of f.flags() and the use of fill is implementation-defined. The required instantiations time_put<char> and time_put<wchar_t> do not use them; formatting is controlled by the pattern only.

Returns an iterator pointing immediately beyond the last character produced.

```
iter_type put(iter_type s, ios_base& f, char_type fill,
         const tm* tmb, char form, char mod = 0) const;
```

Calls do_put(s,f,fill,tmb,form,mod) and returns the result of this call.

locale

PROTECTED MEMBER FUNCTIONS

virtual **~time_put**();

Destroys an object of type time_put_byname<charT,OutputIterator>.

virtual iter_type **do_put**(iter_type s, ios_base& f,
                      char_type fill, const tm* t,
                      char format, char modifier) const;

Produces a formatted character sequence that is a representation of the values contained in the tm structure pointed to by t. It interprets format and modifier as conversion specifiers identically as the format specifiers in the string argument to the C library function strftime(). See appendix C for details. The interpretation of the format control parameters f.flags() and the fill character fill is implementation-defined (see below). Returns an iterator pointing immediately beyond the last character produced. Any failures are not directly reported, but must be extracted from the returned iterator.

   Note that the standard does not require that the format parameters or the fill character be used by a time_put facet's do_put() function. The required instantiations time_put<char> and time_put<wchar_t> do not use them; instead, formatting is controlled by the parameters format and modifier only. The reason for providing the format parameters and the fill character as arguments to do_put() is to make them available to overriding versions of do_put() in facet types derived from time_put.

time_put_byname<charT, OutputIterator>

CLASS TEMPLATE

```
template<class charT, class OutputIterator = ostreambuf_iterator<charT> >
```

class **ctype_byname**
header: **<locale>**
base class(es): **time_put**<charT,InputIterator>

DESCRIPTION

time_put_byname is the *byname* time_put facet. It allows the behavior of an object to be specified to conform to a certain localization environment. (See the description of the constructor for more information.)

The following instantiations are required: time_put_byname<char> and time_put_byname<wchar_t>. The time_put_byname template must be instantiable for all character types and output iterator types. The behavior of the instantiations is implementation-specific for character types other than char and wchar_t.

SYNOPSIS

```
namespace std {
 template <class charT, class OutputIterator=ostreambuf_iterator<charT> >
 class time_put_byname : public time_put<charT, OutputIterator> {
 public:
  // type definitions:
  typedef charT          char_type;
  typedef OutputIterator iter_type;
  // constructors:
  explicit time_put_byname(const char*, size_t refs = 0);
 protected:
  // destructor:
  virtual ~time_put_byname();
  // formatting operations:
  virtual iter_type do_put(iter_type s, ios_base&,char_type, const tm* t,
                      char format, char modifier) const;
 };
}
```

locale

PUBLIC MEMBER FUNCTIONS

Implements all public member functions as described for time_put_byname <charT,OutputIterator>, except

```
explicit time_put_byname(const char*, size_t refs = 0);
```

Constructs an object of type time_put_byname<charT,OutputIterator>. The implementation-specific name specifies the localization environment to which the constructed object conforms. If refs==0, the lifetime of this is managed by the locale(s) that contain(s) this. If refs==1, the memory of this must be explicitly managed. The behavior for refs>1 is not defined.

PROTECTED MEMBER FUNCTIONS

Implements all protected member functions as described for time_put <charT,OutputIterator>, except

```
virtual ~time_put_byname();
```

Destroys an object of type time_put_byname<charT,OutputIterator>.

time_base

CLASS

class **time_base**
header: **<locale>**
base class(es): **[none]**

DESCRIPTION

time_base is the base class of all time_get facets. It provides the means to describe the order of elements that form a date.

SYNOPSIS

```
namespace std {
 class time_base {
 public:
  enum dateorder { no_order, dmy, mdy, ymd, ydm };
 };
}
```

TYPE DEFINITIONS

enum **dateorder** { no_order, dmy, mdy, ymd, ydm };

Enumerated type that represents different types of date ordering.

CONSTANT DEFINITIONS

The following list shows the predefined values and their semantics for the nested enumerated type result:

dmy

order: day, month, year

mdy

order: month, day, year

ydm

order: year, day, month

ymd

order: year, month, day

no_order

none of the above

tm

STRUCTURE

struct **tm**
header: **<ctime>**

DESCRIPTION

tm is a structure from the C Library that is used by the time facets and represents a time/date value. The tm structure contains at least the following members, in any order.

SYNOPSIS

```
struct tm {
        int tm_sec;
        int tm_min;
        int tm_hour;
        int tm_mday;
        int tm_mon;
        int tm_year;
        int tm_wday;
        int tm_yday;
        int tm_isdst;
        };
```

PUBLIC DATA MEMBERS

int **tm_sec;**

second after the minute, that is, [0–60]. The range [0, 60] for tm_sec allows for a positive leap second.

int **tm_min;**

minutes after the minute, that is, [0–59].

int **tm_hour;**

hours since midnight, that is, [0–23].

int **tm_mday;**

day of the month, that is, [0–31].

locale

```
int tm_mon;
```

month since January, that is, [0–11].

```
int tm_year;
```

years since 1900.

```
int tm_wday;
```

days since Sunday, that is, [0–6].

```
int tm_yday;
```

days since January 1, that is, [0–365].

```
int tm_isdst;
```

daylight saving time flag. The value of `tm_isdst` is positive if daylight saving time is in effect, zero if daylight saving time is not in effect, and negative if the information is not available.

2
C H A R A C T E R   T R A I T S

header file <string>

FILE NAME

<string>

DESCRIPTION

The header file contains all declarations for the template class `char_traits` and its specialization. It also contains all declarations for the C++ string classes.

SYNOPSIS

```
namespace std {
  // general template:
  template<class charT> struct char_traits;

  // specialization for type char:
  template<>
  struct char_traits<char> {
    typedef char       char_type;
    typedef int        int_type;
    typedef streamoff  off_type;
    typedef streampos  pos_type;
    typedef mbstate_t  state_type;

    static void assign(char_type& c1, const char_type& c2);
    static bool eq(const char_type& c1, const char_type& c2);
    static bool lt(const char_type& c1, const char_type& c2);
```

```
   static int compare(const char_type* s1,const char_type* s2,size_t n);
   static size_t length(const char_type* s);
   static const char_type* find
   (const char_type* s, size_t n, const char_type& a);
   static char_type* move(char_type* s1, const char_type* s2, size_t n);
   static char_type* copy(char_type* s1, const char_type* s2, size_t n);
   static char_type* assign(char_type* s, size_t n, char_type a);

   static int_type not_eof(const int_type& c);
   static char_type to_char_type(const int_type& c);
   static int_type to_int_type(const char_type& c);
   static bool eq_int_type(const int_type& c1, const int_type& c2);
   static int_type eof();
};

// specialization for type wchar_t:
template<>
struct char_traits<wchar_t> {
   typedef wchar_t        char_type;
   typedef wint_t         int_type;
   typedef streamoff      off_type;
   typedef wstreampos     pos_type;
   typedef mbstate_t      state_type;

   static void assign(char_type& c1, const char_type& c2);
   static bool eq(const char_type& c1, const char_type& c2);
   static bool lt(const char_type& c1, const char_type& c2);

   static int compare(const char_type* s1,const char_type* s2,size_t n);
   static size_t length(const char_type* s);
   static const char_type* find
   (const char_type* s, size_t n, const char_type& a);
   static char_type* move(char_type* s1, const char_type* s2, size_t n);
   static char_type* copy(char_type* s1, const char_type* s2, size_t n);
   static char_type* assign(char_type* s, size_t n, char_type a);

   static int_type not_eof(const int_type& c);
   static char_type to_char_type(const int_type& c);
   static int_type to_int_type(const char_type& c);
   static bool eq_int_type(const int_type& c1, const int_type& c2);
   static int_type eof();
};
}
```

character traits

char_traits<charT>

CLASS TEMPLATE

```
template<class charT>
struct char_traits { }
```
header: **<string>**

DESCRIPTION

char_traits is a (possibly empty) struct template and serves as a basis for explicit specializations.

char_traits<char>

TEMPLATE SPECIALIZATION

template<> struct **char_traits**<char>

header: **<string>**

base class(es): **[none]**

DESCRIPTION

`char_traits<char>` contains information and functionality associated with the character type `char`.

SYNOPSIS

```
namespace std {
 template<>
 struct char_traits<char> {
    //  type definitions:
    typedef char        char_type;
    typedef int         int_type;
    typedef streamoff   off_type;
    typedef streampos   pos_type;
    typedef mbstate_t   state_type;

    //  character traits operations:
    static void assign(char_type& c1, const char_type& c2);
    static bool eq(const char_type& c1, const char_type& c2);
    static bool lt(const char_type& c1, const char_type& c2);

    static int compare(const char_type* s1,const char_type* s2,size_t n);
    static size_t length(const char_type* s);
    static const char_type* find
            (const char_type* s, size_t n, const char_type& a);
    static char_type* move(char_type* s1, const char_type* s2, size_t n);
    static char_type* copy(char_type* s1, const char_type* s2, size_t n);
    static char_type* assign(char_type* s, size_t n, char_type a);

    static int_type not_eof(const int_type& c);
    static char_type to_char_type(const int_type& c);
    static int_type to_int_type(const char_type& c);
    static bool eq_int_type(const int_type& c1, const int_type& c2);
    static int_type eof();
 };
}
```

character traits

TYPE DEFINITIONS

Contains type definitions for char_type, int_type, off_type, pos_type, and state_type associated with the character type char.

```
typedef char      char_type;
typedef int       int_type;
typedef streamoff off_type;
typedef streampos pos_type;
typedef mbstate_t state_type;
```

PUBLIC MEMBER FUNCTIONS

```
static void assign(char_type& c1, const char_type& c2);
```

Performs c1 = c2.

```
static char_type* assign(char_type* s,
                         size_t n, char_type a);
```

Performs s[i] = a for each i in the interval [0,n) and returns s.

```
static int compare(const char_type* s1,
                   const char_type* s2, size_t n);
```

Returns 0, if s1[i] == s2[i] for each i in the interval [0,n); else a value < 0, if for some j in [0,n), s1[j] < s2[j] and for each i from [0,j), s1[i] == s2[i]. Otherwise returns a value > 0.

```
static char_type* copy(char_type* s1,
                       const char_type* s2, size_t n);
```

If s2 is not in the interval [s1,s1+n), the operation performs s1[i] = s2[i] for each i in the interval [0,n) and returns s1; otherwise the behavior is undefined.

```
static int_type eof();
```

Returns EOF, which represents end-of-file.

```
static bool eq(const char_type& c1, const char_type& c2);
```

Compares values of type char_type for equality.
     Returns (c1 == c2).

character traits

```
static bool eq_int_type(const int_type& e1,
                        const int_type& e2);
```

Compares values of type `int_type` for equality.

For values `e1` and `e2` that are `int_type` representations of `char_type` values `c1` and `c2`, returns the same as the comparison of the respective `char_type` values would yield, that is, `char_traits<char>:: eq_int_type(char_traits<char>:: to_int_type(c1),char_traits<char>::to_int_type(c2))` yields the same as `c1 == c2`.

For values `e1` and `e2`, which are both copies of (or original) values obtained by `char_traits<char>::eof()`, returns `true`.

If one of `e1` and `e2` is a copy of (or original) value obtained by `char_traits<char>::eof()` and the other is not, returns `false`.

The return value for other combinations is unspecified.

```
static const char_type* find(const char_type* s,
                             size_t n, const char_type& a);
```

Returns the smallest pointer p in the interval [`s`,`s+n`), such that `*p == a`. If no such pointer exists, the return value is 0.

```
static state_type get_state(pos_type pos);
```

Returns the conversion state represented in `pos`.

```
static size_t length(const char_type* s);
```

Returns the smallest value n of type `size_t`, such that `s[n] == char(0)`.

```
static bool lt(const char_type& c1, const char_type& c2);
```

Returns (`c1 < c2`).

```
static char_type* move(char_type* s1,
                       const char_type* s2, size_t n);
```

Performs `s1[i] = s2[i]` for each i in the interval [`0`,`n`) and returns `s1+n`.

character traits

`static int_type` **not_eof**`(const int_type& e);`

Returns `c` if `char_traits<char>::eq_int_type(e,eof())` is `false`. Otherwise returns some other value `f` of type `int_type`, so that `char_traits<char>:: eq_int_type(f,eof()))` is `false`.

`static char_type` **to_char_type**`(const int_type& e);`

Translates a value of type `int_type` into its corresponding representation of type `char_type`, if any such representation exists.

In other words, if for some value `c` of type `char_type`, `char_traits<char>:: eq_int_type(e,char_traits<char>::to_int_type(c))` is `true`, then the value `c` is returned. Otherwise returns some unspecified value.

`static int_type` **to_int_type**`(const char_type& c);`

Translates a value of type `char_type` into its corresponding representation of type `int_type`, if any such representation exists.

In other words, returns some value of type `int_type`, constrained by `char_traits<char>::to_char_type()` and `char_traits<char>:: eq_int_type()`.

char_traits<wchar_t>

TEMPLATE SPECIALIZATION

template<> struct **char_traits**<wchar_t>
header: **<string>**
base class(es): **[none]**

DESCRIPTION

char_traits<wchar_t> contains information and functionality associated with the character type wchar_t.

SYNOPSIS

```
namespace std {
 template<>
 struct char_traits<wchar_t> {
    //  type definitions:
    typedef wchar_t      char_type;
    typedef wint_t       int_type;
    typedef streamoff    off_type;
    typedef wstreampos   pos_type;
    typedef mbstate_t    state_type;

    //  character traits operations:
    static void assign(char_type& c1, const char_type& c2);
    static bool eq(const char_type& c1, const char_type& c2);
    static bool lt(const char_type& c1, const char_type& c2);

    static int compare(const char_type* s1,const char_type* s2,size_t n);
    static size_t length(const char_type* s);
    static const char_type* find
    (const char_type* s, size_t n, const char_type& a);
    static char_type* move(char_type* s1, const char_type* s2, size_t n);
    static char_type* copy(char_type* s1, const char_type* s2, size_t n);
    static char_type* assign(char_type* s, size_t n, char_type a);

    static int_type not_eof(const int_type& c);
    static char_type to_char_type(const int_type& c);
    static int_type to_int_type(const char_type& c);
    static bool eq_int_type(const int_type& c1, const int_type& c2);
    static int_type eof();
 };
}
```

character traits

TYPE DEFINITIONS

Contains type definitions for char_type, int_type, off_type, pos_type, and state_type associated with the character type wchar_t.

```
typedef wchar_t      char_type;
typedef wint_t       int_type;
typedef wstreamoff   off_type;
typedef wstreampos   pos_type;
typedef mbstate_t    state_type;
```

PUBLIC MEMBER FUNCTIONS

static void **assign**(char_type& c1, const char_type& c2);

Performs c1 = c2.

static char_type* **assign**(char_type* s, size_t n, char_type a);

Performs s[i] = a for each i in the interval [0, n) and returns s.

static int **compare**(const char_type* s1, const char_type* s2, size_t n);

Returns 0, if s1[i] == s2[i] for each i in the interval [0, n); or else a value < 0, if for some j in [0, n), s1[j] < s2[j] and for each i from [0, j), s1[i] == s2[i]. Otherwise returns a value > 0.

static char_type* **copy**(char_type* s1, const char_type* s2, size_t n);

If s2 is not in the interval [s1, s1+n), the operation performs s1[i] = s2[i] for each i in the interval [0, n) and returns s1; otherwise the behavior is undefined.

static int_type **eof**();

Returns WEOF, which represents end-of-file.

static bool **eq**(const char_type& c1, const char_type& c2);

Returns (c1 == c2).

character traits

```
static bool eq_int_type(const int_type& e1,
                        const int_type& e2);
```

Compares values of type `int_type` for equality.

For values e1 and e2 that are `int_type` representations of `char_type` values c1 and c2, returns the same as the comparison of the respective `char_type` values would yield; that is, `char_traits<wchar_t>:: eq_int_type(char_traits<wchar_t>::to_int_type(c1),char_traits<char>::to_int_type(c2))` yields the same as c1 == c2.

For values e1 and e2, which are both copies of (or original) values obtained by `char_traits<char>::eof()`, returns `true`.

If one of e1 and e2 is a copy of (or original) value obtained by `char_traits<wchar_t>::eof()` and the other is not, returns `false`.

The return value for other combinations is unspecified.

```
static const char_type* find(const char_type* s,
                             size_t n, const char_type& a);
```

Returns the smallest pointer p in the interval `[s,s+n)`, such that `*p == a`. If no such pointer exists, the return value is 0.

```
static state_type get_state(pos_type pos);
```

Returns the conversion state represented in `pos`.

```
static size_t length(const char_type* s);
```

Returns the smallest value n of type `size_t`, such that `s[n] == char(0)`.

```
static bool lt(const char_type& c1, const char_type& c2);
```

Returns `(c1 < c2)`.

```
static char_type* move(char_type* s1,
                       const char_type* s2, size_t n);
```

Performs `s1[i] = s2[i]` for each i in the interval $[0,n)$ and returns s1+n.

```
static int_type not_eof(const int_type& e);
```

Returns c if char_traits<wchar_t>::eq_int_type(e,eof()) is false. Otherwise returns some other value f of type int_type, so that char_traits<wchar_t>:: eq_int_type(f,eof())) is false.

```
static char_type to_char_type(const int_type& e);
```

Translates a value of type int_type into its corresponding representation of type char_type, if any such representation exists.

In other words, if for some value c of type char_type, char_traits<wchar_t>:: eq_int_type(e, char_traits<wchar_t>::to_int_type(c)) is true, then the value c is returned. Otherwise returns some unspecified value.

```
static int_type to_int_type(const char_type& c);
```

Translates a value of type char_type into its corresponding representation of type int_type, if any such representation exists.

In other words, returns some value of type int_type, constrained by char_traits <wchar_t>::to_char_type() and char_traits<wchar_t>::eq_int_type().

character traits

3
IOSTREAMS

header file <iosfwd>

FILE NAME

`<iosfwd>`

DESCRIPTION

The header file contains forward declarations for the following:

- the specializations of the template class `char_traits`
- all IOStreams class templates
- the type definitions for the narrow- and wide-character stream types
- the template class `fpos`
- the type definitions for specializations of `fpos`

SYNOPSIS

```
namespace std {
        template<class charT> class char_traits;
        template<> class char_traits<char>;
        template<> class char_traits<wchar_t>;

        template<class T> class allocator;

    //   class definitions:

        template <class charT, class traits = char_traits<charT> >
          class basic_ios;
```

```
template <class charT, class traits = char_traits<charT> >
  class basic_streambuf;

template <class charT, class traits = char_traits<charT> >
  class basic_istream;

template <class charT, class traits = char_traits<charT> >
  class basic_ostream;

template <class charT, class traits = char_traits<charT> >
  class basic_iostream;

template <class charT, class traits = char_traits<charT>,
          class Allocator = allocator<charT> >
  class basic_stringbuf;

template <class charT, class traits = char_traits<charT>,
          class Allocator = allocator<charT> >
  class basic_istringstream;

template <class charT, class traits = char_traits<charT>,
          class Allocator = allocator<charT> >
  class basic_ostringstream;

template <class charT, class traits = char_traits<charT>,
          class Allocator = allocator<charT> >
  class basic_stringstream;

template <class charT, class traits = char_traits<charT> >
  class basic_filebuf;

template <class charT, class traits = char_traits<charT> >
  class basic_ifstream;

template <class charT, class traits = char_traits<charT> >
  class basic_ofstream;

template <class charT, class traits = char_traits<charT> >
  class basic_fstream;

template <class charT, class traits = char_traits<charT> >
  class istreambuf_iterator;
```

iostreams

```
template <class charT, class traits = char_traits<charT> >
  class ostreambuf_iterator;
```

// **type definitions:**

```
typedef basic_ios<char>        ios;
typedef basic_ios<wchar_t>     wios;

typedef basic_streambuf<char> streambuf;
typedef basic_istream<char>    istream;
typedef basic_ostream<char>    ostream;
typedef basic_iostream<char>   iostream;

typedef basic_stringbuf<char>       stringbuf;
typedef basic_istringstream<char> istringstream;
typedef basic_ostringstream<char> ostringstream;
typedef basic_stringstream<char>   stringstream;

typedef basic_filebuf<char>  filebuf;
typedef basic_ifstream<char> ifstream;
typedef basic_ofstream<char> ofstream;
typedef basic_fstream<char>   fstream;

typedef basic_streambuf<wchar_t> wstreambuf;
typedef basic_istream<wchar_t>    wistream;
typedef basic_ostream<wchar_t>    wostream;
typedef basic_iostream<wchar_t>   wiostream;

typedef basic_stringbuf<wchar_t>       wstringbuf;
typedef basic_istringstream<wchar_t> wistringstream;
typedef basic_ostringstream<wchar_t> wostringstream;
typedef basic_stringstream<wchar_t>   wstringstream;

typedef basic_filebuf<wchar_t>  wfilebuf;
typedef basic_ifstream<wchar_t> wifstream;
typedef basic_ofstream<wchar_t> wofstream;
typedef basic_fstream<wchar_t>   wfstream;

template <class state> class fpos;
typedef fpos<char_traits<char>::state_type>    streampos;
typedef fpos<char_traits<wchar_t>::state_type> wstreampos;
}
```

header file <iostream>

FILE NAME

<iostream>

DESCRIPTION

The header file contains declarations of the predefined global stream objects, namely `cin`, `cout`, `cerr`, `clog`, `wcin`, `wcout`, `wcerr`, and `wclog`.

SYNOPSIS

```
namespace std {
      extern istream cin;
      extern ostream cout;
      extern ostream cerr;
      extern ostream clog;

      extern wistream wcin;
      extern wostream wcout;
      extern wostream wcerr;
      extern wostream wclog;
   }
```

header file <ios>

FILE NAME

<ios>

DESCRIPTION

The header file contains declarations for the stream base classes `ios_base` and `basic_ios<class charT, class traits>`.

SYNOPSIS

```
#include <iosfwd>

namespace std {
      typedef  OFF_T   streamoff;
      typedef  SZ_T   streamsize;
      template <class stateT> class fpos;

      class ios_base;
      template <class charT, class traits = char_traits<charT> >
        class basic_ios;

   //  manipulators:
      ios_base& boolalpha  (ios_base& str);
      ios_base& noboolalpha(ios_base& str);

      ios_base& showbase   (ios_base& str);
      ios_base& noshowbase (ios_base& str);

      ios_base& showpoint  (ios_base& str);
      ios_base& noshowpoint(ios_base& str);

      ios_base& showpos    (ios_base& str);
      ios_base& noshowpos  (ios_base& str);

      ios_base& skipws     (ios_base& str);
      ios_base& noskipws   (ios_base& str);

      ios_base& uppercase  (ios_base& str);
      ios_base& nouppercase(ios_base& str);

   //  adjustfield:
      ios_base& internal   (ios_base& str);
```

```
    ios_base& left        (ios_base& str);
    ios_base& right       (ios_base& str);

//  basefield:
    ios_base& dec         (ios_base& str);
    ios_base& hex         (ios_base& str);
    ios_base& oct         (ios_base& str);

//  floatfield:
    ios_base& fixed       (ios_base& str);
    ios_base& scientific (ios_base& str);
}
```

IMPLEMENT SPECIFIC TYPE DEFINITIONS

streamoff is an implementation-defined type that can be constructed from an integral value, can be converted to an integral value, and allows checks for equality and inequality. Usually it is a typedef for one of the signed basic integral types.

streamsize is an implementation-defined type that is a typedef for one of the signed basic integral types. In general it is used to represent the number of characters transferred in an I/O-operation, or the size of an I/O-buffer.

header file <streambuf>

FILE NAME

<streambuf>

DESCRIPTION

The header file contains declarations for the stream buffer class template `basic_streambuf<class charT, class traits>` and type definitions for its specializations.

SYNOPSIS

```
namespace std {
      template <class charT, class traits = char_traits<charT> >
        class basic_streambuf;
      typedef basic_streambuf<char>     streambuf;
      typedef basic_streambuf<wchar_t>  wstreambuf;
    }
```

header file <istream>

FILE NAME

`<istream>`

DESCRIPTION

The header file contains declarations for the following:

- the input stream class template `basic_istream<class    charT, class traits>`

- the bidirectional stream class template `basic_iostream<classcharT, class traits>`

- type definitions for their specializations

- the standard input stream manipulators, i.e., the function template ws

SYNOPSIS

```
namespace std {
  template <class charT, class traits = char_traits<charT> >
    class basic_istream;
  typedef basic_istream<char>     istream;
  typedef basic_istream<wchar_t>  wistream;

  template <class charT, class traits = char_traits<charT> >
    class basic_iostream;
  typedef basic_iostream<char>     iostream;
  typedef basic_iostream<wchar_t> wiostream;

  template <class charT, class traits>
  basic_istream<charT,traits>& ws(basic_istream<charT,traits>& is);
}
```

header file <ostream>

FILE NAME

<ostream>

DESCRIPTION

The header file contains declarations for the following:

- the output stream class template `basic_ostream<class charT, class traits>`

- type definitions for its specializations

- the standard output stream manipulators, i.e., the function templates `endl`, `ends`, and `flush`

SYNOPSIS

```
namespace std {
  template <class charT, class traits = char_traits<charT> >
    class basic_ostream;
  typedef basic_ostream<char>    ostream;
  typedef basic_ostream<wchar_t> wostream;

  template <class charT, class traits>
    basic_ostream<charT,traits>& endl(basic_ostream<charT,traits>& os);
  template <class charT, class traits>
    basic_ostream<charT,traits>& ends(basic_ostream<charT,traits>& os);
  template <class charT, class traits>
    basic_ostream<charT,traits>& flush(basic_ostream<charT,traits>& os);
}
```

header file <iomanip>

FILE NAME

`<iomanip>`

DESCRIPTION

The header file contains declarations for the standard manipulators, i.e., for the function templates `resetiosflags`, `setiosflags`, `setbase`, `setfill`, `setprecision`, and `setw`.

SYNOPSIS

```
namespace std {
        // Types  T1,  T2, ... are unspecified implementation types
        T1 resetiosflags(ios_base::fmtflags mask);
        T2 setiosflags  (ios_base::fmtflags mask);
        T3 setbase(int base);
        template<charT> T4 setfill(charT c);
        T5 setprecision(int n);
        T6 setw(int n);
    }
```

header file <sstream>

FILE NAME

<sstream>

DESCRIPTION

The header file contains declarations for the string stream classes:

- the string stream buffer class template `basic_stringbuf<class charT, class traits, class Allocator>`

- type definitions for its specializations

- the input string stream class template `basic_istringstream <class charT, class traits, class Allocator>`

- the output string stream class template `basic_ostringstream <class charT, class traits, class Allocator>`

- the bidirectional string stream class template `basic_stringstream <class charT, class traits, class Allocator>`

- type definitions for their specializations

SYNOPSIS

```
namespace std {
     template <class charT, class traits = char_traits<charT>,
             class Allocator = allocator<charT> >
       class basic_stringbuf;
     typedef basic_stringbuf<char>     stringbuf;
     typedef basic_stringbuf<wchar_t> wstringbuf;

     template <class charT, class traits = char_traits<charT>,
             class Allocator = allocator<charT> >
       class basic_istringstream;
     typedef basic_istringstream<char>     istringstream;
     typedef basic_istringstream<wchar_t> wistringstream;

     template <class charT, class traits = char_traits<charT>,
             class Allocator = allocator<charT> >
       class basic_ostringstream;
     typedef basic_ostringstream<char>     ostringstream;
     typedef basic_ostringstream<wchar_t> wostringstream;
```

```
       template <class charT, class traits = char_traits<charT>,
                 class Allocator = allocator<charT> >
         class basic_stringstream;
       typedef basic_stringstream<char>     stringstream;
       typedef basic_stringstream<wchar_t> wstringstream;
   }
```

header file <fstream>

FILE NAME

fstream

DESCRIPTION

The header file contains declarations for the file stream classes:

- the file stream buffer class template `basic_filebuf<class charT, class traits>`
- type definitions for its specializations
- the input file stream class template `basic_ifstream <class charT, class traits >`
- the output file stream class template `basic_ofstream <class charT, class traits >`
- the bidirectional file stream class template `basic_fstream <class charT, class traits >`
- type definitions for their specializations

SYNOPSIS

```
namespace std {
      template <class charT, class traits = char_traits<charT> >
        class basic_filebuf;
      typedef basic_filebuf<char>    filebuf;
      typedef basic_filebuf<wchar_t> wfilebuf;

      template <class charT, class traits = char_traits<charT> >
        class basic_ifstream;
      typedef basic_ifstream<char>    ifstream;
      typedef basic_ifstream<wchar_t> wifstream;

      template <class charT, class traits = char_traits<charT> >
        class basic_ofstream;
      typedef basic_ofstream<char>    ofstream;
      typedef basic_ofstream<wchar_t> wofstream;

      template <class charT, class traits = char_traits<charT> >
        class basic_fstream;
      typedef basic_fstream<char>    fstream;
      typedef basic_fstream<wchar_t> wfstream;
    }
```

iostreams

global type definitions

HEADER

header: **<iosfwd>**

TYPE DEFINITIONS

```
typedef basic_ios<char>    ios;
typedef basic_ios<wchar_t> wios;


typedef basic_streambuf<char> streambuf;
typedef basic_istream<char>   istream;
typedef basic_ostream<char>   ostream;
typedef basic_iostream<char>  iostream;


typedef basic_stringbuf<char>     stringbuf;
typedef basic_istringstream<char> istringstream;
typedef basic_ostringstream<char> ostringstream;
typedef basic_stringstream<char>  stringstream;


typedef basic_filebuf<char>  filebuf;
typedef basic_ifstream<char> ifstream;
typedef basic_ofstream<char> ofstream;
typedef basic_fstream<char>  fstream;


typedef basic_streambuf<wchar_t> wstreambuf;
typedef basic_istream<wchar_t>   wistream;
typedef basic_ostream<wchar_t>   wostream;
typedef basic_iostream<wchar_t>  wiostream;


typedef basic_stringbuf<wchar_t>     wstringbuf;
typedef basic_istringstream<wchar_t> wistringstream;
typedef basic_ostringstream<wchar_t> wostringstream;
typedef basic_stringstream<wchar_t>  wstringstream;


typedef basic_filebuf<wchar_t>  wfilebuf;
typedef basic_ifstream<wchar_t> wifstream;
typedef basic_ofstream<wchar_t> wofstream;
typedef basic_fstream<wchar_t>  wfstream;


template <class state> class fpos;
typedef fpos<char_traits<char>::state_type>    streampos;
typedef fpos<char_traits<wchar_t>::state_type> wstreampos;
```

iostreams

global objects

HEADER

header: **<iostream>**

OBJECTS

```
extern istream cin;
extern ostream cout;
extern ostream cerr;
extern ostream clog;

extern wistream wcin;
extern wostream wcout;
extern wostream wcerr;
extern wostream wclog;
```

DESCRIPTION

cin is an input stream object that handles characters of type char. Its stream buffer is initially associated with stdin from the C standard I/O. Also, it is initially tied to cout, i.e., cin.tie() returns &cout.

cout is an output stream object that handles characters of type char. Its stream buffer is initially associated with stdout from the C standard I/O.

cerr is an output stream object that handles characters of type char. Its stream buffer is initially associated with stderr from the C standard I/O. Also, it is initially configured to pass the data received by one output operation on the stream level directly to the external device; i.e., cerr.flags() | unitbuf is nonzero.

clog is an output stream object that handles characters of type char. Its stream buffer is initially associated with stderr from the C standard I/O.

wcin is an input stream object that handles characters of type wchar_t. Its stream buffer is initially associated with stdin from the C standard I/O. Also, it is initially tied to wcout; i.e., wcin.tie() returns &wcout.

wcout is an output stream object that handles characters of type wchar_t. Its stream buffer is initially associated with stdout from the C standard I/O.

wcerr is an output stream object that handles characters of type wchar_t. Its stream buffer is initially associated with stderr from the C standard I/O. Also, it is initially configured to pass the data received by one output operation on the stream level directly to the external device; i.e., wcerr.flags() | unitbuf is nonzero.

wclog is an output stream object that handles characters of type wchar_t. Its stream buffer is initially associated with stderr from the C standard I/O.

The predefined global streams listed above are initialized in such a way that they can be used in constructors and destructors of static and global objects.

The predefined global streams are by default synchronized with their associated C standard files. You can switch off the synchronization by calling `ios_base::sync_with_stdio(false)`.

The relationship between the global narrow-character streams and their wide-character counterparts is undefined, which means that you do not know what is going to happen if you use both in the same program.

The difference between `clog` and `cerr` is that `clog` is fully buffered, whereas output to `cerr` is written to the external device immediately after formatting. The same holds for `wclog` and `wcerr`.

basic_filebuf<charT,traits>

CLASS TEMPLATE

template <class charT, class traits = char_traits<charT> >
class **basic_filebuf**
header: **<fstream>**
base class(es): **basic_streambuf**<charT,traits>

DESCRIPTION

basic_filebuf represents an abstraction that handles the bidirectional transfer of characters of type charT between a file stream and an external file. Optionally it buffers the
characters during transfer. Depending on the contained locale, it converts the characters
from the external representation to the internal representation during input operations,
and from the internal representation to the external representation during output
operations.

SYNOPSIS

```
namespace std {
 template <class charT, class traits = char_traits<charT> >
 class basic_filebuf : public basic_streambuf<charT,traits> {
 public:
  //  type definitions:
  typedef charT                    char_type;
  typedef typename traits::int_type int_type;
  typedef typename traits::pos_type pos_type;
  typedef typename traits::off_type off_type;
  typedef traits                   traits_type;
  //  constructors/destructor:
  basic_filebuf();
  virtual ~basic_filebuf();
  //  open/close:
  bool is_open() const;
  basic_filebuf<charT,traits>* open(const char* s,
                                    ios_base::openmode mode);
  basic_filebuf<charT,traits>* close();
 protected:
  virtual streamsize showmanyc();
  virtual int_type underflow();
  virtual int_type uflow();
  virtual int_type pbackfail(int_type c = traits::eof());
  virtual int_type overflow (int_type c = traits::eof());
  virtual basic_streambuf<charT,traits>*
              setbuf(char_type* s, streamsize n);
```

iostreams

```
    virtual pos_type seekoff(off_type off, ios_base::seekdir way,
                 ios_base::openmode which = ios_base::in|ios_base::out);
    virtual pos_type seekpos(pos_type sp,
                 ios_base::openmode which = ios_base::in|ios_base::out);
    virtual int      sync();
    virtual void     imbue(const locale& loc);
  };
}
```

PUBLIC MEMBER FUNCTIONS

basic_filebuf();

Constructs an object of type basic_filebuf<charT,traits>. After the construction this->is_open() == false.

~basic_filebuf();

Destroys an object of type basic_filebuf<charT,traits>.
Calls this->close() during the destruction.

OPEN AND CLOSE

basic_filebuf<char_type,traits_type >* **close**();

If is_open() == true, the associated file is closed and this is returned. Otherwise the return value is 0.

bool **is_open**() const;

Returns true if a previous call to open() succeeded and thereafter no successful call to close() has been processed. Otherwise the return value is false.

basic_filebuf<char_type,traits_type >*
open(const char *filename, ios_base::openmode mode);

Opens the file specified by filename according to the mode. Returns this if successful, otherwise 0.

PROTECTED MEMBER FUNCTIONS

virtual void **imbue**(const locale& loc);

Same functional description as for the base class. Redefined here to deal with the special constraints of a file buffer.

```
virtual int_type overflow(int_type c = traits_type::eof());
```

Makes space available in the put area by transferring characters from the put area to the external file. Depending on the contained locale, the transferred characters are converted to an external character representation. It is implementation-dependent how many characters from the put area are transferred to the external file. It is also implementation-dependent if `c` is transferred to the external file, for `traits::eq_int_type (c,traits_type::eof()) == false`. The return value is `traits_type:: not_eof(c)` if the operation succeeded. Otherwise `traits_type::eof()`.

```
virtual int_type pbackfail(int_type c = traits_type::eof());
```

Same functional description as for the base class. Redefined here to deal with the special constraints of a file buffer.

```
virtual pos_type
seekoff(off_type off, ios_base::seekdir dir,
    ios_base::openmode mode = ios_base::in | ios_base::out);
```

Alters the file position. The requested new file position is described by `off` and `dir` in the following way: `dir` describes the base position and `off` is used to determine the offset relative to the base position. If the code conversion facet of the locale contained in `this` indicates that each internal character is converted to a constant number of external characters (i.e., `use_facet<codecvt<charT,char,typename traits::state_type> >(this->getloc()).encoding() > 0`), the offset relative to the base position will be `off` multiplied by this constant number. Otherwise the repositioning will fail, if `off != 0`. The return value is `pos_type(off_type(-1))` in case of failure.

```
virtual pos_type
seekpos(pos_type pos,
    ios_base::openmode mode = ios_base::in | ios_base::out);
```

Alters the file position. The following table shows how `mode` affects the operation:

CONDITION	EFFECT
`(mode & basic_ios::in) != 0`	sets the file position to `pos`, then updates the input sequence
`(mode & basic_ios::out) != 0`	sets the file position to `pos`, then updates the output sequence
otherwise	operation fails

iostreams

If `pos` is an invalid stream position, the operations fails. If `pos` has not been obtained by a previous successful call to a positioning function, the effect is undefined. If successful the return value is `pos`, otherwise an invalid stream position.

```
virtual basic_streambuf<char_type,traits_type>*
setbuf(char_type* s, streamsize n);
```

If `setbuf(0, 0)` is called before any I/O has occurred, the stream that holds this file buffer becomes unbuffered; i.e., that `pbase()` and `pptr()` always return 0 and output to the file appears as soon as possible. The return value is `this`. For other parameters the operation behaves in an implementation-dependent manner.

```
virtual int showmanyc();
```

Overrides the base class functionality if it is able to determine more available characters.

```
virtual int sync();
```

Same functional description as for the base class. Redefined here to deal with the special constraints of a file buffer.

  If a put area exists, that is, if there are characters that have not yet been written, calls `filebuf::overflow()` to write the characters to the file. If a get area exists, the effect is implementation-defined.

```
virtual int_type uflow();
```

Same functional description as for the base class, except that it uses the mechanisms as described in `basic_filebuf::underflow()` to make characters available.

```
virtual int_type underflow();
```

Reads new characters from the external file and converts them, if necessary, to the internal character representation. The resulting characters, either from the read or the conversion, are put into the get area, and the pointers of the get and put areas are updated. The return value is the first newly read character. If no new characters could be made available, the return value is `traits_type::eof()`.

basic_fstream<charT,traits>

CLASS TEMPLATE

template <class charT, class traits = char_traits<charT> >
class **basic_fstream**
header: **<fstream>**
base class(es): **basic_iostream**<charT, traits>

DESCRIPTION

basic_fstream is a bidirectional stream that can be associated with a file.

SYNOPSIS

```
namespace std {
 template <class charT, class traits=char_traits<charT> >
 class basic_fstream : public basic_iostream<charT,traits> {
 public:
  //  type definitions:
  typedef charT                      char_type;
  typedef typename traits::int_type int_type;
  typedef typename traits::pos_type pos_type;
  typedef typename traits::off_type off_type;
  typedef traits                     traits_type;
  //  constructors:
  basic_fstream();
  explicit basic_fstream(const char* s,
           ios_base::openmode mode = ios_base::in|ios_base::out);
  //  file stream operations:
  basic_filebuf<charT,traits>* rdbuf() const;
  bool is_open();
  void open(const char* s,
           ios_base::openmode mode = ios_base::in|ios_base::out);
  void close();
 private:
  // basic_filebuf<charT,traits> sb; exposition only
 };
}
```

PUBLIC MEMBER FUNCTIONS

basic_fstream();

Constructs an object of type basic_fstream<charT,traits>

```
explicit
basic_fstream(const char* filename,
             ios_base::openmode mode = ios_base::in | ios_base::out);
```

Constructs an object of type basic_fstream<charT,traits>. rdbuf()->open(filename, mode) is called. If this call fails, setstate(failbit) is called.

FILE STREAM OPERATIONS

```
void close();
```

Calls rdbuf()->close(). If this call fails, setstate(failbit) is called.

```
bool is_open();
```

Calls rdbuf()->is_open() and returns the result.

```
void open(const char* filename,
         ios_base::openmode mode = ios_base::in  | ios_base::out);
```

Calls rdbuf()->open(). If this call fails, setstate(failbit) is called.

```
basic_filebuf<char_type,traits_type>* rdbuf() const;
```

Returns the pointer to the private member of type basic_filebuf <char_type,traits_type>. Note the subtle difference from basic_ios<charT,traits>::rdbuf(). basic_ios<charT,traits>::rdbuf() returns the pointer to a stream buffer that is maintained in basic_ios <charT,traits>. For a newly constructed object, both functions return the same pointer. After a call to basic_ios<charT,traits>::rdbuf(basic_filebuf <char_type, traits_type>* sb), basic_ios<charT,traits>::rdbuf() returns the newly set pointer, while basic_fstream<charT,traits>::rdbuf() keeps returning the pointer to its own private member.

basic_ifstream<charT,traits>

CLASS TEMPLATE

template <class charT, class traits = char_traits<charT> >
class **basic_ifstream**
header: **<fstream>**
base class(es): **basic_istream**<charT, traits>

DESCRIPTION

basic_ifstream is an input stream that can be associated with a file.

SYNOPSIS

```
namespace std {
  template <class charT, class traits = char_traits<charT> >
  class basic_ifstream : public basic_istream<charT,traits> {
  public:
    // type definitions:
    typedef charT                    char_type;
    typedef typename traits::int_type int_type;
    typedef typename traits::pos_type pos_type;
    typedef typename traits::off_type off_type;
    typedef traits                   traits_type;
    //  constructors:
    basic_ifstream();
    explicit basic_ifstream(const char* s,
                        ios_base::openmode mode = ios_base::in);
    //  input file stream operations:
    basic_filebuf<charT,traits>* rdbuf() const;
    bool is_open();
    void open(const char* s, ios_base::openmode mode = ios_base::in);
    void close();
  private:
    //  basic_filebuf<charT,traits> sb;        exposition only
  };
}
```

PUBLIC MEMBER FUNCTIONS

basic_ifstream();

Constructs an object of type basic_ifstream<charT, traits>.

```
explicit
basic_ifstream(const char* filename,
               ios_base::openmode mode = ios_base::in);
```

Constructs an object of type basic_ifstream<charT,traits>.
rdbuf()->open(filename, mode) is called. If this call fails, setstate(failbit) is
called.

```
void close();
```

Calls rdbuf()->close(). If this call fails, setstate(failbit) is called.

```
bool is_open();
```

Calls rdbuf()->is_open() and returns the result.

```
void open(const char* filename,
          ios_base::openmode mode = ios_base::in);
```

Calls rdbuf()->open(). If this call fails, setstate(failbit) is called.

```
basic_filebuf<char_type,traits_type>* rdbuf() const;
```

Returns the pointer to the private member of type basic_filebuf<char_type,
traits_type>. Note the subtle difference from basic_ios<charT,traits>::
rdbuf(). basic_ios<charT,traits>::rdbuf() returns the pointer to a stream
buffer that is maintained in basic_ios<charT,traits>. For a newly constructed
object, both functions return the same pointer. After a call to basic_ios<charT,
traits>::rdbuf(basic_filebuf<char_type,   traits_type>*   sb),
basic_ios<charT,traits>::rdbuf() returns the newly set pointer, while
basic_ifstream<charT,traits>::rdbuf() keeps returning the pointer to its own
private member.

basic_ios<charT,traits>

CLASS TEMPLATE

template <class charT, class traits = char_traits<charT> >
class **basic_ios**
header: **<ios>**
base class(es): **ios_base**

DESCRIPTION

basic_ios is the character-type and traits-type-dependent base class for all streams. It encapsulates the common character-type-dependent functionality of a stream, e.g., setting and getting the stream buffer.

SYNOPSIS

```
namespace std {
 template <class charT, class traits = char_traits<charT> >
 class basic_ios : public ios_base {
 public:
  //  type definitions:
  typedef charT                     char_type;
  typedef typename traits::int_type int_type;
  typedef typename traits::pos_type pos_type;
  typedef typename traits::off_type off_type;
  typedef traits                    traits_type;
  //  constructor/destructor:
  explicit basic_ios(basic_streambuf<charT,traits>* sb);
  virtual ~basic_ios();
  //  error state:
  operator void*() const
  bool operator!() const
  iostate rdstate() const;
  void clear(iostate state = goodbit);
  void setstate(iostate state);
  bool good() const;
  bool eof()  const;
  bool fail() const;
  bool bad()  const;
  //  exceptions handling:
  iostate exceptions() const;
  void exceptions(iostate except);
  //  locales:
  locale imbue(const locale& loc);
  char narrow(char_type c, char dfault) const;
```

```
char_type widen(char c) const;
// miscelleaneous:
basic_ostream<charT,traits>* tie() const;
basic_ostream<charT,traits>* tie(basic_ostream<charT,traits>* tiestr);
basic_streambuf<charT,traits>* rdbuf() const;
basic_streambuf<charT,traits>* rdbuf(basic_streambuf<charT,traits>* sb);
basic_ios& copyfmt(const basic_ios& rhs);
char_type fill() const;
char_type fill(char_type ch);
protected:
basic_ios();
void init(basic_streambuf<charT,traits>* sb);
private:
basic_ios(const basic_ios& );          // not defined
basic_ios& operator=(const basic_ios&);      // not defined
};
}
```

PUBLIC MEMBER FUNCTIONS

```
explicit
basic_ios(basic_streambuf<char_type,traits_type>* sb);
```

Constructs an object of type basic_ios<charT,traits>. Additionally, this->init(sb) is called.

```
virtual ~basic_ios ();
```

Destroys an object of type basic_ios<charT,traits>.

ERROR STATE

```
operator void*() const;
```

Returns 0 if this->fail() == true. Otherwise some value != 0.

```
bool operator!() const;
```

Returns this->fail().

```
bool bad() const;
```

Returns true if ios_base::badbit is set in this->rdstate().

```
void clear(iostate state = goodbit) const;
```

Sets the stream state for this to state, if rdbuf()!=0. Otherwise to state | ios_base::badbit.

```
bool eof() const;
```

Returns true if ios_base::eofbit is set in this->rdstate().

```
bool fail() const;
```

Returns true if ios_base::failbit or ios_base::badbit is set in this->rdstate().

```
bool good() const;
```

Returns (this->rdstate() == 0).

```
iostate rdstate() const;
```

Returns the stream state of this.

```
void setstate(iostate state = goodbit);
```

Calls this->clear(rdstate() | state).

EXCEPTION HANDLING

```
iostate exceptions() const;
```

Returns a bitmask that determines which elements in this->rdstate() cause exceptions to be thrown.

```
void exceptions(iostate except);
```

Sets this to cause exceptions for all elements specified in except and calls this->clear(rdstate()).

LOCALES

```
locale imbue(const locale& loc);
```

Calls ios_base::imbue(loc) and if rdbuf()!=0, rdbuf()->imbue(loc). Returns the previous return value of ios_base::imbue().

```
char narrow(char_type c, char deflt) const;
```

Returns the `char` representation that corresponds to `c`, if it exists; otherwise `dflt`, using the `ctype` facet of the stream's locale, i.e., calls `use_facet<ctype<char_type> >` `(getloc()).narrow(c,deflt)` and returns the resulting character.

```
char_type widen(char c) const;
```

Returns the `char_type` representation that corresponds to `c`, using the `ctype` facet of the stream's locale, i.e., calls `use_facet<ctype<char_type> >(getloc())`. `widen(c)` and returns the resulting character.

MISCELLANEOUS

```
basic_ios& copyfmt(basic_ios& rhs);
```

Assigns to the data members of `this` the corresponding data members of `rhs`. `this->` `rdstate()` and `this->rdbuf()` are left unchanged. Before copying any part of `rhs`, all registered callbacks `cb` are called together with their index `ix` as `(*cb)(erase_event,*this,ix)`. After all parts except `this->exceptions()` have been replaced, all callbacks `cb` that were copied from `rhs` are called together with their index `ix` as `(*cb)(copyfmt_event,*this,ix)`. Finally `this->exceptions()` is altered by calling `this->exceptions(rhs.exceptions())`. The return value is `*this`.

```
char_type fill() const;
```

Returns the character used to pad (fill) an output field to the specified width.

```
char_type fill(char_type c);
```

Causes `this` to use the character `c` for padding (filling). Returns the previous value of `this->fill()`.

```
basic_streambuf<char_type,traits_type>* rdbuf() const;
```

Returns the pointer to the stream buffer.

```
basic_streambuf<charT,traits>*
rdbuf(basic_streambuf<char_type,traits_type>* sb);
```

sb replaces the current stream buffer pointer contained in this. Additionally, this->clear() is called. Returns the previous value of this->rdbuf().

```
basic_ostream<char_type,traits_type>* tie() const;
```

Returns the pointer to an output stream that is tied to, i.e., synchronized with, this.

```
basic_ostream<char_type,traits_type>*
tie(basic_ostream<char_type,traits_type>* str);
```

Ties (synchronizes) an output stream to (with) this. Returns the previous value of this->tie().

PROTECTED MEMBER FUNCTIONS

```
basic_ios();
```

Constructs an object of type basic_ios<charT,traits> leaving its data member uninitialized. The object must be initialized by calling its init () member function. If it is destroyed before it has been initialized the behavior is undefined.

```
void init(basic_streambuf<char_type,traits_type>* sb);
```

Initializes this so that

- this->rdbuf()==sb,
- this->rdstate()==ios_base::goodbit, if sb!=0 otherwise this->rdstate()==ios_base::badbit
- this->exceptions()==ios_base::goodbit,
- this->flags()==ios_base::skipws | ios_base::dec,
- this->width()==0,
- this->precision()==6,
- this->fill()==this->widen(' '),
- this->tie()==0,
- this->getloc() returns a copy of the global locale, constructed by locale(), and
- this->iarray and this->parray are null pointers.

basic_iostream<charT,traits>

CLASS TEMPLATE

template <class charT, class traits = char_traits<charT> >
class **basic_iostream**
header: **<iostream>**
base class(es): **basic_istream**<charT,traits>, **basic_ostream**<charT,traits>

DESCRIPTION

basic_iostream represents the abstraction of a bidirectional stream.

SYNOPSIS

```
namespace std {
 template <class charT, class traits = char_traits<charT> >
 class basic_iostream : public basic_istream<charT,traits>,
                        public basic_ostream<charT,traits> {
 public:
  // constructor/destructor
  explicit basic_iostream(basic_streambuf<charT,traits>* sb);
  virtual ~basic_iostream();
 };
}
```

PUBLIC MEMBER FUNCTIONS

explicit **basic_iostream**
(basic_streambuf<char_type,traits_type>* sb);

Constructs an object of type basic_iostream<charT,traits>, which uses sb as its stream buffer. It assigns initial values to its base classes by calling basic_istream<charT,traits>(sb) and basic_ostream<charT,traits>(sb).

    If the pointer sb is zero or points to an invalid stream buffer object, the behavior of operations subsequently performed on the newly constructed stream is undefined.

virtual ~**basic_iostream** ();

Destroys an object of type basic_iostream<charT,traits>. No operations are performed on the stream buffer; i.e., rdbuf() is not called, during destruction.

basic_istream<charT,traits>

CLASS TEMPLATE

```
template <class charT, class traits = char_traits<charT> >
class basic_istream
header: <istream>
base class(es): basic_ios<charT, traits> (virtual)
```

DESCRIPTION

basic_istream represents the abstraction of a general input stream.

SYNOPSIS

```
namespace std {
  template <class charT, class traits = char_traits<charT> >
  class basic_istream : virtual public basic_ios<charT,traits> {
  public:
    // type definitions:
    typedef charT                   char_type;
    typedef typename traits::int_type int_type;
    typedef typename traits::pos_type pos_type;
    typedef typename traits::off_type off_type;
    typedef traits                  traits_type;
    // prefix/suffix:
    class sentry;
    // constructor/destructor:
    explicit basic_istream(basic_streambuf<charT,traits>* sb);
    virtual ~basic_istream();
    // formatted input:
    basic_istream<charT,traits>& operator>>(bool& n);
    basic_istream<charT,traits>& operator>>(short& n);
    basic_istream<charT,traits>& operator>>(unsigned short& n);
    basic_istream<charT,traits>& operator>>(int& n);
    basic_istream<charT,traits>& operator>>(unsigned int& n);
    basic_istream<charT,traits>& operator>>(long& n);
    basic_istream<charT,traits>& operator>>(unsigned long& n);
    basic_istream<charT,traits>& operator>>(float& f);
    basic_istream<charT,traits>& operator>>(double& f);
    basic_istream<charT,traits>& operator>>(long double& f);
    basic_istream<charT,traits>& operator>>(void*& p);
    basic_istream<charT,traits>& operator>>
      (basic_streambuf<char_type,traits>* sb);
```

```
    // unformatted input:
    streamsize gcount() const;
    int_type get();
    basic_istream<charT,traits>& get(char_type& c);
    basic_istream<charT,traits>& get(char_type* s, streamsize n);
    basic_istream<charT,traits>& get(char_type* s, streamsize n,
                                     char_type delim);
    basic_istream<charT,traits>& get(basic_streambuf<char_type,
                                     traits>& sb);
    basic_istream<charT,traits>& get(basic_streambuf<char_type,
                                     traits>& sb, char_type delim);
    basic_istream<charT,traits>& getline(char_type* s, streamsize n);
    basic_istream<charT,traits>& getline(char_type* s, streamsize n,
                                         char_type delim);
    basic_istream<charT,traits>& ignore(streamsize n = 1,
                                        int_type delim =traits::eof());
    int_type                 peek();
    basic_istream<charT,traits>& read    (char_type* s, streamsize n);
    streamsize               readsome(char_type* s, streamsize n);
    // manipulator extractors:
    basic_istream<charT,traits>& operator>>
       (basic_istream<charT,traits>& (*pf)(basic_istream<charT,traits>&));
    basic_istream<charT,traits>& operator>>
       (basic_ios<charT,traits>& (*pf)(basic_ios<charT,traits>&));
    basic_istream<charT,traits>& operator>>
       (ios_base& (*pf)(ios_base&));
    // buffer management:
    basic_istream<charT,traits>& putback(char_type c);
    basic_istream<charT,traits>& unget();
    int sync();
    // positioning:
    pos_type tellg();
    basic_istream<charT,traits>& seekg(pos_type);
    basic_istream<charT,traits>& seekg(off_type, ios_base::seekdir);
};
// character extraction:
template<class charT, class traits> basic_istream<charT,traits>&
  operator>>(basic_istream<charT,traits>&, charT&);
template<class traits> basic_istream<char,traits>&
  operator>>(basic_istream<char,traits>&, unsigned char&);
template<class traits> basic_istream<char,traits>&
  operator>>(basic_istream<char,traits>&, signed char&);
```

```
template<class charT, class traits> basic_istream<charT,traits>&
  operator>>(basic_istream<charT,traits>&, charT*);
template<class traits> basic_istream<char,traits>&
  operator>>(basic_istream<char,traits>&, unsigned char*);
template<class traits> basic_istream<char,traits>&
  operator>>(basic_istream<char,traits>&, signed char*);
// input stream manipulators:
template <class charT, class traits>
  basic_istream<charT,traits>& ws(basic_istream<charT,traits>& is);
}
};
```

CLASS DEFINITIONS
PREFIX/SUFFIX

```
class sentry
{
 public:
  explicit sentry (basic_istream<char_type,traits_type>& is,
                                      bool noskipws = false);
  ~sentry();
  operator bool();
};
```

`sentry` defines a helper class that handles exception-safe preparations for formatted and unformatted input.

The constructor calls `is.tie()->flush()`, if `is.tie()!=0`. If `noskipws==` `false` and `is.flags() & ios_base::skipws != 0`, it extracts and discards each available whitespace character from the input. The locale that is currently imbued in `is` is used to determine if a character from the input is a whitespace character.

If, after these operations, `is.good()==true`, `this->operator bool()` returns `true`, otherwise `false`. The constructor may also call `is.setstate(ios_base::` `failbit)` to indicate an error.

PUBLIC MEMBER FUNCTIONS

```
explicit basic_istream
(basic_streambuf<char_type,traits_type>* sb);
```

Constructs an object of type `basic_istream<charT,traits>`. Additionally, calls `basic_ios::init(sb)` to initialize it.

If the pointer `sb` is zero or points to an invalid stream buffer object, the behavior of operations subsequently performed on the newly constructed stream is undefined.

```
virtual ~basic_istream ();
```

Destroys an object of type `basic_istream<charT,traits>`. No operations are performed on the stream buffer; in particular, `rdbuf()` is not called during destruction.

FORMATTED INPUT

```
basic_istream<char_type,traits_type>&
operator>>(bool& b);
```

Extracts a value of type `bool` and stores it in `b` by using the `num_get<char_type, istreambuf_iterator<char_type> >` facet from the locale contained in `this`. The return value is `*this`. Failures are indicated by the state of `*this`.

```
basic_istream<char_type,traits_type>&
operator>>(short& s);
```

Extracts a value of type `short` and stores it in `s` by using the `num_get<char_type, istreambuf_iterator<char_type> >` facet from the locale contained in this. The return value is `*this`. Failures are indicated by the state of `*this`.

```
basic_istream<char_type,traits_type>&
operator>>(unsigned short& us);
```

Extracts a value of type `unsigned short` and stores it in `us` by using the `num_get<char_type, istreambuf_iterator<char_type> >` facet from the locale contained in `this`. The return value is `*this`. Failures are indicated by the state of `*this`.

```
basic_istream<char_type,traits_type>&
operator>>(int& i);
```

Extracts a value of type `int` and stores it in `i` by using the `num_get<char_type, istreambuf_iterator<char_type> >` facet from the locale contained in `this`. The return value is `*this`. Failures are indicated by the state of `*this`.

```
basic_istream<char_type,traits_type>&
operator>>(unsigned int& ui);
```

Extracts a value of type `unsigned int` and stores it in `ui` by using the `num_get<char_type, istreambuf_iterator<char_type> >` facet from the locale contained in `this`. The return value is `*this`. Failures are indicated by the state of `*this`.

```
basic_istream<char_type,traits_type>&
operator>>(long& l);
```

Extracts a value of type `long` and stores it in `l` by using the `num_get<char_type, istreambuf_iterator<char_type> >` facet from the locale contained in `this`. The return value is `*this`. Failures are indicated by the state of `*this`.

```
basic_istream<char_type,traits_type>&
operator>>(unsigned long& ul);
```

Extracts a value of type `unsigned long` and stores it in `ul` by using the `num_get<char_type, istreambuf_iterator<char_type> >` facet from the locale contained in `this`. The return value is `*this`. Failures are indicated by the state of `*this`.

```
basic_istream<char_type,traits_type>&
operator>>(float& f);
```

Extracts a value of type `float` and stores it in `f` by using the `num_get<char_type, istreambuf_iterator<char_type> >` facet from the locale contained in `this`. The return value is `*this`. Failures are indicated by the state of `*this`.

```
basic_istream<char_type,traits_type>&
operator>>(double& d);
```

Extracts a value of type `double` and stores it in `d` by using the `num_get<char_type, istreambuf_iterator<char_type> >` facet from the locale contained in `this`. The return value is `*this`. Failures are indicated by the state of `*this`.

```
basic_istream<char_type,traits_type>&
operator>>(long double& ld);
```

Extracts a value of type `long double` and stores it in `ld` by using the `num_get<char_type, istreambuf_iterator<char_type> >` facet from the locale contained in `this`. The return value is `*this`. Failures are indicated by the state of `*this`.

```
basic_istream<char_type,traits_type>&
operator>>(void*& p);
```

Extracts a value of type `void*` and stores it in `p` by using the `num_get<char_type, istreambuf_iterator<char_type> >` facet from the locale contained in `this`. The return value is `*this`. Failures are indicated by the state of `*this`.

```
basic_istream<char_type,traits_type>&
operator>>(basic_streambuf<char_type,traits_type>* sb);
```

Extracts characters of type `char_type` from the input stream `*this` and inserts them into the stream buffer `*sb`. Characters are extracted and inserted until extraction from the input stream `*this` or insertion into the stream buffer `*sb` fails, or some other error occurs. Failures are indicated by the state of `*this`. Return value is `*this`.

UNFORMATTED INPUT

```
streamsize gcount() const;
```

Returns the number of characters of type `char_type` extracted by the last call to an input member function of `this`.

```
int_type get();
```

Extracts a character of type `char_type` if one is available and returns it. Otherwise `ios_base::failure` is set in the state of `*this` and `traits_type::eof()` returned.

```
basic_istream<char_type,traits_type>&
get(char_type& c);
```

Extracts a character of type `char_type` if one is available and assigns it to `c`. Otherwise `ios_base::failure` is set in the state of `*this`. Return is always `*this`.

```
basic_istream<char_type,traits_type>&
get(char_type* s, streamsize n, char_type delim);
```

Extracts characters of type `char_type` and puts them into the array of type `char_type[]` whose first element is designated by s. Characters are transferred until extraction fails, n-1 characters are transferred, or the next input character equals `delim` (in which case the delimiter is not extracted). The end-of-string character is written behind the last character stored in the array. When no characters are transferred, failure will be indicated by the state of `*this`, and `*s` will contain only the end-of-string character. Return is `*this`.

```
basic_istream<char_type,traits_type>&
get(char_type* s, streamsize n);
```

Calls `this->get(s,n,widen('\n'))` and returns the result from this call.

```
basic_istream<char_type,traits_type>&
get(basic_streambuf<char_type,traits_type>* sb, char_type delim);
```

Extracts characters of type `char_type` and inserts them into the output stream associated to `*sb`. Characters are extracted and inserted until extraction or insertion fails, some other error occurs, or the next character to be extracted equals `delim` (in which case the delimiter is not extracted). Failures are indicated by the state of `*this`. Return value is `*this`.

```
basic_istream<char_type,traits_type>&
get(basic_streambuf<char_type,traits_type>* sb);
```

Calls `this->get(sb,widen('\n'))` and returns the result from this call.

```
basic_istream<char_type,traits_type>&
getline(char_type* s, streamsize n, char_type delim);
```

Extracts characters of type `char_type` and puts them into the array of type `char_type[]` whose first element is designated by s. Characters are transferred until extraction fails, n-1 characters are transferred, or the next input character equals `delim`. If the transfer is stopped because `delim` equals the next input character, this character is extracted but not stored in the array. The end-of-string character is written behind the last character stored in the array. When no characters are transferred, failure will be indicated by the state of `*this`, and `*s` will contain the end-of-string character. Return value is `*this`.

```
basic_istream<char_type,traits_type>&
getline(char_type* s, streamsize n);
```

Calls `this->getline(s,n,widen('\n'))` and returns the result from this call.

```
basic_istream<char_type,traits_type>&
ignore(streamsize n = 1, int_type delim = traits_type::eof());
```

Extracts characters of type `char_type` and discards them. Characters are extracted until extraction fails, n characters are extracted, or the next input character equals `delim` (in which case the delimiter is extracted). Failures are indicated by the state of `*this`. Return value is `*this`.

```
int_type peek();
```

Returns the next available character without consuming it, that is, returns `this->rdbuf()->sgetc()`, if the stream state is good, and returns `traits_type::eof()` otherwise.

```
basic_istream<char_type,traits_type>&
read(char_type* s, streamsize n);
```

Extracts n characters from the external input device, that is, extracts characters of type `char_type` and puts them into the array of type `char_type[]` whose first element is designated by s. Characters are transferred until extraction fails or n characters are transferred.
Failures are indicated by the state of `*this`. Return value is `*this`.

```
streamsize readsome(char_type* s, streamsize n);
```

Extracts up to n characters that are immediately available from the external input device, that is, extracts characters of type `char_type` and puts them into the array of type `char_type[]` whose first element is designated by s. Characters are transferred until an error occurs during extraction, n characters are transferred, or `this->rdbuf()-> in_avail == 0`. In other words, the number of characters transferred is `min(n, rdbuf()->in_avail())`.

`readsome()` differs from `read()` in that it does not wait for input (from a terminal for instance), but returns immediately.

Failures are indicated by the state of `*this`. If `this->rdbuf()-> in_avail == 0` stops the transfer of characters, `ios_base::eofbit` is set. Returns the number of characters transferred.

MANIPULATOR EXTRACTORS

```
basic_istream<char_type,traits_type>&
operator>>(basic_istream<char_type,traits_type>&
           (*pf) (basic_istream<char_type,traits_type>&));
```

Triggers the invocation of a manipulator function pf by calling `pf(*this)`. Returns `*this`.

```
basic_istream<char_type,traits_type>&
operator>>(basic_ios<char_type,traits_type>&
           (*pf) (basic_ios<char_type,traits_type>&));
```

Triggers the invocation of a manipulator function pf by calling `pf(*this)`. Returns `*this`.

```
basic_istream<char_type,traits_type>&
operator>>(ios_base& (*pf) (ios_base&));
```

Triggers the invocation of a manipulator function `pf` by calling `pf(*this)`. Returns `*this`.

BUFFER MANAGEMENT

```
basic_istream<char_type,traits_type>& putback(char_type c)
```

Inserts `c` into the putback sequence by calling `this->rdbuf()->putback(c)`. Failures are indicated by the state of `*this`. Returns `*this`.

```
int sync()
```

Calls `this->rdbuf()->pubsync()` to synchronize `this` with the external device. Returns −1, if `this->rdbuf()==0`. If `this->rdbuf()->pubsync()` returns −1, `ios_base::badbit` is set.

```
basic_istream<char_type,traits_type>& unget()
```

Makes the last character extracted from `this` available again by calling `this->rdbuf()->unget()`. Failures are indicated by the state of `*this`. Returns `*this`.

POSITIONING

```
basic_istream<char_type,traits_type>&
seekg(ios_base::pos_type pos);
```

Repositions `this` to the location designated by pos, by calling `this->rdbuf()->pubseekpos(pos)`. Failures are indicated by the state of `*this`. Returns `*this`.

```
basic_istream<char_type,traits_type>&
seekg(ios_base::off_type off, ios_base::seekdir dir);
```

Repositions `this` to the location designated by `off` and `dir`, by calling `this->rdbuf()->pubseekpos(off,dir)`. Failures are indicated by the state of `*this`. Returns `*this`.

```
pos_type tellg();
```

If `this->fail()==true`, returns `pos_type(-1)`. Otherwise gets the stream positions by calling `this->rdbuf()->pubseekoff(0,ios_base::cur,ios_base::in)` and returns the result from this call.

GLOBAL FUNCTIONS
CHARACTER EXTRACTION

```
template<class charT, class traits>
  basic_istream<charT,traits>& operator>>
      (basic_istream<charT,traits>& is, charT& c);
```

Extracts a character of type `charT` and stores it in `c`. The return value is `*is`. Failures are indicated by the state of `is`.

```
template<class traits>
  basic_istream<char,traits >& operator>>
      (basic_istream<char,traits >& is, unsigned char& c);
```

Extracts a character of type `unsigned char` and stores it in `c`. The return value is `*is`. Failures are indicated by the state of `is`.

```
template<class traits>
  basic_istream<char,traits>& operator>>
      (basic_istream<char,traits>& is, signed char& c);
```

Extracts a character of type `signed char` and stores it in `c`. The return value is `*is`. Failures are indicated by the state of `is`.

```
template<class charT, class traits>
  basic_istream<charT,traits>& operator>>
      (basic_istream<charT,traits>& is, charT* s);
```

Extracts characters of type `charT` and puts them into the array of type `charT[]` whose first element is designated by `s`. Characters are transferred until extraction fails, `is.width()-1` characters are transferred (if `is.width() >0`), or the next input character is a whitespace character. The end-of-string character is written behind the last character stored in the array. When no characters are transferred, failure will be indicated by the state of `*this`, and `*s` will contain only the end-of-string character. The operation calls `is.width(0)` in any case. Returns `*this`.

```
template<class traits>
  basic_istream<char,traits>& operator>>
      (basic_istream<char,traits>& is, unsigned char* s);
```

Extracts characters of type `unsigned char` and puts them into the array of type `unsigned char[]` whose first element is designated by `s`. Characters are transferred until extraction fails, `is.width()-1` characters are transferred (if `is.width()` >0), or the next input character is a whitespace character. The end-of-string character is written behind the last character stored in the array. When no characters are transferred, failure will be indicated by the state of `*this`, and `*s` will contain only the end-of-string character. The operation calls `is.width(0)` in any case. Returns `*this`.

```
template<class traits>
  basic_istream<char,traits_type>& operator>>
    (basic_istream<char,traits_type>& is, signed char* s);
```

Extracts characters of type `signed char` and puts them into the array of type `signed char[]` whose first element is designated by s. Characters are transferred until extraction fails, `is.width()-1` characters are transferred (if `is.width()` >0), or the next input character is a whitespace character. The end-of-string character is written behind the last character stored in the array. When no characters are transferred, failure will be indicated by the state of `*this`, and `*s` will contain only the end-of-string character. The operation calls `is.width(0)` in any case. Returns `*this`.

INPUT STREAM MANIPULATORS

```
template<class traits>
  basic_istream<char,traits_type>& ws
    (basic_istream<char,traits_type>& is);
```

Manipulator that extracts whitespace characters from the input stream `is`. Extraction stops when the next character in the input stream `is` is not a whitespace character or no more characters are available. If the extraction stops because no more characters are available, `ios_base::eofbit` is set for `is`.

basic_istringstream<charT,traits,Allocator>

CLASS TEMPLATE

```
template <class charT, class traits = char_traits<charT>,
                                class Allocator = allocator<charT>  >
```

class **basic_istringstream**
header: **<sstream>**
base class(es): **basic_istream**<charT, traits>

DESCRIPTION

basic_istringstream is an input stream that is associated with an object of type basic_string<charT,traits,Allocator>.

SYNOPSIS

```
namespace std {
 template <class charT, class traits = char_traits<charT>,
          class Allocator = allocator<charT> >
 class basic_istringstream : public basic_istream<charT,traits> {
 public:
   //  type definitions:
   typedef charT                   char_type;
   typedef typename traits::int_type int_type;
   typedef typename traits::pos_type pos_type;
   typedef typename traits::off_type off_type;
   typedef traits                  traits_type;
   // constructors:
   explicit basic_istringstream(ios_base::openmode which = ios_base::in);
   explicit basic_istringstream(
                    const basic_string<charT,traits,Allocator>& str,
                    ios_base::openmode which = ios_base::in);
   // string stream operations:
   basic_stringbuf<charT,traits,Allocator>* rdbuf() const;
   basic_string<charT,traits,Allocator> str() const;
   void str(const basic_string<charT,traits,Allocator>& s);
 private:
   //  basic_stringbuf<charT,traits,Allocator> sb;    exposition only
 };
}
```

iostreams

PUBLIC MEMBER FUNCTIONS

explicit **basic_istringstream** (ios_base::openmode mode = ios_base::in);

Constructs an object of type basic_istringstream<charT,traits,Allocator>.

explicit **basic_istringstream**
 (const basic_string<char_type,traits_type,Allocator>& s,
  ios_base::openmode mode = ios_base::in);

Constructs an object of type basic_istringstream<charT,traits,Allocator> and initializes its string stream buffer with a call to basic_stringbuf<charT,traits,Allocator>(s, mode | ios_base::in).

STRING STREAM OPERATIONS

basic_stringbuf<char_type,traits_type,Allocator>* **rdbuf**() const;

Returns the pointer to the private member of type basic_stringbuf<char_type,traits_type,Allocator>. Note the subtle difference from basic_ios<charT,traits>::rdbuf(). basic_ios<charT,traits>::rdbuf() returns the pointer to a stream buffer that is maintained in basic_ios<charT,traits>. For a newly constructed object, both functions return the same pointer. After a call to basic_ios<charT,traits>::rdbuf(basic_stringbuf<char_type, traits_type,Allocator>* sb), basic_ios<charT,traits>::rdbuf() returns the newly set pointer, while basic_istringstream<charT,traits>::rdbuf() keeps returning the pointer to its own private member.

basic_string<char_type,traits_type,Allocator> **str**();

Returns the string contained in the string stream buffer by calling this->rdbuf->str().

void **str**(basic_string<char_type,traits_type,Allocator>& s);

Sets the string contained in the string stream buffer to s by calling this->rdbuf->str(s).

basic_ofstream<charT,traits>

CLASS TEMPLATE

template <class charT, class traits = char_traits<charT> >
class **basic_ofstream**
header: **<fstream>**
base class(es): **basic_ostream**<charT, traits>

DESCRIPTION

basic_ofstream is an output stream that can be associated with a file.

SYNOPSIS

```
namespace std {
 template <class charT, class traits = char_traits<charT> >
 class basic_ofstream : public basic_ostream<charT,traits> {
 public:
   //  type definitions:
   typedef charT                     char_type;
   typedef typename traits::int_type int_type;
   typedef typename traits::pos_type pos_type;
   typedef typename traits::off_type off_type;
   typedef traits                    traits_type;
   //  constructors:
   basic_ofstream();
   explicit basic_ofstream(const char* s,
                       ios_base::openmode mode = ios_base::out);
   //  file stream operations:
   basic_filebuf<charT,traits>* rdbuf() const;
   bool is_open();
   void open(const char* s, ios_base::openmode mode = ios_base::out);
   void close();
 private:
   //  basic_filebuf<charT,traits> sb;        exposition only
 };
}
```

PUBLIC MEMBER FUNCTIONS

basic_ofstream();

Constructs an object of type basic_ofstream<charT, traits>.

explicit
basic_ofstream(const char* filename, ios_base::openmode mode = ios_base::out);

Constructs an object of type basic_ofstream<charT,traits>.
rdbuf()->open(filename, mode) is called. If this call fails, setstate(failbit) is
called.

FILE STREAM OPERATIONS

void **close**();

Calls rdbuf()->close(). If this call fails, setstate(failbit) is called.

bool **is_open**();

Calls rdbuf()->is_open() and returns the result.

void **open**(const char* filename, ios_base::openmode mode = ios_base::out);

Calls rdbuf()->open(). If this call fails, setstate(failbit) is called.

basic_filebuf<char_type,traits_type>* **rdbuf**() const;

Returns the pointer to the private member of type basic_filebuf<char_type,
traits_type>. Note the subtle difference from basic_ios<charT,traits>::
rdbuf(). basic_ios<charT,traits>::rdbuf() returns the pointer to a stream
buffer that is maintained in basic_ios<charT,traits>. For a newly constructed
object, both functions return the same pointer. After a call to basic_ios<charT,
traits>::rdbuf(basic_filebuf<char_type, traits_type>* sb), basic_ios
<charT,traits>::rdbuf() returns the newly set pointer while basic_ofstream
<charT,traits>::rdbuf() keeps returning the pointer to its own private member.

basic_ostream<charT,traits>

CLASS TEMPLATE

template <class charT, class traits = char_traits<charT> >
class **basic_ostream**
header: **<ostream>**
base class(es): **basic_ios**<charT, traits> (virtual)

DESCRIPTION

basic_ostream represents the abstraction of a general output stream.

SYNOPSIS

```
namespace std {
 template <class charT, class traits = char_traits<charT> >
 class basic_ostream : virtual public basic_ios<charT,traits> {
public:
  //  type definitions:
  typedef charT                    char_type;
  typedef typename traits::int_type int_type;
  typedef typename traits::pos_type pos_type;
  typedef typename traits::off_type off_type;
  typedef traits                   traits_type;
  //  prefix/suffix:
  class sentry;
  //  constructor/destructor:
  explicit basic_ostream(basic_streambuf<char_type,traits>* sb);
  virtual ~basic_ostream();
  //  formatted output:
  basic_ostream<charT,traits>& operator<<(bool n);
  basic_ostream<charT,traits>& operator<<(short n);
  basic_ostream<charT,traits>& operator<<(unsigned short n);
  basic_ostream<charT,traits>& operator<<(int n);
  basic_ostream<charT,traits>& operator<<(unsigned int n);
  basic_ostream<charT,traits>& operator<<(long n);
  basic_ostream<charT,traits>& operator<<(unsigned long n);
  basic_ostream<charT,traits>& operator<<(float f);
  basic_ostream<charT,traits>& operator<<(double f);
  basic_ostream<charT,traits>& operator<<(long double f);
  basic_ostream<charT,traits>& operator<<(const void* p);
  basic_ostream<charT,traits>& operator<<
       (basic_streambuf<char_type,traits>* sb);
```

```
// unformatted output:
basic_ostream<charT,traits>& put(char_type c);
basic_ostream<charT,traits>& write(const char_type* s, streamsize n);
// manipulator inserters:
basic_ostream<charT,traits>& operator<<
    (basic_ostream<charT,traits>& (*pf)(basic_ostream<charT,traits>&));
basic_ostream<charT,traits>& operator<<
    (basic_ios<charT,traits>& (*pf)(basic_ios<charT,traits>&));
basic_ostream<charT,traits>& operator<<
    (ios_base& (*pf)(ios_base&));
// buffer management:
basic_ostream<charT,traits>& flush();
// positioning:
pos_type tellp();
basic_ostream<charT,traits>& seekp(pos_type);
basic_ostream<charT,traits>& seekp(off_type, ios_base::seekdir);
};


// character inserters:
template<class charT, class traits>
basic_ostream<charT,traits>& operator<<(basic_ostream<charT,traits>&,
                                        charT);
template<class charT, class traits>
basic_ostream<charT,traits>& operator<<(basic_ostream<charT,traits>&,
                                        char);
template<class traits>
  basic_ostream<char,traits>& operator<<(basic_ostream<char,traits>&,
                                         char);
template<class traits>
  basic_ostream<char,traits>& operator<<(basic_ostream<char,traits>&,
                                         signed char);
template<class traits>
  basic_ostream<char,traits>& operator<<(basic_ostream<char,traits>&,
                                         unsigned char)
template<class charT, class traits>
  basic_ostream<charT,traits>& operator<<(basic_ostream<charT,traits>&,
                                          const charT*);
template<class charT, class traits>
  basic_ostream<charT,traits>& operator<<(basic_ostream<charT,traits>&,
                                          const char*);
template<class traits>
  basic_ostream<char,traits>& operator<<(basic_ostream<char,traits>&,
                                         const char*);
```

```
template<class traits>
  basic_ostream<char,traits>& operator<<(basic_ostream<char,traits>&,
                                         const signed char*);
template<class traits>
  basic_ostream<char,traits>& operator<<(basic_ostream<char,traits>&,
                                         const unsigned char*);
// output stream manipulators:
template <class charT, class traits>
  basic_ostream<charT,traits>& endl(basic_ostream<charT,traits>& os);
template <class charT, class traits>
  basic_ostream<charT,traits>& ends(basic_ostream<charT,traits>& os);
template <class charT, class traits>
  basic_ostream<charT,traits>& flush(basic_ostream<charT,traits>& os);
}
```

CLASS DEFINITIONS
PREFIX/SUFFIX

```
class sentry
{
 public:
  explicit sentry (basic_ostream<char_type,traits_type>& os);
  ~sentry();
  operator bool();
};
```

`sentry` defines a helper class that handles exception-safe preparations and follow-up treatment for formatted and unformatted output. The constructor calls `os.tie()->flush()`, if `os.tie()!=0`. If, after these operations, `is.good() == true`, `this->operator bool()` returns `true`, otherwise `false`. The constructor may also call `is.setstate(ios_base::failbit)` to indicate an error. If `((os.flags() & ios_base::unitbuf)`, and there are no uncaught exceptions, the destructor calls `os.flush()`.

PUBLIC MEMBER FUNCTIONS

`explicit **basic_ostream** (basic_streambuf<char_type,traits_type>* sb);`

Constructs an object of type `basic_ostream<charT,traits>`. Additionally, calls `basic_ios::init(sb)` to initialize it.

If the pointer `sb` is zero or points to an invalid stream buffer object, the behavior of operations subsequently performed on the newly constructed stream is undefined.

virtual **~basic_ostream** ();

Destroys an object of type basic_ostream<charT, traits>. No operations are performed on the stream buffer, i.e., rdbuf() is not called, during destruction.

FORMATTED OUTPUT

basic_ostream<char_type, traits_type>&
operator<<(bool b);

Inserts a value of type bool, which is stored in b by using the num_put<char_type, ostreambuf_iterator<char_type> > facet from the locale contained by this. The return value is *this. Failures are indicated by the state of *this.

basic_ostream<char_type, traits_type>&
operator<<(short s);

Inserts a value of type short, which is stored in s by using the num_put<char_type, ostreambuf_iterator<char_type> > facet from the locale contained by this. The return value is *this. Failures are indicated by the state of *this.

basic_ostream<char_type, traits_type>&
operator<<(unsigned short us);

Inserts a value of type unsigned short, which is stored in us by using the num_put<char_type, ostreambuf_iterator<char_type> > facet from the locale contained by this. The return value is *this. Failures are indicated by the state of *this.

basic_ostream<char_type, traits_type>&
operator<<(int i);

Inserts a value of type int, which is stored in i by using the num_put<char_type, ostreambuf_iterator<char_type> > facet from the locale contained by this. The return value is *this. Failures are indicated by the state of *this.

basic_ostream<char_type, traits_type>&
operator<<(unsigned int ui);

Inserts a value of type unsigned int, which is stored in ui by using the num_put<char_type, ostreambuf_iterator<char_type> > facet from the locale contained by this. The return value is *this. Failures are indicated by the state of *this.

```
basic_ostream<char_type,traits_type>&
operator<<(long l);
```

Inserts a value of type long, which is stored in l by using the num_put<char_type, ostreambuf_iterator<char_type> > facet from the locale contained by this. The return value is *this. Failures are indicated by the state of *this.

```
basic_ostream<char_type,traits_type>&
operator<<(unsigned long ul);
```

Inserts a value of type unsigned long, which is stored in ul by using the num_put<char_type, ostreambuf_iterator<char_type> > facet from the locale contained by this. The return value is *this. Failures are indicated by the state of *this.

```
basic_ostream<char_type,traits_type>&
operator<<(float f);
```

Inserts a value of type float, which is stored in f by using the num_put<char_type, ostreambuf_iterator<char_type> > facet from the locale contained by this. The return value is *this. Failures are indicated by the state of *this.

```
basic_ostream<char_type,traits_type>&
operator<<(double d);
```

Inserts a value of type double, which is stored in d by using the num_put<char_type, ostreambuf_iterator<char_type> > facet from the locale contained by this. The return value is *this. Failures are indicated by the state of *this.

```
basic_ostream<char_type,traits_type>&
operator<<(long double ld);
```

Inserts a value of type long double, which is stored in ld by using the num_put<char_type, ostreambuf_iterator<char_type> > facet from the locale contained by this. The return value is *this. Failures are indicated by the state of *this.

```
basic_ostream<char_type,traits_type>&
operator<<(void* p);
```

Inserts a value of type void*, which is stored in p by using the num_put<char_type, ostreambuf_iterator<char_type> > facet from the locale contained by this. The return value is *this. Failures are indicated by the state of *this.

```
basic_ostream<char_type,traits_type>&
operator<<(basic_streambuf<char_type,traits_type>* sb);
```

Gets characters of type char_type from the stream buffer *sb and inserts them in the output stream *this. Characters are read from the stream buffer *sb until its end is reached, insertion to the output stream *this fails, or some other error occurs. Failures are indicated by the state of *this. Return value is *this.

UNFORMATTED OUTPUT

```
basic_ostream<char_type,traits_type>&
put(char_type c);
```

Inserts a character c of type char_type. Failures are indicated by the state of *this. Return value is *this.

```
basic_ostream<char_type,traits_type>&
write(const char_type* s, streamsize n);
```

Inserts characters of type char_type, which are obtained from successive locations of an array whose first element is designated by s. Characters are inserted until n characters are inserted or insertion fails. Failures are indicated by the state of *this. Return value is *this.

MANIPULATOR INSERTERS

```
basic_ostream<char_type,traits_type>&
operator<<(basic_ostream<char_type,traits_type>&
                (*pf) (basic_ostream<char_type,traits_type>&));
```

Triggers the invocation of a manipulator function pf by calling pf(*this). Returns *this.

```
basic_ostream<char_type,traits_type>&
operator<<(basic_ios<char_type,traits_type>&
           (*pf) (basic_ios<char_type,traits_type>&));
```

Triggers the invocation of a manipulator function pf by calling `pf(*this)`. Returns `*this`.

```
basic_ostream<char_type,traits_type>&
operator<<(ios_base& (*pf) (ios_base&));
```

Triggers the invocation of a manipulator function pf by calling `pf(*this)`. Returns `*this`.

BUFFER MANAGEMENT

```
basic_ostream<char_type,traits_type>& flush()
```

Calls `this->rdbuf()->pubsync()` to synchronize this with the external device. Returns −1, if `this->rdbuf()==0`. If `this->rdbuf()->pubsync()` returns −1, `ios_base::badbit` is set.

POSITIONING

```
basic_ostream<char_type,traits_type>&
seekp(pos_type pos);
```

Repositions this to the location designated by pos, by calling `this->rdbuf()->pubseekpos(pos)`. Failures are indicated by the state of `*this`. Returns `*this`.

```
basic_ostream<char_type,traits_type>&
seekp(off_type off, ios_base::seekdir dir);
```

Repositions this to the location designated by off and dir, by calling `this->rdbuf()->pubseekpos(off,dir)`. Failures are indicated by the state of `*this`. Returns `*this`.

```
pos_type tellp();
```

If `this->fail()==true`, returns `pos_type(-1)`. Otherwise gets the stream positions by calling `this->rdbuf()->pubseekoff(0,ios_base::cur,ios_base::out)` and returns the result from this call.

GLOBAL FUNCTIONS

```
template<class charT, class traits>
basic_ostream<charT,traits >& operator<<
      (basic_ostream<charT,traits >& os, charT c);
```

Inserts a character c of type charT the output stream os. Padding is done according to the adjustfield setting in os. After the insertion, width(0) is called. The return value is *os. Failures are indicated by the stream state of os.

```
template<class charT, class traits>
basic_ostream<charT,traits>& operator<<
      (basic_ostream<charT,traits>& os, char c);
```

Inserts a character c of type char into the output stream os. In case c has type char and the character type of the stream is not char, then the character to be inserted is os.widen(c); otherwise the character is c. Padding is done according to the adjustfield setting in os. After the insertion, width(0) is called. The return value is *os. Failures are indicated by the stream state of os.

```
template<class traits>
basic_ostream<char,traits>& operator<<
      (basic_ostream<char,traits>& os, char c);
```

Inserts a character c of type char into the output stream os. Padding is done according to the adjustfield setting in os. After the insertion, width(0) is called. The return value is *os. Failures are indicated by the stream state of os.

```
template<class traits>
basic_ostream<char,traits>& operator<<
      (basic_ostream<char,traits>& os, signed char c);
```

Inserts a character c of type signed char into the output stream os. Padding is done according to the adjustfield setting in os. After the insertion, width(0) is called. The return value is *os. Failures are indicated by the stream state of os.

```
template<class traits>
basic_ostream<char,traits>& operator<<
      (basic_ostream<char,traits>& os, unsigned char c);
```

Inserts a character c of type char into the output stream os. Padding is done according to the adjustfield setting in os. After the insertion, width(0) is called. The return value is *os. Failures are indicated by the stream state of os.

```
template<class charT, class traits>
basic_ostream<charT,traits>& operator<<
     (basic_ostream<charT,traits>& os, const charT* s);
```

Inserts a character array of type `const charT[]` into the output stream `os`. The number of successive characters taken from the array is determined by `traits::length(s)`. (Note: The result of `char_traits<char>::length(s)` is the same as `strlen(s)`.)

Padding is done according to the `adjustfield` setting in `os`. After the insertion, `width(0)` is called. The return value is `*os`. Failures are indicated by the stream state of `os`.

```
template<class charT, class traits>
basic_ostream<charT,traits>& operator<<
     (basic_ostream<charT,traits>& os, const char* s);
```

Inserts a character array of type `const char[]` into the output stream `os`. The number of successive characters taken from the array is determined by `traits::length(s)`. (Note: The result of `char_traits<char>::length(s)` is the same as `strlen(s)`.) In case `s` is a sequence of characters of type `char` and the character type of the stream is not `char`, then the characters to be inserted are widened using `as.widen()`.

Padding is done according to the `adjustfield` setting in `os`. After the insertion, `width(0)` is called. The return value is `*os`. Failures are indicated by the stream state of `os`.

```
template<class traits>
basic_ostream<char,traits>& operator<<
     (basic_ostream<char,traits>& os, const char* s);
```

Inserts a character array of type `const char[]` into the output stream `os`. The number of successive characters taken from the array is determined by `traits::length(s)`. (Note: The result of `char_traits<char>::length(s)` is the same as `strlen(s)`.) In case `s` is a sequence of characters of type `char` and the character type of the stream is not `char`, then the characters to be inserted are widened using `as.widen()`.

Padding is done according to the `adjustfield` setting in `os`. After the insertion, `width(0)` is called. The return value is `*os`. Failures are indicated by the stream state of `os`.

```
template<class traits>
basic_ostream<char,traits>& operator<<
   (basic_ostream<char,traits>& os, const signed char* s);
```

Inserts a character array of type `const signed char[]` into the output stream `os`. The number of successive characters taken from the array is determined by `traits::length(s)`. (Note: The result of `char_traits<char>::length(s)` is the same as `strlen(s)`.)

Padding is done according to the `adjustfield` setting in `os`. After the insertion, `width(0)` is called. The return value is `*os`. Failures are indicated by the stream state of `os`.

```
template<class traits>
basic_ostream<char,traits>& operator<<
   (basic_ostream<char,traits>& os, const unsigned char* c);
```

Inserts a character array of type `const unsigned char[]` into the output stream `os`. The number of successive characters taken from the array is determined by `traits::length(s)`. (Note: The result of `char_traits<char>::length(s)` is the same as strlen(s).)

Padding is done according to the `adjustfield` setting in `os`. After the insertion, `width(0)` is called. The return value is `*os`. Failures are indicated by the stream state of `os`.

OUTPUT STREAM MANIPULATORS

```
template<class traits>
  basic_ostream<char,traits_type>& endl
     (basic_ostream<char,traits_type>& os);
```

Manipulator that calls first `os.put(os.widen('\n'))` and then `os.flush()`. Returns `os`.

```
template<class traits>
  basic_ostream<char,traits_type>& ends
     (basic_ostream<char,traits_type>& os);
```

Manipulator that calls `os.put(traits::eos())` and returns `os`.

```
template<class traits>
  basic_ostream<char,traits_type>& flush
     (basic_ostream<char,traits_type>& os);
```

Manipulator that calls `os.flush()` and returns `os`.

iostreams

basic_ostringstream<charT,traits,Allocator>

CLASS TEMPLATE

```
template <class charT, class traits = char_traits<charT>,
          class Allocator = allocator<charT>  >
class basic_ostringstream
```
header: **<sstream>**
base class(es): **basic_ostream**<charT, traits>

DESCRIPTION

basic_ostringstream is an output stream that is associated with an object of type
basic_string<charT,traits,Allocator>.

SYNOPSIS

```
namespace std {
  template <class charT, class traits = char_traits<charT>,
          class Allocator = allocator<charT> >
  class basic_ostringstream : public basic_ostream<charT,traits> {
  public:
    //  type definitions:
    typedef charT                       char_type;
    typedef typename traits::int_type int_type;
    typedef typename traits::pos_type pos_type;
    typedef typename traits::off_type off_type;
    //  constructors/destructor:
    explicit basic_ostringstream
      (ios_base::openmode which = ios_base::out);
    explicit basic_ostringstream
     (const basic_string<charT,traits,Allocator>& str,
      ios_base::openmode which = ios_base::out);
    //  string stream operations:
    basic_stringbuf<charT,traits,Allocator>* rdbuf() const;
    basic_string<charT,traits,Allocator> str() const;
    void str(const basic_string<charT,traits,Allocator>& s);
  private:
    //  basic_stringbuf<charT,traits,Allocator> sb;   exposition only
  };
}
```

PUBLIC MEMBER FUNCTIONS

```
explicit
```
basic_ostringstream (ios_base::openmode mode = ios_base::out);

Constructs an object of type basic_ostringstream<charT,traits,Allocator>.

```
explicit
```
basic_ostringstream
```
  (const basic_string<char_type,traits_type,Allocator>& s,
   ios_base::openmode mode = ios_base::out);
```

Constructs an object of type basic_ostringstream<charT,traits,Allocator> and initializes its string stream buffer with a call to basic_stringbuf<charT, traits,Allocator>(s, mode | ios_base::out).

STRING STREAM OPERATIONS

basic_stringbuf<char_type,traits_type,Allocator>* **rdbuf**() const;

Returns the pointer to the private member of type basic_stringbuf <char_type,traits_type,Allocator>. Note the subtle difference from basic_ios<charT,traits>::rdbuf(). basic_ios<charT,traits>::rdbuf() returns the pointer to a stream buffer that is maintained in basic_ios <charT,traits>. For a newly constructed object, both functions return the same pointer. After a call to basic_ios<charT,traits>::rdbuf (basic_stringbuf<char_type, traits_type,Allocator>* sb), basic_ios <charT,traits>::rdbuf() returns the newly set pointer, while basic_ostringstream<charT,traits,Allocator>::rdbuf() keeps returning the pointer to its own private member.

basic_string<char_type,traits_type,Allocator> **str**();

Returns the string contained in the string stream buffer by calling this->rdbuf-> str().

void **str**(basic_string<char_type,traits_type,Allocator>& s);

Sets the string contained in the string stream buffer to s by calling this->rdbuf-> str(s).

basic_streambuf<charT,traits>[2]

CLASS TEMPLATE

```
template <class charT, class traits = char_traits<charT> >
class basic_streambuf
header: <streambuf>
base class(es): [none]
```

DESCRIPTION

basic_streambuf represents an abstraction that handles the bidirectional transfer of characters of type charT between a stream and an external device. It provides the functionality to buffer the characters during transfer. No objects can be instantiated from any basic_streambuf template class, because no public constructor is defined; all constructors are protected.

SYNOPSIS

```
namespace std {
 template <class charT, class traits = char_traits<charT> >
 class basic_streambuf {
 public:
  //  type definitions:
  typedef charT char_type;
  typedef typename traits::int_type int_type;
  typedef typename traits::pos_type pos_type;
  typedef typename traits::off_type off_type;
  typedef traits traits_type;
  // destructor:
  virtual ~basic_streambuf();
  //  get area:
  streamsize in_avail();
  int_type snextc();
  int_type sbumpc();
  int_type sgetc();
  streamsize sgetn(char_type* s, streamsize  n);
```

---

2. In the description of basic_streambuf member functions below, we deviate from the notational conventions that we use throughout the rest of the reference section. For the member functions that give access to the pointers to the get and put area we omit the this pointer; that is, we simply say (gptr()!= 0 && eback()<gptr()) instead of (this->gptr() != 0 && this->eback() < this->gptr()). This is done to facilitate readability of the descriptions.

```
//  putback:
int_type sputbackc(char_type c);
int_type sungetc();
//  put area:
int_type   sputc(char_type c);
streamsize sputn(const char_type* s, streamsize  n);
//  buffer management:
basic_streambuf<char_type,traits>* pubsetbuf(char_type* s,streamsize n);
int pubsync();
//  positioning:
pos_type pubseekoff(off_type off, ios_base::seekdir way,
                  ios_base::openmode which=ios_base::in|ios_base::out);
pos_type pubseekpos(pos_type sp,
                  ios_base::openmode which=ios_base::in|ios_base::out);
//  locales:
locale    pubimbue(const locale &loc);
locale    getloc() const;
protected:
//  constructor:
basic_streambuf();
//  put area:
char_type* pbase() const;
char_type* pptr() const;
char_type* epptr() const;
void   pbump(int n);
void   setp(char_type* pbeg, char_type* pend);
virtual streamsize xsputn(const char_type* s, streamsize n);
virtual int_type   overflow (int_type c = traits::eof());
//  putback:
virtual int_type   pbackfail(int_type c = traits::eof());
//  get area:
char_type* eback() const;
char_type* gptr()  const;
char_type* egptr() const;
void   gbump(int n);
void   setg(char_type* gbeg, char_type* gnext, char_type* gend);
virtual int        showmanyc();
virtual streamsize xsgetn(char_type* s, streamsize n);
virtual int_type   underflow();
virtual int_type   uflow();
//  buffer management:
virtual basic_streambuf<char_type,traits>* setbuf(char_type* s,
                                                  streamsize n);
```

```
    // positioning:
    virtual pos_type seekoff(off_type off, ios_base::seekdir way,
              ios_base::openmode which = ios_base::in | ios_base::out);
    virtual pos_type seekpos(pos_type sp,
              ios_base::openmode which = ios_base::in | ios_base::out);
    virtual int sync();
    // locales:
    virtual void imbue(const locale &loc);
  };
}
```

PUBLIC MEMBER FUNCTIONS

virtual **~basic_streambuf** ();

Destroys an object of type basic_streambuf<charT,traits>.

GET AREA

streamsize **inavail**();

Returns the number of bytes available, i.e., egptr()-gptr(). If the get area does not exist or is empty (i.e., gptr()== 0 || eback()>= gptr()), this->showmanyc() is called and returns the result of this call.

int_type **sbumpc**();

Gets one character from the get area and returns this character converted to int_type, i.e., traits_type::to_int_type(*gptr()); additionally, the next pointer of the get area is incremented. If the get area does not exist or is empty (i.e., gptr()== 0 || eback()>= gptr()), this->uflow() is called and returns the result of this call. In contrast to sgetc(), sbumpc() additionally increments the get position in the input sequence, which means that it consumes the character.

int_type **sgetc**();

Gets one character from the get area and returns this character converted to int_type, i.e., traits_type::to_int_type(*gptr()). If the get area does not exist or is empty (i.e., gptr()== 0 || eback()>= gptr()), this->underflow() is called and returns the result of this call.

streamsize **sgetn**(char_type* s, streamsize n);

Calls this->xsgetn(s,n) and returns the result of this call.

iostreams

```
int_type snextc();
```

Calls the function `sbumpc()`. If it returns `traits_type::eof()`, the return value is `traits_type::eof()`. Otherwise `this->sgetc()` is called and the result of this call is returned; i.e., it gets the next character from the input sequence, in contrast to `sgetc()`, which gets the current character.

PUTBACK

```
int_type sputbackc(char_type c);
```

If a putback position is available (i.e., `gptr() != 0 && eback()<gptr()`) and the character in the putback position (i.e., `*gptr()[-1]`) is equal to `c`, the next pointer of the get area is decremented and the element the next pointer is now pointing to is returned. The element is converted to `int_type` before the return. Otherwise calls `this->backfail(traits::to_int_type(c))` and returns the result of this call.

```
int_type sungetc();
```

If a putback position is available (i.e., `gptr() != 0 && eback()<gptr()`), the next pointer of the get area is decremented and the element the next pointer is now pointing to is returned. The element is converted to `int_type` before the return. Otherwise calls `this->backfail()` and returns the result of this call.

PUT AREA

```
int_type sputc(char_type c);
```

Stores the character c in the put area, e.g., `(*pptr()) = c`. If the put area does not exist or is full (i.e., `pptr()==0 || pptr()==epptr()`), `this->overflow()` is called and the result of this call returned.

```
streamsize sputn(const char_type* s, streamsize n);
```

Calls `this->xsputn(s,n)` and returns the result of this call.

BUFFER MANAGEMENT

```
basic_streambuf<char_type,traits_type>*
pubsetbuf(char_type* s, streamsize n);
```

Calls `this->setbuf(s,n)` and returns the result of this call.

```
int pubsync();
```

Calls `this->sync()` and returns the result of this call.

POSITIONING

```
pos_type
pubseekoff(off_type off, ios_base::seekdir dir,
ios_base::openmode mode = ios_base::in | ios_base::out);
```

Calls `this->seekoff(off,dir,mode)` and returns the result of this call.

```
pos_type
pubseekpos(pos_type pos,
ios_base::openmode mode = ios_base::in | ios_base::out);
```

Calls `this->seekpos(pos,mode)` and returns the result of this call.

LOCALES

```
locale getloc() const;
```

Returns the locale of `this`.

```
locale pubimbue(const locale& loc);
```

Sets the locale of `this` to `loc` and calls `this->imbue(loc)`. The return value is the previously used locale.

PROTECTED MEMBER FUNCTIONS

```
basic_streambuf();
```

Constructs an object of type `basic_streambuf<charT,traits>`, which contains a locale that is a copy of the global locale at the point of construction, constructed by `locale()`.

PUT AREA

```
char_type* epptr() const;
```

Returns the end pointer of the put area.

```
virtual int_type overflow(int_type c = traits_type::eof());
```

Handles the situation where c cannot be inserted into the put area, because the put area does not exist or is full (i.e., `pptr() == 0 || pptr() >= epptr()`). The concrete handling depends on the specific derived class. `basic_streambuf<charT,traits>::overflow()` always returns the failure indication `traits_type::eof()`.

```
char_type* pbase() const;
```

Returns the begin pointer of the put area.

```
void pbump(int n);
```

Advances the next pointer of the put array by n. n can also be negative. If `pptr()+n >= epptr()`, the behavior is undefined. The purpose is that derived classes, which manipulate the put area themselves, adjust the next.

```
char_type* pptr() const;
```

Returns the next pointer of the put area.

```
void setp(char_type* beg, char_type *end);
```

Sets the begin pointer and the next pointer to beg and the end pointer to end. This function is typically used by derived classes when they supply a buffer area.

```
virtual streamsize xsputn(const char_type* s, streamsize n);
```

Writes n successive characters beginning with (`*s`) to the put area. It behaves like repeated calls to `this->sputc()`. Writing stops when either n characters have been written or a call to `this->sputpc()` would return `traits_type::eof()`. The function returns the number of written characters.

PUTBACK

```
virtual int_type pbackfail(int_type c = traits_type::eof());
```

Makes a character available that will be returned with the next call to `this->sgetc()`. If c is not equal to `traits_type::eof()`, c is the character to be made available. If c is equal to `traits_type::eof()`, the character that is in the input sequence before the characters that are already in the input area is the character to be made available. The details of *making the character available* are implementation-specific. Returns `traits_type::eof()` if the character cannot be made available. The concrete handling depends on the specific derived class. `basic_streambuf<charT,traits>::` `pbackfail()` always returns the failure indication `traits_type::eof()`.

GET AREA

`char_type* ` **`eback`**`() const;`

Returns the begin pointer of the get area.

`char_type* ` **`egptr`**`() const;`

Returns the end pointer of the get area.

`void ` **`gbump`**`(int n);`

Advances the next pointer of the get array by n. n can also be negative. If `eback()` `>=` `gptr()` `-n`, the behavior is undefined. The purpose is that derived classes, which manipulate the get area themselves, adjust the next pointer accordingly.

`char_type* ` **`gptr`**`() const;`

Returns the next pointer of the get area.

`void ` **`setg`**`(char_type* beg, char_type* next, char_type *end);`

Sets the begin pointer to `beg`, the next pointer to `next`, and the end pointer to `end`. This function is typically used by derived classes when they supply a buffer area.

`virtual int ` **`showmanyc`**`();`

Returns an estimation of the number of characters that are at least available from the input sequence or −1. If the operation returns −1, calls to `this->underflow()` and `this->uflow()` will fail. Otherwise the returned number of characters can be made available by one or more calls to `this->underflow()` or `this->uflow()`. The concrete handling depends on the specific derived class.

> `basic_streambuf<charT,traits>::showmanyc()` always returns 0.

`virtual int_type ` **`uflow`**`();`

Handles the situation where the get area does not exist or is empty (i.e., `gptr()` `== 0 ||` `gptr()` `>= egptr()`) and behaves like `underflow()`, but additionally increments the next pointer of the get area. The concrete handling depends on the specific derived class.

`basic_streambuf<charT,traits>::uflow()` always returns the failure indication `traits_type::eof()`.

`virtual int_type` **underflow**`()`;

Handles the situation where the get area does not exist or is empty (i.e., `gptr()==0 ||` `gptr() >= egptr()`). The concrete handling depends on the specific derived class.

`basic_streambuf<charT,traits>::underflow()` always returns the failure indication `traits_type::eof()`.

`virtual streamsize` **xsgetn**`(char_type* s, streamsize n)`;

Assigns n successive characters from the get area to s. It behaves like repeated calls to `this->bumpc()`. Assigning stops when either n characters have been assigned or a call to `this->bumpc()` would return `traits_type::eof()`. The function returns the number of assigned characters.

BUFFER MANAGEMENT

`virtual basic_streambuf<char_type,traits_type>*` **setbuf**`(char_type* s, streamsize n)`;

The concrete handling depends on the specific derived class.

`basic_streambuf<charT,traits>::setbuf()` does nothing and returns `this`. The purpose of this operation is to allow the specification of special functionality in derived classes.

`virtual int` **sync**`()`;

Synchronizes the put area with the input and output sequence, e.g., takes the characters from the put area and makes them available in the output and input sequence. Pointers to the put area are adjusted. In case of failure, the return value is −1. What constitutes failure is determined by each derived class. `basic_streambuf<charT,traits>::sync()` does nothing but return 0. The effect on the get area is implementation-specific.

POSITIONING

`virtual pos_type` **seekoff**`(off_type off, ios_base::seekdir dir,` `ios_base::openmode mode = ios_base::in | ios_base::out)`;

Alters the position in one (i.e., input or output) or both (i.e., input and output) sequences. The concrete handling depends on the specific derived class. `basic_streambuf<charT,`

```
traits>::seekoff()    always    returns    the    failure    indication
pos_type(off_type(-1)).
```

```
virtual pos_type
seekpos(pos_type pos,
ios_base::openmode mode = ios_base::in | ios_base::out);
```

Alters the position in one (i.e., input or output) or both (i.e., input and output) sequences. The concrete handling depends on the specific derived class. `basic_streambuf <charT,traits>::seekpos()` always returns the failure indication `pos_type(off_type(-1))`.

LOCALES

```
virtual void imbue(const locale& loc);
```

Allows an object of a derived class to be informed that the locale of `this` has changed, by overwriting this function in the respective derived class. `basic_streambuf <charT,traits>::imbue()` does nothing.

basic_stringbuf<charT,traits,Allocator>

CLASS TEMPLATE

```
template <class charT, class traits = char_traits<charT>,
   class Allocator = allocator<charT> >
class basic_stringbuf
```
header: **<sstream>**
base class(es): **basic_streambuf**<charT,traits>

DESCRIPTION

basic_stringbuf represents an abstraction that handles the bidirectional transfer of characters of type charT between a string stream and an array of type charT. It allows getting and setting an object of type basic_string<charT,traits,Allocator>, which corresponds to the characters in the internal buffer.

SYNOPSIS

```
namespace std {
 template <class charT, class traits = char_traits<charT>,
         class Allocator = allocator<charT> >
 class basic_stringbuf : public basic_streambuf<charT,traits> {
 public:
  // type definitions:
  typedef charT                    char_type;
  typedef typename traits::int_type int_type;
  typedef typename traits::pos_type pos_type;
  typedef typename traits::off_type off_type;
  typedef traits                   traits_type;
  // constructors:
  explicit basic_stringbuf(ios_base::openmode which
                                = ios_base::in | ios_base::out);
  explicit basic_stringbuf
              (const basic_string<charT,traits,Allocator>& str,
               ios_base::openmode which = ios_base::in | ios_base::out);
  // get and set:
  basic_string<charT,traits,Allocator> str() const;
  void str(const basic_string<charT,traits,Allocator>& s);
 protected:
  // overridden virtual functions:
  virtual int_type   underflow();
  virtual int_type   pbackfail(int_type c = traits::eof());
  virtual int_type   overflow (int_type c = traits::eof());
  virtual basic_streambuf<charT,traits>* setbuf(charT*, streamsize);
```

iostreams

```
virtual pos_type    seekoff(off_type off, ios_base::seekdir way,
                    ios_base::openmode which=ios_base::in|ios_base::out);
virtual pos_type    seekpos(pos_type sp,
                    ios_base::openmode which=ios_base::in|ios_base::out);
private:
// ios_base::openmode mode;        exposition only
};
}
```

PUBLIC MEMBER FUNCTIONS

```
explicit basic_stringbuf
(ios_base::openmode mode = ios_base::in | ios_base::out);
```

Constructs an object of class basic_stringbuf<charT,traits> and sets the mode data member to mode.

```
explicit basic_stringbuf
(const basic_string<char_type,traits_type,Allocator>& s,
 ios_base::openmode mode = ios_base::in | ios_base::out);
```

Constructs an object of class basic_stringbuf<charT,traits,Allocator> and sets the mode data member to mode. Additionally, copies s into the internal buffer and initializes the get and put area according to mode.

GET AND SET STRING

```
basic_string<char_type,traits_type,Allocator> str();
```

Returns an object of type basic_string<char_type,traits_type,Allocator>, whose content is equal to the characters in the internal buffer. If this is constructed only in input mode (i.e., ((mode & ios_base::in) == true) && ((mode & ios_base::out) == false)), the content of the returned object is equal to the get area. Otherwise the content of the returned object is equal to the put area.

```
void str(basic_string<char_type,traits_type,Allocator>& s);
```

Discards the previous content of the internal buffer and then copies s into the buffer. Initializes the get and put area according to the ios_base::openmode parameter that was passed to the constructor of this.

PROTECTED MEMBER FUNCTIONS

```
virtual int_type overflow(int_type c = traits_type::eof());
```

Allocates a new internal buffer that can hold the characters from the previous internal buffer plus one or more additional write positions. Copies the characters from the previous buffer to the newly allocated one and adjusts the pointers. Then calls `this->sputc(c)` and returns the result of this call.

```
virtual int_type pbackfail(int_type c = traits_type::eof());
```

Same functional description as for the base class. Redefined here to deal with the special constraints of a string buffer.

```
virtual pos_type
seekoff(off_type off, ios_base::seekdir dir,
  ios_base::openmode mode = ios_base::in | ios_base::out);
```

Alters the stream position in the following way. `mode` determines in which controlled sequence the position is altered:

if (mode & basic_ios::in) != 0, positions the input sequence,

if (mode & basic_ios::out) != 0, positions the output sequence,

if (mode & (basic_ios::in|basic_ios::out)) ==(basic_ios::in| basic_ios::out), and dir is either basic_ios::beg or basic_ios::end, positions both the input and the output sequence.

`dir` determines the way in which the position is altered; details are given in the table below:

CONDITION	NEW NEXT POINTER	CONSTRAINTS
dir == basic_ios::beg	begin_pointer + off	fails if off < 0, or begin_pointer + off > end_pointer
dir == basic_ios::cur	next_pointer + off	fails if next_pointer − begin_pointer +off < 0, or next_pointer + off > end_pointer
dir == basic_ios::end	end_pointer + off	fails if end_pointer − begin_pointer +off < 0, or off > 0

Returns pos_type(off_type(-1)) in case of failure. Otherwise the new position.

```
virtual pos_type
seekpos(pos_type pos,
    ios_base::openmode mode = ios_base::in | ios_base::out);
```

Alters the stream position within

> the input sequence, if (mode & basic_ios::in) != 0,

> the output sequence, if (mode & basic_ios::out) != 0,

to correspond to the stream position stored in pos. If pos is an invalid stream position, the operation fails. If pos has not been obtained by a previous successful call to one of the positioning functions (seekoff() seekpos(), tellg(), tellp()), the effect is undefined. Returns pos_type(off_type(-1)) in case of failure. Otherwise pos.


```
virtual int_type underflow();
```

Returns traits_type::to_int_type(*gptr()) if a read position is available in the get area, i.e., gptr() != 0 || gptr() < egptr(). Otherwise returns traits_type:: eof().

basic_stringstream<charT,traits,Allocator>

CLASS TEMPLATE

```
template <class charT, class traits = char_traits<charT>,
          class Allocator = allocator<charT>  >
class basic_stringstream
```
header: **<sstream>**
base class(es): **basic_iostream**<charT, traits>

DESCRIPTION

basic_stringstream is a bidirectional stream that is associated with an object of type basic_string<charT,traits,Allocator>.

SYNOPSIS

```
namespace std {
 template <class charT, class traits = char_traits<charT>,
           class Allocator = allocator<charT> >
 class basic_stringstream : public basic_iostream<charT,traits> {
 public:
  //  type definitions:
  typedef charT                    char_type;
  typedef typename traits::int_type int_type;
  typedef typename traits::pos_type pos_type;
  typedef typename traits::off_type off_type;
  //  constructors/destructors
  explicit basic_stringstream(
          ios_base::openmode which = ios_base::out|ios_base::in);
  explicit basic_stringstream(
          const basic_string<charT,traits,Allocator>& str,
          ios_base::openmode which = ios_base::out|ios_base::in);
  //  string stream operations:
  basic_stringbuf<charT,traits,Allocator>* rdbuf() const;
  basic_string<charT,traits,Allocator> str() const;
  void str(const basic_string<charT,traits,Allocator>& str);
 private:
  // basic_stringbuf<charT, traits>  sb ;  exposition only
 };
}
```

PUBLIC MEMBER FUNCTIONS

```
explicit
basic_stringstream (ios_base::openmode mode =
                    ios_base::in | ios_base::out);
```

Constructs an object of type basic_stringstream<charT,traits,Allocator>.

```
explicit
basic_stringstream
 (const basic_string<char_type,traits_type,Allocator>& s,
  ios_base::openmode mode = ios_base::in | ios_base::out);
```

Constructs an object of type basic_stringstream<charT,traits,Allocator> and initializes its string stream buffer by a call to basic_stringbuf<charT, traits,Allocator>(s, mode).

STRING STREAM OPERATIONS

```
basic_stringbuf<char_type,traits_type,Allocator>* rdbuf() const;
```

Returns the pointer to the private member of type basic_stringbuf<char_type, traits_type,Allocator>. Note the subtle difference from basic_ios <charT,traits>::rdbuf(). basic_ios<charT,traits>::rdbuf() returns the pointer to a stream buffer that is maintained in basic_ios<charT,traits>. For a newly constructed object, both functions return the same pointer. After a call to basic_ios<charT,traits>::rdbuf(basic_stringbuf<char_type, traits_type,Allocator>* sb) the function basic_ios<charT,traits>:: rdbuf() returns the newly set pointer, while basic_stringstream <charT,traits,Allocator>::rdbuf() keeps returning the pointer to its own private member.

```
basic_string<char_type,traits_type,Allocator> str();
```

Returns the string contained in the string stream buffer by calling this->rdbuf-> str().

```
void
str(basic_string<char_type,traits_type,Allocator>& s);
```

Sets the string contained in the string stream buffer to s by calling this->rdbuf-> str(s).

iostreams

fpos<stateT>

CLASS TEMPLATE

template <class stateT> class **fpos**
header: **<ios>**
base class(es): **[none]**

DESCRIPTION

fpos represents an abstraction that maintains the file position information and its associated conversion state.

SYNOPSIS

```
namespace std {
 template <class stateT> class fpos {
 public:
  stateT state() const;
  void state(stateT);
 private;
  // stateT st;  exposition only
 };
}
```

PUBLIC MEMBER FUNCTIONS

fpos(stateT s);

Constructs an object of type fpos<stateT> with a conversion state set to s.

stateT **state**()

Returns the conversion state that is related to the file position described by this.

void **state**(stateT s)

Sets the conversion state that is related to the file position described by this to s.

ios_base

class **ios_base**
header: **<ios>**
base class(es): **[none]**

DESCRIPTION

ios_base is the character-type and traits-type-independent base class for all streams. It encapsulates the common character-type-independent functionality of a stream, e.g., setting and getting formatting / parsing flags.

SYNOPSIS

```
namespace std {
      class ios_base {
      public:
        //  class definitions:
        class Init;
        class failure;
        //  type definitions and constants:
          //  format flags:
        typedef  T1  fmtflags;
        static const fmtflags boolalpha;
        static const fmtflags dec;
        static const fmtflags fixed;
        static const fmtflags hex;
        static const fmtflags internal;
        static const fmtflags left;
        static const fmtflags oct;
        static const fmtflags right;
        static const fmtflags scientific;
        static const fmtflags showbase;
        static const fmtflags showpoint;
        static const fmtflags showpos;
        static const fmtflags skipws;
        static const fmtflags unitbuf;
        static const fmtflags uppercase;
        static const fmtflags adjustfield;
        static const fmtflags basefield;
        static const fmtflags floatfield;
```

```
      // stream state:
typedef  T2  iostate;
static const iostate badbit;
static const iostate eofbit;
static const iostate failbit;
static const iostate goodbit;
      // open modes:
typedef  T3  openmode;
static const openmode app;
static const openmode ate;
static const openmode binary;
static const openmode in;
static const openmode out;
static const openmode trunc;
      // positioning:
typedef  T4  seekdir;
static const seekdir beg;
static const seekdir cur;
static const seekdir end;
      // callback events;
enum event { erase_event, imbue_event, copyfmt_event };


      // destructor
virtual ~ios_base();
      // format control operations:
fmtflags flags() const;
fmtflags flags(fmtflags fmtfl);
fmtflags setf(fmtflags fmtfl);
fmtflags setf(fmtflags fmtfll, fmtflags mask);
void unsetf(fmtfllags mask);
streamsize precision() const;
streamsize precision(streamsize prec);
streamsize width() const;
streamsize width(streamsize wide);
      // locales:
locale imbue(const locale& loc);
locale getloc() const;
      // user storage:
static int xalloc();
long&  iword(int index);
void*& pword(int index);
      // callbacks;
typedef void (*event_callback)(event, ios_base&, int index);
void register_callback(event_call_back fn, int index);
```

```
      //  miscellaneous:
      static bool sync_with_stdio(bool sync = true);
  protected:
      //  constructor:
      ios_base();
  private:
      //  static int index;   exposition only
      //  long* iarray;       exposition only
      //  void** parray;      exposition only
  };


//  ios_base manipulators:
    //  alpha representation of bool:
    ios_base& boolalpha  (ios_base& str);
    ios_base& noboolalpha(ios_base& str);
    //  integer base:
    ios_base& showbase   (ios_base& str);
    ios_base& noshowbase (ios_base& str);
    //  decimal point:
    ios_base& showpoint  (ios_base& str);
    ios_base& noshowpoint(ios_base& str);
    //  sign:
    ios_base& showpos    (ios_base& str);
    ios_base& noshowpos  (ios_base& str);
    //  skip whitespace:
    ios_base& skipws     (ios_base& str);
    ios_base& noskipws   (ios_base& str);
    //  uppercase:
    ios_base& uppercase  (ios_base& str);
    ios_base& nouppercase(ios_base& str);
    //  adjustfield:
    ios_base& internal   (ios_base& str);
    ios_base& left       (ios_base& str);
    ios_base& right      (ios_base& str);
    //  basefield:
    ios_base& dec        (ios_base& str);
    ios_base& hex        (ios_base& str);
    ios_base& oct        (ios_base& str);
    //  floatfield:
    ios_base& fixed      (ios_base& str);
    ios_base& scientific (ios_base& str);
}
```

CLASS DEFINITIONS

```
class Init
{
 public:
  Init();
  ~Init();
};
```

The class `Init` describes an object that controls the construction of the global objects `cin`, `cout`, `cerr`, `clog`, `wcin`, `wcout`, `wcerr` to take place before they are used by any function and the destruction to take place after they are used by any function. That means that the global stream objects can be used in constructors and destructors of static and global objects.

```
class failure
: public exception
{
  public:
    explicit failure (const string& msg);
    virtual ~failure();
    virtual const char* what() const;
};
```

All objects that are thrown as exceptions in the IOStreams library are instances of class `failure`. The member function `what()` returns a message that describes the exception.

TYPE DEFINITIONS

Implementation-specific bitmask types for

fmtflags,	which represent the formatting / parsing information
iostate,	which represents the stream state
openmode,	which represents modes for opening streams

Enumerated types:

```
enum seekdir
{ beg, cur, end };
```

which represents a specified position in a file stream,

```
enum event
{ erase_event, imbue_event, copyfmt_event };
```

which represents an event that causes a callback.

A type definition:

```
typedef  void (*event_callback)(event, ios_base&, int)
```

which represents a callback.

CONSTANT DEFINITIONS

The following list shows the predefined values and the effect gained by setting a certain value for the nested bitmask type fmtflags. The numeric values are implementation-dependent.

FORMAT FLAG CONSTANTS

boolalpha

Extracts and inserts values of bool type in alphabetical format. Relevant for parsing and formatting Boolean values.

showbase

Output contains a prefix that indicates the numeric base of an integral value. Relevant for formatting integral values and parsing and formatting monetary values.

showpoint

Output always contains a point character ('.') as radix separator for floating-point numbers independent of the actual locale. Relevant for formatting floating-point values.

showpos

Output contains a plus character ('+') in front of non-negative numeric output. Relevant for formatting numerical values.

skipws

Input operations skip leading whitespace characters. Relevant for all input operations.

unitbuf

Output is flushed after each output operation. Relevant for all output operations.

uppercase

Output operations replace certain lowercase letters with their respective uppercase equivalents. Relevant for formatting numerical values.

internal

Output contains fill characters at a designated point of certain output operation. Relevant for formatting numerical and monetary values.

left

Output contains fill characters at the left of certain output operations. Relevant for formatting of numerical and monetary values.

right

Output contains fill characters at the right of certain output operations. Relevant for formatting numerical and monetary values.

dec

Extracts and inserts values of any integer type in decimal base. Relevant for parsing and formatting integral values.

hex

Extracts and inserts values of any integer type in hexadecimal base. Relevant for parsing and formatting integral values.

oct

Extracts and inserts values of any integer type in octal base. Relevant for parsing and formatting integral values.

fixed

Output contains floating-point numbers in fixed-point notation. Relevant for formatting floating-point values.

scientific

Output contains floating-point numbers in scientific notation. Relevant for formatting floating-point values.

adjustfield

Defined as left|right|internal. Can be used as a mask to clear the output adjustment specification.

basefield

Defined as dec|oct|hex. Can be used as a mask to clear the numeric base specification.

floatfield

Defined as scientific|fixed. Can be used as a mask to clear the floating-point number output specification.

STREAM STATE CONSTANTS

The following list shows the predefined values and their semantics for the nested bitmask type iostate. The numeric values are implementation-dependent, except that goodbit must be 0.

badbit

Indicates an irrecoverable loss of integrity.

eofbit

Indicates that an input operation reached the end of the input sequence.

failbit

Indicates that either an input operation failed to read the expected input or an output operation was unable to generate the desired output.

goodbit

Indicates that everything is OK.

OPEN MODE CONSTANTS

The following list shows the predefined values and their semantics for the nested bitmask type `openmode`. The numeric values are implementation-dependent:

app

Seek to end before each write operation at system level.

ate

Seek to end immediately after opening.

binary

System-specific conversion, e.g., replacing "\r\n" with "\n", are suppressed.

in

Open for input.

out

Open for output.

trunc

Truncate an existing stream when opening.

POSITIONING CONSTANTS

`seekdir` is an enumerated type that represents a specified position used for seeking in a file stream. The following list shows its values and their semantics:

beg

Seek is relative to the beginning of the file stream.

cur

Seek is relative to the current position in the file stream.

end

Seek is relative to the end of the file stream.

CALLBACK EVENT

`event` is an enumerated type that represents an event that causes a callback. The following list shows its values and their semantics:

copyfmt_event

Indicates that new member data has been set by a call to `basic_ios<charT, traits>::copyfmt(basic_ios<charT,traits>&)`.

erase_event

Indicates that the stream is going to be destroyed or new member data are going to be set by a call to `basic_ios<charT,traits>::copyfmt(const basic_ios&)`.

imbue_event

Indicates that a new locale has been imbued to the stream.

PUBLIC MEMBER FUNCTIONS

~ios_base ();

Destroys an object of class `ios_base`. Each registered callback `cb` and its index `ix` are called as `(*cb)(erase_event,*this,ix)` at such a point during destruction that any ios_base member function called by `cb` has defined results.

FORMAT CONTROL OPERATIONS

`fmtflags` **flags**`() const;`

Returns the current control information for formatting and parsing.

```
fmtflags flags(fmtflags fmtfg);
```

Sets the control information for formatting and parsing to `fmtfg` and returns the previously used control information.

```
streamsize precision() const;
```

Returns the precision, e.g., the number of digits behind the radix separator, that should be generated for certain output operations.

```
streamsize precision(streamsize prec);
```

Sets the precision, e.g., the number of digits behind the radix separator, that should be generated for certain output operations. Returns the previously used precision.

```
fmtflags setf(fmtflags fmtfg);
```

Sets the control information for formatting and parsing to `fmtfg` and returns the previously used control information, i.e., has the same effect as calling `this->flags(fmtfg)` and returning the result from the call.

```
fmtflags setf(fmtflags fmtfg, fmtflags mask);
```

Clears the mask specified by `mask` in the control information for formatting and parsing and then sets the control information to `fmtfg & mask`, i.e., has the same effect as first calling `this->unsetf(mask)` and then `this->setf(fmtfg & mask)`. Returns the previously used control information.

```
void unsetf(fmtflags fmtfg);
```

Clears the mask specified by `fmtfg` in the control information for formatting and parsing, i.e., has the same effect as calling `this->flags((this->flags()) & (~fmtfg))`.

```
streamsize width() const;
```

Returns the minimum field width (counted as the number of characters) that should be generated for certain output operations.

```
streamsize width(streamsize prec);
```

Sets the minimum field width (counted as the number of characters) that should be generated for certain output operations. Returns the previously used minimum field width.

LOCALES

```
locale getloc() const;
```

If no locale was previously imbued, a copy of the global C++ locale is returned. Otherwise the previously imbued locale is returned.

```
locale imbue(const locale& loc);
```

Sets a locale used in the stream to `loc`. After that, all callbacks `cb` are called together with their index `ix` as `(*cb)(imbue_event,*this,ix)`. If no locale was previously imbued, a copy of the global C++ locale is returned. Otherwise the previously imbued locale is returned.

USER STORAGE

```
long& iword(int ix) const;
```

Used to get and set the user storage of type `long` at index `ix`.

```
void*& pword(int id) const;
```

Used to get and set the user storage of type `void*` at index `ix`.

```
static int xalloc();
```

Gets the next available index for the user storage.

CALLBACKS

```
void register_callback(event_callback cb, int ix);
```

Registers a callback function `cb` together with its index `ix`. The callback is invoked when either `ios_base::~ios_base()`, or `ios_base::imbue(locale&)`, or `basic_ios<charT, traits>::copyfmt(basic_ios<charT, traits>&)` is called.

iostreams

MISCELLANEOUS

`static bool` **`sync_with_stdio`**`(bool sync = true);`

If any input or output operation has occurred prior to this call, the effect is implementation-defined. Otherwise, called with a `false` argument, allows the standard C++ stream objects to operate independently of their standard C counterparts. This could improve efficiency. Called with a true argument, the standard C++ streams object are synchronized with their respective C counterparts, which is the default behavior. The return value indicates the previous setting.

PROTECTED MEMBER FUNCTIONS

`ios_base();`

Constructs an object of type `ios_base`. Its members have indeterminate values after the construction.

GLOBAL FUNCTIONS
FMTFLAGS MANIPULATORS

`ios_base&` **`boolalpha`**`(ios_base& s);`

Manipulator that calls `s.setf(ios_base::boolalpha)` and returns `s`.

`ios_base&` **`noboolalpha`**`(ios_base& s);`

Manipulator that calls `s.unsetf(ios_base::boolalpha)` and returns `s`.

`ios_base&` **`showbase`**`(ios_base& s);`

Manipulator that calls `s.setf(ios_base::showbase)` and returns `s`.

`ios_base&` **`noshowbase`**`(ios_base& s);`

Manipulator that calls `s.unsetf(ios_base::showbase)` and returns `s`.

`ios_base&` **`showpoint`**`(ios_base& s);`

Manipulator that calls `s.setf(ios_base::showpoint)` and returns `s`.

`ios_base&` **`noshowpoint`**`(ios_base& s);`

Manipulator that calls `s.unsetf(ios_base::showpoint)` and returns `s`.

`ios_base& `**`showpos`**`(ios_base& s);`

Manipulator that calls `s.setf(ios_base::showpos)` and returns s.

`ios_base& `**`noshowpos`**`(ios_base& s);`

Manipulator that calls `s.unsetf(ios_base::showpos)` and returns s.

`ios_base& `**`skipws`**`(ios_base& s);`

Manipulator that calls `s.setf(ios_base::skipws)` and returns s.

`ios_base& `**`noskipws`**`(ios_base& s);`

Manipulator that calls `s.unsetf(ios_base::skipws)` and returns s.

`ios_base& `**`uppercase`**`(ios_base& s);`

Manipulator that calls `s.setf(ios_base::uppercase)` and returns s.

`ios_base& `**`nouppercase`**`(ios_base& s);`

Manipulator that calls `s.unsetf(ios_base::uppercase)` and returns s.

`ios_base& `**`unitbuf`**`(ios_base& s);`

Manipulator that calls `s.setf(ios_base::unitbuf)` and returns s.

`ios_base& `**`nounitbuf`**`(ios_base& s);`

Manipulator that calls `s.unsetf(ios_base::unitbuf)` and returns s.

ADJUSTFIELD MANIPULATORS

`ios_base& `**`internal`**`(ios_base& s);`

Manipulator that calls `s.setf(ios_base::internal, ios_base::adjustfield)` and returns s.

`ios_base& `**`left`**`(ios_base& s);`

Manipulator that calls `s.setf(ios_base::left, ios_base::adjustfield)` and returns s.

`ios_base& `**`right`**`(ios_base& s);`

Manipulator that calls `s.setf(ios_base::right, ios_base::adjustfield)` and returns `s`.

BASEFIELD MANIPULATORS

`ios_base& `**`dec`**`(ios_base& s);`

Manipulator that calls `s.setf(ios_base::dec, ios_base::basefield)` and returns `s`.

`ios_base& `**`hex`**`(ios_base& s);`

Manipulator that calls `s.setf(ios_base::hex, ios_base::basefield)` and returns `s`.

`ios_base& `**`oct`**`(ios_base& s);`

Manipulator that calls `s.setf(ios_base::oct, ios_base::basefield)` and returns `s`.

FLOATFIELD MANIPULATORS

`ios_base& `**`fixed`**`(ios_base& s);`

Manipulator that calls `s.setf(ios_base::fixed, ios_base::floatfield)` and returns `s`.

`ios_base& `**`scientific`**`(ios_base& s);`

Manipulator that calls `s.setf(ios_base::scientific, ios_base::floatfield)` and returns `s`.

manipulators

HEADER

header: **<iomanip>**

FUNCTIONS

smanip **resetiosflags**(ios_base::fmtflags mask);
smanip **setiosflags**(ios_base::fmtflags mask);
smanip **setbase**(int base);
template<class charT> *smanip* **setfill**(charT c);
smanip **setprecision**(int n);
smanip **setw**(int n);

> *(see also basic_istream<charT,traits>, basic_ostream<charT,traits> and ios_base for manipulators without arguments)*

DESCRIPTION

The type *smanip* is implementation-specific, and the standard allows that it might be a different type for each manipulator.

Additional requirements are that, for a manipulator m that returns *smanip* and an object os of type basic_ostream<charT, traits>, the operation os << m(p); triggers the invocation of the functionality described for this specific manipulator; and for an object is of type basic_istream<charT, traits>, the operation is >> m(p); triggers the invocation of the functionality described for this specific manipulator.

smanip **resetiosflags**(ios_base::fmtflags mask);

Manipulator that calls s.setf(ios_base::fmtflags(0), mask) when applied to an object s of type ios_base.

smanip **setiosflags**(ios_base::fmtflags mask);

Manipulator that calls s.setf(mask) when applied to an object s of type ios_base.

smanip **setbase**(int base);

Manipulator that calls

```
s.setf(base ==  8 ? ios_base::oct :
       base == 10 ? ios_base::dec :
       base == 16 ? ios_base::hex :
       ios_base::fmtflags(0)
       ,ios_base::basefield)
```

when applied to an object s of type `ios_base`.

template<class charT> *smanip* **setfill**(charT c);

Manipulator that calls `s.fill(c)` when applied to an object s of type `basic_ios<charT>&`.

smanip **setprecision**(int n);

Manipulator that calls `s.precision(n)` when applied to an object s of type `ios_base&`.

smanip **setw**(int n);

Manipulator that calls `s.width(n)` when applied to an object s of type `ios_base&`.

4
STREAM ITERATORS

header file <iterator>

FILE NAME

<iterator>

DESCRIPTION

This header file contains all declarations for stream iterators and stream buffer iterators. It also contains all declarations for the container iterators.

SYNOPSIS

The synopsis contains only the part of the header file `<iterator>` that is relevant for stream and stream buffer iterators.

```
namespace std {
 //  primitives:
 template<class Iterator> struct iterator_traits;
 template<class T> struct iterator_traits<T*>;

 template<class Category, class T, class Distance = ptrdiff_t,
          class Pointer = T*, class Reference = T&>
   struct iterator;

 struct input_iterator_tag {};
 struct output_iterator_tag {};
 struct forward_iterator_tag: public input_iterator_tag {};
```

```
struct bidirectional_iterator_tag: public forward_iterator_tag {};
struct random_access_iterator_tag: public bidirectional_iterator_tag {};

//  stream iterators:
template <class T, class charT = char,class traits = char_traits<charT>,
          class Distance = ptrdiff_t>
  class istream_iterator;
template <class T, class charT, class traits, class Distance>
  bool operator==(const istream_iterator<T,charT,traits,Distance>& x,
                  const istream_iterator<T,charT,traits,Distance>& y);
template <class T, class charT, class traits, class Distance>
  bool operator!=(const istream_iterator<T,charT,traits,Distance>& x,
                  const istream_iterator<T,charT,traits,Distance>& y);

template <class T,class charT = char,class traits = char_traits<charT> >
  class ostream_iterator;

//  stream buffer iterators:
template<class charT, class traits = char_traits<charT> >
  class istreambuf_iterator;
template <class charT, class traits>
  bool operator==(const istreambuf_iterator<charT,traits>& a,
    const istreambuf_iterator<charT,traits>& b);
template <class charT, class traits>
  bool operator!=(const istreambuf_iterator<charT,traits>& a,
    const istreambuf_iterator<charT,traits>& b);

template <class charT, class traits = char_traits<charT> >
  class ostreambuf_iterator;
}
```

istreambuf_iterator<charT,traits>

CLASS TEMPLATE

```
template <class charT, class traits = char_traits<charT> >
class istreambuf_iterator
header: <iterator>
base class(es): iterator<input_iterator_tag, charT,
                         typename traits::off_type, charT*, charT&>
```

DESCRIPTION

istreambuf_iterator is an iterator that reads successive characters from the stream buffer for which it was constructed. When the istreambuf_iterator is dereferenced, it provides access to the current input character, if any. Each time istreambuf_iterator is incremented, it advances to the next input character. It is impossible to assign a character via an istreambuf_iterator. An istreambuf_iterator can be used only for one-pass algorithms.

If the end of stream is reached, the istreambuf_iterator becomes equal to the end-of-stream iterator value. Two end-of-stream iterators are always equal. An end-of-stream iterator is not equal to a nonend-of-stream iterator.

SYNOPSIS

```
namespace std {
    template<class charT, class traits = char_traits<charT> >
    class istreambuf_iterator
        : public iterator<input_iterator_tag, charT,
                          typename traits::off_type, charT*, charT&> {
    public:
        // type definitions:
        typedef charT                       char_type;
        typedef traits                      traits_type;
        typedef typename traits::int_type   int_type;
        typedef basic_streambuf<charT,traits> streambuf_type;
        typedef basic_istream<charT,traits>   istream_type;
        // class definition:
        // class proxy;                      exposition only
        // constructors:
        istreambuf_iterator() throw();
        istreambuf_iterator(istream_type& s) throw();
        istreambuf_iterator(streambuf_type* s) throw();
        istreambuf_iterator(const proxy& p) throw();
        // iterator operations:
        charT operator*() const;
```

stream iterators

```
                istreambuf_iterator<charT,traits>& operator++();
                proxy operator++(int);
                //  miscellaneous:
                bool equal(istreambuf_iterator& b);
            private:
                //  streambuf_type* sbuf_;    exposition only
            };
            //  global operators:
            template <class charT, class traits>
                bool operator==(const istreambuf_iterator<charT,traits>& a,
                                const istreambuf_iterator<charT,traits>& b);
            template <class charT, class traits>
                bool operator!=(const istreambuf_iterator<charT,traits>& a,
                                const istreambuf_iterator<charT,traits>& b);
        }
```

CLASS DEFINITIONS (FOR EXHIBITION ONLY)

```
template <class charT, class traits = char_traits<charT> >
class proxy
{
 public:
  charT operator*() { return keep_; }
 private:
  charT keep_;
  basic_streambuf<charT,traits>* sbuf_;
  proxy(charT c, basic_streambuf<charT,traits>* sbuf)
    : keep_(c), sbuf_(sbuf) {}
};
```

This nested class is for exposition only. An implementation of the
istreambuf_iterator is permitted to provide equivalent functionality without providing a class with this name.

Class `proxy` provides a temporary placeholder as the return value of the postincrement operator `operator++(int)`. It keeps the character pointed to by the previous value of the iterator for some possible future access to get the character and allows the creation of a `streambuf_iterator` from the `proxy` object that uses the `proxy` object's stream buffer.

PUBLIC MEMBER FUNCTIONS

istreambuf_iterator() throw();

Constructs the end-of-stream iterator.

istreambuf_iterator(istream_type& s) throw();

Constructs an `istreambuf_iterator` that uses the stream buffer of the stream s, namely `*(s.rdbuf())`. Constructs an end-of-stream iterator if the stream does not have a stream buffer, that is, if `s.rdbuf()` is 0.

istreambuf_iterator(streambuf_type* s) throw();

Constructs an `istreambuf_iterator` that reads from the stream buffer s. Constructs an end-of-stream iterator if the argument s is 0.

istreambuf_iterator(const proxy& p) throw();

Constructs an `istreambuf_iterator` that uses the proxy object's stream buffer.

An implementation of the `istreambuf_iterator` is permitted to provide equivalent functionality without providing a proxy class. In that case, the argument to this constructor must be of the same (or compatible) type as the return code of the postincrement operator `operator++(int)`.

ITERATOR OPERATIONS

charT **operator***() const;

Provides the current input character by returning the character obtained via the stream buffer member `sgetc()`.

The result of `operator*()` on an end of stream is undefined.

stream iterators

```
istreambuf_iterator<charT,traits>& operator++();
```

Advances the iterator advances to the next input character by calling the stream buffer member `sbumpc()`. If the end of stream is reached, the iterator becomes equal to the end-of-stream iterator value. Returns `*this`.

```
proxy operator++(int);
```

Advances the iterator advances to the next input character by calling the stream buffer member `sbumpc()`. If the end of stream is reached, the iterator becomes equal to the end-of-stream iterator value. Returns a proxy object constructed as `proxy(sbuf_->sbumpc(), sbuf_)`, where `sbuf_` is a pointer to the stream buffer from which the iterator reads.

An implementation of the `istreambuf_iterator` is permitted to provide equivalent functionality without providing a proxy class. In that case, an iterator (or iterator-like object) must be returned that provides the character read via `sbumpc()` when it is dereferenced and points to the previous stream buffer, that is, to the stream buffer before the read operation.

MISCELLANEOUS

```
bool equal(istreambuf_iterator& b);
```

Returns `true` if, and only if, both iterators are at end of stream, or if neither is at end of stream, regardless of what stream buffer object they use.

GLOBAL OPERATORS

```
template <class charT, class traits>
bool operator==
(const istreambuf_iterator<charT,traits>& a,
 const istreambuf_iterator<charT,traits>& b);
```

Returns `a.equal(b)`.

```
template <class charT, class traits>
bool operator!=
(const istreambuf_iterator<charT,traits>& a,
 const istreambuf_iterator<charT,traits>& b);
```

Returns `!a.equal(b)`.

istream_iterator<T,charT,traits,Distance >

CLASS TEMPLATE

```
template <class T, class charT = char, class traits = char_traits<charT>,
          class Distance = ptrdiff_t>
class istream_iterator
```
header: **<iterator>**

base class(es): **iterator**<input_iterator_tag, T, Distance, const T*, const T&>

DESCRIPTION

istream_iterator is an iterator that allows an input stream to be seen as a sequence of elements of type T. The iterator reads successive elements from the input stream for which it was constructed, using operator>>(istream&,T&) for reading.

After the iterator is constructed, and every time it is increased, the iterator reads a value of T and stores it internally. When the iterator is dereferenced, a const T& is returned. It is impossible to store things into istream iterators, which can be used only for one-pass algorithms.

If the end of stream is reached, the iterator becomes equal to the end-of-stream iterator value. Two end-of-stream iterators are always equal. An end-of-stream iterator is not equal to a nonend-of-stream iterator. Two nonend-of-stream iterators are equal when they are constructed from the same stream.

SYNOPSIS

```
namespace std {
 template <class T, class charT = char,
           class traits = char_traits<charT>,
           class Distance = ptrdiff_t>
   class istream_iterator
   : public iterator<input_iterator_tag,T,Distance,const T*,const T&> {
   public:
   //   type definitions:
    typedef charT char_type
    typedef traits traits_type;
    typedef basic_istream<charT,traits> istream_type;
   //   constructors/destructor:
    istream_iterator();
    istream_iterator(istream_type& s);
    istream_iterator(const istream_iterator<T,charT,traits,Distance>& x);
    ~istream_iterator();
```

stream iterators

```
    //  iterator operations:
    const T& operator*() const;
    const T* operator->() const;
    istream_iterator<T,charT,traits,Distance>& operator++();
    istream_iterator<T,charT,traits,Distance>  operator++(int);
  private:
    // basic_istream<charT,traits>* in_stream;        exposition only
    // T value;                                       exposition only
};
//  global operators:
template <class T, class charT, class traits, class Distance>
  bool operator==(const istream_iterator<T,charT,traits,Distance>& x,
                  const istream_iterator<T,charT,traits,Distance>& y);
template <class T, class charT, class traits, class Distance>
  bool operator!=(const istream_iterator<T,charT,traits,Distance>& x,
                  const istream_iterator<T,charT,traits,Distance>& y);
}
```

PUBLIC MEMBER FUNCTIONS

istream_iterator();

Constructs the end-of-stream iterator.

istream_iterator(istream_type& s);

Constructs an istream_iterator that reads from the stream s. The first value may be read during construction or the first time it is referenced.

istream_iterator (const istream_iterator<T,charT,traits,Distance>& x);

Constructs an istream_iterator that is a copy of x.

~istream_iterator();

Destroys the istream_iterator.

ITERATOR OPERATIONS

const T& **operator***() const;

Returns the internally stored value.

```
const T* operator->() const;
```

Returns a pointer to the internally stored value by returning `&(operator*())`.

```
istream_iterator<T,charT,traits,Distance>& operator++();
```

Reads the next value from the stream using `operator>>()` and stores the value internally. Returns `*this`.

```
istream_iterator<T,charT,traits,Distance> operator++(int);
```

Reads the next value from the stream using `operator>>()` and stores the value internally. Returns the previous `*this`, that is, a pointer to itself before the read operation.

GLOBAL OPERATORS

```
template <class T, class charT, class traits, class Distance>
bool operator==
(const istream_iterator<T,charT,traits,Distance>& x,
 const istream_iterator<T,charT,traits,Distance>& y);
```

Returns `true` if both iterators are end-of-stream iterators or both iterators were constructed from the same stream.

```
template <class T, class charT, class traits, class Distance>
bool operator!=
(const istream_iterator<T,charT,traits,Distance>& x,
 const istream_iterator<T,charT,traits,Distance>& y);
```

Returns `!(x == y)`.

iterator<Category,T,Distance,Pointer,Reference>

CLASS TEMPLATE

```
template<class Category, class T, class Distance = ptrdiff_t,
        class Pointer = T*, class Reference = T&>
struct iterator
```
header: **<iterator>**
base class(es): **[none]**

DESCRIPTION

iterator is the base class of all iterator types and is used to ease the definition of required types for new iterators. It provides a number of type definitions that are used by derived classes.

SYNOPSIS

```
namespace std {
  template<class Category, class T, class Distance = ptrdiff_t,
          class Pointer = T*, class Reference = T&>
  struct iterator {
        typedef T          value_type;
        typedef Distancee  difference_type;
        typedef Pointer    pointer;
        typedef Reference  reference;
        typedef Category   iterator_category;
  };
}
```

stream iterators

iterator category tags

HEADER

header: **<iterator>**

CLASS TEMPLATES

struct **input_iterator_tag** {};

struct **output_iterator_tag** {};

struct **forward_iterator_tag**
 : public input_iterator_tag {};

struct **bidirectional_iterator_tag**
 : public forward_iterator_tag {};

struct **random_access_iterator_tag**
 : public bidirectional_iterator_tag {};

DESCRIPTION

An iterator category describes an iterator's capabilities. The iterator category tag classes are used for algorithm selection, so that a template function can find out what is the most specific category of its iterator argument and can select the most efficient algorithm at compile time.

ostreambuf_iterator<charT,traits>

CLASS TEMPLATE

template <class charT, class traits = char_traits<charT> >
class **ostreambuf_iterator**
header: **<iterator>**
base class(es): **iterator** <output_iterator_tag, void, void, void, void>

DESCRIPTION

ostreambuf_iterator is an iterator that writes successive characters to the stream buffer for which it was constructed. It is not possible to get a character value out of an ostreambuf_iterator.

SYNOPSIS

```
namespace std {
    template <class charT, class traits = char_traits<charT> >
    class ostreambuf_iterator:
      public iterator<output_iterator_tag, void, void, void, void> {
    public:
      // type definitions:
      typedef charT                          char_type;
      typedef traits                         traits_type;
      typedef basic_streambuf<charT,traits>  streambuf_type;
      typedef basic_ostream<charT,traits>    ostream_type;
      // constructors:
      ostreambuf_iterator(ostream_type& s) throw();
      ostreambuf_iterator(streambuf_type* s) throw();
      ostreambuf_iterator& operator=(charT c);
      // iterator operations:
      ostreambuf_iterator& operator*();
      ostreambuf_iterator& operator++();
      ostreambuf_iterator& operator++(int);
      // miscellaneous:
      bool failed() const throw();
    private:
      // streambuf_type* sbuf_;       exposition only
    };
}
```

stream iterators

PUBLIC MEMBER FUNCTIONS

ostreambuf_iterator(ostream_type& s) throw();

Constructs an `ostreambuf_iterator` that uses the stream buffer of the stream s, namely `*(s.rdbuf())`.

ostreambuf_iterator(streambuf_type* s) throw();

Constructs an `ostreambuf_iterator` that uses the stream buffer `*s`.

ITERATOR OPERATIONS

ostreambuf_iterator& **operator=**(charT c);

If `failed()` yields `false`, writes the character c to the stream buffer by calling the stream buffer member `sputc(c)`; otherwise has no effect. Returns `*this`.

ostreambuf_iterator& **operator*** ();

Returns `*this`.

ostreambuf_iterator& **operator++**();

Returns `*this`.

ostreambuf_iterator& **operator++**(int);

Returns `*this`.

MISCELLANEOUS

bool **failed**() const throw();

Returns `true` if in any previous assignment to the iterator at the end of the stream was reached.

ostream_iterator<T,charT,traits,Distance >

CLASS TEMPLATE

template <class T, class charT = char, class traits = char_traits<charT> >
class **ostream_iterator**
header: **<iterator>**
base class(es): **iterator**<output_iterator_tag, void, void, void, void>

DESCRIPTION

ostream_iterator is an iterator that allows an output stream to be seen as a sequence
of elements of type T. The iterator writes successive elements onto the output stream for
which it was constructed, using operator<<(ostream&,const T&) for writing, and
inserts a delimiter string after the element. It is not possible to get a value out of an
ostream_iterator.

SYNOPSIS

```
namespace std {
    template <class T, class charT = char,
            class traits = char_traits<charT> >
    class ostream_iterator
    : public iterator<output_iterator_tag, void, void, void, void> {
    public:
      //  type definitions:
      typedef charT char_type;
      typedef traits traits_type;
      typedef basic_ostream<charT,traits> ostream_type;
      //  construction/destruction/assignment
      ostream_iterator(ostream_type& s);
      ostream_iterator(ostream_type& s, const charT* delimiter);
      ostream_iterator(const ostream_iterator<T,charT,traits>& x);
     ~ostream_iterator();
      ostream_iterator<T,charT,traits>& operator=(const T& value);
      //  iterator operations:
      ostream_iterator<T,charT,traits>& operator*();
      ostream_iterator<T,charT,traits>& operator++();
      ostream_iterator<T,charT,traits>& operator++(int);
    private:
      //  basic_ostream<charT,traits>* out_stream;      exposition only
      //  const char* delim;                            exposition only
    };
  }
```

stream iterators

PUBLIC MEMBER FUNCTIONS

ostream_iterator(ostream_type& s);

Constructs an ostream_iterator that writes to the stream s. Initializes the delimiter string with 0.

ostream_iterator(ostream_type& s, const charT* delimiter);

Constructs an ostream_iterator that writes to the stream s. Initializes the delimiter string with delimiter.

ostream_iterator(const ostream_iterator<T,charT,traits>& x);

Constructs an ostream_iterator that is a copy of x.

~ostream_iterator();

Destroys the ostream_iterator

ostream_iterator<T,charT,traits>&
operator=(const T& value);

Writes the element t to the stream using operator<<() followed by the delimiter string. Returns *this.

ITERATOR OPERATIONS

ostream_iterator<T,charT,traits>& **operator***();

Returns *this.

ostream_iterator<T,charT,traits>& **operator++**();

Returns *this.

ostream_iterator<T,charT,traits>& **operator++**(int);

Returns *this.

5
O T H E R   I / O   O P E R A T I O N S

bitset<N>

FILE NAME

`<bitset>`

DESCRIPTION

The header file contains a template class and several related functions for representing and manipulating fixed-size sequences of bits, including the following I/O operations:

GLOBAL OPERATORS

```
template <class charT, class traits, size_t N>
basic_istream<charT, traits>& operator>>
(basic_istream<charT, traits>& is , bitset<N>& x);
```

Extracts up to N (single-byte) characters from the input stream `is`. Stores these characters in a temporary object `str` of type `string`, then evaluates the expression `x = bitset<N>(str)`. Characters are extracted and stored until any of the following occurs:

- N characters have been extracted and stored;

- end-of-file occurs on the input sequence;

- the next input character is neither 0 nor 1, in which case the input character is not extracted.

If no characters are stored in str, the failbit is set. Returns a reference to the input stream is.

```
template <class charT, class traits, size_t N>
basic_ostream<charT, traits>& operator<<
(basic_ostream<charT, traits>& os , const bitset<N>& x);
```

Returns the string representation of the bitset object as if obtained by its to_string() member function; that is, the operation returns os <<
x.template to_string<charT,traits,allocator<charT> >().

complex<T>

FILE NAME

`<complex>`

DESCRIPTION

The header file contains a template class and numerous functions for representing and manipulating complex numbers including the following I/O operations:

GLOBAL OPERATORS

```
template<class T, class charT, class traits>
basic_istream<charT, traits>& operator>>
(basic_istream<charT, traits>& is, complex<T>& x);
```

Extracts a complex number x of the form u, (u), or (u, v), where u is the real part and v is the imaginary part. The input values must be convertible to type T. If bad input is encountered, the failbit is set. Returns a reference to the input stream is.

```
template<class T, class charT, class traits>
basic_ostream<charT, traits>& operator<<
(basic_ostream<charT, traits>& os, const complex<T>& x);
```

Inserts the complex number x onto the stream os as if by `os << '(' << x.real() << "," << x.imag() << ')';` using the stream's format flags, precision, and locale. Returns a reference to the output stream os.

other i/o operations

basic_string<charT,traits,Allocator>

FILE NAME

<string>

DESCRIPTION

The header file contains all declarations for strings, including the following I/O operations:

GLOBAL OPERATORS

```
template<class charT, class traits, class Allocator>
basic_istream<charT,traits>& operator>>
(basic_istream<charT,traits>& is,
 basic_string<charT,traits,Allocator>& str);
```

Begins by constructing a sentry object of type basic_istream<charT, traits>:: sentry. If the construction succeeds, it clears the output string str by invoking str.erase() and then extracts characters from the input stream is and appends them to the output string str.

If the stream's field width is.width() is greater than zero, the maximum number of characters appended is the field width is.width() and otherwise the maximum string size str.max_size().

Characters are extracted and appended until any of the following occurs:

- The maximum number of characters are stored.

- End-of-file occurs on the input sequence.

- A whitespace character is found; that is, isspace(c, is.getloc()) is true for the next available input character c.

After the last character (if any) is extracted, the field width is reset to zero and the sentry object is destroyed. Returns a reference to the input stream is.

```
template<class charT, class traits, class Allocator>
basic_ostream<charT, traits>& operator<<
(basic_ostream<charT, traits>& os,
 const basic_string<charT,traits,Allocator>& str);
```

Begins by constructing a sentry object of type basic_ostream<charT, traits>:: sentry. If the sentry construct succeeds, padding is done as follows: If the field width str.width() is nonzero and the string length str.size() is less than the field width,

other i/o operations

fill characters are added according to the adjustfield setting. Then the field width is reset to zero and the sentry object is destroyed. Returns a reference to the output stream os.

```
template<class charT, class traits, class Allocator>
basic_istream<charT,traits>& getline
(basic_istream<charT,traits>& is,
 basic_string<charT,traits,Allocator>& str,
 charT delim);
```

Begins by constructing a sentry object of type basic_istream<charT, traits>:: sentry. If the construction succeeds, it clears the output string str by invoking str.erase() and then extracts characters from the input stream is and appends them to the output string str until any of the following occurs:

- End-of-file occurs on the input sequence, in which case the eofbit is set.

- The next available input character is the delimiter character delim, in which case the delimiter is extracted but not appended to the output string.

- The maximum string size is reached; that is, str.max_size() characters are stored, in which case the failbit is set.

The conditions are tested in the order shown. In any case, after the last character is extracted, the sentry object is destroyed. If the function extracts no characters, the failbit is set. Returns a reference to the input stream is.

```
template<class charT, class traits, class Allocator>
basic_istream<charT,traits>& getline
(basic_istream<charT,traits>& is,
 basic_string<charT,traits,Allocator>& str);
```

Returns getline(is,str,is.widen('\n')).

other i/o operations

Appendices

APPENDIX A

Parsing and Extraction of Numerical and bool *Values*

This section describes comprehensively and in detail how the num_get facet's member functions parse character sequences and what the resulting numerical or bool values are. The num_get facet is represented by the class template:

```
template <class charT, class InputIterator = istreambuf_iterator<charT> >
class num_get;
```

It contains the following member functions:

```
iter_type get(iter_type in, iter_type end, ios_base& str,
                          ios_base::iostate& err, long& val) const;
iter_type get(iter_type in, iter_type end, ios_base& str,
                          ios_base::iostate& err, unsigned short& val) const;
iter_type get(iter_type in, iter_type end, ios_base& str,
                          ios_base::iostate& err, unsigned int& val) const;
iter_type get(iter_type in, iter_type end, ios_base& str,
                          ios_base::iostate& err, unsigned long& val) const;
iter_type get(iter_type in, iter_type end, ios_base& str,
                          ios_base::iostate& err, short& val) const;
iter_type get(iter_type in, iter_type end, ios_base& str,
                          ios_base::iostate& err, double& val) const;
```

```
iter_type get(iter_type in, iter_type end, ios_base& str,
                          ios_base::iostate& err, long double& val) const;
iter_type get(iter_type in, iter_type end, ios_base& str,
                          ios_base::iostate& err, void*& val) const;
iter_type get(iter_type in, iter_type end, ios_base& str,
                          ios_base::iostate& err, bool& val) const;
```

Input streams use these member functions for the implementation of the respective stream extractors. Hence the following text describes not only the num_get facet but also how the stream extractors parse the input and extract a value.

A.1 Parsing Numerical Values

The parsing and extraction for numerical values is done in three stages:

Stage 1: Determine a conversion specifier and an optional length modifier.

Stage 2: Extract characters from in and transform them into chars. Accumulate the characters until extraction terminates.

Stage 3: Convert the accumulated character sequence according to the conversion specifier and length modifier determined in stage 1 and store the results. Indicate the result of the whole operation.

The details of the stages are presented below. The parsing and extraction of a bool value is described thereafter.

STAGE 1

A conversion specifier and an optional length modifier are determined according to str.flags() and the type that will hold the extracted value. The conversion specifier and length modifier used are the same as for the standard C function scanf(). They are described in detail in section A.3, Conversion Specifiers and Length Modifiers below.

The conversion specifier is

%g, if the extracted value is stored as a double or long double,

%p, if the extracted value is store as void*.

The conversion specifiers for an integral value are listed below. The first specifier, whose condition is true, applies.

%o, if (str.flags() & ios_base::basefield) == ios_base::oct

%x, if ((str.flags() & ios_base::basefield) == ios_base::hex)

&& (str.flags() & ios_base::uppercase)

%X, if (str.flags() & ios_base::basefield) == ios_base::hex

%i, if (str.flags() & ios_base::basefield) == 0

%d, if the extracted value will be stored in long

%u, if the extracted value will be stored in an unsigned type: unsigned short, unsigned int or unsigned long

A length modifier is added to the conversion specifier according to the specified type:

h, for short and unsigned short

l, for long and unsigned long

L, for long double

Types not listed add no length modifier.

STAGE 2

As long as in!=end, a character ct of type charT is extracted from in. A related character c of type char is created according to the rules below; the variable loc, which is mentioned in the descriptions below, is the locale contained in str, i.e., loc = str.getloc().

If ct is the radix separator, i.e., ct == use_facet< numpunct<charT> > (loc).decimal_point(), the related character is set to '.'.

If ct can be converted to a character of type char by ctype's member function narrow(), the related character is the character that results from the conversion; otherwise it is ' '; i.e., the result of use_facet< ctype<charT> > (loc).narrow(ct, ' ') is assigned to c.

If ct is the thousands separator, no related character is created.

If a character has been created, it is checked, whether or not it is allowed as the next character of an input field according to the conversion specifier determined in stage 1. If so, it is accumulated; otherwise stage 2 is terminated.

If stage 2 is not terminated, the input iterator is advanced by ++in, and processing continues at the beginning of stage 2.

STAGE 3

If the sequence of chars accumulated in stage 2 caused the standard C function scanf() parameterized with the conversion specifier from stage 1 to report an input failure, ios_base::failbit is assigned to err. This is also done if a position of the discarded thousands separators does not conform to the specification of use_facet< numpunct<charT> >(loc).grouping(). Otherwise the sequence of characters that have been accumulated in stage 2 is converted to a value of the type of val according to the conversion specifier from stage 1. Then this value is stored in val and err is set to ios_base::goodbit.

In any case, if stage 2 processing was terminated by the test for in == end, then err |= ios_base::eofbit is performed.

A.2 Parsing bool Values

If val is of type bool, then the following happens:

If (str.flags()&&ios_base::boolalpha)==0, the input proceeds as it would for a long, except that the value stored into val will be true if 1 is extracted and false if 0 is extracted. In all other cases, no value is assigned to val and err |= ios_base::failbit is performed.

If (str.flags()&&ios_base::boolalpha)!=0, the characters obtained by performing *in++ as long as in!=end must either match use_facet< numpunct <charT> >(str.getloc()).truename() or use_facet< numpunct<charT> >(str.getloc()).falsename(). If truename() was matched, val is set to true and err to ios_base::goodbit. If falsename() was matched, false is assigned to val and ios_base::goodbit is assigned to err. If input was terminated because in != end, val is set to ios_base::eofbit. In all other cases ios_base::failbit is assigned to err.

A.3 Conversion Specifier and Length Modifier

This section describes the semantics of the conversion specifiers and length modifiers that are used in stage 1 of the parsing and extraction of numerical and bool values. Please note that this description does not cover all elements from the C standard, but only those relevant for the description of the num_get facet.

CONVERSION SPECIFIER

%p—The operation matches an implementation-defined sequence of characters, which should be the same as the sequence that may be produced by the %p conversion of the printf function. The interpretation of the input is implementation-defined. If the input represents an item that was produced earlier by an output operation using a %p conversion, the pointer value that results from the input will compare equal to the pointer that was output.

%g—The operation matches a sequence of characters that represent an optionally signed floating-point number. The expected format of the sequence is an optional plus- or minus-sign character, followed by a nonempty sequence of digit characters optionally containing a decimal-point character; then an optional exponent part, consisting of a character e or E and an optionally signed sequence of digit characters. If the sequence has the expected form, the sequence of characters starting with the first digit or decimal-point character (whichever occurs first) is interpreted as a floating-point constant. If neither an exponent part nor a decimal-point character appears, a decimal-point character is assumed to follow the last digit character from the subject sequence. If the character sequence begins with a minus-sign character, the value resulting from the conversion is negated.

%d, %o, %u, %x, %X—The operation matches a sequence of characters that represent an optionally signed octal (for %o), hexadecimal (for %x, %X), or decimal (%d, %u) integer. The expected format of the sequence is an optional plus- or minus-sign character, followed by a nonempty sequence of characters representing an integer. Valid characters depend on the conversion specifier. For %d and %u all digit characters are valid. For %o all digit characters except 8 and 9 are valid. For %x and %X the characters 0x or 0X may precede the sequence of valid characters, which consist of digit characters plus the letters a b c d e f or A B C D E F. The letters represent the values 10 to 15. If the subject sequence has the expected form, the sequence of characters starting with the first digit or letter character (in the case of %x, %X) is interpreted as an octal (for %o), hexadecimal (for %x, %X), or decimal (for %u, %d) integer constant. If the character sequence begins with a minus-sign character, the value resulting from the conversion is negated.

%i—The operation matches a sequence of characters that represent an optionally signed integer. The expected format of the sequence is an optional plus- or minus-sign character, followed by a nonempty sequence of characters representing an integer. The first characters of this sequence determine how the following characters should be interpreted. If the first character is not 0, the following characters are interpreted as representing a decimal integer constant: For the following characters, only digit characters are valid. If the first character is a 0 and the next character is neither an x nor an X, the following characters are interpreted as representing an octal integer constant: For the following characters, all digit characters except 8 and 9 are valid. If the first character is a 0 and the next character is either an x or an X, the following characters are interpreted as representing a hexadecimal integer constant: For the following characters, all digit characters plus the letters a b c d e f or A B C D E F are valid. If the sequence has the expected form, the sequence of characters starting with the first significant digit or letter character is interpreted as an integer constant represented in a radix determined before. If the character sequence begins with a minus-sign character, the value resulting from the conversion is negated.

LENGTH MODIFIER

h—Together with the conversion specifiers %d, %i, the length modifier h indicates that the extracted value is a short rather than an int. Together with the conversion specifiers %o, %u, %x, %X, the length modifier h indicates that the extracted value is an unsigned short rather than an unsigned int.

l—Together with the conversion specifiers %d, %i, the length modifier l indicates that the extracted value is a long rather than an int. Together with the conversion specifiers %o, %u, %x, %X, the length modifier l indicates that the extracted value is an unsigned long rather than an unsigned int.

L—Together with the conversion specifiers %g, the length modifier L indicates that the extracted value is a long double rather than a float.

APPENDIX B

Formatting Numerical and `bool` *Values*

This section describes comprehensively and in detail how the num_put facet's member functions format a numerical or `bool` value to a character sequence. The num_put facet is represented by the class template:

```
template <class charT, class OutputIterator = ostreambuf_iterator<charT> >
class num_put;
```

contains the following member functions:

```
iter_type put(iter_type out, ios_base& str,
                              char_type fill, bool val) const;
iter_type put(iter_type out, ios_base& str,
                              char_type fill, long val) const;
iter_type put(iter_type out, ios_base& str,
                              char_type fill, unsigned long val) const;
iter_type put(iter_type out, ios_base& str,
                              char_type fill, double val) const;
iter_type put(iter_type out, ios_base& str,
                              char_type fill, long double val) const;
iter_type put(iter_type out, ios_base& str,
                              char_type fill, void* val) const;
```

These member functions are used for implementing the inserters of output streams for numerical and `bool` values. Hence the following text describes not only the num_put facet but also how the stream inserters format a numeric or `bool` value.

B.1 Formatting Numerical Values

Formatting numerical values is done in four stages:

> Stage 1: Determine a conversion specification and the characters generated by the standard C function `printf()` given this conversion specification.

> Stage 2: Transform the characters generated in stage 1 to `charT`.

> Stage 3: Determine where padding is required.

> Stage 4: Insert the character sequence generated in stage 3 to `out`.

> Each stage is described in detail below.

STAGE 1

A conversion specification formed by a conversion specifier and an optional qualifier, length modifier, and precision specifier is determined according to `str.flags()` and the type of the value `val` that is formatted. The conversion specifier, the qualifier, and the length modifier used are the same as for the standard C function `printf()`. They are described in detail in section B.3, Conversion Specifiers, Qualifiers, and Length Modifiers, below.

The conversion specifier is `%p` if a value of type `void*` is formatted.

For the two floating-point types `double` and `long double`, the conversion specifiers are

`%f`, if `(str.flags() & ios_base::floatfield) == ios_base::fixed`

`%e`, if `((str.flags() & ios_base::floatfield) == ios_base::scientific)`
            `&& !(str.flags() & ios_base::uppercase)`

`%E`, if `(str.flags() & ios_base::floatfield) == ios_base::scientific`

`%g`, if `!(str.flags() & ios_base::uppercase)`

`%G`, otherwise

For an integral type, the conversion specifiers are

`%o`, if `(str.flags() & ios_base::basefield) == ios_base::oct`

`%x`, if `((str.flags() & ios_base::basefield) == ios_base::hex)`
            `&& !(str.flags() & ios_base::uppercase)`

`%X`, if `(str.flags() & ios_base::basefield) == ios_base::hex`

%d, if the value that is formatted is of type long

%u, if the value that is formatted is of type unsigned long

Both lists above are ordered; i.e., the first specifier whose condition is true applies.

An optional qualifier and a length modifier are added to the conversion specifier according to the rules below. If the type that is formatted is an integral type; that is, either long, unsigned long, double, or long double, the qualifier that is added is

+, if (str.flags() & ios_base::showpos)

#, if (str.flags() & ios_base::showbase)

If the type that is formatted is a floating-point type that is either double or long double, the qualifier that is added is

+, if (str.flags() & ios_base::showpos)

#, if (str.flags() & ios_base::showpoint)

The following length modifiers are added:

l, if the type that is going to be formatted is long or unsigned long

L, if the type that is going to be formatted is long double

All other types add no length modifier.

For type double or long double, precision() is added to the conversion specification as a precision specifier if (str.flags() & ios_base::fixed)!=0 or if precision() > 0.

The result of stage 1 is a character sequence as if generated by a call to the standard C function printf() with the conversion specification determined above and the value val as parameters.

STAGE 2

All characters from the sequence resulting from stage 1 are converted to charT according to the following rules:

If the character is equal to the decimal point '.', the result of the conversion is use_facet< numpunct<charT> >(str.getloc()).decimal_point(); otherwise the character is converted to a character of type charT by the ctype's member function widen(); i.e., if c is a character from this sequence unequal to '.', it is converted via use_facet< ctype<charT> >(loc).widen(c).

If the value that is formatted is of type long or unsigned long, i.e., of an integral type, thousands separators are inserted. They are placed according to the specification returned by use_facet< numpunct<charT> >

`(str.getloc()).grouping()`. The character that is inserted as the thousands separator is specified by `use_facet< numpunct<charT> >` `(str.getloc()).thousands_sep()`.

STAGE 3

If `str.width()` is nonzero and the number of characters in the sequence after stage 2 is less than `str.width()`, fill characters are added to enlarge the length of the sequence to `str.width()`. Otherwise nothing is done in this stage.

The location of padding is determined according to the rules below. The rules are ordered; i.e., the first condition that becomes true determines the rule that applies.

If `(str.flags() & ios_base::adjustfield) == ios_base::left`, padding is done after the character sequence created in stage 2.

If `(str.flags() & ios_base::adjustfield) == ios_base::right`, padding is done before the character sequence created in stage 2.

If `(str.flags() & ios_base::internal) == ios_base::left`, and a sign occurs in the character sequence created in stage 2, padding is done after the sign.

If `(str.flags() & ios_base::internal) == ios_base::left`, and a sign occurs in the character sequence created in stage 1 began with `0x` or `0X`, padding is done after these two characters.

If none of the above conditions applies, padding is done before the character sequence created in stage 2.

The character used for padding is the character passed to the `put()` member function as parameter `fill`.

STAGE 4

The sequence of characters resulting from stage 3 is output to `out`; i.e., if c is a character from the sequence, `*out++ = c` is performed. If at any point during this operation `out.failed()` becomes true, the operation is terminated.

B.2 Formatting bool Values

For values of type `bool` the following happens:

If `(str.flags()&ios_base::boolalpha)==0`, that is, if the `boolalpha` flag is not set, then the value `val` is treated as a numerical value and formatted as described in the previous section.

If (str.flags()&ios_base::boolalpha)!=0, that is, if the boolalpha flag is set, the respective string representation of either true or false is used. The string representation is taken from the numpunct facet that is contained in the ios_base object that was passed to the put() function; that is, the output is

```
val ? use_facet< numpunct<char_type> >(str.getloc()).truename()
    : use_facet< numpunct<char_type> >(str.getloc()).falsename();
```

B.3 Conversion Specifiers, Qualifiers, and Length Modifiers

This section describes the semantics of the conversion specifiers, qualifiers, and length modifiers that are used in stage 1 of the formatting of numerical and bool values. Please note that this description does not cover all elements from the C standard but only those relevant for the description of the num_put facet.

CONVERSION SPECIFIER

%p—The value of the pointer is converted to a sequence of characters in an implementation-defined manner.

%f—The double value is converted to a sequence of characters that represent a decimal notation in the style [-]*ddd.ddd*, where *d* is a digit character. The number of digit characters after the decimal-point character is equal to the specified precision. The default is 6, if no precision is specified. If the precision is zero and the # qualifier is not specified, no decimal-point character appears. The value is rounded to the appropriate number of digits.

%e, %E—The double value is converted to a sequence of characters in the style [-]*d.ddde±dd*, where *d* is a digit character and *e* is the character that introduces the exponent. This is either the character e if the conversion specifier is %e or E if the conversion specifier is %E. There is always one digit character before the decimal-point character, which is not 0 if the value is nonzero. The number of digit characters after the decimal-point character is equal to the specified precision. The default is 6, if no precision is specified. If the precision is zero and the # qualifier is not specified, no decimal-point character appears. The value is rounded to the appropriate number of digits. The exponent always contains at least two digits. If the value is zero, the exponent is 00.

%g, %G—The double value is converted in the same way as if %f or %e (%E in case of %G) is specified. The specifier used depends on the value that is going to be converted. %e (or %E) will be used only if the exponent resulting from such a conversion is less than −4 or greater than or equal to the precision. If the precision is 0, it is taken as 1. Trailing zeros are removed from the fractional portion of the result, and the decimal-point character appears only if it is followed by a digit.

%o, %u, %x, %X—The unsigned int value is converted to a sequence of characters that represent an unsigned octal (%o), unsigned decimal (%u), or unsigned hexadecimal (%x, %X) in the style *dddd,* where *d* is a digit character. To represent hexadecimal digits larger than 9, the characters a b c d e f are used for the conversion specifier %x and A B C D E F for the conversion specifier %X.

%d—The int value is converted to a sequence of characters that represent a signed decimal in the style [-]*dddd,* where *d* is a digit character.

QUALIFIER

+—The resulting character sequence will always begin with a plus- or minus-sign character.

#—For %o conversions the first character of the resulting character sequence is a 0. For %x (or %X) conversions the first two characters of the resulting character sequence are 0x (or 0X). For %e, %E, %f, %g, %G conversions the result will always contain a decimal-point character, even if no digit characters follow it. For %g and %G conversions, trailing zeros will not be removed from the result.

LENGTH MODIFIER

l specifies that the following %d, %o, %u, %x, %X conversion specifier applies to a long or unsigned long value.

L specifies that the following %e, %E, %f, %g, %G conversion specifier applies to a long double value.

APPENDIX C

strftime() *Conversion Specifiers*

The time_put facet, represented by the class template

```
template <class charT, class OutputIterator = ostreambuf_iterator<charT> >
class time_put;
```

contains the following member functions:

```
iter_type put(iter_type s, ios_base& f, char_type fill, const tm* tmb,
                         const charT* pattern, const charT* pat_end) const;
iter_type put(iter_type s, ios_base& f, char_type fill, const tm* tmb,
                         char form, char mod = 0) const;
```

which both use the same conversion specifiers as the standard C function strftime(). The first function parses the interval [pattern, pat_end) and interprets the characters immediately following a '%' character as conversion specifiers. The second function interprets the parameter form as a conversion specifier. The list below shows all valid conversion specifiers and their semantics:

%a—is replaced by the abbreviated weekday name as known to the time_put facet.

%A—is replaced by the full weekday name as known to the time_put facet.

%b—is replaced by the abbreviated month name as known to the time_put facet.

%B—is replaced by the full month name as known to the time_put facet.

%c—is replaced by the time_put facet's appropriate date and time representation.

%d—is replaced by the day of the month as a decimal number, i.e., a number between 01 and 31.

%H—is replaced by the hour (24-hour clock) as a decimal number, i.e., a number between 00 and 23.

%I—is replaced by the hour (12-hour clock) as a decimal number, i.e., a number between 01 and 12.

%j—is replaced by the day of the year as a decimal number, i.e., a number between 001 and 366.

%m—is replaced by the month as a decimal number, i.e., a number between 01 and 12.

%M—is replaced by the minute as a decimal number, i.e., a number between 00 and 59.

%p—is replaced by the time_put facet's equivalent to the AM/PM designations associated with a 12-hour clock.

%S—is replaced by the second as a decimal number, i.e., a number between 00 and 61.

%U—is replaced by the week number of the year (the first Sunday as the first day of week one) as a decimal number, i.e., a number between 00 and 53.

%w—is replaced by the weekday as a decimal number, i.e., a number between 0 and 6, where Sunday is 0.

%W—is replaced by the week number of the year (the first Monday as the first day of week one) as a decimal number, i.e., a number between 00 and 53.

%x—is replaced by the time_put facet's appropriate date representation.

%X—is replaced by the time_put facet's appropriate time representation.

%y—is replaced by the year without century as a decimal number, i.e., a number between 00 and 99.

%Y—is replaced by the year with century as a decimal number.

%Z—is replaced by the time zone name or abbreviation, or by no character if no time zone is determinable.

%%—is replaced by %.

APPENDIX D

Correspondences Between C Stdio and C++ IOStreams

D.1 File Open Modes

Some of the open modes for file streams correspond to the file open modes used in the C stdio for invocation of the `fopen()` function.

The `ios_base::in` flag is equivalent to the C open mode `'r'`, the `ios_base::out` flag is equivalent to `'w'`, the combination `ios_base::in|ios_base::out` corresponds to `'a'`, the `ios_base::binary` flag is equivalent to the `'b'`, and so on. Table D-1 lists all correspondences:

Table D-1: File Stream Open Modes in IOStreams and Their Equivalents in C stdio

IOS_BASE::OPENMODE FLAG COMBINATION					C STDIO EQUIVALENT
binary	in	out	trunc	app	
		+			`"w"`
		+		+	`"a"`
		+	+		`"w"`
	+				`"r"`
	+	+			`"r+"`
	+	+	+		`"w+"`
+		+			`"wb"`
+		+		+	`"ab"`
+		+	+		`"wb"`
+	+				`"rb"`
+	+	+			`"r+b"`
+	+	+	+		`"w+b"`

D.2 Stream Positions

The symbolic stream positions used as arguments to the `tellg()` and `tellp()` functions correspond to the argument that is passed to the C stdio function `fseek()`. Table D-2 shows the correspondences:

Table D-2: Symbolic Stream Positions in IOStreams and Their Equivalents in C stdio

IOS_BASE::SEEKDIR VALUE	C STDIO EQUIVALENT
beg	SEEK_SET
cur	SEEK_CUR
end	SEEK_END

APPENDIX E

Differences Between Classic and Standard IOStreams

Standard IOStreams stands in the tradition of the classic IOStreams library that has been around since the first days of C++. Before the advent of the standard IOStreams, several implementations of the classic IOStreams library were available to the C++ community, all of which were similar, yet slightly different. One goal of the standardization was formally to specify the IOStreams, as well as to improve and enhance it. Potentially dangerous features, like assignment of streams, were removed, and new capabilities, such as internationalization support, were added. This appendix provides an overview of the differences between the classic and the standard IOStreams, which are particularly interesting to those developers who have existing IOStreams applications and want to migrate to the standard IOStreams.

To make this chapter understandable even if you have not yet read the entire book, we include short reviews of topics that are covered in detail elsewhere in the book. Take a deeper look at the sections given as references if you would like further information.

Here is an overview of the major differences:

The standard IOStreams is a template taking the character type as a parameter.

The base class `ios` is split into character-type-dependent and character-type-independent portions.

Standard IOStreams optionally throws exceptions.

Standard IOStreams is internationalized.

Assignment and copying of streams are prohibited.

File descriptors are no longer supported.

The character-array-based `strstreams` are replaced by string-based streams.

Additional virtual functions have been added to the stream buffer interface.

E.1 Templatizing the IOStreams Classes

When you look at the new IOStreams header files, you immediately notice that most classes that you might know from the classic IOStreams are turned into class *templates* in the standard IOStreams. The template parameters are the character type and the character traits type. Here is an example:

```
class ostream    turned into
template <class charT, class Traits = char_traits<charT> >
class basic_ostream.
```

The classic IOStreams classes allowed input and output of text that could be represented as a sequence of narrow characters of type `char`. This was seen as a restriction, because not all alphabets and their corresponding character encodings can be conveniently expressed in terms of narrow characters. Sequences of wide characters of type `wchar_t` are needed to represent larger alphabets, like the Japanese one for instance. The standards committee decided to turn the traditional IOStreams classes into class templates in order to eliminate the restriction of narrow-character I/O. The stream class templates take two template arguments: the character type and an associated·character traits type. Character types and trait types are described in greater detail in section 2.3, Character Types and Character Traits. Here is a brief summary:

The *character type* is usually one of the built-in character types `char` or `wchar_t`. The instantiations for the narrow-character type `char` are designed to cover the traditional functionality of classic IOStreams. The instantiations for the wide-character type `wchar_t` operate on wide-character sequences and can convert them to external multibyte character encodings. The character type can also be of any other conceivable user-defined type.[1]

The *character traits type* describes the properties of the character type. These include information such as the end-of-file value, which is an integral constant called `EOF` for type `char`, and a constant called `WEOF` for type `wchar_t`, the meaning of equality, or comparison of two characters.

For ease of use, and for backward compatibility, the standard defines type definitions for the stream class templates instantiated with the character types `char` and `wchar_t`. For type `char` these are

---

1. "User-defined" here stands for any character type that is not built into the language. A user-defined character can be added by a library vendor as well as by a user.

```
typedef basic_istream<char> istream;
typedef basic_ostream<char> ostream;
typedef basic_iostream<char> iostream;
typedef basic_ifstream<char> ifstream;
typedef basic_ofstream<char> ofstream;
typedef basic_fstream<char> fstream;
```

Note that these typedefs define names identical to the class names in the traditional IOStreams. In other words, there is still an `ostream`; the only difference is that it now stands for a `basic_ostream<char, char_traits<char> >`.

While these typedefs help to migrate an implementation that uses classic IOStreams to the use of standard IOStreams, some points still need attention:

As already mentioned, all definitions of the standard IOStreams reside in the namespace `::std`. This is also true for the typedefs listed above; as a result, either a using declaration or using directive must be used to refer to the typedefs, or the typedefs must be qualified with their namespace, e.g., `::std::fstream`.

Since the typedefs are not classes anymore, they cannot be used in forward declarations, as they could with the classic IOStreams where these names depicted classes. We recommend using the include file `<iosfwd>` instead.

E.2 Splitting Base Class `ios`

In the process of transforming the IOStreams classes into class templates, the base class of all traditional IOStreams classes, class `ios`, was split into (1) a common, character-type-independent part: `ios_base`, and (2) a character-type-dependent class template: `basic_ios<class charT, class Traits>`, having the character type and the character traits type as template parameters.

The stream base classes are described in greater detail in section 2.1.1, Class Hierarchy. Here is a brief summary:

`ios_base` is the base class of `basic_ios<class charT, class Traits>`, which again is the base class template of all remaining stream classes. `ios_base` contains all the stream properties that are independent of the stream's character type, such as the flags that are used for formatting control, error indication,[2] open modes, and stream position-

---

2. One might expect that the functionality error handling, not only the flag definitions, would be contained in `ios_base` because error handling is character-independent. However, error indication is done in `basic_ios<class charT, class Traits>`, because `ios_base` is also used in the locale section of the standard library, where it serves as an abstraction for passing formatting information to the locale. If `ios_base` contained the error handling, which in the standard IOStreams includes the indication of errors by throwing exceptions (see subsequent sections for details), these exceptions could also be raised by the standard locale. This effect was neither intended nor acceptable. Hence, `ios_base` contains only the definition of all flags for error indication; the raising of exceptions and the indication of error states are located in `basic_ios<class charT, class Traits>`.

ing. It also manages the user-allocable storage (`iword`/`pword`), handles registration and invocation of callbacks, and allows imbuing of locales.

The advantage of splitting class `ios` into class `ios_base` and class template `basic_ios<class charT, class Traits>` is that all behavior independent of the template parameters is factored out into a nontemplate. This minimizes the binary code size of the library as well as user programs.

Besides the split, the behavior of the new stream base classes differs from the behavior of the classic IOStreams base class `ios`. Stream callbacks are a completely new feature of the standard IOStreams provided by `ios_base`. They help implement proper resource management when streams get copied via `copyfmt()` or destroyed by their destructor. Another point is the open modes. While classic IOStreams' implementations typically offered a `nocreate` open mode in their `ios` base class, this mode no longer exists in the standard IOStreams.

E.3 Indicating Errors

One of the advantages of IOStreams is its intuitive use of the `operator<<()`. This is particularly convenient for grouping output operations; for instance, you can put into one line of source code all operations that are needed to produce one line of output. Here is an example:

```
int value;
 // some calculation
 ...
cout << "The calculated value is: " << value << '\n';
if (!cout)
   handle_error();
```

As convenient as it may be, it has one drawback: In the example above it is not possible to check the stream state, which accumulates the stream errors after each output operation. C++ exceptions can help in this situation, because they allow a more active error indication. For this reason the standard IOStreams optionally allows error indication via exceptions. The mechanisms for error indication are described in greater detail in section 1.3, The Stream State. In particular, IOStreams exceptions are explained in section 1.3.3, Catching Stream Exceptions. Here is a brief review of both mechanisms:

In IOStreams each stream maintains a stream state that indicates the success or failure of a operation. The stream state can either be *good,* or one of the following:

end-of-file; an input operation reached the end of an input sequence.

fail; an input operation failed to read the expected characters, or an output operation failed to generate the desired characters.

bad; the stream or the underlying input or output sequence lost its integrity.

Errors are accumulated in the stream state and must be actively checked by calling certain member functions such as good(), fail(), bad(), etc.

The standard IOStreams provides means for enabling or disabling exceptions. An exception mask specifies which of the stream state flags should trigger an exception. If, for instance, the fail bit is set in the exception mask, an operation that sets the fail bit in the stream state will also raise an exception of type ios_base::failure. By default, all exceptions are disabled. The user of IOStreams can actively enable exceptions by modifying the exception mask. The stream classes offer the exceptions() member function for retrieval and modification of the exception mask.

Note that there is no guarantee that all exceptions will be suppressed, even if all bits in the exception mask are turned off. Errors detected by the stream and the stream buffer themselves are not indicated via exceptions if the exception mask does not allow it, but exceptions raised by user-provided operations will be propagated. Examples of user-provided operations are overridden virtual functions of derived stream buffer classes, registered callback functions, and operations of user-defined locales and facets.

E.4 Internationalizing IOStreams

The standard library includes a component for internationalization, which consists of locales and facets. Each facet has information or services for a certain set of cultural conventions such as representation of date and time. Internationalization services for a cultural area, that is, the corresponding facets, are bundled into a so-called locale object. A locale acts as a container of facets. The standard IOStreams is internationalized in the sense that it uses standard locales for formatting and parsing numerical values, recognition of whitespace characters, and conversion between character encodings.

The internationalization support in the standard C++ library is described in part II. The relationship between streams and locales is described in sections 2.1.4, How Streams Maintain Their Locale, and 2.1.5, Collaboration with Stream Buffers and Locales, in part I. The parsing and formatting of numerical values are described in appendix A, Parsing and Extraction of Numerical and bool Values, and appendix B, Formatting Numerical and bool Values. Here is a brief summary:

Each stream holds a locale object in its base object ios_base. The stream has an additional locale object in its stream buffer. Usually, both the stream and the stream buffer hold copies of the same locale. The streams use their locales for the parsing and formatting of numerical values and for recognition of whitespace character, digits, etc. The stream buffer uses its locale for character code conversion between the internally held representation and the external encoding.

E.5 Removing _withassign Classes

In the standard IOStreams the classes basic_istream, basic_ostream, and basic_iostream have a *private* copy constructor and assignment operator to prevent copy and assignment for objects of these classes, because there are no "right" semantics for copying or assigning a stream with respect to its stream buffer. There are different possibilities, e.g., sharing the stream buffer after the assignment, flushing the stream buffer during the assignment and then providing both streams with entirely independent buffers, and so on. None of these possibilities is intuitively right, though. Consequently, copying and assigning are prohibited.

On the other hand, streams need to be assigned. The most convincing example is the wish to redirect standard output (or any of the other standard I/O objects) by assigning a valid stream object to `cout`. In order to satisfy this requirement, the classic IOStreams had the classes `istream_withassign`, `ostream_withassign`, and `iostream_withassign`. It implemented a *public* copy constructor and assignment operator, which let both streams share the stream buffer after the copying or assignment. This imposed dependencies between the lifetime of the two stream objects used in the copy constructor or assignment operator, and the correct use of the `_withassign` classes was rather complicated.

For this reason the classes `istream_withassign`, `ostream_withassign`, and `iostream_withassign` no longer exist in the standard IOStreams. To perform operations equivalent to the copy constructor and the assignment operator of the old `_withassign` classes, the user of the standard streams has to explicitly implement this functionality. Standard streams have the following member functions defined in `basic_ios<class charT, class Traits>`, that can be used for this purpose:

`iostate rdstate()`, which allows retrieval of the stream state

`void clear(iostate state = goodbit)`, which allow setting of the stream state

`basic_streambuf<class charT, class Traits>* rdbuf()` and `basic_streambuf<class charT, class Traits>* rdbuf (basic_streambuf<class charT, class Traits>* sb)`, which allow setting and retrieval of the stream buffer,

`basic_ios<class charT, class Traits>& copyfmt(basic_ios<class charT, class Traits>& rhs)`, which allows setting of all other data members of `rhs`

The correct use of these functions is discussed in detail in section 2.1.3, Copying and Assignment of Streams.

E.6 Removing File Descriptors

In the traditional IOStreams all file streams offered a member function `fd()`, which returned the file descriptor of the file that was associated with the file stream. This feature was helpful when some functionality of the underlying file system was needed that was not available in IOStreams. For example, the function `int ftruncate(int fd, off_t` length) is available on some UNIX platforms and allows a file to be set to a defined length; however, this feature was not directly supported by the traditional IOStreams, but accessible only indirectly through the file descriptor.

The `fd()` function is omitted from the C++ standard. The simple reason is that the C++ standard does not want to exclude operating systems without file descriptors from providing a standard-conforming IOStreams library.

On the other hand, vendors of the standard C++ library are free to extend the library, as long as these extensions do not conflict with the standard. Hence it is quite possible that a functionality like `fd()` will be included as a nonstandard extension in some library implementations.

E.7 String Streams: Replacing `strstream` by `stringstream`

The purpose of string streams is to facilitate text input and output to memory locations. The string stream classes in the traditional IOStreams, class `strstream`, `istrstream`, `ostrstream`, and `strstreambuf`, allow input and output to and from character arrays of type `char*`. In the standard IOStreams, these classes are replaced by corresponding `stringstream` classes that allow input and output to and from strings of type `basic_string<charT>`. The most obvious difference is that instead of providing character arrays to a `strstream`, you now provide string objects to a `stringstream`. As you can convert character arrays into string objects and vice versa, there are no major restrictions regarding the functionality of string streams. The classic `strstream` classes are deprecated features in the standard IOStreams, which means that they are still provided by implementations of the standard IOStreams but will be omitted in the future.

The usage of string streams is described in section 1.5, In-Memory Input/Output, and the related string stream buffer classes are explained in detail in section 2.2.3, String Stream Buffers. The classic `strstream` classes, as they are deprecated, are not described in the book. Following is a brief description of the subtle differences between the deprecated classic `strstream` classes and the new standard `stringstream` classes.

String streams are dynamic, which means that the internal character buffer is resized and reallocated once it is full. String streams also allow retrieval of the content of the internal character buffer by calling the member function `str()`.

In most of the traditional IOStreams implementations, `str()` returns a pointer to the internal character buffer. After such a call to `str()` the string stream is *frozen;* i.e., the buffer is no longer resized. This modification is very sensible, since every reallocation would invalidate the buffer pointer.

In the standard IOStreams, string streams are always dynamic; they do not freeze. A call to `str()` provides a string object that is a copy of the internal buffer but does not allow access to the buffer itself.

A similar difference occurs with regard to the construction of string streams. There are constructors taking a character array or a string for use as the internal character buffer. In the traditional IOStreams this character array was actually used as the internal buffer, and the string stream constructed this way was frozen. In the standard IOStreams the string is not used as an internal buffer; only its content is copied into an independent internal buffer area. Again, the internal buffer is not accessible from outside the string stream, and freezing is not necessary.

E.8 Changes to the Stream Buffer Classes

`setbuf()`

The semantics of `setbuf()` changed. For string stream buffers, the semantics of `setbuf()` are implementation-defined, except that `setbuf(0,0)` has no effect. For file stream buffers, too, the semantics of `setbuf(0,0)` are defined: If `setbuf(0,0)` is called on a stream before any I/O has occurred on that stream, the stream becomes unbuffered. Otherwise the results are implementation-defined.

This was different in the classic IOStreams, where one could use `setbuf()` for providing a character buffer that the respective stream buffer object then used as an internal buffer. The reason for removing the `setbuf()` functionality from the standard IOStreams is that it introduced lifetime dependencies between the stream objects and their externally provided character buffer, which was seen as error prone. Also, the need for replacing a stream buffer's internal character buffer was generally questioned.

If you want to control which character array is used by a stream buffer, you have to implement specialized stream buffer classes.

`uflow()`

In the classic IOStreams, the main virtual function for the input direction in stream buffers used to be `underflow()`. In the standard IOStreams, a second virtual function `uflow()` was added for input of characters from an external device.

Typically, when a new stream buffer class was derived for a new external device, `underflow()` had to be overridden. The required functionality for `underflow()` was, and still is, to make available a character from the external device without consuming it. In the classic IOStreams, the nonvirtual stream buffer functions `sgetc()` and `sbumpc()`, both defined in the stream buffer base class `streambuf`, used to call `underflow()`. `sgetc()`, which is basically a peek at the next character without consuming it, only calls `underflow()`, whereas `sbumpc()`, which consumes the next character, peeks at the character by calling `underflow()` *and* increments the get area's next pointer. With these implementations of `sgetc()` and `sbumpc()` it was sufficient to override `underflow()` for a new derived stream buffer class, as long as the new stream buffer used an internal character array for buffering the input characters. Stream buffer classes, which were unbuffered, could not be implemented, because the implementation of the nonvirtual function `sbumpc()` unconditionally tried to increment the get area's next pointer, although there is no get area in an unbuffered stream buffer.

To allow for greater flexibility, the standards committee added another virtual function to the stream buffer base class `basic_streambuf`, namely, the function `uflow()`. `uflow()` is similar to `underflow()` in that it makes available a character from the external device, but in contrast to underflow(), it consumes the character. The nonvirtual stream buffer functions sgetc() and sbumpc() in the standard IOStreams call different functions: sgetc() calls underflow(), as it used to do in the classic IOStreams; sbumpc() was changed and now calls uflow(). With these changes, unbuffered stream buffers too can be derived, because sbumpc() does not require that an internal character buffer exists. Instead, the functionality of peeking at the next and consuming it is virtual and can be overridden for a derived stream buffer class. The default implementation of uflow() provided in the base class basic_streambuf is built on top of underflow(): uflow() calls underflow() and increments the next pointer, which is a reasonable default behavior for buffered stream buffers.

The net effect of this change to the stream buffer base class is that for derived stream buffer classes with an internal character buffer, only underflow() must be overridden, pretty much as it was in the classic IOStreams. See section 3.4.1.1.2, A Stream Buffer for Buffered Character Transport, for an example. For a stream buffer class that does not buffer the characters internally, underflow() *and* uflow() must be overridden. See section 3.4.1.1.1, A Stream Buffer For Unbuffered Character Transport, for an example.

pbackfail()

In the classic IOStreams, the stream buffer function sputbackc(char) directly accessed the internal character buffer. In the standard IOStreams, sputbackc(char) invokes a virtual member function spbackfail() instead.

In the classic IOStreams, the nonvirtual member function sputbackc(char) allowed a character to be put back into the input sequence. That character could either be the previously extracted one or a different character that had not been obtained from the external device. As sputbackc(char) was a nonvirtual function, it was impossible to override its behavior in any derived stream buffer class. Moreover, sputbackc(char) was implemented so that it directly accessed the internal character buffer in order to store the putback character in the previous position. This implementation naturally does not work for stream buffers that do not maintain an internal character array. It also does not work if the next pointer points to the beginning of the internal character buffer, although for certain stream buffers it might be possible to make available additional putback positions even in such a situation.

To overcome these limitations, the standards committee introduced a virtual member function called pbackfail(), and sputbackc() calls this function if a character different from the previously extracted one is put back into the input sequence. In such a case, write access to the internal character buffer, or any equivalent functionality, is provided by pbackfail(). sputbackc() also calls pbackfail() if the next pointer points to the beginning of the internal character buffer. In that case, pbackfail() makes available additional putback positions.

Additionally, a second nonvirtual member function sungetc() was introduced into the stream buffer classes. Its functionality is a subset of sputbackc()'s functionality, namely, putting back the previously extracted character into the input sequence.

sungetc() also calls the virtual pbackfail() function if no putback positions are available.

A side effect of these additions is that under certain circumstances uflow(), underflow(), *and* pbackfail() must be overridden in a derived stream buffer class, because these three functions are semantically interdependent. Specifically, underflow(), which is a peek without consumption of the character, must have the same semantics as uflow(), which is a peek with consumption, followed by pbackfail(), which represents ungetting the consumed character. The implementation of uflow() in the stream base class basic_streambuf provides a reasonable default behavior that works for buffered stream buffer classes: uflow(), the peek with consumption, is implemented as underflow(), which is a peek without consumption, plus increment of the get area's next pointer, which means consumption of the character. For this reason, it is enough to override underflow() for a buffered stream buffer class. (See section 3.4.1.1.2, A Stream Buffer for Buffered Character Transport, for an example.) For unbuffered stream buffers, in contrast, all three functions must be redefined. (See section 3.4.1.1.1, A Stream Buffer for Unbuffered Character Transport, for an example.)

E.9 Minor Changes

NAME CHANGES

In addition to the differences explained above, there are a couple of minor deviations from the traditional IOStreams. Some items are renamed, for instance, such as the type io_state from the traditional IOStreams, which is now named iostate. The same holds for open_mode and seek_dir, which are now openmode and seekdir. Also, the names of the include files have changed; for instance, the header <iostream.h> is now <iostream>.

APPENDIX F

Relationship Between C and C++ Locales

The internationalization supports defined in standard C and standard C++ have a lot in common. In particular, they both provide services and information for the same range of cultural differences. There is also a relationship between the global C++ locale and the global C locale.

F.1 Locale Categories in C and C++

The parallels between the C and C++ internationalization supports are most visible in the way localization information and services in a locale are grouped together into categories.

There is almost a one-to-one relationship between the five C locale categories and the six C++ locale categories. In fact, the relationship is so close that the C locale categories can be passed as arguments to C++ locale constructors in lieu of C++ categories. Table F-1 shows the parallels:

Table F-1: Locale Categories in C and C++

C++ CATEGORY	C LOCALE CATEGORY	C++ FACET TEMPLATES	FUNCTIONALITY
ctype	LC_CTYPE	ctype	character classification and conversion
		codecvt	code conversion
collate	LC_COLLATE	collate	string collation
message		messages	retrieving localized message strings from message catalogs
numeric	LC_NUMERIC	numpunct	information about the format and punctuation of numerical and Boolean expressions
		num_get	parsing of character sequences that represent a numerical or Boolean value
		num_put	generation of formatted character sequences that represent a numerical or Boolean value
monetary	LC_MONETARY	moneypunct	information about the format and punctuation of monetary expressions
		money_get	parsing of character sequences that represent a monetary value
		money_put	generation of formatted character sequences that represent a monetary value
time	LC_TIME	time_get	parsing of character sequences that represent a date and/or time
		time_put	generation of formatted character sequences that represent a date and/or time

F.2 The Global Locale in C and C++

The main difference between the C and C++ locales is that in C there is exactly one locale, which is global, whereas in C++ locales are objects. Arbitrarily, many C++ locale objects can be created, and they typically exist in a local scope and are passed around if needed.

In C, internationalized functions such as strcoll(), which performs locale-sensitive string comparison, use the information they find in the global C locale. In C++, internationalized operations do not use the global C++ locale. String comparison in C++ can be performed by means of the locale::operator()(), and this operation uses the locale for which it is invoked. Similarly, the inserters and extractors for numerical values in IOStreams use the locale object that is attached to the stream they work on.

There is a global locale in C++ too. It is used as a default locale for operations that do not explicitly choose a locale object. Streams, for instance, are created with a snapshot of the global C++ locale and use this snapshot unless another locale is explicitly attached.

The difference between the global locale in C and the global locale in C++ becomes visible when we consider that the global locale can be changed. In C, when the current global C locale is replaced by another locale, all internationalized operations from then on use the new global locale and silently change their behavior accordingly. In C++, when the current global C++ locale is replaced by another locale, all internationalized operations work as before. The change affects only new snapshots that are taken of the global locale. Existing snapshots taken of the previous global locale are not affected. In other words, snapshots of the global C++ locale are not transparent and do not reflect any replacement of the global locale.

Under certain circumstances, setting the global C++ locale has an effect on the global C locale. If the C++ locale provided has a name, the `setlocale()` function from the standard C library is called. As a result, C functions, which are called from a C++ program, will be using the same global locale as the calling C++ functions. Note that the reverse is not true. Setting the global C locale has no effect on the global C++ locale. If the global C++ locale does not have a name, the effect on the C locale is implementation-defined.

The C++ locale model has the advantage that working with several cultural environments in one program is much easier than in C. In C, the global locale must be switched back and forth each time another cultural area is relevant. In C++, several locale objects can be used in parallel, and each internationalized operation can use its own locale. Here is an example:

```
cin.imbue(locale(""));      //  the native locale
cout.imbue(locale::classic());
double f;
while (cin >> f) cout << f << endl;
```

In a German locale, with input 3.456,78, output is 3456.78.

Traditional C-style localization using the global locale is still easy. Simply use snapshots of the global C++ locale in all places:

```
locale::global(locale(""));         //  set the global locale
                                    //  imbue it on all the std streams
cin.imbue(locale());
cout.imbue(locale());
cerr.imbue(locale());
wcin.imbue(locale());
wcout.imbue(locale());
wcerr.imbue(locale());

double f;
while (cin >> f) cout << f << endl;
```

On a "German" computer, all input and output will be parsed and formatted according to German conventions.

The most important difference between the C and C++ locales is that the C++ locale also provides an extensible framework into which user-defined internationalization services can be integrated. The C locale does not allow any extensions.

APPENDIX G

New C++ Features and Idioms

G.1 Bitmask Types

A bitmask type represents the abstraction of a bit field. A bit field is an object that contains a combination of bits or flags. Each of the bits can be set, cleared, or tested.

The bitmask type is the type of such a bit field. Each bitmask type is defined along with a set of predefined values; such a value may represent a single bit in the mask or a combination thereof or zero, that is, no bit at all. Combinations of the predefined values are valid bitmask values themselves and can be stored in an object of the bitmask type.

Bits can be set, cleared, or tested by applying the following operations to objects (the bit fields) and values (the bits) of bitmask types:

To set a value Y in an object X is to evaluate the expression X |= Y.

To clear a value Y in an object X is to evaluate the expression X &= ~Y.

The value Y is set in the object X if the expression X & Y is nonzero.

Bitmask types can be implemented in several ways. A bitmask type can be an integer type, a bitset,[1] or an enumerated type that overloads certain operators. As a user,

---

1. bitset is a class template defined in the standard C++ library in the header file <bitset>. The template class bitset<N> represents a fixed-sized sequence of N bits.

you need not know what it really is. All you need to care about is the name of the bitmask type and the names of the associated predefined bit values. It is guaranteed that you can set, clear, and test the flags as outlined above, and that you can assign combinations of bits to an object of the bitmask type.

Bitmask types are used in various places throughout the standard C++ library. Examples in IOStreams are the format flags, the stream state, and the open modes. All of these bitmask types are implementation-defined.

G.2 POD—Plain Old Data

The POD stands for Plain Old Data. A POD type is basically a C-style structure as opposed to a C++ structure.

In C++, a structure is almost the same as a class. The only difference between a structure and a class is that the members and base classes of a structure are `public` by default, whereas the members and base classes of a class are `private` by default.

A POD is different. It must not have any user-defined constructors, copy assignment operators, or destructors; virtual functions; base classes; private or protected nonstatic data members; nonstatic data members of type pointer to member; nonstatic data members of type non-POD (or array of such types); or nonstatic data members that are references.

A structure (or class) with these properties has a storage layout that is compatible with that of a structure in C; that is, an object of POD type occupies contiguous bytes of storage and can be copied bitwise—using, for instance, the `memcpy()` library function. Also, PODs can be initialized using a brace-enclosed, comma-separated list of initializers.

G.3 Explicit Constructors

One-argument constructors can be used to perform a conversion from the type of the constructor argument to the type of the constructed object. In C++ the compiler can choose to incorporate such converting constructors into any implicit conversion sequence that it must generate. Implicit conversions are performed, for example, when the type of an argument passed to a function does not match the required argument type. Let us study the example of a class that has two different one-argument constructors:

```
class MyString
{
public:
   MyString(const char* cString);
   MyString(unsigned int capacity);

   MyString& add(MyString anotherString);

   // ... other members ...
};
```

The first one-argument constructor of class `MyString` takes a `const char*` argument representing a C-style string, which is a pointer to an array of characters terminated with a `'\0'`. An automatic conversion by means of this constructor is very convenient, because it allows use of a C-style string wherever a `MyString` object is required. This is a desired effect. For example, when we call the `add()` member function, we do not have to explicitly construct a `MyString` object from the C-style string that we intend to pass as an argument, but we can directly use the C-style string itself, as shown below:

```
X s("Hello ");
s.add("world !");
```

The second one-argument constructor of class `MyString` takes an `unsigned int` argument specifying the initial capacity of the `MyString` object under construction, though initially the constructed object will not contain any text. With this constructor it is now possible to use an `unsigned int` where a `MyString` object is required. Consider the following example:

```
MyString s("test");
s.add(5); // oops, supposedly the C-string "5"
```

Let us suppose we forgot to put the integral value 5 into quotes so that it would be a C-string literal. Unfortunately, the compiler will not catch this mistake, because it can implicitly convert the (unsigned) int literal 5 to a `MyString` object using the second constructor. In fact, a `MyString` object with the capacity to hold five characters containing no text is constructed, and this temporary `MyString` object is passed to the `add()` function. This effect is certainly not desired and illustrates the typical pitfall that stems from implicit conversions based on one-argument constructors. Often, only some constructors are meant as conversions, while others have entirely different semantics; and use of the nonconverting constructors for implicit conversions is usually not desired, yet it cannot be suppressed.

The function-specifier `explicit` was invented to remedy this shortcoming of the language. A one-argument constructor that is specified `explicit` is not included in any implicit type conversion that is automatically generated by the compiler. By means of the `explicit` specification, a programmer can distinguish between one-argument constructors that have conversion semantics and one-argument constructors that are not meant as conversions. We can benefit from this language improvement by changing our example to

```
class MyString
{
public:
    MyString(const char* cString);
    explicit MyString(unsigned int capacity);

// ... other members ...
};
```

With this modification the previous example will not compile any longer and the supposed error (passing an integer literal in lieu of a C-style string) will now be detected by the compiler:

```
MyString s("test");
s.add(5); // error: cannot convert integer to MyString
```

Note that the use of `explicit` prevents use of the one-argument constructor in implicit conversions performed by the compiler, but the programmer can still use them for explicit conversions if needed. For illustration, let's assume we have a class X that can be constructed from a `MyString` object:

```
class X {
public:
   X(const MyString& s);

// ... other members ...
};
```

Then the compiler will not accept the following code:

```
X x(5); // wrong !!!
```

because it involves an implicit conversion from an `integer` to a `MyString` object, and this conversion is available only via the one-argument constructor of class `MyString` that is specified `explicit`. Yet the compiler will accept the following:

```
X x(MyString(5)); // okay
```

Here, the `explicit MyString` constructor is explicitly invoked by the programmer in order to create a temporary object which is then passed to X's constructor. The compile also accepts the following:

```
X x(static_cast<MyString>(5)); // okay
```

Here the programmer uses a `static_cast` to tell the compiler that it should do an explicit conversion from `integer` to `MyString` based on the `MyString`'s explicit constructor.

In sum, nonconverting constructors must be specified `explicit`; all one-argument constructors without an `explicit` specification are treated as converting constructors, and the compiler may use them in implicit conversion sequences.

G.4 Template Specialization

Class templates can be specialized; that is, a special version of a template can be provided for a particular set of template arguments. Let us consider an example:

```
template <class T>
class Order {
public:
  bool less()(const T& lhs, const T& rhs) const
  { return lhs < rhs; }
  bool equals()(const T& lhs, const T& rhs) const
  { return lhs == rhs; }
};
```

Such a class template can be instantiated for all types T that can be ordered by means of operator < and compared for equality by means of operator ==. We can, for instance, use it for sorting or finding objects of type T as in the find() function below:

```
template<class T, class Strategy>
T* find(T* array, size_t siz, const T& val, Strategy eq)
{ for (size_t i=0; i < siz; ++i,++array)
      if (eq.equals(*array,val))
          return (array);
   return 0;
}
```

When we invoke the find() function, we can pass an object of type Order<T> as an argument, shown below for type int:

```
int buf[1024];
// fill the integer buffer
if (find(buf, 1024, 0, Order<int>()))
    // integer 0 found
```

The example above also works for strings:

```
string buf[1024];
// fill the string buffer
if (find(buf, 1024, string("xyz"), Order<string>()))
    // string "xyz" found
```

However, it does not work as expected for C-style strings of type const char*, because the operations provided by class Order<const char*> would compare the pointers to the C-style strings for equality. Two C-style strings with the same content, but stored at different memory locations, would not compare as equal. Hence a call to find() with an Order<const char*> object will find only *identical* C-style strings, that is, C-style strings with the same address, but will not be capable of identifying *equal* C-style strings, that is, C-style strings with the same content.

```
const char* buf[1024];
// fill the string buffer
if (find(buf, 1024, "xyz", Order<const char*>()))
    // will never get here; strings equal to "xyz" are only found,
    // if stored at same memory location as the string literal "xyz"
```

What we would need here to make our find() function work is a special version of the Order class template for C-style strings. This is what template specialization is for. We can define a version of the class template Order for type const char*, see below:

```
template <>
class Order<const char*> {
public:
  bool less(const char* lhs, const char* rhs) const
  { return strcmp(lhs,rhs)<0; }
  bool equals(const char* lhs, const char* rhs) const
  { return strcmp(lhs,rhs) == 0; }
};
```

If we now call find(..., Order<const char*>()), the specialization of the Order class template for type const char* would be used instead of an instantiation of the general class template Order.

PARTIAL SPECIALIZATION

C++ also allows partial specialization of templates. A partial specialization differs from a full specialization in that it is still a template. If, for instance, we have a class template with two template parameters and we provide a specialization that binds only one of the two template arguments, we have partial specialization. If we bind both template parameters, we have full specialization.

```
template <class S, class T>    // the actual class template
class X { ... };
template <class S>             // a partial specialization
class X<int> { ... };
template <>                    // a full specialization
class X<int,string> { ... };
```

We can use partial specialization in our example above and provide a specialization of the Order class for pointer types, which compares the objects being pointed to rather than the pointers themselves. Such a specialization is a partial specialization, because it is still a template; it just has a different kind of template parameter; that is, it uses its template argument differently. Here is the partial specialization Order<T*> for pointers:

```
template <class T>
class Order<T*> {
public:
  bool less(const T* lhs, const T* rhs) const
  { return *lhs < *rhs; }
  bool equals(const T* lhs, const T* rhs) const
  { return *lhs == *rhs; }
};
```

This template would be instantiated whenever a version of the Order class for any pointer type is needed, except for pointers of type const char*, because the full specialization Order<const char*> is even more specialized than the partial specialization Order<T*>.

```
template <class T>              // the actual class template
class Order { ... };
template <class T>              // a partial specialization
class Order<T*> { ... };
template <>                     // a full specialization
class Order<const char*> { ... };
```

VARIABILITY AMONG TEMPLATE SPECIALIZATIONS
In principle, specializations of class templates need not even have the same structure. A specialization can have different data and function members. It is, for instance, possible to add or remove member functions. Below is yet another specialization for the Order class template for strings, where we implement a culture-sensitive string comparison using C++ locales. It has a constructor and a function call operator in addition to the member functions less() and equals():

```
template <>
class Order<string> {
public:
  Order(locale l=locale()) : _l(l) {}
  bool operator<(const string& lhs, const string& rhs) const
  { return less(rhs,lhs); }
  bool less(const string& lhs, const string& rhs) const
  { return _l(rhs,lhs); }
  bool equals(const string& lhs, const string& rhs) const
  { return !_l(rhs,lhs)&&!_l(lhs,rhs); }
private:
  locale _l;
};
```

Here is a specialization for complex numbers. Complex numbers cannot be ordered, but only compared for equality. In this specialization the `less()` member function is removed from the template:

```
template <class Float>
struct Order<complex<Float> > {
  static bool equals
  (const complex<Float>& lhs, const complex<Float>& rhs)
  { return lhs == rhs; }
};
```

Moreover, the `equals()` operation is a static member function in this specialization, but a nonstatic member function in the general class template.

The differences between a class template and its specializations can be even more drastic. The standard character traits class template `char_traits`, for instance, is an empty class template; only its specializations are meaningful classes. In comparison, we could decide that we cannot provide a meaningful `Order` template for all types in general, but only for specific types. Following this line of logic, we could implement our `Order` template and its specializations like this:

```
template <class T>
class Order {};

template <>
class Order<string> {
public:
  Order(locale l);
  bool operator<(const string& lhs, const string& rhs) const;
  bool less(const string& lhs, const string& rhs) const;
  bool equals(const string& lhs, const string& rhs) const;
private:
  locale _l;
};

template <>
class Order<const char*> {
public:
  bool less(const char* lhs, const char* rhs) const;
  bool equals(const char* lhs, const char* rhs) const;
};
```

```
template <class Float>
struct Order<complex<Float> > {
  static bool equals();
};

template <class Numeric>
struct Order<Numeric> {
  static bool less(Numeric lhs, Numeric rhs);
  static bool equals(Numeric lhs, Numeric rhs);
};
```

With this implementation of Order and its specializations, the find() function can be invoked only on types for which a specialization of Order is defined, because the instantiation of Order for an arbitrary type would not yield a meaningful class.

SPECIALIZATION OF FUNCTION TEMPLATES

Function templates can be specialized, too. We talk of function template overloading, instead of function template specialization, because special versions of a function template simply contribute to the set of overloaded functions. Here are some overloaded versions of an equals() function template:

```
template <class T>
bool equals(const T& lhs, const T& rhs)
{ return lhs == rhs; }

template <class T>
bool equals(const T* lhs, const T* rhs)
{ return *lhs == *rhs; }

template <class StringT>
bool equals(const StringT& lhs, const StringT& rhs, locale l)
{ return !l(rhs,lhs)&&!l(lhs,rhs); }

bool equals(const char* lhs, const char* rhs)
{ return strcmp(lhs,rhs) == 0; }

bool equals(const wchar_t* lhs, const wchar_t* rhs)
{ return wcscmp(lhs,rhs) == 0; }
```

Depending on the actual function arguments, either a function or an instantiation of one of the function templates would be invoked. Here are some examples:

```
int i=1, j=2;
wstring s(L"abc"),t(L"xyz");
```

```
equals(i,j);      // equals<int>(const int&, const int&) instantiated from equals<T>

equals(&i,&j));   // equals<int>(const int*, const int*) instantiated from equals<T*>

equals("a","b");  // equals(const char*, const char*) function

equals(s,t);      // equals<wstring>(const wstring&, const wstring&)
                  // instantiated from equals<T>

equals(s,t,locale()); // equals<wstring>(const wstring&, const wstring&, locale)
                      // instantiated from equals<StringT>
```

Functions generated from any of the `equals()` function templates as well as normal functions with the name `equals()` can be invoked. The compiler chooses the "best match." Given the choice between a function generated from a template and a normal function, if these are otherwise equally good matches, the compiler prefers the normal function.

G.5 Default Template Arguments

Templates can have three different kinds of arguments: type arguments, nontype arguments, and template arguments. Here are examples from each of the arguments categories.

The class template `Buffer` below has a type template parameter `T`, which denotes the type of elements stored in the buffer; and a nontype template parameter `s` of type `size_t`, which represents the size of the buffer:

```
template <class T, size_t s>
class Buffer {
 public:
    ...
 private:
   T _buf[s];
};
```

The class template `Stack` below has a template template parameter `Container`, which is the container template on top of which the stack is implemented.

```
template <class T, template <class T> class Container>
class Stack {
 public:
    ...
 private:
   Container<T> c;

};
```

All three different kinds of template parameters can have default values. The default value for a nontype template argument is a constant value of the respective type; the default for a type template argument must be suitable for instantiation of the class template, and the default for a template template argument is a class template. Only trailing parameters can be omitted. Here are examples.

Let us first examine defaults for nontype template parameters:

```
template <class T, size_t s = 256>
class Buffer {
 public:
    ...
 private:
   T _buf[s];
};
```

With the default value of 256 specified for the buffer size, the size argument can be omitted when the Buffer template is instantiated. A Buffer can be specified as

```
Buffer<string, 100>
```

in which case it would have 100 entries, but also as

```
Buffer<string>
```

in which case the buffer would have the default size of 256 entries.

Here is an example of a default value for a type template argument:

```
template <class CharType = char>
class String {
 public:
   CharType& operator[](size_t idx);
    ...
 private:
   CharType* _str;
};
```

With the default value of type char specified for the character type of this String class, the type argument can be omitted when the String template is instantiated. A Buffer can be specified as

```
Buffer<wchar_t>
```

in which case it would be handling a wide-character string, but also as

```
String<>
```

in which case the string would handle tiny characters of type char. Note that the empty brackets <> are needed in order to indicate that we refer to the String class template, not just to a class named String.

Even template template parameters can have a default. Here is the previously mentioned Stack example:

```
template <class ElemT, template <class T> class Container = deque>
class Stack {
 public:
   ...
 private:
   Container<ElemT> c;

};
```

With the container template deque specified as a default value for the container template, the template template argument can be omitted when the Stack template is instantiated. A Stack can be specified as

```
Stack<string, vector>
```

in which case it would be built on top of a vector container, but also as

```
Stack<string>
```

in which case the Stack would use a deque container.

Default template arguments can depend on previous template arguments. One of the most prominent examples is the string class from the standard library.

```
template <class charT, class Traits = char_traits<charT> >
class basic_string;
```

The default for the type template argument Traits is an instantiation of the standard character traits template for type charT, where charT is the first type argument of the string template. Hence, if charT is wchar_t, the Traits parameter would have the default char_traits<wchar_t>, and if charT is MyCharType, the default for the Traits type would be char_traits<MyCharType>. If the default traits type fits the need, the string template can be referred to as

```
basic_string<char> or
```

```
basic_string<MyCharType>.
```

If nonstandard traits are needed, the defaulted template parameter must be explicitly specified, as shown in the example below:

```
basic_string<char, caseInsensitiveTraits<char> >
```

Note that only class templates can have default template arguments. Defaults cannot be provided for any argument of a function template. The following would be illegal:

```
template<class InputIterator, class Predicate>
InputIterator find_if
 (InputIterator first, InputIterator last,
  Predicate pred =
          equal_to<typename iterator_traits<InputIterator>::value_type>
 );
```

Instead, an overloaded version of the `find_if()` function template must be provided, which implicitly uses a default. The overloaded version of the function template `find_if` takes a value, not a predicate, and it considers comparison with the specified value by means of `operator()` as the predicate:

```
template<class InputIterator, class T>
InputIterator find
 (InputIterator first, InputIterator last, const T& value);
```

G.6 Explicit Template Argument Specification

Traditionally, function template arguments are deduced from the function arguments. If you have a function template

```
template <class T> void foo (T t)   { /* ... */ }
```

you usually do not care about instantiation of the function template. You simply use this function template as in the following example:

```
int i = 5;
foo(i);
float x = 1.5;
foo(x);
```

The compiler does the work for you; it examines the arguments to these function calls, determines the argument types, and deduces that in the above cases the function templates need to be instantiated for type `int` and for type `float`.

Now let's take a look at the `use_facet` function template. It is declared as

```
template <class Facet> const Facet& use_facet(const locale& loc);
```

Different from the example above, the template parameter `Facet` does not appear as a type of function parameter. The only function parameter to `use_facet` is the locale. Now consider a call to this function template:

```
locale loc;
const numpunct<char>& fac = use_facet(loc);   // will not compile !!!
```

The function argument `loc` does not allow the template argument to be deduced, because its type has nothing to do with the template argument `Facet`. The return type of the function template is not considered for template argument deduction. Hence in the call to `use_facet` above, the template argument `Facet` cannot be deduced. It has to be explicitly specified.

Explicit template argument specification is done like this:

```
locale loc;
const numpunct<char>& fac = use_facet<numpunct<char> >(loc);
```

Note that the syntax for explicit template argument specification of a function template is similar to template argument specification of class templates. If you have a class template

```
template <class T> class list;
```

you naturally specify the template arguments whenever you need an instantiation of the class template:

```
list<int> counters;
list<float> sizes;
```

With a function template

```
template <class T> void foo();
```

you do exactly the same:

```
foo<int>();
foo<float>();
```

if you have to. If the template argument appears in the function argument list, it is more convenient to let the compiler deduce the template argument for you.

G.7 The `typename` **Keyword**

The `typename` keyword is one of the language features that was introduced into the C++ programming language during the standardization process. Its addition enables the compiler to check the syntax of the definition of a template before it is instantiated.

When a compiler parses a template definition, it needs to know what a plain (i.e., nonqualified) name means when it sees it in the template. Before the invention of the `typename` keyword, the compiler could not tell whether a nonqualified name was a type name or not, and therefore it could not further analyze the template definition. With the `typename` keyword, the rule is that a name used in a template is assumed not to name a type unless it has been explicitly declared to refer to a type in the context enclosing the template declaration or is qualified by the keyword `typename`. For illustration, let us examine a couple of examples:

```
template <class T>
class B {
  void f()
  {
    T* a;                //1
    typename T::A* b;  //2
    T::A* c;             //3
  }
};
```

//1   Here, `T` clearly is a type in the context of the template declaration; it is the type provided as a template argument to this class template `B`. Hence, this is a declaration; a is declared a pointer to `T`.

//2   Here, `T::A` is qualified as a type by using the `typename` keyword. Hence, this is a declaration too; b is declared a pointer to `T::A`.

//3   Here, `T::A` is not a type name. It is assumed to be a data member of class `T`. Hence, this is an expression: multiply `T::A` by `c`.

So far, so good. A couple of surprises pop up once inheritance is involved. Consider the following:

```
template <class T>
class B {
  public:
    typedef int someType_t;
};
```

```
template <class T>
class D : public B<T> {
  public:
    typename someType_t foo();
};
```

This does not compile, because a name following a typename keyword must be a qualified name that depends on the template parameter. In general, a qualified name is a name that is preceded by a scope operator; in this case it must be a qualifier containing a template parameter or a template class name. Therefore, we have to correct our example to

```
template <class T>
class B {
  public:
    typedef int someType_t;
};

template <class T>
class D : public B<T> {
  public:
    typename B<T>::someType_t foo();
};
```

One might have expected that the derived class D inherits the type definition of someType_t. However, when a base class of a class template depends on a template parameter, as is the case in our example, the compiler cannot inspect the base class while parsing the template definition of the derived class to see if a name like someType_t is defined there. Hence we have to reference the type someType_t using a qualified name such as B<T>::someType_t. The reason is that although the compiler might have seen the definition of the base class template B, it does not know whether the actual B that will be used will be an instance from the template or a specialization that the compiler has not yet seen.

All this makes for funny effects that are somewhat surprising. Here's an example from the standard library, the base class for binary function objects:

```
template <class Arg, class Result>
struct unary_function
{
    typedef Arg argument_type;
    typedef Result result_type;
};
```

Its purpose is to inherit the two types argument_type and result_type to its derived classes, so that these types are available in every function object. However, although you derive from the unary_function base class you cannot use any of these types unless you fully specify them. Here's an example of a typical function object. What you might expect to find is

```
template <class T>
struct negate : public unary_function<T, T>
{
 result_type operator() (const argument_type& x) const { return -x; }
};
```

However, here is what you probably *will* find in your header file:

```
template <class T>
struct negate : public unary_function<T, T>
{
 typename unary_function<T,T>::result_type
 operator() (const typename unary_function<T,T>::argument_type& x) const
   { return -x; }
};
```

The types `argument_type` and `result_type` have to be fully specified. Here they are specified in terms of the base class `unary_function<T, T>`. An alternative would be to specify them in terms of the derived class, i.e., as `typename negate<T,T>::argument_type` and as `typename negate<T,T>::result_type`. Also, you might find implementations of the derived class `negate<T,T>` that repeat the base class's type definitions for `argument_type` and `result_type`:

```
template <class T>
struct negate : public unary_function<T, T>
{
    typedef typename unary_function<T,T>::argument_type argument_type;
    typedef typename unary_function<T,T>::result_type result_type;
    result_type operator() (const argument_type& x) const { return -x; }
};
```

In any case, the point is that although you inherit the type definitions from the `unary_function` base class, you have to fully qualify them.

The parameter class in our article is a similar case. Fortunately, it is pretty simple; it does not use the types it defines and inherits. Still, if you wanted to use any of the types defined in the base class somewhere in the definition of the derived class, you would have to fully specify the type names or repeat the base class's type definitions. We defined the base class as

```
template<class Collection, class Iterator = Collection::iterator>
struct iterParam
{
   typedef Iterator    iterator;
   typedef Collection  collection;
   typedef typename Collection::value_type    value_type;
   typedef typename Collection::difference_type    distance_type;
};
```

If we wanted to allow unqualified references to these types in the derived classes, we would have to repeat the type definitions:

```
template<class Collection, class Iterator>
struct constIterParam : public iterParam<Collection,Iterator>
{
   typedef typename IterParam<Collection,Iterator>::iterator      iterator;
   typedef typename IterParam<Collection,Iterator>::collection    collection;
   typedef typename IterParam<Collection,Iterator>::value_type    value_type;
   typedef typename IterParam<Collection,Iterator>::distance_type distance_type;

   typedef typename Collection::const_pointer      pointer;
   typedef typename Collection::const_reference    reference;

   // use, for instance, type "iterator"
};
```

G.8 Dynamic Cast

C++ allows all kinds of conversions between objects, pointers, and references of different type. Some of these conversions are performed implicitly; others must be forced by means of an explicit cast operator. Among types that belong to the same inheritance tree, we distinguish between upcasts and downcasts.

UPCASTS

An upcast is a cast up the inheritance tree, i.e., from a derived class to a base class. Here is a simple example:

```
class Base {};
class Derived : public Base {};
Derived* dp = new Derived;
void foo(Base*);
foo(dp); // upcast
```

A pointer to a derived class object is passed to a function that expects a base class pointer. For argument passing, the derived class pointer is implicitly cast to a base class pointer. Implicit casts are considered harmless, and indeed an upcast is always well defined, because an object of a derived class type contains a subobject of the base class type. For that reason, it cannot happen that the function `foo()` accesses any members that do not exist.

DOWNCAST

A downcast is a cast down the inheritance tree, i.e., from a base class to a derived class. Here is an example:

```
class Base {};
class Derived : public Base {
 public:
  int cnt;
};
Base* bp = new Derived;
void foo(Base* p)
{ ((Derived*)p)->cnt = 0; } // downcast and access to data member of derived
                            // class
```

A function taking a base class pointer accesses a member that is available solely in the derived class. An explicit cast is needed to convert the base class pointer to the desired derived class pointer. Different from an upcast, a downcast is never performed automatically by the compiler. Instead, the programmer has to cast explicitly, which in our example is done using the old-style cast notation.

In our example, the base class pointer points to an object of the derived class type, so nothing harmful can happen. All access to members of the object pointed to via the derived class pointer is well defined in this case. However, a downcast is potentially dangerous. Consider the following example:

```
class Base {};
class Derived : public Base {
 public:
  int cnt;
};
Base* db = new Base;
void foo(Base* p)
{ ((Derived*)p)->cnt = 0; } // downcast and access to data member of derived
                            // class
```

In this case, the base class pointer does not point to a derived class object, only to a base class object. Accessing the data member `cnt` in function `foo()` is likely to lead to a program crash, because the object pointed to does not have the required data member.

SAFE DOWNCAST

As an alternative to the potentially hazardous language construct of an old-style down-cast, C++ has a new language feature, the `dynamic_cast`, which is a safe downcast. It does not simply perform the required cast, regardless of the actual type of object pointed to, but instead allows checking of whether the object pointed to really is of the expected derived class type. In the previous example, one would rewrite the function `foo()` so that it checks the pointer's runtime type information before it attempts access to any members of the object pointed to. The rewritten function would look like this:

```
void foo(Base* ptr)
{
 Derived* dp = dynamic_cast<Derived*>(ptr);
  if (dp == 0)
    { /* whatever is appropriate, but do not access any members
        of the derived class */
    }
  else
    dp->cnt = 0;
}
```

AVOIDING DOWNCASTS

Usually, the use of downcasts is considered poor programming style, because it can almost always be avoided and replaced by proper use of virtual functions and polymorphism. Instead of using `dynamic_cast`, we could fix the base class and introduce virtual functions that give access to the data member in question. The base class versions of the access functions would not do anything but return a default value; the derived class versions of the access functions would really access the data member.

```
class Base {
 public:
  virtual int cnt() { return 0; }
  virtual int cnt(int i) { return 0; }
};
class Derived : public Base {
 public:
  virtual int cnt() { return _cnt; }
  virtual int cnt(int i) { int tmp = _cnt; _cnt = i; return tmp; }
 private:
  int _cnt;
};
Base* db = new Base;
void foo(Base* p)
{ p->cnt(0); } // polymorphic call of access function
```

It is not always possible to modify an inheritance hierarchy as suggested above. If, for instance, the base class is part of a third-party library, which you are neither able nor willing to modify, you might end up in a situation where you cannot circumvent the downcast. Deriving from the stream classes in the standard library is such a case and was the example that convinced the standards committee to include the dynamic_cast language feature.

THE DYNAMIC_CAST OPERATOR

The dynamic_cast operator comes in two flavors: (1) for casting pointers and (2) for casting references. If the dynamic cast of a pointer fails, a zero pointer value is returned. If the dynamic cast of a reference fails, an exception of type std::bad_cast is raised. Here are the two alternatives:[2]

```
void foo(Base* ptr)
{
 Derived* dp = dynamic_cast<Derived*>(ptr);
  if (dp == 0)
     { /* whatever is appropriate, but do not access any members of the
         derived class */
     }
  else
     dp->cnt = 0;
}
```

and

```
void foo(Base& ref)
{
 try { Derived& dr = dynamic_cast<Derived&>(ref); }
 catch (bad_cast)
 { /* whatever is appropriate, but do not access any members of the
     derived class */
 }
 dr.cnt = 0;
}
```

Only pointers and references to polymorphic types can be cast via the dynamic_cast operator. A polymorphic type is a class type that has at least one virtual member function, either directly defined or inherited from a base class. This is because only

---

2. Include directives and using statements are omitted, as usual. The standard exception bad_cast is defined in the header file <exception>.

polymorphic types contain runtime type information. The `dynamic_cast` operator needs the runtime type information in order to perform the required type check.

PEER CAST

The `dynamic_cast` operator can also be used for upcasts, which is not terribly useful in the first place. It is, however, interesting in the case of multiple inheritance. In that context it allows safe peer class casts such as the following:

```
class Base_1 {};
class Base_2 {};
class Derived : public Base_1, public Base_2 {};
Base_1* b1p = new Derived;
Base_2* b2p = dynamic_cast<Base_2*>(b1p); //is the pointed to object
                                          //also derived from Base_2?
```

In this case, a pointer to a derived object with multiple base classes is cast from a base class pointer type to another base class pointer type. The cast fails if the object pointed to is not of a type that is derived from both base classes. This kind of cast is neither an upcast nor a downcast, but a cast from one branch of the inheritance tree to another. It is sometimes referred to as a peer class cast.

G.9 Function `try` Blocks

To eliminate a deficiency of prestandard C++, the standards committee added the language construct of a function try block to the language. Without function try blocks, it was not possible to catch exceptions from operations invoked in a constructor initializer list. Now, with the function try block, a constructor can catch and handle all exceptions, including those raised during construction of base classes and data members.

Below is an example that shows the problem in prestandard C++ and how the function try block can be used to solve it. Let us assume we have a class X that is defined as

```
class X : public Y
{
public:
   X(int i, int j) : Y(i), z(j)  { ... some other code here ... };

   ... other members ...

private:
   Z z;
}
```

In prestandard C++ we could only wrap the whole function body of the constructor into a try block:

```
X(int i, int j) : Y(i), z(j)
{
   try
   {
      ... some other code here ...
   }
   catch (...) // this ellipsis is correct C++ syntax
   {
      ... do something about the error ...
   }
}
```

It was not possible to include the initialization list in the try block. As a result, it was impossible to add any functionality that would react to an exception thrown from the initialization list, i.e., from the base class constructor of Y(int) or the member constructor of Z(int). For this reason the standards committee added the function try block to the C++ programming language.

X's constructor can be improved in the following way, using a function try block:

```
X(int i, int j) try : Y(i), z(j)
{
   ... some other code here ...
}
catch(...) // this ellipsis is correct C++ syntax
{
   ... do something about the error ...
}
```

As usual in a failed constructor, the fully constructed base classes and members are destroyed. This happens before the handler is entered, meaning that base classes and non-static data members cannot be accessed in the handler. Only the arguments to the constructor are still accessible.

It is not possible to "handle" the exception and finish the creation of the object, because it is not possible to "return" from the handler. We must exit from the handler either via an explicit throw statement or a call to exit(), abort(), or the like. If we try to leave the handler via a return statement or by flowing off the end of the handler, pretending we had handled the exception, the caught exception is automatically rethrown.

Function try blocks can be used not only with constructors but also with destructors and normal functions. Here is an example in which the function try block is used for a destructor:

```
~X() try
{
    ... some code here ...
}
catch(...) // this ellipsis is correct C++ syntax
{
    ... do something about the error ...
}
```

The function try block for a destructor behaves similarly to that of a constructor: It is not possible to prevent the throwing of an exception once the control flow has entered the exception handler, because the handler can be left only by either an explicit throw or an automatic rethrow.

Finally, let us explore how a function try block behaves together with a normal function. Here is an example of this kind of use:

```
void foo() try
{
    ... some code here ...
}
catch(...) // this ellipsis is correct C++ syntax
{
    ... do something about the error ...
}
```

The code above is mostly equivalent to

```
void foo()
{
    try
    {
        ... some code here ...
    }
    catch(...) // this ellipsis is correct C++ syntax
    {
        ... do something about the error ...
    }
}
```

Unlike constructors and destructors, the handler of a function try block for a normal function can be left with a return statement; it does not trigger an automatic rethrow. Not explicitly returning from the handler, but flowing off the end of the catch block, is equivalent to a return with no value, which results in undefined behavior in the case of a value-returning function. Like the function try block for a constructor, the scope and lifetime of the parameters extend into the handler of the function try block.

When applied to main() or main(int argc, char* argv[]), the function try block catches all exceptions raised during execution of the main() function, but it does not catch exceptions thrown by constructors or destructors of global objects.

G.10 Standard Exceptions

The C++ standard defines a number of standard exception types. The IOStreams exception, class `ios_base::failure`, is an example. The standard exception types fall into two categories:

LANGUAGE EXCEPTIONS. Exceptions that are thrown by language constructs such as the `dynamic_cast` operator or operator `new`. They are declared in the header file `<exception>`. These exceptions are the following:

`bad_alloc`	—exception raised by `new` expressions
`bad_cast`	—exception raised by `dynamic_cast` expression
`bad_exception`	—exception raised by `unexpected()`

LIBRARY EXCEPTIONS. Exceptions that are thrown by operations of the standard library components. They are either declared in the header file `<stdexcept>` or in the header file of the component they belong to. `ios_base::failure`, for instance, is defined in the header file `<ios>`.

The standard library exceptions belong to a hierarchy of exception types that follow a certain error model. Errors are divided into two broad categories: logic errors and runtime errors. The distinguishing characteristic of logic errors is that they are due to errors in the internal logic of the program. In theory, they are preventable. By contrast, runtime errors are due to events beyond the scope of the program. They cannot easily be predicted in advance. The hierarchy of standard exception types contains the following:

```
class logic_error
    class domain_error
    class invalid_argument
    class length_error
    class out_of_range
class runtime_error
    class range_error
    class overflow_error
    class underflow_error
```

The IOStreams exception `ios_base::failure` is the only standard library exception that is not embedded into this hierarchy of exception types.

All C++ standard exception types are derived from the class `exception`:

```
class exception
{
public:
    exception() throw;
    exception(const exception&) throw;
    exception& operator= (const exception&) throw;
```

```
    virtual ~exception() throw;
    virtual const char* what() const throw;
};
```

Hence all exception objects contain a message, which is retrievable via the what()
function. The content of this message is not standardized.

G.11 Numeric Limits

The standard C++ library defines a component numeric_limits that provides information about various properties of the fundamental types in C++. It is defined in the header
file <limits>. The numeric_limits is a class template that is specialized for the built-
in floating-point and integral types, including bool. Information can be retrieved via static members. Typically provided in numeric_limits are the minimum and maximum
value for a type, or information specific to floating-point numbers, such as the maximum
rounding error or the rounding style.

Numerous values defined in numeric_limits<class T> are equivalent to values
defined in the C library. For instance, numeric_limits<int>::max() is equivalent to
INT_MAX and numeric_limits<char>::min() is equivalent to CHAR_MIN, and so
on. In principle, in does not make a difference whether you use information from
numeric_limits or its equivalent defined by the C library. However, if you need to
determine a property of an implementation-specific type, such as the maximum
streamsize value, for instance, you have to use the numeric_limits. All you know
about the streamsize type is that it is guaranteed to be one of the built-in integral types,
but you do not know which one. On the other hand, there is a specialization of the
numeric_limits template available for each of the built-in types. Hence,
numeric_limits<streamsize>::max() will return the maximum streamsize
values no matter which integral type streamsize equates to in a given implementation.

G.12 C++ Strings

In C++ there are two types of strings:

C STRINGS. They are a generalization of the string representation in C. As in C, they
are character arrays of type charT[ ] with a terminating end-of-string character, which is
charT('\0').

C++ STRINGS. They are objects of a type instantiated from the class template
basic_string <class charT, class Traits = char_traits<charT>, class
Allocator = allocator<charT> >.

The class template basic_string<class charT, class Traits, class
Allocator> is defined in the library header file <string>. There are type definitions
string (= basic_string<char>) and wstring (= basic_string<wchar_t>) for
the narrow- and wide-character string types.

C++ strings differ from C strings in a number of ways:

MEMORY MANAGEMENT. C++ strings automatically allocate and deallocate their memory. The memory management is encapsulated into the string class template. The memory of a C string has to be allocated and deallocated explicitly.

DYNAMIC SIZE. A C++ string internally maintains a character buffer, which is dynamically resized as needed, whereas C strings are character arrays of fixed size.

RANGE CHECK. C++ strings have access functions that check for range violations and throw exceptions to indicate such violations. C strings are accessed directly via pointers; no range check is possible.

VALUE SEMANTICS. C++ strings behave like values, which means that copies of a C++ string object can be treated as independent of each other. Copies of C strings have to be explicitly created via C library functions like `strcpy()`.

COPY ON WRITE. You can pass a C++ string around without worrying about the overhead of avoidable copying. Duplication of a C++ string object's internal data is performed only if needed; i.e., it is automatically delayed to the actual write access. (*Copy on write* is not a feature required by the standard. However, it is permitted optimization that is likely to be present in a reasonable implementation.)

ALLOCATORS. C++ strings support different memory allocation models by means of so-called allocators.

FUNCTIONALITY. C++ strings offer numerous operations for accessing and manipulating strings. Here is an overview.

element access: `operator[]()`, `at()`

manipulation: `operator+()`, `append()`, `assign()`, `insert()`, `erase()`, `replace()`, `copy()`

searching: `find()`, `find_first_of()`, `find_last_of()`, `substr()`

comparison: `compare()`, `operator<()`, `operator()>`, `operator==()`

convertibility to C strings via constructor for `charT*` and `c_str()`

BIBLIOGRAPHY

THE ISO/ANSI C++ LANGUAGE STANDARD

International Standard ISO/IEC 14882
Programming Language C++

THE CLASSIC IOSTREAMS LIBRARY

Eggink, Bernd, *Die C++ iostreams-Library* (Munich: Hanser Publishers, 1995).
Teale, Steve, *C++ IOStreams Handbook* (Reading, Mass.: Addison-Wesley Publishing Company, 1993).

INTERNATIONALIZATION

Kano, Nadine, *Developing International Software for Windows 95 and Windows NT* (Redmond, Wash.: Microsoft Press, 1995).
Lunde, Ken, *Understanding Japanese Information Processing* (Sebastopol, Calif.: O'Reilly, 1993).
Unicode Consortium, *The Unicode Standard: Version 2.0* (Reading, Mass.: Addison-Wesley Publishing Company, 1996).

THE C++ PROGRAMMING LANGUAGE

Lippman, Stanley B., and Josee Lajoie, *C++ Primer, Third Edition* (Reading, Mass.: Addison-Wesley Publishing Company, 1998).
Stroustrup, Bjarne, *The C++ Programming Language, Third Edition* (Reading, Mass.: Addison-Wesley Publishing Company, 1997).

THE STANDARD TEMPLATE LIBRARY (STL)

Ammeraal, Leen, *STL for C++ Programmers* (New York: John Wiley & Sons, 1997).

Austern, Matthew H., *Generic Programming and the STL: Using and Extending the C++ Standard Template Library* (Reading, Mass.: Addison-Wesley Publishing Company, 1998).

Breymann, Ulrich, *Designing Components with the C++ STL: A New Approach to Programming* (Reading, Mass.: Addison-Wesley Publishing Company, 1998).

Glass, Graham, and Brett L. Schuchert, *The STL Primer* (Upper Saddle River, N.J.: Prentice Hall, 1996).

Josuttis, Nicolai M., *The C++ Standard Library* (Reading, Mass.: Addison-Wesley Publishing Company, 1999).

Musser, David R., and Atul Saini, *STL Tutorial and Reference Guide: C++ Programming with the Standard Template Library* (Reading, Mass.: Addison-Wesley Publishing Company, 1996).

Nelson, Mark, *C++ Programmer's Guide to the Standard Template Library* (New York: IDG Books, 1995).

PATTERNS

Gamma, Erich, Richard Helm, Ralph Johnson, and John Vlissides, *Design Patterns: Elements of Reusable Object-Oriented Software* (Reading, Mass.: Addison-Wesley Publishing Company, 1994).

INDEX

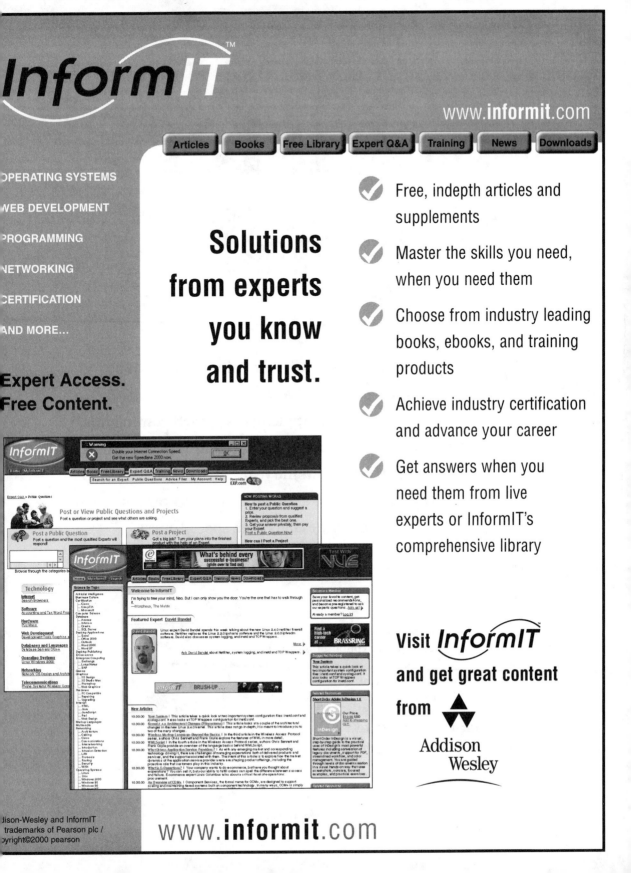

Register
Your Book
at www.aw.com/cseng/register

You may be eligible to receive:

- Advance notice of forthcoming editions of the book
- Related book recommendations
- Chapter excerpts and supplements of forthcoming titles
- Information about special contests and promotions throughout the year
- Notices and reminders about author appearances, tradeshows, and online chats with special guests

Contact us

If you are interested in writing a book or reviewing manuscripts prior to publication, please write to us at:

Editorial Department
Addison-Wesley Professional
75 Arlington Street, Suite 300
Boston, MA 02116 USA
Email: AWPro@aw.com

Visit us on the Web: http://www.aw.com/cseng